Cross-Border Transactions and Environmental Law

Cross-Border Transactions and Environmental Law

Edited by
Mark Brumwell LLB(Hons), AMI Env. Sc.
Solicitor, Partner, Planning and Environmental
Group, SJ Berwin & Co

Butterworths
London, Dublin, Edinburgh
1999

United Kingdom	Butterworths, a Division of Reed Elsevier (UK) Ltd, Halsbury House, 35 Chancery Lane, LONDON WC2A 1EL and 4 Hill Street, EDINBURGH EH2 3JZ
Australia	Butterworths, a Division of Reed International Books Australia Pty Ltd, CHATSWOOD, New South Wales
Canada	Butterworths Canada Ltd, MARKHAM, Ontario
India	Butterworth India, NEW DELHI
Ireland	Butterworth (Ireland) Ltd, DUBLIN
Malaysia	Malayan Law Journal Sdn Bhd, KUALA LUMPUR
New Zealand	Butterworths of New Zealand Ltd, WELLINGTON
Singapore	Butterworths Asia, SINGAPORE
South Africa	Butterworths Publishers (Pty) Ltd, DURBAN
USA	Lexis Law Publishing, CHARLOTTESVILLE, Virginia

© Reed Elsevier (UK) Ltd 1999

All rights reserved. No part of this publication may be reproduced in any material form (including photocopying or storing it in any medium by electronic means and whether or not transiently or incidentally to some other use of this publication) without the written permission of the copyright owner except in accordance with the provisions of the Copyright, Designs and Patents Act 1988 or under the terms of a licence issued by the Copyright Licensing Agency Ltd, 90 Tottenham Court Road, London, England W1P 0LP. Applications for the copyright owner's written permission to reproduce any part of this publication should be addressed to the publisher.

Warning: The doing of an unauthorised act in relation to a copyright work may result in both a civil claim for damages and criminal prosecution.

Any Crown copyright material is reproduced with the permission of the Controller of Her Majesty's Stationery Office.

A CIP Catalogue record for this book is available from the British Library.

ISBN 0 406 90807 9

Typeset by M Rules
Printed in Great Britain by Redwood Books, Trowbridge, Wiltshire

Visit us at our website: http://www.butterworths.co.uk

PREFACE

If you can fill the unforgiving minute with sixty seconds' worth of distance run.
Yours is the Earth and everything that's in it.
And, which is more, you'll be a Man, my son!

If, Rudyard Kipling

The core of maturing environmental law practice in most commercial law firms is based on company mergers and acquisitions and the sale and purchase of real property. Environmental practice revolves around an assessment of the environmental issues applying to the transaction and the provision of contractual terms to apportion risk. Advising on environmental liabilities attaching to the funders of transactions and how to divide environmental risks in joint ventures and other commercial projects is also becoming increasingly important.

Many of the more substantial transactions involve sites in a number of countries with the lead law firm working with individual firms in each of those countries to provide a comprehensive suite of legal advice. While the lead law firm may have substantial environmental expertise, the individual firms in each jurisdiction are not always so equipped. The lead firm will in any event need to have an understanding in outline of the environmental regimes applying in each jurisdiction, to ensure that the correct questions are asked of the individual firms in each jurisdiction and that those firms make all the necessary due diligence inquiries in conjunction with appropriately experienced environmental consultants. Only then can the lead law firm ensure that the contractual provisions take full account of the law applying in every jurisdiction covered by the transaction.

This book is designed primarily to fill that information need by providing a simple guide to the basics of environmental law in other jurisdictions which will generally be applicable for cross-border transactions. It will also be of use to specialist and non-specialist in-house lawyers and to non-lawyers in multinational organisations who need a basic guide to environmental law applying in the countries in which their company operates.

Although there are a variety of books on international environmental law and on EU environmental law, none looks at the national law which applies in each jurisdiction and the way in which international and EU regimes are applied nationally. The national law is in fact likely to be the most significant type of law and its diversity between jurisdictions makes it challenging for the practitioner to identify all the essential points for a given transaction. Even within the EU, there is little co-ordination of environmental regimes. Most member states have developed sophisticated liability regimes independent of any EU initiatives.

Preface

This book is the work of many authors and my greatest thanks must go to the contributors from all over the world who agreed to participate in the first edition of a new publication and who then gave up so much time to produce a set of excellent contributions. This book is by practitioners for practitioners and I am especially grateful to everyone for successfully juggling the demands of busy practices with the requirements of the editor and publisher.

I must also thank so many other people within SJ Berwin & Co who encouraged and supported me in producing this work. Thanks must go first of all to my fellow Environment Group partners Pat Thomas and Michael Rose for initial advice and encouragement and for putting me in touch with several of the contributors. Thanks are also due to Matthew Hudson for his encouragement from the Corporate Finance Department. My assistants Stuart Wardlaw, Andrea Muirhead, Juliette Glubb and John Faulks also provided invaluable help with the editing process over the two-year period which it took to produce the book and Sara Davies undertook sterling work on typing the text and taking expert care of numerous administrative details.

Last, but certainly not least, thanks go to my wife Dr Lynn Myers who accepted the distractions of the book during evenings and weekends for so long. I was fortunate that, as the editor of a prestigious book herself, Lynn appreciated the extent of the task involved and I remain eternally grateful for her support and encouragement throughout the project.

The legal position set out in each chapter is up to date as of mid-1999 when the final version of the contributors' scripts was received by me.

Mark J Brumwell
SJ Berwin & Co
August 1999

CONTENTS

Preface	v
Table of National Statutes	xi
Table of Statutory Instruments	xxi
Table of European and other Legislation	xxiii
Table of Cases	xxv

Chapter 1 Comparative Environmental Laws 1
   Introduction 1
   Outline of law 3
   Transactional issues 8
   Management of issues 11
   Conclusion 13

Chapter 2 The United States of America 15
   Introduction 15
   Outline of US environmental law relevant to mergers and acquisition transactions 20
   Particular environmental issues relevant to transactions 29
   Managing environmental issues in transactions 33
   Conclusion 35

Chapter 3 Germany 37
   Introduction 37
   Outline of environmental law relevant to merger and acquisition transactions 39
   Particular environmental issues relevant to transactions 44
   Managing environmental issues in transactions 49
   Conclusion 54

Chapter 4 The United Kingdom 57
   Introduction 57
   Outline of environmental law relevant to merger and acquisition transactions 59

Contents

Particular environmental issues relevant to transactions	68
Managing environmental issues in transactions	73
Conclusion	77

Chapter 5 The Netherlands — 79
- Introduction — 79
- Outline of environmental law relevant to merger and acquisition transactions — 81
- Particular environmental issues relevant to transactions — 93
- Managing environmental issues in transactions — 98
- Conclusion — 103

Chapter 6 Australia — 105
- Introduction — 105
- Outline of environmental law relevant to merger and acquisition transactions — 110
- Particular environmental issues relevant to transactions — 123
- Managing environmental issues in transactions — 128
- Conclusion — 134

Chapter 7 Belgium — 137
- Introduction — 137
- Outline of environmental law relevant to merger and acquisition transactions — 138
- Particular environmental issues relevant to transactions — 148
- Managing environmental issues in transactions — 156
- Conclusion — 159

Chapter 8 Sweden — 161
- Introduction — 161
- Outline of environmental law relevant to merger and acquisition transactions — 164
- Particular environmental issues relevant to transactions — 172
- Managing environmental issues in transactions — 178
- Conclusion — 181

Chapter 9 Spain — 183
- Introduction — 183
- Outline of environmental law relevant to merger and acquisition transactions — 186
- Particular environmental issues relevant to transactions — 198
- Managing environmental issues in transactions — 202
- Conclusion — 205

Chapter 10 Austria — 207
- Introduction — 207
- Outline of environmental law relevant to merger and acquisition transactions — 209
- Particular environmental issues relevant to transactions — 220
- Managing environmental issues in transactions — 223
- Conclusion — 229

Contents

Chapter 11 Switzerland — 231
  Introduction — 231
  Outline of environmental law relevant to merger and acquisition
    transactions — 234
  Particular environmental issues relevant to transactions — 243
  Managing environmental issues in transactions — 245
  Conclusion — 249

Chapter 12 France — 251
  Introduction — 251
  Outline of environmental law relevant to merger and acquisition
    transactions — 256
  Particular environmental issues relevant to transactions — 264
  Managing environmental issues in transactions — 266
  Conclusion — 268

Chapter 13 Portugal — 269
  Introduction — 269
  Outline of environmental law relevant to merger and acquisition
    transactions — 270
  Particular environmental issues relevant to transactions — 278
  Managing environmental issues in transactions — 282
  Conclusion — 282

Chapter 14 Greece — 283
  Introduction — 283
  Outline of environmental law relevant to merger and acquisition
    transactions — 286
  Particular environmental issues relevant to transactions — 297
  Managing environmental issues in transactions — 303
  Conclusion — 305

Chapter 15 Israel — 307
  Introduction — 307
  Outline of environmental law relevant to transactions — 311
  Particular environmental issues relevant to transactions — 323
  Managing environmental issues in transactions — 328
  Conclusion — 330

Chapter 16 Norway — 331
  Introduction — 331
  Outline of environmental law relevant to merger and acquisition
    transactions — 334
  Particular environmental issues relevant to transactions — 339
  Managing environmental issues in transactions — 347
  Conclusion — 350

Contact Details — 351
Index — 357

TABLE OF NATIONAL STATUTES

References in this Table are to Chapter and paragraph. The Chapter number is in **bold** type followed by the paragraph number within that Chapter.

PARA

AUSTRALIA
Airports Act 1996 .... **6** 2.5, 3.9
Commonwealth of Australia Constitution
   Act 1990
   s 9 .... **6** 1.2
   51 .... **6** 1.2
     (xxix) **6** 1.3.1
   52 .... **6** 1.2
   75, 76 .... **6** 1.2
   90, 109 .... **6** 1.2
Company Law Review Act 1998
   s 299 (1) (f) **6** 4.5
Environment Protection and Biodiversity
   Conservation Act 1999 .... **6** 1.3.1,
                                1.3.5, 2.2.2, 5.1
Environment Protection (Impact of
   Proposals) Act 1974 .... **6** 2.2.2
Environment Protection (Impact of
   Proposals) Administrative Procedures
   Act 1987
   s 3.1.2 .... **6** 2.2.2
Foreign Acquisitions and Take-overs Act
   1975 .... **1** 3.2;
                                     6 2.2.1
Income Tax Assessment Act 1935
   s 82BI **6** 3.8
   82BM (2) **6** 3.8
Trade Practices Act 1974
   s 52, 59 .... **6** 4.3

New South Wales
Carbon Rights Legislation Amendment
   Act 1998 .... **6** 3.7
Clean Air Act 1961 .... **6** 2.3.1
Clean Waters Act 1990 .... **6** 2.3.1

PARA

Contaminated Land Management Act
   1997 .... **6** 3.4, 3.5
   s 5, 12, 17..................... **6** 2.4.1
   23, 36, 60 .... **6** 2.4.1
Dangerous Goods Act 1975 .... **6** 2.4.6
Environmental Planning and Assessment
   Act 1979 .... **6** 2.4.9
Environmentally Hazardous Chemicals
   Act 1985 .... **6** 2.4.6
Land and Environmental Court Act 1979: **6** 1.2
Mining Act 1992 .... **6** 2.5
Noise Control Act 1975 .... **6** 2.3.1
Pollution Control (Load Based Licensing)
   Act 1997 .... **6** 3.7
Protection of the Environment Admin-
   istration Act 1991 .... **6** 1.3.2
Protection of the Environment Operations
   Act 1997 .... **6** 1.3.2, 2.3.2, 2.4.2,
                              2.4.4, 2.4.5
   s 55 .... **6** 3.6
   116 .... **6** 2.3.1
   118 .... **6** 2.3.1, 3.4
   119–146 .... **6** 2.3.1
Road and Rail Transport (Dangerous
   Goods) Act 1997 .... **6** 2.4.6
Waste Minimisation and Management Act
   1995 .... **6** 2.4.5

Queensland
Carriage of Dangerous Goods by Road
   Act 1984 .... **6** 2.4.6
Environmental Protection Act 1994 .... **6** 1.3.2,
                              2.4.2, 2.4.5
   s 5A **6** 2.3.2
   15–17 .... **6** 2.3.1

Table of National Statutes

	PARA
Environmental Protection Act 1994 – contd	
s 18	**6** 3.7
39–41	**6** 2.3.2
44 (c)	**6** 2.3.2
47 (4)	**6** 2.3.2
48 (4)	**6** 2.3.2
55–58	**6** 3.6
63	**6** 2.3.2
80	**6** 4.5
81	**6** 3.7, 4.5
82–100	**6** 4.5
118J (5)	**6** 3.5
118v (3)	**6** 3.5
120	**6** 2.3.1, 2.4.1
122, 123	**6** 2.3.1
Sch 4	**6** 3.7
Explosives Act 1952	**6** 2.4.6
Integrated Planning Act 1997	**6** 1.2, 2.4.9
Mineral Resources Act 1989	**6** 2.5
Road Transport Reform (Dangerous Goods) Act 1995	**6** 2.4.6

South Australia

Dangerous Substances Act 1979	**6** 2.4.6
Development Act 1993	**6** 2.4.9
Environment Protection Act 1993	**6** 1.3.2, 2.3.2, 2.4.1, 2.4.2
s 3 (1)	**6** 3.5
35	**6** 2.4.9
36	**6** 2.3.2
44	**6** 4.5
79–84	**6** 2.3.1
93, 99, 100	**6** 2.3.1
Sch 1	**6** 2.3.2
Environment Resources and Development Court Act 1993	**6** 1.2
Mines Works and Inspections Act 1929	**6** 2.5

Tasmania

Environmental Management and Pollution Control Act 1994	**6** 2.3.1
s 38	**6** 3.7

Victoria

Dangerous Goods Act 1985	**6** 2.4.6
Environment Protection Act 1970	**6** 1.3.2
s 4	**6** 2.4.1
(3) (c)	**6** 3.5
13 (1)	**6** 2.3.1
19A	**6** 2.3.2, 2.4.9
20	**6** 2.3.2
25	**6** 3.6
62A	**6** 2.3.1, 2.4.1
64A, 66B	**6** 2.3.1
Health Act 1958	**6** 2.3.1
Local Government Act 1989	**6** 2.3.1
Mineral and Resources Development Act 1990	**6** 2.5
Planning and Environment Act 1987	**6** 2.4.9
Water Act 1989	**6** 2.3.1, 2.4.2

Western Australia

Environmental Protection Act 1986	**6** 2.3.1

AUSTRIA

Administrative Offences Code (*Verwaltungsstrafgesetz*)	
s 9	**10** 3.3
Air Pollution Law for Boiler Facilities (*Luftreinhaltegesetz für Kesselanlagen*)	**10** 2.5.3
Chemicals Law (*Chemikaliengesetz*)	**10** 2.8
Civil Code (*Allgemeines Bürgerliches Gesetzbuch*)	**10** 2.3.4, 2.9, 3.1.1, 3.1.2
s 1409	**10** 3.2.1, 3.2.2
Commercial Code (*Handelsgesetzbuch*)	
s 25	**10** 3.2.2
Criminal Code (*Strafgesetzbuch*)	**10** 2.2.2
Environmental Impact Assessment Law 1993 (*Umweltverträglichkeitsprüfungsgesetz*)	**10** 2.11
Fertilisers Law (*Dünghemittelgesetz*)	**10** 2.10
Fishing Laws (*Fischereigesetze*)	**10** 2.10
Forest Law (*Forstgesetz*)	**10** 2.5.5, 2.10, 3.1.1
Hazardous Substances Act 1983	**10** 2.6
Hazardous Waste Law 1990	**10** 2.3.2, 2.6, 3.1.1
Hunting Laws (*Jagdgesetze*)	**10** 2.10
Impact of Air Emissions Law 1997 (*Immissionsschutzgesetz-Luft*)	**10** 2.5.2
Laws on the Preservation of Natural Beauty (*Naturschutzgesetze*)	**10** 2.10
Mining Law (*Berggesetz*)	**10** 2.5.5, 2.10
Old Waste Sites Act	**10** 2.3.2, 2.3.4, 3.1.1, 4.1.2
Ozone Law 1992 (*Ozongesetz*)	**10** 2.5.4
Plant Protective Agents Law (*Pflanzenschutzmittelgesetz*)	**10** 2.10
Trade Code (*Gewerbeordnung*)	**10** 1.3, 2.1, 2.3.2, 2.5.1, 2.5.5, 3.1.1, 4.4
Waste Management Act	**10** 2.3.3
s 18	
para 3	**10** 2.6
32	**10** 2.6
Water Law (*Wasserrechtsgesetz*)	**10** 2.3.2, 2.3.4, 2.4, 3.5
s 31, 138	**10** 2.3.3

BELGIUM

Civil Code	
art 544	**7** 2.3.2, 3.2.1, 3.2.4
1382–1384	**7** 2.3.2, 3.2.1, 3.2.4
Federal Statute on Toxic Waste 1974	**1** 2.6
art 7	**7** 2.3.2, 3.2.1
Federal Statute (26 March 1971)	**7** 2.3.3
Federal Statute (12 July 1985)	**7** 2.2
Federal Statute (21 January 1987)	**7** 2.2
Federal Statute (12 January 1993)	**7** 3.2.3
Federal Statute (15 April 1994)	**7** 2.2

Table of National Statutes

	PARA
Brussels Metropolitan Region	
Ordinance of the Brussels Metropolitan Council (5 June 1997)	7 2.5.1
Ordinance on Town Planning (29 August 1991)	7 2.5.3
Statute on the Protection of Surface Water against Pollution 1971	7 2.5.3
Flemish Region	
Implementing Decree for the Regional Statute on the Environmental Permit 1991 (*Vlarem I*)	7 2.3.1, 2.3.3
art 42	7 3.3.2
Implementing Decree for the Regional Statute on the Environmental Permit 1995 (*Vlarem II*)	7 2.3.1, 2.3.3
Regional Statute (19 April 1995)	7 2.3.3
Regional Statute on Environmental Care within Companies 1995	7 3.2.4
Regional Statute on the Environmental Permit 1985	7 2.3.1
Regional Statute on Groundwater Management 1984	7 2.3.3
Regional Statute on Planning 1996	7 2.3.3
Regional Statute on Soil Clean-Up 1995	1 2.2, 3.1; 7 2.3.2, 3.3.1, 4.2, 4.5, 5
Regional Statute on Waste Prevention and Management 1981	7 2.3.3
Regional Statute on Zoning 1996	7 2.3.3
Regional Statute on Zoning 1999	7 2.3.3
Walloon Region	
Regional Statute (27 November 1997)	7 2.4.3
Regional Statute on the Protection and Exploitation of Groundwater and Drinking Water 1990	7 2.4.3
Regional Statute on the Protection of Surface Waters Against Pollution 1985	7 2.4.3
Regional Statute on Waste 1996	7 2.4.3
Regional Statute Regulating Access to Environmental Information 1991	7 2.4.3
Walloon Zoning Code 1984	7 2.4.3
ENGLAND AND WALES	
Alkali etc Works Regulation Act 1906	1 1.1, 2.5
Ancient Monuments and Archaeological Areas Act 1979	4 2.7
Environment Act 1995	1 2.2; 4 2.1, 2.2, 3.1, 3.5, 4.2, 5
Environmental Protection Act 1990	4 2.1, 3.5
Pt I (ss 1–28)	4 2.4, 2.5
Pt II (ss 29–78)	1 2.6, 4.1; 4 2.6
Pt III (ss 79–85)	4 2.1
s 7 (4)	4 2.4
9 (2)	4 3.6
13, 14, 23	4 2.4
33, 34	4 2.6
40, 74	4 3.6
75	4 2.6
78A (2)	4 2.1

	PARA
Environmental Protection Act 1990 – *contd*	
s 78F, 78M	4 2.1
79	4 2.1, 2.9
80, 82	4 2.9
Sch 2B	4 2.6
European Communities Act 1972	4 1.1
Health and Safety at Work etc Act 1974	4 2.8
Planning (Hazardous Substances) Act 1990	4 2.7, 2.8
Planning (Listed Buildings and Conservation Areas) Act 1990	4 2.7
Pollution Prevention and Control Act 1999	4 2.4
Radioactive Substances Act 1993	
s 6, 13, 14	4 2.8
Town and Country Planning Act 1947	4 2.7
Town and Country Planning Act 1990	
s 55, 172, 183	4 2.7
Water Industry Act 1991	1 2.4
Water Resources Act 1991	
s 24	4 2.3
85, 88	4 2.2
104	4 2.2
161A–161D	4 2.2
Sch 10	4 2.3
FRANCE	
Air Law (1996)	12 2.2, 2.2.1
art 12, 13, 21	12 2.2.5
Barrier Law (2 February 1995)	12 2.1.3, 2.2
Civil Code	
art 1134	12 2.1.2
1382	12 2.1.1, 3.3
1383	12 3.3
1384	12 3.2, 3.3
Classified Installations Law (1976)	1 2.2, 2.4; 12 2.2, 2.2.7, 2.2.9, 3.2, 3.3, 3.6
art 18–20	12 2.2.1
Decree (2 February 1971)	12 1.1.3
Decree (19 August 1977)	12 2.2.6
Decree (12 October 1977)	
art 2	12 2.1.3
Decree (21 November 1989)	12 2.2.6
Decree (7 December 1990)	12 1.1.3
Decree (1 April 1992)	12 2.2.6
Decree (25 February 1993)	12 2.1.3
Decree (13 July 1994)	12 2.2.6
Decree (18 April 1995)	12 2.2.9
Decree (15 May 1997)	12 2.2.8
Decree on Insalubrious, Awkward or Hazardous Facilities 1810	1 2.5; 12 1.1.1
Environment Protection Reinforcement Law (1995)	12 2.2
Integration Order (2 February 1998)	12 2.2.4
Law of 2 August 1961	12 2.2.5
Law of 12 December 1964	
art L.20, L.21	12 2.2.2
Law of 30 December 1991	12 2.2.8
art 13	12 1.1.3
Ministerial Order (4 November 1991)	12 1.1.3
Ministerial Order (14 November 1991)	12 2.2.2
Nature Law (10 July 1976)	12 2.1.3, 2.2, 2.2.3

xiii

Table of National Statutes

	PARA
Noise Law (1992)	**12** 2.2, 2.2.9
Public Inquiries Law (1983)	**12** 2.2
Sea Bed Mineral Resources Law (1981)	**12** 2.2
Sea Pollution Laws (1976, 1977, 1983)	**12** 2.2
Waste Law 1975	**12** 2.2, 2.2.1
art 1	**12** 2.2.6
8	**12** 2.2.8
Water Law (1992)	**12** 2.2, 2.2.1, 2.2.2
art 2	**12** 2.2.3

GERMANY

Bavarian Water Act (*Bayrisches Wassergesetz*)	**3** 3.2
Civil Code (*Bürgerliches Gesetzbuch*)	**1** 4.2; **3** 3.1
s 459	**3** 4.2
823, 852	**3** 3.1.1
906	**3** 3.1.1
Criminal Code (*Strafgesetzbuch*)	
s 14	**3** 3.1.3
324–330	**3** 3.1, 3.1.3
Economic Circulation and Waste Disposal Act 1996 (*Kreislaufwirtschaftsund Abfallgesetz*)	**1** 2.6; **3** 2.4
s 24	**3** 2.3
53, 54	**3** 3.4
Environmental Impact Act (*Gesetz über die Umweltverträglichkeitsprüfung – UVPG*)	**3** 2.1
Environmental Liability Act (*Umwelthaftungsgesetz*)	**3** 3.1, 3.5
s 1, 6	**3** 3.1.1
8–10	**3** 3.1.1
Federal Chemicals Act (*Chemikaliengesetz*)	**3** 2.6
Federal Immission Control Act (*Bundesimmissionsschutzgesetz*)	**1** 2.4; **3** 1.2, 2, 3.5
s 5	**3** 2.1
14	**3** 3.1.1
52a, 53	**3** 3.4
Federal Planning Code (*Baugesetzbuch*)	**3** 2.5
Federal Soil Protection Act (*Bundesbodenschutzgesetz*)	**1** 3.1, 3.3; **3** 3.2, 3.3
Federal Waste Act (*Abfallgesetz*)	**3** 2.3, 2.4
Federal Water Act (*Wasserhsushaltsgesetz*)	**1** 4.5; **3** 1.2, 2.2, 2.4
s 19a	**3** 3.5
21a	**3** 3.4
22	**1** 2.3; **3** 3.1.1, 4.5
Fourth Ordinance for the Implementation of the Federal Immission Control Act (*4.BlmSchV-Verordnung über genehmigungsbedürftige Anlagen*)	**3** 2.1
Hazardous Substances Ordinance (*Gefahrstoffverordnung*)	**3** 2.6
Packaging Ordinance (*Verpackungsverordnung*)	**3** 2.3
Reorganisation Act (*Umwandlungsgesetz*)	**1** 3.1; **3** 2.4, 3.3
State Planning Code (*Landesbauordnung*)	**3** 2.5

	PARA
GREECE	
Civil Code	
art 57, 59	**14** 3.1.2
281, 914	**14** 3.1.2
984, 989	**14** 3.1.2
1000, 1003–1005, 1108	**14** 3.1.2
Constitution 1975 (amended 1986)	
art 24	**14** 3.1.2
para 1	**14** 1.1
2	**14** 2.6
28	
para 1	**14** 1.1
43	
para 2, 4	**14** 1.1
44	
para 1	**14** 1.1
Law 360/76	**14** 1.1, 1.2
Law 743/77	**14** 2.3
Law 855/78	**14** 2.3
Law 947/79	**14** 2.6
Law 1032/80	**14** 1.2
Law 1147/81	**14** 2.3
Law 1269/82	**14** 2.3
Law 1337/83	**14** 2.6
Law 1360/83	**14** 2.5
Law 1558/85	**14** 1.2
Law 1577/85	**14** 2.6
Law 1650/86	**14** 1.1, 2.1, 5
art 3–5	**14** 2.10
6	**14** 2.10, 3.2
7, 8	**14** 2.4
9, 10	**14** 2.3
11	**14** 2.2
12	**14** 2.5
13	**14** 3.2
15	**14** 2.7
17	**14** 2.7
18–22	**14** 2.6
23	**14** 2.6, 3.2
24	**14** 2.6
25–27	**14** 1.2
28	**14** 2.3, 2.4, 2.5, 2.7, 2.8, 3.1.1, 3.3
29, 30	**14** 2.3, 2.4, 2.5, 2.7, 2.8, 3.1.1
Law 1733/87	
art 28	**14** 2.9
Law 1739/87	**14** 2.3
Law 2496/97	
art 23	**14** 4.4
Law 2508/97	**14** 2.6
art 30	**14** 3.1.1
Legislative Decree (17 July 1923)	**14** 2.6
Legislative Decree 854/1971	**14** 2.9
Ministerial Act 144/2/11/1987	**14** 2.3
Ministerial Act 77/1980	**14** 2.3
Ministerial Act 98/1987	**14** 2.4
Ministerial Act 99/1987	**14** 2.4
Ministerial Act 25/1988	**14** 2.4
Ministerial Decision 221/1965	**14** 2.2, 2.3
Ministerial Decision 72751/3054/1985	
art 17	**14** 2.5

Table of National Statutes

	PARA
Ministerial Decision 463/1352/1986 art 9	14 2.3
Ministerial Decision 49541/1424/1986	14 2.5
Ministerial Decision 18187/272/1988	14 2.7
Ministerial Decision 26857/533/1988	1 2.3; 14 2.3
Ministerial Decision 69001/1921/1988	14 2.8
Ministerial Decision 69269/5387/1990	14 2.10
Ministerial Decision 8243/1113/1991	14 2.4
Ministerial Decision 55648/2210/1991	14 2.3
Ministerial Decision 11294/1993	14 2.4
Ministerial Decision 11535/1993	14 2.4
Ministerial Decision 58751/2370/1993	14 2.4
Ministerial Decision 90461/2193/1994	14 2.3
Ministerial Decision 69728/824/1996	14 2.5
Ministerial Decision 11481/523/1997	14 2.8
Ministerial Decision 113944/1997	14 2.5
Ministerial Decision 114218/1997	14 2.5
Ministerial Decision 19396/1546/1997	14 2.5
Ministerial Decision 5673/400/1997	14 2.3
Ministerial Decision 16190/1335/1997	14 2.2
Penal Code art 15	14 3.3
23	14 3.1.1
279, 417	14 3.1.2
427, 428	14 3.1.2
Presidential Decree 1180/1981	14 2.10
Presidential Decree 22/1997	14 2.9
Presidential Decree 55/1998	14 2.3

ISRAEL

Aviation Regulations (Noise of Aircraft), 5737–1977	15 2.5.2
Aviation Regulations (Transportation of Hazardous Substances), 5743–1983:	15 2.2.1
Beverage Container Deposit Law, 5757–1999	15 2.1.3
Business Licensing Law, 5728–1968	15 2.2.1, 2.8
s 20–22	15 3.3.1
Business Licensing Regulations (Hazardous Plants), 5753–1993	15 2.2.2
Business Licensing Regulations (Removal of Waste of Hazardous Substances), 5750–1990	15 3.1
Business Licensing Regulations (Removal of Waste of Toxic Substances), 5750–1990	15 2.2.3, 2.8
Business Licensing Regulations (Sanitary Conditions at Petrol Stations), 5729–1969	15 2.4.2
Gaza-Jericho Agreement on Protection of the Environment (4 May 1994)	15 1.2
Hazardous Substances Law, 5753–1993	15 2.2.1, 3.5
Hazardous Substances Regulations (Import and Export of Waste of Hazardous Plants), 5754–1994	15 2.2.4
Hazardous Substances Regulations (Registration of Preparations for the Extermination of Pests Harmful to Man), 5754–1994	15 2.2.5

	PARA
Israel-Jordan Agreement on the Environment (19 July 1994)	15 1.2
Law for the Collection and Removal of Waste for Recycling, 5753–1993	15 2.1.2
s 11	15 3.1
Law for the Preservation of Cleanliness, 5744–1984	15 2.1.1
s 8 (3)	15 2.1.2
21a	15 3.3.3
Law for the Prevention of Disturbances, 5721–1961	15 2.5.2, 2.7, 3.3.1
s 11e	15 3.3.3
Law for the Prevention of Environmental Disturbances (Civil Claims), 5752–1992	15 2.1.1
s 2, 8	15 3.2
Law for the Prevention of Pollution to the Sea from Land Sources, 5748–1988	15 2.4.1
s 6	15 3.3.3
9	15 3.1
11	15 2.8, 3.3.3
Law for the Prevention of Sea Pollution (Dumping of Waste), 5743–1983	
s 9	15 3.1
Law of Criminal Procedure	
s 68	15 3.3.3
Municipalities Ordinance (New Version)	
s 235–242	15 2.5.1
249 (15)	15 2.4.2
255	15 2.4.2
Operation of a Vehicle Motorised by Petrol Order, 5721–1961	15 2.7
Operation of Vehicles Law (Engines and Petrol), 5721–1961	15 2.7
Ordinance for the Prevention of Oil Pollution to Sea Water (New Version), 5740–1980	15 2.4.1, 3.1
Penal Law, 5737–1977	
s 23	15 3.1
63 (a)	15 3.1
72	15 3.1
77 (a)	15 3.1
222	15 2.7
223	15 2.5.2
Pharmacists Regulations (Radioactive Elements and their Products), 5740–1980	15 2.3.1
Planning and Building (Environmental Impact Study) Regulations 1982:	15 2.10.2
Planning and Building Law 1975	15 2.10.1
Planning and Building Law (Reviews of the Effects on the Environment), 5742–1982	15 2.10.1
Planning and Building Regulations (Application for a Permit, its Terms and Fees), 5730–1970	15 2.3.2
Preservation of Cleanliness Law, 5744–1984	
s 14	15 3.1
15	15 3.1

XV

Table of National Statutes

	PARA
Protection of Flora Regulations (Arrangement for Import and Sale of Chemical Preparations), 5754–1994:	**15** 2.2.5
Public Health Ordinance 1940	**15** 3.1
s 53	**15** 2.5.2
Public Health Regulations (Determination of Standards for Sewage Water), 5752–1992	**15** 2.4.2
Public Health Regulations (Emission of Pollution from Vehicles), 5740–1980:	**15** 2.7
Public Health Regulations (Mineral Water and Spring Water), 5746–1986 s 221	**15** 2.4.2
Public Health Regulations (The Sanitary Quality of Drinking Water), 5734–1974	**15** 2.4.2
Regional Councils Order s 63 (c)	**15** 2.5.1
Regulations for the Preservation of Cleanliness (Levy for the Preservation of Cleanliness), 5747–1987:	**15** 2.1.3
Regulations for the Prevention of Disturbances (Emission of Molecular Substances into the Air), 5732–1972	**15** 2.7
Regulations for the Prevention of Disturbances (Pollution of the Air by Motor Vehicles), 5723–1963	**15** 2.7
Regulations for the Prevention of Disturbances (Quality of the Air), 5752–1992	**15** 2.7
Regulations for the Prevention of Disturbances (Unreasonable Noise from Building Equipment), 5739–1979	**15** 2.5.2
Regulations for the Prevention of Oil-Pollution of the Sea (Levy for the Preservation of Cleanliness), 5747–1987	**15** 2.11.2
Regulations for the Prevention of Oil Pollution to Sea Water (Implementation of the Treaty, 1987	**15** 2.4.1
Regulations for the Prevention of Pollution to the Sea from Land Sources, 5750–1990	**15** 2.4.1
Regulations for the Prevention of Sea Pollution (Dumping of Waste), 5744–1984	**15** 2.4.1
Standard Byelaw for Local Authorities (Discharge of Industrial Sewage into Sewerage Water), 5741–1981	**15** 2.4.2
Telecommunications Regulations (Standards and Specifications for Cable Networks), 5747–1987	**15** 2.3.2
Torts Ordinance (New Version) s 44, 45	**15** 2.5.1
48	**15** 2.6
71, 74	**15** 3.2
Traffic Regulations, 5721–1961	**15** 2.7
Transportation Services Law, 5737–1977	**15** 2.2.1
Water Law, 5719–1959	**15** 1.3.6, 3.3.1
s 20 (22), (24)	**15** 3.1
20b	**15** 2.4.2

	PARA
Water Regulations (Prevention of Pollution to Water) (Fumigating in the Proximity of Water Sources), 5751–1991	**15** 2.4.2
Water Regulations (Prevention of Pollution of Water) (Reduction of the Use of Salts in the Refreshing Process), 5754–1994	**15** 2.4.2
Water Regulations (Prohibition on Hard Detergents), 5734–1974	**15** 2.4.2

NETHERLANDS

	PARA
Air Pollution Act 1970 (*Wet inzake de luchtverontreiniging*) art 13	**5** 2.3.2
Chemical Substances Act 1985 (*Wet milieugevaarlijke stoffen*) art 1	
para 1	**5** 2.3.5
2, 3	**5** 2.3.5
24	
para 1, 2	**5** 2.3.5
26, 32	**5** 2.3.5
Chemical Waste Substances Act (*Wet chemische afvalstoffen*)	**5** 2.3.1
Civil Code (1992)	**5** 1.1, 1.2
art 6:175	
para 1, 6	**5** 2.3.5
6:176–6:178	**5** 2.3.5, 3.3.1
7:17	**5** 4.1, 4.2
8.6.4, 8.11.4	**5** 2.3.5, 3.3.1
8.14.1, 8.19.4	**5** 2.3.5, 3.3.1
Environmental Control Act 1979 (*Wet milieubeheer*)	**1** 2.7; **5** 2.3.1
art 8.2	**5** 2.3.1
8.20	
para 1, 2	**5** 3.6
8.28-8.34	**5** 2.2.2
8.36	**5** 2.3.1
10.2, 10.5A	**5** 3.3.3
10.20, 10.31	**5** 3.3.3
10.35, 10.44a	**5** 3.3.3
18.4–18.18	**5** 3.3.3
General Act on Administrative Law 1992 (*Algemene wet bestuursrecht*)	**5** 2.3.1
Ground Water Act 1981 (*Grondwater wet*)	**5** 2.2.2
art 14	
para 3	**5** 2.2.2
14a, 15	**5** 2.2.2
34–42	**5** 2.3.5
Housing Act 1991(*Woningwet*) art 43	**5** 2.3.4
Interim Soil Clean-Up Act 1982 (*Interimwet bodemsanering*)	**5** 2.1.2
art 21	**5** 2.1.1, 2.1.2
Mining Act 1810	**5** 2.3.5
Noise Control Act 1979 (*Wet geluidhinder*)	**5** 2.3.6
Nuclear Accident Liability Act 1979	**5** 2.3.5
Nuclear Energy Act 1963	**5** 2.3.5
Nuisance Act (*Hinderwet*)	**5** 2.3.1

Table of National Statutes

Oil Tanker Liability Act 1975 (*Wet aansprakelijkheid olietankschepen*)
art 3
    para 2 .... **5** 2.3.5
Planning Act 1962 (*Wet op de ruimtelijke ordening*) **5** 2.3.4
Soil Protection Act 1987 (*Wet bodemsanering*) **1** 2.2; **5** 2.1.2, 5.2
art 6–11 .... **5** 2.1.2
    13 .... **5** 2.1.2
    27–29 .... **5** 2.1.2
    37 .... **5** 2.1.2
    39 .... **5** 2.1.2
    43 .... **5** 2.1.2
    46 .... **5** 2.1.2, 2.2.1
    63 (k) **5** 2.2.1
    75 .... **5** 2.2.1, 3.2
    para 6 .... **5** 2.1.2, 3.3.2
Surface Water Contamination Act 1969 (*Wet verontreiniging oppervlaktewateren*) **5** 2.2.1
art 1
    para 1, 2 .... **5** 2.2.2
    7b–7d **5** 2.2.2
    17 .... **5** 2.2.2
Waste Substances Act (*Afvalstoffenwet*) . **5** 2.3.1

NORWAY
Maritime Act, 24 June 1994, no 39 (*Sjøloven*) **16** 1.3.5, 2.2.2
Neighbour Act, 16 June 1961, no 15 (*Granneloven*) **16** 1.3.3, 2.2.8, 3.2.10
s 2 .... **16** 3.1.2
Petroleum Act, 29 June 1996, no 72 (*Petroleumsloven*) **16** 1.3.4, 2.2.2, 3.2.10
Planning and Building Act, 14 June 1985, no 77 (*Plan-og bygningsloven*) **16** 1.3.2
Pollution Control Act, 13 March 1981, no 6 (*Lov om vern mot forurensning og om avfall*) **16** 1.3.1, 2.1.1, 2.1.2, 2.1.3, 2.1.5, 2.1.6, 2.2.1, 2.2.4, 2.2.7, 3.1, 3.1.2, 3.2.1, 3.2.4, 3.2.8, 3.2.9, 3.3, 4.6
s 7 .... **16** 3.2.5, 4.2
  11 .... **16** 3.4
  17 .... **16** 3.5.2
  18 .... **16** 3.4
  55 .... **16** 3.1.3, 3.2.3, 3.2.5
  74, 75 .... **16** 2.3
  76 .... **16** 2.3, 3.2.5
Tort Act
s 2–1 .... **16** 3.2.10

PORTUGAL
Basic Law on the Environment 11/87 (*Lei de Bases do Ambiente*) **13** 1.1, 2.1, 2.4, 3
art 41 .... **13** 3.1
    42 .... **13** 3.3
Basic Law on Soils 794/76 (*Lei de Solos*): **13** 2.1.1

Basic Law on Water 74/90 (*Lei das Aguas*): **13** 2.2, 2.3
Civil Code **13** 2.1, 3.6
  art 483 .... **13** 3.1
Criminal Code **13** 2.1, 3.2, 3.6
  art 272 .... **13** 3.2.1
    273 .... **13** 3.2.2
    275 .... **13** 3.2.3
    278 .... **13** 3.2.4
    279 .... **13** 3.2.5
    280 .... **13** 3.2.6
    281 .... **13** 3.2.7
    282 .... **13** 3.2.8
Decree-Law 38.382 .... **13** 2.7
Decree-Law 13/71 .... **13** 2.7
Decree-Law 90/71 .... **13** 2.2
Decree-Law 468/71 .... **13** 2.1.1
Decree-Law 343/75 .... **13** 2.1.1
Decree-Law 271/84 .... **13** 2.9
Decree-Law 488/85 .... **13** 2.6
Decree-Law 28/87 .... **13** 2.10
Decree-Law 251/87 .... **13** 2.9
Decree-Law 280-A/87 .... **13** 2.8
Decree-Law 138/88 .... **13** 2.10
Decree-Law 176-A/88 .... **13** 2.7
Decree-Law 221/88 .... **13** 2.8
Decree-Law 292/89 .... **13** 2.9
Decree-Law 348/89 .... **13** 2.10
Decree-Law 8/90 .... **13** 2.10
Decree-Law 47/90 .... **13** 2.8
Decree-Law 69/90 .... **13** 2.7
Decree-Law 90/90 .... **13** 2.1.2
Decree-Law 121/90 .... **13** 2.10
Decree-Law 186/90 .... **13** 2.7, 2.10
Decree-Law 352/90 .... **13** 2.5
Decree-Law 88/91 .... **13** 2.8
Decree-Law 109/91 .... **13** 2.7
Decree-Law 445/91 .... **13** 2.7
Decree-Law 204/93 .... **13** 2.8
Decree-Law 296/95 .... **13** 2.6
Decree-Law 322/95 .... **13** 2.10
Decree-Law 153/96 .... **13** 2.10
Decree-Law 239/97 .... **13** 2.6
Decree-Law 278/97 .... **13** 2.7, 2.10
Decree-Law 236/98 .... **13** 2.2
Government Directive 624/90 .... **13** 2.3
Government Directive 879/90 .... **13** 2.9
Government Directive 286/93 .... **13** 2.5
Government Directive 53/94 .... **13** 2.5
Government Directive 77/96 .... **13** 2.9
Government Directive 125/97 .... **13** 2.5
Government Directive 399/97 .... **13** 2.5
Regulatory Decree 55/81 .... **13** 2.1.1
Regulatory Decree 10/91 .... **13** 2.7

SPAIN
Air Protection Act 38/1972 .... **9** 2.5
Basque Country Act 3/1998
  art 55–66 .... **9** 2.1
Canary Islands Act 1/1998 .... **9** 2.1
Catalan 13/1990 .... **9** 2.11
Catalan Act 3/1998 .... **9** 2.1

xvii

Table of National Statutes

	PARA		PARA
Catalan Air Protection Act 22/1983	**9** 2.5	Packaging and Waste Act 11/1997	**9** 2.6
Civil Code 1889		Spanish Constitution 1978	**9** 1.1
art 590	**9** 2.11	Waste Act 10/1998	**1** 2.2, 3.5;
1484	**9** 3.2, 4.2		**9** 2.6, 3.2
1490	**9** 3.2	art 3, 9	**9** 2.6
1902, 1908	**9** 2.11	9.4	**9** 3.5
1968	**9** 3.2	11–13	**9** 2.6
Coast Act 22/1988	**9** 2.3	13.4	**9** 3.5
art 57, 58	**9** 2.4.2	21, 22	**9** 2.6, 4.5
91.2	**9** 2.3.2	27.1, 27.4	**9** 2.2
92	**9** 3.2	27.6	**9** 3.4
93	**9** 2.4.2	28	**9** 2.2
(b)	**9** 3.3	32, 33	**9** 2.6
95.1	**9** 2.3.2	35.1	**9** 2.2
97.1 (a)	**9** 2.3.2, 2.4.2	36	**9** 2.6
100.2	**9** 2.3.2	Water Act 29/1985	**9** 2.3
Corporations Act		art 61	**9** 3.5
art 133	**9** 3.3	85, 89	**9** 2.3.1
Criminal Code		92, 95	**9** 2.4.1
art 31	**9** 3.3	108, 110	**9** 2.3.1
325	**9** 2.10		
Decree 2414/1961 (Harmful, Unsanitary, Noxious and Dangerous Activities):	**9** 1.4.2, 2.1	**SWEDEN**	
		Act on Working Environment (SFS1997: 1160)	**8** 2.7
Annex I	**9** 2.1	Environmental Code (SFS1998:808)	**1** 2.4;
Decree 833/1975			**8** 1.2, 5
art 56	**9** 2.5	Ch 2	**8** 2.3, 2.4, 2.7, 2.4.9
61	**9** 3.6	s 1	**8** 2.4.1
72	**9** 2.5	2	**8** 2.4.2
Annex II	**9** 2.5	3	**8** 2.4.3, 2.4.4
Decree 2187/1978 (Planning Disciplinary Regulation)	**9** 2.7	4	**8** 2.4.5
		5	**8** 2.4.6
Decree 2519/1982 (Health Protection Against Ionising Radiation Regulation)		6	**8** 2.4.7
		7	**8** 2.4.8
		8	**8** 3.2
art 59	**9** 2.8	Ch 3	**8** 2.6
Decree 1613/1985	**9** 2.5	Ch 4	**8** 2.6, 2.4.5
Decree 717/1987	**9** 2.5	Ch 5	**8** 2.4.5
Decree 833/1988 (Hazardous Waste Regulation)		Ch 9	
		s 3	**8** 3.5
art 10.1	**9** 2.6	Ch 10	**8** 2.1
Decree 1131/1988	**9** 2.7	Ch 11	**8** 2.3
Decree 258/1989		Ch 14	**8** 2.4.7, 2.7
art 7, 8	**9** 3.6	Ch 15	**8** 2.5
Annex II	**9** 2.4.2	Ch 16	**8** 1.3, 2.4.9
Decree 108/1991	**9** 2.5	s 2	**8** 3.7
Decree 1/1992	**9** 2.7	3	**8** 3.6, 4.4
Decree 1088/1992	**9** 2.5	4	**8** 2.6
Decree 1321/1992	**9** 2.5	Ch 17	
Decree 363/1995 (Hazardous Substances Regulation)	**9** 2.8	s 1	**8** 1.3
		Ch 18–23	**8** 1.3
Decree 484/1995	**9** 3.6	Ch 24	**8** 1.3
Decree 1800/1995	**9** 2.5	s 3	**8** 3.6
Decree 1302/1996 (Environmental Impact Assessment)	**9** 2.7	5	**8** 3.7
		Ch 26	
Decree 952/1997	**9** 2.6	s 20	**8** 4.1
Land Act 6/1998	**9** 2.7	Ch 29	**8** 3.1
Licence of Classified Activities	**1** 2.4	s 6	**8** 3.6
Nuclear Energy Act 25/1964		Ch 30	**8** 2.4.10, 3.1
Ch V	**9** 2.8	Ch 32	**8** 2.2
art 31	**9** 2.8	s 1	**8** 3.3
55	**9** 4.5	Ch 33	**8** 4.5

Table of National Statutes

	PARA
Environmental Protection Act 1969 (SFS1969:387)	**8** 1.2, 2.4, 3.2
Nature Conservancy Act 1964 (SFS1964: 822)	**8** 1.2
Ordinance on Dangerous Waste	**8** 2.5
Ordinance on Environmentally Hazardous Activity and Health Protection s 32	**8** 3.6
Ordinance on Working Environment (SFS1997:1166)	**8** 2.7
Planning and Building Act 1987 (SFS1987:10) Ch 2 s 1	**8** 2.6
Rescue Service Act (SFS1986:1102)	**8** 2.7

SWITZERLAND

	PARA
Civil Code 1907	**11** 2.4, 3.1
art 679	**11** 3.2
684	**11** 3.2
Code of Obligations	**11** 3.1
Federal Act Concerning Administrative Criminal Law 1974 (*Bundesgesetz*)	**11** 3.3
Federal Constitution art 22	**11** 2.7
Federal Law on Protection of Surface and Groundwaters 1991 (*Bundesgesetz über den Schutz der Gewässer Gewässerschutzgesetz*) art 36	**11** 2.4
Federal Law Relating to the Protection of the Environment 1983	**1** 2.2; **11** 1.2, 5
art 1	**11** 2.1.1
s 2	**11** 2.1.2, 2.10
2	**11** 2.1.3
7	**11** 4.3
s 2, 4	**11** 2.1.5
9	**11** 2.10
10	**11** 2.11
11 s 1	**11** 2.1.3
2, 3	**11** 2.1.5
12, 14	**11** 2.1.5
16	**11** 4.4
29d, 29f, 29h	**11** 2.12
31a–31c	**11** 2.6
32a	**11** 2.6
32c	**11** 4.4
para 1	**11** 2.3
32d	**11** 2.3
para 3	**11** 4.4
32e	**11** 2.3
33 s 2	**11** 2.2
34	**11** 2.2
35a, 35b	**11** 2.1.3
39 s 3	**11** 2.1.4
41a	**11** 2.1.4
42	**11** 1.3
43, 43a	**11** 2.1.4

	PARA
Federal Law Relating to the Protection of the Environment 1983 – *contd*	
art 46	**11** 2.3, 4.4
59a	**11** 3.1
60, 61	**11** 3.3
Federal Law Relating to Regional Planning 1979 (*Raumplanungsgesetz*)	**11** 2.2
Federal Zoning Statute 1979 (*Bundesgesetz über die Raumplanung*) art 14	
para 2	**11** 2.7
15	**11** 2.7
27	**11** 2.7
Ordinance on Air Pollution Control 1985 (*Luftreinhalteverordnung*)	**11** 2.5
Ordinance on Contamination of the Soil 1998 (*Verordnung über Belastungen des Bodens*) art 1	
para 1	**11** 2.2
7 para 4b	**11** 2.2
Ordinance on Disaster Prevention 1991 (*Verordnung über den Schutz vor Störfallen*)	**11** 2.11
Ordinance on Environmental Impact Assessments 1988 (*Verordnung über die Umweltverträglichkeitsprüfung*)	**11** 2.10
Ordinance on Noise Abatement 1986 (*Larmschutz Verordnung*)	**11** 2.9
Ordinance on the Restoration of Contaminated Sites 1998 (*Verordung über die Sanierung von belasten Standorton, Altlastenverordnung*)	**11** 2.3
Ordinance on the Return, Taking Back and Disposal of Electrical and Electronic Appliances	**11** 2.6
Ordinance on Wastewater Discharge 1975 (*Verordnung über Wassereinleitungen*)	**11** 2.4
Ordinance relating to Environmentally Hazardous Substances 1986 (*Verordnung über umweltgefährdende Stoffe Stoffverordnung*) art 12, 31	**11** 2.8

UNITED STATES OF AMERICA
Federal Laws

	PARA
Clean Air Act	**2** 1.2, 1.2.1, 2.2.3, 2.2.6, 2.3.1
Clean Air Acts Amendments 1990	**2** 2.2.5, 3.5
Clean Water Act	**2** 1.2, 2.1.6, 2.2.1, 2.3.1
Comprehensive Environmental Response, Compensation and Liability Act	**1** 2.2; **2** 1.6, 2.1.1, 2.6.2, 3.2, 3.6, 3.7, 3.8, 5
Emergency Planning and Community Right-To-Know Act	**2** 2.6.3
Oil Pollution Act	**2** 2.1.5

xix

Table of National Statutes

	PARA
Resource, Conservation and Recovery Act	**2** 2.1.2, 2.1.7, 2.3.1, 2.6.2, 3.8
Safe Drinking Water Act	**2** 2.1.6
Securities Act 1933	**2** 2.6.4
Securities Exchange Act 1934	**2** 2.6.4

State Laws
California

	PARA
Safe Drinking Water and Toxic Enforcement Act 1986	**2** 1.3.5

New Jersey

Industrial Sites Recovery Act	**2** 1.3.1, 2.6.5

TABLE OF STATUTORY INSTRUMENTS

References in this Table are to Chapter and paragraph. The Chapter number is in **bold** type followed by the paragraph number within that Chapter.

	PARA
England and Wales	
Control of Major Accident Hazard Regulations 1984, SI 1984/1902	**4** 2.8
Groundwater Regulations 1998, SI 1998/2746	**1** 2.3
Planning (Hazardous Substances) Regulations 1992, SI 1992/656	**4** 2.7
Producer Responsibility Obligations (Packaging Waste) Regulations 1997, SI 1997/648	**4** 2.6
Town and Country Planning (Environmental Impact Assessment) (England and Wales) Regulations 1999, SI 1999/293	**4** 1.1
Sch 1	**4** 2.7
Sch 2	**4** 2.7

TABLE OF EUROPEAN AND OTHER LEGISLATION

References in this Table are to Chapter and paragraph. The Chapter number is in **bold** type followed by the paragraph number within that Chapter.

	PARA		PARA
PRIMARY LEGISLATION		Council Directive 83/513	**14** 2.3
Agreements, Conventions and Treaties		Council Directive 84/156	**9** 1.3; **14** 2.3
Single European Act 1987		Council Directive 84/360	**15** 2.7
art 130r–130t	**3** 1.2	Council Directive 84/491	**9** 1.3; **14** 2.3
Treaty Establishing the European Community (Rome, 1957)		Council Directive 84/533	**14** 2.8
		Council Directive 84/535	**14** 2.8
art 3 (k)	**3** 1.2	Council Directive 84/536	**14** 2.8
130r–130t	**12** 1.1.2	Council Directive 84/537	**14** 2.8
169	**9** 1.3	Council Directive 84/631	**14** 2.7
		Council Directive 85/203	**14** 2.4
SECONDARY LEGISLATION		Council Directive 85/337	**1** 2.7; **4** 1.1, 2.7;
Directives			**5** 2.3.1; **9** 2.7; **12** 2.1.3;
Council Directive 75/439	**12** 2.2.6		**13** 2.7, 2.10; **14** 2.10;
Council Directive 75/440	**14** 2.3		**15** 2.10.1
Council Directive 75/442 (Waste Framework Directive)	**1** 2.6; **4** 2.6; **14** 2.5	Council Directive 85/406	**14** 2.8
		Council Directive 85/407	**14** 2.8
Council Directive 76/160	**14** 2.3	Council Directive 85/408	**14** 2.8
Council Directive 76/403	**14** 2.5	Council Directive 85/409	**14** 2.8
Council Directive 76/464	**9** 1.3, 2.4.2	Council Directive 85/469	**14** 2.7
Annex	**14** 2.3	Council Directive 85/513	**9** 1.3
Council Directive 78/319	**14** 2.5	Council Directive 86/279	**14** 2.7
Council Directive 78/659	**14** 2.3	Council Directive 86/280	**9** 1.3, 2.4.2
Council Directive 79/831	**5** 2.3.5	Annex II	**14** 2.3
Council Directive 79/869	**14** 2.3	Council Directive 86/662	**14** 2.8
Council Directive 79/923	**14** 2.3	Council Directive 87/101	**12** 2.2.6
Council Directive 80/68	**1** 2.3; **14** 2.3	Council Directive 87/112	**14** 2.7
Council Directive 80/778 (Water Intended for Human Consumption)	**4** 3.3	Council Directive 87/216	**14** 2.7
		Council Directive 87/217	**14** 2.4
Council Directive 80/779	**14** 2.4	Council Directive 88/347	**14** 2.3
Council Directive 82/176	**9** 1.3; **14** 2.3	Council Directive 88/609	**9** 2.5; **13** 2.5;
Council Directive 82/501 (Major Accident Hazards of Certain Industrial Activities)	**4** 2.8; **8** 2.7;		**14** 2.4
		Council Directive 88/610	**13** 2.8
	11 2.11; **14** 2.7	Council Directive 89/369	**9** 2.5; **13** 2.5
Council Directive 82/884	**14** 2.4	Council Directive 89/427	**13** 2.5
		Council Directive 89/429	**9** 2.5

xxiii

Table of European and Other Legislation

	PARA
Council Directive 91/156	**1** 2.6; **14** 2.5
Council Directive 91/271 (Urban Waste Water Treatment)	**4** 3.7; **14** 2.3
Council Directive 91/676	**14** 2.2
art 3, 4	**9** 1.3
Council Directive 91/689	**14** 2.5
Council Directive 92/32	**5** 2.3.5
Council Directive 94/62	**4** 2.6; **9** 2.6; **13** 2.10
Council Directive 96/61	**1** 2.4; **3** 5 **4** 2.4; **9** 3.6
Council Directive 97/11	**1** 2.7

Regulations

Council Regulation 259/93 (Shipment of Waste)	**5** 3.3.3; **16** 2.2.7
Council Regulation 1836/93 (EMAS Regulation)	**10** 4.4; **11** 2.1.4

Other Legislation

Basel Convention 1989 (International Shipment of Hazardous Waste)	**10** 1.1; **11** 2.6
Fund Treaty 1992	**16** 1.3.5
International Convention on Civil Liability for Oil Pollution Damage (Brussels, 1969)	**5** 2.3.5; **15** 2.4.1
International Convention on the Prevention of Marine Pollution from Ships 1973	**14** 2.3
International Convention on the Protection of the Mediterranean Sea Against Pollution 1976	**14** 2.3
International Convention on the Protection of the Mediterranean Sea Against Pollution by Dumping from Ships and Aircraft 1972	**14** 2.3
Kyoto Protocol to the UN Convention on Climate Change	**15** 2.7
Liability Treaty 1992	**16** 1.3.5
Montreal Protocol on Substances that Deplete the Ozone Layer	**10** 1.1; **12** 1.1.2; **15** 1.2, 2.7
Protocol (to the Barcelona Convention) for the Protection of the Mediterranean Sea against Pollution from Land-Based Sources and Activities	**15** 2.4.1
Rio de Janeiro Convention on Biological Diversity	**15** 1.2
United Nations Framework Convention on Climate Change	**15** 1.2
Vienna Convention for the Protection of the Ozone Layer	**15** 1.2

TABLE OF CASES

References in this Table are to Chapter and paragraph. The Chapter number is in **bold** type followed by the paragraph number within that Chapter.

PARA

AUSTRALIA

Burnie Port Authority v General Jones Pty Ltd (1994) 120 ALR 24 .... **6**.2.4.1
EPA v Caltex Refining Co Pty Ltd (1993) 92 LERA 51 .... **6**.3.4
Environment Protection Authority v McMurty (9 March 1995, unreported) **6**.3.4
Environment Protection Authority v White (1996) LGERA 263 .... **6**.3.4
Fletcher v Rylands and Horrocks (1866) LR 1 Exch 265, 30 JP 436, 4 H & C 263, 35 LJ Ex 154, 12 Jur NS 603, 14 LT 523; affd sub nom Rylands v Fletcher LR 3 HL 330, 33 JP 70, 37 LJ Ex 161, 14 WR 799, [1861-73] All ER Rep 1, 19 LT 220 .... **6**.2.4.1
Leatch v National Parks and Wildlife Service and Scholhaven City Council (1993) 81 LGERA 270, NSW Land and Environment Court **6**.2.2.1
Rylands v Fletcher. See Fletcher v Rylands and Horrocks
State Pollution Control Commission v Kelly (1991) 5 ACSR 607 .... **6**.3.5

ISRAEL

Society for the Protection of Nature v National Council for Planning and Building Takidan – Elyon, vol 91 (2), at p 53 .... **15**.2.11

NETHERLANDS

Algemeen Burgerlijk Pensioenfonds, Beleggingsmaatschappij Heerlen BV and BV Galgenwaard v FGH and Breevast, Nederlandse Jurisprudentie 1996, nr. 300 .... **5**.4.1
Bato's Erf v State, Nederlandse Jurisprudentie 1996, nr. 214 .... **5**.3.4
Durlinger c.s. v Laura Bakens, Nederlandse Jurisprudentie 1997, nr. 527 .... **5**.2.1.3
Gravenhage v Bensal and Bohemen, Nederlandse Jurisprudentie 1988, nr. 139 .... **5**.2.1.3
Groningen v Zuidema, Nederlandse Jurisprudentie 1994, nr.290 .... **5**.2.1.3
Luycks v Kroonenberg, Nederlandse Jurisprudentie 1998, nr. 659 .... **5**.2.1.3
Maassluis, Nederlandse Jurisprudentie, Re 1994, nrs. 286 – 289 .... **5**.2.1.3
Mines de Potasse d'Alsace SA v Onroerend Goed Maatsschappij Bier BV, firma Gebr. Strik and Handelskwekerij Jac. Valstar BV, Nedrlandse Jurisprudentie 1989, nr. 743 .... **5**.2.2.2
Sijpesteijn c.s. v Oyens c.s., Nederlandse Jurisprudentie 1997, nr. 527 .... **5**.2.1.3
State v Akzo Resins, Nederlandse Jurisprudentie 1993, nr 644 .... **5**.3.2
State v Holdoh Houtunie, Tijdschrift voor Milieu-aansprakelijkheid 1994-1, p 28 .... **5**.3.4
State v Roco and Rouwenhorst, Nederlandse Jurisprudentie 1996, nr. 215 .... **5**.3.4
State v Van Amersfoort, Nederlandse Jurisprudentie 1991, nr. 462 .... **5**.3.2
Van Wijngaarden v State, Nederlandse Jurisprudentie 1993, nr. 643 .... **5**.3.2, **5**.3.7

Table of Cases

PARA

SPAIN

EC Commission v Spain: C-71/97 [1998] ECR I-5991, ECJ	**9**.1.3
EC Commission v Spain: C-92/96 [1998] ECR I-505, ECJ	**9**.1.3
EC Commission v Spain: C-214/96 [1998] ECR I-7661, ECJ	**9**.1.3
Puigneró, Re (1 February 1998, unreported), Supreme Court	**9**.3.4

UNITED KINGDOM

Cambridge Water Co Ltd v Eastern Counties Leather plc [1994] 2 AC 264, [1994] 1 All ER 53, CA; revsd [1994] 2 AC 264, [1994] 1 All ER 53, [1994] 2 WLR 53, [1994] 1 Lloyd's Rep 261, [1994] 11 LS Gaz R 36, [1994] NLJR 15, 138 Sol Jo LB 24, HL ...	**4**.3.3
Empress Car Co (Abertillery) Ltd v National Rivers Authority [1997] JPL 908, [1997] Env LR 227; affd sub nom Environment Agency (formerly National Rivers Authority) v Empress Car Co (Abertillery) Ltd [1999] 2 AC 22, [1998] 2 WLR 350, sub nom Empress Car Co (Abertillery) Ltd v National Rivers Authority [1998] 1 All ER 481, [1998] 08 LS Gaz R 32, [1998] NLJR 206, [1998] EGCS 16, 142 Sol Jo LB 69, HL	**4**.2.2
Environment Agency (formerly National Rivers Authority) v Empress Car Co (Abertillery) Ltd. See Empress Car Co (Abertillery) Ltd v National Rivers Authority	
Fletcher v Rylands and Horrocks (1865) 3 H & C 774, 34 LJ Ex 177; revsd LR 1 Exch 265, 30 JP 436, 4 H & C 263, 35 LJ Ex 154, 12 Jur NS 603, 14 LT 523; affd sub nom Rylands v Fletcher (1868) LR 3 HL 330, 33 JP 70, 37 LJ Ex 161, 14 WR 799, [1861-73] All ER Rep 1, 19 LT 220	**4**.3.3
Midland Bank Tyres Case unreported	**4**.3.5
National Rivers Authority v Yorkshire Water Services Ltd [1995] 1 AC 444, [1995] 1 All ER 225, [1994] 3 WLR 1202, 159 JP 573, [1995] NLJR 17, HL	**4**.2.2
R v Swale Borough Council and Medway Ports, ex p Royal Society for the Protection of Birds [1991] 1 PLR 6, [1991] JPL 39	**4**.2.7
Rylands v Fletcher. See Fletcher v Rylands and Horrocks	

UNITED STATES OF AMERICA

United States v Best Foods 524 US 51 (1998)	**2**.3.6

Chapter 1

COMPARATIVE ENVIRONMENTAL LAWS

Mark J Brumwell

SJ Berwin & Co

1 INTRODUCTION

1.1 Origins and structure of environmental law

Environmental issues affect a great many areas of business life. The environment is everywhere and the effects of emissions into the environment are many and complex. Reflecting this, a feature of environmental law common to all jurisdictions in this book, is the complexity of its origins and current composition.

The origins of environmental law in most jurisdictions are diverse. The typical pattern is for general legal provisions, whether of a statutory or judicial origin, to be the first having the effect of a body of environmental law, albeit in a generalised way. Subsequently, as environmental issues have become more readily acknowledged and problems have become apparent, more specific provisions have been introduced, overlaid onto the general law.

However, the systems of law in each county have significant structural differences, some having a great deal of centralisation, while others give considerable power to local law makers, so that the overall jurisdictional position is often complex. Typically, this reflects the constitutional position of the country involved and the relative political power of its various components. In the USA, both federal and state provisions are important, in Germany the *Bund*, *Länder* and *Gemeinden* have a role and in the UK, the national Parliament has the primary legislative role although assemblies for Wales and Scotland have recently taken a degree of devolved power. The position in the USA is particularly complex as the different political perspectives of the federal and 52 state administrations has led to both layers of government developing detailed environmental controls. The resulting variety of state mechanisms makes it essential to obtain advice on each state's provisions applying in any transaction, as well as the federal position. The picture is further complicated by certain inter-state provisions, typically dealing with trans-boundary contamination.

In every jurisdiction covered in the book, there is a growing awareness of environmental issues both within business communities and the general public. Some jurisdictions, for example Sweden, Germany and Austria have a long-standing, well-developed system of environmental law with a high degree of co-ordination, and environmental issues have been at the forefront of many legislative and judicial minds for some time. Other jurisdictions such as Portugal and Israel show less interest in implementing a separate, co-ordinated system of law to reflect the holistic nature of environmental issues, although the influence of foreign investment in Portugal is starting to change this. Australia is particularly interesting in that environmental issues have only been the subject of specific legislation within the last 10 years, but this has enabled the government to start with a virtually 'clean sheet' and introduce a modern and effective environmental regulatory system. Much regulation is undertaken at state level and most states are now looking at further co-ordination, moving away from topic-based controls to holistic environmental regulation. In mid-1999, the federal government also passed a consolidating statute, replacing several individual environmental provisions.

The UK forms a middle ground. Its national legislation on environmental issues goes back many years with the Alkali etc Works Regulation Act of 1906 being an early example and several Public Health Acts predating this. Common law on environmental matters has also developed steadily, though relatively unspectacularly, but environmental law was only widely recognised as a separate legal discipline with reform and consolidation of the UK's legislation in the late 1980s and early 1990s. Since then, further developments have dealt with specific aspects of environmental protection, such as contaminated land, and with implementation of a large number of EU provisions.

Although the European Union has had a very significant effect on environmental law in member states, its influence in terms of co-ordinating and unifying law has not been as great as may perhaps be perceived. EU law has tended to tackle issues on a topic-by-topic basis, dealing with specific problems with focused regulations and directives addressing particular issues. For most member states, this has then meant that pre-existing national provisions have been modified to comply with EU requirements and the extensive use of directives rather than regulations for EU environmental law has allowed individual member states, when implementing those directives, to retain national characteristics to the particular issue as an embellishment to the EU requirements. Consequently, the systems of law which actually apply to a given environmental issue in member states are anything but unified.

1.2 Enforcement of environmental law

The way in which environmental issues are actually enforced in practice and the diversity of institutions involved in enforcement also varies. In many jurisdictions, there is a particularly complex web of institutions with a variety of different and sometimes conflicting enforcement powers. A notable example is France, which besides giving overall environmental responsibility to the Ministry of the Environment, also has four general Regional Environmental Departments, a separate Regional Department for Industry, Research and the Environment, 11 specialised agencies (some organised nationally, some regionally) and various other important environmental institutions and advisory bodies. Many jurisdictions have a main regulator, such as the UK's Environment Agency, with more minor controls being dealt with by other regulators, sometimes at a more localised level. The UK divides its more minor enforcement roles principally between local authorities and sewerage undertakers.

The actual standard of enforcement varies widely. For some states, such as Greece and Spain, although a significant number of environmental provisions are in place, the relative lack of priority given to enforcement makes actual day-to-day control of limited effect. For example, in Spain, although a number of provisions exist for directors' liability, there has so far been only one example of a director actually being prosecuted. The Swiss system of regulation and enforcement is different again. The law itself is quite stringent in a number of respects but actual enforcement is characterised by a high degree of co-operation between regulators and business, with voluntary enforcement by agreement being commonplace. In the UK, enforcement is by and large more pragmatic than some other countries, such as the USA, but the Environment Agency frequently exercises pressure for greater and more effective enforcement provisions and larger budgets to go with them.

1.3 Third party and contractual rights

In nearly all jurisdictions, in addition to administrative and public law regulation, the system of private civil law also has a significant influence. Switzerland is a notable exception. In all other jurisdictions, third party citizens and others adversely affected by environmental conditions have the ability to use general civil law and other remedies to take action.

Citizens' constitutional rights have an important role to play in some jurisdictions. In contrast to the UK which has no written constitution, Greece, Austria, Australia and Norway have basic environmental rights and duties enshrined in their constitutions, although the actual influence of constitutional rights again varies widely. For instance, in Greece, economic factors almost always outweigh environmental constitutional arguments, whereas Australia has particularly significant and wide-ranging aspirations in its constitution, including the precautionary principle, intergenerational equity, conservation of biological diversity and ecological integrity, and improved valuation, pricing and incentive mechanisms.

2 OUTLINE OF LAW

2.1 General

Most jurisdictions have a basic system of environmental law covering protection for the elements of soil, water and air. The sophistication of these controls depends upon the perceived importance of environmental issues within the jurisdiction and whether, for example, the country has a strong industrial base with a history of frequent and serious pollution.

2.2 Land contamination

Most jurisdictions now have a specific contaminated land regime, though others rely on general controls or specific controls in other areas which have a subordinate contaminated land element, for example the French Classified Installations Law. Some countries, such as Spain through its Waste Act of 1998, have introduced a contaminated land system which is similar in some respects to that in the UK and other countries. Switzerland also has contamination clean-up provisions, in the Federal Law relating to Protection of the Environment, but these apply only to waste disposal sites, although they incorporate a polluter and owner hierarchy of responsibility similar to many other provisions.

Most focused land contamination regimes rely on the central principal of 'the polluter pays', though there are many detailed differences in the way in which the regimes can also impose liability on innocent parties, such as the person acquiring ownership of a polluted site. This is an area where local advice is crucial.

In the UK, specific contaminated land controls are about to be enforced following statutory provisions introduced, but not yet brought into effect, pursuant to the Environment Act 1995. These place responsibility for pollution, whether current or historic, on the person who 'caused or knowingly permitted' the pollution to occur or, if such a person cannot be found, on the current owner or occupier of the land which has been contaminated.

Of particular importance are the controls applying in the Flemish Region of Belgium which are unique in a number of important respects and can have a very significant effect on the mechanics of a transaction involving land. These are summarised in para 3.1 below. Also of note is the system applying in some states of Australia where liability applies first to the original cause of pollution, then to the owner of the polluted site and, in the third instance, specifically to the mortgagee in possession or another party with vested rights in the property.

The Netherlands also has a particularly well-developed and stringent contaminated land system. The Soil Protection Act provides that for prescribed potentially polluting activities, a soil quality survey should be carried out and the results filed with the regulatory authorities, although the requirement is suspended for companies involved in a prescribed voluntary programme of investigation and clean-up. Receipt of the soil quality survey by The Netherlands regulator can lead to a clean-up requirement. In contrast to the majority of contaminated land instruments which adopt a 'suitable for use' approach or a similar concept, the clean-up standards imposed in The Netherlands are not related to the proposed use of the land but are standards deemed suitable for all end uses. Some limited exceptions to the multi-functional standard apply and regulatory authorities now have some discretion to accept a lower standard of remediation on grounds of efficiency, but the multi-functional approach may well impose higher clean-up standards for contaminated land in The Netherlands than would be imposed for equivalent land in many other jurisdictions.

One aspect of The Netherlands' system which is of some comfort is the limited ways in which an innocent owner or occupier of contaminated land can find themselves liable for remediation. An owner or leaseholder will not be liable if they had no long-term relationship with the polluter when pollution was caused, they were not directly or indirectly involved in the pollution and they did not know and could not reasonably have known of the pollution when acquiring title to the polluted property.

In contrast, the US Comprehensive Environmental Response, Compensation and Liability Act (CERCLA) deserves special mention. The system introduced by this Act, more frequently referred to as Superfund, has been the subject of extensive litigation as the US courts have moved from their original expansive interpretation of the provisions to their recent, more restrictive position. Liability under the Act for land contamination is joint and several and non-fault based. The categories of potentially liable persons are also very wide, encompassing not only the original polluter and the current owner of contaminated land but also persons arranging for the disposal of hazardous substances at a contaminated property and even transporters of hazardous substances to the property. The combined effect of these principles can have apparently inequitable results, with persons having had little practical connection with a contaminated site subsequently fixed with disproportionate liability for remedying its condition.

Some jurisdictions have specific mechanisms applying on the transfer of land, intended to control the transfer of contaminated sites with a view to clean-up being undertaken where necessary. An example is the Flemish Regional Statute on Soil Clean-up (see para 3.1 below).

Although the UK has a land contamination system enshrining many concepts common to other jurisdictions, such as 'the polluter pays' principle and the 'suitable for use' approach, it contains no general obligation to advise the regulatory authorities of known pollution problems with land. However, some other jurisdictions do have such an obligation. Examples include Sweden and Australia (New South Wales and Queensland).

2.3 Water

Most jurisdictions have controls over direct pollution of water and a permit system for discharges governing the content, quality and quantity of output. The scarcity of water resources in a particular country affects how frequently the controls are used.

In general, the principles by which liability is allocated for water pollution are simpler than those for contaminated land. The law is usually designed to deal with immediate rather than gradual pollution incidents where a responsible person is easier to identify. Nevertheless, in the UK, liability for pollution of water resources falls on the person who 'caused or knowingly permitted' polluting material to enter water. A number of uses have illustrated the variety of persons who, without any positive act on their part, may be regarded as having 'caused or knowingly permitted' polluting material to enter water. Examples have included the sewerage system operator whose system, unknown to the operator, carried polluting material into a river or the garage proprietor who maintained oil tanks without locks on the stop cocks, enabling trespassers to release the oil into a watercourse.

EU member states should all have implemented groundwater protection controls under Directive (EEC) 80/68 but actual transposition into national legislation varies. The UK has only just introduced the Groundwater Regulations 1998, some 17 years after the Directive required this. Greece implemented the Directive with Ministerial Decision 26857/533/1988.

Germany is unusual in having specific obligations under its Federal Water Act to make economical use of water. There is also civil liability for substances discharged to water under the Federal Water Act, s 22.

2.4 Integrated pollution control

Despite the increasing acknowledgment of the holistic nature of environmental issues, relatively few jurisdictions have a comprehensive integrated pollution control regime. One of the earliest integrated systems is from Sweden which introduced integrated control in 1969. These early provisions have now been subsumed into a new consolidating Environmental Code which came into force on 1 January 1999 and which incorporates a general precautionary principle into Swedish environmental law as well as requirements to use 'best possible technology' and the 'best possible location' for the facility.

Sweden has perhaps one of the most stringent environmental regimes in the countries studied. Extensive retrospective liability for pollution exists, remaining with the polluter when a business has been sold on. The Swedish Environmental Code includes requirements that collateral be provided for pre-closure clean-up of land, all permits under the Code are now time limited and subject to review on renewal, with regular audits as the operation continues. Regulatory non-compliance may prejudice an operator's ability to obtain renewal of his permit. Environmental sanction charges may be imposed on an operator for non-compliance, even if negligence is not proved and no environmental harm has been caused.

Integrated pollution prevention and control will be introduced into member states of the European Union by Directive (EC) 96/61 which should be implemented in member states by 30 October 1999. For jurisdictions without integrated control, this provision is likely to have a tremendous impact, but even for countries such as the UK and Sweden which have had integrated control for some time, the additional requirements to use 'best available techniques' for raw material and energy consumption will be significant, as will the new post-closure land remediation obligations which introduce concepts different to existing national provisions.

Germany also has an integrated pollution control system under its Federal Immission Control Act (see para 2.5 below for an explanation of the 'immission' concept). This grants one permit for all immissions from a facility, apart from water, extending even to the building control permission, in contrast to the UK, where planning permissions continue to be granted under a different procedure. In the UK, integrated pollution control permits include discharges to rivers and other water bodies but not to drains which continue to require a permit under the Water Industry Act 1991.

Some countries have systems of regulation which apply a general permit requirement to most or a large proportion of polluting activities. Examples include the Spanish Licence of Classified Activities and the French Law of Classified Installations. These should not be confused with integrated pollution control systems. Permits granted under these provisions do not necessarily authorise all significant discharges from a particular installation. The Spanish Licence of Classified Activities in particular is only the first of many permits required for installations with multiple discharges to the environment.

2.5 Atmospheric emissions

Most jurisdictions tackle air pollution by controlling the amount and composition of 'emissions', in other words the substances being released into the air. However, Germany has a different concept by analysing 'immissions', meaning the amount and composition of substances being received by an environmental receptor which may be harmed by those substances. 'Emissions' are only controlled to the extent that they have an unacceptable 'immission' effect.

Air emissions in most jurisdictions are controlled through a permit system for polluting activities, similar to that used for water discharges, controlling the quantity and composition of emissions. Acceptable air quality is sometimes determined by quality standards, although the availability of accepted standards varies from one jurisdiction to another.

Air quality is becoming an increasingly important issue for many countries, as public knowledge of the health effects of air pollution becomes more widespread. In the UK, air quality indices are now regularly incorporated in weather forecasts and media stories on air issues are frequent. Although emissions to air have been controlled under atmospheric pollution control and integrated pollution control permits and their predecessors for many years (the UK's Alkali etc Works Regulation Act 1906 and the French Decree on Insalubrious, Awkward or Hazardous Facilities of 1810 being early examples), the effect of non-industrial sources such as transport is only now starting to be tackled. Some jurisdictions, such as Austria and France, already have powers to prevent private car use when air quality is poor and Austria has a public warning system for excessive ozone levels.

2.6 Waste

It is fair to say that there is no real unified approach to waste management across the jurisdictions covered in the book. There is a great diversity in approach. Each jurisdiction has developed its own laws depending on its individual focus on the waste issues and the particular types of waste produced by each jurisdiction which are considered problematic. However, the European Union is a major force in co-ordinating waste management policy, at least among its member states, although, even the EU has generally focused on specific waste streams when introducing detailed controls, for example packaging waste and electronic waste. The UK, for one, has had to do a great deal of work to modify its pre-existing waste management legislation to conform with the requirements of the Waste Framework Directive (Directive (EEC) 75/442) as amended by Directive (EEC) 91/156. This necessitated the introduction of a much more sophisticated waste management control in the Environmental Protection Act 1990, Pt II.

Recycling and re-use obligations vary between jurisdictions. Most have no overall recycling and re-use obligations applied by law, although many have policy developments in this area. Germany is an exception, having general producer responsibility obligations applying to all waste under the Economic Circulation and Waste Disposal Act 1996. Greece also obliges waste disposers to provide plans for waste reduction, recycling, re-use and recovery including the production of energy from waste.

In some countries, the particular hazards presented by waste have led to strict liability regimes of some stringency. The Belgian Federal Statute on Toxic Waste of 1974 provides that a generator of toxic waste remains liable for it even if he no longer has control over the waste. In contrast, the Spanish and UK waste systems absolve a generator from liability, provided that the waste was passed to a properly authorised person and correct hand-over procedures were observed.

2.7 Land use planning

Controls of land use planning apply in all jurisdictions covered. Generally, the issue is taken seriously in most jurisdictions and the commercial importance of this control has been appreciated for some time, pre-dating the focus on wider environmental provisions.

The UK has probably the most sophisticated and stringent control of land use planning of the various jurisdictions examined, reflecting its particular population pressures on land uses. There are also land use legacies in some jurisdictions. For example, past practice in Belgium has led to industrial installations being located in proximity to sensitive neighbours leading to frequent neighbour relation problems.

Directive (EEC) 85/337 on Environmental Impact Assessments, as amended by Directive (EEC) 97/11 applies in all EU member states and similar assessments are also undertaken in some non-member states. The practical implementation of the provisions, however, varies quite significantly. Some countries, such as the UK, have incorporated the provisions as part of the land use planning system, whereas others treat them as a free-standing requirement. In Austria, the composition of an environmental impact assessment (EIA) is centrally controlled, the assessment being undertaken by individuals chosen by the state authority and all necessary environmental permits for EIA projects then being granted together under one streamlined process. In Australia, the EIA provisions are not an implementation of the EU Directives, but are particularly wide ranging and are often applied to Australian government investments abroad. In The Netherlands, EIAs are dealt with as part of their integrated pollution control system under the Environmental Control Act 1979.

3 TRANSACTIONAL ISSUES

3.1 Acquisition of historical liabilities—contaminated land

As a general principle, historical liabilities will be acquired when purchasing shares in a company, as the shareholding will bring with it all the assets and liabilities, whether historical or present, associated with the legal entity comprised by that company.

Acquisition of assets will not necessarily attract liability for all historical liabilities associated with the asset, although this is increasingly the trend with respect to environmental issues. Some jurisdictions, such as Germany, express this distinction through the concept of the 'universal successor' who acquires liability under the German Federal Soil Protection Act where the 'single successor' does not. A purchaser will be the 'universal successor' if it acquires the entire business of its predecessor and carries it on under another name, if all or almost all the assets of its predecessor are acquired or if the successor is a surviving company after a reorganisation under the Reorganisation Act. This means that all historical liability can be acquired on an asset purchase as well as a share purchase. In the UK, some environmental legislation now places specific liability on successor owners for historical problems with any assets which they buy. For example, both the water pollution and prospective land contamination controls place liability on a person who 'caused or knowingly permitted' pollution or contamination to occur. Judicial interpretation of this phase is so wide that successor owners are likely to be caught in some circumstances. The contaminated land controls also contain direct liability provisions for owners or occupiers of contaminated land where no 'causer or knowing permitter' of pollution can be found. In general, therefore, it is safest in most jurisdictions to assume that historical liabilities will be acquired on an assets purchase as well as a share purchase.

However, detailed local provisions can have a significant effect on the acquisition of historical liabilities and local advice in this area is always wise. One of the most notable sets of provisions are the land contamination controls applying in the Flemish Region of Belgium (the Regional Statute on Soil Clean-up 1995). Particular care needs to be used for any Flemish transaction involving contaminated land. Although pollution occurring before the Statute came into force (1995) requires treatment only if a 'serious threat', this protection does not apply to contamination occurring or continuing after this date. The operator or owner of the contaminated land can be made liable for clean-up unless an 'innocent possessor' within the meaning of the Statute. For any transfer of land occurring after 1 October 1996, a soil certificate must be provided under supervision from OVAM, the local regulator. Failure to obtain a certificate can render a transaction void, although curiously, the provisions do not appear to apply when shares in a company owning a property are transferred, thus making a major difference between share sale and asset sale transactions in the Flemish Region.

Contaminated land in the Netherlands should also be considered particularly carefully due to the stringent clean-up standards applied in many cases (see para 2.2 above).

3.2 Other national issues

Foreign investments in Australia may also require particular care of environmental issues. The Foreign Acquisitions and Takeovers Act 1975 can require environmental issues to be investigated with the federal agency, Environment Australia, being consulted.

Various peculiarities of local provisions should be borne in mind. In Greece, although the general standard of enforcement is low, the court in civil cases may order that publicity is given to the defendant's conduct. This can have ramifications for a company's public image beyond the direct effect of compensation for any losses incurred. Similar provisions apply when large fines for environmental offences are imposed in Portugal.

3.3. The corporate veil

In most cases, traditional principles of corporate law will apply to compartmentalise liability for environmental issues, making the specific company causing pollution responsible alone. However, where environmental issues are concerned, some jurisdictions are more ready to pierce the corporate veil than others. For example, in The Netherlands, a parent company may be liable for environmental problems not only where it has specifically directed a polluting subsidiary to carry out a polluting act, but also where it has become aware of pollution and either failed to direct its subsidiary to stop the pollution or has extracted funds from the polluting subsidiary to frustrate the recovery of damages. In Germany, the new Federal Soil Protection Act, in force from March 1999, also makes provision for the corporate veil to be pierced so that responsibility for contaminated land may lie not only with the legal entity owning the site, but also with its parent company where the two companies are regarded as 'de facto consolidated'.

3.4 Liability of directors and managers

Liability of directors and managers, particularly for legislative non-compliance, is provided for in most jurisdictions. However, the degree to which directors and managers find themselves liable in practice varies. In some jurisdictions, liability can be managed away by a specific process of delegation which will in itself be sufficient to avoid the general directors and managers being liable for environment problems. In Austria, this is often achieved by the appointment of a 'responsible agent' who is then solely responsible for complying with all administrative requirements.

Provisions of general corporate law are of equal application in terms of environmental liability as to other types of liability. In Belgium, a company's shareholders can take action against the directors of the company for losses caused by 'ordinary management faults' and this can cover losses related to environmental problems. This is an additional right specifically given to shareholders over and above their civil rights as citizens. In the Flemish Region, the position of the designated 'environmental co-ordinator' is also important, such person having some liability for environmental problems in addition to the directors and managers of the company.

In a few cases, liability of directors and managers is specifically extended. For example, in Australia, the New South Wales legislation on land contamination provides for personal liability for former directors where a company is wound up to avoid liability for contaminated land.

3.5 Liability of financiers

One of the common elements to nearly all the jurisdictions concerned are the principles which govern financiers' liability. Even the stringent provisions of Swedish

3.5 *Chapter 1*

environmental law do not provide that financiers will acquire liability by virtue only of lending money to polluting companies. However, financiers will generally become liable if they become involved in the management of a polluting company and make decisions or give advice to the company which leads to or is connected in some way to pollution which is then caused. They will also become liable if they enforce security and go into possession of the property, although the French hypothèque system of charges is a notable exception. In contrast to a mortgage, the lender holding such a charge does not actually acquire ownership of the asset concerned even when enforcing their security.

In some countries, application of the general law is modified in favour of financiers when dealing with environmental liabilities. Australian provisions remove or limit a financier's liability for contaminated land when going into possession under a charge. The Spanish Waste Act 1998 provides that a lender taking possession of contaminated land may hold it for a year without attracting any liability under that Act. An unusual exception to this picture is in the USA, where some state provisions can impose liability on financiers even where they have neither taken possession of property, nor become involved in managing the activities of a polluting borrower. However, the US courts are now moving away from imposing CERCLA liability on non-foreclosing lenders.

Despite the difficulty of financiers' acquiring direct liability, environmental problems will still affect their interests in all jurisdictions by reducing the value of the assets against which they have security and by making it difficult for them in practice to enforce security over any assets which have environmental problems, without attracting direct liability on themselves. Consequently, environmental issues are of crucial importance to financiers in all jurisdictions.

3.6   Transfer of permits

In all jurisdictions, there is a basic distinction between the position on a transfer of shares in a company holding permits and the transfer of assets. In the former case, no transfer of permits is required as the identity of the company holding the permits remains unchanged, whereas a specific transfer of permits is necessary in the latter case. No jurisdictions have widespread controls bringing permits to an end or requiring a transfer on any change in control of a company enjoying those permits.

There are no common principles for the process of permit transfer. Even within jurisdictions, the diversity of origin of many environmental controls means that different types of permit have to be transferred in different ways and different principles apply in each case. The ease of transfer therefore depends upon the particular control and circumstances involved in each individual case.

On an asset transfer, this specific point will need attention for each jurisdiction involved but for share transfers, the identity of the company holding the permits remains the same so that, in general, no transfer of the permit or other action is required. There does not appear to be any widespread use of provisions requiring any administrative process to be undertaken for permits where there is only a change of control in the company holding those permits.

3.7   Ongoing compliance requirements

Some environmental controls, such as the UK's integrated pollution control and atmospheric pollution control systems, include an overriding obligation to operate processes in accordance with best available techniques not entailing excessive cost, or a similar concept (for example, Australia uses 'best practice environmental management' and the EU integrated pollution prevention and control system implements 'best available techniques'). As the techniques change, so can the cost of complying with this requirement so that, for example, emission abatement equipment upgrades can be required by regulators without any need for the operational permit itself to change. In the UK, it is therefore important to consider the compliance of a process with the latest and anticipated future guidance notes describing the application of 'best available techniques' to the particular process concerned and there will often be equivalent technical papers in other jurisdictions.

The introduction of economic incentives to encourage regulatory improvements is an increasing trend. In Australia, New South Wales permit charges are now based on the level of pollutants emitted and a permit trading system is to be introduced for water resource use and rights to pollute. Permit trading of nitrogen oxide and sulphur dioxide emission has been in place for some time in the USA and there are moves to introduce other national and international emissions trading systems as a response to the Kyoto Protocol targets to address climate change.

4 MANAGEMENT OF ISSUES

4.1 Assessment of risk

The practice for assessment of risk varies greatly between jurisdictions. This is not necessarily based solely on the intrinsic relative importance of environmental law in each jurisdiction, but also on the generally accepted degree of focus on environmental issues in commercial transactions in a particular jurisdiction. Even if local practice is not to give environmental provisions special attention, it is still worth considering when undertaking transactions in that jurisdiction whether due diligence should be required to a greater degree than the local practice would suggest and establishing whether there are specific risks in this area in a local context. In any event, a company operating in a jurisdiction with relatively lax controls may, as a matter of internal policy, require the undertaking of as full a due diligence investigation as is possible in the circumstances, and certainly greater than local practice would dictate.

Some jurisdictions such as the US have a long history of concentration on environmental issues and treat this as one of the most important aspects of many transactions. Other jurisdictions such as Israel or Portugal tackle environmental issues on a commercial basis relatively rarely.

There is no unified practice for the amount of environmental due diligence undertaken in transactions. However, in most jurisdictions, environmental issues are now acknowledged as of increasing importance in commercial terms and due diligence practice in this area is improving. In some jurisdictions, it is now becoming commonplace for soil, water and ground water physical testing to be undertaken as a matter of routine for any transaction where there is any risk of contamination. Given the stringency of environmental control in Sweden, a soil and groundwater investigation is normally carried out on any significant land transaction and this is also the case in The Netherlands, Switzerland and the USA. In the USA, it is now commonplace for at least a Phase I environmental consultant's report to be provided by the seller. In the UK, each transaction differs but it is becoming gradually more frequent to expect Phase I reports for all industrial properties and a Phase II report where there is an indication of potentially significant contamination liabilities. Some legislative procedures also require this as a matter of course, for example, the Flemish soil protection legislation.

4.1 *Chapter 1*

There are examples of jurisdictions where there is now a clear incentive on the seller of contaminated land to reveal to the buyer all the information it has on this fact, irrespective of any warranty terms which may be included in the sale contract. In Spanish law, the vendor will be liable for any hidden defects in any asset which make it unsuitable for use, reduce its value or would have resulted in the purchaser not buying the asset if he had known of the defects. In the UK, although the general concept of 'the buyer beware' still applies, the new contaminated land regime under Pt II of the Environmental Protection Act 1990 can, in some cases, remove liability for remediation of contaminated land from a seller who passes the land to a buyer who is made aware, expressly or constructively, of its contaminative status. In The Netherlands, there is a civil duty to disclose contamination and in some circumstances, the courts will imply a warranty that land is fit for the purpose for which it was sold.

4.2 Warranty and indemnity terms

In all jurisdictions, warranty and indemnity provisions are dealt with on an ad hoc basis for each transaction. Generally speaking, there is no clearly understood 'basic' set of warranties or principles for indemnities in any jurisdiction. Warranties and indemnities are tailor-made for each transaction depending on the nature of the business involved, the sensitivity of the buyer and seller to commercial issues, the degree to which due diligence in environmental issues has been undertaken, the outcome of any due diligence and any specific environmental provisions applying.

However, in some jurisdictions, the general law will apply warranties into the sale and purchase contract. The German Civil Code, for instance, will imply a warranty of the value of the asset, the absence of defects, fitness for purpose and adequacy of description. These can be modified by specific sale terms.

4.3 Practice of financiers

Financiers adopt a 'hands off' approach for the environmental aspects of most business transactions. Although involved in the initial assessment of the company or asset being financed, financiers are generally content with a basic set of environmental provisions in the funding documentation which does not give them any day-to-day role in management of the assets or companies concerned. The provisions are designed to give funders some security that the value of any security will not be eroded by environmental problems, although some funders are now taking this further and requiring a better level of environmental performance from their investments to comply with ethical lending policies. For lenders who are particularly environmentally sensitive, this can even extend to requiring their borrowers to implement an environmental management system or to submit to the lender a regular report on their environmental performance. Funders are now influencing environmental performance in a number of jurisdictions, often as a response to stakeholder pressure, and raising environmental issues as an important part of their lending policies.

4.4 Environmental management systems

The provision of environmental management systems (EMSs) is far from widespread. They are seen as the exception rather than the norm, even in environmentally sophisticated jurisdictions such as Germany. Pressure to implement EMSs often comes from a company's customers or its financiers as frequently as it results from the company management's own perception of this as a worthwhile exercise.

4.5 Insurance

Insurance is generally not perceived as having a significant role in most jurisdictions. In the USA, there is a history of litigation surrounding the coverage of environmental issues in general insurance policies. As a result of this, most insurance companies have pulled away from environmental coverage, although some jurisdictions, such as in the UK, are now seeing the development of specialised insurance policies specifically to provide cover against environmental risks. In Sweden, insurance provision is required as a condition for obtaining permits under the Environmental Code.

Insurance provision in Germany has been a particular issue in the recent past. In contrast to most other jurisdictions, specific environmental policies to cover strict liability for water pollution under the Federal Water Act have been available since the 1960s. However, the subsequent history of disputes between insurers and insured reduced the popularity of those policies significantly and, since 1992, a new model of environmental insurance policy has been available instead. Although more flexible than the Federal Water Act policies, the cover is fundamentally restricted in a number of ways and premiums are relatively expensive so that its popularity is likely to be limited.

5 CONCLUSION

Although some general principles emerge from our examination of comparative environmental law provisions (for example, financiers' liability, share purchase as opposed to asset purchase liabilities, issues of the corporate veil) there are sufficient detailed differences with each regime covered in this book to make it important to obtain local advice from an environmental specialist for most significant cross border transactions.

Contaminated land is a particularly important issue. The liabilities which can arise are considerable and a large number of jurisdictions have particularly complex regimes. There are a significant number of structural differences between each country's provisions to catch the unwary.

Environmental issues are of increasing importance in most commercial transactions and this trend is likely to continue. The business community is increasingly alive to the environment as a 'hot topic' in terms of stakeholder and financier acceptability as well as the adverse effect on company performance of unexpected environmental liabilities. The environment is a crucial issue in transactions and it is here to stay.

Chapter 2

THE UNITED STATES OF AMERICA

Andrew A Giaccia

Chadbourne & Parke LLP, Washington DC

1 INTRODUCTION

1.1 Overview

Environmental law clearly plays an important role in virtually any type of merger, acquisition and new project development or construction in the US. With one of the most comprehensive environmental regulatory structures in the world, it is quite likely that the relevant industrial operations, real estate holdings or planned development which are the subject of the transaction may need to comply with requirements on at least three regulatory levels (federal, state and local) and may perhaps face requirements from regional regulatory authorities as well. The following chapter will provide an overview of environmental requirements in the US with an emphasis on how they affect, and should be managed in, transactions.

1.2 Federal environmental laws and requirements

The federal government is the source of a considerable body of environmental law which is applicable throughout the US. For example, the centerpieces of US environmental law in the areas of air pollution control and water are the federal Clean Air Act (CAA) and the federal Clean Water Act (CWA) respectively. Each of these laws mandates the US Environmental Protection Agency (EPA) to develop standards of clean air and clean water and to develop requirements for the protection and, as necessary, improvement of air and water quality. Nevertheless, the preferred method of implementation of many of these requirements under both statutes is through EPA-approved state regulatory programmes.

1.2.1 *Approved state programmes*

In essence, the US federal government defines the basic requirements that must be met by particular state programmes and the states, in turn, develop programmes (referred to as state implementation plans under the CAA) which must be approved by the federal EPA. The EPA reviews these programmes to ensure that they meet the minimum requirements that it has specified for the compliance of state programmes and then, upon approval, delegates enforcement authority to the state under the relevant federal law. This pattern is followed to some extent in several other federal environmental laws as well. States are free to impose standards or requirements that are more restrictive than the relevant federal programme, but they cannot receive approval if their plans are less restrictive. As the EPA develops new standards or requirements under these federal laws, the EPA will periodically require that the relevant state implementing authorities and regulations be updated, specifying deadlines within which such updates must be submitted to the EPA for approval.

1.2.2 Non-conforming state plans

Where a state programme is not approved, the EPA may nevertheless allow the state to implement the relevant programme but may retain a greater direct control over implementation decisions, including the issuance of relevant permits and approvals. In addition, a state programme may be approved in part but may have elements that are not approved.

The EPA's ability to become directly involved in permitting decisions is generally quite limited, consisting primarily of a consultative role prior to issuance of the permit. EPA does have much more say over state permitting decisions in partially delegated programmes and usually controls any administrative appeals of state permitting decisions. There are some exceptions to this rule, including under the fairly new federal CAA Operating Permit Programme (also known as the Title V Programme), where the EPA retains the authority to veto the permit decision even though the state programme has been approved.

1.2.3 EPA enforcement jurisdiction

Even in instances where a programme delegation has occurred, however, the EPA does retain enforcement jurisdiction. The EPA's use of such enforcement jurisdiction in a particular state context is often defined by memoranda of understandings negotiated between the EPA and the relevant state. Nevertheless, the EPA may periodically become dissatisfied with the adequacy of state enforcement in a particular area and may then either attempt to place enforcement pressure on the relevant state agency (with the implicit threat of revoking the state's delegated authority in whole or in part) or may directly engage in enforcement action against relevant companies or on an industry-wide basis.

1.2.4 Other federal programmes

Other federal programmes have little or no state delegation. One example is the federal Superfund Programme where the EPA still takes a lead role in the enforcement of clean-up requirements concerning sites sufficiently contaminated to qualify for the federal National Priorities List.

1.3 Consistency between state environmental programmes

Because of the substantial amount of federal involvement in each state environmental programme, there is a considerable degree of consistency between the environmental programmes of various states. Thus, for example, it can be expected that virtually every state programme has air permitting and air pollution control requirements relating to both stationary emission sources and mobile air emission sources, as well as waste water permitting requirements, wetlands regulations, and hazardous and solid waste management programmes. There may also be significant variations between the detail of state programmes as a result of regional or local differences in environmental quality and degradation. Areas with poor air quality, for example, are more likely to have stricter air regulations and are typically obliged to impose stricter standards under the federal CAA. Common differences between state environmental programmes include the following.

1.3.1 State transfer laws

A handful of states have significant transfer statutes that require notification to the state environmental agency when an industrial facility is being sold or transferred. The most well-known transfer law is the New Jersey Industrial Sites Recovery Act, which requires detailed submissions to the New Jersey Department of Environmental Protection (NJDEP) when a transfer or even a closure of a facility is about to occur, and in some instances requires that detailed environmental assessment reports be prepared and submitted for the NJDEP to review. The NJDEP even has the ability to require follow-up investigation and remediation before it will approve the sale. Other states, such as Connecticut and Illinois, have less comprehensive reporting or buyer notification requirements.

1.3.2 Contamination reporting requirements

There is considerable variability in environmental reporting requirements between states. Some states, such as New York, have very little in the way of mandatory reporting requirements, whereas other states, such as Massachusetts and North Carolina may require environmental impairment reporting by both the property owner and by environmental consulting firms. In the case of North Carolina, there is typically a requirement associated with the issue of groundwater well permits that the permitee must disclose to the state the results of the sampling investigation performed pursuant to such permits.

1.3.3 Remediation standards and requirements

There is still considerable variability among state laws concerning the imposition of environmental remediation responsibilities on private parties. Most states have developed 'trigger' levels which, if exceeded, are likely to require some sort of responsive action. States are increasingly embracing risk-based approaches to environmental remediation but few have succeeded in making the application of site-specific risk-based remedial standards a sufficiently predictable proposition to enable parties in a transaction to evaluate adequately the potential cost of remedial actions without extensive and time-consuming governmental input.

1.3.4 Permit procedures

While most states follow certain general outlines concerning the nature of permits to be obtained and the basic process for obtaining permits (application, review, public notice, etc), there can be considerable variability from one state to another on the length of time it takes to obtain basic permits. The level of public participation in the permitting process may also vary greatly, especially with respect to the categories of individuals with the ability to challenge or appeal permitting decisions. This right of

1.3 *Chapter 2*

appeal (known as 'standing') is accorded in some states only to individuals who are directly impacted by a particular project or permitting decision. In other states, such as Connecticut, there are much broader rights of appeal extending to any party with an interest in protection of the environment, health, or natural resources. There are also differences among states and even between various permitting programmes, with respect to permit transfer requirements. In some instances, for example air permits in New York, an existing air permit may not be transferred but must instead be reissued to the new operator.

1.3.5 Enforcement

While enforcement efforts by state agencies are frequently monitored by both the federal EPA and a variety of environmental groups, there can still be considerable differences between states with respect to environmental enforcement. The differences can also be considerable between programmes in the same state. Recently the US EPA, for example, objected to the lack of what the Agency viewed as adequate enforcement by the state of New York Department of Environmental Conservation of the state's CAA compliance programme. These EPA complaints have resulted in a very substantial increase in CAA enforcement actions by the State of New York over the last year.

Many states also recognise a variety of citizens enforcement rights which may not be present elsewhere. For an extreme example, the State of California authorises citizens to enforce industry obligations under the Safe Drinking Water and Toxic Enforcement Act 1986, which entitles successful citizen enforcers to keep 25% of fines and sanctions collected pursuant to such actions.

1.4 Regional law

The vast majority of environmental law and regulation in the US has been developed at the federal and state level. Nevertheless, there are also regional authorities with jurisdiction over environmental issues, especially involving the protection of natural resources. Among such authorities are the following.

1.4.1 River Basin Commissions

A number of the major rivers in the US, such as the Delaware River and the Susquehanna River, have River Basin Commissions created by inter-state compacts. The task of these commissions, among other things, is to regulate the use of waters from certain rivers and their tributaries. Typically, the commissions require that an approval be obtained for any intended use of the waters from the basin and that entities using such waters mitigate the impacts of such use.

1.4.2 Ozone Transport Commission

The 1990 Clean Air Act Amendments established the entire northeastern region of the US from Northern Virginia through Maine as a non-attainment area for ozone pollution. As a result, the northeastern states were required to take a variety of actions to reduce emissions of pollutants that were considered precursors to ozone pollution (specifically volatile organic compound emissions and nitrogen oxide emissions). Because the impacts of such pollution are manifestly inter-state in nature, the northeastern states joined together to form the Ozone Transport Commission

(OTC). It is the work of this commission to ensure that the northeastern states coordinate their efforts to control emissions of ozone precursors. As a consequence of the efforts of the OTC (as well as the EPA and individual states), the northeastern US faces some of the strictest and most expensive air pollution control requirements in the country.

1.4.3 Air quality management districts

In some parts of the country, primarily California, air pollution is regulated by regional authorities with jurisdiction over areas that share common meteorological impacts. These regional air quality management districts promulgate their own regulations and are essentially the air permitting authority for sources within their territory.

1.5 Requirements of local law

The degree of regulation from local governmental authorities can vary considerably depending on the location. For example, the Dade County, Florida environmental agency performs most of the functions associated with state government environmental jurisdiction in other areas of the country, including air and water permitting. In most cases, however, local jurisdictions typically regulate environmental impacts from projects through land use and zoning laws. Often locally issued zoning permits or special use permits (in the case of uses that do not conform to standard zoning requirements) include a review of environmental impacts from the proposed project or development and a series of restrictions and conditions that are intended to mitigate those impacts to the maximum extent possible. Other common examples of local environmental regulation include wetlands protection in which 'buffer zones' are added to jurisdictional wetlands, to restrict development in or impacts to such areas further.

1.6 Judicial sources of environmental law

Judicial rulings play an important role in supplementing both statutory environmental law and the implementing regulations of governmental agencies. One area in which such judicial rulings have played a very important role has been under the federal Superfund law, the Comprehensive Environmental Response, Compensation and Liability Act (CERCLA), in which a substantial body of case law must be considered when determining the nature and scope of potential liability for site contamination. There are noticeable trends in the CERCLA case law as the courts have transitioned from previously more expansive interpretations of CERCLA liability to more narrow interpretations that have developed in recent years. This also means that the scope of CERCLA liability can be different from one court to the next.

Another important area of judicial environmental law arises from common law. One area of common law that has developed especially in the last two decades is 'toxic torts', which generally refers to property damage or injury to human health caused by exposure to hazardous or toxic substances. Toxic tort principles and standards vary from state to state and are created by both the federal and state judicial systems, as courts attempt to impose duties and liabilities on entities which the courts view as responsible to some extent for environmental harm.

A variety of common law principles may be applicable in a particular jurisdiction, including principles of negligence and strict liability. Many states impose absolute

1.6 *Chapter 2*

liability, without regard for fault, on entities engaging in what are considered 'abnormally dangerous activities'. For this reason, basic due diligence, especially for companies with existing operations, requires an assessment of whether any hazardous substances or wastes used, generated or disposed in connection with a company's operations may have harmed individuals by, for example, polluting their drinking water supplies, contaminating their property through airborne contamination or otherwise diminishing the value of the victim's property as a result of potential health risks or remedial costs.

1.7 Other sources of US environmental law

Additional potential sources of environmental duties and requirements include international treaties and conventions to which the US is a signatory or a participant. Examples of such sources of requirements include the International Joint Commission established by the US and Canada by treaty to regulate the impacts of trans-boundary pollution in the Great Lakes region. Since most of the impacts involve airborne and waterborne pollutants emanating from the US, most of the Commission's focus is upon US facilities.

1.8 Structure of environmental regulatory agencies

In general federal and state environmental agencies in the US are divided into regional offices where some autonomy is vested for permitting and enforcement. The US EPA, for example, is divided into nine regions. There can be considerable differences in the approach and attitude of different regional offices of the EPA and varied approaches to the same issues can also be experienced in regional offices within state agencies. The central office of each agency may provide some recourse for companies seeking redress from actions or decisions of the regional offices, but this is typically quite limited.

The offices of most US environmental regulatory agencies are organised according to environmental media (eg air, water, solid and hazardous waste). There are also typically separate administrative groups for permitting and compliance enforcement.

Administrative enforcement is normally handled through attorneys employed by the agency itself. However, judicial actions are usually managed by the State Attorney General or, in the case of the federal government, the federal Department of Justice. Numerous more specialised functions are commonly performed by specific offices or sub-groups, including offices of legislative affairs, toxic substances control, and advisory science. Thus, while routine matters may be managed by a single office or department within a region, more complex issues may require or involve the actions of numerous groups of regional and central office regulators.

2 OUTLINE OF US ENVIRONMENTAL LAW RELEVANT TO MERGER AND ACQUISITION TRANSACTIONS

The laws of the various jurisdictions described above are quite comprehensive. There is essentially no form of emission or release or discharge of any pollutant or control and management of hazardous materials that is not regulated in some way within this corpus of legal requirements. Nevertheless, the following is a brief description of a number of areas in which environmental regulation can be expected.

2.1 Contaminated land, water and groundwater

2.1.1 CERCLA

As discussed in para 1.6 above, the federal CERCLA is widely used to assign liability where property contamination has occurred. Because CERCLA liability is primarily status-based, rather than fault-based, its requirements can be extremely onerous. Under CERCLA, the liable parties include the current owner or operator of the contaminated land, former owners and operators of the same property to the extent that releases of hazardous substances occurred during the period of their ownership or operation, persons who arranged for the disposal of hazardous substances at the property (whether wittingly or unwittingly) and transporters of hazardous substances to the property. Liability to the government under CERCLA is joint and several and without regard to fault. In addition, private parties can also bring claims for contribution and indemnification of costs that they incur or may incur in responding to contaminated conditions (or the threat thereof). A number of states also have CERCLA-type laws. Further discussions of CERCLA liability and its ramifications in transactions appear in paras 3.1–3.2 and 3.7–3.8 below.

2.1.2 Resource Conservation and Recovery Act (RCRA)

The federal RCRA and its state counterparts require permits for the operation of a regulated 'hazardous waste' treatment, storage, or disposal facility. Hazardous wastes are substances that are either produced by specific processes (such as metals degreasing) and waste materials exhibiting certain characteristics (toxicity, corrosivity, flammability, and reactivity). Facilities where hazardous wastes have been disposed of can be required to apply for and obtain a closure permit, which is an extremely onerous process, typically involving elaborate permitting requirements and strict remedial standards, along with long-term groundwater monitoring requirements. Violations of permitting requirements are subject to 'reasonable' penalties up to $25,000 per day, per violation.

RCRA also authorises actions both by the government and private parties where the severity of contamination involving hazardous waste (considering the proximity of potential receptors) indicates that there is an 'imminent and substantial endangerment' of human health or the environment. In such circumstances, any person who has contributed to the hazardous conditions can be required to perform remediation and take other corrective measures. 'Knowing' violations of RCRA are punishable by criminal penalties of up to $50,000 per day of violation and up to two years in prison.

2.1.3 Voluntary remediation and brownfields laws

There is a growing trend in the US toward the recognition of the value of a co-operative approach toward the remediation of contaminated property, especially in areas that have previously been developed for industrial activities. Many states have recognised that the redevelopment of such 'brownfields' is advantageous both to the economy of the state and to the environment, because it encourages the re-use of industrial property rather than the development of new land for industrial purposes. Typically such programmes involve the negotiation of a voluntary agreement (such as in West Virginia, Pennsylvania, or New York) or a self-implementing process in which all of the 'regulatory' work is essentially delegated to environmental professionals who are licensed by the state to perform remedial work and must certify that the work was done correctly and that the property was brought into compliance with applicable requirements (such as in Massachusetts and Connecticut). In each case, these programmes encourage voluntary action based upon the use of risk-based approaches to developing remediation standards, rather than merely applying rigid numerical standards regardless of the lack of any potential impacts to human health or the environment.

To the extent that these programmes are voluntary, the governmental sanctions, if any, will be set forth in the voluntary action agreement with the state, such as penalties for failure to meet contractual deadlines. While sanctions can sometimes include monetary penalties, the most common governmental enforcement action involves taking over the remediation itself.

2.1.4 State groundwater protection laws

In a number of states, such as North Carolina, environmental remediation requirements may be driven by laws establishing standards for groundwater quality and prohibiting releases of contaminants to groundwater. Thus, where groundwater impacts are present, these states use their jurisdiction to require remediation of contaminated conditions, possibly using pre-existing background levels as the relevant standards. These clean-up requirements are typically imposed directly against entities that may have caused the pollution. The use of penalties in such situations is not common, especially when the focus relates to contamination occurring in the past.

2.1.5 The federal Oil Pollution Act

The federal Oil Pollution Act (OPA) prohibits petroleum discharges to waters of the US and establishes standards of responsibility for owners and operators of vessels and onshore facilities from which releases of oil pollution may occur. Owners and operators may be liable under the OPA for both the costs of removing the oil and for damages to natural resources and property (subject to certain liability caps if the responsible party is not guilty of gross negligence or wilful misconduct). The OPA has a number of state counterparts, some of which take even stricter liability approaches. For example, its counterpart under Florida law also imposes liability upon the owner of a petroleum product who merely arranged for a ship to transport the substance, if the owner failed to determine whether the ship operator possessed the financial resources necessary to remediate a spill and was otherwise in compliance with the requirements of the OPA.

2.1.6 Clean Water Act

The federal CWA and its state counterparts authorise the issuance of orders requiring the remediation of spills to federal jurisdictional waters. In addition, under the Safe Drinking Water Act, the EPA has established standards for contaminants in drinking water known as 'maximum contaminant levels'. While such standards have not been established for all substances, they have been used historically not only as a standard for safe drinking water, but also as a default standard for remedial action.

Violations of the CWA are subject to civil penalties of up to $25,000 per day of violation. Certain negligent violations of the CWA are punishable by criminal fines of between $2,500 and $25,000 per day and up to one year in prison, with doubling for repeat offences. Knowing violations can result in criminal fines of between $5,000 and $50,000 per day and up to a year of incarceration, again with doubling for repeat violations. Some violations are also subject to enforcement by private citizens.

2.1.7 Underground storage tanks

There are both federal and state laws relating to releases of contaminants from underground storage tanks. Under the federal requirements (which are part of RCRA), such tanks must either have been closed or upgraded to comply with modern performance standards, including leak detection systems, by December 1998. Although this requirement was phased in during a 10-year period, a considerable amount of enforcement activity concerning non-compliant tanks is expected over the next few years. This is an area in which vigilance during due diligence is important. In addition, many states have special standards for leaks from underground tanks, which are treated differently than other types of contamination and are often regulated by separate departments within state and local environmental agencies. Both the EPA and states have jurisdiction to issue orders requiring clean-up of tank leaks and may impose administrative or judicial penalties on violators of up to $25,000 per day.

2.2 Water and air permit requirements

As discussed above, both federal and state law typically requires facilities to obtain permits for all but the most minor air and water emissions. The division of responsibilities between the federal government and state agencies under such programmes has already been discussed (see paras 1.1–1.8). The following summarises some types of air and water permits that are often required under applicable law.

2.2.1 National Pollutant Discharge Elimination System (NPDES) permits

The Clean Water Act requires that any facility discharging to navigable waters must first obtain an NPDES permit authorising such discharge. Typically, such permits contain standards for content, toxicity, and thermal values as well as other characteristics that may be relevant to the discharge in question. They require periodic monitoring and self-reporting of the discharge quality, especially if the discharge is not in compliance with the permit, and the results of such monitoring may be used in enforcement proceedings against a non-compliant facility. Penalties for violations of the CWA are given in para 2.1.6 above.

2.2.2 Stormwater permits

One sub-set of the NPDES programme concerns the discharge of stormwater. Stormwater permits are required for construction activities and for the management and discharge of stormwater from industrial sites above certain size restrictions. Typically it is possible to satisfy these requirements by submitting a notification that the discharges qualify for and will comply with certain 'general permits' that have already been developed and published by the federal and state agencies. However, if the characteristics of the stormwater differ from the requirements of the general permit (for example if such discharge includes stormwater run-off from a coal pile storage area) an individual NPDES permit must be obtained. (See para 2.1.6 above concerning CWA penalties.)

2.2.3 Federal Clean Air Act permits

The federal CAA requires the EPA to develop air quality standards which define safe or appropriate levels of pollutants in the ambient air and new source emission control programmes to limit emissions of pollutants from industrial and other sources. These two programmes interrelate in that areas where air quality standards have not been met (known as 'non-attainment areas) have much stricter permitting requirements than areas that comply with ambient air standards. Major sources of air pollution in non-attainment areas will be required to comply with additional control technology requirements and other restrictions, usually implemented at the state or local level, intended to reduce overall emissions of the non-attainment pollutant(s) so that the area can be brought into attainment. Among these restrictions may be requirements to purchase expensive emission offsets, credits, or allowances that can exceed $3,000 per ton of emissions (in the case of nitrogen oxide allowances in the northeast).

Unlike NPDES permits, new source permits under the CAA are a prerequisite to the commencement of construction of a facility requiring such a permit. In addition, modifications of such a facility may also trigger such new source permitting, which can be both elaborate and time-consuming.

Violations of the CAA, including the failure to obtain a CAA permit or to comply with the requirements of such a permit, can result in civil penalties of up to $25,000 per day. Criminal penalties for knowing violations of CAA requirements and for negligently releasing air pollutants may include fines and up to one year in prison. Enforcement actions may be commenced by the EPA or state agencies or by, in some instances, private citizens.

2.2.4 Acid rain permits

Another permitting programme under the CAA involves the control of emissions of air pollutants which are precursors to acid rain deposition, namely sulphur dioxide (SO_2) and nitrogen oxides (NO_x). Sources of such emissions, particularly power plants burning fossil fuels, are required to obtain acid rain permits and are required to hold SO_2 allowances in a quantity that is at least equivalent to the total actual acid rain emissions from such facility. Each allowance is equivalent to one ton of SO_2. The allowance programme is designed to cap total SO_2 emissions at 8.9 million tons by the year 2000. On the whole, the programme has been very cost-effective, with SO_2 allowances currently trading in the range of $200 per ton. This price is expected to increase dramatically in the next decade given that a larger variety of sources will be subject to the programme starting in the year 2000. NO_x emissions will typically be limited to a specific emission rate in an acid rain permit. (See para 2.2.3 above for a discussion of penalties.)

The acid rain programme contrasts with other types of emissions trading programmes in the US because it is not restricted geographically. SO_2 allowances are allocated (typically in insufficient quantities) to certain large power plants, which, in turn, are free to sell them if they are not needed (whether because the plant has shut down or because it has installed a scrubber or changed to lower sulphur fuel). A facility regulated under the programme in Pennsylvania, for example, is free to buy the allowances from plants as far away as California or Florida, because the programme is primarily designed to control country-wide global impacts rather than local acid deposition. By contrast, other types of US allowance or offset programmes that allow for emissions banking and trading, such as the NO_x allowance programme in the northeast, are much more restrictive geographically and cover many more types of emission sources. Consequently, they produce much higher allowance prices (ie currently over $3,000 per ton for northeastern NO_x allowances).

2.2.5 Operating permits

The 1990 Clean Air Act Amendments also created a federal operating permits programme. The development of this programme has been quite slow, and facilities throughout the country are only now beginning to obtain CAA operating permits. The purpose of the operating permit programme is not to impose new operating requirements on specific facilities but rather to consolidate all applicable federal and, hopefully, state air emission standards and requirements within a single permit document. Nevertheless, operating permits have become vehicles for imposing new restrictions in the context of administrative orders or enforcement actions and for uncovering past violations of applicable regulatory requirements. Applicants are required to certify compliance with applicable requirements under threat of potential criminal sanctions for false certifications. A responsible official must also continue to provide a certification of compliance in future years under the programme. (See para 2.2.3 above for a discussion of CAA penalties.)

2.2.6 State and local air permits

While not all facilities have in the past held federal CAA permits (either because they are not significant enough sources of air emissions or because they were grandfathered from applicable federal programme requirements), most sources of air pollution do typically possess a state air permit. Such state and local programmes may contain a variety of process-specific emission standards and other operating restrictions, including restrictions on the use of certain chemical substances or on methods or hours of operation. The types of sanctions available under these programmes are typically similar to those under the CAA (see para 2.2.3 above), although the penalties are more likely to be lower and citizen enforcement rights are unusual.

2.3 Waste management requirements

2.3.1 Management of hazardous waste

As discussed in para 2.1.2 above, RCRA and its implementing EPA regulations include extensive requirements with respect to the management, treatment, storage, or disposal of materials that qualify as 'hazardous wastes'. Such requirements can profoundly affect the methods and costs of waste management and disposal at industrial facilities.

There are special requirements for the segregation, length of storage, and method of appropriate disposal of various types of hazardous waste. Some hazardous wastes can be disposed of directly in landfills, but others must be treated to meet certain land disposal standards before such disposal can take place.

In addition, an originating facility must prepare and sign manifests identifying the hazardous wastes it is shipping and their disposal location. If the disposal facility is later determined to be contaminated, the originating facility would have a well-documented liability for the materials that it sent there.

As with the CAA and CWA, much of the hazardous waste programme is implemented by the states, which can sometimes be more stringent than the applicable federal regulations require. Because of the extensive regulations and standards that are imposed on hazardous waste disposal facilities, the costs of hazardous waste disposal, are quite high, frequently exceeding $200 per ton.

Engaging in any activity that would qualify as the treatment, storage, or disposal of a hazardous waste without a permit is strictly prohibited under RCRA. Statutory penalties for such conduct can exceed $25,000 per day per violation, but they are rarely enforced at this level. Nevertheless, such permits can be difficult to obtain, requiring extensive applications and layers of governmental review and public scrutiny, and may impose costly compliance requirements. Once a particular operation falls within the jurisdiction of the hazardous waste programme, it typically cannot be discontinued without an additional 'closure permit'. Closure permits, in turn, can require long-term groundwater monitoring and other information, even if no impacts to the environment have been observed. For all of these reasons, most industrial facilities try to avoid RCRA permitting requirements.

2.3.2 Recycled materials

The definition of hazardous waste excludes certain materials that are recycled, particularly those that are re-used in the original process in which the wastes were generated. While such recycling/re-use exceptions can greatly reduce waste management costs with respect to such materials, the categories provided in the applicable regulations are quite limited. In addition, most states have programmes that provide exemptions from solid waste disposal requirements for solid wastes that are beneficially re-used. For example, combustion ash from a coal- or wood-fired power boiler may often be re-used in the manufacture of cinder block, in road beds, or as a structural fill material. Such beneficial re-use in lieu of disposal in an approved solid waste disposal facility typically requires a permit.

2.3.3 Solid wastes

While federal law and regulations impose requirements on the operation of solid waste disposal facilities themselves, most solid waste regulation is a creature of state law. The term solid waste is itself somewhat deceiving since it includes liquid, semi-solid and even contained gaseous materials resulting from industrial, commercial, and other activities. State laws typically prohibit the disposal of solid waste materials in unregulated facilities. Penalties for violation of state solid waste regulations can vary considerably, with administrative abatement orders being among the most common remedies. Monetary penalties are usually much lower than those applicable to hazardous waste violations.

2.3.4 Radioactive materials

Activities involving radioactive materials typically fall under the jurisdiction of the Nuclear Regulatory Commission (NRC). Except with respect to nuclear power plants and other activities that specifically involve considerable quantities of radioactive materials, the most common experience with NRC regulations involves the use of equipment, primarily laboratory equipment, that contains radioactive materials. The use and operation of such equipment is regulated by the NRC and some states, with a requirement that a licence or licences be obtained and that any operation of such equipment be conducted by specially trained individuals. The NRC has also established remediation standards and requirements for sites that are contaminated with radioactive materials.

2.4 Land use planning and zoning

Environmental requirements relating to the types of permissible land use are typically creatures of local law, especially local zoning laws. Such laws often require that significant new developments obtain special zoning approvals, which are often controversial and result in litigation. Zoning approvals, or special zoning exception approvals, where the zoning ordinance does not contemplate the intended use, may include dozens of environmental requirements regulating everything from dust emissions to water usage. Not all localities have zoning ordinances, but where a zoning approval is required, it is inevitably a prerequisite to construction activities. Violations can result in fines, cease and desist orders, and even revocation of the zoning approval itself.

2.5 Noise and other nuisance

Permissible noise emissions from the operation of a facility are typically regulated under state and/or local law. The most common form of noise regulation requires compliance with specific noise levels based upon the nature of adjoining property uses, with the strictest standards involving residential properties, particularly at night. Noise compliance can often be difficult to predict, particularly for new construction and for long-term operation of existing facilities where noise performance may deteriorate over time. The risks of noise non-compliance can vary greatly, from the imposition of relatively minor penalties to cease and desist orders, tort claims, and actions for violations of permits where noise standards have been directly incorporated. Other types of project emissions, especially odour, to the extent they are not otherwise prohibited by applicable regulatory standards, may nevertheless form the basis of private common law tort claims for injury or property damage.

2.6 Environmental disclosure requirements

A number of federal and state environmental laws require self-reporting with respect to chemical usage, waste generation and violations of applicable requirements. Such self-reporting provides valuable documentation of past facility operations and should be reviewed in connection with transactional due diligence.

2.6.1 Air and water compliance reporting

The most typical form of self-reporting involves requirements under air and water permits, which require self-monitoring and reporting of emissions and special reporting when emissions exceed permit limitations. Such self-reporting documents can then be used as evidence against the regulated entity in enforcement proceedings. (See paras 2.1.6 and 2.2.3 above for a discussion of CWA and CAA penalties.)

2.6.2 Spill and leak reporting

There are also self-disclosure obligations under laws relating to spills, including requirements relating to releases to land, surface water or groundwater under CERCLA. For example, there is an obligation under CERCLA to report immediately a release in excess of certain threshold quantities specified for each type of hazardous substance (known as 'Reportable Quantities') within any 24-hour period.

CERCLA imposes criminal penalties of up to 3 years in prison for failing to provide such a report (or providing a false or misleading report). Other programmes such as the Underground Tank Programme under RCRA, also require self-reporting of spills or releases. There are also unique programmes under certain state laws, such as North Carolina, which require anyone wishing to investigate the condition of groundwater in the state to obtain a permit to install a groundwater monitoring well and, as a condition of such permit, to report the results of the testing of the groundwater in the well.

2.6.3 Chemical usage reporting

Other laws, such as the Emergency Planning and Community Right-To-Know Act (EPCRA), require facilities that use or store hazardous materials in quantities exceeding certain specified thresholds to report their chemical storage and use and to develop emergency response plans. EPCRA also requires that certain facilities report all releases of regulated substances on an annual basis (whether or not such releases were authorised under specific permits). Such self-reporting requirements are designed to assist fire departments and other emergency service agencies in dealing with emergencies at the facilities in question and to assist the general public in understanding the substances that are used at neighbouring facilities and the quantities in which they are used, as well as chemical usage in industries as a whole. Failure to comply with reporting obligations could lead to substantial civil and criminal penalties under EPCRA and similar state and local laws.

2.6.4 Reporting under US securities laws

Another significant form of self-reporting with respect to environmental matters involves the US securities laws. The federal Securities and Exchange Commission (SEC) has issued guidance documents on what it views to be the disclosure obligations of companies that are registrants under such laws. In particular, the SEC has noted that registrants should discuss 'known trends or any known demands, commitments, events or uncertainties that will result in or that are reasonably likely to result in the registrant's liquidity increasing or decreasing in any material way'. Such disclosure may include liabilities at Superfund sites and in other environmental litigation as well as expected trends in environmental regulation. In view of the above requirements, it is sometimes useful in transactional due diligence to review disclosure documents created under the Securities Act 1933 and the Securities Exchange Act 1934. Nevertheless, these documents usually include only generic or limited environmental disclosures, rarely containing information that is not readily available from other sources.

Although the SEC has not conducted many enforcement actions with respect to disclosures required under the securities laws violators could face monetary penalties of up to $500,000 for each violation or the gross amount of the company's pecuniary gain from its actions. In addition, shareholders may bring a cause of action for loss arising out of a failure to disclose material information. The SEC staff and some watchdog groups have for some time given indications that enforcement activities will increasingly focus upon the adequacy of environmental disclosures. Thus this remains an important area to consider from an environmental compliance standpoint.

2.6.5 State transfer laws

There also may be self-reporting requirements under the various state transfer laws discussed in para 1.3.1 above. The majority of the states with transfer laws require only that the presence of certain types of regulated activities or of known contamination be provided either directly to a purchaser or in the form of a deed of notification. Typically, such laws require the seller to make the required disclosure, even if the buyer is willing to concede that no representations or warranties are made with respect to the property. Sanctions range from imposition of penalties to statutory liability for a buyer's damages to even voiding the transaction entirely (in the case of New Jersey's Industrial Sites Recovery Act).

2.7 Criminal liability

Almost every environmental law includes or is subject to criminal penalties (criminal fines and imprisonment). Typically, such liabilities are based upon knowing and intentional violations of environmental laws or at least willful actions that cause a violation of an environmental law. Another common category involves actions which result in a reckless endangerment of human health or safety.

Criminal liability for actions of environmental consequence is not limited to provisions in environmental statutes. For example, in situations where self-reporting is required, criminal prosecution can result where knowing false statements are made to the government. Federal and state agencies are bringing record numbers of environmental crime cases. The US Department of Justice has an environmental crimes section as does the EPA, and many State Attorney's offices have specialised environmental prosecution sections. In view of the above, this continues to be an area of growing importance.

3 PARTICULAR ENVIRONMENTAL ISSUES RELEVANT TO TRANSACTIONS

In view of the framework of extensive environmental regulation and the prospect of substantial liability, every transaction, no matter how environmentally benign the relevant business activities may be, will need to address a number of potential environmental issues. A brief discussion of some of the most common issues appears below.

3.1 Site contamination issues

Under CERCLA, a company may have liability for contamination that is present on real property either because it is the current owner of the property or because it conducts operations currently on the property. Other entities that may have liability include former owners and former operators of the property, but only to the extent that releases of hazardous substances occurred on the property during the period of their ownership or operation. It does not matter whether the current owner or operator of the property actually knows of or in some way caused the contamination that is present. As a result, liability for site contamination is a prominent concern in most transactions.

Site conditions can also play a role with respect to planned changes in a facility after it is acquired, including an expansion or a completely changed use. For example, asbestos (or lead-based paint) that may be present at the facility in various building materials usually does not require remediation if the materials are kept in good condition and repaired where necessary. Nevertheless, if a plant expansion is planned, such that these materials would be disturbed, an asbestos remediation may be triggered.

3.2 Off-site contamination

Applicable environmental laws may also impose liabilities for contamination that is present at off-site locations, such as off-site disposal facilities or neighbouring properties. To the extent that the contamination on such off-site properties arose on a company's facility and has simply migrated off-site, the liability concepts discussed with respect to on-site contamination would still apply. In addition, there may be tort liabilities or injury to human health as a result of the migrating materials.

With respect to contamination that was originally disposed off-site, CERCLA may impose liability even though the company that generated the hazardous materials was entirely unaware of their ultimate disposal location. By virtue of giving hazardous materials to a waste haulier or recycler, for example, a company will have liability for any foreseeable acts of such haulier or recycler, including illegal acts. Thus, the company generating the wastes may be held liable even if the haulier does not remove the wastes to a licensed disposal facility but instead illegally dumps them by the side of the road. The generator may also have liability even though the facility that receives the waste is licensed and fully regulated but nevertheless mismanages the materials and releases them to the environment. Moreover, CERCLA does not provide clear standards for distinguishing between the liabilities of various parties at third-party disposal sites such as landfills. If, for example, the government chooses a generator as one of the parties that it wishes to sue for recovery of clean-up costs with respect to the disposal facility, the generator could suffer joint and several liability for the costs of clean-up (which could be in the tens of millions of dollars) and will have to identify and bring claims against other parties who may have sent wastes to the site. In such circumstances, the cost of merely defending a claim can easily exceed the actual liability.

3.3 Liability for past non-compliance

As discussed above, there are a variety of environmental regulatory regimes that may be applicable to a single facility and a variety of potential enforcement authorities, including federal, state, and local agencies and public-interest groups. Because of long-term statutory limitation periods, which take seven years or more to expire (or possibly decades in the case of some clean-up liabilities), past violations must be carefully evaluated, especially where the violation is documented (such as in past emissions reports). Liabilities for past violations are not automatically assumed if the transaction is structured as an asset purchase, but they do automatically transfer with the stock in a stock sale. Thus, in the context of an asset purchase, the assumption of existing environmental liabilities becomes an important point of negotiation. If the asset purchaser is nevertheless willing to assume such liabilities, it is necessary that an indemnification be provided since the seller will still remain nominally liable for them.

3.4 Permit requirements and restrictions

Careful consideration in any facility acquisition must be given to the restrictions and requirements in facility permits, as well as the risks associated with permits and approvals that have yet to be obtained. Permit conditions, for example in air permits, can result in restrictions on hours of operation or fuel usage and, therefore, plant capacity. It can also result in the imposition of costly operating requirements such as the periodic acquisition of emission allowances or offsets. Moreover, if a facility has had a history of non-compliance with a permit restriction or requirement, there may be future consequences, even if the prior owner has agreed to retain past liabilities. Future violations of the same requirement may result in enforcement action that has not been taken by the government in the past (in view of the cumulative effect of chronic violations of the relevant standard) or could result in new permit restrictions and operating requirements imposed by the relevant agency to ensure more consistent compliance in the future. In addition, whenever new permits need to be obtained, there are permitting risks that must be carefully considered. Such risks include the nature of the restrictions that may appear in the permits, delays associated with obtaining the relevant permits (sometimes a year or more with respect to certain major source air permits) and the possibility of public opposition or appeals resulting in a denial of the permit.

Transfers and renewals of existing permits typically do not pose the same level of permitting risk, even though the relevant regulatory agencies generally retain the discretion to deny the permit transfer or renewal or to make unilateral modifications. Regulatory agencies do not typically want to be perceived as creating restrictions on the alienation of property by virtue of such permitting requirements and will usually only consider the suitability of the new owner in terms of past non-compliance history in the relevant jurisdiction for purposes of permit transfer or reissuance to a new owner.

3.5 Change in law risks

There has been no major federal environmental legislation since the Clean Air Act Amendments of 1990. There have, however, been a number of significant programmatic developments at the state level, particularly in the area of brownfields redevelopment and voluntary remedial action. On the whole, the trend has been toward more lenient remedial standards with respect to site contamination issues, but stricter standards with respect to air and water pollution. The latter, however, are typically areas of future regulatory risks that are accepted by a buyer because they relate to the future operation of the facility. The prospect of change in law with respect to site contamination is a different matter and must be addressed by the parties in their negotiations.

3.6 Parent, shareholder and director liability

In the late 1980s and early 1990s, there was tremendous uncertainty under US environmental law concerning the extent to which environmental liabilities of a subsidiary corporation could be passed on to the directors of that corporation or its shareholders, including a parent corporation. While there are still some courts that occasionally appear to expand the particular principles, the general rule is that officers and shareholders will have no direct liability for site contamination if they are not directly involved in the operation of a particular facility, especially with respect to environmental management decisions. To the extent that they are directly involved, they may be considered to have 'operator' liability under CERCLA (see para 2.1.1 above).

In certain circumstances, a court will pierce the corporate veil of a corporation to impose the clean-up liability of a corporation on its shareholders or on its parent corporate entity. The principles most often applied for piercing the corporate veil are, on the whole, not unique to environmental law. They include an analysis of whether the parent is excessively involved in the governance of the subsidiary, whether the subsidiary is adequately capitalised and is able to make basic financial decisions about its operation, whether the corporate forms of the subsidiary have been observed (ie meetings of shareholders, elections of directors, etc), and whether there are any other factors that suggest that the subsidiary is merely an alter ego of the parent. The US Supreme Court has recently ruled in the *Best Foods*[1] case, however, that without piercing the corporate veil, a parent corporation cannot be liable even if it exercises actual control over a facility that was responsible for the operation of the contaminated property unless the parent corporation was directly involved in the operations specifically related to the pollution itself.

3.7 Successor liability

In the context of an asset acquisition, the purchaser can still find itself liable under environmental laws for contamination in two circumstances, namely

(1) where the assets include the contaminated land or at least operations on contaminated land such that purchaser becomes an owner or operator under CERCLA; and
(2) where the contamination is only off-site or at a former site but the purchaser is considered to be the 'successor-in-interest' to the selling corporation.

There are several tests of successor liability, with the most commonly applied being the 'continuity of enterprise' principle. Courts have held that this principle requires more than a purchase of assets and a continuation of the prior business enterprise itself. Successor liability requires that there are substantial ties between seller and purchaser and less than fair market value was paid or at least the purchaser had full knowledge of past practices.

3.8 Lender liability

In the early 1990s and late 1980s, a series of expansive judicial interpretations of CERCLA liability strongly suggested that lenders in normal financing transactions could find themselves liable for environmental mismanagement by their customers, even without foreclosing on the borrower's property. CERCLA and RCRA have since been amended by Congress to provide a safe harbour for lenders and clarify what actions lenders may take without running a foul of CERCLA liability.

Under current federal law, lenders can engage in normal transactional due diligence and both retain and even exercise remedies over the borrower under the loan agreement without fear of liability, as long as the lenders do not become directly involved in operations in such a way as to lead to the conclusion that they exercised control over the management of hazardous substances at the facility. Lender's may also foreclose on a property and even operate the asset to maintain its value, as long as they actively pursue the sale of the asset in good faith.

The changes to CERCLA do not, however, change applicable state law, including individual state CERCLA-type laws. While most states have developed policies to protect lenders and other innocent third parties from contamination liabilities merely because they hold security interests in contaminated property, lenders are still well advised to be cautious in exercising their default remedies because of the risk of liability under state law.

1 *United States v Best Foods*, 524 U.S. 51 (1998).

4 MANAGING ENVIRONMENTAL ISSUES IN TRANSACTIONS

A number of structures and techniques have been developed to address many of the issues and concerns discussed above, including the following.

4.1 Environmental site assessments

It is common practice in the US for sellers to provide at least a Phase I environmental site assessment outlining the history of a site and any areas of concern or issues identified based upon a non-intrusive examination of the facility and an examination of files and regulatory databases. State agencies and the US EPA maintain databases recording a considerable amount of information about the facility in question, including any past releases of hazardous substances or management of hazardous wastes at that location, and concerning neighbouring properties whose operations may have resulted in impacts to the facility's site. The use of Phase II assessments involving soil and water sampling and analysis has also become virtually standard with respect to site investigations. Fewer transactions go forward without Phase II investigations than was the case in the late 1980s. This is in part due to quicker response and turn-around times for environmental sampling and analysis, including the use of environmental sampling techniques such as geo-probes and hydropunches that can provide environmental sampling data in a very short period of time and at much less cost than was previously possible. The Phase II assessments will more often be performed on behalf of the seller but there is nothing absolute about this approach.

4.2 Representations and warranties

Whether the transaction involves a stock purchase or an asset purchase, it is standard to find both representations concerning environmental compliance and conditions at the relevant operations of the seller and indemnities concerning either non-compliance with the environmental warranties or simply addressing environmental liabilities in general. There is no magic to these provisions, which are not significantly influenced by differences in state laws. It should be noted, however, that if parties do not address environmental issues in their contractual provisions, the courts have interpreted the laws as allocating environmental liabilities based upon statutory principles. Thus, for example, the seller of contaminated property may still have liability to the purchaser even though it makes no representations and warranties and agrees to provide no contractual indemnification with respect to contaminated property, but only if the contamination occurred during the period of the seller's ownership or operation of the property. Nevertheless, a seller who attempts to limit its liability with respect to environmental conditions in a sale agreement must still be careful to clarify that the environmental liability provisions provide the only remedies with respect to environmental conditions or non-compliance with environmental laws.

Where a state transfer law comes into play (see para 1.3.1 above), there may be a whole series of obligations that must be complied with in order for the transaction to go forward. Parties typically allocate responsibilities between themselves for the necessary filings and any ongoing compliance obligations under such laws. Otherwise, those obligations are the burden of the seller of the property.

4.3 Escrow agreements

In many instances, the parties simply cannot come to an agreement as to the significance and scope of environmental liabilities that may be identified at the time of sale. This is often the case when an adverse environmental condition has been identified through site sampling in connection with the sale, but there is no understanding of the likely reaction of relevant regulatory authorities to such condition. The parties inevitably argue about what may be required, and when. If the differences are substantial, they can sometimes proceed by placing a portion of the purchase price in escrow pending resolution of the environmental issues. This is often accompanied by a type of arbitration proceeding involving the use of an independent environmental consultant paid by each of the parties to evaluate the conditions and in some instances to remediate them or negotiate with applicable authorities. While the escrow approach makes it possible to close the deal, the resolution of the arbitration can be time-consuming and expensive.

4.4 Indemnification agreements

When the seller agrees to indemnify the purchaser for environmental liabilities, a common issue involves who should control the remedial programme. Thus the sale agreement sometimes may contain a lengthy and detailed outline of each party's respective rights and responsibilities if an adverse environmental condition occurs or is identified. Difficulties arise where there is no clear guidance under US environmental laws with respect to what actions must be taken in order to respond to an adverse environmental condition at a property. In order to avoid having purchasers perform elaborate and unnecessarily expensive remediations, sellers will sometimes attempt to define carefully what is acceptable for indemnification purposes or they may even insist on retaining responsibility for performing any remedial work themselves. In either case, it is likely that conflicts will arise concerning interference with ongoing plant operations and remedial strategies. Another approach favoured by some companies is not to attempt to define what must be done but rather to provide for a sharing of costs between the parties on a percentage basis. Thus, for example, the parties may each pay 50% of all remedial costs. The assumption here is that if the purchaser must pay a significant percentage of all costs incurred with respect to the remedial action, it will have less incentive to go beyond what is essentially required to deal with the situation.

4.5 Environmental management systems

Although the use of certified environmental management systems is certainly not as popular in the US as it is in parts of Europe and elsewhere, the existence of such systems and, hopefully, their effective use is a source of comfort in the environmental due diligence process. A common documentary manifestation of such systems is the internal environmental audit report. Unfortunately, there are severe limitations on the ability of companies to protect internal audit documents from disclosure in litigation or to governmental authorities. The EPA and a number of states have attempted to develop policies intended to encourage the use of such internal audit documents by clarifying when they are entitled to protection, but such policies are generally inadequate and, as a consequence, the internal audit documents tend to resort to generalisations and avoid discussing in any substantive way, serious issues or concerns.

4.6 Role of environmental insurance

Up until a few years ago, environmental insurance was virtually non-existent in the US. The insurance that was available was extremely limited and expensive. More recently, insurance companies have begun to develop more aggressive products that are intended to play a role in the allocation of environmental liabilities in the context of transactions. This area is evolving very quickly, and, at this time, the use of insurance policies to assist parties in resolving disputes about the size and scope of environmental liability remains rare. One of the obstacles involves the standard insurance disclaimer for 'known' conditions and circumstances that the insured has failed to disclose to the insurer. The fear is that whenever a condition is ultimately discovered, there will be some information source, including long-time employees, that the insurer can identify as having been available to the insured but not disclosed at the time of the policy. There are other disclaimers that are also too open-ended for most transactions. However, insurers have recently begun to give indications of a willingness to negotiate these clauses and still provide insurance policies that are relatively affordable.

5 CONCLUSION

As discussed above, the allocation of environmental responsibilities and liabilities remains a central consideration in any transaction, including cross-border transactions involving assets in the US. Methods for assessing the nature and scope of environmental liabilities and conditions including the use of computer databases and new types of sampling equipment, have been growing increasingly sophisticated, but less expensive and, as a consequence, it is possible to enter into acquisition transactions (or mergers) with much more information at the disposal of the purchaser than ever before.

In addition, there has been some relaxation in the liability regime, but the most important trend in this regard has been an increasing reliance by state regulatory agencies on the use of self-implementing remedial programmes. In many cases, these include the use of licensed professionals who are authorised by the state agency (as in Connecticut and Massachusetts) to assess conditions, apply the applicable standards, perform any necessary remedial actions, and certify closure of the facility without obtaining input or approval from the regulators themselves. This streamlined process makes it possible to understand much more quickly the scope of an environmental problem that has been identified at a particular site. Other states are relaxing their remedial standards to better reflect the nature of potential property uses and human exposure and have created brownfields programmes to promote redevelopment of distressed properties. Thus the overall cost or potential cost of some environmental liabilities has decreased in recent years. Finally, as noted above, the use of environmental insurance is a growing trend and potentially a very promising way of further securing the interests of the seller and purchaser with respect to unresolved environmental problems.

At this stage, there are no major changes anticipated at the federal level in the US. CERCLA reform has been discussed in Congress for years, but no major changes appear to be on the horizon. Any such changes would primarily relate to remediation of large, multi-party CERCLA sites, rather than to the liability provisions that typically haunt sellers and purchasers of potentially contaminated properties. Most of the significant new developments continue to be in the area of air regulation. There are prospects for increasingly stringent restrictions on emissions of certain types of air pollutants, such as acid rain precursors in the northeast and ozone-causing agents in various areas of the US, including the northeast. Some additional restrictions are already embodied in programmes with upcoming implementation dates such as the commencement of Phase II of the acid rain programme in the year 2000 and the commencement of the ozone-season NO_x allowance requirements on 1 May 1999. Other restrictions are further on the horizon, including global warming legislation which has received a lot of attention but, so far, little action in Congress. All of these programmes have the potential of increasing costs very substantially for major air pollution sources, especially in the northeastern US. Ozone-season NO_x allowances, for example, are already trading at over $3,000 per ton, which could result in very significant expenditure to purchase allowances necessary to offset ozone-season NO_x emissions in facilities that are subject to that programme. These and other potential future compliance costs should be carefully considered in evaluating potential acquisitions or mergers of companies operating in the US.

Chapter 3

GERMANY

Dr Gerhard Limberger and Dr Stefanie Birkmann

Bruckhaus Westrick Heller Löber,
Attorneys at Law, Frankfurt am Main

1 INTRODUCTION

1.1 General principles of the German legal system

As is the case with most continental European countries, Germany has a codified legal system. Court decisions supplement the statutory framework and provide guidelines for the interpretation of legal provisions.

According to the *Grundgesetz*, ie the Constitution of the Federal Republic of Germany, legislative power is allocated to different bodies at the federal level (*Bund*), state level (*Länder*) and local level (*Gemeinden*). In principle, legislative power is allocated to the 16 states. However, the constitution contains several exceptions to this rule. Depending on the area of law, federal bodies may be entitled to issue general parameters (framework legislation) which will be supplemented by state laws (eg water law, natural protection) and in some cases may regulate the area as a whole to the exclusion of the states (eg immission control). Finally, in areas of special relevance to the local community the local bodies are entitled to enact the necessary provisions (*Satzungen*) for the community, provided that they are in line with federal and state laws.

At the federal level as well as at the state level, supplementary to the statutes passed by Parliament (*Bundestag/Landtag*), ordinances (*Rechtsverordnungen*) may be enacted by administrative bodies (eg the federal or state government or a minister of the government) if such power is delegated in the relevant statute. In addition to this, especially in areas requiring a high standard of technical or scientific specification, administrative regulations (*Verwaltungsvorschriften*) provide for guidelines to define statutory requirements and threshold values in greater detail (eg *TA Luft, TA Lärm, TA Abfall*). A large part of German environmental law consists of ordinances and administrative regulations. This is due to the fact that alterations in environmental standards are more swiftly implemented by means of such statutory instruments than would be possible with the enactment of formal legislation.

Similar to the legislative power, the executive power is not allocated exclusively to central agencies. Rather, a number of different authorities at the federal level, state level and local level implement the legal provisons (eg *Stadtverwaltung, Landkreis,*

1.1 *Chapter 3*

Regierungspräsidium, Ministerium). Except for particular areas listed exclusively in the constitution, the organisation of the administrative authorities and the applicable procedures is within the states' competence. The organisation of environmental administration is therefore not uniform. In addition, the individual area of environmental protection (eg water law, immission control, waste law, zoning law) determines the competent authority. In each case, a careful investigation of the circumstances and the statutory requirements is necessary in order to determine the competent authority.

1.2 Characteristics of German environmental law

In the last 30 years Germany has developed a high degree of public regulation in environmental matters. Due to the allocation of legislative power and the fact that the environment as a whole has been perceived only very recently as an object of legal protection, there is no uniform legislation covering the field with respect to the protection of the environment. Rather, public environmental law in Germany consists of a vast number of different statutes, ordinances and administrative regulations which have gradually been enacted by various competent bodies over the last 30 years. Part of this regulation deals with the erection and operation of production plants and is therefore installation-related (eg the federal Immission Control Act; the federal Water Act). In addition, there are product-related environmental laws regulating the quality and the marketing of products (eg the Packaging Ordinance; the laws on hazardous substances).

In its early stages, environmental legislation was primarily designed along media lines, such as air and water, aiming at the warding off of dangers from these media and the management of particular environmental problems. Since 1980 environmental problems caused by extensive soil and groundwater contamination, especially on industrial sites and premises used for the storage of waste, have increasingly attracted public attention and posed a new threat to the environment. Legislators as well as the competent authorities were challenged to find remedies for environmental damage, often caused by a lack of knowledge and insensitivity towards environmental matters in the past. A new dimension was added to this problem by the reunification of Germany. As it emerged, the large number of contaminated areas and the extent of soil and groundwater contamination in East Germany required technical and financial measures which could not be made available without public assistance.

Following the regulation of environmental law over the last three decades, environmental debate in Germany now primarily focuses on how to complete and refine the existing legal instruments (eg by prescribing threshold values and technical procedures for the determination and assessment of environmental impact in greater detail). Additionally, draft legislation has been prepared aimed at the harmonisation of the various statutes with respect to the environment and their integration into one statute for the protection of the environment as a whole (*Umweltgesetzbuch—UGB*).

However, the development of German environmental law cannot be seen in isolation from the EC laws on the environment. Although originally a comprehensive basis of authority of the European Community in the field of environmental protection did not exist, since the 1960s European institutions have enacted nearly 180 legal instruments (regulations, directives, decisions etc) concerning the environment. The vast majority of German environmental law has, thus, to a greater or lesser extent been influenced by EC law.

Finally, within the framework of the Single European Act, which came into force on 1 July 1987, arts 130r–130t have been inserted into the EC Treaty expressly authorising the European Community in the field of environmental law. A high level of environmental protection is to be striven for, although the varying existing circumstances in the individual member states is to be taken into consideration. Furthermore, environmental protection has now been established as an objective in art 3 (k) of the EC Treaty. The legislative projects to be pursued by the European Community are outlined in the programmes of action of the European Community for environmental protection. These programmes of action are non-binding political declarations of intent of the Community organs. However, they furnish a comprehensive overview of future activities in the field of environmental law.

With regard to the incorporation of EC law into national law, a distinction must be made between the regulation and the directive. Whilst the regulation constitutes law which is directly applicable in the member states, the directive is merely a binding instruction to the member states to implement the content of the directive into national law. Generally, the legislator has a discretion as to how a directive is incorporated into German law. However, in the sphere of environmental law the European Court of Justice has ruled that the implementation of a directive by means of an administrative provision (in this case the Technical Instruction on the Preservation of Clean Air—*TA Luft*) is not a suitable means of implementing EC law into German law because of its lack of commitment, certainty and precision. Thus, formal legislation is required.

2   OUTLINE OF ENVIRONMENTAL LAW RELEVANT TO MERGER AND ACQUISITION TRANSACTIONS

German environmental law comprises numerous statutes, ordinances and administrative regulations, part of it installation-related and part of it product-related.

Frequently, not only one area of environmental law will be pertinent to the erection and operation of a plant but rather various ones. In such a case, various approvals may be required from various competent authorities. Generally, each of the approval procedure has to be carried out independently. An exception to this rule applies only if the relevant statute provides that the permission granted thereunder shall render other official decisions under public law unnecessary (eg permission under the Federal Immission Control Act; plan approval procedures). However, this so called 'concentration' does not release the operator of the plant/owner of the premises from complying with all material requirements. Rather, compliance with all material requirements imposed by applicable law is a precondition for licensing and will be checked by the authority in the course of the licensing procedure.

The following outline contains a basic description of the most important areas of environmental law relevant to merger and acquisition transactions:

2.1   Immission control; noise and nuisance

Immission control is an area of environmental law mainly governed by federal law. The Federal Immission Control Act (*Bundesimmissionsschutzgesetz—BImSchG*) contains installation-related provisions for the protection of people, animals, plants and other receptors of emissions from air pollution, noise, vibration, light, heat and similar effects. Harmful effects on the environment (*schädliche Umwelteinwirkungen*), the central concept of the Act, are defined as immissions which, according to their nature, extent or duration, are likely to cause hazards, considerable disadvantages or considerable nuisance to the general public or the neighbourhood. Immissions, as opposed to emissions originating from an installation, are measured at the place where they affect the human being or the object of protection.

2.1 Chapter 3

Industrial plants must be constructed and operated so that harmful environmental impact or other hazards, significant detriments or significant nuisance are not caused. In addition, precautions have to be taken against causing harmful environmental impact by applying state of the art technology (*Stand der Technik*) for restricting emission levels which cannot be questioned by cost considerations.

The establishment and operation of an installation which, by its nature or operation, is particularly liable to cause harmful effects on the environment or otherwise endanger or cause considerable disadvantage or considerable nuisance to the general public or the neighbourhood, is subject to licensing under the Federal Immission Control Act. The installations subject to licensing are designated exclusively in the Fourth Ordinance for the Implementation of the Federal Immission Control Act (*4.BImSchV—Verordnung über genehmigungsbedürftige Anlagen*).

The licence under the Federal Immission Control Act is a non-discretionary consent decision. It shall be granted provided that the obligations set out in s 5 of the Act (*§ 5 BImSchG*) and the requirements imposed under certain ordinances are met. In this context guidelines such as the Technical Instruction on the Preservation of Clean Air (*TA Luft*) and the Technical Instruction on Noise (*TA Lärm*), which add detail to the general statutory obligations, are of crucial importance. A further precondition is that the establishment and operation of such installation does not conflict with any other provisions under public law or labour law.

Depending on the lay-out of the plant and the chemicals used either a formal procedure or a simplified one has to be carried out. As part of the formal procedure a thorough public notification and participation procedure takes place. After the submission of the complete application documents, the licensing authority will give public notice of the project and the application (except for documents containing trade or industrial secrets) will be made available for public inspection for a period of one month. Third parties may submit written objections for up to two weeks after the expiry of the inspection period. The licensing authority will discuss the arguments against the project with the applicant and with those raising objections. A private discussion which is not open to the public will be scheduled for this purpose. After the conclusion of the investigations, which include the results of the discussion, the licensing authority shall decide on the application within seven months.

According to the Environmental Impact Act (*Gesetz über die Umweltverträglichkeitsprüfung—UVPG*), certain projects which are listed in the Appendix to the Act require an assessment of the impact on the environment. This assessment, if required, is integrated into the licensing procedure under the Federal Immission Control Act. The environmental impact assessment takes place in three stages: In the first stage (the 'Scoping') the operator and the competent authority discuss the implementation of the assessment and the probable measures of examination. The opinions of other public authorities whose sphere of responsibility is affected by the project are obtained in the second stage of the environmental impact assessment. If the project may have repercussions in other member states of the European Union, the public authorities of those countries are also involved. In the final stage, the competent authority draws up a summary description of the effects of the project, in particular the effects on human beings, animals, plants and environmental media. The assessment of the effects are to be taken into consideration when the decision whether or not to grant permission for the project is made, but it does not have a binding effect.

If a licence under the Federal Immission Control Act is required, this licence will cover other official decisions concerning the installation (eg building permission), provided that the material requirements of the applicable laws are met. A licence or permit under the Federal Water Law is still, however, required as an exception to this.

According to the Federal Immission Control Act, the competent authority shall give orders to close down or dismantle an installation if it is established, operated or materially altered without having been licenced to do so. In addition to this, the competent authority may prohibit all or part of the operation provided that the operator of the installation does not comply with conditions imposed, an enforceable subsequent order given or a conclusive obligation ensuing from an ordinance.

2.2 Water law

Under German administrative law, there are federal and state laws that govern the use of water bodies. In accordance with the constitutional allocation of powers, the federal government may only issue general parameters for the regulation of water resource management. The Federal Water Act (*Wasserhaushaltsgesetz—WHG*) provides a framework for the management of bodies of water, which is supplemented and detailed by regulations of the states (*Landeswassergesetze*).

According to the principles laid down in the Federal Water Act, water, as an integral part of the ecosystem, shall be managed in a manner that serves the common good and also benefits the individual user. Every avoidable harmful impact to bodies of water shall be prevented. Where activities can have an impact on water, there is an obligation for everyone concerned to take the care necessary in the circumstances to prevent contamination of the water or any other detrimental change in its properties and to ensure the economical use of water.

The use of surface water, coastal water and groundwater (eg the withdrawal or diversion of water, the introduction or discharge of substances into water) as well as any measures which are likely to cause, either permanently or to a not merely insignificant degree, harmful changes in the physical, chemical or biological properties of water require an official permit or licence. The licensing procedure, as well as the measures which can be taken to enforce compliance with applicable law, are regulated by state water law.

Finally, the discharge of waste water into public sewage systems is subject to licensing under water law. A permit shall only be granted if the pollutant load of the waste water is kept as low as possible and if the processes in question are carried out in line with the statutory requirements. There are federal guidelines with respect to the minimum requirements for the discharge of waste water into stretches of water (*Rahmen-Abwasserverwaltungsvorschriften*) which contain certain requirements for specific industries as well as technical standards for analysis and measurement. The states must implement the necessary measures to ensure that no hazardous substances are discharged into the public sewage system. Independent of the state regulations, standards for the discharge of waste water may be set by municipal byelaws in order to maintain and protect the safety of the public sewage system.

2.3 Waste management including recycling/re-use obligations

On 7 October 1996 the Economic Circulation and Waste Disposal Act (*Kreislaufwirtschafts und Abfallgesetz—KrW-/AbfG*) entered into force and replaced the Federal Waste Act (*Abfallgesetz—AbfG*). Its intention is to promote the conservation of natural resources, the re-use of waste and the environmentally compatible waste disposal. It further aims at reducing the accumulation of waste requiring disposal and reducing the burden on public disposal facilities by increasing the responsibilities of producers and consumers (Producer Responsibility Principle). Based on the principle of prevention, it contains a hierarchy for the treatment of waste in the order: 'Avoidance—Re-use—Disposal of Waste'.

Whilst waste disposal and removal services from private households are performed by public authorities, such authorities are obliged to dispose of waste generated by economic enterprises only in certain cases. Producers of commercial waste are responsible themselves to the extent that they possess their own systems or have assigned their waste disposal legal obligations to private disposal operators. This is the case if waste is subject to a reacceptance or return obligation on the basis of the Producer Responsibility Principle. The party with the obligation to dispose of the waste is also responsible, not only for re-use of waste and removal, but also for preparatory and accompanying measures such as collection, conveyance, storage and treatment. Whether they fulfill this obligation in facilities of their own or assign it to a contractor is left to their discretion. The applicable principle of public waste disposal, therefore, takes second place behind this obligation of producers and owners.

On the basis of the Federal Waste Act (*AbfG*) implementing the Producer Responsibility Principle, in 1991 the federal government issued the Packaging Ordinance (*Verpackungsverordnung*). It obliges producers, fillers and distributors to take back packaging from consumers. To meet their obligation to take back and dispose of packaging, producers and distributors founded the *Duales System Deutschland* (DSD). DSD is a private limited liability company formed by German industry. The sole purpose of the company is to take over and fulfil the obligations of producers to take back and dispose of packaging waste. DSD renders this service on behalf of the obligated parties on payment of a licence fee. The producers and distributors involved mark their products with the so-called 'green dot' to designate them for collection and disposal by DSD. The Packaging Ordinance is continuing in force under s 24 of the Economic Circulation and Waste Disposal Act (*§ 24 KrW-/AbfG*).

2.4 Contaminated land

At the federal level, until recently Germany did not have a general legal and technical standard applicable to contamination of soil and groundwater. Damages were handled on the basis of the Economic Circulation and Waste Disposal Act (*KrW-/AbfG*)/Federal Waste Act (*AbfG*), the Federal Water Act (*WHG*) and the state laws regulating water protection and waste management. If these laws did not provide for sufficient authorisation, clean-up, remediation or reimbursement orders had been issued on the basis of the states' general police laws (*Polizei und Sicherheitsrechtrecht*). Due to these legal uncertainties, the general principles applicable to the environmental liability for a contaminated site were developed by German administrative practice and related court decisions. On the basis of such practice and decisions it could be concluded that in all German states potential liability for remediation and clean-up costs resulting from environmental damage existed for the following parties: the polluter; the current, and in some states the former owner of a site; the operator of an existing/former plant on the site; and the person/entity who is in actual possession of the site.

This situation underwent major changes when the new Federal Soil Protection Act (*Bundesbodenschutzgesetz—BBodSchG*) entered into force on 1 March 1999. The Act not only aims at the protection of the soil against future detriment but also contains special provisions for the treatment of existing contamination.

For the first time uniform standards for liabilities and remediation measures resulting from harmful effects on the soil apply. This is considered an important improvement, since more than 30 different lists of risk and threshold values had been issued during the previous years which varied widely from state to state, sometimes even from one city to another. An ordinance issued on the basis of the Federal Soil Protection Act contains the relevant values and, thus, enables those potentially liable to better foresee and evaluate the risk of remediation measures as well as the quality and extent of such measures.

Compared with the former principles of liability, the Federal Soil Protection Act led to a considerable tightening-up of liability. Not only might the polluter and the current owner of the site or the person/entity who is in actual possession be responsible for remediation measures to be taken, but also the universal successor of the polluter (*Gesamtrechtsnachfolger des Verursachers*) may be liable.

Under German law, a person/entity becomes the universal successor of the polluter if he, by virtue of law, assumes all the polluter's rights and obligations. Universal succession exists, for instance, by inheritance or in cases where a surviving company exists after a merger has taken place under the provisions of the Reorganisation Act (*Umwandlungsgesetz*).

If title to the property was transferred after 1 March 1999, the former owner of the site is liable, too. Furthermore, liability is extended under the new Act from the current owner of the site to the person/entity responsible under general principles of company law for the legal entity owning the contaminated site. By doing so, the rule of a strict separation between the corporation (GmbH or AG) as a legal entity and its shareholders may be disregarded, allowing the corporate veil to be pierced under the same principles which have been developed in a company law context. According to pertinent court rulings, however, shareholder liability may arise in exceptional cases only if reference to the legal personality of the corporation is deemed to contravene the principle of good faith. The Federal German Supreme Court ruled that if the controlling company permanently manages the business of the controlled company (GmbH or AG) in such a way that isolated detrimental acts can no longer be determined and the creditors thus need to be protected by a general loss compensation, the controlling company will be responsible. The companies then are regarded as 'de facto consolidated companies' (*qualifiziert-faktischer Konzern*).

2.5 Land use planning/zoning

The statutory requirements to be met by a building project under public law are specified in the Federal Planning Code (*Baugesetzbuch*) and the State Planning Code (*Landesbauordnung*). In addition to this, at the local level, the municipal council is empowered to enact a zoning plan (*Bebauungsplan*), a local statute which details the planning measures taking into account the special circumstances of a certain area of the city.

Before the commencement of construction, the builder (*Bauherr*) must seek planning permission (*Baugenehmigung*). Once the application for the planning permission, together with the necessary specifications, has been submitted, the building authority decides independently whether the project complies with the legal requirements and therefore whether planning permission can be granted.

If the builder starts construction without the planning permission being issued, he runs the risk that the competent authority may require dismantling of the building. The authority is entitled to do so unless the requirements for the issuance of a planning permission are met.

2.6 Use and storage of hazardous substances

The use and storage of hazardous substances is governed by the Federal Chemicals Act (*Chemikaliengesetz—ChemG*) and a number of subsidiary ordinances (eg Hazardous Substances Ordinance—*Gefahrstoffverordnung*), which are crucial to define and implement the statutory requirements. The laws on hazardous substances form part of an area of German environmental law which has been strongly influenced by EC law.

The Federal Chemicals Act aims at the protection of human beings and the environment from harmful effects of hazardous substances and preparations, in particular by ensuring these are adequately labelled and controlled. In order to achieve these objectives, the Act provides for certain measures which apply to hazardous substances, preparations and products. The manufacturer and the importer of such substances are primarily subject to the statutory requirements with respect to the bringing into circulation and use of these substances.

The Federal Chemicals Act contains duties of notification and testing. With respect to those duties a distinction has to be drawn between 'existing' and 'new' substances. The manufacturer or importer of a new substance may only bring it into circulation or import it 60 days after it is registered and evidence of it having been tested has been submitted to the notification authority. If no objections are raised by the authority within the 60-day period, the substance can be intoduced into circulation, but the notification authority may within this period require additional testing for particular dangerous characteristics. However, there is no notification requirement if a substance is already produced in or imported into another member state of the European Union and has undergone an equivalent procedure there.

In addition to notification and testing obligations, the Federal Chemicals Act, together with the Hazardous Substances Ordinance, imposes classification, packaging and labelling requirements on the manufacturer or importer of hazardous substances and preparations. Generally, packaging must be such that none of the contents can accidentally escape. Moreover, the packaging must be capable of safely withstanding the expected stresses on it and must be made from material which cannot be attacked by the substance or preparation and which cannot form a dangerous reaction with it.

Finally, the federal government is entitled by means of an ordinance to determine existing and new substances which must not, or may only under certain conditions, be used and brought into circulation, provided that such regulation is necessary to attain the objectives of the Act.

3 PARTICULAR ENVIRONMENTAL ISSUES RELEVANT TO TRANSACTIONS

3.1 Common principles of liability

When participating in a merger and acquisition transaction in Germany, the purchaser of a company is confronted with three major categories of environmental liability: private liability, public liability and criminal liability. Private liability (*zivilrechtliche Haftung*) concerns liability to private parties for damages caused by an incident harmful to the environment. The person/entity suffering damage may be able to claim compensation or apply for an injunction. Private liability is governed by the German Civil Code (*Bürgerliches Gesetzbuch—BGB*) and by special statutes such as the Environmental Liability Act (*Umwelthaftungsgesetz—UmwHG*) and is a matter of federal law. Public liability (*öffentlich-rechtliche Verantwortung*) enables local and state agencies to issue orders (*Anordnungen*) demanding investigation and/or remediation measures to be taken or, if these measures turn out not to be sufficient to protect the environment adequately, prohibiting the operation of the site. Finally, the wrongdoer may be responsible under criminal law (*strafrechtliche Verantwortlichkeit*). The German Criminal Code (*Strafgesetzbuch—StGB*), ss 324–30d contains special provisions dealing with offences against the environment. Penal sanctions can be imposed for the offence such as imprisonment or a fine.

3.1.1 Private liability for environmental damage

Section 906 of the German Civil Code *(§ 906 BGB)* and s 14 of the Federal Immission Control Act *(§ 14 BImSchG)* govern the relationship between neighbours with respect to emissions from one parcel of land to another. Generally, one may seek to have the emission (eg the intrusion of gases, vapours, smells, smoke, soot, heat, noises, shocks and similar interferences) discontinued. If, however, the emission is localised and cannot be prevented through commercially viable means, then the injured party may not seek an injunction to stop such conduct, but may demand monetary compensation instead. While statutory liability in this case does not depend on fault, the scope of these provisions is limited to real property damage. Bodily injury, impairment to one's health and damage to personal property are not covered.

In the case of an incident harmful to the environment, tort law *(§ 823 BGB)* may be relevant. Under this provision, a person is liable for any injury caused to the life, limb, freedom or property of another. Liability under this rule, however, is based on wilful or negligent conduct. Although significant practical problems often arise in proving the necessary elements of this cause of action, the Federal German Supreme Court (*Bundesgerichtshof*) has greatly improved the prospects of obtaining relief in the area of environmental liability by easing the rules of evidence and reversing the burden of proof. As a result, for liability to be imposed, the injured party need only establish a causal link between the emission of a substance and the damage or injury.

Another provision for compensation in cases of damage to the environment is s 22 of the Federal Water Act *(§ 22 WHG)*: any person who introduces or discharges any substance into water or takes any action which results in a change in its physical, chemical or biological properties shall be liable to compensate for damage caused to any other person as a result of this action. If several persons were responsible for the action, they shall be jointly and severally liable for any damage. As this is strict liability, there is no requirement to prove unlawful or culpable conduct. Rather, the liability is based on an underlying policy of social responsibility for acceptable risks.

Section 1 of the Environmental Liability Act *(§ 1 Umwelthaftungsgesetz— UmwHG)*, which entered into force on 1 January 1991, is another strict liability provision with respect to harmful effects on the environment. If any person is killed or suffers bodily injury or damage to health, or if property is damaged, as a result of an effect on the environment caused by an installation listed in the Appendix to the Act, the operator of the installation shall be under an obligation to compensate the injured party for the resulting damage. Compared to the provisions on liability described above, the Environmental Liability Act contains a series of far-reaching provisions which lead to an extension of liability. According to s 6 of the Act *(§ 6 UmwHG)*, if, in view of the circumstances of a given case, an installation is likely to have caused identified damage, it shall be presumed that the damage has been caused by the facility. Sections 8–10 of the Act *(§§ 8–10 UmwHG)* provide for special access to information concerning the operation of the installation.

Under the German Civil Code, the right to demand an act or an omission from another person is subject to a limitation period. The usual period is 30 years. However, various regulations provide for an exception to this rule. According to s 852 of the German Civil Code (*§ 852 BGB*), a claim for compensation for any damage arising from tort (*§§ 823 ff BGB*) is barred in three years from the time at which the injured party has knowledge of the injury and of the identity of the person responsible, and without regard to such knowledge, in 30 years from the doing of the act. The same limitation period applies for claims under s 22 of the Federal Water Act (*§ 22 WHG*) and s 1 of the Environmental Liability Act (*§ 1 UmweltHG*).

3.1.2 *Public liability for harmful effects on the environment*

Since German environmental law is made up of a vast number of statutes, ordinances and administrative regulations at the federal, state and local level, liability may lie under various legal provisions. If, however, special regulations do not exist or do not provide for sufficient authorisation (which has been true for most contaminated sites where investigation and remediation measures need to be taken) the competent authority may issue the necessary orders (*Anordnungen*) on the basis of the states' general police laws. The principles by which liability can accrue are basically the same in all states and can be summarised as follows:

If there is a situation which poses a threat to public safety and order (*Gefahr für die Öffentliche Sicherheit und Ordnung*) the person/legal entity who directly caused this situation (*Handlungsstörer*) is responsible for remedying it. Also, the person/legal entity who owns or is in actual possession of the premises, the facility, or the site (*Zustandsstörer*) can be held responsible for investigation and remediation measures or subject to cost recovery actions. The liability, which is irrespective of fault, is joint and several, ie each responsible party is liable for the full amount of environmental damage. The competent authority has a broad discretion with respect to imposing liability between the parties involved. Generally, the most efficient measure is to be taken in order to remedy the danger immediately.

In principle, the party responsible can be called to account by the competent authority for an unlimited period of time. Limitation, as understood in a civil law context, is not recognised in public law and the competent authority does not waive its right to issue the necessary orders by reason of inactivity or lapse of time.

3.1.3 *Responsibility under criminal law for offences against the environment*

As previously mentioned, the German Criminal Code (*Strafgesetzbuch—StGB*), ss 324–330d contain special provisions dealing with offences against the environment.

Due to the growing sensitivity in terms of environmental protection, the number of criminal cases in this field has increased significantly in the last 10 to 15 years. In most cases producing enterprises have been accused of conduct harmful to the environment. The prosecuting authorities were frequently faced with the problem of allocating environmental duties and the failure to perform such duties to individuals within the company. In German criminal law, a company cannot be held responsible, rather fault can only lie with individual persons. Pursuant to s 14 of the German Criminal Code (*§ 14 StGB*), the environmental duties of an enterprise are allocated to the company management. In principle, all members of the management are jointly and extensively liable for any failure to perform the environmental obligations prescribed by law. German criminal law does not draw a distinction between a company manager and a company director. According to relevant court decisions, the overall responsibility for environmental damage occurring in the course of the operation lies with the company's management.

This joint liability of the company management can partly be limited by clearly specifying in advance the areas every manager is responsible for. Moreover, the company management may discharge itself, to some extent, by downward delegation of responsibility. This, however, does not result in a transfer of obligations to subordinate company levels. Rather, the obligations of corporate management are transformed into selection and monitoring obligations. However, high standards are set for such allocation of tasks and in situations of crises, the general responsibility and overall competence of the management remains.

Although in the past a number of charges of offences against the environment have been dismissed, the risk of prosecution should not be underestimated. The selection and monitoring obligations a company manager/director has to fulfil in order to limit his criminal responsibility have been prescribed in great detail by court decisions. Furthermore, administrative authorities are increasingly aware of the criminal responsibility which might exist in the case of an environmental incident and are then prepared to initiate a prosecution.

3.2 Liability of those financing businesses

Liability of those financing businesses for conduct harmful to the environment (lender liability) is, in general, not recognised in the German legal system.

However, an exception to this rule may apply, first of all, if the lender exercises influence on the operation of the plant to an extent enabling him to be classified as the person/entity who directly caused a threat to the public safety and order (*Handlungsstörer*). While these requirements in most cases will not be met, special attention should be directed to the relevant financing agreements. If it can be concluded that, according to these agreements, the financing party has substantial control over the business, no statutory exception to the lender liability will apply.

Moreover, the lender may be held liable if, in the case of a conditional sale or a lease financing transaction, the lender is the legal owner of the plant and as such responsible under general police laws (*Zustandstörer*). A lender secured by a mortgage on the property is generally not responsible for environmental damage which has been caused on the property because, under German law, he does not acquire legal title to the property. This may change, however, if an event of default occurs under the loan agreements and the lender forecloses and acquires the property in order to protect its position (*Rettungskauf*).

Finally, the Bavarian Water Act (*Bayrisches Wassergesetz*), which entered into force in 1994, allows in certain cases for costs to be imposed resulting from remediation measures for soil and water contamination upon the person/entity secured by a property lien. The provision presumes that remediation measures carried out by a public institution such as the *Gesellschaft zur Altlastensanierung in Bayern mbH* lead to an increase in the value of the property and that it is justified to hold the secured party financially responsible. The new federal Soil Protection Act, however, provides for such a compensatory claim for publicly financed remediation measures to be made only against the owner of the premises. It can therefore be concluded that, under applicable law, the principle of lender liability remains restricted to the abovementioned categories.

3.3 Liability of the purchaser for existing environmental damage

When purchasing a company in Germany, the issue may arise as to whether responsibility for environmental damage caused whilst the seller (or a predecessor) was owner, passes to the successor-in-title.

This issue is, however, irrelevant with respect to the liability of the owner and the legal possessor of the site under states' general police laws (*Zustandsstörerhaftung*), since the liability applies afresh to each purchaser of the site.

Nevertheless, the purchaser of a company may also be confronted with environmental liability as a result of his position as successor-in-title to the person/entity who performed conduct harmful to the environment (*Rechtsnachfolge in die Handlungsstörerhaftung*). A number of state laws regulating water and soil protection and waste management expressly provide for the responsibility of the successor-in-title. The new Federal Soil Protection Act enables the competent authority to hold the universal successor (*Gesamtrechtsnachfolger*) to the party who caused the contamination liable. The liability of the universal successor is of importance if the polluter no longer exists or if he does not have the financial capacity to perform the necessary investigation and remediation measures. The parties to cross-border transactions are qualified as universal successors, however, only under certain conditions, for instance, if an entire business is acquired and continued under its previous name, if all or substantially all of the seller's assets are acquired, or in cases where a surviving company exists after a merger has taken place under the provisions of the Reorganisation Act (*Umwandlungsgesetz*). The singular successor (*Einzelrechtsnachfolger*), ie a person who only acquires a single object but does not assume the legal position of the seller as a whole, is generally not liable under German law. The liability of the universal successor under the new Soil Protection Act basically corresponds to the general principles of liability which have been developed by German administrative practice and related court decisions.

3.4 Obligations concerning corporate organisation

In order to ensure that environmental safety requirements are met, German environmental laws increasingly provide for obligations concerning the corporate organisation in addition to material requirements for the erection and operation of an installation. The objective of these provisions is not only to give the competent authorities a better insight into the corporate structure and the production flow but rather to enhance the company's internal ability to control and assess compliance with all relevant regulatory requirements.

A number of environmental laws (eg *§§ 53 ff BImSchG; §§ 54 ff KrW-/AbfG; §§ 21a ff WHG*) provide for enterprise delegates to be appointed by the operator of a plant. These employees monitor compliance with specific environmental obligations by the company and strive for constant improvement of the environmental performance of the company. The delegates must have the requisite technical qualification and reliability to perform the duties properly and are not bound by the instructions of corporate management. The independent monitoring function implies that these employees stand outside the general corporate hierarchy and have no independent decision-making power. Before taking any decisions regarding the introduction of processes and products as well as any investment decisions, however, the operator of the plant must seek the delegate's opinion on such matters. Furthermore, the operator shall ensure by means of internal organisational measures that the delegate can submit his proposals or objections direct to the corporate management.

In addition to the appointment of enterprise delegates for environmental matters, certain environmental laws (*§ 52a BImSchG; § 53 KrW-/AbfG*) provide for further organisational obligations. Corporate enterprises whose representative body consists of several members may be obliged to notify the competent authority as to which of them performs the duties of the operator of the installation subject to licensing in accordance with the regulations. By these means the competent authority is informed about the person internally in charge of the performance of environmental obligations. If the installation is subject to licensing under the federal Immission Control Act, the operator/managing director in charge of environmental matters shall also communicate to the competent authority whether and in which way the regulations and orders providing protection against harmful effects on the environment are being observed during operation. These regulations do not detail the independent organisational obligations of the company, but such obligations are, according to general opinion, presumed by this regulation. This means that a company is principally obliged to take organisational measures which guarantee fulfilment of the environmental law obligations. These are, in particular, measures of in-house monitoring, immediate reporting of incidents, instant measures of hazard avoidance etc.

3.5 Transferability of permits and licences

Whether the purchaser of a company can continue to enjoy environmental permits and licences which have been granted to the target company depends, first of all, on the method of acquisition the purchaser has decided upon.

In a merger and acquisition transaction, the purchaser may decide upon the acquisition of the company's shares (share purchase transaction). In this case there is no need for a conveyance of individual assets. Title to the assets and liabilities constituting the business is unaffected and the assets and liabilities remain within the company. Since the legal entity operating the business is the same, the existing permits remain effective.

If, alternatively, the purchaser acquires all the assets of the target company (asset purchase transaction) the assets and liabilities of the business to be acquired have to be transferred to the new owner. With respect to the transferability of permits and licences a distinction has to be drawn between installation-related permits/licences (*Realkonzession*) and holder-related permits (*Personalkonzession*). Whereas installation-related permits pass automatically with the acquisition of ownership to the new owner of the premises/operator of the plant, holder-related permits expire with the discontinuance of the operator's business.

Most permits required under German environmental law are installation-related (eg permission under federal Immission Control Act and Federal Water Act; building permission). As long as the operation of the plant, ie the production flow, the materials used etc, does not deviate from the permit granted to the target company, the competent authority will not need to review the permit. In some areas of environmental law there is at most a notification requirement (eg *§ 19a WHG*).

4 MANAGING ENVIRONMENTAL ISSUES IN TRANSACTIONS

Due to the high demands set by environmental legislation on the erection and operation of an installation and the different routes of environmental liability, it is important to direct special attention to the management of environmental matters before entering into a cross-border transaction.

Prior to any final decision on the financial investment in and the acquisition of the target company respectively, an investigation should be carried out with respect to the target company's compliance with environmental requirements. Only by this means can potential risks resulting from the former erection and operation of the plant be identified and, if necessary, adequately settled in the acquisition agreement. Moreover, the environmental assessment will have a considerable impact on the valuation of the target company. Aspects of environmental law also increasingly play a greater part in the banks' investigation of credit-worthiness.

In addition to an investigation into the former operation of the site, an analysis should be conducted as to the requirements which have to be met which respect to the future operation. If the installation cannot be operated in line with all requirements imposed by applicable law, the purchaser runs the risk that the competent authorities will issue subsequent orders or, at worst, will prohibit all or part of the operation. This may lead to increasing costs for legal compliance. Furthermore, uncertainties about the company's environmental situation may entail the risk of environmental incidents happening in the future for which the corporate management will be held liable. In this context, the issue may arise as to whether insurance coverage is available for environmental matters and which damages are covered.

In the following paragraphs, a number of crucial points concerning the management of environmental requirements in the course of a cross-border transaction are described in greater detail.

4.1 Environmental audits/environmental due diligence

An environmental audit should be performed in all significant transactions involving industrial facilities in order to evaluate the extent of potential liabilities. Such audits typically involve a review of documents and, as appropriate, site visits and contact with public authorities to ascertain the extent of compliance with environmental safety standards. Special attention should be directed to the permits/licences obtained by the company, hazardous substances used in the production, environmental incidents in the past, on-site soil or groundwater contamination, the organisational structure with regard to environmental safety standards, and insurance policies held by the target company.

The extent to which environmental due diligence is undertaken in Germany varies widely from case to case. In the course of a bidding process, due diligence of the target company is usually restricted to the review of documents made available to the interested parties in a data room. Even if the potential investor obtains knowledge of environmental incidents occurring during the former operation of the site, it is quite rare that soil or groundwater testing is undertaken to determine the extent of the contamination. More often, the parties involved insert special provisions into the acquisition agreement in order to allocate the risks associated with potential environmental liability.

4.2 The acquisition agreement

Public environmental liabilities may be imposed on a purchaser of a company, despite an agreement between the seller and the purchaser that the seller will retain all such liabilities. Although public law duties cannot be influenced by private law contracts, the consequences resulting from such duties can be regulated by private law in the relationship between the parties.

Under German law, environmental risks and liabilities between the contracting parties are, first of all, allocated by the provisions regarding liability under applicable law. Without any special clauses being inserted into the acquisition agreement the seller warrants under ss 459 ff of the German Civil Code (*§§ 459 ff BGB*) that, at the time when the risk passes to the purchaser, the asset sold is free from defects which diminish or destroy its value or its fitness for its ordinary use, or the use provided for in the contract. Additionally, the seller warrants that the asset has the promised qualities. The seller will not be responsible if the purchaser knew of the defect at the time of entering into the contract. If the defect has remained unknown to the purchaser as a consequence of gross negligence, the seller will be responsible only if he has fraudulently concealed it, unless he has guaranteed that the asset is free from defect. These general rules also apply to the acquisition of a company. Since environmental damage relating to the company, such as soil or groundwater contamination on the premises, constitute a defect of quality, the purchaser may demand cancellation of the sale or reduction of the purchase price. However, the claim for cancellation or reduction is subject to a limitation period, unless the seller has fraudulently concealed the defect, in the case of land, one year after the transfer.

In most cases it is advisable to modify or supplement the statutory provisions with regard to environmental liabilities in the acquisition agreement. First of all, the purchaser should demand that the seller expressly warrants that he has operated the site in accordance with the requirements imposed under applicable law; that he has obtained all permits and licences necessary for the operation of the site; and that, according to his knowledge, there have been no environmental incidents which may lead to the purchaser's liability.

If environmental incidents are known to the parties or indications of soil and/or groundwater contamination on the premises exist, the responsibility for investigation and clean-up measures as well as the cost burden for such measures should be clearly identified and allocated between the parties. Additionally, the agreement may contain special provisions enabling the purchaser to claim compensation from the seller if the competent authority holds the purchaser liable for environmental damage. Alternatively, the agreement can provide for a right of the purchaser to withdraw from the contact if contamination is found on the premises and the cost of necessary remediation measures exceeds a certain sum of money. Since contamination often only becomes apparent after the statutory limitation period has expired, the parties should consider extending this period in the contract. However, depending on the parties' bargaining power, the purchaser might have to accept that the seller will only assume the liability for a specific period of time or up to a specific amount. If the parties agree that remediation measures shall be borne by one party, it is advisable that the scope of remediation and the intended use of the premises after the remediation has been completed are specified in the acquisition agreement.

4.3 Management of environmental responsibility through corporate structuring

As mentioned above, a number of environmental laws prescribe certain minimum requirements for the corporate organisation in order to ensure compliance with environmental safety standards. Before entering into the acquisition agreement, the potential purchaser should investigate whether the target company meets these statutory requirements.

However, as the case may be, the issue of corporate structuring with respect to environmental matters may be of relevance during the cross-border acquisition even beyond these statutory minimum requirements. First of all, the existence of a corporate structure which ensures the company's compliance with environmental safety standards influences the valuation of the target company. A company which is capable of proving that clear responsibilities have been established as well as certain procedures in order to handle environmental matters is likely to be more attractive to any

4.3 Chapter 3

potential purchaser or investor. The company's environmental situation may be presented in an understandable way, enabling the purchaser to perform a reliable risk analysis.

The issue of a corporate structure concerning environmental matters may arise, secondly, after the acquisition of the target company has been completed. Considering circumstances such as the size of the company, its line of business, the chemicals used, and the production flow, it may be advantageous to implement a corporate structure which, beyond the statutory requirements with respect to the company's organisation, ensures compliance with environmental safety standards. The clear identification of addressees of environmental standards and their respective areas of responsibilities is essential to prevent environmental incidents during the future operation of the site. Furthermore, if the corporate management can demonstrate a duly performed and supervised delegation of environmental duties, it may discharge itself from its principal environmental obligations and therefore reduce the risk of being held liable under public, civil and criminal law. Finally, such corporate structure can be integrated into the process of analysing and optimising the production flow and thus contribute to an ecologically and economically reasonable use of natural resources such as water, energy etc.

To implement an organisational structure which ensures compliance with environmental safety standards, different organisation models are principally available. At the level below corporate management, it is possible, within the context of a 'specialist solution', to establish a specialised unit (an expert unit or environmental safety department), which is responsible for the implementation and monitoring of environmental protection measures throughout the company. In the 'integration solution', on the other hand, employees and departments or other organisational units are assigned the tasks of environmental protection alongside their other responsibilities. The assignment of responsibility to the respective employee should be formulated and documented with sufficient precision. In relation to management, reporting and notification duties should be specified. Delegation to subordinate company levels is possible.

4.4 Environmental management systems

In order to prove compliance with environmental safety standards and to establish an organisation enabling the company to analyse and improve its situation, companies in Germany have increasingly been participating in environmental management systems such as EMAS (European Union's Eco-Management and Audit Scheme) or ISO 14000 et seq (drafted by the International Standards Organisation). Of all EU member states, it seems that EMAS has found the highest degree of acceptance in Germany, although initially German business was opposed to the introduction of EMAS. By 1 October 1997, 836 German sites had been registered under EMAS and 280 sites under ISO 14001.

Whereas the environmental auditing guidelines as drawn up in ISO 14000 et seq are primarily meant for internal management purposes, EMAS provides for validation by external auditors and accredited environmental verifiers, environmental statements designed for distribution to the public, and the registration of the site, and therefore a higher degree of communication with the public. Furthermore, under EMAS the company has to aim for the continuous improvement of environmental performance, with a view to reducing environmental impact to levels not exceeding those corresponding to the economically viable application of the best available technology.

The participation in both management systems is, however, voluntary. Although the issue has been raised as to whether the participation in EMAS should, to some extent, entail a withdrawal of public control, until today at the federal level an easing of statutory requirements or notification obligations has not been agreed upon. The company's participation in a management system nevertheless makes it more attractive to the purchaser and might be beneficial with respect to the insuring of environmental risks.

4.5 Insurance

The insurability of environmental liability in Germany is considered one of the greatest problems in environmental law. To understand the insurance coverage currently available in the market it is helpful to take a look at the historical development of environmental insurance.

Originally, environmental liability for personal injury and damage to property was covered by the employer's regular liability insurance (*Betriebshaftpflichtversicherung*), which was supplemented in the late 1970s by the Policy 78 insurance (insurance protection against damage to property or pecuniary loss on the basis of soil, water and air pollution resulting from a hazardous incident on the plant site).

Additionally, since the beginning of the 1960s a special insurance policy has been available to cover strict statutory liability for damage to water (*Gewässerschadenshaftpflichtversicherung*) under s 22 of the federal Water Act *(§ 22 WHG)*. Initially, this insurance was well received by operators of facilities which posed a threat to water, not least because such policies were quite reasonably priced. This changed, however, in the beginning of the 1980s when differences began to emerge between insurance companies and policy-holders with respect to the coverage of damages arising from pre-existing contamination. As such damage often came into being as a result of decades of polluting the environment, ascertaining the time at which the damage was caused and thus the occurrence of the event insured against was at best difficult and in many cases impossible. The insurance industry argued with the so-called 'theory of the first drop', according to which the sweeping of harmful substances into the water is the decisive moment to determine the occurrence of damage. Accordingly, the person liable was eligible to claim insurance payments only if insurance cover existed at this point in time. Several more theories have been developed, however, on how to determine whether insurance cover exists in a certain case and which of several subsequent insurers has to pay out.

After the Environmental Liability Act came into force in 1991, which led to a considerable tightening-up of liability, the call increased for a change in the insurability of environmental damage. At the end of December 1992 the new 'environmental insurance model' (*Umwelthaftpflichtmodell*) of the insurance business was approved. This model provides for a uniform insurance cover for damages caused by effects on the environment (ie soil, air and/or water) pursuant to the Environmental Liability Act. The model consists of seven risk components of which the individual insurance contract may be composed. Each component describes an actual risk scenario, and the party to be insured can select the component which corresponds to its situation as the basis for its insurance policy.

The scope of insurance is limited to those risks which are expressly and clearly described in the insurance policy. This places considerable demands on the insured party. In order to obtain sufficient insurance cover, he must ascertain and specify the installations to be insured in an exact and correct way. Furthermore, any increase and expansion of risk after an insurance policy is taken out is excluded, provided it is not

4.5 *Chapter 3*

merely an increase in the quantity of the substances concerned. Therefore, an insured party must continually notify the insurer of all increases in risk which may be associated with an increase in administrative costs.

The new environmental insurance model provides a completely new definition of the occurrence of the event insured against. It takes into account the particular nature of the long-term developments in the environment. In the case of environmental damage, there are frequently long intervals between the cause of a damage, the actual occurrence of the damage, and the discovery of the damage. Thus, the new environmental insurance model deems the verifiable first discovery of the personal injury, damage to property, or pecuniary loss by the party who suffered damage, a third party or the insured party as decisive. This permits a clear temporal classification of the occurrence of the event insured against, which should ease the proof of insurance protection for the insured party.

Compared to the former insurance, the coverage for expenditure prior to the occurrence of the event insured against (so-called rescue costs) has been reduced significantly. Only expenditure necessary for measures after a disruption in operations or in accordance with an order of a public authority will be covered in future. Furthermore, the expenditure to be reimbursed is limited to a certain amount per occurrence and the insured party is required to retain part of the uninsured risk. Despite the reduction of the scope of insurance coverage, the tariffs have been raised under the new insurance model.

Any environmental damage caused by the normal operation of an installation is excluded from insurance protection, although the operator of an installation is liable for such damage under the terms of the Environmental Liability Act. An exception to this rule applies only if the insured party proves that he was not in a position where he ought to have recognised the possibility of such damage, judging by the state of technology at the time of the effect on the environment.

In summary, it can be stated that insurability of environmental risks is limited. In each case it needs a thorough investigation of all relevant installations and risk components. Moreover, one should keep in mind that the new environmental liability insurance model excludes certain risks and provides for maximum amounts payable per occurrence of an event insured against.

5   CONCLUSION

Over the last three decades, German environmental law has developed at such a rate and with such density and complexity that it is criticised as unclear and confusing. German environmental law can be characterised as a system predominated by public control and sanction in case of non-compliance with statutory requirements. Primarily, the environmental laws are designed along single media such as air, water, soil. In this context, a high standard of environmental protection is striven for by prescribing threshold values and technical requirements for the relevant media combined with very detailed testing procedures.

As already mentioned, German environmental law is increasingly influenced and overlapped by directives enacted by the European Community. EC law, however, has a direction in many ways different from the German approach. The IPPC Directive (Directive (EC) 96/61) for instance, which entered into force on 30 October 1997, aims at an integrated appoach to pollution prevention and control. It is based on the assumption that, despite its complexity, for pollution control purposes the environment must be perceived as a single interrelated medium. Therefore, the effects of activities and substances on the environment as a whole, and the complete commercial and environmental lifecycles of substances shall be taken into account when assessing the risks they pose and when developing and implementing controls to limit their release. By providing for licensing procedures which follow this integrated approach to protect the environment effectively and prevent the movement of substances from one medium to another, the IPPC Directive goes beyond the already existing environmental impact assessment.

Another approach increasingly stressed by European Community's legislation in the field of environmental law is the mobilisation of the public in order to influence the compliance with environmental standards. Accordingly, special access to information has been provided for, detached from any administrative procedure.

Finally, market oriented instruments and the strengthening of the companies' own responsibilty for the protection of the environment have gained more and more importance. A management system such as EMAS, in which the participation is based on voluntary conduct, carries with it the assumption that the participation in the system can be used as a marketing tool, thus making it attractive to companies to join the system.

Taking into account these developments at the EC level it can be expected that, at least to some extent, the German environmental system will be adapted in the near future. In which way this will happen remains to be seen. The discussions stimulated by the enactment of the IPPC Directive show that integrating the new EC approaches into the existing German system will require considerable effort and may lead to major changes in the field of environmental law. Furthermore, the issue as to whether public control can, to some extent, be withdrawn and replaced by consensual measures is also being discussed increasingly in Germany. To promote Germany as a place of business it is deemed necessary to shorten the licensing requirements and to make them more flexible. For companies doing business in Germany this could mean that in the future a degree of discretion will be left as to how the company ensures that it complies with environmental safety standards. The strengthening of the companies' own responsibility for environmental compliance should not be conceived, however, as a reduction of the material requirements to protect the environment. On the contrary, due to the growing sensitivity in terms of environmental protection and the use of indirect measures of control (eg environmental taxes and levies) it can be expected that companies will increasingly be required to implement the necessary steps to comply with and, sometimes even to be ahead of, environmental safety standards. Thus, environmental law will remain of crucial importance when performing a cross-border transaction involving a German company.

Chapter 4

THE UNITED KINGDOM

Mark J Brumwell

SJ Berwin & Co

1 INTRODUCTION

'A sleeping giant, just stirring from his slumber.' That was a colleague's recent description of UK environmental law. He was expressing the wide-ranging nature of environmental law and the multitude of legislative and common law provisions in UK domestic law, as well as the ever-increasing importance of EU law.

The epithet 'sleeping' is open to misinterpretation, as UK environmental law is a very lively and dynamic body of law. There is great potential for the law to impose substantial liabilities and obligations on both the corporate world and individuals, but so far, practical application of the law has been characterised by wide-ranging pragmatism and realism by UK regulatory bodies and the UK has also had relatively few high-profile civil suits concerning pollution and other environmental problems compared, for example, with the US.

The first part of this chapter looks at the framework within which this 'slumbering giant' of law is applied in this country, with later discussion concentrating on the specific legal controls and how they are dealt with in transactions.

1.1 Origin of environmental law

United Kingdom law originates from both domestic institutions and the European Union. European Union environmental law primarily arises from directives issued by the European Commission which are then brought into force in the UK by domestic regulations made under the European Communities Act 1972. For example, Directive (EC) 85/337 on the Assessment of the Effects of Certain Public and Private Projects on the Environment is applied in the UK primarily by the Town and Country Planning (Environmental Impact Assessment) (England and Wales) Regulations 1999, SI 1999/293.

Despite the undoubted influence of EU environmental law, the majority of the more important controls in the UK originate from domestic law, primarily from two sources:

(1) Acts of Parliament (also known as statutes) enacted by the legislature in London; and
(2) common law, which is the body of decisions made by the judiciary, originating with general legal principles such as negligence, nuisance and trespass.

1.1 Chapter 4

The majority of the most frequently applied environmental provisions come from one or both of these domestic sources. Consequently, an understanding of EU environmental law gives only a patchy view of the environmental law which actually applies in the UK on a day-to-day basis. Important areas such as pollution of rivers, streams and groundwater and contaminated land are all dealt with primarily by UK domestic law, with EU environmental law introducing additional requirements or enhancements without fundamentally altering the basic principles which apply.

In addition to these primary sources, a certain amount of environmental law originates at local level, with byelaws enacted by local authorities, water and sewerage companies and other bodies under an element of statutory control. Typically, byelaws can govern areas such as rivers, canals, docks and public parks or activities such as the provision of flood defences.

The organisation of legal affairs within the UK is divided into three main geographical areas:

(1) England and Wales;
(2) Scotland;
(3) Northern Ireland.

The Channel Islands, Isle of Man and Isles of Scilly have separate legal regimes, but space precludes their examination.

At the time of writing, the UK is going through a process of political re-examination and reform as a result of the election of a Labour government in May 1997 after 18 years of Conservative control, during which the balance of power moved away from local to central government. Devolution for the UK is now taking place with new legislative assemblies being established for Scotland and for Wales and the transfer of some law making power away from London.

At present, virtually identical systems of law apply in England and Wales. Scotland and Northern Ireland's systems are different at a technical level, in that separate statutes sometimes apply in Scotland as opposed to England and Wales, while legislation in Northern Ireland is provided by Orders in Council. However, although the technical law is different, in general quite similar principles apply, although the timing of the introduction of new legislation is often different. However, property law applying in England and Wales on the one hand and Scotland on the other is radically different and this always needs to be borne in mind when dealing with issues in both jurisdictions, given that environmental matters frequently have a property-based context. Both the concepts of property interests and the mechanics of purchase and sale transactions for land are markedly different.

1.2 Enforcement of environmental law

Enforcement of environmental regulation in England and Wales is the responsibility of a number of environmental regulators, principally:

(1) the Environment Agency which administers the more wide-ranging and important controls such as water pollution, waste management and integrated pollution control;
(2) local authority environmental health departments which control atmospheric pollution permitting, statutory nuisance and a variety of more minor controls;
(3) sewerage undertakers which, despite now being private companies, retain statutory powers to regulate the discharge of trade effluent to the drainage system;

(4) the Nuclear Installations Inspectorate which deals with the specialised control of nuclear power stations and other radioactive sources.

Areas related to environmental controls, such as workplace health and safety, have additional regulators. The Health and Safety Commission is responsible for promoting legislation and guidance, advised by the Health and Safety Executive (HSE). The HSE and local authorities are jointly responsible for enforcement of the law with local authorities dealing with certain categories of workplaces, mainly distribution, retail, office, leisure and catering premises.

In Scotland, a separate regulator, the Scottish Environmental Protection Agency (SEPA), has the majority of controls covered in England and Wales by the Environment Agency. However, in contrast to England and Wales, waste management licensing remains with local authorities and trade effluent control is enforced by SEPA.

In Northern Ireland, responsibility for environmental enforcement lies largely with the Environment & Heritage Service, an agency of central government.

The Environment Agency became operational in 1996 as an amalgamation of the National Rivers Authority, Her Majesty's Inspectorate of Pollution and the waste regulation arm of local authority environmental control. It has a staff of over 7,000 and is organised on a regional basis, although there is a significant degree of central control in terms of policy making and practice, with the Agency issuing codes of practice covering its activities on matters such as enforcement.

The Environment Agency is not an elected body, its board being appointees of the central government Department of Environment, Transport and the Regions and Ministry of Agriculture Fisheries and Food. In contrast, local authority regulators are highly political and while individual council officers dealing with day-to-day issues are not elected, they report to elected council members who make or endorse all the major decisions of the council. Sewerage undertakers are organised as companies with shareholder owners and management by a board of directors. However, to protect the interests of its customers, the companies are subject to overall regulation by the Director General of Water Services.

In this chapter the specific law applying in England and Wales will be examined, although many of the principles will be of equal application in the other areas of the UK.

2 OUTLINE OF ENVIRONMENTAL LAW RELEVANT TO MERGER AND ACQUISITION TRANSACTIONS

Although environmental law in the UK is a mixture of statutory and common law, the common law is based on existing principles such as negligence, nuisance and trespass. In contrast, statute law has been developed specifically to deal with environmental issues and, as such, provides a number of legal principles of particular application to environmental matters and of special interest in transactions. This section of the chapter inevitably concentrates on statute law, although the importance of common law liability should also be remembered.

2.1 Contaminated land

At the time of writing, the UK is still awaiting the introduction of a statutory regime specifically dealing with the allocation of liability for contaminated land. The issue is an important one, as this country has a long history of industrial development, much of it undertaken at a time when the importance of caring for the environment was

2.1 Chapter 4

unrecognised. In addition, the cost of dealing with serious land contamination problems is often considerable. Although the law in this area is still developing, this has not prevented land contamination liabilities becoming a highly significant issue in the UK, both on redevelopment of contaminated land and in the ongoing management of day-to-day environmental risk.

The Environment Act 1995 (EA 1995) introduced a set of principles to deal with this problem, the statutory rules being amplified in guidance issued in draft by the Department of the Environment in September 1996 and successively updated in 1998 and 1999. The regime is likely to be brought into force in April 2000, with guidance in a similar form to the draft issued in September 1996.

The EA 1995 introduces the contaminated land controls by incorporating a new Pt IIA into the UK's principal environmental statute, the Environmental Protection Act 1990 (EPA 1990). The controls will apply retrospectively without any time limit so that liability is attracted for land contaminated by past as well as future actions.

The regime will be operated jointly by the Environment Agency and local authorities, the Agency dealing with Special Sites, classified as such by their greater likely significance, with local authorities dealing with all other sites.

To take action, the relevant authority has first to identify property as being 'contaminated land' which is defined by EPA 1990, s 78A(2) as being, in that authority's opinion, in such a condition due to the presence of substances in, on or under it that either:

(a) significant harm is being caused; or
(b) there is a significant possibility of significant harm being caused; or
(c) pollution of controlled waters is being or is likely to be caused.

Once 'contaminated land' has been identified, the relevant authority has a duty to serve a remediation notice requiring the property to be brought into a satisfactory condition. The remediation notice can only be served on an 'appropriate person', defined by EPA 1990, s 78F as being either:

(1) any person or persons who caused or knowingly permitted the substances or any of the substances by virtue of which the land is regarded as 'contaminated land' to be in, on or under the land; or
(2) if no such person can be found after reasonable inquiry, the current owner or occupier of the property.

Failure to comply with a remediation notice without reasonable excuse constitutes a criminal offence under EPA 1990, s 78M, with a fine of up to £20,000 plus a daily penalty for a continuing failure to comply.

Two particular features of this regime are worthy of special note:

(1) a person (and this phrase includes a company, a partnership and any other recognised legal entity) can remain liable for the condition of property which he caused or knowingly permitted to be contaminated, even if he has disposed of the property to another party. Although he may no longer own or even occupy the property, he can still be served with a remediation notice in respect of it, although there are various mechanisms whereby a person may become released from this continuing liability in practice; and
(2) an owner or occupier of property can become liable for its contaminated condition even if he did not cause its pollution and even if he did not know that it was contaminated.

The United Kingdom 2.2

Until the regime in Pt IIA of the EPA 1990 comes into force, contaminated land remains within the general ambit of Pt III of that Act which controls statutory nuisance. The operation of this regime is described more fully below, but EPA 1990, s 79 of the Act confirms that a statutory nuisance can include:

'any premises [being] in such a state as to be prejudicial to health or a nuisance'.

Notices to require the nuisance to be abated can be served by the local authority on the person responsible for the nuisance or, where such a person cannot be found, on the owner or occupier of the premises.

Traditionally, the law of statutory nuisance has been used infrequently to address contaminated land problems. Land contamination is a legally complex issue in terms of identifying the origin and effects of pollution and who should be made responsible for any clean-up. The statutory nuisance controls are essentially simple tools more appropriate for use against factory or domestic noise and smell emissions.

2.2 Pollution of water resources

In contrast to the developing nature of the contaminated land regime, controls over water resource pollution have been in existence for some time and have been used frequently by environmental regulators. In common with contaminated land, this is an area where considerable liability issues often arise. Statute law on this subject is now encapsulated in the Water Resources Act 1991 (WRA 1991) which deals with the pollution of 'controlled waters', defined in WRA 1991, s 104 as:

(a) territorial waters up to 3 miles from the coastline;
(b) waters inland from territorial waters, meaning all saltwater and freshwater surface resources including rivers, streams, lakes, ponds and docks;
(c) groundwaters, meaning water in any underground strata.

Under WRA 1991, ss 85 and 88, it is an offence to cause or knowingly permit any poisonous, noxious or polluting matter or solid waste to enter controlled waters, other than in accordance with the terms of a relevant permit.

The phrase to 'cause or knowingly permit' is again used in this legislation and it is in this context that the phrase has been most frequently the subject of judicial opinion. Many cases have concentrated on the extent to which a person has to be associated with a chain of events leading to pollution for the person to be said to have 'caused or knowingly permitted' the pollution. Two cases are of particular interest and give a flavour of the general approach.

In *National Rivers Authority v Yorkshire Water Services*,[1] a company was operating a sewage works which discharged the contents of treated effluent to a river by gravity. An unknown person discarded a quantity of iso-octonal into the sewer system which passed through the works and into the river. The company had not acted positively to discharge the iso-octonal into the river and it was accepted that, as the iso-octanol disposal was an isolated instance, the company could not have reasonably foreseen it, but the High Court nevertheless considered that it was open to the Crown Court to conclude that, through mere passive operation of the sewage works, the sewage company had 'caused' the discharge.

Similarly, in *Empress Car Company (Abertillery) Ltd v National Rivers Authority*[2] a stopcock on a diesel tank was opened by an unknown person and the contents of the

1 [1995] 1AC 444.
2 [1997] Env LR 227.

tank drained into a local river. The company which owned the tank was successfully prosecuted for causing pollution under WRA 1991, s 85 because the company had created a situation where contamination could occur and the act of the third party which had actually led to the release was an ordinary rather than extraordinary event which had not interrupted the causal link to the company.

A person committing an offence of 'causing or knowingly permitting' a discharge is liable to a fine which is not subject to a financial limit if action is taken in the Crown Court rather than the Magistrates' Court. A prison sentence of up to 2 years can also be imposed on a Crown Court action, with a lower limit of 3 months for an offence tried in the Magistrates' Court. The average penalties imposed by the courts for these offences are increasing and in spring 1998 ICI was fined £300,000 for a water pollution incident occurring from its Runcorn plant.

However, the more substantial penalty in many cases is the cost of cleaning up the pollution, particularly if, as is sometimes the case with general UK insurance policies, the polluter has only limited insurance cover against the cost. Section 161 of the Water Resources Act 1991 allows the Environment Agency to carry out work to clean up or prevent pollution and then serve a notice to recover the cost from the person who 'caused or knowingly permitted' the pollution to occur or to be in a position where pollution was likely to occur. In practice, this provision has been of limited use since the Agency is reluctant to take action where there is the possibility that it will be unsuccessful subsequently in recovering costs, so ss 161A–161D of the WRA 1991 were introduced by EA 1995, now allowing the Agency to serve a works notice requiring the person who 'caused or knowingly permitted' the pollution to occur to carry out clean-up or preventative works themselves.

2.3 Water resource discharge and abstraction licensing

Consents for the discharge of substances into controlled waters are granted under WRA 1991, Sch 10. Discharges may also be permitted under a variety of other legislation including waste management licences and integrated pollution control consents. Discharge consents can prescribe the point of discharge and the quantity and composition of the effluent.

Abstraction of water from inland rivers, streams, lakes and ponds or from groundwater is permitted only by a licence issued under s 24 of the WRA 1991. The licence will usually prescribe the maximum quantity and rate of flow of the abstraction and the purpose for which the water is to be used.

For industrial processes with substantial water requirements, abstraction licences can be vital for their operations and are valuable assets, although they are subject to an overriding ability of the Environment Agency to modify or even revoke licences in certain circumstances.

The UK government is currently looking at options for increasing the cost of water discharge consents to provide an added incentive to reduce harmful discharges. A consultation paper was issued in January 1998 containing proposals for the introduction of market-based instruments for future water discharges or a more straightforward taxation charge grafted on to the existing permit system.

2.4 Integrated pollution control

For particularly complex or hazardous operations with a combination of discharges, an integrated pollution control (IPC) permit is required under provisions in Pt I of the

EPA 1990. These permits are granted by the Environment Agency and typically govern discharges to the air and water and of solid waste.

Part I of the EPA 1990 also controls air emission permitting through atmospheric pollution control (APC) permits for a variety of lesser operations (see para 2.5 below). However, many of the principles of IPC are of application also to APC.

The concept of IPC permitting is similar to the integrated pollution prevention and control system (IPPC) being introduced to member states of the European Union by Directive (EC) 96/61. This also governs a variety of discharges in a single permit but takes an even more holistic approach to environmental permitting by bringing matters such as the installation's energy consumption under control. IPC is solely concerned with the 'outputs' from an installation. IPPC governs certain of the 'inputs' as well. In the UK, IPPC has been introduced by the Pollution Prevention and Control Act 1999. The new control is due to be implemented in October 1999.

A central principle of IPC is that every process should be operated using the best available techniques not entailing excessive cost to minimise pollution (BATNEEC). Section 7(4) of the EPA 1990 provides that every IPC permit is subject to this requirement as a general condition. The specific requirements of BATNEEC for any process are determined having regard to the best practicable environmental option for minimising the release of any particular substance. Numerous guidance notes issued by the Environment Agency and its predecessor regulator are relevant to how these principles are applied for any given industry or process. IPC permits are also subject to reviews every four years, giving the Environment Agency the opportunity to impose tougher discharge restrictions as long as they are within the concept of BATNEEC. Holders of IPC permits may therefore be subject to periodic equipment upgrading requirements with consequent cost implications.

Section 23 of the EPA 1990 provides for a variety of offences including the operation of a prescribed process without an IPC permit or failure to comply with the conditions of a permit. Fines and imprisonment can be imposed, with unlimited fines and up to two years' imprisonment for serious offences tried in the Crown Court. However, in addition to the criminal penalties applied by EPA 1990 s 23, an administrative enforcement regime is available under EPA 1990, ss 13 and 14, which will often be used by the Environment Agency instead of or before criminal proceedings. EPA 1990, s 13 allows the Environment Agency to serve an enforcement notice on an IPC operator where the process is not operating in accordance with the conditions of the consent, specifying steps which the operator should take to become compliant. In particularly serious cases, where the Environment Agency believes that the process is causing an imminent risk of serious pollution of the environment, the Agency can serve a prohibition notice under EPA 1990, s 14, withdrawing the authorisation until the steps set out in the notice are taken. An operator receiving a prohibition notice must suspend operation of the process until the terms of the notice are complied with, otherwise he risks prosecution for carrying on an unauthorised process.

2.5 Emissions to atmosphere

Part I of the EPA 1990 also governs industrial and other processes which have significant emissions to the atmosphere but are not prescribed for IPC consents. The APC authorisation process is policed by local authorities rather than the Environment Agency. Although there are a variety of centrally issued guidance notes which describe how APC control should be applied, it is fair to say that there is relatively little consistency in the practical application of this regime from one local authority area to another. Some local authorities have the expertise to deal with the control

2.5 Chapter 4

particularly effectively while others often find it difficult to resource this area of their work leading to widespread non-compliance. An audit of 50 local authority regulators by Cardinal Environment for the Department of Environment, Transport and the Regions published in May 1998 indicated that 90% of air pollution improvements required by government guidance by March 1998 had been implemented, but noted that many authorities were failing to carry out the required level of systematic inspection and that a significant proportion of upgrading programmes required by APC consents were behind their time schedules.

The powers described in para 2.4 above as available to the Environment Agency are also available to local authorities for APC processes and equivalent offences can also be committed by process operators.

2.6 Waste management including recycling/re-use obligations

Waste management is governed primarily by the provisions of Pt II of the EPA 1990. It is a particularly complex area of UK environmental law and has been influenced significantly by the development of EU waste management law.

Section 33 of the EPA 1990 prohibits the deposit, treatment, keeping or disposal of 'controlled waste' other than in accordance with a waste management licence and provides that an offence is committed by anyone 'causing or knowingly permitting' the deposit etc of waste in this way. It is a further offence for a person to treat, keep or dispose of waste in a way likely to pollute the environment or cause harm to human health.

A range of criminal penalties is available in this area, similar to those described above for IPC, APC and water pollution, but the civil enforcement and prohibition notice procedures are absent in waste management control. However, the level of criminal penalties is high with an unlimited fine and up to five years' imprisonment available for serious offences involving 'Special Waste', a prescribed category of particularly hazardous or polluting substances. Prosecutions under the waste management legislation are relatively frequent compared with other areas of environmental control, although this is partly a feature of the waste industry in the UK where there are still a significant number of small businesses operating with insufficient environmental management.

'Controlled waste' is now defined in accordance with the requirements of Directive (EEC) 75/442 (as amended), commonly known as the Waste Framework Directive, by reference to the holder discarding it, intending to discard it or being required to discard it. The various categories of substance within this overall description are now incorporated in Sch 2B to the EPA 1990 (EPA 1990, s 75).

Waste is an area of environmental law which touches most businesses in the UK which may otherwise be unaffected by environmental law, at least on a day-to-day basis. The application to many businesses is through the requirements of the waste duty of care introduced by s 34 of the EPA 1990. This applies to any person importing, producing, carrying, keeping or disposing of controlled waste and provides that the person has a duty to take all applicable measures to prevent others from contravening EPA 1990, s 33, to prevent the escape of waste from his control and to transfer waste only to authorised persons with a sufficient written description of the waste.

The practical application of the duty is explained in a code of practice issued by the Department of the Environment in March 1996. However, there is still widespread failure to comply with the duty and code of practice, particularly by businesses which have low level environmental impacts and are subject to little other environmental control. However, prosecutions for uncompounded failures to comply with the waste management duty of care are relatively rare.

At present, the UK does not apply wide-ranging waste recovery or recycling obligations to companies or individuals, although there are government policy initiatives in this area. However, the UK's overall performance in recycling and re-use of waste is poor compared to many other EU member states and the country has also been reliant traditionally on landfill sites for the disposal of much domestic and industrial waste. Use of landfill is likely to decline following the introduction in October 1996 of the UK's first overt environmental tax, the landfill tax, and also from the introduction of the Directive on Landfill Sites which will introduce stringent landfill reduction targets and prevent disposal of putrescible and non-putrescible waste at the same landfill site.

A notable exception is provided by the Producer Responsibility Obligations (Packaging Waste) Regulations 1997, SI 1997/648, which were introduced in June 1997. These regulations transpose the requirements of Directive (EC) 94/62 into UK law and impose obligations on 'obligated persons' to recover and recycle a specified proportion of packaging waste, with existing targets increasing from 2001 onwards. The regulations are complex and their implementation has proved difficult for the Environment Agency which is tasked with policing the regime. Many obligated businesses have still failed to register either with the Agency or with one of several approved collective compliance schemes and the Agency is concentrating on getting the existing registered businesses to perform properly rather than chasing those which have failed to respond at all.

2.7 Land use planning/zoning

Land use planning control in the UK has a long history, commencing with the Town and Country Planning Act 1947. The control is operated primarily by local authorities and is subject to a considerably greater degree of political influence than other environmental regimes. Controversial planning applications frequently attract local interest and objections which the local authority must deal with, always bearing in mind that the authority's councillors are elected individuals who will be conscious of the popularity of their decisions within the local area.

In addition to local authorities, the Secretary of State for Environment, Transport and the Regions has a role, primarily to determine appeals by applicants for planning permission where permission had been refused by the local authority or where the authority has failed to take a decision within the prescribed timescale, and through calling in for his own determination planning applications of more than local significance.

In 1990, land use planning legislation was consolidated into three main Acts:

(1) Town and Country Planning Act 1990 (TCPA 1990);
(2) Planning (Listed Buildings and Conservation Areas) Act 1990; and
(3) Planning (Hazardous Substances) Act 1990.

The central provisions are contained in the TCPA 1990 which provides that planning permission is required for 'development', defined by s 55 of the TCPA 1990 as either:

(a) 'the carrying out of building, engineering, mining or other operations in, on, over or under land' or
(b) 'the making of a material change of use of any buildings or other land'.

2.7 *Chapter 4*

Carrying out development without planning permission or other than in accordance with planning permission can result in the service of an enforcement notice under TCPA 1990, s 172 which specifies the steps required to remedy the breach of planning control. An appeal against an enforcement notice will suspend its application until the appeal is determined, so s 183 of the TCPA 1990 provides that where the local authority deems it expedient, it may serve a stop notice requiring the steps to be taken before the enforcement notice comes into effect. However, if an appeal is launched against the related enforcement notice and is successful, the local authority may in certain circumstances be required to pay compensation for losses arising from compliance with the stop notice, so this procedure is used relatively infrequently.

The Planning (Listed Buildings and Conservation Areas) Act 1990 is essentially concerned with the protection of historical buildings and areas. It contains particularly stringent controls over demolition, alteration or extension of historic buildings contained in a list maintained by the Historic Buildings and Monuments Commission (known as English Heritage). These are known as Listed Buildings.

Also dealing with the preservation of the built environment is the Ancient Monuments and Archaeological Areas Act 1979 which provides additional protection for scheduled and ancient monuments as well as designated areas of archaeological importance.

The Planning (Hazardous Substances) Act 1990 provides a control regime operated by the local authority whereby a licence is required for the keeping on, over or under land of more than a particular quantity of specified hazardous substances. Licences are granted by local authorities and the substances and quantities to which the control applies are set out in the Planning (Hazardous Substances) Regulations 1992, SI 1992/656.

The long history of UK planning control has meant that the system has evolved with relatively little influence from the European Union. However, there is one area of planning control which has been significantly affected and which is now prominent in more substantial projects, namely environmental impact assessments (EIAs).

EIAs originate from Directive (EEC) 85/337 on the Assessment of the Effect of Certain Public and Private Projects on the Environment. This directive has been brought into force by a variety of UK statutory instruments, principally (and most recently) the Town and Country Planning (Environmental Impact Assessment) (England and Wales) Regulations 1999, SI 1999/293. For projects listed

(a) in Sch 1 to the 1999 Regulations; and
(b) in Sch 2 to the 1999 Regulations and which are likely to give rise to significant effects on the environment by virtue of factors such as their nature, size or location;

planning consent should not be given without an assessment of the environmental impacts having been made.

The UK has seen several high profile court actions in the UK concerning the need for an EIA for particular projects. These types of cases were particularly prevalent when regulations first came into force, but the issues are still very significant and are often used by environmental pressure groups, a particularly notable case being *R v Swale Borough Council and Medway Ports, ex p Royal Society for the Protection of Birds*[3] in which the Royal Society for the Protection of Birds challenged the lack of an EIA for proposals connected with expansion of the Port of Sheerness.

---

3 [1991] 1 PLR 6.

2.8 Use and storage of hazardous substances including radioactive material

The control of hazardous substances is an area where environmental, employee health and safety and land use planning classifications overlap, the two main legislative provisions being:

(1) the Control of Industrial Major Accident Hazard Regulations 1984, SI 1984/1902 (COMAH Regulations); and
(2) the Planning (Hazardous Substances) Act 1990.

The COMAH Regulations made under the Health and Safety at Work etc Act 1974 implement the 'Seveso' Directive (EEC) 82/501 which was a response to an accident near Milan, Italy in 1976 in which a large release of dioxins occurred from a chemical plant, leading to widespread contamination in the vicinity of the plant and evacuation of the local population. The COMAH Regulations provide that persons in control of specified industrial activities which are capable of producing a major accident hazard should identify those hazards and take adequate steps to prevent their occurrence. Should a major accident occur, the person in control must notify the Health and Safety Executive (HSE).

For certain sites which present a greater level of risk, the COMAH Regulations impose additional obligations to provide, before commencing operations:

(1) a report on the use and storage of the hazardous substances involved which should include the number of people present, the management system used to control the activity, and any preventative measures adopted;
(2) an emergency plan describing how major accidents will be dealt with; and
(3) information to members of the public who may be affected by an accident, including procedures for warning of an accident and action to be taken in the event of an emergency.

The COMAH Regulations are policed by the HSE who have prosecution powers under the Health and Safety at Work Act 1974 for criminal offences involving a compliance failure.

In contrast to the COMAH Regulations, the Planning (Hazardous Substances) Act 1990 provisions are entirely domestic in origin (see para 2.7 above).

Control over the keeping and use of radioactive sources and the accumulation of radioactive waste is provided by the Radioactive Substances Act 1993. A person keeping or using radioactive material at any premises for the purposes of an undertaking is required to be registered or covered by an exemption (Radioactive Substances Act 1993, s 6). Similar provisions apply to radioactive sources in mobile equipment. Sections 13 and 14 provide that the disposal or accumulation with a view to subsequent disposal of radioactive waste is prohibited unless pursuant to an authorisation from the Agency or an appropriate exemption. Enforcement and prohibition notices can be served for compliance failures (similar to the notice provisions for IPC control outlined above) and there are criminal penalties for failing to obtain or comply with the terms of authorisations or registrations. For serious offences tried before the Crown Court, penalties can be unlimited fines and imprisonment for up to five years.

2.9 Noise and nuisance

Noise and nuisance are issues both in UK statute law and in common law, the common law predating statutory involvement. Common law gives a right of action in private nuisance arising from unlawful interference with another person's use or enjoyment of land and damages can be awarded by the civil courts as well as an injunction to prevent continuance of the action causing nuisance. The ability to take action is dependent on an interference with property rights, so action is limited to those with a recognised ownership or occupation interest in land.

Statutory nuisance, in contrast, does not suffer from such restrictions. Section 80 of the EPA 1990 obliges a local authority which is satisfied that a statutory nuisance exists to serve an abatement notice either on the person responsible for the nuisance or where they cannot be found on the owner or occupier of the premises, or where the nuisance arises from a structural defect, on the owner of the premises. The abatement notice must specify the steps required to abate the nuisance and if the person receiving the notice fails without reasonable excuse to comply with it, he may be liable to a fine of up to £20,000.

The term 'statutory nuisance' is defined by s 79 of the EPA 1990 to include a number of alternative elements including the state and condition of premises, the emission of smoke, fumes, gases, steam or smells and the emission of noise. To constitute statutory nuisance, the matter complained of must be sufficiently serious to be 'prejudicial to health or a nuisance'.

Section 82 of the EPA 1990 contains a useful further provision allowing a person aggrieved by the nuisance to commence proceedings to require the court to make an order to abate the nuisance, rather than relying on the local authority to do so. To many litigants, this can be an attractive alternative to taking civil proceedings in that action is taken in the magistrates' court which has simplified procedures, with a significantly lower cost.

3 PARTICULAR ENVIRONMENTAL ISSUES RELEVANT TO TRANSACTIONS

There are a number of common themes and principles arising from these areas of law which are particularly relevant for commercial transactions and which will often dictate how a transaction is to be structured and the extent to which pre-transaction due diligence should be undertaken.

3.1 Assumption of liabilities—routes and basis for liabilities

A common general principle of commercial transactions in the UK is that acquisition of shares in a company will result in the assumption by the purchaser of that company's entire liabilities, whereas acquisition of a company's assets will only attract the liabilities which the law applies directly to those assets. Environmental law is no exception and reinforces the principle in that much environmental liability in the corporate world is applied to companies rather than assets.

A common theme of statutory environmental law is that a person who 'causes or knowingly permits' a state of affairs to exist is primarily liable to prosecution or for clean-up requirements imposed by the regulatory authorities. This applies for example to contaminated land, water resource pollution and waste management.

In general, this type of liability applies retrospectively without a specific time limit within which the authorities must take action. This is entirely consistent with the nature of many environmental problems which do not become apparent for some considerable period following the originating incident. However, this means that particularly thorough due diligence exercises are needed if the full extent of any historical problems are to be assessed.

Unfortunately, purchase of assets rather than shares will not necessarily solve the problem, as UK environmental law imposes liability on assets in a number of important areas. An asset purchase will require the transfer of all relevant operating permits (a process which in itself may add significantly to the proposed timetable for the transaction). The acquiring company will assume liability for compliance with the terms of those licences following the purchase. Additionally, the contaminated land controls in the EA 1995, when brought into force, will impose liability on the current owner or occupier of contaminated land where no person 'causing or knowingly permitting' contamination can be identified or found. Furthermore, the company which acquires property knowing that it is contaminated or having had the opportunity to investigate the property in this respect may also find itself liable as a 'knowing permitter' in respect of the contaminated land, with the regulatory authorities serving remediation notices on them rather than the original polluter. The purchaser of property from which a contaminating substance is being emitted may also find itself liable in civil proceedings to those who are adversely affected. Also, the statutory nuisance provisions impose liability on the person causing nuisance or, if that person cannot be found, on the owner or occupier of the property which is causing the nuisance.

Thus, although an asset purchase may reduce the areas of liability which may be acquired, it does not obviate the need for a thorough assessment of the assets which are being purchased.

3.2 Historical liabilities—past practices and procedures, including those of former site owners

As outlined above, an element of liability can be retained for previously owned assets, particularly land, and can strike many years after the asset has been sold. Naturally, there are problems of proof in demonstrating that a historical problem was caused by a particular company at a particular time, but the law does provide for this possibility in some circumstances.

This area of liability needs to be addressed in many transactions but, by its nature, it is often very difficult to quantify. Although desk top due diligence investigations can be undertaken, these will not provide as much information on lurking problems as a site inspection, and any physical investigation is usually impractical as neither party has any access to previously owned sites. However, it is still possible for the transaction itself to apportion responsibility for this area of liability through contractual provisions.

3.3 Liabilities for off-site activities or impacts

A company can become liable for the off-site effects of its activities either through the civil law or through regulatory action under statute law.

Civil law will give a third party adversely affected by the activity the right to take action to recover damages equating to the loss suffered and, in appropriate cases, to seek an equitable remedy such as an injunction whereby the court orders that the offending activity be stopped. The principle of such an action will be based on established common law causes of action such as nuisance, negligence, trespass or the rule in *Rylands v Fletcher*.[4] The leading case in this area is *Cambridge Water Co v Eastern Counties Leather*[5] in which a water company took action in respect of the ingress over a number of years into the aquifer of a solvent, PCE, from a tannery. The process causing the PCE escape had stopped in 1976, but the PCE eventually reached a borehole from which the water company extracted water for public supply, the PCE concentration being too high to allow the company to use the water according to Directive (EEC) 80/778 on Water Intended for Human Consumption. The House of Lords ruled that the consequences of the PCE escape were not foreseeable in 1976 and on that basis declined to award damages to the water company. This result is based on the unusual nature of the spilled substance, as it would have been possible to have used the water for its intended purpose if the directive had not set a concentration limit for public water supplies. Had a more conventional contaminant been spilled, the court would have been more likely to have found that the adverse consequences of the spillage were foreseeable.

Statute law imposes liability for the off-site impact of activities in various ways as described above, with liability being crystallised either as a clean-up obligation or as a criminal offence. Indeed, the statutory provisions go further than the civil law and impose liability in respect of the unowned environment. Civil remedies protect private ownership interests whereas statute is not so dependent and deals with damage caused or likely to be caused to water in aquifers, rivers or streams or to the ecological balance of nature conservation areas.

In some jurisdictions, notably the USA, additional liabilities are imposed through the waste management chain with responsibility for substances disposed of at landfill sites passing back to the originator of the waste. It is unlikely that such liability would be attracted in the UK as long as the originator of the waste had discharged his duty of care obligations and passed the waste to a properly authorised person with the appropriate paperwork.

3.4 Liability of directors and managers

Directors and senior managers of companies can be liable personally for offences along with the company itself. Most of the principal environmental statutes include a director's liability clause with many providing further that if a company commits an offence with the consent or connivance of another person or which is attributable to that person's neglect, that other person can be liable as well.

In practice, the regulatory authorities have tended to use these provisions mostly in cases where a small company is involved and the day-to-day operations are in practice conducted by a particular individual or group of individuals who are also directors of the company. However, the statutes certainly allow the directors liability provisions to be used more widely and it is possible that the directors of larger companies with some personal culpability in an offence could be the target of a prosecution in the future.

3.5 Liability of those financing businesses

There are two basic types of environmental liability with which the financier will be concerned:

---

[4] (1865) 3 H & C 774; revsd LR 1 Exch 265; aftd LR 3 HL 330.
[5] [1994] 2 AC 264.

(1) liabilities which attach to the financier directly and which he will be responsible for discharging; and
(2) indirect liabilities which will result in a reduced value for the investment and consequently reduced security for the financier should he need to foreclose and go into possession.

Direct liability for environmental problems is likely to fall initially on the company operating the business itself. However, in a situation where a company's financial health is perhaps under threat and typically where the prospect of insolvency is looming, there is a very real risk that direct liability will attach to the financiers concerned. The danger arises primarily from the statutory phrase to 'cause or knowingly permit'.

The potential for financiers to attract liability through being regarded as 'causers or knowing permitters' was reviewed in the draft guidance to the EA 1995 contaminated land regime. This suggests that the mere act of lending money to a company which then pollutes the environment will not mean that the lender has caused or knowingly permitted that pollution. However, if the lender has some direct control over the activities taking place which have caused pollution, that could mean that it is regarded as a causer or knowing permitter. In the typical relationship between a lender and borrower, it is thought that a sufficient degree of control will generally arise only once the lender has foreclosed on the loan, gone into possession of property and started to exercise day-to-day control over the borrower's business. However, there is a danger that the lender which instead provides a significant amount of management assistance to a borrower could, as a result, be regarded as a causer or knowing permitter.

Clearly, once the lender goes into possession and continues to operate the assets over which it took security, there is every prospect that it will assume direct liability at that point. In addition to the application of the 'causing or knowingly permitting' test, liability may be attracted by virtue of the lender being the owner or occupier of property. For example, the EA 1995 contaminated land regime applies a clean-up obligation on the owner or occupier of contaminated land if no person who caused or knowingly permitted contamination can be identified or found. Additionally, the statutory nuisance regime under the EPA 1990 imposes a liability on the person in control of the property from which a nuisance is originating.

A salutary lesson is provided in the *Midland Bank Tyres* case (unreported). Midland Bank foreclosed on a loan and took possession of a property without conducting any site inspection or environmental audit. Subsequently, the local authority environmental health department identified that a statutory nuisance was occurring at the property as a result of 13,000 degrading tyres having been dumped there. Some of the tyres were contaminated with oil. It served a statutory nuisance abatement notice on Midland Bank who were then required to clean-up the site and remove the tyres for proper disposal elsewhere. The cost of this operation is believed to have been close to £100,000.

Passing to indirect liability, the lender's interest will be to ensure that the borrower does not cause environmental problems which result in a reduction in the value of the investment or which would be sufficiently serious to prevent the lender using the assets as security in a foreclosure. It will therefore be important for the lender to ensure that an appropriate range of contractual controls applies to the borrower to reduce the possibility of this happening (see para 4.3 below).

3.6 Transferability of permits and licences

In general, an asset purchase (in contrast to a company share purchase) will not automatically transfer to the purchaser the environmental permits associated with

3.6 Chapter 4

the asset being purchased. Specific contractual provisions will be needed to manage the transfer. There is no universal transfer process under statute for the various environmental permits which a company may hold. Transfer of the principal environmental permits likely to be encountered must be arranged as follows:

(a) *IPC/APC permits* IPC and APC permits can simply be transferred to a successor by the current holder. Under Section 9(2) of the EPA 1990, the transferee is obliged to notify the relevant regulatory authority within 21 days of the transfer, otherwise an offence is committed.

(b) *Waste management licences* Waste management licences are transferable under s 40 of the EPA 1990 on joint application by the current and proposed new owner. Amongst other things, the Environment Agency will be concerned to see that the proposed new holder is a 'fit and proper person' within the meaning of EPA 1990, s 74. The new holder will have to demonstrate that they have the necessary level of financial resources and technical expertise at their disposal to discharge the licence obligation.

(c) *Water abstraction and discharge permits* In general, when a person occupies land which has the benefit of a water abstraction licence, the licence automatically transfers to the successor provided that the successor notifies the Environment Agency within 15 months of the transfer taking place. It is particularly important that this notification occurs as the licence rights will be lost by the new occupier if he fails to do so.

Discharge licences are treated differently. These must be subject to an express transfer by the existing holder to the new holder and the transferor must give notice to the Environment Agency within 21 days of the transfer. It is an offence for the transferor to fail to give this notice.

(d) *Land use planning (zoning)* In general, planning consents attach to the land in respect of which they give permission for development. They automatically transfer to the succeeding owner of the land concerned. However, their transferability can be restricted by conditions attaching to the consents which may provide that the consents are only enjoyable by named individuals or by a specific class of persons.

3.7 Mechanisms for compliance cost increases

The cost of regulatory compliance can obviously be affected by changes in the law. Changes can originate both from the UK government and from the implementation of EU requirements. For example, significant compliance costs have been imposed on certain sectors of UK industry in the recent past by the UK government's introduction of the landfill tax and by the introduction of Directive (EC) 91/271 concerning Urban Waste Water Treatment.

However, the existing law and existing environmental permits may also impose upgrading requirements, even though the level and type of operations is static. For example, IPC consents are subject to a review every four years which may lead to the imposition of more stringent conditions or the prescription of more onerous requirements to comply with the overall obligation to use 'best available techniques not entailing excessive cost'. Similarly, trade effluent consents may be reviewed by sewerage authorities periodically leading to different effluent volume and composition limits being set.

Increasing compliance costs may also be imposed indirectly through the regulatory authorities taking action in response to identified operational problems. For example, an operation may become the subject of a significant number of complaints by local residents such that the local authority serves an abatement notice under the EPA's statutory nuisance provisions. The abatement notice may, for example, require the installation of air emission control mechanisms to reduce smell and chemical emissions from the process.

4 MANAGING ENVIRONMENTAL ISSUES IN TRANSACTIONS

4.1 Current practice for assessment of risk

Acquisition of a company which has an impact on the environment will usually now involve a significant degree of due diligence work by the acquirer and its advisers. The nature and extent of this will depend on whether the company is involved in a potentially contaminative activity as its core operation or whether environmental hazards are an ancillary aspect of its main activity. For example, due diligence activity on the acquisition of a portfolio of newly constructed leisure parks is likely to be directed chiefly to identifying whether the parks are constructed on potentially contaminated land or perhaps whether there are neighbouring occupiers who are likely to interfere with their operations. In contrast, the acquisition of a number of engineering businesses which have been operating since the 19th century and which now include metal galvanising and paint spraying processes will clearly need to cover historical contamination issues in some depth, but will also need to concentrate on the current management of the business and its general regulatory compliance.

The acquirers' legal advisers will generally be responsible for reviewing environmental information provided on the company and for raising pre-contract inquiries specifically directed to obtaining as much additional information as possible on the company's past and present activities. Legal advisers may also conduct statutory register searches and reviews of commercially available information on previous contaminative land uses. They will also advise on the need for environmental consultants to be involved to conduct further investigations.

Depending on the likely importance of environmental liabilities for the transaction, consultants may be asked to undertake either:

(a) a desk top search, involving a review of database records on the company and its properties from sources such as ordnance survey mapping, geological and hydrogeological surveys, trade directories and regulatory authorities' database records;
(b) a Phase 1 audit, involving the desk top element plus a site walkover visit to examine the operations currently being undertaken and to identify any visual evidence of contamination;
(c) a Phase 2 audit, involving a borehole and/or trial pit examination of soil and water under and possibly adjacent to the site for evidence of contaminative substances.

For acquisitions involving a portfolio of potentially contaminative industrial processes, the Phase 1 audit is now usually the minimum requirement and Phase 2 audits, although considerably more expensive than Phase 1 audits, are becoming more frequent, sometimes even used as a precaution where a Phase 1 audit has not identified a particular problem requiring further investigation.

4.2 Warranty or indemnity terms

In a corporate acquisition, a good set of environmental warranties given by the seller to the buyer is sometimes still seen as a substitute for conducting a comprehensive due diligence exercise. However, environmental warranties are increasingly viewed as supplementary to due diligence rather than as an alternative. Although the purchaser may start out the transaction envisaging that it will obtain a comprehensive and unqualified set of warranties, this is very rarely the case by the time the transaction has closed. The coverage and extent of warranties is usually reduced in negotiation and made subject to important qualifications, such as the vendor's awareness, strict time limits for claims and overall financial caps for liability. In most cases, it is therefore essential to ensure that adequate due diligence is undertaken irrespective of the warranty cover which is anticipated at the outset.

There is no standard set of environmental warranties for UK transactions, but warranties may typically cover some if not all of the following areas:

(1) compliance with environmental law and the terms and conditions of environmental consents;
(2) revocation, suspension, modification or non-renewal of environmental consents;
(3) compliance with the terms of any insurance policies against environmental liability;
(4) whether any environmental consents are personal to the company concerned;
(5) the condition of the property and in particular any requirement to clean-up the property imposed by or agreed with regulators;
(6) the use, release or emission of hazardous substances;
(7) actual, pending or threatened claims by regulatory authorities or third parties;
(8) use of the property for waste management activities;
(9) underground storage tanks or pipework; and
(10) PCBs, lead, asbestos or other deleterious materials on the property or in the fabric of buildings.

Additional warranties may be required in particular cases and clearly not every type of warranty will be applicable to each business.

At the time of writing, the EA 1995 contaminated land provisions were still not in force, but these provide a very significant future area of liability. It is increasingly common to expect warranty cover against liability arising under this regime, with the vendor warranting in respect of the guidance issued in draft in September 1996 and subsequently updated.

Since the acquisition of shares in a company rather than the company's assets means that liability in respect of previously owned and occupied sites may potentially be assumed, warranties should cover such sites if possible. Indeed, this is likely to be particularly important since only very limited due diligence can generally be undertaken at such sites. It may well be appropriate in such cases for the purchaser to be indemnified by the vendor against such liabilities or for an arrangement to share liability between vendor and purchaser for a specific period to be agreed.

Indemnities are also used frequently where specific problems are identified in the due diligence process for which the purchaser is unwilling to assume liability. Often, these will be problems arising from mismanagement of the business which has led to permit compliance requirements being overlooked or where there has been an incident leading to pollution of land or water for which there is an ongoing liability. In many North American transactions, it has become commonplace for the vendor to give the purchaser a comprehensive indemnity against any possible environmental liability arising prior to the purchase. In UK transactions, such a provision would be unusual, although indemnities for specific, identified problems are becoming more common.

4.3 Issues for those lending money to businesses

As the financiers of transactions are normally removed from day-to-day operational considerations, their contractual protection will be slightly different, although it originates from similar considerations. In UK transactions, the lenders' interests will generally be protected in the finance documents by a set of conditions precedent, representations and warranties and undertakings specifically relating to environmental issues. Typical provisions are:

Condition precedent
(a) that a certified copy of an Environmental Report on the borrower be provided to the lender and approved by the lender prior to the loan being advanced;

Representations and warranties
(a) the borrower is in compliance with and has no actual or contingent liability under environmental law;
(b) the borrower has obtained and is in full compliance with the terms and conditions of all environmental consents;
(c) the borrower has no liens or any other charge or restriction on the assets of the borrower's business for any liability under environmental law;
(d) no releases or emissions from the business have occurred in breach of environmental law; and
(e) there has been no notice of any other indication of any actual, pending or threatened claim, complaint, assessment or litigation against the borrower under environmental law.

Undertakings
Undertakings will generally repeat the representations and warranties on a regular basis but some additional clauses may be required by some lenders. For instance, some may require that the lender is provided with a report on the environmental condition of the business and assets on a regular basis. Sometimes the report can be by the company itself, especially if it has significant in-house environmental inspection and auditing experience. If the lender is taking this provision particularly seriously, an external audit by environmental consultants will be necessary. To supplement this, further undertakings may cover:

(a) allowing the lender's representatives to inspect the borrowers' records and its assets, properties and business to assess any environmental risk;
(b) the borrower notifying the lender of any circumstances which may lead to a breach of the environmental undertakings; and
(c) the borrower notifying the lender if it becomes aware of any proposals to register the property as contaminated land.

Typically, the finance documents will also contain a comprehensive indemnity by the borrower of the lender against any environmental liabilities, although this is not a particularly effective provision given that the indemnity will often be relevant only in circumstances where the financial state of the borrower is insufficient to discharge any significant indemnity obligations.

Events of default must also deal with environmental issues. Typical events of default are:

(a) if the borrower fails to comply with environmental law or attracts liability under environmental law or fails to obtain or fully comply with an environmental consent so that there is a material adverse affect on the value of the assets, the financial condition of the borrower or the ability of the borrower to discharge its obligations under the lending agreements;
(b) where a change occurs in environmental law which may result in the imposition of liability on the lender under environmental law or which may cause the rights of another person to rank ahead of the rights of the lender against the borrower; and
(c) if any property is registered as contaminated land.

4.4 Role of environmental management systems

Some lenders may now ask for an environmental management system (EMS) to be introduced by the borrower as a condition of the loan being advanced. In the UK, such a requirement is unusual but it may be a requirement for entry to certain lenders' preferential loan facilities, available for businesses which satisfy environmental performance criteria. Additionally, in certain industries, an EMS is sometimes a prerequisite for the small or medium-sized company seeking to supply a larger business.

Following the adoption of an International Standards Organisation (ISO) standard, the former British standard for EMSs was withdrawn so that there are now two recognised types:

(1) ISO 14001; and
(2) the EU (Eco-Management and Audit Scheme EMAS).

In the UK, the ISO standard has proved more popular, being more flexible and less site specific than EMAS. Its similarity to the former British standard has also encouraged its wider acceptance. In addition, EMAS involves a greater degree of information being made available for public inspection, although both systems provide for an environmental statement of the company's performance to be made available for inspection by anyone.

4.5 Insurance

Until relatively recently, the UK insurance industry had a negative attitude to environmental risk, concentrated on ensuring that their exposure for this potentially vast area of liability was reduced. Most insurers backed away from environmental coverage in general policies, although some adopted the North American model of covering liability only for the consequences of 'sudden and accidental' incidents. However, this attitude is now changing as practice in underwriting has developed so that specific environmental risk policies are increasingly available and can be used to manage risk.

The market for environmental insurance is becoming increasingly active with a variety of new policies being introduced. The trend is towards policies covering specific environmental risk areas such as the discovery of contamination risk in redevelopment projects and building contractors environmental risk, although policies against long-term land contamination problems are also becoming available.

4.6 Structuring the management of companies, ownership of assets and operation of businesses

Liability for environmental issues can attach to the corporate entity carrying out operations, to its directors and senior managers, to the person holding an environmental permit or to the person owning or occupying land on which operations are being or have been carried out or which is now causing an environmental problem. This complex web of potential liabilities must be borne in mind when structuring any transaction where apportionment of environmental liabilities is important. This is particularly important where liabilities are an issue for an ongoing business relationship such as a joint venture.

For example, if in a joint venture arrangement, environmental liability is to be placed with one party alone, it may be necessary for that party to assume entire management responsibility for the operation, with no effective day-to-day control remaining with its joint venture partner. The first party will need to own and occupy all the land used for the operation and ensure that all environmental permits are applied for and taken in its name.

However, if responsibility is to be divided between two parties, perhaps with the first party being liable for problems from historical pollution of the land, whilst the second party is to be liable for the ongoing operation concerned, the first party may perhaps retain a freehold interest in the land and grant a lease of it for operational purposes to the second party, the lease ensuring that none of the tenant's covenants impose a liability on the second party for historical pollution and incorporating an indemnity of the second party against losses arising from such problems. The second party will again apply for and obtain all operational permits.

The possibilities for transactional structuring are enormous and their full extent is beyond the scope of this chapter, but the potential cost of environmental liabilities now makes these issues of such importance in many commercial situations that they should be considered of equal importance to issues such as taxation which have driven transactional structuring for many years.

5 CONCLUSION

UK environmental law and practice is a constantly changing and fluid system. Politically, environmental issues assume an ever-higher profile.

In the near future, the following legal and political developments are likely to be increasingly influential:

(1) The contaminated land provisions of the EA 1995 coming into force. These are long awaited, but have the potential to make a dramatic difference to liability for historically contaminated land, if the regulatory authorities are given sufficient resources to police the regime properly.
(2) The introduction of more environmental taxes. Given public support for environmental issues, these have the potential to achieve something of a paradox: a popular form of taxation. The landfill tax has proved successful and the government has consulted on proposals to introduce a tax on recovery of primary aggregates and to tax discharges to watercourses.

(3) The policy emphasis on development of derelict and possibly contaminated land (known as 'brownfield sites) in preference to building in open countryside. The government aims to ensure that 60% of the nation's new housing requirements are satisfied on brownfield areas. This is likely to lead to greater interest and understanding of redevelopment of brownfield sites, and probably greater pragmatism in this area by developers, financiers and regulators.

(4) The emphasis away from use of the private motor car and towards alternative modes of transport including trains, buses, cycling and walking. A White Paper has been issued heralding road pricing and taxation of workplace car parking spaces. Further measures to improve air quality in towns and cities are likely.

(5) A gradual increase in the level of fines imposed and damages awarded by the courts for environmental offences and losses. Regulatory authorities are increasingly willing to prosecute for indictable rather than summary offences where serious pollution has occurred or where regulations have been deliberately and consistently flouted and fine levels are higher as a result. Developing experience with civil cases for environmental losses and the publicity attaching to those is also attracting greater interest in this area.

(6) More cases where public interest groups or individuals seek to challenge the decisions of environmental regulators and government. Although the success rate for these actions has been poor, the ability of aggrieved individuals and groups to organise such challenges seems undiminished.

Environmental considerations are becoming gradually more and more central to business decision-making, with companies appreciating the importance of their public profile in this area as well as their legal compliance requirements. The downside of environmental issues is becoming more significant, but so are the advantages from taking a responsible and forward-looking stance.

Chapter 5

THE NETHERLANDS

Willem Th. Braams and Mark R Birnage

Pels Rijcken & Droogleever Fortuijn

1 INTRODUCTION

1.1 Scope of chapter

The Kingdom of The Netherlands consists of The Netherlands, the Netherlands Antilles and Aruba.

This chapter describes the laws of The Netherlands. The Netherlands Antilles and Aruba have a separate legal system, which is based on Dutch law. This means that much of the law is similar to that of The Netherlands. However, there is often no equivalent to more recent and detailed Dutch legislation. Little specific environmental legislation exists. Where specific environmental legislation does exist, notably in the area of protection of the marine environment, this is a result of international environmental conventions to which the Netherlands Antilles and Aruba are party through the Kingdom of The Netherlands.

Civil law is similar to Dutch civil law dating from before the introduction of a new Civil Code in The Netherlands in 1992. The Supreme Court of The Netherlands (*Hoge Raad*) also acts as the final appeal court for civil cases in the Netherlands Antilles and Aruba. Civil law has not often been used as a basis for action in environmental matters in the Netherlands Antilles and Aruba.

1.2 Basic structure of the law

The principal sources of Dutch law are:

(1) legislation;
(2) international conventions;
(3) custom.

Most Dutch law is laid down in comprehensive legislation. The principal sources of Dutch law are interpreted in judge-made law. The courts are not bound by precedents. Even the *Hoge Raad* can deviate from its earlier decisions. However, in practice, lower courts will follow decisions of higher courts. Well-established judge-made law has been subsequently codified, for example in the new Civil Code of 1992.

1.2   Chapter 5

A hierarchy in legislation exists. Statutes (Acts of Parliament) take precedence over subordinate legislation known as general administrative measures (*algemene maatregelen van bestuur* or *AMVBs*) and royal decrees (*koninklijke besluiten* or *KBs*) made by government, and over bye-laws and regulations of lower public authorities, such as provinces and municipalities. The courts can consider whether lower legislation conflicts with statutes. The courts may not, however, consider whether statutes conflict with the constitution. This is viewed as the responsibility of Parliament when adopting a statute.

International conventions generally require parliamentary approval and ratification. After this, conventions can be applied by the Dutch courts. Provisions of international conventions may be considered by the courts to have 'direct effect', so that individuals can rely on them. International conventions take precedence over statutes, including the constitution. As a result, the courts may consider whether statutes conflict with international conventions.

EU directives must usually be incorporated into Dutch legislation to become effective. EU regulations and some parts of directives have direct effect.

Environmental law can be civil, administrative or penal. Where remedies under both civil and administrative law are open to a public authority, the public authority is free to choose between these, unless using civil law remedies unacceptably infringes on the administrative powers of the authority concerned. Environmental penal law is not covered by this chapter.

The basic structure of the court system in civil matters in ascending order of hierarchy is: *Kantongerecht* (Cantonal Court), *Arrondissementsrechtbank* (District Court), *Gerechtshof* (Court of Appeal) and *Hoge Raad* (Supreme Court of The Netherlands).

In administrative matters, the body which has taken the decision must generally first be requested to review that decision. The decision on review is then open to appeal to the District Court, Administrative Department. A right of appeal of the decision of the District Court exists to the Administrative Judicial Department of the Council of State (*Afdeling Bestuursrechtspraak van de Raad van State* or *ABRS*). Some administrative decisions are open to direct appeal to the *ABRS*, without first appealing to the District Court. This is the case for many administrative decisions on environmental matters.

1.3   Structure of environmental authorities

Various environmental authorities exist in The Netherlands.

Where the State is the competent authority, responsibility will usually rest with the Minister of Housing, Spatial Planning and the Environment. In some cases, licences will be granted in co-ordination with another minister, such as the Minister for Economic Affairs and the Minister for Social Affairs and Employment for licences to operate nuclear facilities.

The Provincial Executive is the competent authority for the Soil Protection Act, except in the cities of Amsterdam, Rotterdam, The Hague and Utrecht, where responsibility rests with the Municipal Executive.

The Municipal Executive is competent with respect to many planning and zoning issues and generally under the Environmental Control Act. Specialised bodies exist in inter alia the area of water management.

2 OUTLINE OF ENVIRONMENTAL LAW RELEVANT TO MERGER AND ACQUISITION TRANSACTIONS

2.1 Contaminated land

2.1.1 Introduction

The problem of contaminated land is one of the most important issues in environmental law in The Netherlands. As a densely populated country where industrial activities and housing compete for the limited space available, The Netherlands has found itself regularly confronted with the consequences of soil pollution. As a result, a legal system through which this issue is addressed was developed relatively early.

In 1978 the first major case of soil pollution came to light. A housing estate was found to have been built on seriously contaminated land. The State cleaned up the pollution, preserving the houses, at a cost of 160 million guilders. The problem of contaminated land in The Netherlands was subsequently investigated by the government. The conclusion was reached that nationwide action on a statutory basis was necessary. This led to the first statute on contaminated land, the Interim Soil Clean-up Act[1] (*Interimwet bodemsanering*) of 29 December 1982, which came into force in 1983.

Cases brought by the State on the recovery of costs of soil quality surveys and clean-up under art 21 of the Interim Soil Clean-up Act have lead to a number of landmark decisions of the *Hoge Raad*. The main issue has been that of responsibility for historical pollution. The most important cases are described at paras 3.2 and 3.3 below.

2.1.2 The Soil Protection Act[2]

(a) Introduction

The Soil Protection Act (*Wet bodembescherming*) came into force in 1987. The Act did not contain provisions on soil clean-up at the time. This was regulated by the *Interimwet bodemsanering*). Comprehensive clean-up regulations replacing the Interim Soil Clean-up Act (*Interimwet bodemsanering*) were incorporated into the Soil Protection Act by an Act of 15 May 1994.[3]

Where the *Interimwet bodemsanering* assumed the State would fund the clean-up cases of serious pollution and would recover its costs from the polluter, the intention of the Soil Protection Act (SPA) is that the polluter himself, or the owner or leaseholder of contaminated land, undertakes the necessary clean-up action.

The SPA provides for regulations to be made for use and protection of the soil by *AMVB* (arts 6–11). *AMVBs* have been introduced in a number of areas, such as the storage of substances in underground tanks.[4] Also by *AMVB*, certain listed categories of companies carrying out potentially polluting activities are required to carry out a preliminary soil quality survey on their premises and report the results to the authorities.[5] The list of companies contains some 450 categories, ranging from oil refineries and pesticide factories to advertising agencies and clog makers. The obligation to carry out a survey is suspended if the company takes part in a voluntary programme for investigation and clean-up of soil pollution of active business premises, known as

---

1 *Staatsblad* 1982, nr 763.
2 Act of 3 July 1986, *Staatsblad* 1986, nr 374.
3 *Staatsblad* 1994, nrs 331 and 332.
4 The *Besluit opslaan in ondergrondse tanks 1998* (BOOT) of 1 July 1998, *Staatsblad* 1998, nr 414.
5 The *Besluit verplicht bodemonderzoek bedrijfsterreinen* of 25 September 1993, *Staatsblad* 1993, nr 602.

2.1   Chapter 5

the BSB programme. Under this programme, companies taking part carry out soil quality surveys and—if necessary—soil clean-up, according to a timetable set by a body (*BSB-stichting*) founded by local industry and monitored by the authorities.

The SPA contains a general duty of care for anyone carrying out potentially polluting activities to take all necessary measures to prevent soil pollution and to clean up the soil if any pollution occurs (art 13). New cases of pollution must be reported to the competent authorities (the Provincial Executive or, in Amsterdam, Rotterdam, The Hague and Utrecht, the Municipal Executive) as soon as possible (art 27).

Anyone wishing to clean up or to have an effect on the state of any existing soil pollution must notify the authorities of their intended activities.[6] The results of any soil quality survey must be produced with this notification (art 28).

(b)   Soil clean-up

The authorities will decide on the basis of the results of a soil quality investigation whether a 'case of serious pollution' exists, in which case clean-up is necessary (art 29). The authorities will also determine the term within which the pollution must be cleaned up (so-called 'urgency', see art 37).

The criteria for determining a 'case of serious pollution' and the 'urgency' to clean-up are to be set by proposed *AMVB*s. These *AMVB*s have not yet come into force. In the mean time, the criteria are stated in a governmental policy document.[7] This document gives so-called 'intervention values' and 'target values' for a great number of polluting substances. If an 'intervention value' is exceeded, clean-up will usually be necessary. The 'target value' forms the maximum acceptable concentration after cleaning up.

Decisions of the competent authority under SPA, arts 29 and 37 are open to administrative review by that body, followed by appeal to the *ABRS* (see para 1.2 above).

Before clean-up of the soil actually takes place, a clean-up plan must be submitted for approval to the competent authority (art 39). The clean-up standard to be achieved is that the functional properties of the soil for man, plant or animal life are maintained or restored. This is known as the principle of multi-functionality, and makes all end uses possible.

Under certain circumstances, an exception to the rule that clean-up should achieve multi-functionality exists. The pollution may then be isolated, controlled and monitored. The objective is then to continue current use without unacceptable risk. This is the case if measures to achieve full restoration would be:

(1) extremely dangerous to the surrounding area, or if these would only mean moving a landfill from an existing to a new location;
(2) technically impossible; or
(3) extremely costly compared to isolation of the pollution.[8]

Recently, governmental policy has shifted away from strict adherence to these circumstances as the only exceptions to the rule of multi-functionality. The competent authorities may now decide to permit deviation from these circumstances for efficiency reasons.

---

6   Exceptions to this duty to notify are made in the *Besluit niet-meldingplichtige gevallen bodemsanering* of 29 November 1994, *Staatsblad* 1994, nr 844.
7   The *Circulaire Saneringsregeling Wet bodembescherming, beoordeling en afstemming* of 19 December 1997.
8   See Annex 6 to the *Circulaire saneringsregeling Wet bodembescherming, beoordeling en afstemming*.

After clean-up has taken place, a report of the result achieved must be submitted for approval to the competent authority.

(c) Enforcement

Not all cases of pollution are cleaned up on a voluntary basis. If voluntary clean-up does not take place, the authorities have the power to issue the following orders (SPA, art 43) to carry out:

(1) a further soil quality survey;[9]
(2) temporary measures to prevent soil pollution spreading;
(3) a clean-up survey;
(4) clean-up of a case of serious pollution.

An order to carry out a further soil quality survey and to take preventative measures can be issued to anyone who has a right to a polluted property and is using or has used the property for business purposes. The polluter, the leaseholder and owner of the polluted property can be issued with all four of the orders mentioned above. However, according to SPA, art 46, a clean-up order cannot be issued to the owner or leaseholder who proves that:

(a) he had no long-term legal relationship with the polluter during the period in which pollution was caused;
(b) he was not directly or indirectly involved in causing the pollution; and
(c) he did not know or could nor reasonably have known of the pollution at the time he acquired title to the polluted property.

An owner or leaseholder who does not satisfy the first two of these requirements, but who was not involved in causing a substantial part of the pollution, can avoid a clean-up order by payment to the competent authority of an amount corresponding to the clean-up costs of the part of the pollution which he was involved in causing. The same applies to a minor polluter.

Orders are open to review by the issuing authority, followed by appeal to the *ABRS*. Orders can be enforced by an administrative fine, or by carrying out the measures ordered at the cost of the addressee (see para 2.3.1(b) below).

As yet, not much use has been made of the power to issue orders. The *ABRS* has considered two orders to carry out soil quality investigations, and has upheld both of these.

The authorities can also decide to carry out soil quality investigations and soil clean-up measures themselves, using predominantly state funds. Article 75 of the SPA, which is the successor to art 21 of the *Interimwet bodemsanering* (see para 2.1.1 above), provides for the recovery of the costs incurred by the State through the civil courts.

Under art 75, the State can recover the costs from anyone who committed a tort which caused the pollution, or who is otherwise non-contractually liable for the consequences of the pollution under civil law. The State can also recover the costs from anyone who is 'unjustly enriched' by the measures taken. Unjust enrichment occurs if a person profits from the measures taken without reasonable grounds, eg if he acquired the property cleaned up at the expense of the State with knowledge that the property was polluted.

---

9 The SPA differentiates between the preliminary or orientation survey, the further survey and the clean-up survey, which take place successively before clean-up commences.

2.1 Chapter 5

In reaction to decisions of the *Hoge Raad*, which ultimately established that causing pollution before 1 January 1975 generally does not constitute a tort against the State, para 6 of art 75 was introduced. This paragraph provides that under certain circumstances the State can recover the costs of soil quality surveys and clean-up measures from the polluter, even if he did not commit a tort against the State in causing the pollution. The polluter is liable under para 6 if, at the time of causing the pollution, he knew of or should have known of the serious dangers related to the substances involved, and was grossly negligent in not refraining from the polluting activities, considering the available technology and practice of the industry at the time. Liability for pollution caused before 1 January 1975 on the basis of this provision has been accepted in some lower court decisions.

A large number of cases have been brought before the courts by the State on the basis of art 75, and its predecessor, art 21 of the Interim Soil Clean-up Act.

2.1.3 Sale of contaminated property

The sale of contaminated property can lead to liability of the seller under certain circumstances. Liability can be contractual or in tort. As a rule, the purchaser must make reasonable inquiries about the condition of the property he is purchasing. The seller must disclose information he has about the condition of the property, which he reasonably knows to be relevant to the purchaser.

The question whether the sale of contaminated land forms a tort against the purchaser must be answered according to the standards and knowledge prevalent at the time of the sale.[10] In a case on the sale of land for building purposes which had taken place in 1980, the *Hoge Raad* decided that a municipality had committed a tort against the purchaser of the land by not giving any warning of contamination present on the land, which the municipality caused in the past, and therefore knew about or should have known about.[11] In a series of cases concerning the sale of contaminated land in the period between 1976 and 1982, the sellers were held to be under an implicit duty to guarantee that the land was fit for the building purposes for which the land was purchased.[12]

On the other hand, the *Hoge Raad* has held that a non-professional seller did not have to know before or around 1990 that a sub-soil oil tank on the property could mean an increased risk of soil pollution, and did not have to warn the purchaser of its presence.[13] Before or around 1990, the purchaser could not rely on an implicit duty for the seller to guarantee the property was fit for building purposes, if the seller only knew of the presence of a sub-soil oil tank but did not know of any soil pollution.[14]

Given the level of knowledge which parties involved in business real estate transactions may currently be assumed to have, specific contractual provisions on responsibility for possible soil pollution will be necessary where real estate changes hands (see para 4.2 below). It should be noted that under certain circumstances, such provisions may not have effect. For example, the courts may consider it unreasonable to hold a party to discharge fully a guarantee to clean-up soil pollution, if both parties are under a misapprehension about the extent of the measures necessary to achieve this.[15]

---

10 HR 19 February 1993 in *Groningen v Zuidema*, Nederlandse Jurisprudentie 1994, nr 290.
11 HR 13 November 1987 in *s-Gravenhage v Bensal and Bohemen*, Nederlandse Jurisprudentie 1988, nr 139.
12 HR 9 October 1992, four decisions in *Re Maassluis*, Nederlandse Jurisprudentie 1994, nrs. 286–289.
13 HR 22 November 1996 in *Sijpesteijn c.s. v Oyens c.s.*, Nederlandse Jurisprudentie 1997, nr 527.
14 HR 28 November 1997 in *Durlinger c.s. v Laura Bakens*, Nederlandse Jurisprudentie 1998, nr 658.
15 HR 28 November 1997 in *Luycks v Kroonenberg*, Nederlandse Jurisprudentie 1998, nr 659.

2.2 Water contamination

2.2.1 Liability for the pollution of underwater soil

Until 1997, the clean-up regulations of the SPA (see para 2.1.2 above), like the earlier *Interimwet bodemsanering*, applied to both the contamination of dry land and the contamination of underwater soil. Special regulations for national waters under the SPA came into force on 15 April 1997, followed by the regulations on regional waters on 1 August 1997.[16]

Like the clean-up regulations for dry land discussed in para 2.1.2 above, the recent special regulations for underwater soil are aimed at the removal of serious contamination, and more specifically seriously contaminated dredger spoil.[17]

For the underwater soil of national waters, the water quality manager for these waters, the Minister of Transport, Public Works and Water Management, is the competent authority to issue a clean-up order. For regional waters, the Provincial Executive is the competent authority; the Municipal Executive does not play any role here.

The water quality managers of regional waters are not only responsible for carrying out surveys and clean-up of underwater soil. They also have to contribute to financing these operations, to the extent that the clean-up has not been carried out by the polluter, the owner or the leaseholder at his own cost (possibly prompted by the threat or issue of a clean-up order). The water quality managers of regional waters have been given the power to recover their costs in civil law under SPA, art 75 (see para 2.1.2 above). The Minister of Transport, Public Works and Water Management has the same power for the beds of national waters.

As explained in para 2.1.2 above, an owner or leaseholder of dry land can avoid a clean-up order under the SPA if he satisfies the conditions of art 46. Article 63(k) of the SPA provides the conditions which the owner or leaseholder of a watercourse bed, whether this is under national water or regional water, must satisfy to avoid a clean-up order. The owner or leaseholder of a watercourse bed cannot be issued with a clean-up order if he demonstrates that (a) he had no long-term legal relationship with the polluter(s) during the period in which the pollution was caused. If a long-term legal relationship did exist, he must demonstrate that the legal relationship consisted only of making the watercourse bed available to the polluter, and that the pollution was caused by a discharge which did not contravene the Surface Water Contamination Act, or by a discharge which the water quality manager was or should reasonably have been aware of. The owner or leaseholder must further demonstrate (b) that he was not directly or indirectly involved in causing the pollution, and (c) that he was not and should not reasonably have been aware of the pollution at the time he acquired the property, or that the owner or leaseholder of the property on 1 August 1995—and (where applicable) the successors in law to that owner or leaseholder—satisfied conditions (a) and (b).

2.2.2 Liability for pollution of surface water

Emissions of harmful substances can not only cause contamination of the beds of watercourses, but also pollution of surface water. This can lead to problems in the supply of drinking water.

---

16 Act of 30 January 1997, *Staatsblad* 1997, nr 86, the *AMVB* of 8 April 1997, *Staatsblad* 1997, nr 156, and the *AMVB* of 22 July 1997, *Staatsblad* 1997, nr 351.
17 Seriously contaminated dredger spoil is generally referred to as class 4 dredger spoil.

2.2   Chapter 5

The Netherlands is situated in a delta region which is fed by a large number of rivers originating in foreign countries. As a result, much of the water pollution is not caused within The Netherlands, but is in fact imported. This was true in the case which lead to the judgment of the *Hoge Raad* on the contamination of the River Rhine by the potash mines in France, Les Mines de Potasse d'Alsace SA (MDPA).[18] The salination of the river's water caused damage to vegetable growers in the Westland region of the province of South Holland. They chose to sue MDPA in tort for the damage suffered.

Although the ruling of the *Hoge Raad* was passed in an international setting, it would certainly also seem to be of indicative importance within the national context. In assessing the illegality of the activities carried out by the polluter, the *Hoge Raad* held that the interests of the polluter should be weighed against the interests of those using the river's water downstream. In balancing these interests, particular attention must be paid to the nature, the seriousness and the duration of the damage suffered and the circumstances of the case, as well as the extent to which the use of downstream water is vulnerable to the substances discharged. Special consideration must be given to the interests of users downstream as, in principle, they may reasonably expect the river not to be excessively contaminated by large-scale discharges.

2.2.3   Discharges to water and removal of water from natural resources

(a)   Introduction

Dutch law not only has instruments for recovery of the costs of clean-up of watercourse (bed) contamination from those responsible for the contamination (see para 2.2.1 above), but also has instruments which aim to prevent contamination of water and the beds of watercourses.

(b)   Surface Water Contamination Act[19]

The Surface Water Contamination Act (*Wet verontreiniging oppervlaktewateren*) contains regulations which are aimed at combating and preventing the contamination of surface water, taking into account the various functions which watercourses fulfil. In case law, the term 'surface water' is broadly interpreted. As a result, the protection of watercourse beds also falls within the terms of the Surface Water Contamination Act (SWCA).

The SWCA operates a licensing scheme. It is prohibited to discharge waste matter, contaminated or harmful substances by a drain etc. into surface water in whatever form without a licence (SWCA, art 1, para 1). Discharge of these substances is permitted if the conditions specified in a licence are satisfied. These conditions may concern the amount of substances permitted to be discharged, the decontamination procedures to be taken before discharge and the sampling of waste water.

The Act creates the possibility of establishing rules by *AMVB* to replace the licence obligation, and to prescribe conditions over and above those of individual licences. The licensing authority may also be instructed to include specific conditions in licences. Furthermore, the SWCA includes the possibility of an absolute discharge prohibition: the discharge of certain specified substances in surface water may be forbidden by *AMVB*.

---

18   HR 23 September 1988, in *Mines de Potasse d'Alsace SA v Onroerend Goed Maatschappij Bier BV, firma Gebr. Strik and Handelskwekerij Jac. Valstar BV, Nederlandse Jurisprudentie* 1989, nr 743.
19   Act of 13 November 1969, *Staatsblad* 1969, nr 536.

In principle, the SWCA only relates to *direct* discharges to surface water. *Indirect* discharge by a drain etc into, for example, local authority sewers, generally does not require a licence (SWCA, art 1, para 2). The same provision makes an exception to this exemption, for substances specified by *AMVB*. Regulations may also be made by *AMVB* for these indirect discharges on the basis of art 8.40 of the Environmental Control Act.

In practice, often not only will a SWCA licence be necessary, but also a licence under the Environmental Control Act. The complex rules of harmonisation between these Acts can be found in arts 8.28–8.34 of the Environmental Control Act and arts 7b–7d of the SWCA.

The competent authority under the SWCA for surface water under state administration, is the State itself; for other surface water this is the Provincial Executive of the province in which the surface water is situated. However, the provinces have passed this authority on to the water boards and the local authorities. Article 6 of the SWCA permits this.

Article 17 of the SWCA allows the competent authority to raise certain levies. In short, the proceeds of these levies serve to offset the costs of taking measures to combat or prevent the contamination of surface water.

(c)   Groundwater Act[20]

The Groundwater Act (*Grondwaterwet*) is primarily intended to promote good management of groundwater. The Act sets out rules for extraction of groundwater as well as for infiltration (artificial permeation of soil with water).

The Groundwater Act (GWA) contains a system of licensing: the first paragraph of art 14 stipulates that it is prohibited to extract water from land or infiltrate land with water without a licence. A licence may contain conditions in the interests of groundwater management. These conditions may provide for prior notification of termination or reduction of extractions or infiltrations. The Provincial Plan for Water Management must be taken into account when issuing, withdrawing or amending the licence (GWA, art 14, para 3). Article 14a of the GWA sets out rules on the prevention of soil pollution in case of infiltration of water.

The licensing authority is the Provincial Executive in each of the provinces. Article 15 of the GWA stipulates that exceptions to the obligation to obtain a licence may be made in cases specified by provincial byelaw.

2.3   Other issues

2.3.1   Integrated pollution control

(a)   Environmental Control Act[21]

The Environmental Control Act (*Wet milieubeheer*) contains general provisions which apply to all parts of the environment (water, soil and air). The purpose of the Environmental Control Act (ECA) is to create a legal framework for regulating general environmental matters which used to be dealt with in specific legislation such as the Nuisance Act (*Hinderwet*), the Waste Substances Act (*Afvalstoffenwet*) and the Chemical Waste Substances Act (*Wet chemische afvalstoffen*).

Under the ECA, a licence is required to establish, operate and make changes to a facility. The term facility refers to certain categories of businesses listed in an

20   Act of 22 May 1981, *Staatsblad* 1981, nr 392.
21   Act of 13 June 1979, *Staatsblad* 1979, nr 442.

2.3 Chapter 5

AMVB.[22] An exception exists for some categories of smaller businesses, for which standard requirements are set. For activities which may have a substantial adverse effect on the environment, an environmental impact assessment (*Milieu-effectrapport* or *MER*) will have to be submitted to the competent authority to obtain a licence. The provisions on the submission of environmental impact assessments are an implementation of Directive (EEC) 85/337.[23]

In general, the Executive of a municipality in which a facility is wholly or mainly situated is the authority competent to grant a licence for the facility under the ECA. Two exceptions to this rule exist. Article 8.2 of the ECA provides that by *AMVB* the Provincial Executive or the Minister of Housing, Spatial Planning and the Environment may be appointed as the competent authority. This has taken place in the *IVB* for certain categories of facilities.

For certain categories of facilities, art 8.36 of the ECA states that a licence shall only be granted after a declaration of no objection from the minister. This concerns the disposal from a facility or emission to the soil of certain categories of waste substances. The facilities to which this applies are listed in the *IVB*.

The ECA also allows regulations to be made by *AMVB* which are applicable over and above the conditions of a licence. Such regulations have been made for, inter alia, liquid petroleum gas filling stations, activities in relation to asbestos, and underground tanks.

If waste water is emitted to surface water from a facility, the question whether a SWCA licence is necessary beside an ECA licence requires consideration (see para 2.2.3 above).

The provisions of the ECA for emissions to the atmosphere and for the disposal of waste are discussed in paras 2.3.2 and 2.3.3(a) below.

(b) Administrative enforcement of environmental legislation

The General Act on Administrative Law[24] (*Algemene wet bestuursrecht*), sets out the procedural rules on application for licences, appeal procedures and the application of administrative enforcement measures. The following sanctions are available under the General Act on Administrative Law for the enforcement of the environmental legislation (including licences) mentioned in this chapter.

The competent authority has a choice either to itself redress what has been done in contravention of any legal requirement at the cost of the infringing party (*bestuursdwang*), or to summon the infringing party to cease the infringement subject to a fine (*dwangsom*). The amount of fines is determined by the authority taking the enforcement measures. The amount must be reasonable in relation to the seriousness of the infringement. If the fine is not in the form of a lump sum, the relevant authority must determine a maximum amount above which fines are no longer payable. The competent authority may also decide to repeal a licence. The infringing party has the right to appeal against enforcement measures to the administrative court (see para 1.2 above).

2.3.2 Emissions to atmosphere

Emissions to the atmosphere are dealt with in two acts, the Air Pollution Act[25] (*Wet inzake de luchtverontreiniging*) and the ECA. The Air Pollution Act (APA) is primarily aimed at sources of air pollution outside facilities;[26] the ECA concerns air pollution from within facilities.

22 The *Inrichtingen- en vergunningenbesluit milieubeheer (IVB)* of 5 January 1993, *Staatsblad* 1993, nr 50.
23 OJ 1985 L 175/40.
24 Act of 4 June 1992, *Staatsblad* 1992, nr 315.
25 Act of 26 November 1970, *Staatsblad* 1970, nr 580.
26 For an explanation of the term 'facility', see para 2.3.1 (a) above.

Article 13 of the APA provides that regulations can be set by *AMVB* for certain categories of machines, fuel and polluting activities (mobile sources). Regulations have been made on, inter alia, the type approval of motor vehicles, scooters and motors for mobile appliances, on the sulphur content of fuel, the lead content of petrol and on emission standards for fuel burning installations. These concern, for example, a duty to monitor emissions.

Facilities emitting substances to the atmosphere will require a licence under the ECA. ECA licences are issued by the Provincial Executive. The standards for emission to the atmosphere used by the competent authorities when issuing licence are given in the Dutch Emission Guidelines.[27]

2.3.3 Waste management including recycling and re-use obligations

(a) Legislation—the Environmental Control Act

The disposal of waste is dealt with by the ECA. The term waste is broadly defined under the ECA, and is interpreted in case law of the *ABRS*. Art 10.2 of the ECA creates a general duty of care for the handling of waste. It is prohibited to emit waste to the soil outside a facility. It is also prohibited to handle waste in a way harmful to the environment. Obligations to separate waste and to dispose of this only to authorised collectors can be imposed under the ECA. The ECA also allows for obligations to place deposits on packaging materials or products to be imposed, in order to stimulate the return of these to the producer.

The ECA distinguishes between household waste, industrial waste, hazardous waste, waste water and scrap cars. Removal of household waste is the responsibility of the municipalities. Industrial waste may only be disposed of through licenced collectors and in accordance with provincial notification procedures. The removal of waste over provincial borders is subject to constraints in provincial regulations. Hazardous waste[28] also must be offered to licenced collectors, with notification. Removal of hazardous waste over international borders is subject to prior approval by the Minister of Housing, Spatial Planning and the Environment.

Licences for collectors are issued by the Provincial Executive under the ECA, or in certain cases, by the minister.

(b) Covenants

In The Netherlands, the waste management problem is dealt with not only by legislation, but also by so-called covenants. These are agreements between the public authorities and industry. An example is the covenant to reduce the amount of packaging materials by 10% by the year 2000.

Covenants generally have a voluntary character as they are not easily enforceable.

2.3.4 Land use planning/zoning

An extensive planning and zoning system governs the use of the limited amount of land available in The Netherlands. The most important acts in this field are the Planning Act[29] (*Wet op de ruimtelijke ordening*) and the Housing Act[30] (*Woningwet*).

---

27 The *Nederlandse Emissie Richtlijnen* of May 1992.
28 Hazardous waste is defined in the *Besluit aanwijzing gevaarlijke afvalstoffen* of 25 November 1993, *Staatsblad* 1993, nr 617.
29 Act of 5 July 1962, *Staatsblad* 1962, nr 286.
30 Act of 29 August 1991, *Staatsblad* 1991, nr 439.

2.3 Chapter 5

(a) Planning Act

Under the Planning Act (PA), national, regional and local zoning plans exist. The local zoning plans (*bestemmingsplannen*), drawn up by the executive boards of the Municipal Executive, are the most relevant to companies wishing to establish or change the activities of a business.

The local zoning plan provides regulations on the type of building activities and on the type of use of land and buildings permitted in the area covered by the plan. The local authorities can enforce compliance with a local zoning plan by administrative sanctions (fines, halting of illegal activities or demolition of illegal structures). Users of neighbouring land may request the competent authority to take administrative measures or may bring actions in tort before the civil courts if land use is contrary to a local zoning plan.

Local zoning plans may be altered by the local authorities, on request or of their own accord, although this requires a lengthy procedure. Alterations are generally subject to approval by the relevant Provincial Executive. The decision of the Provincial Executive is open to appeal by interested parties with the *ABRS*. A zoning plan may also provide that exemptions from certain provisions in the plan can be granted. Furthermore, if land use is not in accordance with an existing zoning plan, but conforms to a proposed new zoning plan, an exemption from the existing plan may be granted. This so-called anticipation procedure is often used in practice to allow building activities to start without having to wait for final revision of the relevant zoning plan.

(b) Housing Act

The Housing Act (HA) regulates the issuing of building permits. A building permit is required for most building activities. An exception exists for certain minor building activities, for which notification of the authorities is sufficient,[31] and for very small constructions described in art 43.

Building permits are issued by the Municipal Executive. The provisions of the local zoning plan will be taken into account when deciding on a request for a building permit. Technical standards and conditions for building activities are set in the local Building Regulations (*Bouwverordening*[32]). A condition for granting a building permit may be that a soil quality survey is carried out and soil pollution is cleaned up before building commences. If an ECA licence is required for the activities which are to take place in a proposed building, the applications for a building permit and an ECA licence must be dealt with in a co-ordinated procedure.

The decision by the Municipal Executive on an application for a building permit is open to review by the Municipal Executive itself, followed by appeal to the District Court, Administrative Department and ultimately to the *ABRS*.

2.3.5 *Hazardous substances including radioactive material*

Dutch law pays a great deal of attention to the regulation of activities involving hazardous substances and preparations and liability for damage caused by them. Specific attention is also paid to activities involving radioactive materials.

---

31 The *Besluit meldplichtige bouwwerken* of 27 April 1992, *Staatsblad* 1992, nr 196.
32 See also the *Bouwbesluit* of 16 December 1991, *Staatsblad* 1991, nr 680.

(a) Chemical Substances Act[33]

The preamble to the Chemical Substances Act (*Wet milieugevaarlijke stoffen*) states that this Act aims to protect man and the environment from hazardous substances and also to enforce Directive (EEC) 79/831 of 18 September 1979.[34] In Directive (EEC) 92/32[35] of 30 April 1992, the earlier standards have been tightened and adapted to the creation of the European Economic Area (EEA) on 1 January 1994.

Basic concepts in the Chemical Substances Act (CSA) are 'substances' and 'preparations'. Paragraph 1 of art 1 defines 'substances' as chemical elements and their compounds, occurring naturally or man-made. 'Preparations' are mixtures or solutions of substances.

Article 2 of the CSA contains a general duty of care: anyone who professionally manufactures a substance or preparation, transfers this to others, imports or applies this for use in The Netherlands and who knows or may reasonably suspect that this may present a risk to man or the environment through his activities, is obliged to take all measures which may reasonably be expected of him to limit these risks as much as possible.

The second chapter of the CSA contains an obligation to inform the Minister of Housing, Spatial Planning and the Environment of the intention to produce a new substance, to import this or to make this available to third parties (CSA, art 3).

Chapter 3 of the CSA lists rules on research carried out by the government and by industry.

If there is a reasonable assumption that undesirable effects for man and the environment will arise from activities involving certain substances and preparations, regulations can be set by *AMVB* for the manufacture of these substances and preparations, their import in The Netherlands, their application, their availability to others, their transport, their export and their disposal (CSA, art 24, para 1). These regulations may provide for the prohibition of activities involving substances and preparations without a licence (CSA, art 24, para 2). The procedure for the application for and issuing of licences can be found in the Environmental Control Act (CSA, art 26).

Article 32 of the CSA states that anyone professionally engaged in the manufacture of substances or preparations or their import into The Netherlands, must keep a record of the quantities of the substances or preparations he manufactures, imports or makes available to others.

(b) Nuclear Energy Act[36]

The Nuclear Energy Act was originally an implementation of the Euratom Treaty, but has gradually evolved into an environmental protection Act. Various activities involving nuclear energy require a permit. Permits are issued in concurrence by the Minister of Housing, Spatial Planning and the Environment, the Minister for Economic Affairs and the Minister for Social Affairs and Employment.

(c) Liability under civil law for hazardous substances

A number of years ago, rules on liability for damage caused by hazardous substances were introduced into the Dutch Civil Code. Specific legislation which applies to certain hazardous substances also contains rules on liability.

---

33 Act of 5 December 1985, *Staatsblad* 1985, nr 639.
34 OJ 1979 L 259.
35 OJ 1992 L 154.
36 Act of 21 February 1963, *Staatsblad* 1963, nr 82.

2.3 Chapter 5

(i) Civil Code, arts 6:175–6:178

Article 6:175–6:178 of the Civil Code stipulate special liabilities for damage caused by hazardous substances.[37]

Paragraph 1 of art 6:175 of the Civil Code creates strict liability for commercial users of hazardous substances which cause damage to third parties. The second paragraph adds that anyone commercially storing hazardous substances, the transporter, the forwarder, the loader, the keeper or any similar agent receiving the substance for transport under the terms of a transport-related agreement, can also be strictly liable.

Article 6:175 of the Civil Code does not use the term 'hazardous substance' as such, but describes this as being 'a substance which is known to have properties that present serious danger to persons or objects'. Whether a substance presents 'serious danger' is determined according to the criteria and methods set on the basis of art 34 of the CSA. It is also possible to deem certain substances to be hazardous by *AMVB* (Civil Code, art 6:175, para 6). This procedure has already been used.[38] The list provided in this *AMVB* is explicitly non-exhaustive.

The fourth paragraph of art 6:175 of the Civil Code deserves particular attention. This stipulates that, if environmental damage is caused by hazardous substances, liability rests with the person who, at the start of the incident leading to the contamination, was liable under this provision.

Article 6:176 of the Civil Code creates strict liability for the operator of a landfill. The operator is strictly liable for damage arising before or after the closure of the landfill as a result of air, water or soil pollution by substances disposed of in the landfill before its closure. This does not necessarily have to concern damage by hazardous substances in the sense of art 6:175 of the Civil Code. Art 6:176 refers very generally to 'substances disposed of', whatever these may be.

Article 6:177 of the Civil Code states that the operator of a borehole is strictly liable for damage caused by the outflow of minerals as a result of sub-surface forces when operating or drilling a borehole. Again, this does not necessarily have to involve damage by hazardous substances in the sense of art 6:175 of the Civil Code. Article 6:177 refers to minerals in the sense of the Mining Act of 1810,[39] meaning crude oil and natural gas.

Article 6:178 of the Civil Code limits the scope of strict liability under art 6:175, 6:176 and 6:177 of the Civil Code. The provision lists a number of circumstances in which there is no strict liability under these articles.

Dutch law has contained specific legislation on liability for damage during the transport of hazardous substances for some time now (see, for example, the Oil Tanker Liability Act discussed in (ii) below). However, since 1 February 1995, the Civil Code has a number of general liability provisions in arts 8.6.4, 8.11.4, 8.14.1 and 8.19.4. These sections, which concern transport by ocean-going vessels, inland shipping, road and rail respectively, create strict liability in the same manner as arts 6:175, 6:176 and 6:177 of the Civil Code. In contrast to arts 6:175, 6:176 and 6:177, the transport provisions do include a limited list of hazardous substances.

(ii) Oil Tanker Liability Act[40]

The Oil Tanker Liability Act (*Wet aansprakelijkheid olietankschepen*) is an implementation of the Civil Liability Convention[41] of Brussels 1969.

---

37   Act of 30 November 1994, *Staatsblad* 1994, nr 846.
38   *AMVB* of 15 December 1994, Staatsblad 1994, nr 888.
39   Act of 21 April 1810, *Bulletin des Lois* nr 285.
40   Act of 11 June 1975, *Staatsblad* 1975, nr 321.
41   *Tractatenblad* 1970, nr 196.

Under the Oil Tanker Liability Act, the owner of an oil tanker is exclusively and strictly liable for damage caused by oil escaping or being discharged from a ship as a result of an incident. Paragraph 2 of art 3 of the Act provides certain exceptions to this rule. The owner of a ship can limit his liability (art 4).

(iii) Groundwater Act

In arts 34–42, the GWA (see para 2.2.3(c) above) contains an obligation for the licence-holder to restore damage to real estate resulting from extraction or infiltration of groundwater, as far as reasonably possible. If this is not possible, the party holding title to the real estate must be compensated for the damage. The owner of severely damaged real estate can also demand transfer of ownership of the real estate to the licence-holder.

(iv) Nuclear Accident Liability Act[42]

The Nuclear Accident Liability Act is an implementation of the Treaty of Paris 1960 and the Treaty of Brussels 1963. The operator of a nuclear facility is strictly liable for damage caused by nuclear accidents. The operator is also liable for damage caused in the supply of raw materials to and waste from the facility. Liability is excluded in a number of strictly defined circumstances. At present, liability is limited to an amount of 750 million guilders per incident. The operator must take out compulsory insurance to this amount.

2.3.6 Noise and nuisance

Limits on noise production for business activities will generally be set in the ECA licence which most businesses will require. The Noise Control Act (*Wet geluidhinder*)[43] provides for the establishment of so-called noise zones around certain sources of noise, such as an number of listed noise producing industries. The authorities are required to take measures to protect houses from any excessive amounts of noise. The noise zones will be taken into account when issuing an ECA licence and when drawing up local zoning plans.

The Noise Control Act also sets regulations with respect to certain noise producing appliances, for example by mandatory type-approvals.

Causing noise or other forms of nuisance may form a tort against the person suffering the noise or nuisance under civil law. Whether this is the case depends, inter alia, on the type, seriousness and duration of the noise or nuisance. The courts will weigh the interests of the parties involved. The possession of a licence allowing the activities causing nuisance, does not necessarily form a valid defence against an action in tort by third parties.

3 PARTICULAR ENVIRONMENTAL ISSUES RELEVANT TO TRANSACTIONS

3.1 Assumption of liabilities

In civil law, the burden of proof is on the plaintiff. For the assumption of liability in tort, the plaintiff will have to prove fault on the part of the defendant, damage suffered,

---

42 Act of 17 March 1979, *Staatsblad* 1979, nr 225.
43 Act of 16 February 1979, *Staatsblad* 1979, nr 99.

3.1 Chapter 5

causation between fault and damage and relativity (the *Schutznorm*-theory). The burden of proof may be reversed by the courts. This has been done where there is no reasonably acceptable alternative way in which pollution could have been caused other than by the defendant. The burden of proof has also been reversed where there were strong indications that the defendant has caused the pollution, such as warnings for infringing conditions of environmental licences.

The burden of proof is mitigated in cases of strict liability. Strict liability arises if the conditions of the statutory provision on which liability is based are met. The plaintiff will have to prove this, but will not have to prove fault on the part of the defendant. Strict liability or near strict liability (with a defence introducing a fault element) exists for the following persons in relation to damage caused by:

(1) defective structures: the possessor, the operator (if used by a company);
(2) defective moveables: the possessor, the operator (if used by a company);
(3) employees: the employer;
(4) non-employees: the person issuing instructions to the non-employees;
(5) representatives: the person represented by the representative;
(6) products: the manufacturer;
(7) hazardous substances: the user, the holder, the pipeline owner (if in a pipeline);
(8) landfills: the operator (licence-holder, or in absence of a licence, the actual operator);
(9) drilling holes: the operator (licence-holder, or in absence of a licence, the actual operator);
(10) ships, vehicles and trains carrying hazardous substances: the operator (during loading and unloading, the person responsible for loading and unloading);
(11) mines: the operator;
(12) groundwater pumping installations: the licence-holder;
(13) nuclear installations: the operator;
(14) nuclear powered ships: the operator;
(15) ships carrying oil in bulk: the owner.

More specific liabilities take preference over more general ones.

In administrative law, the public authority taking an enforcement measure will have to provide the grounds for its decision. For example, an order issued under the SPA to clean-up soil pollution will have to provide the grounds upon which the competent authority has established that the addressee is the polluter.

3.2 Historical liabilities

Liability for historical pollution has been the main issue in the cases brought by the State under the *Interimwet bodemsanering* and the SPA. The question was whether causing pollution in the past constituted a tort against the State.[44]

In two decisions of 24 April 1992,[45] the *Hoge Raad* decided that generally it should have been clear from 1 January 1975 to any person commercially using potentially polluting substances, that pollution of the company property would compel the State to take action and cause it to suffer damage in the form of clean-up costs. This means the polluter is, in principle, liable to the State for clean-up costs resulting from pollution caused after 1 January 1975, but not before that date. The *Hoge Raad* held that

---

44 See HR 9 February 1990 in *State v Van Amersfoort, Nederlandse Jurisprudentie* 1991, nr 462.
45 HR 24 April 1992 in *Van Wijngaarden v State; State v Akzo Resins, Nederlandse Jurisprudentie* 1993, nrs 643 and 644.

an exception to this rule exists if the State can prove the polluter was aware before 1 January 1975 that the State would incur clean-up costs. A second, statutory exception has since been introduced in SPA, art 75, para 6 (see para 2.1.2(c) above).

Persons other than the polluter may also become liable for historic pollution. A person acquiring ownership or the leasehold of a polluted property can be liable for the pollution caused by former site owners. He can be issued with an order under the SPA under certain circumstances, the most important being that he knew or ought to have known of the pollution at the time of purchase. An owner who acquired a property with (deemed) knowledge of the pollution present, can also be liable on the basis of unjust enrichment (see para 2.1.2(c) above). Contractual liability for historical pollution may also arise (see para 2.1.3 above).

In takeovers of companies which have undertaken potentially polluting activities, especially after 1 January 1975, the question of possible historical pollution caused on past and present sites will have to be addressed. Investigation of possible pollution of any real estate changing hands will also have to be carried out in connection with contractual liability of the seller or liability under the SPA for the future owner.

3.3 Liabilities for off-site activities

3.3.1 Escape of hazardous or polluting material

For the escape of hazardous substances, the strict liabilities of arts 6:175–6:178 and ss 8.6.4, 8.11.4, 8.14.1 and 8.19.4 of the Civil Code are relevant. These are discussed in para 2.3.5(c) above. Also, the specific legislation discussed in para 2.3.5 above may be applicable.

3.3.2 Liability for the pollution of third party property

The pollution of a third party's property can lead to liability in tort, as this forms an infringement of the third party's rights as owner of the property.

Liability for pollution of a third party's property vis-à-vis the State was dealt with by the *Hoge Raad* in a series of decisions following those of 24 April 1992 (see para 3.2 above).

In its decisions of 24 April 1992 the *Hoge Raad* had left open the question of whether a polluter should have realised before 1 January 1975 that pollution of a third party's property would lead to clean-up costs having to be made by the State. In four decisions of 30 September 1994, the *Hoge Raad* decided that the date of 1 January 1975 must generally also be seen as the date from which foreseeability exists in cases of pollution outside the company's property. The *Hoge Raad* expressly stated that causing soil pollution before 1 January 1975 generally does not constitute a tort against the State. In reaction to these decisions of the *Hoge Raad* - and those of 24 April 1992—para 6 of art 75 was introduced in the SPA (see para 2.1.2(c) above).

3.3.3 Liability through the waste management chain

Since 6 May 1994 Regulation (EEC) 259/93[46] applies, in principle, to the transportation of all waste, whether hazardous or non-hazardous. This means that one set of rules is applicable throughout the entire EU.

---

46 OJ 1993 L 30/1.

3.3 Chapter 5

The rather complicated system of the regulation can be summarised as follows.

(1) The Regulation makes a distinction according to the purpose of the transportation: removal or useful application.
(2) Waste intended for useful application is divided into three categories on the basis of its damaging properties:
    (a) red (annex IV),
    (b) orange (annex III); and
    (c) green (annex II)
    list waste.
(3) A distinction is made between import (and the origin), export (and the destination), transit (and the route) and national transport. Depending on the various categories, different regimes of administrative transport provisions (prohibitions and monitoring procedures) apply under the regulation.

The ECA (s 10.5A) contains additional (implementing) provisions on international transport. An important further elaboration can be found in the *Regeling overbrenging van afvalstoffen (Regeling EVOA)*[47] based on art 10.44a of the ECA.

National transport is left to national legislation, which is contained in arts 10.20 and 10.31–10.35 of the ECA.

Articles 18.4–18.18 of the ECA are applicable to enforcement of Regulation (EEC) 259/93. The Minister for Housing, Spatial Planning and the Environment has the following enforcement powers: to take measures to redress any infringement at the cost of the offender, to impose fines if measures are not undertaken by the offender and to repeal a licence (see para 2.3.1(b) above). The minister may also require payment of a sum as deposit (see the *Regeling EVOA*).

3.4 Corporate issues and liability of directors and managers

The doctrine of piercing the corporate veil has been used on a number of occasions to hold that companies and individuals other than the polluting company are liable for the damage caused. Liability has been accepted for parent companies, successor companies and directors of companies causing pollution.

In general, a parent company is not liable for the debts of its subsidiary. The mere fact that there are close connections between the two is insufficient for liability of the parent company to arise.[48] However, a parent company may be liable for pollution caused by its subsidiary if the parent company has neglected to direct the subsidiary to cease causing pollution.[49] A parent company may also be liable if it has extracted funds from a subsidiary to frustrate recovery of the damage by the injured party from the subsidiary.

A successor company to the polluter may be liable if it was set up to avoid a claim for pollution caused by its predecessor.[50]

Directors of polluting companies may be liable if they actually directed the causing of pollution. In one of the cases of 24 April 1992 (see para 3.2 above), the *Hoge Raad* accepted the decision of the lower courts that a director was personally liable for pollution caused by the company, on the grounds that the director had chosen a

---

47 *Besluit* of 27 April 1994, *Staatscourant* 1994, nr 86.
48 HR 16 June 1995 in *Bato's Erf v State*, *Nederlandse Jurisprudentie* 1996, nr 214.
49 See Rb Assen 27 July 1993 in *State v Holdoh Houtunie*, *Tijdschrift voor Milieu-aansprakelijkheid* 1994–1, p 28.
50 HR 3 November 1995 in *State v Roco and Rouwenhorst*, *Nederlandse Jurisprudentie* 1996, nr 215.

system for the management of waste water which allowed pollution to escape and did nothing to prevent pollution even after he had discovered leakages.[51]

3.5 Liabilities of those financing the business

Lender liability towards third parties is not a well-developed concept under Dutch law. To date, liability for those financing a business which causes environmental damage has never been proposed to the courts.

3.6 Transferability of licences

As is apparent from the previous chapters, a large number of activities that could potentially pollute the environment require permission from the public authorities. In general this permission will be in the form of a licence which is subject to a number of conditions.

In practice, the licence required under the Environmental Control Act (ECA), as already discussed,[52] is the most important one. This licence is transferable in principle, and is issued for the facility within which the activities take place.[53] If ownership of the facility is transferred, the new owner is therefore legally entitled to make use of the licence. A licence under the ECA for the collection of waste products and for a waste disposal plant is, however, not transferable.[54]

As far as licences other than those of the ECA are concerned, it is always necessary to determine whether these are transferable or not.

If an interest in a company is acquired by a transfer of shares, there is no problem with respect to licences. In this case the legal entity holding the licence remains the same. A problem may, however, arise in the case of an asset transaction. A different legal entity will then be carrying out the activities requiring a licence. Licences may have to be transferred or new licences may have to be obtained. The competent authorities may impose more onerous conditions when granting a new licence or approving a transfer of an existing licence.

3.7 Liability attaching to ownership of land and of a business

The owner of a polluted property may be issued with an order under the SPA as described at para 2.1.2 (c) above. If a polluted property is cleaned up by the competent authorities under the SPA, the owner may be confronted with an 'unjustified enrichment' claim by the State. An owner of a polluted property may also be confronted with claims in tort by owners of neighbouring properties, if pollution is spreading to these neighbouring properties.

If a business is conducted through a limited liability company (a *besloten vennootschap* (BV) or a *naamloze vennootschap* (NV)), the owners of the company—the shareholders—are generally not liable for pollution caused by the company (for the doctrine of piercing the corporate veil, see para 3.4 above). If the business is not incorporated, the owners are personally liable for the debts of the business, including those arising from environmental damage. Examples of unincorporated forms of doing business are: the sole trader, the general partnership and the limited partnership.

---

51 HR 24 April 1992 in *Van Wijngaarden v State, Nederlandse Jurisprudentie* 1993, nr 643.
52 See paras 2.3.1 (a), 2.3.2, 2.3.3, 2.3.6 and 3.3.3 above.
53 See ECA, art 8.20, para 1.
54 See ECA, art 8.20, para 2.

3.7 *Chapter 5*

Strict liability exists for owners of certain property posing an increased risk of environmental damage (see para 3.1 above).

4 MANAGING ENVIRONMENTAL ISSUES IN TRANSACTIONS

4.1 Current practice with respect to the assessment of risks

In order to prevent a situation in which unwelcome environmental surprises arise during the process of buying a company, in The Netherlands an investigation is generally carried out into the environmental condition of the assets to be acquired. This investigation is commonly referred to by the English term 'due diligence study'. By carrying out a due diligence study in the field of the environment, the buyer wishes to avoid a number of risks, such as the risk that he is going to be paying over the odds for what he is buying.

The buyer needs to avoid a situation in which he enters into an agreement under the wrong impression, and should furthermore avoid a situation in which a warranty (*garantie*) is interpreted in a manner that is disadvantageous to him because he did not carry out an investigation when he could have done so.[55] This does not alter the fact that the buyer may generally rely on the correctness of the information provided to him by the seller, certainly when it comes to explicitly guaranteed qualities of the object to be sold. See art 7:17 of the Civil Code and the discussion at para 4.2 below.

A number of questions are formulated below (see para 4.2) which should be asked in merger and acquisition transactions from an environmental point of view. From these questions it is apparent that an important part of the due diligence study consists of an investigation into the quality of the soil. If soil pollution is detected, this will often have major financial consequences. Such financial consequences may arise when investments are being made within the framework of extension or construction plans, but also as a result of the attention that the government is paying to soil pollution.

A thorough soil quality survey must start with an investigation into the history of the site in order to ascertain which kind of industrial activities took place on the site in the past. Such an investigation should show whether or not the site could potentially be polluted and, if so, by what kind of substances. In addition to the investigation into the history of the site, an actual soil quality survey will also have to be carried out.

The soil quality survey will generally take place in a number of phases. The first phase is the preliminary or orientation survey, in general based on the NVN 5740 pre-standard[56] which has been designed to establish the soil quality of a site with a minimum amount of effort. This survey will provide a rough idea of the nature, position and concentration of pollutants in the soil. On the basis of the outcome of the preliminary or orientation survey, a further survey may be required. The aim of such a further survey is to establish whether the soil pollution is serious, and serves to provide an insight into the type of pollution and the potential and actual risks involved. If it appears that soil clean-up will have to take place, a clean-up survey will have to be carried out. In this survey, the technical alternatives available for the clean-up of a particular case of soil pollution are compared. Such a survey will furthermore provide an indication of the costs involved in the various clean-up options.

---

55 HR 22 December 1995 in *Algemeen Burgelijk Pensioenfonds, Beleggingsmaatschappij Heerlen BV and BV Galgenwaard v FGH and Breevast, Nederlandse Jurisprudentie* 1996, nr 300.
56 Research strategy to be used in an exploratory soil investigation (*Onderzoeksstrategie bij verkennend bodemonderzoek*), NVN 5740, Netherlands Standardisation Institute (*Nederlandse Normalisatie Instituut*), September 1991.

If soil pollution is detected, a number of questions will have to be answered, such as:

(1) Does the soil pollution make the site unsuitable for the purpose it is intended to be used for by the buyer?
(2) Can and will soil clean-up have to take place and, if so, to what extent and what are the costs involved?
(3) Who is responsible for the costs of the survey and the clean-up?
(4) Which financial consequences does the presence of soil pollution have for the proposed transaction?

The outcome of soil quality surveys will be decisive when it comes to whether or not the transaction will go ahead and for the terms of the purchase agreement.

4.2 Warranty and indemnity terms

Two decades ago, warranty and indemnity terms relating to environmental pollution in merger and acquisition transactions were uncommon. Environmental pollution was not considered an issue. This has since changed dramatically. Environmental matters now play a role not only in transactions concerning potentially polluting businesses, but in any transaction involving the transfer of real property.

The drafting of warranties (*garanties*) will depend not only on the outcome of the due diligence carried out, but may also be used by the purchaser to extract further information from the seller. A warranty will usually take the form of a declaration by the seller that the information contained in a clause is true, accurate and complete. An indemnity (*vrijwaring*) serves to protect the seller against specified claims of third parties in connection with environmental issues dating from before the transaction. Other terms may be included in the transaction documentation, for example an undertaking by the purchaser that he will clean-up certain pollution, given in return for a reduction in the purchase price.

The most important issues to be considered in relation to environmental matters in merger and acquisition transactions are:

(1) Does the target company have all the necessary licences to carry out its activities, and has it done so in the past?
(2) Are the activities of the target company in accordance with the terms of its licences and has this been the case in the past?
(3) Does the target company own or carry out its business from any polluted property and has it received any decisions or orders under the SPA?
(4) Has the target company polluted its property or any property of third parties, including any former company sites, especially after 1 January 1975?
(5) Are the sites on which the target company has disposed of its waste polluted?
(6) Is the target company involved in any environmental litigation or has it received any summons, complaints etc from third parties?
(7) Is the target company party to any covenants, or is any national or EU policy being developed which may restrict the target company's activities in the future?

The transaction documentation should address which party is going to bear which risks, how clean-up costs or costs of necessary environmental expenditures will be divided between the parties and which costs are covered by the warranty terms (eg clean-up costs, legal costs, interest). More specifically, if real property changes hands, contractual provisions should determine the extent of any known pollution, which party bears the risk of unknown pollution at the time of the sale, and, if a clean-up is agreed, which party bears the risk of any setbacks in the costs of clean-up compared to the estimated costs at the time of sale. The risk of increased costs of clean-up can be reduced, but not excluded, by obtaining approval of a clean-up plan from the competent authorities prior to the transaction.

Warranty terms may include restrictions in the time the warranty can be invoked, a maximum amount which can be recovered under the warranty and a threshold amount for claims under the warranty. Maximum and threshold amounts can ensure that it is not in the interest of the purchaser to promote claims for environmental damage during the warranty period.

Indemnifications should be provided not only to the purchaser, but also to the target company itself, so that the target company has a direct course of action against the seller in case of third party claims.

In addition to provision of warranties and indemnifications, it is in the interest of both parties to stipulate in the agreement which qualities the purchaser expects and which use the purchaser intends to make of the business to be purchased. This will assist in answering the question of whether the purchaser obtained what he may have expected according to art 7:17 of the Civil Code. Article 7:17 stipulates that an object delivered by a seller must have the qualities which the purchaser may reasonably have expected. These are the qualities which are necessary for normal use of the object and which the purchaser was entitled to expect to be present, as well as the qualities necessary for specific use of the object contractually provided for.

Obviously a warranty or indemnity is worth only as much as the party providing it. Consideration must be given to the financial situation of the seller. If its financial situation is insufficient, warranties or indemnities may be sought from others, for example from group companies. Amounts of the purchase price may also be retained in escrow, or a bond from a bank may be obtained as security for the warranty and indemnity obligations of the seller.

If the environmental risks in relation to a company are particularly great, an asset purchase transaction may be considered instead of a share purchase transaction. By acquisition of the shares, the purchaser bears the risk of any environmental liability of the target company as the shares will decrease in value as a result. By the purchase of the assets of the company, the risk of environmental liability will, in principle, remain with the seller. The assets must be purchased at a realistic value to ensure the creditors of the company of which the assets are purchased are not disadvantaged. If the assets are purchased at an unrealistic value, the purchaser may be liable in tort to the creditors.

A disadvantage of an asset purchase transaction is that the purchaser does not automatically have the environmental licences necessary to carry out the business (see para 3.6 above).

4.3 Issues for lending money to business

As stated at para 3.5 above, lender liability towards third parties for environmental damage has not been developed in The Netherlands. As a rule, security rights in The Netherlands must be exercised by a public sale of the secured assets. The lender does not itself become the owner of a polluted property when exercising security rights it has over the property. The lender therefore does not acquire the liabilities attaching to ownership of the land.

Lenders may, however, be indirectly confronted with the consequences of environmental damage caused by their debtors. If the costs of clean-up exceed the value of the assets, the lender will not be able to exercise its security rights, as there will be no purchasers for the property. As a result, lenders have in the past given up their security rights and allowed the sale of the polluted property to the State for a symbolic sum. The State can then clean-up the polluted property and recover some of its costs by the sale of the property at its full value.

4.4 Role of environmental management systems

It will be clear that for companies, environmental management is not just a technical but also a management problem. A number of instruments are discussed below which can play an important role in the management of environmental problems. The standards which have been developed within this context and aspects which are of importance in relation to the ECA are also discussed.

4.4.1 *Environmental management systems*

A company environmental management system can be defined as a coherent management system of organisational and administrative measures aimed at identifying the environmental problems of a company, controlling them and reducing them. A proper environmental management system can limit the risk of liability because it makes it possible to pursue a clearly preventative policy.

4.4.2 *Environmental audit*

An environmental audit involves an internal or external systematic investigation into a company's environmental management (and the environmental damage a company causes). An environmental audit in fact forms part of a good environmental management system.

4.4.3 *Environmental reporting*

A growing number of parties, such as customers, consumer and environmental organisations, lenders, shareholders and also employees, are attaching a great deal of importance to a company having a sound environmental management policy. Environmental reporting can contribute towards good relationships and also good communications with these parties and can provide an indication that the company is treating the environment in a responsible manner.

On 1 January 1999 an Act extending the Environmental Control Act with respect to environmental reporting came into force. The companies which are subject to this legislation will have to publish an annual report on the environmental pollution they cause and the attention they pay to the environment for the benefit of the general public and the government.[57] An *AMVB* will determine exactly which companies will be obliged to do so and on what terms.

4.4.4 *Standardisation and certification of environmental management systems*

Regulation (EC) 1836/93 allows voluntary participation by companies in the industrial sector in a Community Eco-Management and Audit Scheme (in short: EMAS).[58]

---

57 Act of 10 April 1997, *Staatsblad* 1997, nr 170.
58 OJ 1993 L 168.

4.4 *Chapter 5*

Companies can take part in this scheme to promote sustained improvements in the environmental performance of industrial activities through the development and implementation of environmental policies, environmental programmes and environmental management systems, by carrying out systematic, objective and periodic evaluations of the environmental achievements of these systems, and by providing information to the general public on environmental performance. The aim is for companies to become aware of the importance of registration as a company that meets all of the requirements of EMAS in order to make them stand out in the market.

Recently (in addition to the amended BS 7750 standard that has generally been applied until now) the ISO 14001 et seq standards have come into regular use in The Netherlands. Both standards have become recognised as possible bases for the application of EMAS. It is important to note that the European Commission has decided that certification according to the ISO 14001 et seq standards does not meet all of the conditions for registration of a site under EMAS.[59] For example, the provisions for publication of results of a company's audit are more limited.

4.4.5 Outline licences

If a company has a properly functioning environmental management system, this can be mentioned in its application for a licence under the ECA. The company can apply for a so-called outline licence, which can have a number of efficiency advantages for the company. In drawing up the conditions of the licence, the relevant authorities can take the environmental management system of the company into account by, for example, setting target requirements instead of detailed requirements. For more general information on licensing under the ECA, see para 2.3.1 above.

4.5 Insurance and financial surety

If a company runs the risk of being held liable for environmental pollution, it should consider whether it should be insuring itself against that risk. Furthermore, various statutory provisions allow for the possibility for the competent authorities to demand financial surety (for example in the form of an insurance) to cover risks of damage arising out of pollution or harmful effects as a result of the activities of the company.

In 1998 the Dutch Association of Insurers presented a new insurance policy for environmental damage (*Milieu Schade Verzekering* or *MSV*). This insurance has a number of clear advantages compared to existing insurances, such as a company liability insurance or an environmental liability insurance. The *MSV*, for example, provides complete cover, which includes compensation for damage to and damage caused from the company's site. It also provides a range of options through different categories offering increasing extents of cover. This insurance is a direct insurance (as opposed to one that offers third party liability cover), which means it is possible to claim under the policy, even if the insured party has not itself been held liable to third parties.

The *MSV* does, however, have a number of important limitations. For instance, cases involving wilful misconduct and evident negligence are excluded from cover. Furthermore, cover is only provided for pollution and material damage that manifest itself before the expiry of 1 year after the insurance has terminated. The *MSV* does not provide cover for third party claims for environmental pollution caused before the insurance was taken out.

---

59 Decision of 16 April 1997, OJ L 104, pp 37 et seq.

4.6 Structuring the management of companies

The risks involved in business activities can be managed by the use of limited liability companies. In this respect, there is no great difference between environmental risks and other business risks. By carrying out different activities in different companies, the activities involving more risk can be separated from those involving less risk. The limited liability company alone will, in principle, be liable for any environmental damage caused. The fact that a company is part of a group does not in itself mean that the other companies in the group are liable.

The doctrine of piercing the corporate veil demonstrates that limited liability companies may not be misused. There is greater scope to argue that the doctrine of piercing the corporate veil should be applied if the management of parent and subsidiary companies consists of the same individuals, if the parent company is intensively involved in the activities of the subsidiary or if funds from the subsidiary are transferred to other group companies without good cause. The management of the company should be structured to avoid this.

Real property is often owned by a separate limited liability company from the company carrying out the business activities. However, this will not prevent actions by the competent authorities under the SPA against the company carrying out the business activities, as these actions can be aimed at the polluter even if it is not the owner of the site.

5 CONCLUSION

5.1 Anticipated developments in the law

The system of environmental legislation has continued to expand in recent years and has become increasingly harmonised, partly under the influence of European legislation. It is therefore not expected that (as far as material content is concerned) any dramatic changes in the law will take place in the short term. It is, however, possible to observe a trend in the thinking about environmental legislation, in which an increasing amount of attention is paid to its effective enforcement.[60]

5.2 Anticipated changes or improvements in practice

In the near future, the most important policy changes can be expected to take place in the area of soil pollution.

In 1997, the government published its views on innovative proposals with regard to its soil clean-up policy (BEVER).[61] A central part of the new approach is the emphasis on increasing both the environmental benefits and the social benefits of the Dutch soil clean-up operation. This includes the introduction of the concept of so-called function-oriented clean-up, which will replace the basic principle of multi-functionalily (see para 2.1.2 (b) above) currently established in the SPA in the medium to long term. Within the framework of increasing the effectiveness of the clean-up regulations of the SPA, improvements of the legal instruments available to the public authorities under this Act are also expected.

---

60 In this context see in particular *Handhaven op niveau, Commissie bestuursrechtelijke en privaatrechtelijke handhaving* (High quality enforcement, Commission for administrative and private enforcement), Deventer 1998.
61 *Tweede Kamer, vergaderjaar* 1996–1997, 25 411, nr 1.

Chapter 6

AUSTRALIA

Martijn Wilder

Baker & McKenzie, Sydney

and

Andrew Beatty

Allen, Allen & Hemsley, Sydney

1 INTRODUCTION

1.1 Introduction

For many US, European, Asian and most recently, South African companies, Australia is a highly attractive investment destination both in its own right and because of its proximity to Asia. Familiar and stable systems of law and government, that encourage foreign investment, have made the acquisition of existing operations and investments, or the establishment of new ones, a regular occurrence. Foreign interests are now well entrenched in a range of major sectors of the Australian economy including mining and resources, property acquisition and development, the ownership of privatised former public utilities and in the retail, media and communications areas.

While certainly encouraged, foreign investment into Australia is carefully regulated at both a threshold and general level. Federal government approval of most foreign investment is required, based on a range of commercial and regulatory criteria and, where appropriate, also subject to environmental impact assessment. Once approved, investment is then subject to the general constraints and requirements of the applicable federal and/or state legal regimes. Interestingly however, even within Australia, transactions that occur in more than one state jurisdiction will also be of a cross-border or cross-jurisdictional nature.

Historically, Australian legal regimes have provided little in the way of environmental regulation. However, with a substantive growth in environmental law, both domestically and internationally, and the emergence of the environment as a major issue of public concern, environmental matters have become one of the key threshold issues for consideration in any transaction. In the most extreme cases, significant threats to the environment, circumstances of historical non-compliance or the cost of environmental remediation may render what was originally an attractive investment, a highly undesirable one.

1.2 The Australian legal system

Like Canada, Switzerland and the US, Australia has a federal system of government based upon a federal constitution which establishes a federal Government (the Commonwealth), commonwealth territories and independent States[1]. Australia currently has six states: Queensland 'QLD'; New South Wales 'NSW'; Victoria 'VIC'; South Australia 'SA'; Western Australia 'WA'; and Tasmania 'Tas'; each with its own constitution, government legislature and legal systems. Australia also has a number of territories under the control of the Commonwealth government including the Northern Territory 'NT'; the Australian Capital Territory 'ACT'; and the Australian Antarctic Territory 'AAT'.

As a former colony of the UK, Australia's legal system is based upon the British model. Law is created through legislation made by Parliament and by courts (common law) in the course of adjudicating disputes or the interpretation of legislation.

Under the Federal Constitution, the Federal Parliament is vested with power to make laws with respect to specific subjects. While most powers are shared with states,[2] there are limited areas over which the Federal Parliament alone has the power to legislate.[3] The parliaments of the states retain the exclusive power to legislate on subjects not included in the federal list of powers. In addition, states also retain a concurrent power to legislate on the subjects in the federal list, other than those over which the Federal Parliament has exclusive power. In this regard, unlike the Canadian Constitution, there are no parallel lists of federal and state powers. Where state legislation is inconsistent with federal legislation, then federal legislation prevails.[4]

The federal/state divide is also evident in the national court structures that exist. The High Court of Australia is the final court of appeal in both federal and non-federal matters. The court holds first instance jurisdiction in some matters[5] and original jurisdiction in others.[6] The High Court is also the final Court of Appeal for decisions made by the Federal Court of Australia and the State Supreme Courts.

The Federal Court has exclusive jurisdiction over matters of a federal nature, as provided for in various Commonwealth legislation, which derives from those areas over which the Commonwealth has direct power under the Federal Constitution. This includes tax, federal administrative decisions (including decisions on environmental matters), trade practices, industrial laws and family law. The Federal Court also acts as the Court of Appeal from the Supreme Courts of territories in both civil and criminal matters.

In relation to all other matters not dealt with directly by the High Court or Federal Court, each state and territory has a Supreme Court which has original and appellate jurisdiction in civil and criminal matters. While the exact nature of Supreme Courts will vary from state to state, in QLD, NSW and VIC, a Court of Appeal also exists as part of the Supreme Court structure to review Supreme Court decisions.[7]

Beneath the Supreme Courts there are also a range of intermediate courts exercising

---

1 Commonwealth of Australia Constitution Act 1990. Section 9 of this Act contains the Federal Constitution.
2 Constitution, s 51 sets out the 'federal list' of powers which includes international trade and commerce, defence, income taxation, external affairs and fisheries beyond territorial limits to name but a few.
3 Constitution, ss 52 and 90. Such exclusive powers are limited to the imposition of customs or excise duties and particular laws relating to the peace, order and good government of the Commonwealth. The full list of concurrent powers is laid out in the Constitution, s 52.
4 Constitution, s 109.
5 Ibid, s 75. This includes matters arising under any environmental treaty.
6 Ibid, s 76.
7 It is important to note that between the Federal and Supreme Courts cross vesting of civil jurisdiction exists. Some state and territory Supreme Courts are vested with the civil jurisdiction of Federal Courts and the Federal Courts are vested with the full jurisdiction of the State and Territory Supreme Courts.

jurisdiction over smaller matters and inferior or lower courts which deal with relatively minor civil and criminal matters.[8]

While matters of an environmental nature are usually heard at the State Supreme Court level, a number of state jurisdictions have dedicated environmental courts for hearing environmental matters. For example, in NSW the Land and Environment Court[9] is of equivalent status to the State Supreme Court, with appeals going directly to the NSW Court of Appeal. It has jurisdiction to hear environment planning and protection appeals, local government and miscellaneous appeals and applications, land tenure, valuation, rating and compensation matters, environmental planning and protection and development contract enforcement and matters relating to convictions for environmental offences.

In QLD, the Planning and Environment Court[10] hears appeals relating to development applications and matters arising from the Environment Protection Act, while in SA the Environment, Resources and Development Court[11] plays a similar role.

The Australian legal system is therefore relatively complex with regulation of activities often taking place at a number of levels and with regulation at the state level varying in each jurisdiction. This adds to the complexity of transactions that occur in more than one state jurisdiction. This chapter will therefore focus on regulation of the environment within the federal context and within the four states of NSW, QLD, VIC and SA.

1.3 Regulation of the environment

The establishment of 'environmental law' as a distinct area of practice within the Australian legal system remains a relatively recent phenomenon, occurring largely over the past decade. Regulation of the environment has therefore evolved mostly through legislative activity rather than by a process of well-documented legal principles undergoing constant refinement by the courts.

1.3.1 Federal regulation

The Federal Government exercises significant legislative power over the environment despite it having no direct or plenary power to do so.[12] Interpretation of the Federal Constitution by the High Court has confirmed that the Commonwealth has legislative power under the Constitution regarding the environment through:

(a) its foreign affairs power which allows it to sign and implement international environmental treaties;[13]
(b) the High Court's general principles of interpretation of the Constitution, which allow the federal government to legislate 'with respect to' those powers specifically identified in the Constitution. For example, in granting an export permit under the power to regulate trade and commerce with other countries the federal government can attach environmental conditions to the permit or require an environmental impact assessment of the export activity;
(c) its ability to make laws for territories (through which it has made numerous environmental protection laws for the Australian Antarctic Territory);
(d) the use of federal financial powers to grant funds for environmental projects or impose 'environmental' taxes; and

---

8 Local courts, magistrates courts, courts of petty sessions.
9 Land and Environment Court Act 1979 (NSW).
10 Integrated Planning Act 1997 (QLD).
11 Environment Resources and Development Court Act 1993 (SA).
12 See James Crawford 'The Constitution and the Environment' (1991) 13(1) Syd LR p 11, March.
13 Constitution, s 51(xxix).

1.3 *Chapter 6*

(e) the use of its constitutional powers to legislate for 'foreign corporations and trading or financial corporations formed within the limits of the Commonwealth'. The corporation's power enables the Commonwealth to regulate the trading and financial activities of trading and financial corporations formed under Australian law, together with all activities of foreign corporations. Therefore, the Commonwealth can impose environmental conditions or requirements on such activities and the power may be used to control the environmental impact of such activities.

Constitutional jurisprudence has therefore enabled the Commonwealth to implement significant environmental regulation over a range of areas including international matters despite the absence of any plenary Commonwealth power over the environment. This includes areas such as climate change, world heritage, the export of hazardous wastes, biodiversity and oceans and the regulation, assessment and approval of the environmental impact of various activities.

Historically, these issues have been dealt with under a range of Acts. However, on 29 June 1999 the federal government passed new legislation (the Environmental Protection and Biodiversity Conservation Act 1999 (Cth)) which will replace much of its existing legislation with a single principal Act. The legislation, which is expected to come into force in mid-2000, provides for the protection of the environment and biodiversity in a more co-operative and less ad hoc manner. It specifically seeks to promote greater inter-governmental control, with the federal government focusing only on matters of national significance or international concern.

Finally, in order to implement its legislation and to advise and implement on government policy and programmes, the federal government has a dedicated agency, 'Environment Australia', under the control of the federal Minister for Environment. Environment Australia works closely with other federal and state agencies including National Parks, customs and the federal police to enforce the federal legislation, impose fines and undertake enforcement actions. The Environment Minister may also appoint appropriate persons to assist in enforcement.

1.3.2 State regulation

Despite the federal government's broad constitutional powers, the states and territories are responsible for the general regulation of all activities with regard to their impact on the environment. State regulation acts to control and regulate the emission of pollutants of environmental harm into receiving environments.

Most Australian states have a principal Environment Protection Act and other relevant legislation under which all activities and operations are carefully controlled so as to minimise any impact upon the environment. Such Acts generally make provision for:

(1) the granting of environmental licences to conduct various activities;
(2) the establishment of various standards relating to the environment (eg air, noise, water);
(3) the creation of offences for breach of the Act; and
(4) the establishment of an Environmental Protection Authority (EPA) or agency to administer and enforce the environmental regulatory framework[14] and with the power to prosecute.

---

14 In NSW, the Environment Protection Authority (EPA) is created under the Protection of the Environment Administration Act 1991 as will be amended by the Protection of the Environment Operations Act 1997 (NSW) (which came into force on 1 July 1999). In SA, the Environment Protection Agency is created under the Environment Protection Act 1993 (SA); in VIC, the Environment Protection Authority is created under the Environment Protection Act (1970) (VIC); and in QLD environmental regulation is carried out by the Department of Environment and Heritage under the Environment Protection Act 1994 (QLD).

Principal responsibility for regulation of such Acts lies with the appropriate state environmental protection authorities. However, other authorities may also have some control over processes which ultimately lead to discharges into the environment. For example, some water boards are empowered to control discharges into sewerage systems and many local governments are responsible for approving activities which will have an environmental impact.

Although most states have similar frameworks of the general nature described above, there are often significant differences between the actual regulatory requirements within each state, and in particular, with respect to the extent to which the relevant regulatory agencies actually enforce state legislation. In NSW, the EPA regularly undertakes prosecutions of environmental offenders. The same cannot, however, be said of all other states.

1.3.3 Local regulation

Mention should also be made of the fact that regulation of some more minor environmental matters also takes place at the local government level. Local councils are usually responsible for the granting of building and development consents and also provide a range of environmental services including waste collection and recycling and control of local vegetation and parks.

1.3.4 Inter-Governmental Agreement on the Environment

Historically, the division of environmental regulation between the Commonwealth and states has caused significant conflict. The ability of the federal government to regulate the environment at all levels, especially in light of the vast differences between different regional environments, has often been questioned.

As a consequence, in 1992, the Commonwealth, states, territories and Australian Local Government Association signed the Inter-Governmental Agreement on the Environment (IGAE) under which a co-operative national approach to the environment was agreed to. This approach is further endorsed in the proposed federal legislation.

Politically, the IGAE represents a retreat by the Commonwealth from using its superior constitutional powers to override the states in favour of a more consultative process based upon broad agreements of principle. It commits all parties to the principle of ecological sustainable development pursued through the further principles of intergenerational equity, the precautionary principle, the conservation of biological diversity and ecological integrity and improved valuation, pricing and incentive mechanisms. It also provides for the creation of a National Environmental Protection Council (NEPC) to implement nationally consistent measures for protection of the environment called National Environmental Protection Measures (NEPMs).

NEPMs are standards, guidelines, goals and associated protocols produced by the National Environment Protection Council (NEPC) to ensure equivalent national protection from air, water, soil and noise pollution. Established under the IGAE, the National Environment Protection Authority (NEPA) can make measures for ambient air quality, ambient marine estuarine and fresh water quality, noise, general guidelines for contamination assessment, the environmental impacts of hazardous waste, motor vehicle emissions and the re-use/recycling of used materials. Once a measure has been made and is enacted by the Federal Parliament, it automatically becomes law in each state jurisdiction. To date the most important measures which have been finalised deal with ambient air quality, the implementation of a national pollutant inventory, the movement of hazardous waste across state and territory borders and the assessment of contaminated sites.

1.3 *Chapter 6*

1.3.5 International environmental law

Finally, and as indicated above, the federal government's foreign affairs power has allowed it to incorporate, into Australian domestic law, a range of international environmental law treaties on issues including world heritage, biodiversity, climate change and endangered species.[15] In doing so, international environmental law treaties, and customary international environmental law principles embodied within them, are increasingly reflected in Australian domestic law, a point further evidenced by the new Environment Protection and Biodiversity Conservation Act 1999 (see para 2.2.2 below) and in those areas covered by the IGAE. Australian courts have also begun to recognise and endorse principles of customary international law such as sustainable development and the precautionary principle.[16]

2 OUTLINE OF ENVIRONMENTAL LAW RELEVANT TO MERGER AND ACQUISITION TRANSACTIONS

2.1 Introduction

The extent to which environmental law will be relevant to merger and acquisition transactions will depend upon both the nature of the transaction and the interests that are being acquired. At the federal level, transactions that involve significant foreign investment into Australia by foreign companies and transactions by, or on behalf, of the federal Australian government or its authorities within Australia, may be subject to a threshold environmental assessment prior to being approved. Such threshold assessment is in addition to the more general operational environmental law requirements that will need to be met at the state level.

Obviously, relatively simple mergers and acquisitions of business interests with little environmental relevance are unlikely to be affected by environmental law requirements. However, merger and acquisition transactions involving operations such as those in the mining, forestry, manufacturing and industrial areas which have a significant impact on the environment, will be subject to a substantial degree of environmental regulation. Where businesses are already operational, compliance with environmental licensing and protection laws will be required. In addition, potential liabilities for both past and current environmental problems may exist both under the legislative regime and at common law. In the case of a new business or project which is part of a merger or acquisition, then development approval and possibility environmental assessment may also be required.

2.2 Threshold approvals for mergers and acquisitions involving foreign interests and the federal government

2.2.1 Foreign Acquisitions and Takeovers Act 1975 (Cth)

The Foreign Acquisitions and Takeovers Act 1975 (Cth)[17] establishes the Foreign

---

15 *Leatch* v *National Parks and Wildlife Service and Scholhaven City Council* (1993) 81 LGERA 270, NSW Land & Environment Court.
16 D Rothwell, and B Boer, 'From the Franklin to Berlin: The Internationalisation of Australian Environmental Law and Policy'(1995) 17 Syd LR 242.
17 This Act was enacted to encourage foreign investment in Australia in a manner that is consistent with the needs of Australia. Small investments do not require approval. However, acquisitions of substantial interests in existing Australian businesses with total assets of $5 million or more ($3 million or more for rural properties); plans to establish new businesses involving a total investment of $10 million or more; and takeovers of offshore companies whose Australian subsidiaries or assets are valued at $20 million or more or account for more than 50% of the company's global assets, are all subject to FIRB approval.

Investment Review Board (FIRB) to approve foreign investment into Australia, including that occurring as a result of acquisitions and mergers. As part of this assessment process, relevant ministries will be consulted, including Environment Australia.

Approval of transactions involving rural properties, agriculture, forestry, fishing, resource processing, oil and gas, mining, manufacturing, non-bank financial institutions, insurance, sharebroking, tourism (hotels and resorts) and most other services, may be made subject to the parties meeting certain conditions. For example, the approval of proposals may be subject to the parties meeting certain environmental protection obligations or undertaking some level of environmental impact assessment.

In addition, where acquisitions involve a new business or project of $50 million and over, it will be necessary in making the FIRB application to describe the environmental impact, if any, of the proposal and to provide details of any environmental studies undertaken. Such details will then form part of the approval process.

While FIRB may grant an approval subject to an environmental assessment being undertaken or certain environmental conditions being met, in practice where such an assessment has already been undertaken, or conditions have already been imposed as part of a state government approval process, then FIRB will endorse these as having met its own requirements. Alternatively, FIRB may simply require that environmental obligations be met at the time when the proposal, if it involves a state government, is assessed by that state government and its environmental authority.

2.2.2 *Environmental Protection and Biodiversity Act 1999 (Cth) and Environment Protection (Impact of Proposals) Act 1974 (Cth)*

On the 29 June 1999, the federal government passed the Environment Protection and Biodiversity Conservation Act, thereby replacing the existing federal environmental assessment process under the Environment Protection (Impact of Proposals) Act 1974. Any matters of national environmental significance and any actions which may have, or are likely to have, a significant impact on a matter of national environmental significance must be approved by the federal Environment Minister under the Act unless some other process (including an accredited state approval process), a bilateral agreement, a declaration or a conservation agreement is already in place.

Matters of national environment significance include world heritage properties, Ramsar wetlands of international importance, nationally threatened species and communities, migratory species protected under each national agreement, nuclear actions, the Commonwealth marine environment and any additional matters specified by regulation after consultation with the states. Furthermore, the federal government has also agreed to investigate the inclusion of greenhouse gas issues as a further matter of national significance that may trigger an assessment.

The new Act is expected to enter into force in mid-2000. Until that time, the current environmental impact assessment procedures under the Environment Protection (Impact of Proposals) Act 1974 will remain operational. Under this Act matters undertaken by, or on behalf of, the federal Australian government and authorities of Australia, either alone or in association with any other government, authority, body or person and which effect the environment to a significant extent, may also be subject to comprehensive environmental assessment. Therefore, where the federal government formulates a proposal, carries out works or other projects, negotiates, operates and enforces agreements or arrangements with other parties (including state governments), makes or participates in the making of decisions and recommendations, and incurs expenditure either alone or in association with any other government, authority, body or person, then the need for an environmental assessment may be triggered. This would include the government selling off a major asset to an investor, entering

2.2 Chapter 6

into a joint venture project with a private investor and the making of a decision to grant some form of licence or approval.

Under the Environmental Protection (Impact of Proposals) Act 1974 and its associated administrative procedures,[18] relevant matters will be referred to the Minister for the Environment who will determine what, if any, environmental assessment is required. In evaluating that assessment the minister will then take into account a range of factors laid out in the administrative procedures which are aimed at determining the extent to which the proposed action will impact on the environment.[19]

As with FIRB approval, where a project involving the federal government has already been approved through a state approval and assessment process then, in most cases, the Federal Minister for the Environment will usually endorse that existing assessment as meeting the Act's requirements if the minister deems it appropriate.

2.3 General environmental regulation of mergers and acquisitions

Although the potential exists for a proposed merger or acquisition to be subjected to comprehensive environmental assessment in the case of foreign investment or transactions involving the federal government, the need for major development approvals and the undertaking of comprehensive environmental impact assessments will be largely reserved for new projects or major alterations to existing operations. General mergers and acquisitions will not attract such threshold assessment and interaction with environmental law will be confined to those ongoing operational aspects such as licensing, pollution control and environmental management.

2.3.1 General environmental protection Acts

Historically, states have regulated the protection of the environment through a range of specific Acts dealing with water pollution, noise pollution, air pollution and so on. However, in recent years there has been a shift by many states, QLD, SA and NSW in particular, towards the establishment of a single broad environmental protection Act.

Victoria was the first Australian state to consolidate its environmental laws with the Environment Protection Act 1970. In other states the relevant Acts are the Environmental Protection Act 1994 (QLD); the Environment Protection Act 1993 (SA); Environmental Protection Act 1986 (WA); the Environmental Management and Pollution Control Act 1994 (Tas). In NSW the Protection of the Environment Operations Act 1997, which came into effect on 1 July 1999 replaces the existing NSW Acts including the Clear Air Act, 1961, Clean Waters Act, 1990 and Noise Control Act, 1975.

(a) South Australia: Environment Protection Act 1993

The SA Environment Protection Act 1993 establishes a general environmental duty under which a person must not undertake an activity that pollutes, or might pollute, the environment unless the person takes all reasonable and practicable measures to prevent or minimise any resulting environmental harm. This duty applies to all forms of pollution whether it be in relation to air, water, noise or some other issue.

---

18 Environment Protection (Impact of Proposals) Act 1974 (Cth) and Environment Protection (Impact of Proposals) Administrative Procedures Act 1987 (Cth).
19 Environment Protection (Impact of Proposals) Administrative Procedures Act 1987, s 3.1.2.

While failure to comply with the duty does not of itself constitute an offence, compliance with the duty may be enforced by the issuing of an environment protection order or through the issuing of a clean-up order or clean-up authorisation issued by the EPA or made by the Environment Resources and Development Court.[20] In determining what measures are required to be taken to prevent or minimise any resulting environmental harm, regard will be had amongst other thing to the nature of the pollution or potential pollution and the sensitivity of the receiving environment, the financial implications of the various measures utilised and the current state of technical knowledge and likelihood of successful application of the measures that might be taken.

Furthermore, in any proceedings (civil or criminal), where it is alleged that a person failed to comply with the general environmental duty by polluting the environment, it would be a defence if pollution levels are within statutory limits or such pollution is authorised by an environmental licence or some form of exemption. Where the environmental duty is breached, and subsequent protection orders or clean-up notices are ignored, the environmental authorities may take steps to ensure compliance, and in doing so, recover the cost of taking such action, including through placing a charge on the land. In addition, non-compliance will also result, in the case of a body corporate, in penalties of up to $120,000.

The SA legislation also provides for the establishment of various environment protection policies which specify mandatory pollution standards, guidelines, controls and other aspects of regulation for a range of environmental matters such as air quality, noise and water discharges. A person who contravenes a mandatory provision of an environment protection policy may face fines of up to $250,000 for a body corporate and $150,000 for a natural person and/or two years' imprisonment. The specific policies are dealt with below.

Finally, the SA legislation also establishes a system of criminal environmental offences which are grouped into three distinct 'tiers'. The first tier offences of intentionally or recklessly causing serious or material environmental harm will attract a penalty of $1 million for corporations and $250,000 and/or four years' imprisonment for individuals.[21] The second tier of causing serious or material environmental harm is a strict liability offence with maximum penalties of $250,000 for corporations and $120,000 for individuals.[22] Finally, the third-tier offences are committing environmental nuisance by polluting the environment intentionally or recklessly and with the knowledge that an environmental nuisance will or might result. Such offences carry a maximum penalty of $30,000.[23]

(b)   Queensland: Environmental Protection Act 1994

Like SA, the QLD Act also establishes a general environment duty not to cause environmental harm unless all reasonable and practicable measures to prevent or minimise the harm are taken. Again, a breach of the general environmental duty is not an offence in itself, but may lead to the commission of other offences under the Act or the issue of an environmental protection order. It may also prevent reliance on certain statutory defences.

In addition, employers are also under a duty to notify the environment authority, as soon as it is reasonably practicable, after becoming aware of serious or material

---

20   Environment Protection Act 1993, Pt 10, ss 93, 99, 100 (SA).
21   Ibid, Pt 9, ss 79–84 (SA).
22   Ibid.
23   Ibid.

2.3 Chapter 6

environmental harm, unless such harm is authorised under the Act. An act or omission causing serious environmental harm, material environmental harm or an environmental nuisance will be unlawful unless done in accordance with an appropriate environmental authorisation.

In this regard, an act or omission causing serious environmental harm, material environmental harm or an environmental nuisance, in the absence of an authorisation, is an offence.[24] Furthermore, releasing a prescribed contaminant into the environment (except under the authority of an emergency direction) or placing a contaminant where it may cause serious or material environmental harm and interfering with any monitoring equipment will also all constitute offences.[25] If convicted of any of these offences, an individual may be fined up to $250,000 and a body corporate up to $1250,000 for the commission of that offence.[26]

(c) New South Wales: Protection of the Environment Operations Act 1997

The NSW legislation does not establish a general environmental duty. Rather, the Act establishes a three-tier level of offences for harming the environment depending upon the degree of severity of the offence.

While minor offences are usually dealt with by way of penalty notices, it is the most serious first-tier and second-tier offences that impose substantial penalties.[27] Under the Act a person who is wilfully and negligently responsible for the disposal of waste in a manner that harms or is likely to harm the environment, and/or causes any substance to leak, spill or otherwise escape in a manner that harms or is likely to harm the environment (including ozone depleting substances) is liable for a first-tier offence. Both the person responsible, and the owner of the substance or any container from which the substance escapes, may be held accountable.[28] A person who is found guilty of a first-tier offence is liable on conviction to a penalty not exceeding $1 million in the case of a corporation or to a penalty not exceeding $250,000 and/or seven years' imprisonment for an individual.[29]

Furthermore, additional offences also exist with respect to water, air and noise pollution.[30] Upon conviction, penalties may again be imposed, with continuing offences incurring a further penalty for each day the offence continues. Again, such penalties may be imposed on both a company and the individual responsible for the pollution.

It is a defence in proceedings against a person for a first-tier offence if the person can establish that the commission of the offence was due to causes over which the person had no control and that the person took reasonable precautions and exercised due diligence to prevent the commission of the offence.[31]

(d) Victoria: Environment Protection Act 1970

The Victorian Act also contains no general environmental duties. Rather, under the Act, the EPA has distinct power, duties and functions concerning the discharge of

---

24 Environment Protection Act 1994 (QLD).
25 Ibid, ss 15–17.
26 Ibid, ss 120–123.
27 Protection of the Environment Operations Act 1997, Chap 5 (NSW).
28 Ibid, s 116.
29 Ibid, s 119.
30 Ibid, ss 120–146. See below.
31 Ibid, s 118.

water, the control of noise and industrial waste and the improvement of the quality of the environment.[32]

It may recommend environment protection policies and specify emissions standards and criteria to protect the environment. Enforcement of these standards may be backed up by abatement notices, injunctions to prevent contraventions of the Act or licences[33] and through the issue of clean-up notices.[34] Clean-up notices may be given to the occupier of a premises from which pollution has occurred or been permitted to occur, a person who has caused or permitted pollution to occur, any person who has abandoned or dumped any industrial waste or potentially hazardous substance and any person who is handling industrial waste or a potentially hazardous substance in a manner likely to cause an environmental hazard.

As in other jurisdictions, amendments have sought to lift the corporate veil, by making each director and each person concerned in the management of the corporation guilty of any contravention by the corporation and liable to the same penalty as the corporation.[35]

Local councils also have responsibilities in relation to the control of noise, water, air and visual pollution under the Local Government Act 1989 and Health Act 1958. Under the Water Act 1989, water authorities may also enforce provisions which forbid the discharge into sewerage systems of anything other than sewerage or permitted trade waste, which would not otherwise be an offence under the Environment Protection Act.

2.3.2 General environmental licence compliance

Provision is made under the relevant state legislation for the granting of environmental authorisations or licences.[36] Activities of environmental significance may not be undertaken without a licence or environmental authorisation, although in some circumstances exemptions may be obtained. The types of activities and industries which need authorisation are generally spelt out in the legislation or the regulations made thereunder and generally encompass the same sorts of activities as those for which formal environmental impact assessment has traditionally been required as part of the development approval process. For example, in South Australia an authorisation will be required for 'activities of environmental significance' which includes a range of industrial and chemical processes and activities, waste treatment and disposal works, extractive industries, food production and animal and plant processing activities and other activities involving aerodromes and marinas.[37] In comparison, the Victorian legislation identifies six types of premises from which activities must be licenced.[38] These include premises from which waste is or is likely to be discharged to the atmosphere, discharged or deposited on to any land or in waters, from which noise is or is likely to be emitted, on which industrial waste is reprocessed, stored or disposed of, where any ozone-depleting substance is handled or where activities might lend to a hazard or require a clean-up of such magnitude that the environment authority requires that prior financial assurances be given.

In determining whether or not to issue a licence, exemption or some other form of

---

32 Environment Protection Act 1970, s 13(1) (VIC).
33 Ibid, s 64A.
34 Ibid, s 62A.
35 Ibid, s 66B.
36 Protection of the Environment Operations Act 1997, Chap 3 (NSW); Environment Protection Act 1993, Pt 6 (SA); Environmental Protection Act 1994, ss 39–41(QLD); Environment Protection Act 1970, ss 19A–20 (VIC).
37 Environment Protection Act 1970, s 36 and Sch 1 (SA).
38 Environment Protection (Scheduled Premises and Exemption) Regulations 1984.

2.3 Chapter 6

approval, an environment authority may be directed to various relevant matters such as furthering the objects of the legislation, ensuring that the general environmental obligations are complied with, the suitability of the applicant to hold such an authorisation, environmental protection policies, environmental assessments, improvement programmes, performance agreements and any obligations that may be imposed under other legislation.[39]

Licence conditions may include those requiring compliance with environmental standards and also longer-term obligations such as the preparation of an environmental management system or ongoing monitoring. In general, licensing authorities are given wide discretion in the determination of licence applications and conditions.

In all jurisdictions, it is an offence to carry out a regulated activity without the appropriate environmental licences or authorisations, and will result in penalties being imposed on either the company or individuals responsible.[40] In addition, contravention of conditions imposed under a licence will also constitute an offence.

2.4 Specific areas of environmental regulation

2.4.1 Contaminated land

The contamination of soil or groundwater will often be the key environmental issue that exists in a transaction. While the general duty not to harm the environment extends to contamination, most Australian jurisdictions have specific statutory provisions or separate regimes for dealing with land contamination. However, there is a real absence of any consistent legal standard to which contaminated sites must be remedied. Various policies and guidelines exist but they vary considerably, particularly in terms of quantifying contamination itself. In practice, those usually relied upon are the 1992 Guidelines for the Assessment and Management of Contaminated Sites produced by the Australian and New Zealand Environment and Conservation Council (ANZECC) and the National Health and Medical Research Council (NHMRC). Importantly, however, the NEPC is currently preparing national guidelines on contaminated sites.

(a) New South Wales: Contaminated Land Management Act 1997

The Contaminated Land Management Act 1997 and associated regulations and guidelines constitute the basic structure for contaminated land management in NSW. The Act gives the Environmental Protection Authority (EPA) wide powers to declare sites to be contaminated or to require further investigation for potential contamination. It also provides the EPA with wide-ranging powers to order the remediation of sites and broadens the categories of persons who may be responsible for carrying out such remediation.

Under the Act, the threshold test for determining contamination is that the contamination must present a 'significant risk of harm to human health or the environment'. Contamination will not be taken to exist merely because in any surface water, standing or running on the land, a substance is present and the concentration above that normally present in, on or under land in the same environment.[41]

Where either a person has reason to believe that his or her activities on land may have contaminated the land in such a way as to present a significant risk of harm or

---

39 Environmental Protection Act 1994, ss 5A, 44(c), 47(4), 48(4), 63 (QLD).
40 Environment Protection Act 1993, s 36 (SA).
41 Contaminated Land Management Act 1997, s 5.

an owner of land has reason to believe that any activity on the land may have contaminated the land (whether before or during the owner's ownership of land) in such a way as to present a significant risk of harm, then there is a specific duty to report such contamination to the EPA.[42]

Furthermore, where the EPA itself is of the view that a site may be contaminated, it has the power to require investigation of sites which it reasonably considers may be contaminated and where necessary to issue a remediation order requiring a person to remediate the land. Where the EPA undertakes the investigation or remediation, it has the right to recover its costs from the owner.[43]

In issuing such orders, the EPA may direct them to a public authority or to an 'appropriate person'.[44] An appropriate person, and therefore the individual liable, is defined in descending order of preference as:

(1) a person who has 'principal responsibility' for the contamination of the land, or if that is not practicable;
(2) an owner of the land (whether or not that person had any responsibility for such contamination), or if that is not practicable;
(3) a 'notional owner' of the land being a mortgagee in possession or another person who has vested rights in relation to the land.

A person is regarded as 'not practicable' if:

(1) there is no such person; or
(2) the EPA cannot, after reasonable inquiry, find out the identity or location of the person; or
(3) the person, in the opinion of the EPA, is unable to pay the person's debts or would, if the person took steps to comply with the order, become unable to pay the person's debts.

Non-compliance within an investigation or remediation order constitutes an offence and penalties will be imposed up to a maximum of $125,000 for corporation and $60,000 for individuals.[45]

The Act forms the cornerstone of the regime for contaminated land management in NSW. Included within this regime is a State Environmental Planning Policy (SEPP 55) which requires all persons who wish to develop potentially contaminated land to prove that the land is suitable for the proposed use or development. Again, as a precondition to consent to such development, councils may require site orders to be carried out or may make remediation a condition of consent.[46]

(b) Queensland: Environmental Protection Act 1994

Chapter 3 of the Environment Protection Act 1994 contains provisions for dealing with the identification, investigation and management of contaminated land in Queensland. As with NSW, the Act contains a hierarchy of liability in the event that it is not practicable to hold the polluter financially liable. But except for the polluter, the liability of other parties is limited. The owner and/or occupier of land must also

---

42 Ibid, s 60.
43 Ibid, s 36.
44 Ibid, s 12.
45 Ibid, ss 17 and 23.
46 See also draft Guidelines on Significant Risk of Harm from Contaminated Land and the Duty to Report (1998) (NSW) Environment Protection Authority.

2.4 *Chapter 6*

notify the relevant authority upon becoming aware that land has been, or is being, contaminated by 'hazardous contaminants'. Upon receipt of such a notice, the EPA must decide whether the land is contaminated and direct that a site investigation of the property be undertaken and that remediation, if required, be carried out. Again, significant financial penalties and imprisonment may be imposed for non-compliance with the Act.[47]

(c) Victoria: Environment Protection Act 1970

Under the Victorian legislation, it is an offence to have polluted land.[48] The EPA may issue a clean-up notice or obtain an injunction to compel compliance. Such notices may be issued against the polluter or occupier of a premises although in practice the EPA tends to target the occupier. The occupier includes a person who has occupation or control of the premises whether or not that person is the owner of the premises. Thus the occupier may be liable regardless of fault.[49]

(d) South Australia: Environment Protection Act 1993

In SA, there are no specific provisions pursuant to the contamination of land. Rather contamination will constitute a breach of the general environmental duty under the Environment Protection Act 1993, which in turn may lead to penalties being imposed by the EPA.[50] Where the EPA is satisfied that a person has caused environmental harm, including contamination, it may issue a clean-up order to the person responsible, requiring them to take specified action, within a specific period, to make good any resulting environmental damage.[51] Various guidelines also exist in relation to remediating and developing contaminated land.

(e) Common law liability

In addition to the statutory regimes that exist, liability, particularly for the off-site migration of contaminants, may arise at common law on the basis of actions in trespass, nuisance or negligence. While regulatory authorities will usually rely on statutory provisions, where one landowner or individual is harmed by the environmental pollution of another, a common law action may be pursued.

Traditionally, companies could be held strictly liable for damage they caused by introducing dangerous substances or carrying out dangerous activities on land they own or occupy based upon the rule in *Rylands v Fletcher*.[52] This is no longer the case. In *Burnie Port Authority v General Jones Pty Ltd*[53] the High Court of Australia has now abandoned *Rylands v Fletcher* holding instead that the normal principles of negligence apply so that a landowner has a duty of care to avoid a reasonably foreseeable risk to a third party. In the case of contamination migrating off-site, this will not be difficult to prove.

---

47 Environmental Protection Act 1994, s 120 (QLD).
48 Environment Protection Act 1970, s 62A (VIC).
49 Ibid, s 4.
50 Environment Protection Act 1993, Pt 4 and Pt 9 (SA).
51 Ibid, Pt 10.
52 (1866) CR 1 EX 265.
53 (1994) 120 ALR 24.

2.4.2 The pollution of water resources

In general, the pollution of waters, including rivers, streams, lakes, groundwater and marine waters, from land-based activities is regulated under the principal state environmental Acts rather than through separate legislation.

In NSW, in addition to the primary first-tier offence of causing environmental harm, the Protection of the Environment Operations Act 1997 provides that a person must not pollute any waters or cause or permit any waters to be polluted. A person who is guilty of such an offence is liable upon conviction to a penalty not exceeding $250,000 in the case of a corporation with a further $120,000 penalty being imposed for each day the offence continues. In the case of an individual, a penalty not exceeding $120,000 will be imposed with a further penalty not exceeding $60,000 for each day the offence continues.

Under the SA Environment Protection Act 1993, pollution of waters will, as a first step, breach the general environmental duty. Furthermore, as a general licence condition all operations have to comply with the Environment Protection (Marine) Policy 1994 under which mandatory standards are set regulating the quality of water which may be discharged into the environment. As indicated in para 2.3.1(a) above, breach of these policies will incur substantial penalties.

In QLD, pollution of water will, depending upon its nature, also constitute a general offence under the principal Environmental Protection Act 1994. Breach of the environment protection policy on water quality may lead to a penalty ranging from $5,000 to $100,000 depending upon the seriousness of the offence.

Finally, in Victoria all discharges into waters are to be licenced under the Water Act 1989 regulating water quality. In addition, specific protection is given to individual waterways, for example by the state environment protection policy for Port Phillip Bay.

2.4.3 Marine pollution

As indicated above, each state and territory regulates marine pollution from land-based sources through its general Environment Protection legislation. In all Australian jurisdictions, there is also a range of legislation which touches upon marine pollution dealing with issues including fisheries, coastal protection, sea dumping and the transport at sea of dangerous goods.

However, there are also specific Acts dealing with marine pollution from vessels. In this regard the legislation seeks to implement those international treaties to which Australia is a party with various state marine pollution Acts implementing the International Convention for the Prevention of Pollution from Ships (MARPOL) and the Convention for the Prevention of Pollution of the Sea by Oil (OILPOL).[54]

2.4.4 Emissions to the atmosphere

As with the pollution of waters, emissions to atmosphere are also regulated under the various state Environment Protection Acts in accordance with conditions imposed under environmental authorisations. For NSW, the Protection of the Environment Operations Act 1997 provides that it is an offence to operate or carry out maintenance on plant so as to cause air pollution or to deal with materials so as to cause air pollution. The same penalties as those for causing the pollution of waters will apply. The Act and associated regulations set out air standards that are to be complied with.

54 For a comprehensive review of the laws dealing with marine pollution in Australia, see G Bates and Z Lipman. *Corporate Liability for Pollution* (1998, Sydney, LBC), Chap 7.

2.4 Chapter 6

In SA, regulation of air emissions is again achieved through Environment Protection policies with policies existing on both air quality and burning, while in QLD policies also exist dealing with air emissions. Breach of these policies will again in most cases constitute a breach of an environmental authorisation and of the general provisions of the respective environmental protection Acts. Finally, in Victoria all discharges into the atmosphere are to be licenced and to comply with the appropriate emission standards.

It is important to be aware also that uniform ambient air quality standards have now been introduced with the National Environmental Protection Measure on Ambient Air Quality.

2.4.5 Waste management and recycling

Waste management is dealt with under separate regulatory regimes in each state jurisdiction. In NSW, the Waste Minimisation and Management Act 1995 establishes a State Waste Advisory Council and contains provisions dealing with regional waste planning and management, industry waste reduction and a waste licensing regime. The Act provides a mechanism to establish waste management regions, to be headed by Waste Planning and Management Boards, with responsibility for co-ordination of waste services in their regions. The Act also provides for the making and enforcement of industry waste reduction plans and for the licensing of occupiers of controlled waste facilities, persons carrying out controlled waste activities and certain transporters of waste. In doing so, it ties in with the first-tier offence under the Protection of the Environment Operations Act 1997 of wilfully or negligently disposing of waste in a manner that harms or is likely to harm the environment.

In SA, the Environment Protection (Waste) Management Policy 1994 provides for the collection and transport of medical waste and establishes duties of councils, hospitals and pharmacies in relation to handling such waste. In addition, it also lays out a duty dealing with the transport of waste generally.

In QLD, the Environment Protection (Interim Waste) Regulations 1996 deal with the storage, removal, collection and disposal of domestic, commercial, industrial and recyclable biodegradable refuse. Regulations require industrial refuse to be stored in appropriate containers and stipulate that all vehicles and equipment used in the removal of industrial waste must be well maintained and clean. The regulations also make provision for waste disposal facilities and, in the case of hazardous waste, require generators and transporters of that waste to notify the local authority of the particulars of the waste. Any breach of the policy may give rise to one of the offences under the Environmental Protection Act 1994.

In Victoria waste is regulated under the Environment Protection (Prescribed Waste) Regulations 1996. The regulations contain a long list of industrial waste including heavy metals, detergents, food processing waste, effluent, pesticides, industrial plant washdown waters, reactive chemicals, vegetable oils and other waste which causes an environmental hazard. A person must not conduct any business, for the purpose of the transportation of prescribed waste or conduct an operation which includes the transportation of prescribed waste, without a permit for each vehicle that is used. In addition, the Industrial Waste Management (Waste Minimisation) Policy, which applies to all Victorian premises at which industrial waste is generated, stored, reprocessed, treated or disposed of, requires that certain licensing applications under the general environmental protection Act be accompanied by a waste management plan. The EPA also requires occupiers of industrial premises to prepare such a plan or undertake a waste audit. Finally, the Environment Protection (Transport) Regulations 1997 establishes a system of certification for the transportation of waste.

2.4.6 Dangerous goods and hazardous substances

As with contaminated land and waste the use, storage and transportation of hazardous goods and dangerous substances including radioactive material and ozone-depleting substances is dealt with under individual State Acts. In general terms, this legislation provides for the issuing of licences to store, handle and transport dangerous and hazardous chemicals and also sets standards for the way in which this is to be done. In addition, the relevant legislation relating to ozone-depleting substances seeks to phase out their use across Australia.

In NSW, licences are issued under the Dangerous Goods Act 1975 to store dangerous goods while the Road and Rail Transport (Dangerous Goods) Act 1997 regulates their movement. Chemicals and chemical wastes are regulated under the Environmentally Hazardous Chemicals Act 1985. The latter Act makes provision for the creation of a list of chemicals and the prohibition of the use of chemicals which are not listed under the Act. The EPA may conduct assessment of chemicals and chemical wastes and make 'chemical control orders' in respect of chemicals and chemical waste assessed. Such orders regulate activities including acts of manufacturing, processing, keeping, distributing, conveying, using, selling or disposing of chemicals or chemical wastes or any act related to such acts.

In SA, the Dangerous Substances Act 1979 regulates the keeping, handling, conveyance, use, disposal and quality of dangerous substances. Administered by the Department on Labour and Industries, the Act imposes a general duty of persons handling dangerous substances to take reasonable precautions and exercise reasonable care. The Act also requires premises on which dangerous substances are kept to be licensed. The Act makes provision for the Department and its inspectors to inspect premises and issue notices requiring remedial activities to be carried out to ensure compliance with prescribed standards of conduct.

In addition, legislation also exists enabling the EPA to prohibit the sale or use within SA of any products of a certain class that have been manufactured using a prescribed substance. This legislation is aimed at protecting the ozone layer and also sets out requirements for labelling of certain products.

In QLD, the Building (Flammable and Combustible Liquids) Regulations 1994 requires licences to be obtained for premises used for storing flammable or combustible liquids. The regulations prescribe certain standards for storage premises. In addition the Carriage of Dangerous Goods by Road Act 1984 regulates the carriage of goods as specified in the Australian Code for the Transport of Dangerous Goods by Road and Rail. This is further supplemented by the Road Transport Reform (Dangerous Goods) Act 1995, which regulates the transportation of dangerous goods. Licences to carry, store, sell or use explosives must be obtained under the Explosives Act 1952.

Finally, in Victoria, the Dangerous Goods Act 1985 regulates the use, handling, storage and conveying of dangerous goods including explosives. Obligations contained in the Act include the requirement to obtain a licence for activities involving dangerous goods and to take all reasonable precautions to prevent tampering, fires and explosions, leakages or any damage to property or danger to the public.

2.4.7 Noise

At the statutory level, noise is again dealt with on the same basis as issues of water and air pollution. In NSW, it is an offence to operate a plant or deal with materials so as to cause noise pollution. A person who is guilty of such an offence is liable upon conviction to a fine of up to $60,000 in the case of a corporation and a further $6,000

2.4 *Chapter 6*

for each day the offence continues and up to $30,000 in the case of an individual with a further $600 for each day the offence continues. In SA and QLD, environment protection policies exist setting out permissible noise levels while in Victoria, premises from which noise is or is likely to be emitted must be licenced.

2.4.8 Common law liability

As is the case with contaminated land, it should be noted that liability for any form of pollution, and in particular noise, air and water pollution, might also arise at common law on the basis of an action primarily in nuisance. Where a third party is affected by the activities that take place on the premises of another, then a common law action may be pursued in nuisance or trespass as described in para 2.4.1(e) above so that third parties may be able to obtain an injunction to stop premises emitting air, noise or water pollution that impacts upon them and, where appropriate, also obtain damages for any loss they have suffered.

2.4.9 Land use, zoning and development control

An expansion of an existing operation or intention to undertake a new activity will require development approval and potentially an environmental impact assessment. Each state has its own development and planning regime, as well as various building regulations which must be complied with. The principal planning Acts are the Environmental Planning and Assessment Act 1979 (NSW), the Integrated Planning Act 1997 (QLD), the Development Act 1993 (SA), and the Planning and Environment Act 1987 (VIC).

A number of states have also now adopted a works approval system under which some environmental authorities will stipulate what equipment or technical requirements must be met to achieve prescribed environmental standards, before new works are constructed, new plant installed, changes made to the method of operation of licenced premises, or alterations to the type of material used and products produced on the premises. The works approval then permits the construction, installation or changes to proceed as opposed to an environmental licence which permits the resulting discharges themselves.[55]

Finally, there is a comprehensive legal regime dealing with heritage protection and issues of native title. Both at the federal level and state level, regulation exists to protect world heritage, national estate, cultural heritage and aboriginal heritage. Federal and state legislation also exists which deals specifically with the issue of native title. In the acquisition of any new property or the undertaking of any new projects, these issues will always have to be considered carefully.

2.5 Specific industry issues

Certain sectors are also subject to specific environmentally related obligations under dedicated legislation. For example, the regulation of all development and environmental matters relating to Australian airports, many of which have now been leased to private operators, are subject to the environmental obligations laid down in the Airports Act 1996.[56] In the case of mining activities, environmental obligations often exist under both the main environmental legislation as well as dedicated mining Acts.

---

55 Environment Protection Act 1993, s 35 (SA); Environment Protection Act 1970, s 19A (VIC).
56 Airports Act 1996 (Cth).

In SA for example, ancillary operations with respect to mining are regulated under an environmental licence, while the major approval and rehabilitation requirements are dealt with under the Mines Works and Inspection Act 1929.[57] With respect to the energy sector, the national privatisation of the electricity and gas markets will see the introduction of specific legislation dealing with sustainable energy, emissions reduction and emissions trading.

3 PARTICULAR ENVIRONMENTAL ISSUES RELEVANT TO TRANSACTIONS

The most attractive transactions will be those in which there is a minimum level of risk and exposure to any form of liability. Nonetheless, in most cases, the acquisition of an operation or the merging with another, will bring with it the need to identify and assess carefully those issues of an environmental nature which give rise to liability. The acquisition of an existing company with historical liabilities or continuing instances of non-compliance and assets that either harm, or have harmed the environment, will have serious implications for a purchaser, and where relevant, financiers.

3.1 Assumption of liabilities—routes and basis for liabilities

The extent to which the historical and continuing liabilities of an existing company will be assumed by an acquiring company will (as discussed later) depend upon the way in which a particular transaction is structured.

In general terms, acquiring a company through purchase of its shares will result in the assumption of all the liabilities associated with that company. This includes both historical liabilities and liability for continuing non-compliance. However, with the exception of land, acquisition of a company's assets will only attract the liabilities which the law applies directly to those assets. Where an asset subject to an environmental authorisation is purchased, and that asset then breaches that authorisation, it is the owner of that asset who will be liable.

In the case of acquiring land however, the person or company in control or possession of the land will be potentially liable, even if not initially. Therefore, acquisition of land, though a share or direct asset purchase will also attract the liabilities arising from control of the land. This includes liability from historical contamination under both statutory and common law as discussed in para 2.4.1 above.

Whatever approach is ultimately adopted, the exposure that arises through the acquisition of a company's shares and assets will need to be carefully assessed. While the structuring of a transaction may enable certain liabilities to be excluded, it will not be possible to exclude all liabilities, therefore reinforcing the need for comprehensive due diligence.

3.2 Historical liabilities—past practices and procedures, including those of former site owners

As discussed above, those acquiring companies and assets such as land, or those subject to environment authorisations, may be liable for past practices or procedures

---

57 See also Mineral Resources Act 1989 (QLD); Mining Act 1992 (NSW); Mineral and Resources Development Act 1990 (VIC).

3.2 *Chapter 6*

associated with that company or asset that cause environmental harm many years after acquistion.

While in some circumstances, an environment authority may first pursue those responsible for the harm, in general it will be the current owner who is in control and possession of the asset who is liable, especially given the difficulties in locating past owners and directors and proving causation.

Furthermore, where environmental harm or non-compliance has been ongoing, both under past and current ownership, it will be the current owners who will face primary liability. The ability to carve out liability for pre-acquisition activities (such as for contamination of land) will be a contractual issue to be determined at the time of sale or one of proving contributory negligence should the matter be subject to litigation.

3.3 Liabilities for off-site activities or impacts

The most common off-site activity or impact for which liability may be attracted is through the off-site migration of contaminants in soil or groundwater. As indicated in para 2.4.1 above such liability may arise either:

(1) under the statutory regimes dealing with contaminated land, which may include the issuing of clean-up orders; or
(2) through the common law avenues of negligence, nuisance and trespass where a third party adversely affected by the activity seeks to recover damages for the harm they have suffered or an injunction to stop the activity.

In addition, the migration off-site of other pollution such as air pollution, waste or damage through some disaster such as the bursting of a holding dam may result in liability arising on a similar basis.

3.4 Liabilities of directors and managers

Within Australian law, there is without doubt an increasing trend towards holding company directors and managers as being responsible for the environmental harm caused by their company's activities. Corporate accountability, and hence that of those who manage and direct a corporation's activities, is now also easier to enforce with the removal of the common law right against self-incrimination (ie to refuse to answer questions or produce documents which would have a tendency to expose a person to criminal liability).[58]

Furthermore, to date a number of company directors have been found criminally liable, with one sentenced to three months' imprisonment[59] and another fined $25,000 and sentenced to 400 hours of community work.[60] While such prosecutions have been limited to more 'hands-on' directors of small businesses, larger blue-chip company directors are now on notice.

---

58 *EPA v Caltex Refining Co Pty Ltd* (1993) 92 LERA 51.
59 *Environment Protection Authority v McMurty* (unreported, 9 March 1995 Court of Petty Sessions, WA).
60 *Environment Protection Authority v White* (1996) 92 LGERA 263. More recently, a number of further prosecutions have taken place in Victoria, see R Baird 'Liability of Directors and Managers for Corporate and Environmental Offences—Recent Prosecutions' (1999) 16(3) *Environment and Planning Law Journal*.

Where a corporation is found guilty of contravening the environmental laws that exist, then as a general rule in nearly all Australian jurisdictions, each person who is a director of the corporation or who is concerned in the management of the corporation is taken to have contravened the same provision[61] unless they can show:

(1) they had no knowledge (actual, imputed or constructive) of the contravention;
(2) they were not in a position to influence the conduct of the corporation in relation to the contravention; or
(3) if in such a position, they used all due diligence to prevent the contravention.[62]

In this respect directors and managers, like all employees, are required to turn their minds to the likely risks of their activities and to exercise a reasonable degree of skill, care and due diligence in the performance of their functions.

For new directors taking over a company for the first time, it is therefore important that they are fully aware of any instances of non-compliance that may exist. While indemnities can be obtained with respect to certain liabilities such as remediation costs, they are not available for criminal liability.

It is also worth noting that under the Contaminated Land Management Act 1997 (NSW), directors and managers of a corporation that contravene the Act are again taken to have contravened the same provision unless they can establish one of the very limited number of defences. Furthermore, where a corporation is wound up to avoid compliance, then a former director or holding company may be ordered by the court to comply with a remediation order. If contaminated land is disposed of to avoid compliance with an order, a director of the corporation who disposed of land may be ordered to comply with the remediation notice personally.

Finally, given the significant levels of attention currently being paid in Australia to developing legal regimes for the abatement of greenhouse gases, some lawyers are already arguing that it would be prudent for companies and their directors to be at least addressing the issue of greenhouse emissions and to consider reporting on their emission levels in accordance with their corporate reporting obligations (as discussed at para 4.5 below).

3.5 Liability of financiers

Although usually removed from the control and management of an acquisition for which financial assistance is provided, financiers remain exposed to potential liability either:

(1) directly, through becoming involved in the continuing management and control of a company, such as in circumstances where a borrower defaults and the financier if required to step in, or
(2) indirectly through environmental liabilities incurred by the company being financed which have the effect of decreasing the security value of the financed asset or which may limit a company's ability to service their loan.

Direct liabilities will usually only arise where it is necessary for a financier to step in and take possession of a company. In such circumstances, continued management of the company, even only until it can be sold, will see the financier exposed to potential liability for breach of environmental law.

---

61 See section 2.5.
62 Protection of the Environment Operations Act 1997, s 118 (NSW); see also *State Pollution Control Commission v Kelly* (1991) 5 ACSR 607.

3.5 Chapter 6

Importantly however, in the case of contaminated land, financiers are afforded some protection under Australian Law. In NSW, the Contaminated Land Management Act 1997 specifically provides that remediation orders may be issued, as a last resort, to 'notional owners' which includes mortgagees in possession of land. However, this does not include financiers acting merely as holders of a security interest in land or financiers who appoint a receiver and/or manager merely to sell the land to a party who undertakes to remediate it.

Under the QLD legislation, liability for contamination lies with the owner of land. This includes a mortgagee of land, where that mortgagee is acting as a mortgagee in possession of the land and has the exclusive management and control of the land. However, despite the classification of mortgagees as 'owners', they are not liable to conduct a site investigation or remediate land, thereby providing financiers with some protection.[63]

In Victoria, the wide definition of 'occupier' encompasses a mortgagee when they take an active and direct management role in the operations of the company. However, the definition also excludes 'a person being a financial institution and acting solely as a holder of a security interest in the premises or as a mortgagee in possession or which is, or appoints a controller of the premises'.[64] Finally, in SA the definition of occupier under s 3(1) of the Environment Protection Act 1993 excludes mortgagees in possession 'unless the mortgage assures active management of the place'.

In the case of more indirect liabilities however, protection is limited. This in itself simply reinforces the role that due diligence investigation and loan conditions and warranties will play.

3.6 The transferability of licences

As a general rule, the transfer of environmental authorisations or licences to a new owner is an administrative procedure. Once the consent of the transferring parties is obtained an application is made to the administering authority who, upon receipt of the relevant fee and transfer form, will cancel the existing licence and issue a new one in the name of the new owner.

In most cases the new licence will be issued on the same terms as the existing licence. However, in Victoria the authority may impose new conditions,[65] while in both NSW[66] and QLD[67] the authority has discretion to refuse the transfer if issues of public safety or the suitability of the new holder arise. It is not possible to transfer trade waste agreements in NSW, Victoria or QLD.

The requirement to transfer a licence will only be triggered where the actual entity in whose name the licence is held is changed or, in Victoria, the person in occupation or control of the premises changes.[68] Therefore, acquisition of a parent company or merger which does not change the name of the licence-holder will not require a transfer of licences. Nonetheless, in such circumstances the normal practice would be to inform the environmental authorities of the changes in ownership at the parent company level.

Finally, unlike environmental licences, development and planning consents benefit the land and not the owner of the land. Transfer of such consents is therefore not required.

---

63 Environmental Protection Act 1994, ss 118J(5), 118V(3) (QLD).
64 Environment Protection Act 1970, s 4(3)(c) (VIC).
65 Environment Protection Act 1970, s 25 (VIC).
66 Protection of the Environment Operations Act 1997, s 55 (NSW).
67 Environmental Protection Act 1994, ss 55–58 (QLD).
68 Environmental Protection Act 1970, s 25 (VIC).

3.7 Mechanisms for compliance cost increases

In most cases, the cost of environmental compliance will be based upon ensuring that operations meet defined standards imposed under environmental laws, licences and applicable policies. However, in some cases the cost of compliance may be of a more flexible or 'uncertain' nature, which has the added effect of potentially increasing the costs of compliance.

In some jurisdictions, regulatory requirements impose the environmental management of an activity which achieves ongoing minimisation of environmental harm through cost-effective measures assessed against currently used national and international best practice standards.[69] The Best Practice Environmental Management (BPEM) approach essentially involves balancing the cost of achieving desirable environmental standards and the risk of environmental harm arising from the activities under consideration. A regulatory authority may set a standard and then require industry to adopt BPEM in relation to its own activities.[70] In addition, in both QLD and SA, environmental improvement programmes may be imposed on licence holders under which measures must be taken to ensure compliance with a specified standard, which may be greater than that normally required.[71]

The regulatory framework is also increasingly shifting towards the adoption of economic instruments and incentives as a means of achieving better environmental outcomes. For example, NSW has recently adopted a load-based licensing system under which licence fees will be determined by the level of pollutants emitted from an operation.[72] Improving environmental performance therefore directly reduces operating costs. Furthermore, the likely introduction of an emissions trading scheme will also allow companies to determine the most cost-effective means of compliance. The purchase of pollution credits or quotas from other parties, may in many cases be more cost-effective than actually upgrading existing operations.

Under the Framework Convention on Climate Change and the Kyoto Protocol, Australia has committed itself to limiting any increase in its greenhouse emissions by the year 2010 to 8% of its 1990 levels. Given that Australia's emissions are expected to grow by 28% by 2010, measures that will effect a 20% reduction in current emissions are therefore required.

The government has introduced a major greenhouse package with a range of measures designed strictly to reduce emission levels.[73] These include the promotion of renewable energy; the reform of the energy market and automotive industries, and the introduction of various energy efficiency codes and standards designed to reduce energy use. In addition, at both federal and state level, work has begun to establish greenhouse gas emissions trading schemes.

The House of Representatives Standing Committee on Environment, Recreation and the Arts has recently completed an inquiry into regulatory arrangements for trading in greenhouse emissions. This parallels work being carried out by both the Australian Bureau of Agricultural and Resource Economics (ABARE) and the National Greenhouse Office on the same issue. While the exact timing and details of such schemes remains to be determined, the NSW Department of Energy has made clear its intention to establish such a scheme and as a first step enacted the Carbon

---

69 Environmental Protection Act 1994, s 18 and Sch 4 (QLD).
70 Environmental Protection Act 1994, s 81 (QLD); Environmental Management and Pollution Control Act 1994, s 38. (Tas)
71 See para 2.5 above.
72 Pollution Control (Load Based Licensing) Act 1997.
73 Commonwealth of Australia, The National Greenhouse Strategy: Strategic Framework for Advancing Australia's Greenhouse Response (1998, Canberra, AGPS).

3.7 *Chapter 6*

Rights Legislation Amendment Act 1998 which will recognise in law the rights associated with carbon sequestrated from the atmosphere by trees and forests.

In addition, the Sydney Futures Exchange has also established the Australian Emissions Trading Forum to encourage active debate on emissions trading and other flexible market mechanisms to reduce greenhouse emissions.

Nonetheless, once established, such schemes will see the issuing of 'tradeable emission permits' that grant the right to produce a given volume of emissions over a specified time period. The total emission rights of the permits are set equal to the overall level of emissions desired by the regulator. Emission sources are then allowed to trade permits. Emittors below their permit levels will therefore be gaining a tradeable asset, while those exceeding their quota will inherit a liability which can only be offset by either the introduction of abatement measures or the purchase of further permits in the market.

3.8 Taxation concessions

It is important to note that the cost of putting in place preventative measures for pollution control and costs of remediation or clean-up may be claimed specifically as a tax deduction. In broad terms the Income Tax Assessment Act 1935 provides that expenditure incurred for the sale or dominant purpose of carrying on an 'eligible environment protection activity' (EEPA) is generally deductible.[74] This includes preventing, combating or rectifying pollution, or treating cleaning up, removing or storing waste.[75] The pollution or waste must have resulted or be likely to result from an income producing activity[76] of the taxpayer or from a business activity of the taxpayer's predecessor on the polluted site.

3.9 Industry specific issues

The liability of companies and their officers for environmental offences and issues such as contamination as outlined above apply to all activities. Nonetheless, in one or two cases specific liability regimes have been implemented by way of legislation, particularly where the disposal of government assets is involved. For example, in 1996 the federal government privatised the operation of Australia's major airports. Under the legislative arrangements invoked, lessors of airport facilities will be liable for any contamination of an airport facility that exists irrespective of whether or not it was pre-existing the privatisation.[77]

4   MANAGING ENVIRONMENTAL ISSUES IN TRANSACTIONS

Introduction

The assessment and management of environmental issues in any transaction, both during the transaction itself and after completion, is fundamental. In some circumstances environmental liabilities may in fact be so significant that they render a transaction unattractive. In others, risks although present may be easily contained

---

74   Income Tax Assessment Act 1935 (Cth), Pt 111, Div 3, Subdiv CA.
75   Ibid, s 82BM.
76   Ibid, ss 82BI, 82BM(2).
77   Airports Act 1996.

through appropriate contractual arrangements. Commercial practice with respect to managing environmental issues is now well developed to the extent that the identification and allocation of liabilities through appropriate due diligence has become a normal part of any commercial transaction.

4.1 Current practice for the assessment of risk

In any transaction, appropriate due diligence inquiries are undertaken of the activities of a company. While historically environmental issues were largely ignored in this context, they now rank as one of the key areas in any due diligence assessment.

The extent of due diligence will vary and will be dependent upon factors such as the nature of the activity concerned, the extent to which a purchaser considers the environment as an issue, the timing of the transaction and the ability to access relevant information. Obviously in some transactions, such as a hostile takeover, it may be difficult to obtain any real information as to the target company. Nonetheless, a preliminary environmental due diligence assessment is one of the first steps to be undertaken.

In practice, due diligence inquiries will generally be the responsibility of the acquirer's legal advisers. As a first step, it is normal practice to review those documents which demonstrate a company's environmental performance. These include previous audit reports, site contamination assessment reports (if any), current operating licences and other authorisations, existing environmental management systems and the records contained therein, internal reporting documentation, records of environmental incidents or prosecutions and general matters of legal compliance.

In many cases, a preliminary due diligence will reveal problems which require further investigation. This is especially the case with sites that may be contaminated. In other circumstances, the information provided may simply be insufficient and therefore further investigation is warranted, or the nature of the industry is such that a far more comprehensive assessment according to the types of risks that are associated with the enterprise is demanded. For example, major industrial activities or those located close to sensitive environments are likely to require some level of auditing and on-site assessments.

In this respect, legal advisers will also often work closely with environmental consultancies to assess further the potential risks that may exist. Consultants will often be engaged to undertake a 'scoping' or 'Phase 1 Audit' to determine what, if any, problems may exist. Such an audit will involve taking composite samples to obtain a profile of potential contamination. Obviously, the nature of the scoping study will depend upon the historical land use of the site.

In circumstances where a scoping study reveals environmental contamination or where, because of the historical use of the site, contamination is expected, a more detailed 'Phase 2 Audit' may be undertaken. This will involve a detailed investigation based upon a full drilling assessment of the site and, where necessary, the preparation of a detailed remediation plan. While Phase 2 audits are more expensive, it is normal practice to carry these investigations out in the case of high risk sites such as an oil refinery to determine the existence of any soil or groundwater contamination.

In all situations, the end result is one that produces a due diligence assessment which identifies:

(1) historical liabilities;
(2) existing liabilities and the current management thereof; and
(3) the likely cost of rectifying or managing any environmental issues that exist.

4.2 *Chapter 6*

4.2 Warranty and indemnity terms

Where due diligence inquiries reveal an absence of any environmental risks, liabilities or instances of non-compliance, the potential for hidden liabilities may still exist. In the case of mergers or takeovers the ability to obtain some form of additional legal protection against hidden liabilities will be difficult. Mergers involving two independent companies leave limited room for warranties and indemnities, while takeovers, particularly those of a hostile nature, will often see little co-operation from the target. However, in the case of acquisition-type transactions, it is usually possible to obtain environmental warranties from the seller, the ultimate form of which will be a matter for negotiation. Purchasers will usually seek warranties from the vendor to the effect that:

(1) all environmental authorisations for the conduct of the operations have been obtained, complied with and remain in full force and effect;
(2) the company and its employees have not committed any environmental offences and that there are no threatened or pending prosecutions;
(3) there are no conditions on any premises which would require work to be carried out operations stopped or clean-up work to be undertaken;
(4) no contamination exists on the site; and
(5) there is no legal action against the company or any of its directors or employees.

As in all cases, the normal commercial risks associated with warranties will always exist and the final form will be the result of contractual negotiations. In addition, where due diligence inquiries bring a particular issue to the purchaser's attention, a warranty to the contrary cannot be relied upon.

Importantly, where a vendor makes warranties of the nature of those outlined above and then it later becomes apparent that the vendor knew them to be untrue, then the vendor may also be liable under the Trade Practices Act 1974[78] for misleading or deceptive conduct or misrepresentation. This simply adds a further level of protection for a purchaser.

Where due diligence inquiries actually reveal the existence of environmental liabilities or suggests a real risk of their existence, further protection will usually be sought through contractual indemnities or specific contractual clauses that 'carve out' the liability. This is particularly the case where a purchaser is unwilling to assume a specific problem.

In terms of environmental indemnities, the most common are a vendor indemnifying a purchaser in respect of any environmental liability that may exist (eg contamination) or against any legal action that may be commenced against the company. Such indemnities may be full or limited to a particular monetary amount. Indemnities will not be available against criminal penalties.

Alternatively, it will also be possible to negotiate other contractual terms by which liability is carved out of the transaction or allocated to one of the parties. For example, contractual provisions are sometimes adopted which allocate all contamination prior to the purchase date to the vendor and all post liability contamination to the purchaser. This will require a comprehensive contamination audit to be carried out prior to sale. The purchase price may then be reduced by taking into account the cost of remediation or a vendor may simply be forced to clean up a site prior to final sale.

---

78 Trade Practices Act 1974 (Cth), ss 52 and 59.

4.3 Issues for those lending money to businesses

In general terms, those lending money for transactions will not be liable for breaches of environmental law where their involvement in the transaction is limited purely to one of a financier. Furthermore, in certain circumstances such as land contamination, specific legislative provisions exist to protect financiers from any liability. However, where financiers take control of an operation or become concerned in the management of it, they will be exposed to potential liability. Furthermore, regardless of their involvement in a company, any significant environmental liabilities that affect the value of the company or the lendor's ability to make repayments will be of serious concern.

It is therefore now standard practice for financiers to incorporate contractual provisions within finance documents. These will usually include:

(1) A precondition on a loan that the borrower provide an independent environmental report on environmental compliance of the company being acquired. In most cases financiers will rely upon the borrower's independent report and due diligence investigations unless an acquisition is of a particularly environmentally sensitive nature.
(2) The incorporation of representations and warranties to the effect that there are no acts or omissions which may give rise to a claim against the company for a breach of environmental law or that there is no requirement for substantial expenditure to remedy an existing environmental liability or none of the assets of the company are contaminated.
(3) An undertaking that the company being acquired, and the acquirer (ie borrower) manage their assets and businesses in an environmentally responsible manner. In this regard, financiers may push for an environmental management system as a condition of lending.

In circumstances involving specific environmental issues, events of default may be incorporated into the contract. However, in most cases financiers will usually rely upon the warranties and indemnities provided for under the finance documents.

It should be noted that a number of major banks, both foreign and domestic, have now established environmental departments to assess carefully major projects in which they become involved.

4.4 The role of environmental management systems

The obligation to ensure environmental compliance and manage the environmental impacts of an acquired entity continue well beyond the completion of the transaction. Increasing regulatory control and enforcement within Australian law has simply reinforced the need for comprehensive environmental management systems capable of minimising and to the extent possible, eliminating, environmental risks and liabilities. Furthermore, companies with a poor environmental record may find it difficult to raise loans or do business with organisations who carefully consider the environmental credentials of their business partners.

Paralleling the increasing enforcement of environmental law, has also been an increase in the significance of defences available under environmental legislation. The primary defence, and in some cases the only available defence, is one of 'due diligence' under which corporations or individuals are able to demonstrate that all

4.4 *Chapter 6*

reasonable and practical measures had been taken to prevent the company committing environmental offences. To this extent, the establishment of the effective environmental management programme and a pro-active approach to the identification, mitigation and management of environmental risks is fundamental, not only to ensure that the defence of due diligence can be established but also for minimising potential risk of environmental harm occurring.

The adoption of an environmental management system is obviously designed to assist the management and staff of a company to understand and comply with their obligations under relevant environmental laws. As indicated earlier, in some jurisdictions, the requirement to establish an environmental management system may be imposed as a licence condition.[79] Certainly many industries are now required to provide a compliance certificate to the environmental authorities at the end of each year. In doing so, a regular review of the compliance of a corporation will ensure that all staff are aware of their obligations.

While the objective of an environmental management system is clear, the actual content and implementation of that system will vary between industries. While internationally recognised systems such as ISO 14001 are regularly adopted, there is no particular required approach under Australian law. Rather to be an effective environmental management system it should be adequately designed so as to:

(1) ensure management and staff turn their minds to the likely risks;
(2) identify the environmental risks which flow from an operation and from the activities carried out within that operation;
(3) evaluate the potential effect of those impacts on the environment;
(4) enable implementation of measures to minimise or prevent those impacts;
(5) guarantee adequate supervision and monitoring of those measures;
(6) provide adequate training for all involved in the operation; and
(7) ensure ongoing environmental improvement through regular reporting on environmental matters, the commissioning of regular performance audits and responding to changing circumstances.

Obviously no system is capable of eliminating all environmental risks. However, the establishment of a comprehensive, efficient and proven environmental management system will go a long way to the long-term environmental management of an operation and the minimising of potential liability for a company, its directors, managers and employees.

While significant provisions exist under the environmental legislative regime for non-compliance, defences do exist where it can be shown that all reasonable care was taken or that effective systems of due diligence exist. The existence within an operation of an effective environmental management system, which is correctly implemented, will both minimise the risk of non-compliance and act as a possible defence to prosecution.[80]

As a general rule, environmental management systems are not compulsory. However in some jurisdictions, particularly QLD, an environmental management programme may be required as a condition of a licence.[81] In addition, in both QLD and SA, environmental improvement programmes which require a licence-holder to improve environmental performance to a specified standard (which may be greater then that normally required) also exist.[82]

---

79 See section 3 above.
80 See section 3 above.
81 Environmental Protection Act 1994, ss 80–100 (QLD).
82 Ibid, ss 85–93; Environment Protection Act 1993, s 44 (SA).

Finally, it is also important that the role of environmental management be utilised to focus on managing potential future risks. While the regulatory framework for the control of greehouse gas emissions is still developing in Australia, the clear signals are that the potential economic impacts and liabilities for industry and business will be significant. In this regard, understanding the debate and the direction of policy and developing an adequate portfolio of responses is critical.

4.5 Environmental reporting

While any effective environmental management system will incorporate reporting provisions, there has been a real shift within regulatory frameworks to increase community awareness through companies being obliged to disclose details of their activities which affect the environment. While many of Australia's listed companies voluntarily provide information relating to environmental performance in annual report documents, from 1 July 1998, mandatory requirements were imposed upon companies to provide information concerning their environmental performance.[83] Under the Company Law Review Act 1998 the company director's report for a financial year must provide details of the company's performance in relation to environmental regulations where that company's operations are subject to any particular and significant environmental regulation under a law for the commonwealth, state or territory.

While the Act does not specifically spell out what is encompassed within the phrase 'particular and significant environmental regulation' it is likely to include environmental licences and approvals, impact assessments, management programmes, the extent of any land contamination, emission levels for pollutants, the outcomes of environmental audits and any environmental prosecutions. Failure to meet these reporting obligations will result in directors being liable to substantial civil penalties and possible removal from office.

4.6 Insurance

Where certain environmental damage has occurred, it may well be that the existing company has some form of insurance to guard against potential liability. In general, insurers are unwilling to take on the potentially enormous risks associated with environmental harm and, as a result, the availability of insurance coverage is both limited and expensive.

Nonetheless, it is possible to obtain specialised cover for certain types of risks such as for pollution from storage tanks or from incidents caused by contractors. In addition, more general insurance coverage, such as under a general environmental impairment liability (EIL) policy, may also be obtained. While such insurance will cover clean-up costs and defending a legal action, it will not cover fines or penalties.[84]

4.7 Structuring the management of companies, ownership of assets and operation of businesses

The acquisition of an operation, by its very nature, will entail parallel acquisition of its assets and liabilities. However, the way in which a transaction, and the management of a company, are structured will enable some flexibility in determining where liabilities may fall.

83 Company Law Review Act 1998 (Cth), s 299(1)(f).
84 G Bates and Z Lipman *Corporate Liability for Pollution* (1998, Sydney, LBC) pp 8–11.

4.7 *Chapter 6*

As discussed in para 3.1 above, acquiring the shares in a company will see the acquirer take full ownership of the company and therefore be responsible for all its actions, including ongoing instances of non-compliance and historical liabilities such as soil or groundwater contamination. Such liabilities may be limited, however, where only the assets of a target company are required. In such cases, historical liability would be retained by the company from which the assets have been purchased. Importantly, in the case of purchasing land, it may still be the owners of that land who may be liable for historical contamination. However, it is possible to acquire a company or its assets and in doing so expressly carve out particular land assets which pose a particular liability.

In the case of joint venture arrangements, the role of each party will also have an effect on the way in which liabilities are allocated. As a general rule, liability will fall on those concerned in the management of a company. In situations where management of a responsibility falls with one party alone, then appropriate arrangements should be made to ensure that any environmental liability is placed entirely upon that party. This will particularly be the case in ventures involving a local participant and a foreign equity partner. The extent to which the foreign equity partner will be liable will depend upon the degree of control they exercise in the decision-making process and management of the company. In this regard, in any joint venture, careful consideration will need to be made as to the responsibilities of the parties, the role they are to play and in whose name assets are to be held and operations conducted.

While Australian law is particularly wide regarding the range of individuals who may attract liability for environmental issues, it is still possible to structure the management of a company in such a way that those more directly involved in the day-to-day operations of a company will be more liable for environmental problems, than other individuals such as non-executive directors, financiers or silent partners.

5 CONCLUSION

5.1 The harmonisation of federal and state regulation of the environment

As indicated throughout this chapter, environmental issues are now accepted as a major issue to be addressed and managed in most commercial transactions. As the level of concern over, and regulation of, the environment continues, attention to environmental issues is only likely to increase. Anticipated developments and trends within Australia simply confirm this.

There has been a concerted effort by Australian governments to harmonise the existing federal and state regulatory frameworks, both in terms of clearly identifying areas of responsibility and in establishing consistent environmental measures, policies and standards applicable to all jurisdictions. Under the IGAE, a number of NEPMs have now been introduced with several others currently being prepared. Furthermore, the new federal Environment Protection and Biodiversity Act 1999 will also see a clearer definition of federal and state involvement in environmental matters with particular attention to:

(1) identifying those areas relating to matters of national environmental significance or which involve the federal government so that they can be appropriately managed by the federal government;
(2) strengthening inter-governmental co-operation and minimising duplication through federal-state bilateral agreements; and

(3) promoting a partnership approach to environmental protection and biodiversity conservation through working with states and territories and appropriate land holders within local communities.

While such moves will hopefully simplify transactions that occur in more than one Australian jurisdiction, they will also have the likely effect of establishing a more uniform regulatory system.

5.2 Increased public accountability and awareness

There are also clear shifts in the law to provide far greater public knowledge of activities that impact upon the environment and the extent to which they do so. The establishment of a National Pollutant Inventory, coupled with the obligation on companies to report annually on their environmental performance, are but two of the measures indicative of such an approach. For companies not wishing to display a poor environmental performance, the added costs of meeting public expectations will have to be addressed.

Suppliers of products and those establishing new operations are also being asked to provide 'lifecycle analysis' of their products or proposals. Such analysis looks at the environmental impacts associated with each product or activity from cradle to grave, including the energy use of products and the decommissioning and rehabilitation implications of major projects.

The demand for increased accountability has to a large extent been driven by the heightened public awareness of environmental issues arising as a result of education of the public, the work of conservation groups and the occurrence of major environmental incidents like French nuclear tests in the Pacific and the Ok Tedi Mine in Papua New Guinea. With conservation groups set to play an increasing participatory role in decision-making processes, public awareness will become even greater.

5.3 The use of market-based incentives

In recent years, a number of State environmental agencies have also begun to adopt market-based mechanisms, or economic incentives, as a way of enforcing environmental laws. While traditionally the emphasis was on 'end-of-pipe' solutions, market-based mechanisms designed to encourage compliance are now emerging.

In NSW for example, a system of load-based licensing has been introduced to replace the traditional standard licence fee system. Under this approach the environmental licence fee to be paid by a corporation relates directly to the load of pollutants which it emits, thereby creating a direct incentive to reduce emission levels and therefore operating costs. Furthermore, rights to utilise certain aspects of the environment such as water resources and rights to pollute are being allocated as part of general tradeable permit schemes.

5.4 The endorsement of international norms and standards

There is also an increasing acceptance and endorsement within Australian law of international norms and standards. While Australia will no doubt continue to become a party to most major environmental treaties, there is increasing acceptance and use of international environmental legal principles such as ecologically sustainable

5.4 *Chapter 6*

development, intergenerational equity and the precautionary principle in state policy documents and in judicial rulings. As transactions become increasingly global, so too will the desire to ensure consistent international standards of regulation.

5.5 Anticipated ramifications

As a consequence of many of the anticipated developments and trends that are now taking place, companies will need to consider carefully the ramifications that arise. For companies that are strong environmental performers, many of the anticipated developments will in fact provide them with a competitive advantage. In addition, the ability to operate efficiently, and with minimal environmental impact, is also likely to decrease the cost of legal compliance. By comparison, companies with poor environmental performance will be faced with higher operating costs and will also come under public pressure to both explain and rectify such poor performance.

Chapter 7

BELGIUM

Francis Van Nuffel

De Bandt, van Hecke, Lagae & Loesch Linklaters & Alliance, Brussels

1 INTRODUCTION

1.1 Constitutional reform

Since the constitutional reform of 1980, the protection of the environment falls mainly within the jurisdiction of the three Regions: the Flemish Region, the Walloon Region and the Brussels Metropolitan Region. Since 1980, each Region has developed a separate body of environmental statutes and regulations, and only a very few environmental matters remain governed by uniform federal legislation. The Regions have the obligation to implement EU directives in the environmental field, without any interference from the federal authorities.

Whereas the Regions have the powers to regulate the protection of the 'outside' environment (eg air pollution, water pollution, waste, soil and groundwater pollution), the 'inside' environment (working conditions; protection of the health and safety of workers) has remained within the realm of the federal authorities.

It should also be noted, however, that contract law, tort law and criminal law, areas of law which are particularly important when dealing with responsibility for environmental harm, have largely remained within the jurisdiction of the federal legislature. The Regions are only allowed to intervene on these areas of law when this is necessary for the exercise of their competence and when the impact on the federal jurisdiction is limited (the so-called 'implied powers). As such, it is permissible for the Regions to impose criminal sanctions for non-compliance with environmental requirements, but they may not significantly change federal criminal procedure law for the prosecution of infringements of Regional law.

1.2 Institutions involved with environmental law

Each Region has its own Environment Ministry and administration. In addition, a number of agencies have been set up to deal with specialised areas such as waste or soil pollution. Some agencies are placed under the direct hierarchical control of the Environment Minister, whereas others enjoy larger freedoms and may even take the form of a commercial company with a hybrid public/private status.

1.2 *Chapter 7*

Local authorities (provinces and municipalities) play an important role in environmental matters as they process operating permit applications. The monitoring of compliance with permit conditions is performed at both local and regional levels. As all environmental laws are criminally sanctioned, the public prosecutor's office also plays an important role in the environmental area.

Law courts play an increasingly important part as more and more cases are brought in which the interpretation of environmental law rules is at stake. Belgium does not have a formal rule of precedent as it is applied in common law systems, but judgments of the highest courts have significant authority. These highest courts are the Court of Cassation (*Hof van Cassatie/Cour de Cassation*) for general civil and criminal law matters, the Court of Arbitration (*Arbitragehof/Cour d'arbitrage*) for constitutional law matters and the Council of State (*Raad van Staat/Conseil d'Etat*) for administrative law matters.

2 OUTLINE OF ENVIRONMENTAL LAW RELEVANT TO MERGER AND ACQUISITION TRANSACTIONS

2.1 Regional similarities and differences

It follows from the constitutional arrangements described above that Belgium does not have one but three separate bodies of law regulating the environment in addition to the few areas of environmental law that have remained at the federal level.

The development of environmental law is unequal in the three Regions. The Flemish Region is ahead in the adoption of environmental legislation, thereby following the example of its neighbours in The Netherlands and Germany.

This means that, generally speaking, the Flemish Region has stricter rules than the two other Regions. On the other hand, in cases where the Brussels Metropolitan Region and the Walloon Region have not yet adopted extensive legislation, the existence of such rules in the Flemish Region provides more legal certainty.

In a number of areas, the three Regions and the federal authorities have concluded Co-operation Agreements to ensure a common policy and regulation in a particular field. Examples are the Co-operation Agreement of 26 October 1994 on the co-ordination of the policy with regard to the import, transit and export of waste, and the Co-operation Agreement of 30 May 1996 on the prevention and management of packaging waste. In some areas, the delimitation of powers between the federal level and the regional level remains unclear. Such is the case with the implementation of the so-called 'Seveso' directive on risks for major accidents in certain categories of industries.

2.2 Environmental laws and regulations at the federal level

All health and safety law concerned with the protection of employees has remained federal law. Most health & safety law is contained in the General Regulations on the Protection of Labour (ARAB or RGPT), which is currently being replaced with a 'Code for the Well-being of Employees'.

These regulations contain, amongst other things, the obligations of the employer with regard to the protection of the employees against the dangers of asbestos. There is no general obligation to remove asbestos but employers must make an asbestos inventory of their buildings and ensure that employees are not directly exposed to asbestos.

Apart from health and safety law, the main area of environmental law that has also remained within the powers of the federal legislature and regulators is the setting of product standards As a result, the law relating to the manufacture, use and transport of hazardous substances and hazardous products has remained at the federal level. As such, the identification, packaging, labelling and notification of dangerous substances that are put on the market, are subject to federal regulations that implement EU directives.

A Royal Decree of 9 July 1986 introduced a ban on the production and trading of products containing PCB or PCT. Existing products may remain in use until the end of their lifecycle. Persons holding products containing PCBs or PCTs must notify the authorities. The handling and transportation of PCB or PCT containing installations is subject to authorisation.

The Federal Statute of 12 July 1985 and its implementing decrees require a permit for the use of machines that cause non-ionising radiation. The federal legislature has also retained power over protection against ionising radiation including radioactive waste in a Federal Statute of 15 April 1994.

The 'Seveso' directive on the risks of major accidents in certain categories of industries has been implemented by a Federal Statute of 21 January 1987.

2.3 Laws and regulations in the Flemish Region

2.3.1 The Vlarem Rules: integrated pollution control and more . . .

The main environmental Acts in the Flemish Region are the Regional Statute of 28 June 1985 on the Environmental Permit and its implementing Decrees of 6 February 1991 (Vlarem I) and 1 June 1995 (Vlarem II).

This Regional Statute has introduced a system of integrated pollution control governed by an 'environmental permit' that has replaced and unified the older permitting systems. Vlarem I contains a list of activities which require an environmental permit to be obtained and the procedures for obtaining it. The covered activities are divided in three 'classes', depending on the level of harm the activity is anticipated to cause. Permits for 'Class 1' activities are granted by the Provincial Government, whereas permits for 'Class 2' activities are obtained from the municipal authorities. For 'Class 3' activities, a notification to the municipality suffices.

Vlarem II contains the general operating conditions that are imposed in every environmental permit, as well as the specific conditions for each type of activity. In addition to these general and 'sectoral' operating conditions, an individual environmental permit may contain other and stricter conditions if these are justified by specific environmental concerns.

The operating conditions that are imposed by Vlarem II are concerned with most of the adverse effects of an ongoing operation, such as air emissions, waste water discharges and noise.

Plants in the Flemish Region may still operate under older permitting systems. Permits that were granted under the old system remain in force for the time period they were granted, up to 1 September 2011. However, transitional provisions gradually impose Vlarem II's operating conditions on existing plants.

2.3.2 Soil and groundwater contamination: Flemish Regional Statute on Soil Clean-up

With the Regional Statute on Soil Clean-up of 22 February 1995 ('the Clean-up Statute'), the Flemish Region also has a comprehensive body of law addressing soil and groundwater contamination and clean-ups. This Statute is quite important when

2.3 Chapter 7

contemplating transactions involving companies established in the Flemish Region, not only because it prescribes when a clean-up is necessary and who is liable for such clean-up, but also because it imposes a number of formalities to be performed at each asset transaction in the Flemish Region. Given the importance of these formalities, they will be addressed in detail in para 3.3.1 below.

The Clean-up Statute entered into force on 29 October 1995, except for a limited series of provisions which became effective on 29 April 1996 and 1 October 1996. The Clean-up Statute was subsequently modified by the Flemish Parliament on 26 May 1998. These modifications entered into force on 25 July 1998. The Statute is being monitored by the Flemish Waste Agency which is better known as 'OVAM'.

(a) When is clean-up necessary?

In the Clean-up Statute, an important distinction is made between 'new pollution' and 'historical pollution', according to whether the soil or groundwater pollution occurred before or after the coming into force of the Statute (29 October 1995). If the pollution occurred partly before and partly after the coming into force of the Statute, the rules relating to 'new pollution' shall be applicable.

New pollution must be cleaned up as soon as the 'clean-up criteria' have been exceeded. These criteria have been established by the Flemish government in its implementing decree of 5 March 1996, relating to the Flemish regulations on soil clean-up, the so-called Vlarebo-decree. For the determination of these clean-up criteria, the characteristics of the soil and its functions are taken into consideration. As a result, the soil clean-up criteria are different according to the composition of the soil (eg clay or gravel) and according to the function of the land (eg natural zone, residential area or industrial land).

Land constituting *historical pollution* is to be cleaned up if the pollution constitutes 'a serious threat'. Such land is designated by the Flemish government upon a proposal by OVAM. Lists of parcels of land which are designated as such by the Flemish government are published from time to time in the *Belgian State Gazette*. These parcels have been further divided into four categories according to the urgency of the clean-up. According to OVAM's internal policy, the clean-up of the parcels that are in the highest category of priority, must be started before 1 January 2006.

(b) To what extent should this clean-up be carried out?

The rules mentioned hereafter are applicable both to historical and new pollution.

A clean-up should aim to achieve the background values for soil and groundwater quality established by the Flemish government in the Vlarebo Decree. The normal background in non-polluted land presenting comparable characteristics is put first and foremost.

However, whenever these background values cannot be achieved by measures corresponding to the best available technology not entailing excessive costs (ie the BATNEEC principle), the clean-up should at least be aimed at achieving a better soil and groundwater quality than is prescribed by the applicable clean-up criteria for new pollution. If this also appears to be impossible by applying the BATNEEC principle, the clean-up should aim at avoiding a soil and groundwater quality which constitutes a serious threat.

Whenever the latter measures cannot be achieved, always on the basis of the BATNEEC principle, restrictions as to use and other preventive measures shall be imposed.

Finally, for those substances for which the Flemish government has not fixed background values, the clean-up shall be aimed at achieving a quality not presenting any adverse effects for persons and the environment, in view of the characteristics of the soil and the functions it serves.

(c) Who should clean up?

When an activity subject to an environmental permit is carried out on the land concerned, the task of cleaning up rests with the operator of the facility that is subject to a permit. If no activity subject to an environmental permit is carried out on this land, the owner is responsible for the clean-up, unless he can prove that another person exercises factual control of the land. If the owner is able to prove this, the clean-up obligation passes to that other person.

These regulations are, however, subject to one exception, ie the 'innocent possessor'. When it appears that the person who should perform the clean-up is an innocent possessor, OVAM shall proceed with the clean-up instead of that person.

Where *new pollution* is concerned (see para 2.3.2(a) above), the person who should carry out the clean-up shall be considered an innocent possessor when this person meets all of the following conditions:

(1) he has not caused the pollution;
(2) at the time he became the operator or owner or obtained factual control of the land, he was not aware or was not supposed to be aware of this pollution;
(3) no activity polluting the soil has been carried out since 1993 on this land.

In case of *historical pollution*, the person who should proceed with the clean-up shall be considered as an innocent possessor if this person meets all of the following conditions:

(1) he has not caused the pollution;
(2) at the time he became the owner or user of the land, he was not aware or was not supposed to be aware of this pollution.

In case of *historical pollution*, the person who should carry out the clean-up, although he was aware or should have been aware of this pollution, and acquired historically polluted land before 1 January 1993, shall not be obliged to clean up the soil if he can prove that he has not caused this pollution and did not use the land as of the date of acquisition for his profession or enterprise.

The question whether a person was aware or should have been aware of pollution at a particular time is to be determined on a case-by-case basis. For all 'transfers of land' that occurred since 1 October 1996, the transfer agreement must include a 'soil certificate' (see para 3.3.1 below), the contents of which are thus considered to be known to the transferee. As for transfers of land occurring prior to that date, case law will have to develop to deal with the issue of the actual or constructive awareness of pollution.

(d) Who must finally pay for the clean-up?

Different regulations are applicable where either new pollution or historical pollution is concerned (see para 2.3.2(a) above).

In the case of *new pollution*, the polluter pays. The person causing pollution of the soil or groundwater by an emission into the atmosphere, soil or water is considered to be the polluter. When this emission is coming from facilities the activities of which are subject to an environmental permit, the operator of these facilities is deemed responsible.

2.3 Chapter 7

In the case of *historical pollution*, the responsibility for the cost of soil clean-up is determined in accordance with the liability criteria applicable before 29 October 1995.

In case of historical soil pollution, the person responsible for the clean-up or OVAM must therefore look for any person who, based on the already existing rules relating to liability, can be considered responsible. Reference should be made to art 1384 of the Civil Code (strict liability of the guardian of a defective object), arts 1382, 1383 of the Civil Code (liability resulting from the violation of a legal, regulatory or permit provision, or from the action (or negligence) which a normally cautious person, placed in the same situation, would not have committed), art 544 of the Civil Code (nuisance) and art 7 of the Statute of 22 July 1974 relating to toxic waste (strict liability of the person producing toxic waste).

Although there is a vast array of existing liability rules, it may be quite burdensome to hold a person liable on the basis of one or more of these liability routes. Prospective plaintiffs may expect exhausting litigation before obtaining a verdict that subsequently may be difficult to enforce if the defendant is insolvent.

2.3.3 Other environmental laws in the Flemish Region

A brief summary of the other main environmental laws in the Flemish Region follows. For each statute, the most significant features that might influence a contemplated transaction, are emphasised.

(a) Water

The Statute of 26 March 1971 on the protection of surface waters against pollution, as adapted by the Flemish legislature, and its implementing decrees, regulate the discharge of substances into the surface waters and public sewage systems of the Region. However, permits for the discharge of waste water are currently granted under the Vlarem Rules (see para 2.3.1 above). The quality of Flanders' surface waters is monitored by the Flemish Environmental Agency (*Vlaamse Milieumaatschappij* or VMM). This Agency also collects taxes that are levied on the authorised discharge of polluting substances in the surface waters. The purification of the sewage waters in the Flemish Region is performed by NV Aquafin, a hybrid public/private company.

(b) Waste

The Regional Statute of 2 July 1981 on waste prevention and management, and its implementing Decree of 17 December 1997 (the so-called Vlarea), contain detailed rules with regard to waste generated by households and industry in the Flemish Region. Companies need to keep waste registers and file a yearly report with OVAM, the Flemish Waste Agency. Waste collectors and transporters must be duly certified by the Flemish government. However, permits for the storage and disposal of waste are currently granted under the Vlarem Rules (see para 2.3.1 above). Taxes are levied on the disposal of waste. A noteworthy feature of Flemish waste law is the 'take-back obligation' that is imposed on the producer, importer, intermediary or seller of a number of products such as electronic equipment and rubber tyres.

(c) Groundwater

The Regional Statute of 24 January 1984 on groundwater management subjects the pumping of groundwater to a specific permit.

(d) Noise

Noise is currently regulated by the Vlarem Rules (see para 2.3.1 above).

(e) Access to environmental information

Such access is guaranteed and regulated by the Vlarem Rules (see para 2.3.1 above).

(f) Environmental impact assessments

Two Decrees of the Flemish Government of 23 March 1989 determine which projects require a prior environmental impact assessment and contain the procedures to perform such assessments.

(g) Land use planning/Zoning

Zoning law in the Flemish Region is governed by the Regional Statute on Zoning dated 18 May 1999. This Statute enters into force on 1 October 1999 and replaces the previous legislation (Regional Statute on Zoning co-ordinated on 22 October 1996 and Regional Statute of 24 July 1996 on Planning). All construction requires a building permit, which will only be obtained if the construction is in accordance with zoning plans at the municipal and regional level. When a project is subject to both a building permit and an environmental permit (under the Vlarem Rules, see para 2.3.1 above), neither permit can be implemented as long as the other has not been obtained.

(h) Environmental care

A Regional Statute of 19 April 1995 has introduced special provisions with regard to environmental care within companies. Companies engaged in an activity that is considered as having an adverse effect on the environment and that is listed as such, must appoint an 'environmental co-ordinator' within the plant who has to show sufficient expertise in environmental matters. This environmental co-ordinator is assigned specific tasks and responsibilities with regard to environmental management of the company and must file a detailed report every year with the authorities.

2.4 Environmental laws and regulations in the Walloon Region

2.4.1 From the operating permit to the environmental permit

Pursuant to the General Regulation on the Protection of Labour of 11 February 1946, (RGPT), as adapted by the Walloon Region, all activities listed as such require an operating permit. The RGPT lays out the procedures to obtain the operating permit, as well as the general operating conditions.

The covered activities are divided in two 'classes', depending on the level of harm the activity is anticipated to cause. Permits for 'Class 1' activities are granted by the Provincial Government, whereas permits for 'Class 2' activities are obtained from the municipal authorities.

The operating conditions that are imposed by the RGPT are concerned with most of the adverse effects of ongoing operation, such as air emissions and noise. In

2.4 Chapter 7

addition to the general operating conditions, an individual operating permit may contain other and stricter conditions if these are justified by specific environmental concerns.

This old system of operating permits will be replaced with a new system of environmental permits by the Regional Statute on Environmental Permits of 3 March 1999. This new system will also integrate a number of other existing permit systems, including the permit for the discharge of waste water, the permit for pumping groundwater and drinking water and the permit to store or to dispose of waste.

The date when the new system will be brought into force will be determined by the Walloon government. Under the new system it is provided that the old permits that were granted under the RGPT will remain valid until their date of expiry. Once the new Walloon Regional Statute on Environmental Permits has entered into force, new permits or the renewal of permits will have to be obtained under the new procedures.

2.4.2 Soil and groundwater contamination: no comprehensive legislation

In the Walloon Region, there is no comprehensive piece of legislation dealing with soil and groundwater contamination and clean-ups. The Walloon government is preparing a Bill to introduce such legislation, but such a Bill has not yet been introduced before the Walloon Parliament, so it is impossible to foresee when a Regional Statute on Soil Clean-ups would be enacted and what its contents would be.

In the meantime, questions of soil and groundwater contamination are dealt with under different provisions in various statutes and regulations. The Regional Statute on waste provides that the person who abandons waste or disposes of waste without complying with the Statute, can be obliged to rehabilitate the site. Another Statute on the taxation of waste imposes taxes on the presence of waste in the Walloon Region, to be paid by the owner of the site. Such an owner can avoid the payment of the taxes by presenting a clean-up plan to the Walloon Waste Agency (*Office régional wallon de déchets*) and perform the clean-up once the plan has been approved. Any person who suffers damage caused by 'waste' and who cannot recover his losses through tort law, may be indemnified by a special fund established from the proceeds of taxes on abandoned waste.

Spaque, a public company, has powers to clean up polluted sites and perform urgent interventions in the Walloon Region. Without a clear statutory basis, the recovery of the costs of such clean-ups and interventions from a responsible party remains problematic.

It follows from the above that the Walloon legislation contains a number of tools to deal with urgent and visible matters of soil pollution, especially with regard to abandoned waste. However, there is no uniform approach for historically polluted land. Liability questions are dealt with under traditional tort and contract law. The absence of clear definitions (are polluting substances in the soil and groundwater to be considered as 'waste'?) as well as the absence of clean-up standards and standard procedures provide for a high level of legal uncertainty.

A specific clean-up regime for service stations was adopted by a Decree of the Walloon Government of 4 March 1999.

2.4.3 Other environmental laws in the Walloon Region

(a) Water

The Regional Statute of 7 October 1985 on the protection of surface waters against pollution, and its implementing decrees, regulate the discharge of substances into the surface waters and public sewage systems of the Region. Permits for the discharge of waste water are currently granted under this Statute, but will in the future be integrated with the environmental permit (see para 2.4.1 above). These regulations also define quality standards and action plans for the improvement of the condition of the Walloon surface waters. Taxes on the discharge of waste water in the Walloon Region are levied pursuant to a Regional Statute of 30 April 1990.

(b) Waste

The Regional Statute of 27 June 1996 on waste, and its implementing decrees, contain detailed rules with regard to waste generated by households and industry in the Walloon Region. Waste collectors and transporters need to be duly certified by the Walloon government. Permits for the storage and disposal of waste are currently granted under this Statute, but will in the future be integrated with the environmental permit (see para 2.4.1 above).

(c) Groundwater and drinking water

The Regional Statute of 30 April 1990 on the protection and exploitation of groundwater and drinking water subjects the pumping of groundwater or drinking water to a specific permit. This permit will in the future be integrated with the environmental permit (see para 2.4.1 above).

(d) Noise

Noise is currently regulated under the R.G.P.T. rules and will be integrated in the new rules concerning the environmental permit (see para 2.4.1 above).

(e) Environmental information

A Regional Statute of 13 June 1991 regulates access to environmental information.

(f) Environmental impact assessments

Environmental impact assessments (EIAs) are governed by the Regional Statute of 11 September 1985. The Walloon EIA system will be changed significantly with the introduction of the environmental permit (see para 2.4.1 above).

(g) Land use planning/Zoning

Zoning law in the Walloon Region is governed by the Walloon Zoning Code of 14 May 1984, which has been modified significantly by the Regional Statute of 27 November 1997. All construction requires a building permit, which will only be obtained if the construction is in accordance with zoning plans at the municipal and regional level.

(h) Environmental care

The Walloon Region has not yet adopted rules related to environmental care. It is expected that such rules will also be introduced under the new environmental permit system (see para 2.4.1 above).

2.5 *Chapter 7*

2.5 Environmental laws and regulations in the Brussels Metropolitan Region

2.5.1 *Integrated pollution control through the environmental permit*

Pursuant to the Ordinance of the Brussels Metropolitan Council of 5 June 1997, all activities listed as such require an environmental permit. The ordinance contains the list of activities that are subject to the requirement of an environmental permit and the procedures for obtaining it. For certain categories of activities, the Brussels Metropolitan Government has enacted general operating conditions.

The covered activities are divided in three 'classes', depending on the level of harm the activity is anticipated to cause. Permits for 'Class I.A' and 'Class I.B.' activities are granted by the Brussels Institute for Environmental Management (BIM/IBGE), a specialised agency under the direct control of the Brussels Metropolitan Government. Class II permits are granted by the municipal authorities.

Each environmental permit contains the operating conditions for the activity it allows. Such operating conditions are concerned with most of the environmental effects that may be caused by an ongoing operation, such as air emissions, waste water discharges and noise.

Plants in the Brussels Metropolitan Region may still operate under older permit systems. Permits that were granted under the old system remain in force for the time period they were granted.

2.5.2 *Soil and groundwater contamination: no comprehensive legislation*

In the Brussels Metropolitan Region, there is currently no comprehensive piece of legislation dealing with soil and groundwater contamination and clean-ups.

Questions of soil and groundwater contamination are currently dealt with under different provisions in various statutes and regulations. The Ordinance on the Environmental Permit provides that the holder of an environmental permit must take all necessary measures to prevent, reduce or remedy all nuisances and dangers caused by the authorised activity. It is also provided that when an activity is stopped or no longer authorised, the holder of the permit must rehabilitate the site to a condition that no longer constitutes a nuisance or a danger.

The Ordinance on Waste provides that the person who produces or retains waste, must ensure its disposal in conformity with the regulations of the Ordinance and by limiting negative effects on soil and groundwater.

The Brussels Institute for Environmental Management (BIM/IBGE) has been granted powers to control the quality of soils and soil clean-ups. The BIM/IBGE uses the provisions mentioned above to impose clean-ups of contaminated sites in the Brussels Metropolitan Region. Soil clean-up criteria have not yet been adopted. The BIM/IBGE currently applies Dutch (not Flemish) intervention standards as guidelines.

A specific clean-up regime for service stations was adopted by a Decree of the Brussels Metropolitan Government of 21 January 1997.

It follows from the above that the Brussels Metropolitan legislation contains a number of tools to deal with soil pollution, but there is no uniform approach for historically polluted land. Liability questions are dealt with under traditional tort and contract law. As is the case in the Walloon Region, the absence of clear definitions as well as the absence of uniform clean-up standards and standard procedures provide for a high level of legal uncertainty.

2.5.3 Other environmental laws in the Brussels Metropolitan Region

(a) Water

The Statute of 26 March 1971 on the protection of surface water against pollution, as adapted by the Brussels Metropolitan Region, and its implementing decrees, regulate the discharge of substances into the surface waters and public sewage systems of the Metropolitan Region. Permits for the discharge of waste water are not granted under this Statute, but are integrated in the environmental permit (see para 2.5.1 above). An Ordinance of 29 March 1996 subjects the discharge of household and industrial waste water to a tax.

(b) Waste

The Ordinance of 7 March 1991 on waste prevention and management, and its implementing decrees, contain detailed rules with regard to waste generated by households and industry in the Brussels Metropolitan Region.

(c) Groundwater

The pumping of groundwater in the Brussels Metropolitan Region is subject to a permit pursuant to Statutes of 18 December 1946 and 26 March 1971, and their implementing decrees.

(d) Noise

Noise is regulated through the conditions of the environmental permit (see para 2.5.1 above), as well as in a number of specific Decrees of the Brussels Metropolitan Government that impose noise limits in the urban area.

(e) Access to environmental information

An Ordinance of 29 August 1991 regulates access to environmental information.

(f) Environmental impact assessment

Environmental impact assessments are governed by the Ordinance of 30 July 1992.

(g) Land use planning/zoning

Zoning law in the Brussels Metropolitan Region is governed by the Ordinance on Town Planning of 29 August 1991. All construction requires a building permit, which will only be obtained if the construction is in accordance with zoning plans at the municipal and regional level. It should be noted that if a project in the Brussels Metropolitan Region requires both a building and an environmental permit, a special procedure to obtain both permits for such 'mixed projects' has to be followed.

(h) Environmental care

The Brussels Metropolitan Region has not yet adopted rules related to environmental care. It is expected that such rules will be introduced under the environmental permit system (see para 2.5.1 above).

3 PARTICULAR ENVIRONMENTAL ISSUES RELEVANT TO TRANSACTIONS

3.1 Belgian particularities

As a response to different kinds of environmental concerns, businesses are nowadays subjected to an ever-increasing number of regulations and operating conditions. A plant that is not in material compliance with such obligations is exposed to important risks in terms of potential financial liabilities and administrative or criminal sanctions. Past practices may also haunt industrial operators and may constitute high potential liabilities for which a company has not necessarily allocated reserves.

These considerations apply to all western industrialised nations and as such are not specific to Belgium. When contemplating a transaction in Belgium, an investor should also be aware of the following additional particular issues.

The first important issue is the existence of a different body of environmental legislation for each of the three Regions. Although the approach to mergers and acquisitions from an environmental law point of view is not very different depending on the Region the plant is located, formal obligations that are imposed on the parties to the transaction (eg notification obligations) may be significantly different. Depending on the level of development of the environmental law body, businesses are confronted with greater or lesser legal uncertainty with regard to potential future liabilities.

While conducting business in Belgium, special attention should always be given to land use planning/zoning law. Belgium is densely populated. The absence of a coherent zoning policy and poor enforcement of zoning law, until the 1980s, have lead to a situation where many industries are located in the vicinity of dwellings, agricultural or natural zones, especially in the Flemish and Brussels Metropolitan Regions. Expansion of such plants is highly problematic. Local environmental groups and individuals are also increasingly active in filing complaints and claims against industrial operations.

3.2 Routes and basis for liability

3.2.1 General principles of civil liability

Any infringement of environmental legislation or regulations is considered to be a 'fault' within the meaning of art 1382 of the Civil Code. This means that all persons who can establish a causal link between a loss they have suffered and the infringement of any environmental regulation, may claim damages.

Even in the absence of any transgression of an environmental regulation, a company can be held liable under arts 1382 and 1383 of the Civil Code if its acts or omissions do not meet the standard of the reasonable and prudent person who is placed in the same situation.

The Belgian courts may also allow damages in the absence of fault or negligence, when the nuisance complained of exceeds the normal and common inconveniences that neighbours have to mutually endure. Such nuisance claims are based on art 544 of the Civil Code.

Pursuant to art 1384 of the Civil Code, the holder of a defective object is strictly liable for all damages caused by such defect. It is generally accepted that contaminated land constitutes such a 'defective object'.

3.2.2 Strict liability under environmental laws

A large number of environmental laws have introduced special liability schemes. The application of such schemes does not exclude the simultaneous application of the general civil liability schemes mentioned above.

The most far-reaching environmental liability scheme is laid down in art 7 of the Federal Statute of 22 July 1974 on toxic waste. This provision obliges the person whose industrial or commercial activity produces toxic waste, to ensure its destruction, neutralisation or elimination at his own expense. Such person remains liable even if he no longer has control over the waste. The list of substances that are considered 'toxic waste' has been enacted by Royal Decree.

All Regions have introduced strict liability systems for persons who illegally dispose of waste. As for soil and groundwater contamination, only the Flemish Region has a specific liability system, making an important difference between 'historical' and 'new' pollution (see para 2.3.2 above).

3.2.3 Criminal liability and enforcement

Nearly all environmental statutes provide for the possibility of criminal sanctions in the event of a violation of the statute and its implementing regulations.

Belgian criminal law traditionally only penalised physical persons. If a violation was committed by a company, only the persons responsible for environmental management of the company were prosecuted. These persons are designated on a case-by-case basis, depending on the internal organisation of the company. In some cases, the day-to-day environmental manager may be targeted, whereas in other cases a CEO will be regarded as ultimately responsible and be convicted. Examples of company executives receiving suspended prison sentences for environmental crimes are becoming increasingly commonplace in Belgium.

A new Statute of 4 May 1999 now provides for criminal punishment of companies.

Environmental crimes are punished by imprisonment and/or fines. The more recent the environmental statute, the more harsh the criminal sanctions that are put into place by the legislators.

Apart from criminal sanctions, most environmental statutes also provide for administrative sanctions such as closing down the operation of installations that are not covered by a permit. Compliance with environmental law is being monitored by both local and regional administration. Officers from environmental administrations or agencies generally have broad powers to access industrial installations, inspect them and take samples.

The enforcement of environmental legislation is being given increasing priority by public prosecutors. Public prosecutors' offices have gained experience and knowledge in environmental law, and often have one or more specialised officers. The environmental administrations also have an increasing number of inspectors.

It should also be mentioned that an increasing number of environmental regulations require self-monitoring by the companies and the regular filing of monitoring results with the administration.

Finally, special attention should be given to a Federal Statute of 12 January 1993 that has granted a special right of action with regard to the protection of the environment. Pursuant to this Statute, the President of the Court of First Instance can order the cessation of any act that constitutes a serious breach of environmental legislation (federal or regional), following summary proceedings. The President can also impose measures aimed at preventing breaches of environmental legislation and at preventing environmental damage. The action can be brought by the public prosecutor, any administrative authority as well as by any association that has been incorporated as a non-profit organisation for more than three years and that has the protection of the environment as one of its goals.

3.2.4 Liability of company directors and of the 'environmental co-ordinator'

Environmental risks directly and indirectly expose company directors and environmental managers to liabilities.

Directors are liable vis-à-vis the company for 'ordinary management faults'. The standard that directors have to meet is that of an ordinary cautious professional, placed in the same circumstances. A normal cautious professional is expected to have an ongoing concern and awareness of the company's impact on the environment. Although no case law is available, it is argued that company directors should be aware of upcoming legislation and should not take measures that unnecessarily increase environmental compliance costs or jeopardise the long-term survival capabilities of the company.

The general assembly of shareholders, as well as individual shareholders or a group of minority shareholders have standing to file a claim against directors for 'ordinary management faults'. Liability for ordinary management faults only exists towards the company, not vis-à-vis third parties. Third parties may only recover if the management fault also constitutes a fault under general civil liability law (art 1382 of the Civil Code).

Company directors are also liable vis-à-vis the company and third parties for damages resulting from a breach of Belgian company law or the company's articles of incorporation. In the environmental field, such a breach may exist for example when a company director provides wrong information to the general assembly of shareholders with regard to environmental management and risks.

Finally, company directors can be held jointly and severally liable for all claims on their company being declared bankrupt when they have committed an 'obvious gross mistake' that contributed to the bankruptcy. Although no case law is available on the subject, it may be argued that the operation of a facility without an operating permit constitutes such an 'obvious gross mistake', where the lack of the permit leads to the closing down of the facility by the authorities or a judge and subsequently to bankruptcy of the company.

Apart from specific liabilities under company law, directors and environmental managers should be aware of the risks they run under criminal law. If a violation of an environmental regulation is committed by a company, the persons who are responsible for environmental management of the company will be prosecuted. These persons are designated on a case-by-case basis, depending on the internal organisation of the company.

Special attention should be given to the position of the 'environmental co-ordinator' in the Flemish Region. Pursuant to the Flemish Regional Statute of 19 April 1995 on environmental care within companies, the operators of facilities that are considered to have a serious adverse effect on the environment and that are listed as such, needed to appoint an environmental co-ordinator at the latest on 4 July 1997. An environmental co-ordinator can be an employee of the company, but can also be an outside consultant. The environmental co-ordinator has the task of monitoring compliance with environmental regulations. He must report to the management of the company on all shortcomings and propose solutions. The environmental co-ordinator also has to perform all specific monitoring and documentary obligations that are imposed by the regulations or the permits. Management must consult with him on all investments related to environmental management of the company.

The environmental co-ordinator is not free from personal liabilities: if he fails to meet his duties, he can become liable both under civil or criminal law. As for civil liability, the environmental co-ordinator who is also an employee of the company, will only be liable vis-à-vis third parties for intentional or gross faults. If his action or omission does not constitute intentional or gross fault, his employer may be held liable if the action or omission constitutes a fault under general civil law (art 1384, third paragraph, of the Civil Code). The environmental co-ordinator who is not an employee of the company, may limit his liability vis-à-vis the company in his consultancy contract. Such co-ordinator will remain liable towards third parties if his actions are regarded as faults or negligence within the meaning of arts 1382 and 1383 of the Civil Code. As for criminal liability, the failure by the environmental co-ordinator to meet the specific duties imposed by the Regional Statute is criminally sanctioned. The environmental co-ordinator may also be identified by the Public Prosecutor's Office as the physical person within the company who is responsible for the environmental offences committed by the company. In order to avoid this risk, the environmental co-ordinator must report to higher management all violations of environmental regulations and submit proposals for remedial action. He must thus be able to show that higher management in the company took ultimate responsibility for non-compliance with environmental obligations.

3.2.5 Liability of those financing businesses

Under Belgian law, a breach of environmental laws by a company that borrows money should in principle not cause the lender to be liable. Indeed, the person who only provides credit and acts as a normal lender cannot normally be held liable. However, the lender—or the physical person appointed by the lender—may in the following circumstances be exposed to environmental liability.

When the lender has fully and effectively taken over the management of the company (including decisions regarding the acts or activities which cause a breach of environmental law or environmental damage), the courts may pierce the corporate veil and/or attribute the acts of the company directly to the lender. In such case, the courts may hold the lender liable under civil law for the breaches of law and the resulting damage and may also hold the lender's physical agents criminally liable for the breaches.

More generally, when it can be proven that the lender has acted negligently with respect to the granting or maintaining of the financing, and the resulting breach of environmental regulations and environmental damage would not have arisen without such negligence, the lender could in principle be held liable vis-à-vis third parties for such damage.

The standard of care the lender is expected to exercise when granting or maintaining credit is that of a normally prudent lender with the same level of professionalism or sophistication in similar circumstances. In addition, the causal relationship between any negligence and the resulting damage may in practice be difficult to prove. In the absence of relevant case law precedents, it is difficult to assess the required due diligence a lender is expected to exercise in practice.

Under Belgian law, a mortgage does not transfer title to the property. The mortgagee does not obtain any right of control over the business conducted within the property. Breach of environmental laws by the company operating on the mortgaged property should therefore not affect the mortgagee. Foreclosure does not transfer title to the mortgagee, but only allows the latter to organise a public sale of the property. Title is transferred directly from the borrower to the purchaser. For real estate situated in the Flemish Region, such a public sale is subject to the performance of a

3.2 *Chapter 7*

number of obligations: in the case of polluted land which requires remediation, the mortgagee will not be allowed to proceed with the public sale unless sufficient financial guarantees are provided for the clean-up of the property.

In those cases where the law does not require a prior clean-up, soil and groundwater contamination may in any case substantially affect the value of the collateral, which in turn may lead to a material decrease in the proceeds from enforcement of the security.

3.3 Formalities imposed on transactions by environmental legislation

3.3.1 *Asset transactions in the Flemish Region: obligations imposed by the Flemish Regional Statute on Soil Clean-up*

Transfer of land located in the Flemish Region triggers certain obligations for the transferor, to be effected prior to the transfer. These obligations are applicable on transfers of land effected on or after 1 October 1996.

(a) Definition of 'transfer of land'

This is a very broad notion, covering:

(1) transfer of ownership rights in land, except on death;
(2) entering into, termination or transfer of a residential lease, commercial lease, farm lease or concession (right to use real estate owned by public authorities) for more than nine years;
(3) entering into, termination or transfer of a residential lease, commercial lease, farm lease or concession for more than one year in the case of land on which an activity is or was carried out which is considered as soil polluting;
(4) entering into, termination or transfer of a long lease (*erfpacht/bail emphytéotique*) or of an agreement related to a building right (*opstal/droit de superficie*) or of an agreement of usufruct (right to occupy a property and use its proceeds—*vruchtgebruik/usufruit*);
(5) grant of a right to use or occupy a property;
(6) entering into a real estate financial leasing agreement or termination of such a leasing agreement (with or without lifting the option to buy);
(7) merger and division of companies owning land;
(8) contribution of a universality of goods or a branch of activity.

It is important to note that the transfer of shares or a majority participation in a company is exempt from the definition, thus creating an important difference between a 'share' and an 'asset' transaction in the Flemish Region.

(b) Obligation applicable to all 'transfers of land': obtaining a soil certificate

Before transferring any plot of land, the transferor must obtain from OVAM a soil certificate and inform the transferee of the contents. The contents of the soil certificate should be referred to in the private transfer agreement and in the notarial deed.

OVAM has 1 month to deliver such a certificate, other than for land on which an activity is or was carried out which is considered as soil polluting, where OVAM has two months to deliver the soil certificate.

Any agreement concluded without complying with this obligation is null and void. The transferee and OVAM can assert the nullity of the agreement. The nullity of a private agreement may not be invoked, however, if the soil certificate was communicated to the transferee before the notarial deed and the transferee waives his right to seek the nullity of the private agreement in the notarial deed.

The soil certificate contains all information relating to the condition of the soil concerned that is available in the Register of Contaminated Soils which is kept by OVAM. This register contains the results of the official soil tests which have been carried out and filed with OVAM. Operators of facilities that are considered to be potentially soil polluting must perform such tests every 5, 10 or 20 years depending on the level of risk the activity is likely to pose. OVAM can also proceed ex officio with the carrying out of orientation soil tests. Finally, soil tests are also carried out at the occasion of a transfer of land on which a potentially soil contaminating activity takes or has taken place, as will be discussed below.

(c) Additional obligation applicable to transfers of 'risk' land: notification of OVAM of an orientation (Phase I) soil survey

Whenever an activity which is considered as potentially soil contaminating is or has been carried out on the plot of land to be transferred, additional formalities must be fulfilled prior to any transfer. The Flemish government has adopted the list of the potentially soil contaminating activities in the annex to the so-called Vlarebo Decree. These activities are hereafter referred to as 'risk activities'. Land on which such activities takes place is 'risk land'.

This list of risk activities is quite long and covers a wide range of industrial activity. It is no exaggeration to say that virtually all large and mid-sized industrial plants in the Flemish Region are covered by this list. Also a number of small businesses are affected, such as printing companies, launderettes and service stations.

Whenever such risk activity is or has been carried out on land, the transferor must notify OVAM of his intention to transfer the land concerned and must at the same time file with OVAM the report of an 'orientation soil test'. The orientation soil test consists of historical research into the potential sources and areas of contamination and limited soil and groundwater sampling.

The transfer can only take place if OVAM has not requested the filing of a 'descriptive soil test', within 60 days of the notification of the report of the orientation soil test. OVAM will request such a descriptive soil test when it finds, on the basis of the orientation soil test, that there are indications that the thresholds for clean-up operations have been exceeded.

The thresholds for clean-up operations are different depending on whether the contamination is regarded as 'new pollution' or as 'historical pollution' (see para 2.3.2 above).

It follows that whenever OVAM finds, on the basis of the orientation soil test, that there are indications that there is new soil pollution that might exceed the soil clean-up criteria, or that there is historical pollution that might pose a 'serious threat', it will request a 'descriptive soil test'. The transfer of land may then not take place unless the transferor has filed the descriptive soil test report.

A descriptive soil test must be carried out by a recognised expert and consists of more extensive sampling and a risk analysis. The expert needs to draft a proposal for the descriptive soil test he intends to carry out, which needs to be declared by OVAM to be in conformity with the statute. Interim reports may also be required during the conduct of the soil investigation, allowing OVAM to readjust the requirements for the descriptive test.

3.3 *Chapter 7*

The transferor who is able to prove to OVAM that he is an 'innocent possessor' (see para 2.3.2 above) can escape the obligation to conduct a descriptive soil test.

Once the final report of the descriptive soil test is filed, OVAM will decide on its conformity with the provisions of the Flemish Statute on Soil Clean-up. Once the report is declared in conformity, OVAM will indicate whether the soil clean-up criteria have been exceeded (new pollution) or whether the contamination poses a serious threat (historical pollution). If this is the case, a soil clean-up project needs to be drafted by the soil expert.

Where the descriptive soil test has shown that the soil clean-up criteria have been exceeded (new pollution) or that the contamination poses a serious threat (historical pollution), the statute provides that the transfer may finally take place if:

(1) a soil clean-up project has been drafted;
(2) the transferor has undertaken in writing to perform the clean-up; and
(3) financial security to cover the clean-up costs has been posted. OVAM provides standard texts for such written undertaking and for the irrevocable bank guarantee, which is the preferred financial security.

All the previous obligations incumbent on the transferor may also, if agreed upon by the parties, be fulfilled by the acquirer or a third party who has the powers to enforce a transfer of land (eg a mortgagee). The relevant agreement must be submitted to OVAM.

(d) Evaluation

The requirement to include a 'soil certificate' in all transfer agreements is primarily intended for the information of the acquirer of a piece of land regarding the soil and groundwater contamination in the plot he wishes to acquire. The aim was to provide an effective tool to prevent in the future what has too often happened in the past: the acquisition by a unsuspecting person of a piece of land on which, at some later date, serious contamination is discovered, reducing the value of the land, without a reasonable possibility of holding anybody liable for the clean-up costs. In the new system, the acquirer will not be able to claim that he did not know or was not supposed to know the property's condition. The soil certificate justifies the imposition of a strict liability on the acquirer if soil contamination has to be cleaned up. The system is not perfect, however, as the soil certificate does not provide the acquirer with any guarantee as to the condition of the soil. The soil certificate includes the information held by OVAM regarding the plot of land in its Register of Contaminated Soils. If no information has ever reached OVAM, the soil certificate will mention this fact, and the acquirer will have to decide whether or not he wishes to conduct his own soil investigation before acquiring the plot.

The transfer formalities regarding risk land were designed not so much to inform the acquirer, but rather to ensure that sufficient funds are available for a clean-up, if one is required. The transfer will only take place if OVAM has given the 'green light'. The 'green light' will be given by OVAM, either after having decided that there is no indication that there is contamination which requires clean-up, or after having obtained financial guarantees to cover the clean-up costs. The rationale is to avoid ownership or control over contaminated land being transferred to insolvent parties. In addition, each acquirer of risk land in the Flemish Region will start with a base-line that is defined by the soil investigations that were performed before the transfer, and if these investigations show contamination above the clean-up standard, the land will be cleaned up at the transferor's expense (unless the acquirer agrees to provide the financial guarantees for the clean-up costs). Only in a case where the transferor is an 'innocent possessor', might OVAM be faced with a situation in which it has to give a 'green light' without having an undertaking for the clean-up works and/or financial guarantees that fully cover the clean-up costs.

In practice, the new regime is often regarded as too burdensome, especially by professional acquirers and vendors. These persons are usually aware of the potential pitfalls that the contamination can pose and will conduct environmental due diligence on their own initiative, within their own time schedule and within the limits of investigation they themselves choose. Now they are faced with a legal system that requires them to perform a due diligence procedure limited to potential soil and groundwater contamination, but within a strict procedure and timetable. Management of these problems will be discussed at para 4.5 below.

3.3.2 The transfer of operating permits

Permits are generally transferable provided certain notification obligations are complied with. These notification obligations are only imposed on an asset transaction, where a new legal personality takes over the operation of the business. Share transactions, where the legal personality of the operator does not change, are not subject to any notification obligation. Administrative authorities are not concerned with the change in ownership of the shares of the operating company.

The transfer of operating permits is not regulated in a uniform way. The obligations of the parties are defined by the regulations applicable to the particular permit.

In a number of cases, regulations do not provide for any specific obligation. This is the case, for instance, for the RGPT that governs the regime for operating permits in the Walloon Region. It is generally accepted that when a regulation remains silent on the issue of transfer, the transfer is allowed, provided the parties inform the permit granting authority in writing of the transfer.

In most cases, regulations explicitly provide for a notification obligation on transfer to a new party. Parties need to pay attention to the form and the time periods in which this notification must be made.

The most important point is the sanction where notification is not made within the prescribed form or time period. In a limited number of cases, the permit will lapse. Such is the case for the permit for the pumping of groundwater in the Flemish Region. A similar rule is laid down in art 42 of Vlarem I with regard to the environmental permit in the Flemish Region. The Council of State has ruled that this severe sanction may not be applied to the environmental permit, however, as the sanction was only enacted in a governmental decree (Vlarem I) without proper delegation by a statute voted in Parliament.

In most cases, non-compliance with the notification obligations does not lead to a lapse of the permit.

There are no specific rules concerning the division of a company, the operations of which are governed by one single permit. The same question arises in the case of the transfer of a branch of activities: is it possible to divide a permit? Generally speaking, the authorities do not oppose a division of a permit and apply the procedures for the transfer of a permit to the division. In the letter of notification, the parties need to detail which activities covered by the permit are transferred to which party and which remain with another party. If parties fail to make such a clear distinction, they run the risk that they will be held liable for permit violations committed by the other party.

4 MANAGING ENVIRONMENTAL ISSUES IN TRANSACTIONS

4.1 Environmental audits

No commercial transaction involving industrial property, whether it be an asset or a share transaction, should proceed without specific environmental provisions.

Environmental concerns are often identified only very late in a transaction, leaving one or sometimes both parties without sufficient understanding of the risks and liabilities that should be addressed, leading to inappropriate wording in the contract. Only an in-depth environmental due diligence exercise, both legal and technical, can adequately protect parties against hidden risks and will enable parties to come to a balanced allocation of the environmental risks in the contract.

Both parties have a duty to act as normal and cautious professionals and have a legitimate expectation that the other party should act in such a way. Environmental auditing is considered increasingly to be part of these pre-contractual duties in mergers and acquisitions. Environmental auditing becomes therefore part of the vendor's duty under general civil law to inform the purchaser of the major defects in his operations, whereas it also becomes part of the acquirer's duty to perform a normal inspection of the assets he acquires.

In recent years, environmental auditing has become a common part of any due diligence exercise involving industrial facilities in Belgium. In particular in the Flemish Region, environmental audits are 'booming' due to various statutory obligations to perform such audits. Pursuant to the Regional Statute of 19 April 1995 on environmental care within companies (see para 2.3.3(h) above), companies in the Flemish Region must file 'environmental year reports' or 'emission year reports'. In addition, they must perform soil and groundwater investigations every 5, 10 or 20 years, depending on the potential impact of the activities on the soil and groundwater condition, as well as at each 'transfer of land' (see para 3.3.1 above). Before ordering a new environmental audit, it is therefore always recommended to verify whether there have not been any recent audits that may already have covered some of the work that is contemplated.

For transactions where a letter of intent precedes a due diligence exercise, it is advisable to include precise wording in such a letter on the scope of the environmental audit that will be performed, as well as on the rights of the parties to review and discuss the work performed by the other party's environmental expert.

Some local companies are still uneasy about a 'hostile' environmental audit of their operations and prefer to perform their own audit and communicate the results to the other party. In those cases, it is important to monitor the work performed by the auditor of the other party, and to appoint, if necessary, a reviewing expert.

4.2 Structuring the transaction

Belgian law on sale and purchase contracts protects the purchaser against the 'hidden defects' of the purchased asset. When it comes to the acquisition of shares, this provision protects the purchaser of shares only against the 'hidden defect' of the shares (eg no voting powers in the general assembly) leaving him unprotected against defects in the assets owned or operated by the company he buys the shares from.

A normal share transaction involving a company that owns or operates industrial land, will therefore always contain environmental representations and warranties, accompanied by disclosure statements from the selling party. Without such provisions, the entire environmental risk will be borne by the purchaser.

Belgium **4.3**

Typical representations include that the company involved in the transaction has obtained all necessary permits and licences to operate its business and that such business is operated in compliance with all applicable environmental laws, including the permit conditions. It is also usual to obtain a warranty from the seller as to the condition of the soil and the groundwater and as to the absence of claims or notices from third parties and public authorities.

Representations are usually made subject to exceptions set out in disclosures. It is also not unusual to add to such representations qualifications that they are limited to 'the best of seller's knowledge', 'material compliance' and/or 'that could give rise to a claim or liability'.

Each contract should also contain clauses that provide for indemnification in case of a breach of a representation. Such indemnification clauses are generally subject to a statute of limitations of two to five years. Notification and co-operation obligations in case of an environmental incident occurring within the period of the statute of limitations are also often provided for.

Contracts whereby assets are transferred are often, unjustly, less sophisticated in their wording on environmental matters in comparison to share transactions. Although the acquirer of assets enjoys legal protection against 'hidden defects' of the land (eg hidden soil and groundwater contamination), such protection is too vague and therefore a source for disputes. It is therefore strongly recommended that detailed wording as to the allocation of environmental risks between the parties is also included in asset transfer contracts.

Asset transactions in the Flemish Region should always take into account the obligations under the Flemish Statute on Soil Clean-up. Specific provisions may be required with regard to the performance of the obligations under the statute (see para 4.3 below). An unwelcome consequence of the Flemish Regional Statute on Soil Clean-up is the fact that sellers of assets in the Flemish Region are often unwilling to provide any guarantee as to the condition of the soil and groundwater, in addition to the circumstances identified in the soil and groundwater investigation reports that were prepared in order for the transaction to go ahead. A cautious purchaser will therefore always try to obtain a second opinion on the soil and groundwater condition before accepting such a limit on the sellers' representations.

4.3 Environmental insurance

Insurance companies are generally not keen on providing very specific coverage for environmental risks. No model insurance policies for such risks exist on the Belgian market, but a number of insurance companies offer tailor-made policies for environmental risks.

In most cases however, a number of environmental risks are covered by the standard policy that insures a company against the damages to third parties caused by its operations. This standard policy requires the existence of an 'accident', ie a sudden and involuntary event causing harm. Therefore, such policies will not cover damages caused by gradual and ongoing pollution. The standard policy covers physical injuries, damage to objects and material losses.

Problems often arise as to the definition of the environmental risk. It is sometimes not clear whether the financial consequences of clean-up notices from public authorities are covered, or whether cover is limited to damage suffered by third parties.

4.4 Environmental management systems

Since 1995, companies in Belgium can be certified under the Eco-management and Audit Scheme (EMAS), but only a handful of companies have felt the need to obtain such certification. The ISO 14001 standard is more popular with Belgian companies. However, these international environmental management systems do not yet play an important role in Belgium.

In the Flemish Region, the Regional Statute on environmental care has obliged a large number of companies to appoint an environmental co-ordinator and draft yearly reports. In addition, a number of regulations impose self-monitoring on environmental aspects of the industrial activity. In order to cope with all environmental obligations and risks, large and mid-sized companies must in practice ensure they have sufficient in-house expertise and the proper reporting and remediating procedures in place.

4.5 Managing the obligations under the Flemish Regional Statute on Soil Clean-up

The above-mentioned obligations (soil certificate and/or soil investigations prior to transfer of land in the Flemish Region) often pose a problem of timing: obtaining a soil certificate may take two months, and carrying out soil investigations may take several months more, resulting in a significant delay for the parties who wish to close a real estate deal. If the parties transfer land without complying with the obligations under the Statute, the transfer contract may be nullified by the civil court at the request of either the transferee or OVAM. The failure to perform an orientation soil test when one is required is also subject to criminal sanctions.

Persons who are contemplating the transfer of real estate situated in the Flemish Region, on which a potentially contaminating activity has taken or takes place, should therefore ensure that their timetable takes account of the possibility that the closing of the transaction may have to be postponed by several months. If the transferor anticipates a problem that may give rise to the request by OVAM for a descriptive soil test, he should conduct an orientation soil test as soon as possible.

The question arises whether the problem of timing can be solved with the conclusion of a contract with a condition precedent for obtaining a 'blank' soil certificate (not containing indications of soil contamination) or with a clause providing for the transfer to take place only when such a soil certificate is obtained. Also, with respect to soil investigations, the question arises whether an agreement related to the transfer can be entered into, with the transfer itself of title, control, etc on the land postponed until all formalities are complied with. In this respect there is a difference between the obligation to obtain the soil certificate and the obligation to perform soil investigations.

As the soil certificate must be notified to the transferee prior to entering into an agreement relating to the transfer of land, an agreement with a condition precedent for obtaining such a certificate, is invalid. This nullity of the transfer agreement without a soil certificate can be covered, however, by the notarial deed relating to the transfer, provided the soil certificate is obtained prior to the notarial deed and the transferee waives his right to invoke such nullity. For agreements that will be notarised, it is therefore possible to conclude the agreement without the soil certificate. The transferor will then have to ensure that he obtains the soil certificate prior to the notarial deed and obtains the waiver from the transferee.

In contrast, soil investigations need to be carried out before the actual transfer of the land. It has therefore been generally accepted that an agreement can be made in which it is stated that the transfer of land will occur at a later date, ie after completion of all the obligations imposed by the Flemish Regional Statute on Soil Clean-up. Such an agreement cannot be notarised, however, as long as the soil certificate has not been obtained.

Land cannot be transferred safely without having completed the entire procedure of soil investigations and the eventual soil clean-up project, if required. Some authors have defended the view, however, that the chances that such a transfer contract would be nullified are quite limited, provided that neither the transferee nor OVAM have an interest in obtaining the nullification of the contract. According to this opinion, OVAM would only have an interest, and therefore standing before a court, where it could show that the transfer agreement concerned potentially contaminated land and no orientation test was filed. Indeed, if the parties agree to transfer 'risk land' and one party agrees to comply immediately with all obligations under the Statute, the potential problems regarding the soil and groundwater will be detected and solved under the supervision of OVAM, so that it is not likely that OVAM will subsequently seek the nullification of the transfer agreement. According to this argument, OVAM would only have standing to seek the nullity of the transfer agreement if the party that agreed to comply with the obligations, subsequently fails to do so.

It remains to be seen whether the courts will easily accept this argument of lack of OVAM's standing in cases where the obligations are performed immediately after the transfer of land has taken place. In the absence of any authoritative case law on the subject, caution is advised and parties should not attempt to transfer actual control or title over land if the obligations under the Flemish Regional Statute on Soil Clean-up are not fully complied with.

Another route that is sometimes used to cope with the 'transfer of land' obligations under the Flemish Statute on Soil Clean-up is the conclusion of a lease agreement for less than one year, with an option to buy the real estate after completion of the full OVAM procedure. During the term of the lease, the transferor (or the transferee) commits himself to the performance of the obligations of the Statute. Leases for less than one year are not covered by the definition of 'transfer of land' and are therefore not subject to the obligations to obtain a soil certificate and to perform soil investigations. As the entire OVAM procedure will generally take less than one year, other than in complicated cases, the go-ahead for a final transaction may be expected within the time period of the one-year lease. As soon as this go-ahead is obtained, the transferor may exercise the option.

There are certain risks involved with the structure of the one-year lease with option to buy. First, it may be argued that the lease cannot be extended beyond one year. Extension of a lease beyond the one-year period can indeed be regarded as falling under the definition of a 'transfer of land'. If the full OVAM procedure has not been completed after one year, the transferor should, according to this interpretation of the Statute, retake possession of the land. Again, case law will have to show whether such is indeed the case. Secondly, it should be taken into account that the transferor can still walk away from the deal after the completion of the term of the lease.

5 CONCLUSION

The Flemish Regional Statute on Soil Clean-up has been referred to throughout this chapter as it has had an enormous impact on transactions involving industrial activity in the Flemish Region. Both the Walloon and the Brussels Metropolitan Regions are said to be preparing legislation in the field of soil and groundwater clean-ups, but as long as this remains in preparation, transactions in these two Regions remain less burdensome.

4.5 *Chapter 7*

Environmental risks do not know any borders, however, and it is therefore fair to state that transactions in any Region in Belgium should be preceded by the same diligent and in-depth approach to environmental concerns related to the industrial activity or the land concerned. Environmental law is rapidly developing and imposes ever-increasing burdens on operators of industrial facilities in all of Belgium's three Regions.

Chapter 8

SWEDEN

Rudolf Laurin

Wistrand Advokatbyrå, Gothenburg

1 INTRODUCTION

1.1 Jurisdiction covered

Sweden is not a federal state. The same legal regime should therefore in principle apply in the whole of Sweden. However, in practice, various provisions of law are applied by municipal and regional authorities in different ways.

In some regulated areas different regimes exist in the different municipalities, eg in the field of waste handling. Different systems for transport or treatment of different waste categories may be created by decisions of the local government. In practice, this may create a practical problem for a purchaser of a company, particularly if the purchaser is a foreign company, not previously active in the region.

1.2 Basic structure of environmental law

Traditionally, Sweden has been considered a very progressive country in the field of environmental protection and legislation. However, a closer study shows that environmental law was comprised in many different pieces of legislation. The Nature Conservancy Act from 1964 (SFS 1964:822) was the first protective legislation enacted. It was then followed by a large number of other provisions aiming at protecting the environment. The most important of those was probably the Environmental Protection Act from 1969 (SFS 1969:387). This Act covered water and air pollution as well as most other nuisances in the environment, including aesthetic impact from stationary sources. It was the first step to integrated pollution control, requiring a permit for production and laying down discharge conditions.

The subsequent approach to legislation has created many problems. Inconsistency when enacting new provisions has created confusion and uncertainty for those applying the legislation. Standards differ and laws overlap or leave gaps where regulation is absent.

The environmental legal system was not designed to embody EU law. When Sweden became a member of the European Union, new questions arose for legislators and operators of environmentally hazardous activities. Such activities were based upon individual permits issued according to procedures laid down in the Environmental Protection Act. Only a limited number of general provisions were in

1.2 Chapter 8

place in the Swedish legislation. The conflict between a discharge condition and a stricter provision in a general applicable EU directive or regulation had to be solved. This was fairly easy for new permits—competent authorities could not issue permits containing more lenient conditions than those prescribed by Brussels. For existing permits, the Environmental Protection Agency was authorised to issue general provisions that would take precedence where necessary.

To address the need for consistency, extensive work to harmonise legislation has been carried out for almost a decade. The first proposal for a comprehensive Act was presented to the Parliament (*Riksdag*) shortly before the election in 1994. This proposal was withdrawn immediately after the election by the winning Social Democratic Government. A new governmental proposal for an Environmental Code was presented to the Parliament in December 1997 (Government Bill 1997/98:45). With the support of the Environmental Party and the Left Party the Code was passed on 11 May 1998 (SFS 1998:808). The Environmental Code entered into force on 1 January 1999. It is accompanied by a large number of Acts, amendments in existing legislation and government ordinances.

Of course, no jurisprudence has yet developed in connection with the new Environmental Code. Not all the content of the Code is new. This is understandable regarding its extent. It contains 33 chapters comprising almost 500 sections. A vast number of existing legislation has been amalgamated in the Environmental Code. Those Acts are:

(1) the Natural Resources Act,
(2) the Nature Conservancy Act,
(3) the Flora and Fauna (Measures Relating to Protected Species) Act,
(4) the Environmental Protection Act,
(5) the Health Protection Act,
(6) the Water Act (in part),
(7) the Agricultural Land Management Act,
(8) the Genetically Modified Organism Act,
(9) the Chemical Products Act,
(10) the Biological Pesticides (Advanced Testing) Act,
(11) the Pesticides (Spreading over Forest Land) Act,
(12) the Fuels (Sulphur Content) Act,
(13) the Public Cleansing Act,
(14) the Dumping of Waste in Water (Prohibition) Act, and
(15) the Environmental Damage Act.

The jurisprudence previously developed may thus to a certain extent be relied upon when interpreting the new Environmental Code. However, one has to be careful. One must always remember to interpret the single provisions of the Environmental Code in the context of the Code and remember that sustainability and a high level of environmental protection are expressly mentioned as objectives of the Environmental Code. This has not always been the case in the different pieces of legislation in force until 31 December 1998.

In this chapter, references are generally made to the Environmental Code and subsequent legislation. For interpretation, a comparison may be made with previous provisions, which have now been repealed.

1.3 Structure of environmental regulatory agencies

The structure of the regulatory bodies will change significantly through the introduction of the Environmental Code. The decision-making procedure in environmental matters has been oriented previously towards political bodies, such as the municipal authorities, the county administrative boards and the government. The Franchise Board (*Koncessionsnämnden*) was an important exception in the otherwise political procedure. Although the Franchise Board was a central administrative body, it operated as if it was a court.

Under the Environmental Code (Chs 16–24), cases, applications for permits and other matters are determined by the government, the county administrative boards and other administrative authorities, the municipalities, environmental courts, the Supreme Environmental Court and the Supreme Court. Cases concerning penalties and forfeiture are considered by the general district courts with appeals to the courts of appeal and the Supreme Court. Although the political and administrative procedures still seem to remain, there are two important innovations in the Environmental Code. First, five regional environmental courts are introduced. Those environmental courts are part of the district courts. Secondly, appeal on judgments from those environmental courts is directed to the Supreme Environmental Court, which is a part of the Svea Appeal Court in Stockholm and then to the Supreme Court also in Stockholm. Previously, decisions of the Franchise Board were appealed to the government.

In summary, the environmental courts will try in the first instance cases concerning the following issues:

(1) permits for environmental hazardous activities according to the annex to the Ordinance on Environmentally Hazardous Activity and Health Protection (SFS 1998:899);
(2) permits for water undertakings;
(3) compensation for intervention by public authorities;
(4) damages for environmental harm and other private claims against the polluter;
(5) distribution of responsibilities for historic pollution;
(6) penalties (not criminal) according to the Environmental Code.

On appeal, the environmental courts will consider decisions of the county administrative boards and other government agencies. There are few limited exceptions with of only little interest to merger and acquisition cases where the appeal is still made to the government.

The county administrative boards and the municipalities act as first instance agencies in a number of matters under the Environmental Code. They consider inter alia questions of permits for those environmentally hazardous activities that are included in the annex to the Ordinance on Environmentally Hazardous Activity and Health Protection. Enumeration in this annex determines what kind of activities are to be considered by the county administrative boards or have to be notified to the municipalities. Another important role of those authorities is their role as 'supervisors' in environmental matters. For a purchaser of a business activity, it may be crucial to establish whether the competent supervising authority has made any criticism of the acquired activity.

Considerations of permissibility of certain new activities hazardous to the environment are reserved to the government under the Environmental Code. Those activities are listed in the Environmental Code, Ch 17, s 1. Examples of such activities include iron and steel works, pulp factories, paper mills, chemical factories, installations for treatment of more than 10,000 tons of hazardous waste per year and

1.3 *Chapter 8*

wind and hydro electricity plants. The consideration by the government takes place as a step in the ordinary permit determination according to the Environmental Code. An application is thus—usually—submitted to the environmental court. After preparing the case, the court will then pass the matter to the government together with its own opinion for considerations of permissibility. An operation in most cases may be vetoed by the municipal assembly in the area where the activity is to be conducted. In cases where the admissibility procedure is applicable, it is therefore necessary that the majority of the local politicians support the project.

2 OUTLINE OF ENVIRONMENTAL LAW RELEVANT TO MERGER AND ACQUISITION TRANSACTIONS

2.1 Contaminated land

It may be said that the regulation of remediation of contaminated land is one of the 'hot topics' in the Environmental Code. In the *travaux préparatoires* it is explicitly stated that as many areas as possible shall be cleaned through the introduction of the Environmental Code without the State having to bear the costs for this clean-up. This objective will leave the operators and landowners with responsibilities for the work and costs occurred. The relevant provisions are to be found in Ch 10 of the Environmental Code.

Before describing the liability provisions, a distinction must be drawn between what is considered in Swedish legislation as an ongoing environmentally hazardous activity and situations considered to be simple land contamination. Land pollution with continuous leakage is considered to be an ongoing activity as long as there is a leakage risk. A closed landfill generating leakage is a typical example of such activity. In this case everyone in possession of the land is considered to be an operator conducting the environmentally hazardous activity. Thus, even a landowner that has acquired the land after termination of the landfill is an operator. On the other hand, in the case of simple land contamination, that is land pollution by, for example, heavy metals or mineral oils where the source of the pollution has stopped and there is no leakage, an 'innocent' landowner is not considered as an operator of any hazardous activities. Only the person or company that has caused the contamination will be considered as the party that has conducted the environmental hazardous activity.

According to the Environmental Code, liability for remediation rests primarily with the party that has conducted or is conducting the environmental hazardous activity. All parties conducting environmentally hazardous activities after 30 June 1969 are in principle joint and severally liable. This applies for all parties even if they have ceased the activities at the time the question of remediation is brought up. Here, the distinction between an ongoing environmental hazardous activity and a simple land contamination, is relevant. In the first case, the landowner—however innocent—is an operator of that activity. He bears the same liability as the person that has actually conducted the activity. In the second case, the landowner is not an operator of any environmental hazardous activity. He is only liable if the preconditions set out below, are fulfilled.

If there is no operator who can conduct the clean-up or compensate for the costs of clean-up measures of contaminated land, the landowner will be made liable. The precondition is that the landowner has bought the contaminated property after 1 January 1999 and knew about or ought to have discovered the contamination. Also in this case, the subsequent landowners' liability will be joint and several.

In addition to the liability of operators and landowners, an 'innocent' party, for example a landowner who has bought the contaminated land before 1 January 1999, may be obliged to contribute to the remediation costs in a case where he would make a profit due to the fact that somebody else had to clean up the land. This provision must, however, be applied with considerable caution.

The remediation liability means that the responsible persons to a reasonable extent must clean up or take other necessary measures to counteract damage or nuisance to the environment or health or pay compensation for such actions. In assessing reasonableness, matters including the length of time elapsed since the contamination, that party's contribution to the contamination or the then applicable obligations to prevent future injurious effects, are to be considered. There is no time-bar for the remediation liability.

Another novelty is the obligation on the owner or user of property to inform the supervisory authority of contamination which is discovered. This obligation is unconditional and applies even if the area where the property in question is situated was previously considered as polluted. The non-fulfilment of this obligation constitutes a criminal offence. If the area is so severely polluted that it constitutes a risk to the environment or human health, the county administrative board must declare such area to be an environmental risk area. Such a declaration will be noted in the land register. The authority will lay down provisions for the use of land in this area. For example, it may be decided that exploitation or even transfer of ownership must be preceded by notification and detailed environmental examination of the property.

2.2 Pollution of water resources

Pollution of water resources is one of the disturbances specially listed in Ch 32 of the Environmental Code. If the pollution of water resources caused by an activity on land leads to personal injury, property damage or pure financial loss of some significance, compensation must be paid to those who have suffered loss. The obligation to pay damages is in principle strict. No intent or negligence has to be shown. The liability is joint and several for the landowner or other occupant of the land and the person who has physically caused the damage.

The operator of the activity leading to the pollution may also face criminal liability. The pollution must either cause a risk of harm to human health or of damage to animals or plants or lead to other substantial nuisance to the environment. If the pollution is caused intentionally or negligently the offence is classified as an environmental crime. The offence is described as *causing environmental disturbance*. Unlike the obligation to pay damages, a physical person must be identified as responsible. If the activity leading to the pollution is conducted by a company, the managing director will normally be held liable. However, this liability may be delegated further down in the organisation.

2.3 Authorisations for discharging and for taking water from natural resources

Authorisations for discharging water are regulated within the framework of the integrated pollution control described at para 2.4 below.

Authorisations for taking water are on the other hand handled within the framework applicable to water undertakings in Ch 11 of the Environmental Code and the Act, with special provisions applicable to water undertakings (SFS 1998:812). A water undertaking is not only taking water from natural resources but also, for example,

2.3 *Chapter 8*

erection and alteration of dams and other installations in water, other operations in surface or groundwater or drainage of water.

There is a duty to obtain a permit for a water undertaking unless it is absolutely clear that neither public or private interests are harmed by the effects of the water undertaking on the water conditions. The burden of proof always lies with the applicant. A permit application is submitted to one of the regional environmental courts.

The integration of water undertakings in the Environmental Code has increased the importance of the environmental aspects when considering permit applications. All the general rules of consideration contained in Ch 2 of the Environmental Code (those rules are described in para 2.4 below) must be fulfilled. Those rules are further supplemented by specific rules applicable to water undertakings. A permit for a water undertaking may only be granted if the advantages from the general and individual point of view exceed the expense and harm caused by the undertaking in question. The water undertaking must be carried out in such a way that future developments of importance to general or private interests concerning the same natural resources are not hindered.

It is a criminal offence to conduct a water undertaking without obtaining a permit. The maximum penalty is two years' imprisonment. If the water undertaking is conducted by a company, the managing director will normally be liable.

2.4 Integrated pollution control

It is not too bold a statement to say that Sweden has been a forerunner in applying integrated pollution control of environmentally hazardous activities. Since 1969, an individual permit determination under the Environmental Protection Act was applied to a large number of industrial activities. The individual environmental permit under this Act deals typically with discharges to water and emissions to the atmosphere, provisions to prevent pollution of water resources and air, prevention of noise and other nuisance etc. However, the environmental permit cannot directly regulate the qualities of the products manufactured in the plant or the resources used for the production. The authorisation for taking water from natural sources was given separately in a judgment from a water court according to the provisions in the Water Act.

With the introduction of the Environmental Code, pollution control is extended to new areas affecting the environment without changing the principle that operators of environmentally hazardous activities must either obtain a permit under the integrated pollution control system or notify the activity to the municipal authorities before its commencement. All activities requiring a permit or notification are listed in the annex to the Ordinance on Environmentally Hazardous Activity and Health Protection.

Except for permits for water undertakings described in para 2.3 above, there are no special permit procedures for emissions to water or atmosphere, noise, nuisance etc. All those issues should, if relevant to the activity in question, be addressed in the permit granted under integrated pollution control.

A number of general principles have been introduced in Ch 2 of the Environmental Code that have to be observed by anyone wishing to conduct or already conducting an activity that may harm the environment. It should be stressed that the application of these rules is not limited to activities requiring a permit or notification under the integrated pollution control system. All activities that may affect the environment or human health are subject to them.

The supervising authorities may use the general rules in Ch 2 in order to regulate activities falling outside the obligation to obtain a permit. Operations that have obtained a permit under the superseded Environmental Protection Act may find themselves facing supplementary requirements in areas that have previously not been regulated in this legislation. For example, additional conditions can be laid down on the chemical substances used when manufacturing products or a requirement can be made on the use of renewable energy.

Because of the importance of these general considerations which should always be addressed in proceedings for obtaining an integrated pollution control permit, it is appropriate to examine the content of those provisions more closely.

2.4.1 The burden of proof (Environmental Code, Ch 2, s 1)

An applicant bears the burden of proof of demonstrating that he has undertaken and fulfilled all the obligations laid down in Ch 2 of the Environmental Code. The applicant bears the risk that an issue of environmental relevance has been sufficiently clarified. This rule may cause considerable problems in a merger or acquisition situation, particularly when a bigger and financially stronger company is taking over a smaller local enterprise. In practice, this may be just the situation the supervising authority has been waiting for to investigate, for example, why a certain kind of butterfly has disappeared from the surroundings of the industrial site included in the acquisition. In order to try to avoid such unpleasant surprises, it is therefore advisable to investigate the nature of the relationship between the target company and the local supervising authority.

2.4.2 Knowledge (Environmental Code, Ch 2, s 2)

A party conducting an activity or intending to conduct an activity is obliged to obtain the necessary knowledge to determine the environmental effects that may arise as a result of the activity. The requirement of knowledge depends on the nature and extent of the activity conducted.

2.4.3 Precautionary measures (Environmental Code, Ch 2, s 3)

This fundamental rule means that anyone wishing to undertake an activity or a measure must perform prescribed protective measures, observe specific limitations and take precautionary measures that are required in order for the activity or the measure not to be harmful to health or the environment. The application of the polluter pays principle can clearly be seen in this provision. As soon as there is a risk of harm, the undertaking of protective measures or observation of limitations is required. The scope of this provision may extend from quite simple and cheap steps, such as the separation of different waste streams, to requirements which may be burdensome, such as limitation of the production process or installation of expensive cleaning devices.

2.4.4 Best possible technology (Environmental Code, Ch 2, s 3)

Operators of commercial activities must apply the best possible technology in order to avoid damage or harm to the environment. The technology must be beyond an experimental stage in order to be considered to be available. Further, it must be industrially feasible for the technology in question to be applied in the particular type of business activity.

2.4.5 Best location (Environmental Code, Ch 2, s 4)

Should the activity demand the use of land or areas of water, a place must be chosen that is suitable having regard to the requirements of resource management provision

2.4   Chapter 8

in Chs 4 and 5 of the Environmental Code. Several places can of course be suitable. The operator has then to choose the place where the activity can be undertaken with the least intrusion and nuisance without incurring unreasonable costs. This test of best location will of course be of greatest significance when considering new production sites. But also the purchaser of existing operations must be aware of this rule. If the validity of the environmental permit runs out or if he wishes to expend or alter the operation, the new or amended permit will be granted only according to the requirement of best possible location.

2.4.6   The resource management and the eco-cycle principles (Environmental Code, Ch 2, s 5)

The provisions described above were generally a part of the examination process prior to issuing an environmental permit under the repealed Environmental Protection Act. The principles under this heading are new requirements under the Environmental Code. There is now a legal obligation on those conducting an activity covered by the Environmental Code to conserve raw materials and energy. In addition, use must be made of existing opportunities of re-use and recycling. There is also an obligation to use renewable energy resources.

How those principles will be applied is not entirely clear. It is evident that the ambit of permit considerations is extended compared with the situation before 1 January 1999. Nevertheless, this does not mean that the environmental court will prohibit the production of petrol driven cars because, when driven, cars use a fossil energy source. However, it is likely that the environmental court may decide that when producing cars, only electricity produced in wind power stations should be used in the car factory. Similarly, the environmental court may take the view that it is possible to use sheet-metal manufactured only from recovered scrap instead of sheetmetal bases from iron ore.

A purchaser should be aware of these principles when assessing the value of an acquired business. Not only may they cause higher production costs when applying for new permits but also activities conducting business under valid permits may find themselves faced with demands from supervising authorities. The legal base for these demands is quite simple: that matters of resource management are not addressed in the existing permit. The likelihood for such demands will increase with the age of the permit: the older the permit under the Environmental Protection Act, the higher the likelihood that new requirements and demands will be presented by the authorities.

2.4.7   The product choice principle (Environmental Code, Ch 2, s 6)

From 1 January 1999, everybody must avoid using or selling chemical products or biotechnical organisms that can harm the environment or human health, if the product may be replaced by another product causing less risk. Corresponding requirements apply to products that contain a chemical product or a biochemical organism or have been treated by such a product. This product choice principle may only be applied in an individual case after appropriate assessment. Prohibition of products by category is possible under special provisions of Ch 14 of the Environmental Code dealing with chemical products. On the base of the product choice principle, the car manufacturer described above may face a requirement to use only cleaning chemicals free of aromatic-based solvents.

2.4.8 Reasonableness rule (Environmental Code, Ch 2, s 7)

The requirements described above can only be applied to the extent that it is not unreasonable to demand the measure in question. When making this assessment, the benefit of the measure is balanced and compared with the cost of it. The nature of the nuisance and its risk are important when assessing reasonableness. The sensitivity of the recipient and protests by the public affected by the hazardous activity are also important. A thorough investigation of those factors should be conducted before the closing of the deal. As pointed out above, it is the obligation of the party wanting to conduct an activity to prove that a measure demanded by the authorities or a third party is either environmentally unjustified or unreasonably burdensome.

2.4.9 Particular considerations for those activities requiring an environmental permit (Environmental Code, Ch 16)

As mentioned at para 2.4 above, the general principles introduced in Ch 2 of the Environmental Code will apply to all activities, irrespective of the obligation on the operator to obtain a permit or to submit a notification. Besides these general rules, Ch 16 of the Code contains further provisions concerning those activities requiring a permit under the integrated pollution control system. Those activities are listed in an annex to the Ordinance on Environmentally Hazardous Activity and Health Protection.

Activities requiring a permit or notification may not be commenced before the permit is issued or the notification has been submitted. Not even the construction or rebuilding of a factory where the operation is to take place is allowed.

A permit may be subject to a condition requiring the applicant to put up collateral to cover the expenses for after-treatment and other restoration measures. Two important new features have been introduced in the Environmental Code. First, a permit for a new activity may not contribute to the contravention of a general environmental quality norm. Secondly, a permit may be refused to a party that has not satisfied its obligations under previous permits or approvals or has failed to apply for such necessary permits or approvals. A connection either by ownership or leadership with a transgressing party may be enough to block an application for a new or amended permit. Finally, a permit may not be issued in contravention of a detailed plan regulating the use of land in the area where the new activity is to be located.

2.4.10 Liability for offences

To commence or conduct an operation requiring a permit or notification in breach of the relevant provisions constitutes a criminal offence if the breach is committed either intentionally or negligently. The managing director will normally be liable if the operator is a company. The crime of *unlawful environmental activity* can lead to a penalty of imprisonment of a maximum of 2 years.

A new sanction has been introduced in Ch 30 of the Environmental Code. Environmental sanction charges may be levied for certain offences. The unlawful environmental activity is one such offence. Environmental sanction charges are directed against the legal person conducting the unlawful activity irrespective of intent or negligence. The charges may amount to substantial sums. To commence an activity that requires a permit without having obtained such a permit may lead to a fine of up to SEK 900,000.

2.5 Waste management

The regulation of general waste management issues such as producer responsibility and other provisions concerning handling of waste is contained in Ch 15 of the Environmental Code. The general resource management and eco-cycle principles obliging everybody to utilise opportunities of re-use and recycling have been described at para 2.4.6 above.

The question of what is 'waste' and what are 'products' has been heavily debated in Sweden. The debate was prompted first, by the fact that there was no legal definition of waste, and secondly, by the fact that exclusive rights to handle substantial amounts of waste streams was given by the legislation either to municipalities or producers. The European definition of waste has now been incorporated in the Environmental Code. The possibility for municipalities to monopolise handling of industrial but not dangerous waste is abolished from 1 January 2000. After this date the municipalities may retain the monopoly for transportation and/or handling of dangerous waste only and will retain their monopoly on the handling of household waste. In a similar way, there is a legal monopoly for the producers to handle waste falling under the different provisions of producer responsibility. To date, producer responsibility has been introduced for recycled papers, tyres, packages and automobiles. Producer responsibility for electronic waste is to be introduced shortly.

When waste is to be transported away through the agency of a municipality or a producer, no person who is not properly authorised by the municipality or the producer may do so. Moreover, general permits authorising the handling of waste may be required. All persons transporting waste must obtain, according to the Cleaning Ordinance, a special permit from a county administrative board. Transport and handling of dangerous waste requires another permit pursuant to the Ordinance on Dangerous Waste.

Further, when doing business in Sweden, it should also be noted that from 1 January 2002, combustible waste no longer may be disposed of in landfills. The same prohibition applies for organic waste from 1 January 2005. This is particularly important to be aware of when acquiring a company which has a production process creating organic sludge containing metals. It can be assumed that handling of this kind of waste will be considerably more expensive in the near future.

The generator of waste has to control who will do the transporting of the waste. He has an obligation to ensure that the carrier has the necessary permits for transport of that particular kind of waste. If the waste is dangerous, in addition, the generator of waste has to make sure that the person receiving it for disposal or recycling has obtained the necessary permits for the activity. Those who generate waste will be criminally liable if they allow persons not having those permits to handle their waste. Should the waste be dangerous, an environmental sanction amounting to a fine of SEK 10,000 will be levied.

2.6 Land use planning/zoning

The use of land is regulated in the Planning and Building Act (SFS 1987:10) from 1987. The purpose of this Act is to promote a social development based on equal and favourable social conditions for the people of today's society and for future generations in a manner consistent with the freedom of the individual. In s 1 of Ch 2 of the Act it is stated that land and water areas must be used for those purposes for which the areas are most suited. Regard shall be taken to the areas' nature and location of the area together with existing needs. Preference will be given to the kind of use that involves good management from the public viewpoint.

When planning or considering a building permit application, Chs 3 and 4 of the Environmental Code containing fundamental provision for management of land and water areas must be applied. Also possible environmental quality norms must be observed.

The use of land is quite strictly regulated. Normally any significant industrial activity will require the competent municipality to take a planning decision on how the land shall be used. A so-called detailed plan may often be required. A detailed plan must precede any more substantial development of an area that has previously not been exploited. This rule of planning applies both to housing developments and industrial developments. A detailed plan has to be adopted by the municipal authority.

Once the necessary plan has been adopted, an individual building permit may be issued on the basis of an application and consideration of the provisions of the plan. There is an interaction between the provisions in a detailed plan and an application for an environmental permit. For a purchaser wanting to change or adapt an existing activity or erect new buildings, it is crucial to check the plans covering the geographical area of business. Following an explicit provision in the Environmental Code (Ch 16, s 4) an environmental permit contravening provisions in a detailed plan may not be granted. The detailed plan must in such cases first be amended. The amendment procedure is normally a political route and, as such, is very often time-consuming and costly. Existing discrepancies between an ongoing activity and provisions in a detailed plan will not prevent the existing activity from being carried on. The requirement to amend the plan will not arise until the operator wishes to develop or change his activity.

It is no longer a criminal offence to erect buildings or change activities without obtaining the necessary building permits. The person guilty of the offence will be subject to an administrative charge calculated on the building area affected by the measures that have been taken. In addition, a rectifying order will be issued by the municipal authority.

2.7 Chemical products and hazardous substances

Dealing with chemical products, biotechnical organisms and hazardous substances including radioactive material is covered by the general principles in Ch 2 of the Environmental Code described in paras 2.4.1–2.4.8 above. When an accident is likely to cause serious damage to the environment or health, a special security regime to minimise accident risk will apply to premises where such activities are conducted. The regime is laid down together with the rescue force according to provisions in the Rescue Service Act (SFS 1986:1102). The handling of chemical products and biotechnical organisms is further regulated in Ch 14 of the Environmental Code.

The Seveso Directive on the Major Accident Hazards of Certain Industrial Activities (Directive (EEC) 82/501 as later amended) is incorporated in Swedish law through the Act on Working Environment (SFS 1977:1160) and the Ordinance on Working Environment (SFS 1997:1166). Empowered by those two pieces of legislation, the central authority on protection of workers' health has issued on ordinance which in detail implements the Seveso Directive.

Everybody who manufactures or imports chemical products and biotechnical organisms is under a strict obligation to ensure that there is a satisfactory environmental and health investigation. The investigation duty applies continuously as long as the product in question remains on the Swedish market. All chemical products and biotechnical organisms must be registered in a product register kept by the Chemicals Inspectorate. Chemical products and biotechnical organisms that have previously not

2.7 *Chapter 8*

been used in Sweden, will have to be notified in advance. The importation of especially dangerous products and organisms from outside the European Union may require a permit. Corresponding obligations may be prescribed for commercial transfer and other handling of particularly dangerous substances.

In principle, it is a criminal offence to be in breach, intentionally or by negligence, of the different pieces of legislation on chemical products and hazardous substances. In the absence of specific delegation within a company, the managing director will assume liability for those offences. Also the company itself will face administrative fines in the form of an environmental penalty when in breach of certain provisions. As an example, the Chemical Inspectorate has already fined companies being in breach of their obligations to register chemical products or update the information in the register. The fines amount to SEK 5,000–25,000.

3 PARTICULAR ENVIRONMENTAL ISSUES RELEVANT TO TRANSACTIONS

3.1 Assumption of liabilities

Liability for environmental crimes has been consolidated in Ch 29 of the Environmental Code. The overall aim is to improve environmental control and ensure that persons infringing the law will receive appropriate punishment. Several changes have been made through the introduction of the Environmental Code in order to achieve this goal. More infringements of law are penalised, accompanied by the introduction of more severe sanctions.

There is a general principle in the Swedish legislation that only physical persons can be liable for criminal acts. It will normally be the managing director of a company that will be the object of criminal proceedings. However, depending on the type of infringement, the liability may fall upon the members or a particular member of the board of directors. On the other hand, a person lower down in the company organisation can also be found liable. Such delegation of liability will usually require a written instruction to the employee coupled with corresponding power and means to take action to prevent the infringement.

For criminal liability to occur, the person responsible must have committed the act either intentionally or by grave or simple negligence. In this context, grave negligence means a recklessness that almost amounts to intention. The specific requirements differ between the different crimes. It should be noted that ignorance of the provisions of law will not normally be a useful defence.

It is an offence not to observe the provisions of environmental legislation or the decisions made under this legislation. It is particularly relevant to merger and acquisition transactions to note that it is an offence of *unlawful environmental activity*, to intentionally or negligently commence or conduct an activity without having obtained the necessary permits or other approvals, or to violate the conditions laid down in a permit. Imprisonment for a maximum of two years is the most severe sanction for this offence. Another equally important provision is the risk of liability for *impeding environmental control* and *inadequate environmental information* in the case of providing incorrect written or oral information to the authorities or defective labelling of products. The maximum penalty is one year's imprisonment. Chemical products and other property that have been the subject of offences and any enhanced value of property or other gain from environmental offences may be declared forfeited unless such forfeiture would be manifestly unreasonable.

Probably the most important novelty in the Environmental Code is the introduction of environmental sanction charges in Ch 30. These administrative charges are imposed for failure to comply with the environmental legislation and are payable irrespective of intention or negligence. The supervisory authority decides on the environmental sanction charge. Imposing this charge does not prevent prosecution for a criminal proceeding for the same offence. The various kinds of violation that will lead to the imposition of an environmental sanction charge are determined by the government. For example, a charge is to be paid by a business operator who commences an activity which requires a permit or notification before the permit is given or notification made. It is of no relevance whether or not the operator has had any economic benefit from the infringement. No nuisance or harm to the environment or health has to occur.

The charges are set down by the government between a minimum of SEK 5,000 and a maximum of SEK 1,000,000. As an example, to commence an operation without obtaining a permit will cost between SEK 250,000 and 900,000 depending on whether the permit is to be issued by a environmental court, where relevant for certain activities after consideration of permissibility by the government, or by a county administrative board. The charges are not tax deductible.

3.2 Historical liabilities

Historical liabilities deriving from the conduct of an environmentally hazardous activity must be seen in the light of the clear objective expressed in the Environmental Code that clean-up measures should be borne by the operators and landowners and not by the state. The principles applying to remediation of contaminated land has been described in para 2.1 above.

The leading principle is that the operator that has caused pollution bears the liability to remedy this pollution. As from 1 July 1989 this principle was explicitly mentioned in s 5 of the now superseded Environmental Protection Act. According to this provision, anyone conducting an environmentally hazardous activity is under an obligation to take measures for the protection of the environment even after he has ceased to conduct the activity in question. It was generally assumed that this obligation existed implicitly since the promulgation of the Environmental Protection Act on 1 July 1969. However, in 1996 the Supreme Administrative Court (judgment RÅ 1996 Ref 57) declared that this assumption was incorrect. The court started by explaining that before 1 July 1989 there was no express obligation in the Environmental Protection Act to take measures after the termination of an activity. Further it was noted that there was no provision in the 1989 amendment of the Environmental Protection Act laying down a retrospective liability. Hence, the court concluded, there was no continuing obligation to undertake protective measures in respect of pollution caused by an activity terminated or sold before 1 July 1989. Only the person or persons conducting an activity after 1 July 1989 would be obliged to take clean- up or protective actions regarding pollution caused before this date. If it could be shown that the nuisance that was to be remedied was not caused by them but by a previous operator, there would be no liability for such pollution.

The situation with regard to liability created by the judgment was not approved and resulted in two provisions being inserted into the Environmental Code. First, anyone who conducts or has conducted an activity causing harm to the environment is responsible for remediation (Environmental Code, Ch 2, s 8). Secondly, the obligation to remedy pollution applies to an environmentally hazardous activity that has been conducted after 1 July 1969 (Environmental Code transitional provisions (SFS 1998: 811), s 8).

To sum up, all operators conducting an environmentally hazardous activity after 1 July 1969 are in principle jointly and severally liable for all pollution caused by that activity unless they can prove that they have had no part in the pollution. The time for causing the pollution is not relevant. Only those operators who have sold the activity before 1 July 1969 are not liable.

As explained in para 2.1 above, previous, current and future operators of a site are in principle jointly and severally liable to clean- up contaminated land or take other appropriate protective measures. The concept of ongoing environmentally hazardous activity in the case of continuous leakage from landfill and other industrial sites means that the landowner of such a site is also regarded as an operator, bearing the same liability as the actual operators. In the case of a simple land contamination, eg contamination by metals, only the landowner who has acquired the property after 1 January 1999 may be held liable for historical pollution.

The consequences of those provisions are of crucial importance both to a purchaser and seller of any business conducting environmentally hazardous activity. It is increasingly important to obtain evidence of any pollution at the time of purchase or lack of pollution at the time of transfer of the business. The liability of an operator who cannot clearly demonstrate that he has not contributed to the pollution will generally extend both to historical pollution caused by previous operators and to future pollution caused by successors.

At the same time, the purchaser or a seller of a business has to bear in mind that the remediation responsibility will only affect those persons, whether natural or legal, conducting the activity. If the activity is conducted by a company with limited liability, in Sweden an *AB*, in principle no one other than the legal entity of the company can be liable. Thus, the liability disappears with dissolution of the company. The consequence of this provision is clear. An operator who has not obtained evidence that he has not contributed to pollution may be held liable for the entire clear-up operation or for the costs of such an operation.

The proposal for the Environmental Code contained a provision giving liability not only to the company, but also to those companies or persons controlling the company. If this provision had been inserted in the adopted legislation, it would have meant a new approach to the principle of limited liabilities in certain companies. Following criticism, it was withdrawn from the final legislation. However, the government explicitly stated in the *travaux préparatoires* that this question would be dealt with in the process of a general revision of company law and, should this not be the case, the government would revert to a new proposal on liability in the environmental field for owners of limited liability companies.

3.3   Liabilities for off-site activities or impacts

Compensation for damage caused by off-site impacts from activities conducted on real property, eg through escape of hazardous or polluting material, is regulated in Ch 32 of the Environmental Code. According to section 1, damages are payable for personal injury, property damage and for purely financial loss. Financial loss that is not connected to personal injury or property damage is only compensated if the financial damage is of some significance.

The responsibility is strict for off-site impacts. However, damage that has not been caused intentionally or through negligence can only be compensated if:

(1) the disturbance should not reasonably be tolerated having regard to the situation in the area; and
(2) the disturbance generally does not occur under comparable circumstances, ie a certain level of disturbance must be tolerated from industrial activities.

Compensation shall be paid for damage caused by any of following disturbances:

(1) pollution of water areas;
(2) pollution of groundwater,
(3) change of groundwater level;
(4) air pollution;
(5) land pollution;
(6) noise;
(7) vibration; or
(8) other similar disturbance.

The causal link between the damage and the disturbance does not have to be absolutely proven. It is enough that there is a likely causal connection between the damage and the disturbance having regard to the nature of the damage and disturbance, other possible reasons for the damage and the circumstances in general. The person conducting the activity that has caused the damage will be held liable. There is no need for this person to be the owner of the property. In contrast to liability to remediate pollution, the liability to pay damages will become time-barred 10 years after the damaging event has taken place.

Liability for pollution in a waste management chain is not clearly regulated in the Swedish environmental legislation. There is no clear provision giving the responsibility to the waste generator. Once the waste generator has handed over the waste to an independent waste collector, it may in most cases be assumed that it is the collector and thereafter the treater of the waste that will be responsible for the pollution or other damage caused by this waste. This would at least be the case if the collector and subsequent treater have necessary permits to conduct their business.

The situation will become more complicated if the activity of, for example, the waste collector is conducted unlawfully. Consider the following: the collector of waste buries oil barrels in a forest instead of delivering them to a recycling facility. As regards the waste generator, it may be assumed that the general principles of liability to pay damages will apply. Thus, there must be intent or carelessness on his part. If he knew that the barrels were buried instead of treated, there might be an obligation to pay damages. There is also the possibility that the waste generator might also be considered as an operator of an environmentally hazardous activity, ie storage of waste. This would mean that he may be obliged to undertake measures to protect the environment according to the provisions of Chs 2 and 9 of the Environmental Code.

3.4 Liability of directors and managers

Intentional or negligent infringement of environmental legislation will trigger criminal liability for the directors and managers of the business. Primarily, it will be the managing director who will be assumed to be liable for any infringement. This presumption may be rebutted by presenting a written delegation plan within the company. If the infringement can be attributed rather to an organisational deficiency than lack of supervision in the day-to-day business, the members of the board may also be liable for this infringement. A general description of those issues has been given in para 3.1 above.

Criminal liability does not automatically constitute financial liability. Such liability presupposes causation of personal injury or property damage as a consequence of the crime. Many, if not most, of the infringements of environmental legislation will not lead to any such direct injury or damage. The commencement of environmentally hazardous activity requiring a permit or violation of an emission condition laid down

3.4 *Chapter 8*

in a permit are typical examples of such infringements. A director or manager who has committed this offence intentionally or negligently may have to face criminal liability. This does not mean that the environmental sanction charge imposed for the same offence has to be paid by the director or manager. The operator of the activity is liable for the charge. Thus the charge would remain unpaid, should the company go bankrupt and the receiver is left with no means to pay the charge.

3.5 Liability of those financing businesses

No lenders' liability has been introduced under the Environmental Code. There was a proposal for introduction of such liability, but it was withdrawn after massive lobbying from the financial institutions. Furthermore, there is an express exemption for banks assuming the liability of landowners in s 3 of Ch 9 of the Environmental Code. Banking institutions are free from this liability if they have assumed ownership of the polluted property with the aim of protecting their loans and the property in question serves as a collateral for the loan.

This lack of direct liability is not a carte blanche for those, particularly the banks, financing acquisitions or conducting business. Even though there is no direct liability, financial institutions will be indirectly concerned by the existence of pollution. It is conceivable that the introduction of the far-reaching provisions of the Environmental Code concerning the obligation to undertake remediation of polluted areas may cause negative real estate values. This may, of course, affect the likelihood of the financier getting his money back from the lender who is liable for remediation.

3.6 Transferability and other issues on validity of permits

The general description in section 2 above, particularly in para 2.4, clearly shows that the Swedish approach to regulating emissions and controlling environmentally hazardous activities is through individual applications and notifications and issuing of permits. Integrated pollution control can be said to be the leading star of the environmental legislation. The idea of one control mechanism has been accentuated by the introduction of the Environmental Code.

Since most environmentally hazardous activities are subject to the terms of a permit, the question whether the purchaser of a company may continue to enjoy the environmental permit or other concessions granted to the target company is of crucial importance not only to the purchaser but also to the financial providers and other parties that may be involved in the acquisition. The superseded Environmental Protection Act was silent on this point. The solution used in practice was a simple notification to the supervisory authority of the transfer of the business. No notification was required when only the ownership of the operating company was transferred and the identity of the legal person remains unchanged.

This practical solution was the consequence of the purpose behind the application procedure. The approval procedure determined whether an activity could be allowed having regard to its environmental consequences. The identity of the person applying for the permit was not that important. For example, a permit would not be refused on the grounds that the applicant previously had disregarded its obligations under environmental legislation or to demand that the applicant provided collateral for the potential expenses of cleaning up.

The Environmental Code now provides for specific control over the latter situations. The question of collateral is regulated in Ch 16, s 3 and the possibility to refuse the grant of a permit on grounds of previous infringements in s 6 in the same Chapter. This would suggest that a purchaser of a business or a part of business, where the identity of the person conducting the environmentally hazardous activity is changed, cannot automatically assume that he may enjoy the environmental permit granted to the seller. However, this interpretation is contradicted by a provision in s 32 of the Ordinance on Environmentally Hazardous Activity and Health Protection. According to this provision the supervisory authority has to be informed as soon as possible if an activity which is subject to a permit or a notification is conducted by somebody other than the person who has obtained the permit or made the notification. It is not clear if this provision for information is subject to the penal provision in the Environmental Code on impeding environmental control (Ch 29, s 6). However, the provision in the Ordinance shows that a purchaser normally can assume that he may enjoy the environmental permit granted for the conducted activity. The provision also indicates, although not explicitly, that no information has to be given to the supervisory authority if the identity of the party conducting the activity remains unaffected by the acquisition. Also a permit for taking water from natural resources or for other water undertaking may continue to be enjoyed by the purchaser after an acquisition.

According to the provisions of s 3 of Ch 24 of the Code, a permit may be completely or partially revoked in a number of situations. This may happen, for example, if the applicant has misled the permit authority and this is of significance for the permit. That could be the case if an acquisition is planned and it would be of importance to know the identity of the purchaser, as this may have affected whether or not a permit should have been issued. Another reason for revoking the permit may be non-compliance with a condition laid down in the permit. Collateral may be demanded according to s 3 of Ch 16 of the Code. The question of collateral must then be solved in the transaction between the parties in order to secure the continuous validity of the permit.

What is said above applies only to permits for environmentally hazardous activities or for taking water from natural sources. As indicated in para 2.5 above, transport of waste and handling of dangerous waste requires permits under the provisions of the Cleaning Ordinance and the Ordinance on Dangerous Waste. Under those ordinances, the county administrative boards are the permit authorities. They will have to consider whether the applicant for a permit has the personal, technical and financial resources to conduct the activities applied for. Thus, the permits are connected closely to the applicant. A purchaser of an activity will not enjoy the continuous validity of the permits; new applications have to be submitted. However, the validity of the permits is not affected if the identity of the operator remains unchanged after the acquisition.

3.7 Compliance cost increases

A permit for environmentally hazardous activity would appear to continue to be valid as regards the purchaser of such an activity. However, the purchaser should be aware of other provisions in the Environmental Code that may limit the validity of the permit and cause an increase of the environmental compliance costs:

(1) According to s 2 of Ch 16 of the Code, a permit may be issued for a limited period of time. The *travaux préparatoires* suggest that the aim of the legislation is that time limited permits should be the rule rather than the exception. This would be a major shift in comparison with permits issued under the Environmental Protection Act. Upon expiry of the permit, there will be an automatic reconsideration of the entire operation in conjunction with the application for a new permit.

3.7 *Chapter 8*

(2) A permit may be revoked or conditions may be changed if this is necessary in order to fulfil Sweden's obligations as a member of the European Union.
(3) A permit may be reconsidered for a number of reasons (see the Code, Ch 24, s 5), for example, where more than 10 years have passed since the issuing of the permit. Other reasons are, inter alia, the contravention of environmental quality norms and the possibility of obtaining a substantial improvement in health or the environment by using a new process or abatement control technique.

4   MANAGING ENVIRONMENTAL ISSUES IN TRANSACTIONS

4.1   Practice for assessment of risk

Assessment of environmental risks from an activity that may be hazardous to environment can be divided in two parts. First, there is the issue of monitoring effects on the environment in the ordinary course of ordinary business. Secondly, there is a need to assess the risks when selling or acquiring a company in Sweden or at the time of the formation of a joint venture.

Concerning the first question, there is so far no formal legislation concerning, for example, environmental audits. More and more companies have started to publish regularly a document that is called an environmental audit. However, such an audit is usually a informal presentation of the environmental effects connected with the activity of the company rather than an formal audit with figures stating the environmental liabilities or assets of the company. Of course, the audit will give the reader some idea about the environmental status of the company, but the value of such audits is for the time being limited and will remain so as long as there are no commonly accepted values for the use of air, water, natural resources etc.

A better way of checking the environmental status of an activity which requires environmental permits according to the provisions of the Environmental Code is the environmental report that must be submitted under s 20 of Ch 26. In the report, which is rather technical, the operator has to give information about the emissions and discharges caused by the activity. Also the use of, for example, water, chemical products and the production and management of waste must be accounted for. The report must state incidents and disturbances which occurred during the year.

The environmental report is also of great importance to the second question above. It has in practice proved to be an extremely useful instrument not only for the supervisory authorities, but also for a purchaser of the business. The report will enable, to some extent, an assessment of the technical status of the production facilities and will indicate the need of future investments. For example, in the past years, the information in the report on the use of CFCs assisted calculation of the costs of adopting the equipment necessary to comply with anticipated legislation on the banning of CFCs. In a similar way, the report can help to assess whether or not the activity is conducted according to relevant permits and other regulations.

At the time of an acquisition, the study of the environmental report and other available information should be combined with a more thorough investigation of the land where the activity is conducted. Samples and analysis of soil and water including groundwater should be undertaken. This is particularly important when there is a risk that the activity acquired may have caused or contributed to soil or water contamination. But also in other cases, this issue should be given special consideration. A remediation responsibility has been introduced in the Swedish legislation for the 'innocent' landowner acquiring the property when he should have known of the contamination. In addition, there is an obligation to inform the supervisory authority immediately of discovered contamination and failure to do this is subject to criminal charges. When considering whether or not to undertake an environmental investigation of land subject to acquisition, the purchaser should remember that it is the goal of the legislation to clean up as many contaminated areas as possible without the State or municipalities having to pay for this clean-up.

4.2 Contractual provisions

The joint and several liability for remediation of pollution for those conducting an environmental hazardous activity and for the landowners of contaminated land requires, besides the investigations described in para 4.1 above, attention when drafting an acquisition or merger agreement. This issue is equally important for the seller and the purchaser.

The principle of freedom of contract applies also to the regulation of environmental responsibilities. The parties can agree which one of them is going to be finally responsible for claims for remediation or damages or they can divide the responsibility between them as they see fit. However, the freedom of contract only extends as far as the relationship between the parties. Contractual arrangements will not limit the responsibility of the parties in respect of investigation and remediation claims from the authorities or claims for damages from third parties. The 'deepest pocket' principle prevails for those claims. The environmental investigation conducted on the occasion of the purchase showing the environmental status of the property at that time becomes crucial for the 'innocent' party's ability to limit as far as possible the extent of the claims that can be made by authorities and third parties.

There is another issue that should be addressed in the contract. The seller should guarantee that the activity has been conducted in accordance with permits and that all necessary permits and the like have been applied for and granted. This issue is connected with the importance of compliance with environmental legislation. First, non-compliance of the previous owner may cause the revocation or reconsideration of permits. Secondly, permits or other approvals may be refused if the operator has not satisfied its obligations under previous permits or has failed to apply for necessary permits. Thirdly, substantial environmental sanction charges may be imposed even if the infringement was caused by the previous owner.

4.3 Role of environmental management systems

There is an increasing tendency among the operators of environmentally hazardous activities to introduce environmental management systems. Two official systems may be chosen. Either registration in EMAS (Eco-management and Audit Scheme), a voluntary scheme of the EU, or certification according to ISO 14000. Generally, the certification under ISO 14000 is the preferred method.

Beside the positive image effects that follow the introduction of any recognised environmental management system, other positive effects are likely to follow. It will become easier to monitor compliance with environmental regulations since the operator is obliged to introduce a monitoring system working on a continuous basis. It is conceivable that such compliance saves money for the operator and makes it possible to better foresee the need for amendments or applications for permits. The latter is very important considering the time taken for applications.

There is another advantage in introducing an environmental management system.

4.3 Chapter 8

Depending on the activity, the operator may have to pay substantial yearly supervision fees to the authorities even though no supervision is actually conducted in a particular year. For example, the fee for a paper pulp plant with a production of more than 200,000 tons a year amounts to SEK 113,000 and for an incineration plant designed for dangerous waste, SEK 250,000. A proposal has been presented that the supervision fees may be reduced by half for operators certified according to ISO 14000 or registered in EMAS.

4.4 Structuring of companies

As described at para 3.2 above, liability for environmental costs is limited to the person conducting the business. Liability can then be limited, particularly for future clean-up costs, by conducting the environmentally hazardous activity in the form of a limited company, which is very common. Utilising a limited company which does not conduct any other business is a further possibility, but is quite rare. In order to limit to some extent the possibility of circumventing the obligations to undertake remediation measures according to the different provisions of the Environmental Code, the provision of collateral for such expenses has been introduced. According to s 3 of Ch 16 of the Code, the provision of collateral may be made a condition for the grant of the environmental permit.

Another issue connected to the structuring of companies is the question of an internal delegation plan. Without the existence of such plan, the managing director and/or the board will be held liable for infringements of the environmental legislation. Such infringements often constitute criminal offences. As a general rule, liability cannot be delegated without the necessary power to make appropriate decisions to avoid the infringements. A delegation plan must be written and the delegation itself should be expressly accepted by the person to whom the liability is delegated.

4.5 Insurance

Chapter 33 of the Environmental Code provides for the continuation of an environmental damage insurance introduced under the superseded Environmental Protection Act and for the establishment of clean-up insurance. Everybody conducting an environmentally hazardous activity that requires a permit or has to be notified is under a duty to pay a yearly insurance contribution. The insurance is handled by a pool of private insurance companies. Compensation from the insurance schemes will be paid for personal injury and property loss caused by environmentally hazardous activity respectively for the remediation of contaminated land. A precondition in both cases is that the party liable for the damage cannot pay.

A company conducting environmentally hazardous activities is advised to enter into an insurance contract concerning the environmental liability. This private contract will not affect the obligation to pay contributions under the compulsory schemes described above. The policy cost of the company's own insurance will of course vary considerably depending on the nature and extent of the conducted activity. There will normally be a limit to the compensation paid under the insurance. Damage caused intentionally or by gross negligence will generally be excluded from the insurance cover.

5 CONCLUSION

Through the introduction of the Environmental Code from 1 January 1999 there has been a major shift in the Swedish environmental legislation. More areas are now covered. The concept of integrated pollution control has been widened to accommodate matters such as those relating to resource management and the eco-cycle principles. At the same time, the general rules of consideration are now applicable to all measures affecting the environment or health.

The new legislation will now have to be consolidated. There is a need for new jurisprudence explaining how the different provisions of the Code should be interpreted and applied. This need applies both for provisions that have been left seemingly unchanged and for new or amended provisions. The application of the new waste definition will have to clarified. In addition, the practical work of the new environmental courts has to be established.

The substantial legislation changes have already been undertaken. However, it is clear from legislative statements that the very important question of environmental liability of owners of limited companies will be revised. Finally, future adaptation of the Swedish legislation to European rules will be necessary. The pending directive on landfills is a specific example of the work that remains to be done.

Chapter 9

SPAIN

Bernat Mullerat

Bufete Mullerat

1 INTRODUCTION

1.1 Jurisdiction over environmental protection

Under the Spanish Constitution of 1978 jurisdiction over environmental protection is broadly divided between the State and 17 autonomous communities (*Comunidades Autónomas*).

The State has exclusive jurisdiction to enact basic environmental legislation. In addition, the State has exclusive jurisdiction over criminal and civil law, without prejudice to the power of some autonomous communities to preserve and develop existing civil laws.

At present, all autonomous communities have power to develop the State's basic legislation, to pass stricter laws and regulations and to execute policy on the management of environmental protection. The autonomous communities' environmental legislation has two main features: (a) it is only applicable in the territory of the relevant autonomous community, and (b) it may not contradict the State's basic legislation.

Thus, Spanish environmental law is made up of:

(1) Criminal and civil law, which may only be enacted by the State, although some autonomous communities are entitled to preserve and develop existing civil laws.
(2) Basic administrative laws and regulations passed by the State which are applicable throughout Spain.
(3) Administrative laws and regulations passed by the autonomous communities.

Finally, it should be pointed out that local authorities are entitled to regulate a number of issues relating to the protection of the urban environment, including noise limits. Such controls are normally enacted in the form of local regulations (*ordenanzas municipales*). However, the main role of local authorities is basically the enforcement of environmental protection under the terms of the state and autonomous communities' legislation.

1.2 Similarities with law applying in associate jurisdictions

As stated above, the State's environmental laws and regulations constitute the common ground of Spanish environmental law. However, autonomous communities have, to a varying degree, used their power to develop the State's legislation and to adopt stricter rules within their jurisdiction. For instance, whilst some autonomous communities (such as the Basque Country and Murcia) have enacted a framework Act on environmental protection, others (such as Catalonia) have passed highly developed provisions on waste management and atmospheric pollution, whilst their most active role is mainly the setting up and enforcement of environmental policies.

In broad terms, it may be argued that most autonomous communities rely on the State's environmental protection laws and regulations.

1.3 Basic structure of law

Spanish environmental law is based entirely on statute. The main sources of environmental law are Acts enacted by the State or the autonomous communities' parliaments which may in turn be developed by governmental regulations (*reglamentos*) and orders (*órdenes ministeriales*). In some cases, legislation requires implementation by regulations before it may be enforced (eg see para 2.2 below).

Spanish law does not have a principal environmental protection Act from which other more specific laws and regulations are derived. Instead, legislation takes a piecemeal approach by separately regulating each area (eg water, waste, air and noise). However, some areas such as waste are regulated through a framework Act that provides the basic principles and general provisions, which are then developed through other Acts and which may, in turn, be developed by regulations and orders.

Even though Spanish environmental law is based on statute, the case law of the Supreme Court provides a complementary source of law which constitutes an essential tool in anticipating the courts' interpretation of environmental laws and regulations.

EC law has had a decisive influence on Spanish environmental law. New legislation has been introduced to implement EC directives as well as the adoption of various maximum standards. For instance, Directive (EEC) 76/464 on pollution caused by hazardous substances discharged to water (and Directives (EEC) 82/176, 84/156, 84/491, 85/513 and 86/280) have given rise to detailed national standards on the discharge of certain hazardous substances to water.

European directives are implemented through Acts or regulations. Controversy may, however, arise in cases where the implementation of directives should be made by the autonomous communities whilst only the State is responsible for implementation vis-à-vis the EU. For instance, in *Commission v Spain*[1] the Commission brought an action against Spain under art 169 of the EC Treaty for failure to fulfil its obligations under arts 3 and 4 of Directive (EEC) 91/676 on the protection of waters against pollution caused by nitrates from agricultural sources. Spain argued that such delay resulted, inter alia, from the fact that the State and the autonomous communities have concurrent powers in the fields covered by that directive. The European Court of Justice rejected the arguments of the Spanish defence and held that 'a State may not plead provisions and practices or circumstances existing in its internal legal system in order to justify a failure to comply with the obligations and time-limits laid down in a Directive'.

As with most EU member states, not all EC directives have been implemented properly or on time. Nonetheless, the level of implementation of EC law in Spain may be considered acceptable although the European Court of Justice has, on a number of

---

1 Case 71/97 *Commission v Spain* [1998] E.C.R. I-5991.

occasions, condemned Spain for failing to implement directives adequately (eg ECJ Judgments of 12 February 1998,[2] 1 October 1998[3] and 25 November 1998[4]).

1.4 Structure of environmental regulatory agencies

Jurisdiction over environmental protection is divided among the various levels of public authorities: the State, the autonomous communities and the local authorities. The State and the autonomous communities exercise their powers over environmental protection either directly or through specialised autonomous agencies.

1.4.1 The State

The Ministry of Environment (MoE) was created in 1996 and is located in Madrid. The MoE has the major responsibility within government for environmental matters. It is not only responsible for setting the government's environmental policy but also for the exercise of those powers granted to the government.

The MoE is internally divided into the following departments: Secretary of State for Water and the Coast, the Subsecretary of Environment and the General Secretary of Environment.

However, other government ministries, such as the Ministry of Public Works, the Ministry of Agriculture, Fisheries and Food and the Ministry of Industry and Energy, retain powers in relation to certain environmental matters.

In addition, there are a number of different agencies involved in environmental protection, including:

(1) Environmental Advisory Council (*Consejo Asesor de Medio Ambiente*), which advises the State Government on environmental protection and is attached to the Ministry of Public Works.
(2) Water Boards (*Confederaciones Hidrográficas*), which exercise the powers of the State over rivers flowing through more than one autonomous community. Such powers include the grant of discharge permits and of authorisations to take water from natural resources. Water boards are attached to the MoE.
(3) Nuclear Energy Council (*Junta de Energía Nuclear*), which exercises certain powers over nuclear energy and is attached to the Ministry of Industry and Energy.

1.4.2 Autonomous communities

The structure of autonomous communities' environmental authorities is not homogeneous. However, the structure of regional environmental authorities follows two major trends:

(1) Autonomous communities with a Department of Environment (La Rioja, Aragon, Valencia, Catalonia, Andalucia and Murcia).
(2) Autonomous communities where environmental regulators are within different departments, such as the Department of Public Works, the Department of Agriculture or other departments (Cantabria, Canary Islands, Navarra, Basque

---

2 Case 92/96 *Commission v Spain* [1998] E.C.R. I-505.
3 Case 71/97 *Commission v Spain* [1998] E.C.R. I-5991.
4 Case 214/96 *Commission v Spain* [1998] E.C.R. I-7661.

1.4 *Chapter 9*

Country, Castilla–Leon, Castilla–La Mancha and Asturias). In some instances, there is a specific Environmental Protection Agency within the Department of Public Works (Madrid and Extremadura).

Some autonomous communities have created independent agencies within the Department of Environment with powers over specific areas. In Catalonia, for instance, the Catalan government's policy and enforcement powers over waste are exercised by the Waste Board (*Junta de Residuos*), whilst powers over water quality are exercised by the Water Agency (*Agencia Catalana del Agua*).

1.4.3 Local authorities

Jurisdiction over local environmental matters falls upon the municipality (*Ayuntamiento*). In greater metropolitan areas, some regulatory and enforcement powers are delegated to a supra-municipal entity.

2 OUTLINE OF ENVIRONMENTAL LAW RELEVANT TO MERGER AND ACQUISITION TRANSACTIONS

When conducting a merger or an acquisition transaction, it is essential to look into the various areas of environmental law which may affect a given target. In addition, particular attention should be drawn to the location of such target since (1) the applicable environmental regulations may differ depending on the autonomous community involved, and (2) the level of enforcement may vary.

2.1 Classified activities licence

Under Decree 2414/1961 of 30 November on Harmful, Unsanitary, Noxious and Dangerous Activities, those activities classified as harmful, unsanitary, noxious and dangerous are subject to a prior authorisation: the licence of classified activities (*licencia de actividades clasificadas*).

Facilities or activities are considered as 'classified' if they are deemed to be:

(1) harmful (ie if the noise, vibration, smoke or smell produced may cause a discomfort);
(2) unsanitary (ie if they give rise to substances that may adversely affect human health);
(3) noxious (ie if they may cause damage to agriculture, forestry, stockbreeding or fish-farming); or
(4) hazardous (ie if they involve the manufacture, management or storage of substances capable of causing serious risks of explosion, combustion, radiation and the like).

Annex 1 to Decree 2414/1961 contains a non-comprehensive list of activities which are considered as 'classified activities'. Most commercial and industrial facilities fall under the category of classified activities, from cafeterias and cinemas to nuclear energy installations.

The licence of classified activities must be applied for prior to the commencement of operations and is granted by the municipality where the facility is to be located or the activity undertaken. The application must include a technical report and a memorandum describing the activities to be carried out, their potential impact on the environment and the technical measures to prevent or reduce such impact, including safety measures.

The licence of classified activities seeks to control those effects of a given activity which alter the safety or hygiene of the environment or which may cause damage or create risks for persons or property. The licence covers a broad range of areas such as noise, location of the facility, safety measures and air pollution.

Any facility carrying out classified activities without this licence is considered unlawful and may be closed down by the municipality. The Supreme Court has consistently upheld municipalities' orders to close down facilities in the absence of a licence of classified activities, even if the facility has been in operation for many years and with the acquiescence of the municipality or other public authorities (Supreme Court Judgments of 5 May 1987, 17 October 1989, 26 May 1996 and 26 June 1998).

It should be pointed out, however, that the licence of classified activities is not effective unless the municipality has inspected the facility to ensure that the conditions and corrective measures imposed in the licence have been complied with and that the relevant corrective measures have been installed effectively.[5] Thus, facilities which have been granted a licence of classified activities may not start operations until such inspection takes place and confirms that the facility satisfies the licence conditions. This control or inspection is generally referred to as a 'checking minute' (*visita de comprobación* or *acta de puesta en marcha*).

The licence of classified activities must be amended and updated when there is a change in the factual background on which the licence was granted. Thus, the incorporation of new equipment or industrial processes to a facility requires the grant of an amendment or expansion of the licence.

The licence of classified activities is granted without prejudice to other authorisations or permits covering specific matters under the applicable legislation, such as waste management, discharge permits, air pollution controls, and so on.

Decree 2414/1961 is applicable in the absence of autonomous communities' regulation on this matter. Until recently, it has been applied over the whole territory of Spain. However, a few autonomous communities have recently passed legislation derogating from Decree 2414/1961:

(1) Canary Islands Act 1/1998 of 8 January on Public Events and Classified Activities. This Act provides a new licensing regime for classified activities and existing facilities were required to adapt to this new regime no later than 14 January 1999.
(2) Catalan Act 3/1998 of 27 February on Integrated Intervention of Environmental Authorities. This Act came into force on 13 April 1999 and provides that facilities with a licence of classified activities granted in accordance with Decree 2414/1961 must apply for a new licence within a given term under the provisions of the Catalan Act.
(3) Basque Country Act 3/1998 of 27 February on Environmental Protection, arts 55–56, provide a new regulation of licensing classified activities.

2.2 Contaminated land

The Spanish regulation of contaminated land is contained in two articles of Act 10/1998 of 21 April on Waste ('the Waste Act').

---

5   Decree 2414/1961, art 34. See Supreme Court Judgments of 30 May 1989 and 18 October 1989.

2.2 Chapter 9

According to art 27.1 of the Waste Act, each autonomous community shall issue an inventory of contaminated properties ('the Contaminated Land Inventory') on the basis of the criteria and standards approved by the Spanish government. The Contaminated Land Inventory will be used to prepare a list of priority actions taking into consideration the risk posed by contaminated properties on human health and the environment.

The main consequence of the inclusion of a property in the Contaminated Land Inventory is the obligation to clean the property up under the terms and conditions imposed by the autonomous community. Such obligation, however, is not automatic but requires the autonomous community's prior clean-up order.

The obligation to clean-up falls, first, upon polluters. Where two or more polluters have contributed to the contamination of a property, they are jointly and severally liable for the clean-up obligations contemplated in the Waste Act. Therefore, if there is more than one polluter, the autonomous community may order any of them to clean-up the land. Such polluter may subsequently recover from other liable parties the clean-up costs attributable to their actions.

In the event that the polluter cannot be identified, then the occupier and, subsequently, the landowner are liable for the clean-up of the land.

According to art 28 of the Waste Act, those responsible for the clean-up of contaminated land (ie polluters, possessors and landowners) may enter into voluntary agreements in order to determine each party's contribution to the remediation operations. If public authorities participate in such agreements, tax incentives may be granted for the financing of clean-up operations.

Public funds may only be granted for the financing of clean-up provided that the parties involved agree that any increase in value on the property will revert to the funding authority.

It should be noted that in Spain there are no soil quality standards analogous to the Dutch standards. However, some autonomous communities (eg Catalonia and the Basque Country) have issued provisional standards for soil quality evaluation. These have no binding effect but may only be used for guidance purposes.

On the other hand, the Waste Act provides that the government shall publish a list of potentially polluting activities.[6] Owners of properties where any potentially land polluting activity has been carried out must disclose this fact in the event of a transfer of the ownership of the property. Once this list is published, property transactions involving contaminated land will need to take environmental considerations into account. Over time, this will change Spanish legal practice on property transactions.

The Waste Act provides that failure to execute clean-up operations pursuant to a clean-up order, and breach of the terms of voluntary clean-up agreements constitute very serious violations. Such violations are subject to a fine of between Pta 5 million and Pta 200 million, save if they involve hazardous waste, in which case the fine will range from Pta 50 million to Pta 200 million.[7]

However, the enforcement of the contaminated land provisions of the Waste Act require regulatory development both at the State and autonomous community level. For instance, autonomous communities must issue the Inventory of Contaminated Land and the Spanish government must publish the list of potentially polluting activities. At the time of writing, no such regulatory development has been enacted and it is difficult to anticipate how, if at all, these provisions will be developed and enforced.

---

6 Waste Act, art 27.4.
7 Ibid, art 35.1.

2.3 Pollution of water resources

The basic regulation of water resources is (a) the Water Act 29/1985 of 2 August, covering continental waters and developed mainly through the Regulation on the Public Hydrological Zone, and (b) the Coast Act 22/1988 of 28 July, broadly covering the coastline and the territorial sea and developed through the Coast Regulation.

2.3.1 Continental waters

In principle all continental water resources (including surface and groundwater) are integrated in the so-called public hydrological zone (*dominio público hidráulico*), which belongs to the State.

Article 89 of the Water Act prohibits:

(1) carrying out any direct or indirect discharges which pollute water resources,
(2) storage of solid waste, rubbish or any substance which constitutes or is capable of constituting a risk of pollution of water resources or their surroundings,
(3) carrying out any operations on the physical or biological water environment which adversely affect or are capable of adversely affecting the water environment, and
(4) carrying out any activity within the protection zones, which may pose a contamination risk or cause an impairment of the public hydrological domain.

Water contamination is defined as 'the action and effect of introducing substances or forms of energy or conditions into water which may, directly or indirectly, adversely affect the quality of water in relation to the future use or the ecological purpose of water'.[8] In addition, the concept of the impairment of the public hydrological zone includes adverse alterations of the zone's surroundings.

According to art 108 of the Water Act, acts (and omissions) which damage the public hydraulic domain constitute an administrative violation subject to a fine of up to Pta 100 million depending on the amount of the damage. In addition to the payment of the relevant fines, water authorities may require polluters of water resources to repair and restore environmental conditions to their state prior to the damage.[9] Such obligations fall on the wrongdoer and, subsequently, on the accomplices and accessories.[10]

2.3.2 Marine water

Under the Coast Act, the public marine zone comprises the coastline, the beaches, the territorial sea and the natural resources of the economic zone and the continental shelf.

Unauthorised discharges as well as the acts and omissions which damage or impair the coastline or marine water or the use thereof constitute an administrative violation,[11] subject to a fine of up to Pta 50 million.[12]

Without prejudice to the applicable administrative and/or criminal liability, the wrongdoer shall restore environmental conditions to their state prior to the damage and pay for the damage caused.[13] If such restoration is not feasible and, in any event, if irreparable damage persists, the wrongdoer is liable to pay a compensatory sum as determined by the government. The following criteria is used to assess this sum:

---

8 Water Act, art 85.
9 Ibid, art 110.
10 Regulation on the Public Hydrological Zone, art 325.2.
11 Coast Act, art 91.2.
12 Ibid, art 97.1(a).
13 Ibid, art 95.1.

2.3 Chapter 9

(1) hypothetical cost of restoration;
(2) value of damage to property;
(3) cost of the damaging activity or project; and
(4) profit obtained from the wrongdoing activity.[14]

2.4 Authorisations for discharges to water and for taking water from natural resources

2.4.1 Continental waters

According to art 92 of the Water Act, any activity capable of polluting or impairing the public hydrological zone and in particular the release of waste water or substances that may pollute continental waters requires prior authorisation (the discharge permit or *permiso de vertidos*).

The discharge permit covers, at a minimum, the following items:

(1) the water treatment equipment and control systems necessary for the operation;
(2) maximum limits imposed on the discharged effluent;
(3) the amount of pollution tax due;
(4) the actions to be adopted by the permit holder in case of emergency;
(5) the term of validity; and
(6) the events of revocation.

The permits and authorisations required for the establishment, amendment or transfer of polluting or potentially polluting facilities or industries (eg the licence of classified activities) must be made conditional on the grant of the discharge permit.[15]

The discharge permit may be amended or provisionally suspended if the circumstances that led to its grant are altered or if new events arise that would have justified the refusal of the permit or its grant with different conditions. In addition, the discharge permit may be revoked in the event of breach of its conditions.

The discharge of waste water without a discharge permit capable of causing damage of up to Pta 750,000 constitutes a serious administrative violation subject to a fine of up to Pta 15 million.

With respect to the taking of water from natural resources, in principle, landowners are entitled to use up to 7,000m^3 of water from on-site surface or underground sources without prior authorisation.[16] The use of water in excess of 7,000m^3 requires either an express legal provision or an administrative concession (*concesión administrativa*). Administrative concessions are granted for a maximum period of 75 years, although they may expire prior to the due date in the event of (a) breach of conditions imposed in the concession, (b) public taking of the concession, or (c) the title holder's waiver.

2.4.2 Marine water

The Coast Act generally provides that all discharges from land to the sea require a prior discharge permit.[17] However, if such discharges contain polluting substances, applicants must demonstrate the impossibility or difficulty of using an alternative

---

14 Ibid, art 100.2.
15 Water Act, art 95.
16 Regulation on the Public Hydrological Zone, arts 83 et seq.
17 Coast Act, art 57.

solution for the elimination or treatment of waste water. Under no circumstances may substances or forms of energy be introduced into marine water which may present an unacceptable risk for the environment and human health, under applicable legislation.

The discharge permit must contain conditions governing the discharge, including:

(1) the term (which may not exceed 30 years);
(2) the treatment and discharge equipment and control systems to be used;
(3) the authorised annual volume of discharge;
(4) discharge quality standards;
(5) an assessment of the impact of the discharge on the marine environment and water quality objectives; and
(6) the applicable discharge fee, which is based on the polluting substances contained in the discharge.[18]

These conditions may be amended by the licensing authority (without compensation to the permit holder) when the circumstances surrounding the grant of the permit have changed or new circumstances have arisen.

According to the Coast Regulation, the discharge permit may require, under certain circumstances, that the management of the facility be undertaken by a technical specialist or that a company co-operating with the government is retained to maintain the facility.[19]

The discharge of hazardous substances from land to the sea is regulated by Royal Decree 258/1989 of 10 March, which implements Directives (EEC) 76/464 and 86/280. The discharge of hazardous substances (listed in annex II to Royal Decree 258/1989) requires a prior authorisation from the relevant autonomous community, which is reviewed every 4 years. Furthermore, Royal Decree 258/1989 sets out control procedures to monitor compliance with the maximum discharge limits imposed in the authorisation.

Discharging waste water without a discharge permit constitutes a serious administrative violation subject to a fine of up to Pta 50 million.[20]

According to the Coast Act, liability for administrative violations falls upon the following natural or legal persons:

(1) in the event of a breach of an administrative authorisation, on the holder of the authorisation,
(2) in other cases, on the operator of an activity or facility, the contractor and the technical supervisor.[21]

2.5 Emissions to the atmosphere

The Air Protection Act 38/1972 of 22 December constitutes the framework legislation on air pollution and is further developed by Decree 833/1975 of 6 February. These framework rules are applicable throughout Spain, although specific regional legislation has been passed in Catalonia (ie Catalan Air Protection Act 22/1983 of 21 November), where such legislation applies in addition to the national framework rules insofar as it does not contravene the national rules.

---

18 Ibid, art 58.
19 Coast Regulation, art 118.
20 Coast Act, art 97.1(a).
21 Ibid, art 93.

2.5 Chapter 9

Annex II to Decree 833/1975 contains a list of potentially air polluting activities. Such activities are required to comply with the maximum emission levels prescribed in annex IV without any prior order or act on the part of public authorities.

The commencement, amendment or relocation of a potentially air polluting activity requires the prior review and assessment of the technical project by public authorities (except for those activities included in category C of annex II). Public authorities must certify that the technical project complies with the necessary conditions and the maximum emission limits.[22] The air pollution assessment issued by public authorities is binding for the grant or refusal of the licence of classified activities and the imposition of conditions on potentially air polluting activities.[23]

With respect to monitoring compliance, art 72 of Decree 833/1975 provides that the competent authority may require the installation of equipment to monitor compliance with maximum emission limits. In addition, activities in category A of annex II must measure the pollutants discharged into the air twice a month and carry out other weekly measurements. Activities in category B are only required to perform periodic emission controls.

In view of the air quality standards, public authorities must assess the amount of contamination caused by each industrial area and take appropriate measures to correct any anomaly observed and initiate administrative proceedings, if applicable.[24]

Violations of the provisions of the Air Protection Act or Decree 833/1975 are subject to a fine of up to Pta 500,000. In the case of repeated serious violations, public authorities may opt for imposing a fine of Pta 500,000 or may order the provisional closure of the facility until the breach has been corrected through the adoption of the appropriate corrective measures. In addition, if violations are committed in areas declared as highly polluted or in emergency situations, the amount of the fine may be doubled or tripled.

There are also a number of regulations setting out maximum allowable limits for specific substances in the atmosphere. Such regulations were adopted to implement EC directives. Air quality standards have been established for sulphur dioxide (Royal Decree 1613/1985 of 1 August[25]), nitrogen dioxide and lead (Royal Decree 717/1987 of 27 May) and asbestos (Royal Decree 108/1991 of 1 February).

With respect to the control of air pollution from specific activities or installations, the main regulations relate to large fuel-burning installations and waste incinerators. Large fuel-burning installations are regulated by Royal Decree 646/1991 of 22 April,[26] which brings Spanish law in line with the requirements of Directive (EC) 88/609. Royal Decree 1088/1992 of 11 September implements Directives (EEC) 89/369 and 89/429 and provides the technical parameters to be applied to municipal waste incinerators and maximum emission limits for certain heavy metals, chloridric and fluoridric acids.

2.6 Waste management

The basic legislation on waste is the Waste Act 10/1998 of 21 April, which provides common regulation for all types of waste and may be developed through regulations on specific categories of waste. In addition, Royal Decree 833/1988 of 20 July[27] (the

---

22 Decree 833/1975, art 56.
23 Ibid, art 57.
24 Ibid, art 76.2.
25 As amended by Royal Decree 1321/1992 of 30 October.
26 As amended by Royal Decree 1800/1995 of 3 November.
27 As amended by Royal Decree 952/1997 of 20 June.

Hazardous Waste Regulation) provides a detailed regulation of hazardous waste producers, carriers and managers.

As a general principle, waste management activities must be performed without endangering human health or using methods which may adversely affect the environment or constitute a risk to water, air, land, fauna or flora or be capable of creating nuisance.[28]

According to art 9 of the Waste Act and art 10.1 of the Hazardous Waste Regulation, the installation, amendment or relocation of facilities producing or importing hazardous waste[29] are subject to prior administrative authorisation. Such authorisation shall determine, inter alia, the conditions and requirements of the waste production activity as well as the maximum production amount per unit and the characteristics of the hazardous waste to be produced.[30] In addition, the licensing authority may require hazardous waste producers to obtain insurance coverage for any liability arising from the waste production activities.

According to art 21 of the Waste Act and the Hazardous Waste Regulation, hazardous waste producers are required to comply with the following obligations:

(1) Formal obligations:
 (a) to keep a record of the produced or imported hazardous waste and the destination thereof,
 (b) to submit an annual report prior to 1 March to the competent authority indicating, at a minimum, the volume, nature and final destination of the produced or imported hazardous waste,[31]
 (c) to inform public authorities in the event of the disappearance, loss or release of hazardous waste,
 (d) to provide authorised waste managers with the necessary information to ensure appropriate treatment and elimination,
 (e) to complete the hazardous waste control and monitoring documents from the place of production until delivery to the collection, treatment or elimination centres, and
 (f) to request from the hazardous waste manager a formal acceptance of any waste intended for transfer.

(2) Material obligations:
 (a) to separate hazardous waste adequately, avoiding any mixing which may increase the danger or difficulty of management,
 (b) to comply with packaging and labelling requirements,
 (c) to label the containers or packaging containing hazardous waste in a clear, legible and indelible manner, and
 (d) to have available storage areas for the subsequent treatment of hazardous waste.

Those possessing waste are required to transfer it to a waste manager for the purposes of its recovery or elimination.[32] The activities of waste recovery or elimination require

---

28 Waste Act, art 12.
29 Article 3 of the Waste Act defines hazardous waste as those types of waste included in Royal Decree 952/1997 as well as the containers thereof and those types of waste classified as hazardous waste by law or by the Spanish government pursuant to European regulations on international conventions.
30 Small producers of hazardous waste (ie those producing less than 10,000 kg per year) who are registered in a specific registry created by the autonomous communities may be exempted from holding such prior authorisation.
31 Small producers of hazardous waste may be exempted from this requirement.
32 Waste Act, art 11.

2.6   Chapter 9

a prior administrative authorisation, although the autonomous communities may, under certain circumstances, exempt on-site facilities for recovery or elimination of non-hazardous waste from such requirement. In any event, licenced recovery or elimination facilities must keep a record of the nature, origin, destination, frequency of collection, transportation and treatment method of the managed waste.[33]

Article 22 of the Waste Act provides that the collection, storage and, under certain circumstances, the transportation of hazardous waste are subject to prior administrative authorisation. Such authorisation, as well as the authorisation of recovery and elimination of hazardous waste, is granted only if the waste process operator obtains civil liability insurance coverage and provides a guarantee for an amount to be determined in the authorisation.

Transportation of hazardous waste requires, in addition to the relevant licence, compliance with the documentary requirements set out in the Waste Act.

Violations are classified into three categories: minor, serious and very serious. Very serious violations include the carrying out of an activity without the required licence or breach of licence conditions, uncontrolled abandonment of hazardous waste or of non-hazardous waste provided there is a risk to human health or the environment, and the delivery or transfer of hazardous waste to persons other than those specified in the Waste Act. Very serious violations are subject to a fine of up to Pta 5 million to Pta 200 million, save if they involve hazardous waste, in which case the fine will range from Pta 50 million to Pta 200 million and a prohibition against carrying out any of the activities contemplated in the Waste Act in the future.

According to art 32 of the Waste Act, liability under the Act is joint and several if (a) the waste possessor or manager delivers such waste to persons other than those specified in the Act, or (2) there are various liable parties and it is not feasible to determine the contribution of each to the violation.

With respect to administrative liability, art 33 of the Waste Act states that no administrative liability shall attach to those who transfer waste to an authorised manager provided that such delivery is performed in compliance with the legal requirements and, in any case, is evidenced in writing.

Finally, art 36 of the Waste Act provides that, without prejudice to criminal and administrative liability, violators shall restore environmental conditions to the state prior to when the violation took place.

With respect to the management of packaging and packaging waste, Act 11/1997 of 24 April on Packaging and Packaging Waste has brought Spanish law in line with the requirements of Directive (EC) 94/62.

In broad terms, Act 11/1997 puts in place a deposit and return scheme which is compulsory for packagers, traders of packaged products and, under certain circumstances, those responsible for selling packaged products. The final possessor of packaging waste or used packaging must deliver such materials to a business for its re-utilisation, recovery or recycling.

However, packagers, traders of packaged products and, under certain circumstances, those responsible for selling packaged products may be exempted from their obligations to adopt a deposit and return scheme provided they participate in an integrated management system (IMS). The IMSs are agreements between businesses for the purposes of periodical collection of used packaging and packaging waste at the consumer's residence or in the nearby area.

The IMSs are financed through the packagers' payment of a charge for each packaged product placed in the national market. Participating packagers are entitled to identify the packaging included in the IMS with a logo.

---

33   Ibid, art 13.

2.7 Land use planning/zoning

Planning law is a highly regulated area in Spain. The framework legislation is Act 6/1998 of 13 April on Land ('the Land Act') and certain provisions of Royal Legislative Decree 1/1992, of 26 June, as well as the various Acts passed by the autonomous communities. In addition to these generally applicable Acts, attention must be drawn to the local planning regulations (*Plan General de Ordenación Urbana*, *Plan Parcial*) issued by the municipality where the facility is located.

According to the Land Act, local planning regulations may classify land into three main categories:

(1) Urban land—where infrastructure works are already completed and the land is ready to be developed. Urban land is generally regulated in great detail, particularly with respect to the permitted use, volume and hygienic conditions of the properties.
(2) Developable land—which may be developed in accordance with specific local planning regulations called partial plans. Partial plans set out the different permitted uses of the land, the zoning of each sector into areas based on the permitted uses, as well as the public interest services and infrastructure (eg schools, health centres, parks, sports facilities). Partial plans also determine the percentage of property which landowners must assign to the municipality for the purposes of locating public services and infrastructure.
(3) Non-developable land—which local planning regulations consider worthy of special protection due to its agricultural, forestry, historic, cultural or environmental value.

Once the local planning regulations have been adopted, the municipality may initiate, at its own initiative or on request by the landowners concerned, the undertaking of development. The development may be carried out through any of the following systems (*sistemas de actuación*):

(1) *Compensación*: the planning initiative is led by landowners organised in a Compensation Board (*Junta de Compensación*). Landowners must not only bear the cost of urbanisation works but also execute such works themselves. In addition, landowners must transfer the land required for locating public services and infrastructure to the municipality.
(2) *Cooperación*: landowners transfer the land required for locating public interest services and infrastructure to the municipality and the municipality in turn executes the urbanisation works at the landowners' expense. In addition, landowners must transfer the land required for locating public interest services and infrastructure to the municipality.
(3) *Expropiación urbanística*: the public authority undertakes a compulsory purchase of property for the purposes of executing the planning of a given area.

Building as well as other works on the land (eg interior works, removal of soil and demolition) are subject to a prior licence from the planning authority ('the licence of works'). The licence of works is essentially aimed at ensuring that the projected works comply with the local planning regulations. In general the licence of works must be applied for subsequent to or simultaneously with the licence of classified activities in order to avoid the possibility that a building or facility is completed but may not become operational due to the lack of a licence of classified activities.

In addition to the planning requirements, a number of projects are made subject to compulsory environmental impact assessment as provided by Royal Legislative Decree 1302/1996 of 28 June on Environmental Impact Assessment and Royal Decree 1131/1988 of 30 September,[34] which implement Directive (EEC) 85/337. The projects in the mandatory list include: crude oil refineries, thermal power stations and nuclear power stations, facilities for asbestos extraction, chemical installations, special roads, long distance railway lines, airports, ports and hazardous waste incineration installations.

Planning violations are governed by the Planning Disciplinary Regulation.[35] In broad terms, planning violations may be classified in two main categories:

(1) *Formal violations* which constitute a breach of the procedural requirements and may be remedied.
(2) *Material violations* which constitute a breach of the applicable planning requirements and may not be remedied.

The main violations include the execution of works without the necessary permit and the execution of works in breach of the planning regulations. The fines attached to planning violations are generally calculated on a percentage of the value of the works performed and may, under certain circumstances, include restoring the physical elements altered as a consequence of the illegal act.

2.8 Use and storage of hazardous substances including radioactive material

The use of hazardous substances in Spain is mainly governed by the Regulation on Notice of New Substances and Classification, Packaging and Labelling of Hazardous Substances[36] (the Hazardous Substances Regulation).

Under the Hazardous Substances Regulation, new substances must be subject to a risk assessment (including health and environmental risks) and certain notification requirements prior to being marketed. Such information on the new substance will allow the Ministry of Health to determine whether the substance falls under the category of 'hazardous substance'. Hazardous substances may only be marketed provided they comply with a number of packaging and labelling requirements set out in the Hazardous Substances Regulation.

Violations of the Hazardous Substances Regulation are classified into three categories: minor, serious and very serious. Without prejudice to other measures imposed on the wrongdoer (eg temporary or permanent closure of facility, seizure of products) very serious violations may be subject to a fine of up to Pta 100 million.

With respect to radioactive material, Ch V of the Nuclear Energy Act 25/1964 of 29 April provides the basic licensing requirements for the installation of nuclear energy facilities as well as for the possession and use of radioactive materials. In particular, art 31 of the Nuclear Energy Act states that radioactive materials may not be used or stored by persons or entities which have not been expressly authorised by the Ministry of Industry.

According to the Regulation on Health Protection Against Ionising Radiation,[37] radioactive materials must be stored in containers which provide sufficient protection

---

34 Note that legislation on environmental impact assessment has been passed by the autonomous communities.
35 Decree 2187/1978 of 23 June.
36 Royal Decree 363/1995 of 10 March.
37 Royal Decree 2519/1982 of 12 August.

against radiation, taking into consideration the characteristics of the place and the potential leakage of radioactive materials. Storage containers should be adequately identified and a record of the stored material should be made in duplicate.

In addition, art 59 of the Regulation on Health Protection Against Ionising Radiation provides that all activities relating to radioactive materials are subject to inspection by authorised personnel appointed by the Nuclear Energy Council. Violations of nuclear energy provisions may be subject to a fine of up to Pta 100 million and may constitute a criminal offence.

2.9 Noise

In Spain there is no general provision regulating noise pollution. Indeed, this matter is mainly dealt with through local regulations, which set out maximum noise limits on the basis of the use of the area involved (eg industrial, residential). It should be noted, however, that not many municipalities have adopted local regulations on noise pollution.

Despite the regulatory lacuna on noise pollution, the licence of classified activities may impose maximum noise limits or the adoption of corrective measures to prevent noise pollution as a condition for the operation of industrial and other facilities, if appropriate. In addition, any excessive noise could be the subject of a civil claim for damages and even for cessation of operation, although the outcome of the case obviously depends on the characteristics of the noise and the surrounding circumstances.

2.10 Criminal law

The Spanish Criminal Code contains various Chapters dealing with criminal liability arising from offences against the environment and/or human health. Besides the Chapter on environmental criminal offences, the Criminal Code covers the protection of fauna and flora, the risk to people or the environment caused by management of explosives and inflammable or hazardous substances and the causing of forest fires.

The basic criminal offence is regulated under art 325 of the Criminal Code, which provides that:

> 'those who, in breach of environmental protection Acts or regulations, cause or produce, directly or indirectly, emissions, discharges, radiations, extractions or excavations, terracings, noise, vibrations, injections or deposits to the atmosphere, soil, subsoil, or to continental, sea or groundwater, capable of causing serious damage to the environment's balance'

shall be subject to a penalty of 6 months to 4 years of imprisonment, a fine of between Pta 48,000 to Pta 36 million (depending on the circumstances of the offence and the financial capacity of the offender) and be professionally disqualified for 1 to 3 years.

Furthermore, art 326 of the Criminal Code provides that such penalties may be increased where:

(1) the facility operates without the necessary authorisation or permit;
(2) the criminal behaviour is performed contrary to express orders from public authorities;
(3) information on environmental performance is falsified or hidden;
(4) inspection by public authorities is hindered;
(5) environmental impairment is regarded as irreversible or catastrophic; or
(6) illegal abstraction of water is carried out in times of restriction.

2.10 *Chapter 9*

In any of the above cases, the judge may order (a) the temporary or permanent closure of the company's premises or (b) the administrative supervision of the company in order to preserve the rights of employees and creditors.

The Criminal Code also contains criminal offences relating to the release of nuclear energy and ionising radiation provided that it puts human health or property at risk. Therefore, such criminal offences are not directly related to damage to the environment although such damage may arise as a consequence.

Delivery, receipt, transport and possession of radioactive materials or nuclear substances and the management of nuclear waste without the necessary administrative authorisation constitutes a criminal offence with a penalty of 1 to 5 years' imprisonment.

2.11 Civil law

Spanish civil law does not expressly cover environmental considerations. However, the following provisions of the Spanish Civil Code 1889 may be used in order to protect private parties' rights in environment-related cases:

(1) Article 590: No one may build wells, sewage drains, chimneys, deposits of hazardous substances or dangerous facilities near another person's property unless the appropriate regulatory or reasonable distances and measures are adopted.
(2) Article 1902: A person who, by act or omission, causes damage to another by fault or negligence, must repair the damage caused. This provision is the basis for non-contractual or tortious liability.
(3) Article 1908: Owners shall be liable for the damage caused by the explosion of machines that were not cared for with due diligence, by excessive smoke that is harmful to persons or properties, by the fall of trees and by the emanations of sewers or deposits of hazardous substances when constructed without the proper precautions.

In addition to the above, Catalan Act 13/1990 of 9 July on Cessation Action, Trespass, Easements and Neighbourhood Relations constitutes an important instrument allowing landowners to request the cessation of nuisance and to claim damages.

3 PARTICULAR ENVIRONMENTAL ISSUES RELEVANT TO TRANSACTIONS

3.1 Assumption of liabilities—routes and basis for liabilities

In broad terms, civil and administrative liabilities attach to the owner or operator of a facility or land. If that owner or operator is a corporate entity, then, in general, civil and administrative liabilities will attach to the company involved rather than to its shareholders, managers or employees.

However, Spanish case law has, under certain circumstances, applied the doctrine of 'piercing the corporate veil' whereby the company's separate legal entity is disregarded in order to protect private or public interests or to prevent an abusive use of the corporate personality to prejudice third parties. Thus, it is possible—albeit difficult—that a majority shareholder or a parent company be held liable for damages caused by an affiliated company to a third party provided that (a) the parent company exercised control over the affiliate, and (b) the damaging conduct is carried out fraudulently or through wilful misconduct.

To the author's knowledge, however, there is no case law regarding piercing of the corporate veil on the basis of environmental damage. Spanish courts are reluctant to disregard the separate corporate entity unless they are confronted with fraudulent or malicious conduct (Supreme Court Judgment of 28 May 1984).

With respect to criminal liability, companies may not be held criminally liable. In principle, the company's directors, managers or whoever is responsible for the criminal conduct within the company's structure will be criminally liable.

3.2 How historical liabilities are dealt with

Historical liabilities are under-regulated in Spain. As a result, until recently when conducting transactions involving, directly or indirectly, real estate property, little attention was paid to historical pollution. However, the increasing concern over environmental liabilities and the enactment of the contaminated land provisions in the Waste Act[38] have brought greater caution when purchasing property or industrial premises.

When confronted with historical liabilities in any given transaction it may be useful to examine whether the potential claims would be time-barred. To this effect, it is necessary to distinguish between civil, criminal and administrative liability:

(1) *Civil liability*. According to art 1968 of the Civil Code, non-contractual or tortious liability claims are time-barred one year after the plaintiff had knowledge of the damage. In principle, the limitation period starts when the damaged party knew or should have known of the damage.

   In cases of continuing or gradual pollution, the case law has held that the limitation period (*dies a quo*) does not start at the time the plaintiff knew or should have known of the damage, but when the last damage is caused (Supreme Court Judgment of 24 May 1993).

   With respect to contractual liability, the general limitation period is 15 years. However, specific limitation periods may apply, for instance, in case of hidden defects of the purchased property.[39]

(2) *Criminal liability*. Environmental criminal offences are subject to a limitation period of five years if the penalty of imprisonment is between six months and three years, or ten years if the penalty of imprisonment is between three and five years.

(3) *Administrative liability*. As a general rule, administrative liability claims by public authorities are subject to the following limitation periods:
   (a) very serious violations: three years,
   (b) serious violations: two years, and
   (c) minor violations: six months.

There are, however, some administrative provisions that provide special limitation periods. For instance, claims for serious violations of the Coast Act provisions are time-barred after four years, whilst minor violations are time-barred after one year.[40]

---

38 See para 2.2 above.
39 Civil Code, arts 1484 and 1490.
40 Coast Act, art 92.

3.3 Liability of directors and managers

Under Spanish corporate law, the directors of a limited liability company may be held personally liable vis-à-vis the company, shareholders and the company's creditors provided that the damages arise from unlawful acts, acts in breach of the company's articles of association or acts performed without the necessary diligence.[41] Case law on directors' liability for damages to the environment is almost non-existent.

On the other hand, criminal liability may only be attached to individuals since companies may not commit criminal offences (*societas delinquere non potest*). Article 31 of the Criminal Code provides that those acting as the company's de jure or de facto directors are liable personally for the criminal conduct of the company. On its part, the Supreme Court has held that those persons who perform the conduct considered to be a criminal offence or those in control shall be held criminally liable for the company's actions (Supreme Court Judgment of 4 October 1972). This is without prejudice to the company's civil liability for damages arising from the offending conduct.

In broad terms, criminal liability for environmental offences is attached to the company's general manager and/or those who have control over the environmental performance of the company (eg head of environmental and safety department, plant manager, etc). However, the determination of who is criminally liable for the company's environmental performance is greatly dependent on the factual background of the case.

In a recent case, the Supreme Court upheld a judgment of the Barcelona Court of Appeal (Audiencia Provincial de Barcelona), which sentenced the general manager and shareholder of a company to four years and two months of imprisonment and a fine on the basis of an environmental criminal offence.[42] The company had discharged highly polluting substances into a river over several years. The general manager was the first person to be imprisoned in Spain for committing an environmental criminal offence.

With respect to administrative liability, in principle the company is liable for the acts or omissions giving rise to administrative liability. Thus, managers and directors are unlikely to be held personally liable for the infringement of administrative rules. Despite the general rule, some Acts specifically provide that administrative liability may go beyond the corporate entity and attach to directors or managers who are directly involved in the company's environmental policy. For instance, art 93(b) of the Coast Act provides that administrative liability may attach to, inter alia, the technical manager of any activity.

3.4 Lender liability

Under Spanish law, it is unlikely that those who provide financing for a transaction will be held liable for environmental damage caused by the borrower. It may be arguable that lenders exercising significant control over a facility's operation could be held liable for civil damages and possibly criminal offences. However, there is no case law on this matter.

The regulation on contaminated land provides that the obligation to clean-up falls first upon polluters, secondly upon occupiers and, lastly, on the landowner.[43]

---

41 Corporations Act, art 133.
42 *Re Puigneró*, Supreme Court Judgment of 1 February 1998.
43 See para 2.2 above.

Therefore, if a lender enforces its security by way of foreclosure or becoming a mortgagee in possession, the lender may become an occupier or landowner, thus becoming liable for clean-up costs. However, art 27.6 of the Waste Act reduces a lender's exposure to contaminated land liability provided that the lender transfers the property within 1 year from the enforcement of the security.

3.5 Transferability of permits and licences

Under Spanish law there is no general provision regulating the transferability of permits and licences. Therefore, the possibility of transferring a permit or a licence should be examined on a case-by-case basis, taking into consideration the specific legal measure regulating the authorisation at stake.

In principle, the provisions allowing for transferability of permits may establish as a condition for such transfer that the licensing authority checks the transferee's compliance with the relevant requirements (eg Waste Act, arts 9.4 and 13.4). In some cases, the transfer shall be expressly authorised by the licensing authority (eg Water Act, art 61).

In any event, when structuring an operation, whether a corporate transaction or an acquisition of assets, it may be important to take into account whether the contemplated transaction will require the transfer of permits or licences. In principle, if assets are acquired permits will need to be transferred, whilst in share acquisitions that may not be the case.

3.6 Mechanisms for compliance cost increases

Under Spanish law, licensing authorities are rarely entitled to amend the conditions imposed in licences or permits unless the licence-holder is in breach of the licence conditions or any extraordinary event or the public interest require this. Indeed, it may be argued that the concept of best available techniques not entailing excessive costs (BATNEEC) is only occasionally used in Spanish environmental regulations since, at the time of writing, Spain has not implemented Directive (EC) 96/61 on integrated pollution and prevention control.

One of the instances where BATNEEC may be required is in connection with atmospheric pollution. Under art 61 of Decree 833/1975 of 6 February no authorisation may be granted for the enlargement of facilities unless (a) the maximum emission limits are observed, or (b) BATNEEC is employed with respect to the existing installation.[44]

Although dynamic permits allowing for compliance cost increases are rarely used, attention should be drawn to two ways in which cost increases may be experienced:

(1) In some instances, regulations set out specific procedures to bring non-compliant sewage discharges in line with the regulatory requirements within a time frame. Thus, those facilities which do not hold a discharge permit or which discharge sewage above the maximum limits, may, under certain circumstances, submit a gradual decontamination programme (GDP) allowing them to reduce the discharging of polluting substances progressively and, ultimately, to bring discharges into compliance with the regulatory limits.[45]

In principle, the licensing authority's acceptance of a GDP entails the granting of a provisional discharge permit, and—if the reduction of the discharges

---

44 Decree 833/1975, art 61.
45 For discharges from land to sea, see Royal Decree 258/1989, arts 7 and 8; for discharges to continental waters, see Royal Decree 484/1995 of 7 April.

takes place within the agreed time frame—the licensing authority will grant a final discharge permit.
(2) From 1 January 1998, investments in certain pollution abatement equipment or installations may be subject to a 10% deduction from corporate tax. Such equipment or installations must be aimed at avoiding or reducing atmospheric pollution or the polluting substances in discharges to water, or to allow an appropriate reduction, management or recovery of industrial waste.

This deduction is intended for investments aimed at complying with regulatory requirements in the execution of programmes or agreements with public authorities. In addition, the installation or equipment must be in use for at least five years, unless the useful life is less than five years.

4 MANAGING ENVIRONMENTAL ISSUES IN TRANSACTIONS

4.1 Current practice for assessment of risk[46]

The parties to a transaction should take all available measures to prevent unexpected risks or liabilities from arising once the closing documents are signed. Thus, the target of a transaction must be scrutinised, to the fullest extent possible, to identify potential risks and liabilities. Such scrutiny is generally done through a due diligence investigation and an environmental assessment. Spanish law does not generally contemplate the undertaking of a due diligence investigation in any type of transaction. Therefore, it is entirely at the client's discretion whether due diligence investigations should be carried out before entering into any asset or property transaction. However, it is the lawyer's duty to inform the client of the advisability or not to undertake a due diligence for a specific project. This will obviously depend on the nature and size of the transaction and the circumstances of the case.

In Spain, due diligence investigations are an increasing practice, in particular in projects of significant size and almost always where a foreign element is involved. In such cases, it is frequently the client who requests that a due diligence investigation be undertaken for two purposes: first, to assess the legal status of the target, identifying potential risks and liabilities; secondly, foreign clients wish to comprehend fully the nature and extent of such potential liabilities under Spanish law and practice. For instance, the lack of a specific licence may, strictly speaking, constitute a serious administrative violation, subject to a fine and/or the adoption of the relevant corrective measures (eg installation of pollution abatement equipment, temporary closure). However, it may be the case that a large percentage of facilities in the region are in a similar situation and, therefore, regulators take a rather lenient approach to such issues.

It should be pointed out, however, that due diligence techniques are instruments that started to be used mainly as a result of a significant number of acquisitions that occurred in Spain during the 1980s. These have been imported mainly from Anglo-Saxon countries and, consequently, Spanish companies with limited experience in international projects may not be well acquainted with due diligence investigations and their procedures and requirements.

---

46 The discussion contained in this section is based on a paper entitled *Due Diligence in Natural Resources Projects: Practical Implications for Lawyers in Spain* presented by the author at the XLII UIA Congress in September 1998.

Besides the general common areas that need to be covered in any due diligence report (eg corporate issues, tax, intellectual property, labour, contract, insurance, litigation), the environmental practitioner must look at a number of issues, including:

(1) *Applicable laws and regulations*: Bearing in mind the increasing regulation of environmental protection, the due diligence report should list the main laws and regulations affecting the project.[47]
(2) *Licensing*: It is of the utmost importance to determine whether the target of the transaction is in compliance with the relevant authorisations, licences and permits. Obviously, the type of licences depend on the nature of the business and its location.

    However, two key aspects need to be outlined in this respect. First, most licences require an update when the factual grounds on which the grant was based are changed. It is not sufficient to ensure that a relevant permit has been granted. It must also be determined that no additional updates or amendments are required, otherwise the cost of compliance may constitute a serious risk or an additional liability for the business. Secondly, the approach towards compliance with licensing requirements should be flexible, depending on the level of enforcement of the national, regional and local regulators. In practice, this means that lawyers should, to the fullest extent possible, provide advice on the legal requirements for strict compliance as well as informing clients of the regulators' practical approach.
(3) *Fines and other penalties*: If the project involves, directly or indirectly, a facility or plant in operation, the due diligence report should also cover the fines and other penalties imposed or threatened on such facility.
(4) *Findings*: The due diligence report must explore the legal effects, if any, of the factual findings arising from an environmental assessment.

4.2 Warranty or indemnity terms

Under Spanish law, the vendor is required to compensate for the hidden defects of the goods sold if such defects make the goods unsuitable for use or if they reduce such use so that, had the purchaser been aware of them at the time of the purchase, he would not have purchased them or would have paid less (art 1484 of the Civil Code). However, for our purposes, claims under this provision face two important limitations: (a) no liability may arise if the purchaser has expert knowledge on the matter and could have easily gained knowledge of the defects, and (b) there is a limitation period of 6 months. In any event, it may be difficult for a purchaser to rely on this provision in the event that due diligence was carried out. This, however, does not mean that vendors commission an environmental audit or disclose information on the environmental condition of the sold goods to prevent a claim against the vendor on the grounds of hidden defects. In practice, vendors usually provide rather basic information on the environmental status of the target and it is for the purchaser to inquire further or to conduct due diligence.

On the other hand, it should be borne in mind that, with respect to transactions consisting of the acquisition of shares, shares may not have any defects, charges or encumbrances. However, assets owned by the company the shares of which are transferred may suffer from defects from an environmental or other perspective. Therefore, representations and warranties and relevant indemnity clauses are advisable.

---

47 This is of particular importance in Spain given that different legal provisions may apply depending on the autonomous community where the project will be carried out.

4.2 *Chapter 9*

Without prejudice to the effect of the liability for hidden defects provision on any particular transaction, it is increasing practice in Spanish transactions to include representations and warranties, particularly where a foreign element is involved.

The drafting of environmental representations and warranties in an agreement will depend on the type of target involved. Generally speaking, such representations and warranties should include that the target complies with the relevant regulatory requirements, that no hazardous materials are included in a given process, that there is no notice of non-compliance or litigation and that the vendor is not aware of the existence of any hazardous substance on the site.

If representations and warranties are included in the first draft agreement, the chances are that no unsuspected issues will arise at a later stage.[48]

If the target's potential liabilities identified in the due diligence are likely to arise, it may be advisable for the client to obtain indemnities, that is, contractual protection against the consequences of the potential liability. For instance, the purchaser of an industrial facility may ask to be indemnified against any damage, cost, claim or liability arising from the presence of hazardous materials on the plant.

Indemnities must achieve a clear risk allocation, from the perspective of all the parties involved, capable of withstanding challenge and judicial scrutiny in the context of future litigation.[49]

Particular attention should be drawn to the fact that such liabilities may be discovered at any time in the future, whilst contractual provisions may have express temporal limitations. On the other hand, indemnities may become useless over time as parties cease to exist or are insolvent.[50]

4.3 Issues for those lending money to businesses

Lenders, investors and financial institutions are showing a fair amount of concern over environmental liability. As a result, there is greater pressure to ensure that no significant environmental liability may be attached to the borrower which could undermine its solvency and could, eventually, constitute the basis of a claim against the financing institution (eg upon foreclosure of a loan).

The level of concern from lenders differs depending on the target of the project being financed. Whilst in real estate transactions, lenders are particularly keen to seek assurances and environmental investigations (particularly where property has been used for industrial purposes), in mergers and acquisitions of companies less attention is commonly paid to environmental issues.

The fact that lenders may only be held liable for damages caused by their own acts or omissions guarantees a great degree of protection to those providing finance for projects.

4.4 Role of environmental management systems

In merger and acquisition transactions where the target company has achieved accreditation under EMAS, ISO 14001 and the like, it may quite straightforward to identify the key environmental issues. In principle, a company's certification under an environmental

---

48 John R Salter, *Corporate Environmental Responsibility: Law and Practice* 1992, (Butterworths) p 157.
49 Elizabeth A Poyck *Environmental Indemnities: Drafting out the Defects* from the web page of Milbank, Tweed, Hadley & McCloy (http:\www\milbank.com).
50 Model Stock Purchase Agreement with Commentary, Committee on Negotiated Agreements, Section on Business Law (1995, ABA).

quality system shows not only that the company complies with environmental regulations but also that it has a detailed environmental policy which is being implemented.

In practice, few Spanish companies have successfully implemented an environmental management system. Indeed, early in 1998 approximately 60 companies complied with ISO 14001 and only 10 were registered under EMAS.[51]

4.5 Insurance

At present, insurance is compulsory only for operators of nuclear installations (Nuclear Energy Act 25/1964, art 55) and for hazardous waste producers, managers and eliminators (Waste Act 10/1998, arts 21 and 22).

General liability insurance policies restrict the coverage of pollution or environmental risks to sudden and accidental damage (expressly excluding gradual pollution coverage). Most insurance companies do not provide coverage against civil claims for environmental damage.

In 1995, the Spanish insurance market organised a pool to cover environmental risks, although there is still limited availability of specific environmental insurance policies.

5 CONCLUSION

Environmental law in Spain is an emerging field that has developed mostly as a result of EU influence. The speed of development of environmental laws and regulations has resulted in a complex and patchy set of rules and regulations. In addition, the division of jurisdiction for the passing of environmental protection laws and regulations among the State and the autonomous communities often make the task of determining the applicable requirements to a given scenario a difficult one.

Environmental considerations are not always taken into account when conducting a property or asset transaction. This is due to the fact that the enforcement of environmental laws and regulations has, in the past, not been consistent. However, public authorities are taking a more active role in the enforcement of environmental protection policies. In addition, companies are growing increasingly aware of the costs of compliance with environmental requirements.

One of the most recent legal developments is the passing of the contaminated land provisions in the Waste Act. Although such provisions may not be fully applicable until the State government and the autonomous communities issue the Contaminated Land Inventories and list of potentially polluting activities, it appears that this new scenario may draw increasing attention to environmental matters when acquiring property or assets in Spain.

---

51 Expansión, 24 March 1998.

Chapter 10

AUSTRIA

Paul Luiki and Gernot Thanner

Bruckhaus Westrick Heller Löber, Vienna

1 INTRODUCTION

1.1 Governmental Structure

Austria is a federal republic, and under its constitution, governmental responsibilities are divided between the federal government (*Bund*), the nine federal provinces (*Bundesländer*) and the local authorities (*Gemeinden*).

The federal government plays the dominant role in the initiation of environmental legislation in Austria as, under the constitution, it is the function of this branch of the government to legislate and enforce laws regulating business and industrial activity. Moreover, the constitution provides the federal government branch with authority to pass regulations governing water (including groundwater) and hazardous waste and to enact measures to counteract the impact on the environment from excessive emissions.

Pursuant to this broad authority, the federal government has passed laws on hazardous waste management, waste, water discharges, air emissions, plant licensing procedures (under the Trade Code) and the clean-up of hazardous waste sites.

Despite the predominant role of the federal government, the provinces have residual authority to legislate on certain environmental matters such as non-hazardous waste management and air pollution. In addition, local authorities (*Gemeinden*) have some powers relating to environmental matters under their local police provisions.

Since 1 January 1995, when Austria became a full member of the European Union, an additional source of environmental legislation has been the European Community. Being a member of the EU, Austria is obliged to implement EC environmental directives into its national law, although in various areas, Austrian environmental law is more stringent than EC law.

Finally, Austria is signatory to various international conventions (eg the Basel Convention which regulates the international shipment of hazardous waste and the Montreal Protocol concerning ozone layer issues) and has enacted legislation implementing its obligations under such conventions.

1.2 Environmental policies and principles

As is the case with other industrialised nations in Europe, growing environmental awareness in Austria has acted as a catalyst for the enactment of new environmental

1.2   Chapter 10

laws. The importance Austria has attached to the pursuit of environmental objectives is reflected in its constitution. In 1984, the federal government adopted the principle of comprehensive environmental protection which is defined as the protection of the natural environment against the harmful effects of human activity. Comprehensive environmental protection includes measures to prevent the pollution of air, water and soil as well as the prevention of noise nuisances. This is clearly a guiding principle (*Staatszielbestimmung*) for federal activity and serves as a general interpretative device.

Several of the basic principles guiding Austrian environmental law are as follows:

(1) the principle of precaution and protective exploitation with prevention of environmental damage and protection of natural sources;
(2) the repair of environmental damage;
(3) the polluter pays principle which provides that those persons causing environmental pollution are responsible for repairing any damage and bearing the costs for such repair;
(4) the principle of social responsibility and democratic decision-making, which seeks the participation of citizens in decisions impacting on the environment;
(5) the integration of environmental considerations into all areas of social and economic policy.

Extensive environmental legislation in Austria has created an increasingly complex web of statutes and regulations, which, in turn, generally translate into higher costs for industry than in other countries. In today's global economy, the argument is increasingly being made that those countries which force domestic industry to spend a disproportionately large amount on environmental controls may run the risk of harming their industry's international competitiveness.

1.3   Structure of environmental law

Since Austria has a civil law system, only statute law creates legally binding obligations and rights. Case law, however, plays an important practical role in interpreting statutory provisions. In the area of environmental law, there is no single comprehensive environmental statute, nor could such an all-encompassing statute be enacted under Austria's constitutional system. Accordingly, different statutes and regulations govern waste water discharges, air emissions and the disposal of hazardous waste. One major exception to the media-specific approach is the Trade Code's (*Gewerbeordnung*) plant licensing procedure, which grants broad powers to legislative and administrative authorities to regulate a facility's impact on the local environment and its neighbours. Virtually all facilities are subject to these regulations and the consent of the relevant authorities is required to both build and operate them.

The three general categories of Austrian law governing environmental matters are:

(1) public environmental law, which primarily encompasses the regulation of industrial activity;
(2) private environmental law, which includes claims for damages as well as injunctive relief; and
(3) criminal law, which imposes fines and/or imprisonment for environmental infringements.

1.4 Structure of environmental regulatory agencies

The Federal Ministry of Environment, Youth and Family Affairs (*Bundesministerium für Umwelt, Jugend und Familie*) is the federal agency primarily responsible for overseeing the implementation and enforcement of federally enacted environmental laws. Other important federal authorities for regulation of the environment are the Federal Environment Agency (*Umweltbundesamt*), the Ministry of Agriculture and Forestry (*Bundesministerium für Land und Forstwirtschaft*) and the Federal Ministry of Economic Affairs (*Bundesministerium für wirtschaftliche Angelegenheiten*), which implements various Trade Code provisions.

The states are primarily responsible for administering state law (eg nature preservation and the management of household waste) and assist in the enforcement of various federal laws (eg the Old Waste Sites Law, the Trade Code, and the Water Law), despite their otherwise subordinate position in Austria's constitutional division of powers.

Finally, it is important to emphasise the decentralised nature of federal law enforcement in the environmental area. Local government authorities are generally responsible for implementing not only local and state laws and regulations but also federal laws and regulations.

1.5 Judicial system

A unique aspect of Austria's constitution is that federal courts have exclusive jurisdiction over all matters. The federal courts are divided into general courts (*ordentliche Gerichte*) and special courts (*außerordentliche Gerichte*). General courts are further divided into county courts (*Bezirksgerichte*) and courts of first instance (*Gerichtshöfe erster Instanz*). The general courts have jurisdiction over civil and criminal matters, with the highest appellate general court being the Supreme Court (*Oberster Gerichtshof*).

The special courts have a more limited jurisdiction and consist of two types: the Administrative Court (*Verwaltungsgerichtshof*), which reviews decisions (*Bescheide*) issued by administrative authorities, and the Constitutional Court, which deals with questions of constitutional law. Unlike other legal systems, Austria's constitution generally forbids an overlap between administrative authorities and non-administrative authorities. Thus, subject to a few exceptions, ordinary courts do not have jurisdiction to review decisions made by administrative agencies.

If a party to an administrative proceeding has exhausted all administrative remedies, it may file a petition with either the Constitutional Court or the Administrative Court. The Constitutional Court has jurisdiction only if the petitioner pleads that fundamental rights granted by the constitution were violated or if he contends that the statute applied by the administrative agency was unconstitutional. The Administrative Court has jurisdiction if the petitioner pleads either that a decision of the highest administrative authority has violated rights other than fundamental rights or that an administrative agency has breached its obligation to decide a case within a given period.

2 OUTLINE OF ENVIRONMENTAL LAW RELEVANT TO MERGER AND ACQUISITION TRANSACTIONS

2.1 Trade Code

The licensing process under the Trade Code is the most effective and comprehensive governmental means of regulating industrial activity in environmental matters. The

2.1 Chapter 10

Trade Code is drafted in a flexible manner to allow the incorporation of rapidly developing environmental law and technology and outlines permit requirements and notification obligations. Unlike most other environmental laws in Austria which focus on a particular type of environmental impact, the Trade Code employs a broader multi-faceted approach. Facilities applying for a Trade Code licence also have to obtain licences under all other applicable environmental laws simultaneously.

Before a plant (*Betriebsanlage*), as defined under the Trade Code, can be constructed or become operative, the owner is required to apply for a facility permit (*Betriebsanlagengenehmigung*) from the trade authority (*Gewerbebehörde*) if the plant, because of its machinery, equipment or other circumstances, is likely to:

(1) endanger life, health or property of employees or neighbours;
(2) cause inconvenience to neighbours with respect to noise, dust, smoke or other pollution;
(3) endanger water quality.

Austrian courts have interpreted the term 'plant' broadly to include virtually all commercial and industrial activities. Thus almost all facilities are required to obtain a permit prior to constructing or operating a facility. When issuing a plant permit after a compulsory hearing at which typically other authorities and neighbours are present, the trade authority usually imposes a number of conditions which the owner of the plant has to fulfil during its operation. Additional conditions may also be imposed by the trade authority in light of new security or pollution considerations as state-of-the-art technology changes. Additional conditions imposed on operators already having licences are, however, subject to a reasonableness test which incorporates economic considerations. In making the determination of whether a facility endangers the life or health of employees or neighbours, the test is based on the best available and proven control technology as well as existing medical and other scientific knowledge. Additionally, a facility will not receive a licence if nuisances, impairments or other impacts related to specifically listed categories (including neighbours and water quality) cannot be limited to a reasonable amount. Similar to the endangerment of life and safety test, the 'reasonable' determination is based on the best available and proven control technology as well as existing medical and scientific knowledge. Specifically the Trade Code provides that the trade authority must limit air emissions by requiring facilities to use the best available and proven control technology, and obligations must be imposed for the storage and other treatment of facility waste to the extent necessary.

Pursuant to the Trade Code the Federal Ministry of Economic Affairs has promulgated a regulation governing incidents of malfunction for potentially dangerous facilities. Under this regulation, such facilities are obliged to take necessary preventive measures to ensure that malfunction events (eg equipment failure resulting in excess air emissions) do not occur. If such an event nevertheless does occur, facilities must immediately notify the relevant authority and provide a written statement within 1 week, describing the event, its causes, the impact on human life and safety, property and the environment, and the emergency measures undertaken to limit its impact.

Trades may be carried on either by entrepreneurs, legal entities, partnerships under commercial law or professional partnerships. Since the latter cannot personally carry on a trade, a representative under trade law (*Gewerberechtlicher Geschäftsführer*) must be nominated by the legal entity or partnership. The representative under trade law is responsible for compliance with trade law provisions and regulations vis-à-vis the trade authorities. Administrative fines of up to ATS 50,000 may be imposed on the representative if trade law rules or regulations are violated. Furthermore, companies are jointly and severally liable for such monetary penalties. The holder of the trade permit (*Gewerbetreibender*) may also be held directly liable if he knowingly consented to the administrative offence or he acted negligently in choosing the representative under trade law.

2.2 Offences under environmental laws

2.2.1 Introduction

Austrian law distinguishes between crimes prosecuted before courts and administrative offences enforced by administrative authorities. In general, under both the Criminal Code and the various administrative laws, only natural persons can be subjected to criminal or administrative penalties. However, a legal entity is jointly liable for imposed fines and repayment with the offender where the offender is the entity's officer.

2.2.2 Criminal offences

Austria has a fairly comprehensive set of criminal provisions dealing with environmental matters. The Criminal Code (*Strafgesetzbuch*) includes the following primary substantive areas that may give rise to criminal liability:

(1) contamination of water (including groundwater), air and soil;
(2) environmentally dangerous operation of a facility;
(3) environmentally dangerous disposal of waste; and
(4) causing of severe noise nuisances.

Causing the above circumstances may trigger criminal liability where two conditions are satisfied: (a) the person acted negligently or intentionally; and (b) the action causing the circumstance was in violation of law or an administrative order. The maximum penalty under the Criminal Code for environmental matters is three years' imprisonment or a criminal penalty of ATS 1.62 million (the allowable criminal penalty is calculated according to the transgressor's personal circumstances, including income, and is based on a 360-day time period).

The environmental crimes provisions of the Austrian Criminal Code are, however, applied fairly infrequently in practice. This is in part due to evidential difficulties that may arise during a trial. Therefore, it is more common to impose administrative criminal penalties for serious violations of environmental laws (mainly under the Water Law) rather than to prosecute an offender under criminal law.

2.2.3 Administrative offences

The criminal provisions dealing with environmental matters are supplemented by administrative offences for which penalties can be imposed pursuant to various environmental laws (eg Trade Law, Water Law, etc). Administrative offences by definition are handled by administrative authorities. Compared to court proceedings, the procedure before a local administrative authority is generally more informal. All administrative decisions resulting in the imposition of a fine or a prison sentence may be appealed to the 'independent panels of administrative review' (*Unabhängige Verwaltungssenate*). The procedure of these panels is very similar to court proceedings.

2.2   Chapter 10

In most cases only fines can be imposed, but prison sentences of up to 6 weeks may be imposed either for failure to pay the fine or in certain serious cases. Apart from the fines imposed, non-compliance with administrative regulations may also have other adverse consequences for a business, such as forced plant closure or trade permit revocation.

2.3   Contaminated land

2.3.1   Introduction

There is no single law in Austria which comprehensively governs the clean-up of contaminated land. Instead, a variety of mechanisms are employed to encourage clean-up activity. The three most commonly used mechanisms are liability under administrative law, liability under civil law and funding from tax incentives.

In practice, the Water Law is by far the most frequently utilised source of environmental law under which administrative clean-up orders are issued. General civil law provisions also provide a basis for clean-up liability. However, civil lawsuits forcing clean-up activity have not played a significant role in the past. Finally, Austria finances the clean-up of old waste sites in part through a special tax placed on operators of disposal sites and exporters of waste. A fund has been created from taxes to finance the clean-up of waste sites appearing on the list of sites requiring clean-up activity (*Altlastenatlas*). This fund is, however, wholly inadequate to address the clean-up of hazardous waste sites properly. The focus of governmental authorities is therefore on issuing administrative orders to responsible parties.

2.3.2   Old Waste Sites Act

The Old Waste Sites Act uses a two-tiered approach to imposing liability. The Act relies primarily on other federal laws to provide the necessary basis for legal liability, although it does contain provisions which impose liability independently of other federal laws.

Once a contaminated site is on the list of sites requiring clean-up under the Old Waste Sites Act, the state authority examines whether a person or entity can be held liable for clean-up under other federal laws, specifically the Water Law (see para 2.3.3 below), the Trade Law (see para 2.2 above) and the Hazardous Waste Law (see para 2.6 below). A party held liable for contamination under one of these federal laws must then undertake the necessary clean-up activity.

If, however, a responsible party cannot be identified under the listed federal laws, or if the responsible party cannot or will not undertake the clean-up, the federal government is obliged to initiate the necessary steps under the Old Waste Sites Act.

Where the federal government has performed a clean-up, the Old Waste Sites Act entitles the government to recover its costs from certain parties, without reference to other federal laws. The Act provides that whoever (1) negligently, and in violation of law, caused the creation of a waste site or (2) is the owner of a waste site or who allowed the waste site to be created or tolerated its existence, is obliged to reimburse the federal government for costs incurred in securing or remediating the waste site.

Due to the complex nature of these provisions, they are generally regarded as wholly inadequate to remedy this situation. The creation of a new class of parties who could be held secondarily liable under the Old Waste Sites Act has not proven effective in practice.

2.3.3 Clean-up liability under the Water Law

The Water Law is the most effective tool by which the governmental authorities impose clean-up obligations. Under this law, administrative authorities can require those parties undertaking or failing to undertake action causing or threatening water contamination to perform corrective measures based on a strict liability standard (Water Law, ss 31 and 138). Groundwater/aquifers are considered as receptors within the text of the Austrian Water Law, which states in s 30 that waters (including groundwater) are not to be impaired and are to be maintained as drinking water. Therefore any impairment in the quality of water resulting from site activities is deemed to be contamination.

The fact that soil contamination is not defined under the pertinent Austrian clean-up laws is often regarded as one of the weaknesses of Austrian clean-up laws. However, in practice, soil contamination clean-ups are often chosen to protect water (including groundwater) from contamination.

Section 31 of the Water Law provides that each person is obliged to ensure, through the exercise of due care, that his action or inaction does not cause water contamination. If any person causes or threatens to cause water contamination, including groundwater contamination, despite the exercise of due care, this person must nevertheless undertake all necessary steps to prevent contamination, and must also immediately notify the relevant authorities. The water authorities may order the person causing the contamination to undertake all steps to prevent, contain and/or remedy the contamination. If the responsible party does not undertake such steps, and the water authority performs the necessary clean-up activity itself, the water authority is authorised to recover its costs from the party causing the contamination.

In addition to s 31 of the Water Law, the other major source of clean-up enforcement is s 138 of the same Law which provides that, independent of penalties and damage claims by third parties, a person who violates the Water Law (eg by causing groundwater contamination without a water permit) is responsible for costs incurred with respect to the following where required by the public interest or the affected parties:

(1) the removal of the innovations (*Neuerungen*) that have been created or undertaking activities that should have been done;
(2) the containment of the contamination in the form of disposals or soil contamination through pertinent measures in the event that removal under (1) is either not possible or is possible only with disproportionate difficulties measured in costs when compared to preventing further contamination;
(3) the remediation of the adverse consequences of the water contamination; and
(4) the re-establishment of damaged hydrological installations.

In addition to the party causing the contamination, ie the *Verursacher*, property owners not causing the contamination can also be held liable in certain circumstances. Such liability, however, is only secondary to the liability of the party causing the contamination. The introduction of secondary liability of property owners occurred in 1990 through major amendments to the Water Law and the Waste Management Act.

A property owner who did not cause water contamination may be held secondarily liable only if he (a) expressly permitted the activity or inactivity that caused or threatened to cause the water contamination or, (b) approved of or voluntarily acquiesced in the disposal activity which caused contamination and neglected to undertake preventive measures that could reasonably be expected of the property owner. In addition,

2.3 Chapter 10

such property owner's successor-in-title may be held secondarily liable if the successor knew or should have known of the situation causing the water contamination.

The Water Law contains an additional limitation regarding a property owner's potential liability for actual or threatened water contamination prior to 1 July 1990. In these circumstances, the property owner not causing the water contamination can be held secondarily liable only if he expressly approved of the means by which the contamination was caused and in addition received compensation for such property use. In any event, the property owner's liability for water contamination caused prior to 1 July 1990 is limited to the amount by which the value actually derived from the property use exceeded the value normally obtained under market conditions. These beneficial limitations on liability do not apply to property owners causing contamination, but only to those who have land which was contaminated by others.

Furthermore, the Austrian Constitutional Court held in a groundbreaking decision in 1993, which was confirmed in 1996, that liability costs imposed on a property owner not causing water contamination cannot be excessive due to a constitutional barrier founded in an owner's property rights.

2.3.4 Civil law liability

Apart from the Old Waste Sites Act, the Water Law and other federal laws, various provisions contained in the Civil Code may impose liability on a party causing contamination. These provisions include tort law (*Schadenersatzrecht*) and neighbouring property owners' rights (*Nachbarrechte*, see para 2.9 below).

2.4 Water law

The Austrian Constitution assigns the legislation and administration of water law to the federal branch. The federally enacted Water Law (*Wasserrechtsgesetz*), which was substantially revised in 1990, forms the basis for the regulation and protection of water in Austria. This law not only regulates the consumption of water resources in general, but also sets out the protective measures required of water users.

One of the principal features of the Water Law is the strict regulation of industrial waste water discharges. In reviewing licence applications, the relevant authority must at least impose best available and proven control technology as a permit condition in order to limit discharges of water contaminants. In addition to the general waste water discharge regulation (*Allgemeine Abwasseremissionsverordnung*) promulgated by the federal Ministry of Agriculture and Forestry, specific waste water discharge regulations are in force for a variety of industry branches. Furthermore, the Water Law contains provisions regulating the use of all kinds of water, including rivers, lakes, groundwater and drinking water. Among other areas, the Water Law impacts on the construction of electric power plants, the maintenance of the water quality in tourist areas and the construction of drinking water facilities. As discussed above, the Water Law also provides a mechanism by which the government can impose liability for clean-up activities.

Under the Water Law administrative fines of up to ATS 500,000 may be imposed on offenders under the relevant provisions of the Water Law. If the administrative offence is committed in connection with the operation of a hydrological installation (*Wasseranlage*), the holder of the water licence as well as his works manager may also be held liable if they have not supervised the plant with due care, have negligently chosen or supervised the person responsible for the supervision of the plant or if the offence was committed with their knowledge. An administrative fine may not be imposed if violation of the Water Law provisions constitutes a crime which has to be dealt with by criminal courts.

2.5 Air pollution law

2.5.1 *Introduction*

The Austrian federal and state branches share jurisdiction over air pollution regulation. In addition to the Trade Code which is an important source of air pollution regulation, other major federal legislation exists which also regulates air pollution. A constitutional amendment was passed in 1988, substantially expanding the federal parliament's authority to pass legislation on air pollution. This broadened authority has lead the somewhat decentralised Austrian air pollution law gradually to become more centralised.

2.5.2 *Impact of Air Emissions Law*

One of the primary goals of the Impact of Air Emissions Law (*Imissionsschutzgesetz—Luft*), a major new federal law enacted in 1997, is to identify and take remedial action in respect of those areas in Austria which have heightened concentrations of certain components of concern such as sulphur dioxide, carbon monoxide and lead. The new law also foresees the detailed listing of individual emission sources.

Once basic measurements have been taken, each provincial governor is authorised and required to promulgate a regulation containing, amongst other things, the following information: (1) the time within which remedial measures are to be taken and (2) the measures that are to be taken, primarily with respect to major sources of emissions and taking into account the potential for reduction and costs involved. However, remedial measures cannot be required where the benefit is out of proportion to the costs involved. Finally, there is an opt-out clause where it is established from a remedial measure catalogue that no measures taken within Austria would have a substantial impact on reducing the impact of emissions in Austria. The last point is particularly interesting in that it recognises the effect of emission sources arising from territories outside of Austria.

Under the Impact of Air Emissions Law administrative fines of up to ATS 500,000 may be imposed on operators of plants who do not comply with the provisions of this newly enacted law. Again, administrative fines are subordinate to proceedings under criminal law.

2.5.3 *Air Pollution Law for Boiler Facilities*

The Air Pollution Law for Boiler Facilities (*Luftreinhaltegesetz für Kesselanlagen*) is a major federal law dealing exclusively with air pollution. This law sets uniform emission standards for boiler facility emissions throughout Austria irrespective of individual facilities' current emissions. Specific emission levels are to be fixed according to best available and proven technology for pollution control.

An unusual provision in the Air Pollution Law for Boiler Facilities states that a boiler facility must comply not only with applicable air emission limits, but also that its emissions cannot impose a danger or nuisance to neighbours. Thus, compliance with emission standards is not sufficient where a danger or nuisance to neighbours is present. Nuisance or danger will, of course, depend on the facility's particular location and emission pathways.

2.5 Chapter 10

Administrative fines of up to ATS 500,000 may be imposed on persons not complying with the relevant provisions of the Air Pollution Law for Boiler Facilities. These rules do not apply where the offence falls under the jurisdiction of criminal courts.

2.5.4 Ozone Law

A central aspect of the federal Ozone Law (*Ozongesetz*), enacted in 1992, is the requirement to reduce ozone precursors (nitrogen oxides and volatile organic compounds) in stages. The Ozone Law anticipates the following ambitious reduction goals: (a) 40% by the end of 1996; (b) 60% by the end of 2001; and (c) 70% by the end of 2006. The base years against which emission reductions are to be measured are 1985 for nitrogen oxides and 1988 for volatile organic compounds.

Furthermore, the Ozone Law provides that it is the State government's duty to warn the population in the event that ozone measurements exceed prescribed levels. Three separate warning levels exist (pre-warning, warning level I and warning level II). Warning level II represents the greatest danger to human health. If warning level I or II are exceeded, the state government is authorised to issue emergency orders, which may include the shutting down of facility operations and a prohibition on automobile traffic.

Under the Ozone Law administrative fines up to ATS 500,000 may be imposed on offenders if the offence does not constitute a crime which has to be dealt with by criminal courts.

2.5.5 Other air pollution laws

The states have also enacted air pollution laws which enhance federal provisions. Furthermore, various other laws (eg the Trade Code, the Mining Law and the Forest Law) contain relevant requirements, although these laws do not principally regulate air pollution issues. Two other important air pollution regulations are:

(1) federal parliamentary constitutional approval of the Agreement on Air Quality Levels (*Immissionsgrenzwertevereinbarung*) between the federal government and the individual states, which sets allowable air quality levels for a variety of chemical substances; and
(2) the Smog Alarm Law (*Smogalarmgesetz*).

2.6 Waste management

Pursuant to its constitutional competence, the federal parliament in 1990 passed a Hazardous Waste Law, establishing a greater degree of uniformity in this area of environmental law. Prior to this Law, various federal laws as well as individual state laws governed the treatment, storage and disposal of hazardous waste.

One progressive aspect of the Hazardous Waste Law is the emphasis on waste prevention. The waste prevention provisions of the Hazardous Waste Law set out a detailed framework of administrative measures that the federal government may impose on industry. In addition, the Hazardous Waste Law also contains detailed provisions regarding the treatment, storage and disposal of hazardous material.

Furthermore, under the Waste Management Act, administrative authorities are also entitled to issue clean-up orders. Section 32 of the Waste Management Act provides that where waste materials are not properly disposed of, stored or treated or where clean-up of waste material and contaminated ground is necessary to prevent danger to plant life or human health and safety, the local authority must require the responsible party to undertake necessary measures. In the event of imminent danger, the local authority itself must take action and seek reimbursement of its costs from the responsible party. The term 'responsible party' has been interpreted by case law decisions as the party causing the contamination. In the event that the responsible party cannot be located, is not legally in a position to undertake clean-up activity or cannot be held accountable for other reasons, the owner of the property may be held secondarily liable for the clean-up costs.

The circumstances where a secondary liability of property owners can be established are set out in s 18 of the Waste Management Act. This section provides that where hazardous waste or used oil have been disposed of on an owner's property illegally with their approval or where they have voluntarily tolerated such activity and have not undertaken reasonable preventive measures, the owner is liable for the proper disposal of the hazardous waste at their own cost. Where successor owners have knowledge of the disposal activity or where they should have had such knowledge, they can also be held liable. Where waste materials which are not hazardous substances within the meaning of the Hazardous Substances Act 1983 are disposed of, and where such disposal activity took place prior to 1990, a property owner's liability as an approver or tolerator of the activity is limited to the extent that the property owner explicitly approved of the disposal activity and received value for it, resulting in a benefit. The liability of the property owner is limited to the value of the benefit in excess of the income realisable for normal use of the property.

Moreover, the Waste Management Act contains a provision imposing a primary liability on property owners in certain circumstances. Paragraph 3 of s 18 of the Waste Management Act provides that the owner of a property where hazardous wastes (within the meaning of certain provisions of the Hazardous Substances Act 1983) were disposed of between 1983 and 1 July 1990 is responsible for the proper treatment of the hazardous waste material if the possessor of the waste material used the property for the collection or storage of hazardous waste with the approval of the property owner or his predecessor.

Finally, it has to be emphasised that the regulation of non-hazardous waste principally falls within the jurisdiction of the individual states, which have enacted respective state Waste Management Acts.

The violation of provisions contained in the Waste Management Act may result in an administrative fine of up to ATS 500,000 where the respective action or omission is not subject to proceedings before the criminal courts.

2.7 Town and country planning/zoning

2.7.1 Town and country planning

Since 1954, when the Constitutional Court ruled that town and country planning (*Raumplanung*) is a state power, the states have enacted planning laws (*Raumordnungsgesetze*). Although there are nine different state laws in existence, there are some common aspects and procedures. The laws distinguish between planning on a state level (*überörtliche Raumplanung*) and on community level (*örtliche Raumplanung*). Planning on the state level principally consists of regulations by the state governments or development programmes (*Entwicklungsprogramme*) containing basic planning principles important for larger regions, such as traffic planning and determination of areas which will be used for a particular purpose (eg agricultural areas etc). Based on the state level regulations, the city councils (*Gemeinderat*) enact planning regulations at a local level. The enactment of community planning regulations is one of the most important powers of the city councils.

In order to ensure that the city councils take into account various planning issues, the state planning laws provide for a complicated procedure to be followed. This procedure includes:

(1) the investigation of all issues relevant for planning at a local level;
(2) the determination of planning policies by the city council;
(3) the promulgation of a draft regulation for the area indicating how the area may be developed;
(4) the opportunity for each individual resident of the community to review the draft regulation and to comment on it in writing;
(5) the city council must review all comments;
(6) the city council enacts the planning regulation;
(7) the State government (*Landesregierung*) approves the regulation; and
(8) the final regulation is promulgated.

However, the entire approval procedure often takes years and there are some areas of Austria which still only have a draft regulation. If relevant circumstances change, the planning laws allow for amendment of the regulations. If a landowner believes that the planning regulation is illegal, he may file an application with the Constitutional Court, asking it to declare the regulation invalid. One particular aspect of the illegality of planning regulations is the non-adherence to the required, yet complicated, procedure before issuing the regulation.

2.7.2 Zoning law

Each of the nine Austrian provinces has its own zoning law and numerous differences exist between these laws. The planning regulations of the city councils contain provisions for the designation of specific areas of the land for specific purposes, such as construction areas, traffic areas, housing areas, industrial areas, recreation areas, etc (*Flächenwidmungspläne*). For construction areas, the planning laws determine the various principles (*Bebauungspläne*) that have to be followed by an applicant for a construction permit. A construction permit is issued only after a hearing at which the neighbours and all authorities who may wish to comment on the construction (eg fire department) are invited. The neighbours are allowed to raise objections against the construction if their subjective public rights (protection against pollution, distance of the construction from the neighbor's land, etc) would be violated by the construction. Construction permits are issued by the mayor of the community and have an extensive appeals process. First, the approval can be appealed to the city council. Secondly, the city council's decision may be brought before the authority of the state which supervises the municipality (*Gemeindeaufsichtsbehörde*). Finally, if there is still disagreement, a petition against the decision of the state authority may be filed with the Administrative Court or with the Constitutional Court by the aggrieved party.

2.8 Use and storage of hazardous substances—Chemicals Law

The primary intention of the federal Chemicals Law (*Chemikaliengesetz*) is to ensure that the producers and importers of chemicals which have potential to cause damage to human health or the environment are subject to regulatory supervision. The

Chemical Law's principal regulatory tool is the obligation to notify all new chemical products. Producers wishing to introduce new chemicals into commercial business must first notify the federal Ministry of Environment, Youth and Family Affairs. The ministry has the authority to limit or absolutely prohibit the use of dangerous chemicals, and has made use of this authority in the past. Chemicals are also regulated through a variety of other Austrian product-related standards which exceed the relevant EC law standards.

Under the Chemicals Law administrative fines of up to ATS 400,000 may be imposed on offenders if the relevant action or omission does not constitute a crime which has to be dealt with by criminal courts.

2.9 Noise and nuisance

The general rule concerning noise and nuisance is contained in ss 364 and 364a of the Austrian Civil Code (*Allgemeines Bürgerliches Gesetzbuch*), which provide for limited strict liability.

A property owner can obtain injunctive relief against a neighbour only if the impact (eg water, noise, smoke, heat, smell, vibrations etc) from the neighbour's property exceed those which are customary for the area and, in addition, if the usual use of the owner's property is substantially impaired. If, on the other hand, the impairment is caused by a mining operation or by a plant with a valid administrative permit that exceeds its allowable emissions, the property owner is only entitled to claim damages (ie the property owner cannot seek injunctive relief). It is important to note, however, that the definition of 'allowable emissions' may be more stringent than standards contained in a licence issued by an administrative authority. In a groundbreaking decision in 1995, the Austrian Supreme Court held that facility owners complying with an outdated permit were not automatically shielded from a neighbour's damages claim.

2.10 Other environmental laws

In addition to the Austrian environmental laws described above, the federal Law of the Forests (*Forstgesetz*), Mining Law (*Berggesetz*), Fertilisers Law (*Düngemittelgesetz*) and Plant Protective Agents Law (*Pflanzenschutzmittelgesetz*), as well as the respective state laws such as the Fishing Laws (*Fischereigesetze*), Hunting Laws (*Jagdgesetze*) and the Laws on the Preservation of Natural Beauty (*Naturschutzgesetze*) illustrate Austria's commitment to comprehensive environmental protection.

2.11 Environmental Impact Assessment Law

In 1985, the European Community adopted a directive on environmental impact assessment which requires member states to assess the environmental impacts of certain public and private projects. Austria implemented this EC directive into national law in 1993 by adopting the Environmental Impact Assessment Law (*Umweltverträglichkeitsprüfungsgesetz*).

This law provides the following essential rules:

(1) persons proposing to build or substantially modify certain listed categories of activity (eg oil refineries and disposal sites) must submit an environmental impact statement to the state authority;

2.11   Chapter 10

(2) the state authority must establish a project group, which assesses its potential environmental impact and drafts an environmental impact opinion;
(3) this opinion must be published and be available for public scrutiny; and
(4) other administrative authorities, to which the project might also be subject, must take into consideration the environmental impact opinion.

Furthermore, the Environmental Impact Assessment Law provides that all permit proceedings under the various environmental laws are to be concentrated into one proceeding. It is also possible to obtain a clearance order from the authorities confirming that the law is not applicable.

Non-compliance with the provisions of this law may result in administrative fines of up to ATS 200,000 if the violation does not constitute a crime which is subject to proceedings before the criminal courts.

2.12   Law on environmental information

The explicit goal of the Law on Environmental Information is to inform the public about the environment, in particular by guaranteeing free access to environmental data held by the administrative authorities as well as through the publication of environmental data. Environmental data is defined very broadly under the Law to include among other things information on the condition of air, water, and soil, remedial plans and sampling results. Furthermore, the Law on Environmental Information states that access to environmental data is not dependent upon demonstrating a legally recognised interest in it.

Administrative fines of up to ATS 200,000 may be imposed if obligations under this Law are neglected. Again, these provisions only apply if the relevant action or omission does not constitute a crime which comes under the jurisdiction of the criminal courts.

3   PARTICULAR ENVIRONMENTAL ISSUES RELEVANT TO TRANSACTIONS

3.1   Assumption of liability

3.1.1   Liability under administrative laws

Since there is no single comprehensive environmental statute which encompasses all areas of environmental law in Austria, there is no single liability rule for environmental contamination. However, all the different provisions mentioned thus far imposing liability follow a certain concept. The general rule with respect to liability under environmental administrative laws is that a person causing contamination may be held liable for the prevention of further contamination and the clean-up of the contamination which has been caused and/or related costs *(Prinzip der Verursacherhaftung)*. In the event that a party does not undertake such steps and the relevant authority performs the necessary measures, the authority is able to recover its costs from the party causing the contamination. Provisions imposing *Verursacherhaftung* are found in the Water Law, the Hazardous Waste Law and the Law of the Forests.

The general rule with respect to property owners is that they can also be liable under certain circumstances *(Liegenschaftseigentümerhaftung)* even if they did not cause the contamination. Provisions imposing secondary liability on property owners are found in the Water Laws and the Hazardous Waste Law.

Furthermore, certain environmental provisions (eg the Hazardous Waste Law, the Old Waste Sites Act and the Law of the Forests) provide that public authorities have to bear the clean-up costs in the event that neither the party who has caused the contamination nor the property owner can be held liable.

The administrative authorities have to apply the various environmental law provisions cumulatively if all elements of the relevant provisions are fulfilled. Thus, a single clean-up or remedial order could, for example, be based on the Water Law, the Old Waste Sites Act and the Law on the Forests.

The person that has the actual and legal power of control (*Verfügungsmacht*) over the enterprise is responsible for compliance with the provisions of the Trade Code. If a trade is carried on by a legal entity, a representative under trade law (*gewerberechtlicher Geschäftsführer*) must be nominated. This person is then responsible for compliance with the provisions of the Trade Code. According to s 309 of the Austrian Civil Code, any person or entity actually exercising custodial powers over the facility will be deemed to be an operator of an enterprise. In the event that a facility terminates its operation, the operator of the facility is liable for compliance with the respective administrative provisions.

3.1.2 Civil law liability

Since Austria operates a Civil Code, private environmental claims are based on statutory provisions, and judicial decisions play an important role in refining the scope of broadly worded statutory provisions. However, while civil law aspects have received a great deal of attention, it is fair to say that civil law suits regarding environmental matters are fairly rare. One of the reasons undoubtedly is the difficulty of establishing causal connection between activities and impacts. Thus, Austrian environmental law is still dominated by administrative law.

3.2 Dealing with historical liabilities

3.2.1 Liability under the Civil Code

Whenever an acquisition of assets or of shares in an Austrian company is contemplated, the question of liability for past practices and procedures arises.

In share transactions, since the target company remains in place and only changes at the shareholder level occur, the target company will continue to be liable for past practices and procedures. In short, the share transfer does not change the potential scope of liability of the target company.

In asset transactions, the general statutory provision governing the liability of the purchaser of an enterprise is s 1409 of the Civil Code. According to this provision, the purchaser of a company can be held jointly and severally liable with the seller towards the company's creditors for any pre-existing liabilities (including those relating to environmental matters) of the acquired enterprise. Without prejudice to the creditor's rights against the seller, a person acquiring a company only becomes liable for such liabilities of the acquired enterprise of which he knew or should have known at the time of the acquisition. However, the purchaser's liability is limited to the value of the assets actually acquired. In the event that the seller of a company is a corporate relative (*naher Angehöriger*) of the acquirer, the seller may be held liable for any previous debts of the company insofar as he cannot prove that he neither knew nor should have known of the debts at the time of the acquisition. Any agreements between the seller and the purchaser of a company to the prejudice of creditors are invalid.

3.2 *Chapter 10*

3.2.2 Liability under the Commercial Code

In asset transactions, pursuant to s 25 of the Commercial Code (*Handelsgesetzbuch*), a person or legal entity acquiring a commercial business and continuing the business under the former company name, with or without indicating the legal succession, is liable for all debts (including those relating to environmental matters) incurred in the course of business by the former proprietor. In contrast to s 1409 of the Civil Code outlined above, the liability under the Commercial Code is not limited to the value of the assets taken over by the purchaser. However, it is permissible to restrict the liability of the purchaser by agreement and thereby exclude liability under s 25 of the Commercial Code. The validity of any such agreement vis-à-vis third party creditors necessitates its entry in the commercial register (*Firmenbuch*) and publication, or individual notification to each third party creditor. However, an agreed upon exclusion of liability is only allowable within the limits set out in s 1409 of the Civil Code. If the company name is not continued, the purchaser of a business can be held liable for the previous business debts only under the provisions of the Civil Code.

3.3 Liability of managers and directors

As outlined in para 2.2.1 above, only natural persons can be subject to administrative penalties under the various administrative laws. However, a legal entity is liable for imposed fines and repayment jointly with the offender if the offender was the company's representative.

For corporations and partnerships, the general rule is that the person authorised to represent the company bears responsibility for compliance with the provisions of administrative law. In large companies, managing directors are often not in a position to ensure compliance and a need arises to allow for delegation. Section 9 of the Austrian Administrative Offences Code (*Verwaltungsstrafgesetz*) provides for the possibility of appointing a 'responsible agent'. The agent is solely responsible for compliance with applicable administrative law provisions. The administrative authorities may even request corporations or partnerships to appoint such an agent.

The responsible agent may also be authorised to represent the company vis-à-vis third parties, although this is not necessary. Thus, the managing directors may define their fields of responsibility and then appoint one managing director as the responsible agent or may appoint other persons (eg employees) as responsible agents for specific aspects of the operations of the company. The administrative authorities will only accept the nomination of a responsible agent who is either granted powers to execute documents on behalf of the company or who actually works for the company.

For the appointment of a responsible agent to have full force, the following four requirements must be met:

(1) The person chosen must have his legal residence in Austria.
(2) The responsible agent must be subject to criminal punishment; thus only persons with full legal capacity can be appointed as responsible agents. Persons who do not have full legal capacity or who are exempted from prosecution for any other personal reason (eg diplomatic immunity status) cannot act as a responsible agent.
(3) There must be proof that the person appointed as responsible agent agreed to the appointment. This requirement is of particular importance. Therefore, in employment contracts or in the case of the subsequent assignment of a certain task, the scope of responsibility should be described in detail and the agent should

draw up a certificate as proof that he agreed to the assignment of responsibility.
(4) A responsible agent must have the power to give out instructions for his scope of activity. Thus, formal appointment is not sufficient. The responsible agent must be in a position to prevent infringements of administrative regulations.

Despite the appointment of a responsible agent, a managing director, a member of the managing board or an individual entrepreneur may still be liable for prosecution under administrative criminal law if:

(a) the responsible agent can prove that he acted within the scope of and in accordance with instructions given and that he was thereby unable to observe the administrative law;
(b) the managing director, a member of the managing board or the individual entrepreneur deliberately failed to act to prevent a prohibited act which he knew was occurring.

3.4 Liability of those financing businesses

Under present Austrian law, financial providers cannot become directly liable for environmental problems arising from the businesses in which they invest. Nevertheless, those financing businesses are indirectly affected by environmental laws. Environmental risks could become business risks, and subsequently jeopardise the financier's investments. Following the motto 'the cleaner competition will win the business', financial providers are increasingly concentrating on businesses which reduce environmental risks through an active environmental management system. Another issue for financial providers is the fact that investments in projects that cause severe damage to the environment could adversely affect the public image of the financier of such projects.

3.5 Transferability of permits and licences

Applying the Austrian rules of legal succession to asset transactions, while the acquirer of a business may be held liable for pre-existing liabilities of the business as outlined above (see para 3.2 above), it is generally entitled to continue to utilise environmental permits and licences granted to the target business. Furthermore, certain permits under the Water Law or the Plant Licensing Procedure are so-called orders in rem (*dingliche Bescheide*) which are effective for any person/entity who holds certain rights over the object which is addressed by an order.

4 MANAGING ENVIRONMENTAL ISSUES IN TRANSACTIONS

4.1 Assessment of environmental risks in transactions

4.1.1 General remarks

Environmental issues have assumed increasing importance in Austrian business transactions. In acquiring a business, purchasers must maintain a fairly broad perspective. A purchaser of a business should always be aware of the seller's existing environmental liabilities regarding past activities that may be passed on. Furthermore, a purchaser should also be aware of the seller's current operating practices and whether such practices comply with existing regulations as well as likely future regulations. With regulations imposing ever more stringent and expensive control technology, purchasing an 'outdated' facility may involve substantial initial environmental expenditure.

Due to the fact that various environmental law provisions impose liability on parties causing contamination and on property owners, it is important for potential buyers to assess the risk of soil and/or groundwater contamination in respect of the target property that may have resulted from past operations.

4.1.2 Environmental audits

Buyers who want to be provided with comprehensive information about the condition of the target enterprise or property often undertake an environmental due diligence investigation. The scope of such an investigation may vary from a simple visual on-site inspection to a detailed and intrusive sampling protocol depending on the likelihood of contamination and the size of a transaction.

In order to be able to assess the environmental risks of the target enterprise or property, a buyer should and generally does conduct due diligence which often covers the following information:

(1) schedule of all real property owned;
(2) current and past use of all real property as well as the surrounding property;
(3) description of facilities including all material governmental permits and licences;
(4) pending governmental permit or licensing proceedings;
(5) summary of material areas of non-compliance with permits or licences;
(6) material concerning compulsory internal reporting under the Trade Code;
(7) information about existing water licences;
(8) information about existing waste sites;
(9) information on air emissions;
(10) summary of malfunctions or facility breakdowns;
(11) information on material or suspected contamination of soil and/or groundwater
(12) information on pending or possible administrative or court proceedings with respect to contamination or negative environmental impacts;
(13) existing environmental assessments, reviews or audits; and
(14) information on close-down orders.

On the basis of the information provided, the following examinations and inspections could be undertaken by a potential buyer:

(1) inspection of the list of suspected contaminated sites and the list of old waste sites under the Old Waste Sites Act. However, the lists under the Old Waste Sites Act are not comprehensive. Accordingly, if the property does not appear on either of these lists, this does not mean that the property is not contaminated;
(2) inspection of the Land Register (*Grundbuch*) and the Water Book (*Wasserbuch*)
(3) determination of whether the target company operates in compliance with issued governmental permits and licences;
(4) evaluation of administrative clean-up or remedial orders as well as environmental claims raised or threatened by third parties; and
(5) testing of soil and groundwater.

In any event, the buyer will need to ensure that appropriate environmental warranty and indemnification clauses are included in the contracts. In drafting contractual provisions, it is important to be aware of potentially applicable Civil Code and related provisions (eg warranty, *laesio enormis*, fraud/error, tort law, guarantees).

4.2 Important Civil Code provisions

4.2.1 Warranty

The warranty (*Gewährleistung*) provision is one of the most important in the Austrian Civil Code in the context of environmental issues on the sale of a business or property.

A warranty is the liability of a seller or a contractor for the quality of the goods sold or services provided. The statutory provisions govern that the seller warrants to the buyer that the item which is to be sold contains the normal characteristics of such an item. The warranty provision does not distinguish between defects in the goods (*Sachmängel*) and defects in title (*Rechtsmängel*), but does distinguish between material and non-material defects. A defect is considered material if the goods sold cannot be used for their contracted or normal use (eg due to extensive soil and groundwater contamination). Furthermore, the warranty provision distinguishes between defects which can be remedied and those which cannot. A defect is considered as not remediable if (a) the repair is technically impossible, (b) the repair would be technically possible but not economic, or (c) a repair cannot be made within a reasonable period of time.

The legal consequences depend on the nature of the defect. If the defect is material and not remediable (*Unbehebbarer Mangel*), the purchaser has the right to rescind the contract. Accordingly, the purchaser must return any goods already delivered to him and the seller must return the purchase price. If the defect is material but remediable, the purchaser has the right to request either repair (*Mängelbehebung*) or a reduction in the purchase price (*Preisminderung*). If the defect is non-material and not remediable, the purchaser can only demand a price reduction. If the defect is non-material but remediable, the purchaser may demand either the repair of the defect or a price reduction.

While the statutory warranty provisions substantially protect buyers, it is generally advisable to set out contractual rights and remedies in detail as part of the purchase agreement. The parties to a contract are free to deviate from the statutory warranty provisions. Generally, a statutory warranty claim must be raised within the period of six months for moveable property or 3 years for immoveable property. This period runs from the delivery of the moveables or the transfer of title (*Abnahme*) of immoveables. Companies are regarded as immoveable items, which means that under statutory provisions the three-year statute of limitations would apply. Since environmental defects may remain hidden for many years, buyers must be aware of the statutory time limitation when negotiating contractual provisions. In commercial transactions, the purchaser has a statutory obligation to notify the seller of his claim immediately after the delivery of the object of purchase or after identification of the defect which was not identifiable at the delivery.

The warranty liability is imposed by the law and is not dependent on the negligence of the seller. Liability exists even if the contract does not contain an express warranty clause. However, the parties to a contract are free to modify and, to a large extent, even to waive the warranty provisions under the Civil Code. It is also important to note that in the event that (1) contamination was readily evident (*in die Augen fallen*) to the purchaser, or (2) the purchaser knew of contamination on the property purchased, the warranty provisions under the Civil Code do not apply.

According to Austrian jurisdiction a plaintiff may base his claims concerning defects of the goods or in title cumulatively on the statutory warranty provisions or in tort law; the Austrian courts have held that there exists a 'real concurrence' (*Echte Konkurrenz*) between these two areas of civil law. The advantage of the tort law provisions is that the statutory period of limitation is three years from the date the damage and the person who has caused the damage is known to the aggrieved person.

4.2.2 Fraud/error

If a contracting party has concluded a contract because of the fraudulent conduct (*Betrug*) of the other party, the contract is invalid if this party, knowing the real facts, would not have concluded the contract. It should be noted that, unlike in criminal law, fraud does not require an intent to cause damage or unlawfully enrich oneself.

Contrary to fraud, an error (*Irrtum*) by a contracting party does not automatically invalidate a contract. An error as to the motivation of a party is irrelevant in contract law unless agreed upon separately. An error going to the substance of a contract is an error about the nature of the transaction itself or about the object of the transaction (eg what is sold as clean property later turns out to be contaminated). A contract may be rescinded by the prejudiced party if it was concluded due to an error in expression or an error going to the substance of a contract, and, in addition if:

(1) the error was caused by the other contracting party;
(2) the other contracting party must have noticed the error; or
(3) the error was promptly detected by the prejudiced party and the other party was notified.

In the event of errors regarding conditions of minor importance, the contract may not be rescinded, but the party in the wrong is obliged to pay reasonable compensation.

A claim grounded in error must be raised within the period of three years from the date the contract was concluded. The statutory period of limitation for a claim based on fraud is 30 years beginning with the conclusion of the contract.

4.3 Contractual provisions

Considering the fact that contamination or other environmental risks could lead to enormous remedial or clean-up expenses for the buyer, it is very important to address clearly the issue of liability in contracts concerning real property or merger and acquisition transactions. Thus, the following contractual clauses could be negotiated between the parties to such contracts. However, in most transactions either one of the following clauses, or a combination thereof is included in the contracts.

4.3.1 Purchase price

If contamination or other environmental risks are obvious to both parties to a contract, this could be considered in determining the purchase price for the target enterprise or object. In such an event, the warranty obligation of the seller could be excluded from the contract.

4.3.2 Definitions

In any event the parties should attempt to define clearly the relevant terms (eg contamination, waste site) in the contract, in order to minimise the risk of a misinterpretation of the contractual provisions. This is particularly important in light of the fact that there are not clearly defined clean-up targets under Austrian law.

4.3.3 Escrow of purchase price

If a contract is concluded at a time when contamination is expected, but no information as to the intensity or potential clean-up costs is available, one option is to hold a part of the purchase price in escrow until the relevant information has been received by the buyer or the representation and warranty period has expired.

4.3.4 Bank guarantee

The risk of future clean-up or remedial costs may also be covered by a bank guarantee which is issued in favour of the buyer of the target enterprise or property.

4.3.5 Guarantee

A guarantee as to the non-existence of contamination is the optimal contract clause from the purchaser's perspective. If a seller agrees to such a guarantee, he should at least attempt to include a maximum limit for price reduction or damages as well as a time frame within which claims must be made.

In addition, a guarantee as to the completeness and correctness of the target company's balance sheet is a common clause in share purchase agreements or asset deals. If the target company has not created reserves in the balance sheet, although it would have been obliged legally to do so due to impending clean-up or remedial costs, the buyer of assets or shares may demand a price reduction or claim damages from the seller. It should be emphasised, however, that a contractual balance sheet guarantee does not always provide adequate protection. There is a large grey area as to when reserves need to be made in the balance sheet for potential future environmental costs. Therefore, a cautious buyer should always insist upon a separate environmental guarantee clause.

4.3.6 Exclusion of warranty provisions

From the seller's perspective a contractual clause excluding the application of the Civil Code's warranty provisions is of course desirable. However, a waiver by the purchaser of the Civil Code warranty provisions is not enforceable if the seller has at the same time guaranteed the non-existence of contamination. Such waivers are usually interpreted rather strictly. In addition, such waivers do not exclude the purchaser from choosing other legal remedies unless these remedies have also been permissibly waived by the purchaser.

4.3.7 Statement of absence of knowledge

The statement of absence of knowledge is occasionally used in connection with a waiver by the purchaser concerning the warranty provisions. In this statement the seller declares that neither he nor persons related to him is/are aware of any contamination or imminent administrative proceedings. In the event this statement turns out to be untrue, the purchaser is entitled to contest the contract based on error or fraud.

4.3 *Chapter 10*

4.3.8 Indemnification clause

Where the party to be responsible for clean-up or remedial costs is agreed upon in the contract, an indemnification clause should also be included. The reason for this indemnification clause is that administrative authorities may still hold a person liable under applicable administrative laws even if another party has contractually agreed to finance the clean-up costs.

4.3.9 Statutory warranty period

The parties to a contract are free to prolong or shorten the statutory warranty period in the contract.

4.4 Management of environmental responsibility and corporate structuring

The Austrian environmental laws contain many provisions which cover different aspects of modern environmental management. The Trade Code provides that the operator of a facility is obliged to determine periodically whether the facility operates in compliance with the terms of its licence and environmental laws (*Eigenüberwachung*). Furthermore, a facility security analysis must be carried out and is the basis for a contingency plan in the event of a malfunction at certain facilities. In addition, almost all environmental laws impose record-keeping obligations with respect to environmental matters, to facilitate supervision by the respective authorities.

Under Austrian law, there is no general environmental agent (*Umweltbeauftragter*) who is responsible for all environmental matters in relation to a businesses. Instead, numerous provisions assign specific environmental responsibilities to various agents and thus create the framework for an internal structure in respect of businesses. Important positions are the representative under trade law (*Gewerberechtlicher Geschäftsführer*), the waste officer (*Abfallbeauftragter*), the waste water officer (*Abwasserbeauftragter*) and the safety adviser (*Sicherheitsvertrauensperson*).

As opposed to the rather rigid Austrian environmental management instruments outlined above, Council Regulation (EEC) 1836/93 of 29 June 1993 allowing voluntary participation by companies in the industrial sector in a Community Eco-Management and Audit Scheme (EMAS) follows the principle of voluntary participation. The objective of this regulation is to promote continuous improvements in the environmental performance of industrial activity by (1) the establishment and implementation of environmental policies, programmes and management systems by companies in relation to their sites, (2) the systematic, objective and periodic evaluation of the performance of such systems and (3) the provision of information to the public in respect of environmental performance. To attain these goals, each participating company has to perform certain tasks including adopting a company environmental policy, introducing an environmental programme subsequent to an environmental review of the site, and carrying out their own environmental audits or having them undertaken by another firm.

4.5 Insurance

Currently Austrian companies do not generally conclude insurance contracts to cover the risks of potential clean-up or remedial costs. Insurance costs are regarded as prohibitive. However, sudden environmental damage resulting from the operation of a business may to some extent be covered by regular professional liability insurance. Austrian insurance contracts generally contain a clause excluding insurance coverage for environmental damages which do not result from sudden events such as the explosion of a tank, but rather from a continuous leakage over a longer time period. Specific environmental liability insurance for enterprises is not yet compulsory, albeit a previous draft of a general civil law on environmental liability provided for such an insurance obligation.

5 CONCLUSION

A major change to Austrian environmental law has been under discussion for more than 5 years concerning the enactment of a general civil law on environmental liability. This purportedly would ease evidentiary burdens for plaintiffs in respect of such matters as causation and would probably also provide for strict liability. This law would not be limited to clean-up law in the traditional sense of soil and groundwater contamination, but would also relate to general emission issues. Currently no action is contemplated to push for the enactment of such a law, and accordingly it cannot be foreseen whether the draft will become law in the near future.

Austria is a country in which both law-making bodies and enforcement authorities have taken environmental issues very seriously. The result is a broad array of environmental laws and regulations, non-compliance with which can result in substantial increased costs of compliance along with administrative and other penalties. Given the potential liabilities involved for purchasers, environmental due diligence investigations have become a standard practice of Austrian merger and acquisition transactions. Purchasers should in particular be aware of potential groundwater contamination issues given that groundwater is a very important source of water in Austria, the protection of which is enforced vigorously by Water Law authorities.

Chapter 11

SWITZERLAND

Dr Hans U Liniger
Attorney at Law, Wallisellen

1 INTRODUCTION

1.1 General legal system

Switzerland has a federal structure. There are three levels in the hierarchy of powers: the federation, the cantons and the communities. The responsibilities of these levels are delineated by two basic rules:

(1) Powers are divided between the federation and the cantons by elaboration of the Federal Constitution. This means that the federation is only responsible if the constitution explicitly says so.
(2) Powers are divided between the cantons and the communities by the cantonal constitutions and laws. This means that the Communities are responsible as long the cantons do not regulate the area in question.

Switzerland is a country with a codified system of law. The main sources of the law are statutes and regulations, both federal and cantonal, and municipal ordinances. Decisions rendered by the courts are not binding on other courts. However, the lower courts generally follow the principles established by the Swiss Federal Court and other higher courts. Thus, precedents of higher courts and in particular of the Swiss Federal Court are becoming a more important source of Swiss law. The cantonal constitutions govern the procedure of introducing, passing and enacting cantonal statutes and regulations as well as municipal ordinances.

On the federal level, Bills may be introduced by the Federal Council, by each of the two houses of Parliament and any of its members, and by any canton. Bills enacted are either federal statutes or federal decrees. They can only be enacted if both houses of Parliament approve the same wording. If 50,000 voters or eight cantons so require, within three months of publication of a federal Bill, a referendum is held and the Bill may take effect only if it is approved by the majority of the voters in the referendum.

An amendment of the constitution may be proposed by 100,000 voters, but the amendment becomes law only if a majority of the voters and of all cantons adopt the amendment in a referendum.

1.2 History of environmental law

In Switzerland, the early origins of environmental law can be traced from private tort, real estate, and trespass remedies in civil law to pioneering legislation in forest protection in the early 1900s. However, the modern era of environmental law, can be said to have had its genesis in 1972, beginning with the amendment of federal legislation addressing water pollution control, and strengthened with the entry into force on 1 January 1985 of the Federal Law relating to the Protection of the Environment of 7 October 1983 (*Bundesgesetz über den Umweltschutz, Umweltschutzgesetz*, SR 814.01—LPE).

Since this time, attention has primarily been directed at executory responsibilities and therefore on the drafting of executory laws and regulations on all levels. Experience quickly revealed, however, that rapid technological developments and continuing high levels of environmental pollution made additional regulations, as well as modifications of already existing regulations, unavoidable. Furthermore, environmental legislative policy received new stimuli from the UN Conference on the Environment and Development of June 1992 in Rio de Janeiro as well as from the concept of sustainable development. The principle of co-operation between the environment and industry has thus also developed into a central issue. Of particular importance is the need to supplement instruments of environmental policy with economic measures.

The final voting on the revision of the Federal Law relating to the Protection of the Environment (LPE) was held on 21 December 1995 (entry into force 1 July 1997). Due to this revision, several ordinances have been changed or newly enforced as set out below.

Selection of newly existing, amended and planned ordinances pertaining to the Federal Law relating to the Protection of the Environment

Wastes

Ordinance on the Movements of Special Wastes	Amended
Technical Ordinance Relating to Waste	Amended
Ordinance on Beverage Packaging	Amended
Ordinance on the Recycling and Disposal of Electric and Electronic Equipment (ORDE)	New

Contaminated sites

Ordinance on the Restoration of Contaminated Sites (Contaminated Sites Ordinance (CSO))	New
Ordinance on the Financing of Restoration Costs of Contaminated Sites	New

Soil protection

Ordinance on Soil Pollutants	Amended

Substances

Ordinance on Substances (New Battery Annex)	Amended
Safety Data Sheet Ordinance	New
Ordinance on Good Laboratory Practices	New

Organisms

Ordinance on the Handling of Organisms in Closed Systems (Confinement Ordinance)	New
Ordinance on the Handling of Organisms in the Environment (Release Ordinance)	New
Ordinance on the Federal Board of Experts for Biological Security	New

Pollution control

Ordinance on Air Pollution Control	Amended
Ordinance on Noise Abatement	Amended
Ordinance on the Protection against Non-ionising Radiation (OPNR)	New

Economic instruments

Ordinance Relating to Financial Incentives on VOC	New
Ordinance Relating to Financial Incentives on the Sulphur Content of Superlight Fuel Oil (SFO)	New
Ordinance on the Promotion of Environmental Technologies	New

Now Switzerland is equipped with a modern system of environmental law which is internationally progressive. This first revision of the LPE introduces financial incentives and instruments, incorporates regulations concerning the handling of environmentally hazardous organisms (genetic technology), adopts a stringent liability system as well as establishing new strategies to deal with waste disposal. The realisation of the co-operation principle is also furthered by the insertion of an article, which regulates co-operation between the federal authorities and private industry.

1.3 Structure of environmental law

Legislative competencies are traditionally, and by constitutional law, vested with the cantons. The maturity of the environmental law system marks a major shift towards federal legislative competence.

Since 1971, the protection of the environment has been a federal duty. Article 24 of the constitution vests broad power in the Swiss Confederation to enact rules and regulations to protect the human being and the natural environment against harmful influences, especially noise and air pollution.

Environmental law is therefore mainly federal law which vests broad power in the Confederation to enact rules and regulations to protect the environment. The Swiss Federal Office of Environment, Forests and Landscape (FOEFL) is of major importance. The legal division prepares reports for the Federal Court, Federal Council and the departments. It is also responsible for preliminary examination and approval of cantonal legislation on implementation.

Each canton however establishes its own policies towards enforcement of environmental law. The cantonal administrative and organisational autonomy remains largely untouched by LPE. Due to the differences in each cantonal system's administration, competence, and jurisdiction, enforcement of environmental law has become a major issue of concern. While most cantons have established departments to implement and enforce environmental law as mandated by LPE (art 42), co-ordination between both cantonal and federal agencies remains difficult.

1.4 *Chapter 11*

1.4 Impact of environmental law on business

Swiss environmental law has developed rapidly since 1985. It now constitutes an imposing body of mainly administrative law that creates significant regulatory compliance risks. However, legislative action has almost exclusively taken the form of coercive regulation (compulsory standards, licences, permits, specific technical measures, performance standards, specification standards etc) rather then venturing into the new and unproven area of economic instruments. Uncertainty for business planning is thus somewhat reduced, costs have become determinable and the risk of non-compliance penalties falls on a relatively determinable class. Also, a common law civil litigation system, to allow the general public to intervene in favour of the environment, does not exist.

2 OUTLINE OF ENVIRONMENTAL LAW RELEVANT TO MERGER AND ACQUISITION TRANSACTIONS

2.1 Federal Law relating to the Protection of the Environment (LPE)

2.1.1 Introduction

Whilst the Federal Law relating to the Protection of the Environment (LPE) is the keystone of environmental law, it is by no means a comprehensive codification. It addresses the following areas which were not, or were insufficiently, dealt with by pre-existing federal statutes, namely air pollution, noise abatement, vibrations, radiation, substances and organisms dangerous to the environment, soil protection and waste management.

The central purpose of LPE is 'to protect persons, animals, and plants, their biological communities and habitats against harmful effects or nuisances and to maintain the fertility of the soil' (LPE, art 1). LPE establishes fundamental principles, furnishes definitions and guidelines, describes specific areas subject to environmental protection, and, most importantly, provides the Federal Government with statutory powers to issue regulations on air pollution, noise abatement, radiation, insulation, toxic substances, waste and soil protection.

2.1.2 Principle of prevention

The principle of prevention states that early preventive measures shall be taken in order to limit effects which could become harmful or a nuisance (LPE, art 1, s 2). The obvious importance of this provision is qualified by the fact that existing pollution shifts the focus from prevention to mandatory improvements.

2.1.3 The polluter pays principle

The actual impact of the 'polluter pays' principle (LPE, art 2) is less important than might be imagined. LPE holds that only the costs of measures taken to comply with its provisions are to be paid by the one who causes the pollution. Most measures are to be taken at the source of the pollution (LPE, art 11, s 1) and are therefore automatically to be carried out by the polluter. Article 2 should not be misconstrued as the basis of a strict tort system for environmental damage. Also, this provision does not introduce alternative legal instruments, such as economic incentives to reduce pollution, into the main system of legislative and administrative regulation of environmental law.

The revised LPE, however, introduced the use of economic incentives only for volatile organic compounds (VOCs) (LPE, art 35 a), such as solvents, the sulphur content of 'extra light' heating oil and agricultural fertilisers (LPE, art 35 b).

2.1.4 The principle of co-operation

The principle of co-operation establishes the necessity for authorities and private individuals to work together towards the common goal of environmental protection. A separate provision in the LPE now also settles the question of co-operation with private industry (LPE, art 41 a). It does not stipulate, however, comprehensive co-operation with the sectors of industry concerned, but the possibility of a case-specific co-operation in matters relating to the *implementation* of legal provisions.

The term 'inter-sector agreement', which is mentioned in the LPE, art 41a, para 2, provides a possible tool. Swiss legislators count, at least partly, on the self-regulating capacity of the individual sectors, which are also encouraged to contribute to meeting environmental protection standards. According to the new provision, if the agreements proposed by a sector prove suitable in attaining the legal objectives, these could be incorporated in the Implementation Law. However, inter-sector agreements must not lead to anti-trust competitive restrictions—a conflict which indeed will not be easy to resolve. However, it is in the interest of most if not all sector members to join an agreement.

To apply such self-supervisory models, the Federal Council is authorised to issue provisions on the introduction of a voluntary system for eco-labels and environmental management and audit (LPE, art 43 a). The system was modelled on Council Regulation (EEC) 1836/93 of 29 June 1993 allowing voluntary participation by companies in the industrial sector in a Community Eco-Management and Audit Scheme (EMAS), and on ISO 14001. As a non-member country, Switzerland will, for the time being, not be able to participate in EMAS. Full participation of Swiss companies in EMAS is only possible through international treaties. Article 43 a constitutes a fall-back position in case the bilateral negotiations should fail. Nonetheless, it provides the Federal Council with the necessary freedom of action to apply such a system.

The duty of the Federal Council to consult with interested parties before enacting ordinances (LPE, art 39, s 3) and the power of public authorities to entrust private entities with their enforcement and implementation (LPE, art 43) are examples of this principle. Increasing difficulties with implementation and enforcement due to lack of qualified civil servants, excessively complicated procedures and restricted public budgets will have a profound impact on the importance of the principle of co-operation in the near future. It is important to note that authorities are more and more willing to negotiate solutions with interested parties, instead of enforcing the law by executive order. Despite several successful precedents it is still questionable whether this practice is covered by the principle of co-operation and the Federal Constitution.

2.1.5 Environmental pollution control system

LPE uses the terms 'emission' and 'immission' standards. While 'emissions' (art 7, ss 2 and 4) are measured at the source, for example, noise or smell emerging from a factory, 'immissions' (art 7, ss 2 and 4) are measured at their place of impact, for example, at neighbouring areas of the factory.

LPE establishes a two-tier system of pollution control. In the first stage harmful effects and nuisances are to be limited, irrespective of existing pollution. This limitation of 'emissions' (see definition above) is based on the availability of state-of-the-art technology and economic acceptability (LPE, art 11, s 2).

2.1 Chapter 11

The second stage involves impact thresholds 'immission' quality standards which define the level at which potentially harmful effects actually become harmful (LPE, art 11, s 3, art 14). In these circumstances, no reference to available technology or economic constraints is relevant.

In order to render the above system operational, the Federal Council is obliged to redefine maximum emission limits continuously (LPE, art 12) by promulgation of respective ordinances, regulations and executive orders.

2.2 Soil protection

The protection of soil quality is regulated in the Federal Law relating to Regional Planning of 22 June 1979 (*Raumplanungsgesetz*, SR 700). The LPE deals with the protection of soil quality against hazardous substances from air pollutants, auxiliary materials such as fertilisers, soil conditioners and pesticides, and wastes which are deposited in waste disposal sites.

The Ordinance on Contamination of the Soil of 1 July 1998 (*Verordnung über Belastungen des Bodens*, SR 814.12—VBBO) aims to ensure long-term soil fertility (VBBO, art 1, para 1). This provision affects only the top, unsealed and rooted soil layer (LPE, art 7, para 4b). This ordinance establishes different values for assessment of the need for restoration of a property. Soil restoration is only prescribed in development planning areas for horticulture, agriculture and forestry exploitation.

Actual soil protection is also regulated in various ordinances (LPE, art 33). Impact thresholds for air pollutants set in OPAIR (see para 2.5 below) also takes the fertility of the soil into account. OSUBST (see para 2.8 below) and other ordinances provide prohibitions and restrictions for the application of fertilisers and pesticides.

Should these measures prescribed by federal legislation be insufficient to meet the guidelines and levels for soil quality, the cantons are required to provide for stricter measures (LPE, art 34).

Soil is endangered also by surface degradation in the form of physical and mechanical damage. The revised LPE limits physical and mechanical damage. It introduces a directly applicable and universal regulation, which stipulates that soil may only be worked or cultivated in a manner so as not to cause lasting damage to its structure (LPE, art 33, s 2). This regulation prevents, for example, forest or agricultural vehicles flattening or compressing the soil to such an extent that the fertility of the soil or the ability of the soil to retain water is permanently affected. This prohibition is not applicable to the use of the soil for construction (LPE, art 33, s 2).

2.3 Liability for restoration of contaminated sites

The 1995 revision of the LPE also includes a provision on restoration of contaminated sites in connection with waste disposal (LPE, arts 32 c–32 e). The cantons are responsible for the restoration of contaminated sites if they represent damage or a risk to the environment. Restoration comprises putting the site into a condition in which risk of damage to the environment, especially to the groundwater, is removed.

Moreover the LPE now offers a solution to the problem of allocation of costs for the restoration of contaminated sites. It provides a veritable plethora of cost liabilities as established by Federal Supreme Court rulings. The first to be held liable for the restoration costs is the polluter, the second is the owner of the landfill or contaminated site. The owner is only liable for any costs incurred if he/she cannot prove that, even through exercising due diligence, he/she could not have been aware of the contamination, that he/she did not derive benefit from the contamination and that he/she will not derive any benefit from restoration. These three prerequisites must be met cumulatively in order for him/her to be exempted from the costs incurred. If several polluters or innocent landowners are involved, they share the restoration costs according to their respective degrees of culpability. A cost distribution provision will be issued on request by the authorities to establish the allocation of costs to the individual polluters or landowners.

The Ordinance on the Restoration of Contaminated Sites of 26 August 1998 (*Verordnung über die Sanierung von belasteten Standorten, Altlastenverordnung*, AltlV, SR 814.60—CSO) was brought into force on 1 October 1998. It contains regulations related to site identification, assessment of the need for restoration and surveillance.

The general duty to disclose information necessary for the enforcement of environmental law is established in LPE, art 46. This obligation serves as a basis for establishing whether a site owner can be obliged to conduct an environmental assessment.

Restoration liability established in LPE, art 32 c, para 1 affects all waste contaminated sites leading to detrimental or undesirable environmental effects or constituting an imminent environmental danger. Liability for restoration is only compulsory upon assessment of the corresponding *need for restoration*. Such an assessment requires several sometimes very costly investigations. Once a contaminated site is recorded in the contaminated sites register, the authorities may automatically request a preliminary investigation from the property owner. He/she is also provisionally liable for the investigation costs, although, he/she can claim them back as soon as the polluter is identified.

The basic steps in a compulsory site restoration are as follows:

(1) Recording and preliminary assessment by the authorities, listing in the register.
(2) Historical and technical preliminary investigation and intermediate assessment, determining whether the emissions from the contaminated site endanger a protected area.
(3) Detailed investigation determining the objective and urgency of restoration (based on a risk assessment).
(4) Restoration project.

The contaminated sites register, compiled by the cantons and open to the public, is a key tool for surveillance and control of contaminated sites. Once a surface contaminated with environmentally hazardous substances (eg waste oil) is recorded in the contaminated sites register, only meeting stringent standards will clear it from the register after remediation. This factor has a significant influence on the value of property. A mere listing in the sites register will act as a deterrent to potential buyers, quite apart from the resulting costs incurred by restoration liability.

The system pertaining to the prescribed investigation steps does not concur with the American ASTM standard (American Society for Testing and Materials, Standard Practice for Environmental Site Assessments: Transaction Screen Process). The preliminary investigation (Step 2) goes beyond Phase I of ASTM, inasmuch as it prescribes not only a historical investigation, but also the taking of soil samples.

According to the outcome of the preliminary investigations, the site in question will either have to be restored or merely monitored. The CSO contains differential threshold values for the assessment of hazardous substances in water, air and soil. The main focus is, however, placed on water pollution hazards. In case water is already contaminated and the pollutants exceed the concentration values defined in Annex 1 of

2.3 Chapter 11

the CSO, immediate application of restoration measures is generally prescribed. Restoration measures can also be imposed if the registered soil contaminants could potentially be released and constitute a corresponding danger. A contaminated site is also liable to be subject to restoration if the concentration value stipulated in Annex 2 for soil gas is exceeded and the emissions released in places regularly visited by people over a prolonged period of time.

The main matter of dispute associated with the restoration of contaminated sites relates to the question of cost liability. The issue of an Ordinance on the Financing of Site Restoration Costs is in fact anticipated, but a draft resolution has yet to be submitted.

2.4 Federal Law on Protection of Surface and Groundwaters

Apart from the LPE and respective ordinances, there are other laws and statutes pertaining to environmental protection. The Federal Law on Protection of Surface and Groundwaters of 24 January 1991 (*Bundesgesetz über den Schutz der Gewässer, Gewässerschutzgesetz*, SR 814.20—WPA) encompasses all natural, artificial, ground and surface water, both public and private. Unlike the water protection legislation of the European Union, the WPA does not focus on the different functions of water. Switzerland has not only established emission standards for the discharge of waste water, but also immission standards. The Ordinance on Wastewater Discharge of 8 December 1975 (*Verordnung über Wassereinleitungen*, SR 814.225.21) establishes quality standards for watercourses on the basis of 52 parameters, for example, heavy metals. The law and its ordinances are presently undergoing substantial structural revision.

Liability under the WPA is extensive. WPA, art 36, includes a general strict liability that goes beyond the general liability in the Swiss Civil Code or particular liability regimes in other fields (eg road traffic). Under the WPA, anyone who pollutes a watercourse through his industrial plant or by his own act or omissions is liable for the damage caused. Only a person who can prove force majeure, contributory blame, or the fault of a third party will be exonerated from liability.

The penal provisions in the WPA are detailed and quite severe. In the case of wilful or serious infractions, the penalty provides for a prison term of between three days and three years and a fine of up to CHF 40,000. When committed negligently the penalty is imprisonment of up to three months or a fine of up to CHF 5,000.

2.5 Air pollution

The Ordinance on Air Pollution Control of 16 December 1985 (*Luftreinhalteverordnung*, SR 814.318.142.1—OPAIR) came into effect on 1 March 1986, and is directly based on the LPE, which follows closely the two-stage system described above. OPAIR establishes maximum emission levels for approximately 150 toxic substances, and 40 different types of stationary sources and installations. This ordinance also provides impact thresholds for eight toxic substances. Cantonal authorities enforce OPAIR, and may set even stricter local standards, if they feel there is danger to the environment. Newly established industrial installations must meet and comply with established emission standards, while existing industrial installations have a 5-year grace period for compliance with these standards.

Owners of existing or planned installations must provide authorities with an emission declaration, containing detailed information concerning type, amount, and location of the emission. In certain cases, immission prognosis is required as well.

Switzerland aims to reduce its overall air pollution to the level of pollution which existed in 1955.

2.6 Environmentally sound waste disposal

The revision of the LPE in 1995 provided Switzerland with an up-to-date waste management law based on waste prevention and recycling. The owners of waste are responsible for the appropriate disposal of waste, except for municipal waste which has to be disposed of by the municipalities (LPE, arts 31 b and 31 c).

In 1986 the Federal Commission for Waste Economy issued a Federal Waste Management Model, the aim of which is a waste disposal system which must be conceived as environmentally sound in its entirety. Articles 31 and 31 a–c of the revised LPE incorporate the following objectives: autonomous disposal, reduction of environmental pollution (preservation of resources) and safety of disposal. The following four strategies must be applied:

(1) Prevention of waste at source.
(2) Reduction of hazardous substances in goods and hazardous substances created during production.
(3) Reduction of waste through reclamation.
(4) Environmentally sound treatment (incineration) and disposal of waste within the country.

A pre-payable disposal fee is placed on certain products which are either to be reclaimed or which require special treatment after use (LPE, art 32 a^{bis}). This fee serves to finance the disposal of the products. The purchase price of the product will thereby be increased by the amount of this fee, and the consumer will bear the cost for the disposal of the product at the time of purchase. This method attempts to ensure that the user actually does deliver this waste to the appropriate collection areas. If, for example, the user did not have to pay the disposal fee until he returned the product, the likely result would be that a great deal of this waste would end up mixed with normal household waste. The advance disposal fee is in keeping with the co-operation principle established in the LPE, whereby the costs of disposal measures are borne by the producer of the waste and not by the State.

An additional change has been introduced by moving responsibility for waste away from the State. Responsibility for the appropriate disposal of waste more frequently rests with private parties, for example industry (LPE, art 31 b, 31 c; Ordinance on the Return, Taking Back and Disposal of Electrical and Electronic Appliances—ORDEA). The cantons themselves are required to take measures only in the event that the desired goals are not achieved (principle of subsidiarity).

Specific regulations deal with special wastes and are contained in the Ordinance on Movements of Special Wastes of 12 November 1986 (*Verordnung über den Verkehr mit Sonderabfällen*, SR 814.014—OMSW) as well as in the Basel Convention on Control of Transboundary Movement and Disposal of Special Wastes (*Basler Konvention über die Kontrolle des grenzüberschreitenden Verkehrs mit Sonderabfällen und ihrer Beseitigung*), and pertain to:

(1) release (identifying/labelling of waste and release, only to licenced recipients with consignment notes),
(2) export (with registration form), transit and transport requirements, including
(3) acceptance (consignee requires authorisation and is subject to special duties of practice and care, respectively).

2.6 *Chapter 11*

The revised LPE, which contains a separate section on special waste disposal, first stipulates the polluter pays principle and then provides the legal basis for a pre-paid disposal fee for certain products.

2.7 Land use planning/zoning

The constitutional basis for zoning law is art 22 of the Federal Constitution. The Federal Zoning Statute of 22 June 1979 (*Bundesgesetz über die Raumplanung*, SR 700—RPG) was brought into force on 1 January 1980.

Federal zoning law, including the Federal Zoning Statute, mainly contains general principles. The protection of the component parts of the environment such as soil, air, water, trees and the landscape is one of the main objectives of the Federal Zoning Statue. Others are the support of harmonious growth by establishing agricultural, construction and protection zones, the encouragement of economic and social development in different parts of the country, safeguarding the basis for a sufficient production of food and ensuring national defence.

The cantons implement the principles stated in the Federal Zoning Statute through a utilisation zoning statute. Such statutes are usually general building statutes and zoning statutes regulating municipal zoning regulations. Cantons are increasingly using the general building and zoning statutes to secure an appropriate mixture between business and housing areas.

Municipal laws and regulations are mostly composed of various technical provisions for the construction of buildings and installations. These concern mainly safety, traffic safety (eg separate access for pedestrians and motor vehicles), health (eg air vents in staircases), equipment (eg type of heating) and amenities (eg children playgrounds).

General zoning and planning instruments are:

(1) *General zoning directives (Richtplan)*: These indicate in maps and text, how a particular area will be developed. They are binding only on official bodies.
(2) *Utilisation plans (Nutzungspläne)*. Utilisation plans regulate all activities which impact on the territory at local level. The Federal Zoning Statute establishes only three zones: construction, agriculture and protection zones (RPG, art 14, para 2). However, the cantons are free to provide for additional zones for uses such as residential, industrial or public recreation.

   The construction zone is particularly important. Land that is already developed or that is suitable and needed for construction within the next 15 years is to be included in the construction zone (RPG, art 15). The utilisation plans are binding on private owners of land and on official bodies.

   Legal protection for landowners is regulated at cantonal level. However, federal law provides that decisions and plans based upon the Federal Zoning Statute and corresponding cantonal laws and regulations may be appealed.
(3) *Planning zones and other zoning measures*: The Federal Zoning Statute provides for planning zones and allows the cantons to adopt other planning measures (RPG, art 27). The objective of a planning zone is to safeguard ongoing or future zoning and planning activities.

Zoning laws have a significant impact on the rights of a real property owner and on the value of land. Zoning laws and regulations can easily increase or decrease the value of the land, in particular as regards inclusion in or exclusion from the construction zone.

2.8 Hazardous substances

On 1 September 1986, the Ordinance relating to Environmentally Hazardous Substances of 9 June 1986 (*Verordnung über umweltgefährdende Stoffe, Stoffverordnung*, SR 814.013—OSUBST) entered into force. Its purpose is to protect persons, animals, and vegetation, as well as their natural habitats, against environmentally hazardous substances. OSUBST maintains a broad definition of 'substances' and 'handling' which includes several types of basic materials, simple mixtures, and products, which directly or indirectly produce a biological effect. OSUBST regulates production, transportation, import, and marketing of such substances. The basic principle established is that of self-supervision. Any potentially hazardous substance not included in specific lists, must undergo detailed environmental impact assessments in order to be registered with the Federal Office for Environmental Protection (OSUBST, arts 12 f, 31 ff). Similar procedures are envisaged for currently listed and recognised substances. Further procedural rules regulate labelling, customer information, and instructions for use, as well as market supervision by cantonal authorities. Some substances (eg cadmium, asbestos, fluorinated and chlorinated hydrocarbons etc) are not only closely scrutinised and regulated, but may be prohibited as well.

OSUBST is a large, complex and very detailed administrative regulatory programme, closely linked to occupational safety and health, toxic and toxic tort law, agricultural law, and food and drug law. In order to facilitate, support the implementation and enforce the laws of OSUBST, the Federal Office of Environmental Protection has issued several annexes and guidelines. Amongst these, the guideline on self-supervision is especially helpful for manufacturers and other private entities which must comply with OSUBST.

With the revision of the LPE and the resulting changes in the ordinances, Swiss law will be harmonised with EU law. This harmonisation will lead to further changes in the hazardous substances legislation.

2.9 Noise abatement

The Ordinance on Noise Abatement of 15 December 1986 (*Lärmschutz-Verordnung*, SR 814.41—ONA) came into effect on 1 April 1987. ONA has three separate levels of standards: planning, immission and emergency standards and these may differ according to the time of day, type of noise and local zoning parameters. Based upon measurements according to these impact thresholds, emission levels are set for both stationary and mobile sources.

2.10 Environmental impact assessment

Article 9 of LPE introduced the environmental impact assessment (EIA) as a truly fundamental instrument of environmental law, and as a direct conversion of the principle of prevention as set out in LPE, art 1, s 2. According to LPE, art 9, authorities shall, before taking any decision regarding the planning, construction, or alteration of installations which may appreciably affect the environment, assess their impact on the environment. The Federal Council enacted the Ordinance on Environmental Impact Assessments of 19 October 1988 (*Verordnung über die Umweltverträglichkeitsprüfung*, SR 814.011—OEIA) on 1 January 1989, in order to expedite the implementation of the EIA scheme.

2.10 Chapter 11

OEIA designates 70 types of installations as being subject to an EIA and the administrative regulatory procedures. Instead of creating a new administrative procedure, OEIA has relied upon the respective existing federal or cantonal procedures applicable for each type of installation. Initially this was considered as a step towards practicability and simplification. However, it now seems to be a source of complication and fundamental incompatibilities.

The procedure in accomplishing an EIA is not a independent procedure, but is mostly integrated in the construction permit issuing process. The specific EIA report has to be prepared by the applicant for the project or by the environmental consultant of his choice. It then has to be provided to the competent authorities together with the request for a construction permit. The report will also be submitted to the respective federal or cantonal environmental agencies, which will assess it and propose the necessary measures to the competent decision-making authority. Anyone may consult the report and the results of the EIA, unless overriding public or private interests require secrecy. Based on the submitted EIA report, the competent authority will decide whether the expected impact of the installation is acceptable or not.

2.11 Disaster prevention and risk management

Article 10 of LPE states that anyone who operates or intends to operate installations, or stores substances which, in exceptional circumstances, could seriously damage persons or the environment, must take proper steps to protect the population and the environment. However, it took Chernobyl and the severe pollution of the Rhine River after the Schweizerhalle accident, to bring about real enforcement of this LPE provision. The Ordinance on Disaster Prevention of 27 February 1991 (*Verordnung über den Schutz vor Störfällen*, SR 814.012—ODP) focuses on prevention of disasters which could occur in relation to manufacturing, production, storage, and transportation of chemical substances, special waste and biologically active micro-organisms. The Seveso Directive (Directive (EEC) 82/501) was the model for this ordinance. According to the general principles of environmental law, the envisaged regulatory system is a mixture of self-supervision and a two-stage control procedure. Operators have to provide authorities with risk analyses which may vary in depth according to the potential damages. Based on each risk analysis, ordinary and extraordinary safety measures will then be decreed by executive order.

2.12 Other environmental controls, genetically modified organisms (so-called organisms hazardous to the environment)

Simply put, genetic technology involves the re-combination of genetic material. Through this process genetic alterations of organisms can be achieved more rapidly, much more precisely and far more extensively than with conventional methods. Today, genetically altered organisms are being introduced into the environment with increasing frequency as a result of experiments in which they are purposely released into the environment, and through the introduction of these organisms in products.

The new regulations concerning organisms hazardous to the environment distinguish between their use in closed systems (laboratories and production installations), and their use in the environment itself, ie outside of a closed system.

When organisms are to be used in closed systems (LPE, art 29 f), the person in charge of the procedure must ensure, with technical, organisational and biological measures, that the organisms do not escape from the premises and thereby endanger the environment. All industrial projects and all research projects involving organisms that are not recognised as harmless must be reported to the authorities.

Before such organisms may be used in the wider environment, whether for experimental purposes or for the introduction of products, the responsible persons must conduct preliminary studies and experiments and be plausibly able to prove that no damaging or detrimental effects on the environment can be expected.

It is the federal authorities who are to decide on the execution of such applications in the environment after thoroughly reviewing these preliminary studies and experiments and by holding hearings of a committee of experts at which the various interested parties are represented (LPE, art 29 h). If necessary, additional experts may be called upon.

Furthermore, the public is to be informed when experiments are conducted which involve the release of environmentally hazardous organisms into the environment (LPE, art 29 d). All experiments are to be monitored and documented.

This regulatory concept corresponds to that of the EU and was agreed with the Organisation for Economic Co-operation and Development (OECD).

3 PARTICULAR ENVIRONMENTAL ISSUES RELEVANT TO TRANSACTIONS

3.1 Liability under the Federal Law relating to the Protection of the Environment

Environmental liability law regulates the liability to provide compensation for damage which private parties have caused through negative effects on the environment. Before the revision of LPE, that law did not contain any provisions concerning liability. Liability for damages arising as a consequence of effects on the environment were subject to various provisions of general liability within the Swiss Civil Code (CC), the Code of Obligations (OR) and elsewhere. In this configuration, Swiss liability law was not an effective means of ensuring environmental protection. The revised LPE greatly improves this situation as it includes a provision for absolute liability without proof of fault. This provision makes a considerable contribution to environmental protection by increasing the risks of liability for environmental transgressors (LPE, art 59 a).

Before the revision of the LPE, the damaged party bore the burden of proof, which entailed not only proving that the damaging party committed an actual breach of duty (such as a defect in workmanship, or exceeding a proprietary right), but also establishing fault on the part of the damaging party. This presented considerable difficulties for the damaged party. In the revised LPE, the damaged party only has to prove that the damage occurred and show the party responsible for the damage and is not required to establish irregularity or fault on the part of the damaging party.

On the one hand, the introduction of a liability without fault provision improves the legal position of the damaged party, whereas on the other hand it increases the risk of having to provide compensation for damage caused to the environment. However, the law limits the application of this provision of strict liability to owners of industrial plants and installations. The possibility that an average household would be subject to this liability is eliminated right from the outset. This differentiation is justified by the fact that substances which could have particularly hazardous effects on the environment may only be produced or utilised lawfully in industrial plants and installations.

In spite of the increased liability resulting from the revisions of the LPE, Swiss legislation is still far from establishing an actual environmental liability law along the lines of the German example. The particular problems of environmental liability are

3.1 Chapter 11

best dealt with in conjunction with the pending total revision of the area of general liability law.

3.2 Civil Code provisions

The Swiss Civil Code of 10 December 1907 (*Schweizerisches Zivilgesetzbuch*, SR 210—CC) provides some tools against environmental nuisance. The law of neighbours generally prohibits excessive emissions and grants various rights of action.

Anyone exercising his property rights, in particular, operating a business on his own land, is obliged to refrain from causing excessive emissions that affect his neighbours' property. The Civil Code expressly prohibits all detrimental emissions, including smoke, annoying smells, noise, or vibration, that cannot be justified, taking into account the location and characteristics, as well as the normal use of surrounding properties (CC, art 684). The term 'excessive' is not defined, but it is a well-established concept developed by the courts. Whether a noise, for example, is excessive depends on the sensitivity of an average person living or working in the particular neighbourhood.

If a property owner exceeds his property rights and thus causes damage or threatens to cause damage to another person, that person may bring an action aimed at restitution or take steps to prevent imminent damage. He may also sue for compensation (CC, art 679). The courts have construed narrowly the capacity to sue, limiting it to direct and indirect neighbours.

Bringing an individual case may thus prove worthwhile, but it does not suffice for the purposes of systematically fighting environmental pollution. Often a party will refrain from bringing action because of the cost and time required. Another serious obstacle to individual action is the fact that one may have to sue several polluters simultaneously and may have difficulty in attributing liability for the damage to one particular source. It is possible that each individual polluter does not exceed the legal limits in his own right, thus giving no ground for complaint, but that all the polluters taken together do exceed them. Given the fact that any civil law action brings considerable risks and may, in case of defeat, lead to extensive costs for the plaintiff, civil law remedies remain of limited value in order to prevent or fight environmental pollution.

3.3 Criminal liability of directors and managers

A proper environmental criminal law is not provided for in the Swiss Penal Code. Criminal provisions provided by other pieces of legislation, in particular the LPE, do, however, secure numerous orders and prohibitions at the penal level. These are intended to prevent misconduct under the threat of a penalty and reinforce the administrative sanctions aimed at preventing such conduct. Nevertheless, criminal and administrative sanctions are often aimed at different legal subjects. Administrative sanctions usually apply to the owners or operators of facilities (eg a company), whereas criminal sanctions are usually directed at the natural persons (eg officers and employees of the company operating the facility).

The LPE classifies criminal acts as misdemeanours or contraventions. Actions punishable according to art 60 of LPE can be met with a prison term of three days to 3 years or a fine of up to CHF 40 000. For the contraventions listed in LPE, art 61, the law provides for prison terms of one day to three months or a fine of up to CHF 5,000. Nevertheless, if the polluter has received a benefit, the amount of any fine may be unlimited, in the case of both misdemeanours and contraventions. In addition, the Swiss Penal Code provides for confiscation of assets in addition to any fine or prison term.

Additional provisions of environmental criminal law can be found in the Water Protection Act, Federal Pipeline Act etc. As a general rule, it can be assumed that where several articles of the Swiss Penal Code and accessory criminal laws apply, all penalties provided for by such statutes must be applied cumulatively.

The Federal Act concerning Administrative Criminal Law of 22 March 1974 (*Bundesgesetz über das Verwaltungsstrafrecht*, SR 313—VStrR) is applicable according to LPE, art 62, to the criminal proceedings regulated by LPE, arts 60 and 61. According to VStrR, art 7 a company may be obliged to pay a fine on behalf of the perpetrator of the offence (eg a director of the company).

3.4 Liability of those financing businesses

Swiss liability regulations do not contain a so-called 'lenders liability'. Thus, action cannot be taken against mortgagees for example. However, creditors should be fully aware of environmental risks as these influence credit-worthiness. Particularly contaminated sites have an effect on the adjustment of property value, since restoration costs of a severe contamination may exceed the actual value of property.

4 MANAGING ENVIRONMENTAL ISSUES IN TRANSACTIONS

4.1 Assessment and management of risk

Diligent assessment and management of environmental risks is now considered mandatory in the conduct of normal business operations in Switzerland. Any entrepreneur in Switzerland, as well as in any other environmental high risk country, must track the two types of environmental risks (regulatory compliance risk and liability risk) in a well-defined procedure. While it is normally not possible to eliminate fully the risks associated with environmental issues, such procedures can help to identify, analyse, manage and allocate risks so that normal business operations and business deals can go forward.

In the last few years, environmental management has developed into a well-defined area of legal, engineering and business practice. Environmental management procedures differ substantially, whether they are used as part of a corporate citizenship policy, and therefore as an ongoing management tool (environmental management), or whether they are used in business transactions to identify, analyse, manage and allocate environmental risks so that the deal can go forward (environmental due diligence).

4.2 Environmental management systems

Environmental awareness has led environmentally sensitive Swiss firms to integrate environmental techniques fully into their corporate citizenship programmes. Such environmental management systems (EMS) usually but not necessarily encompass a sound structural scheme and well-defined corporate policies.

ISO 14001 is the most popular environmental management system utilised in Switzerland today. Some 300 companies are currently certified. A much higher number is striving for certification.

To date, experience with this system reveals that, as far as legal compliance is concerned, it does not meet the quality standard of the EMAS system used within the EU. The reason for this weakness can be attributed to a lack of legal expertise of the auditors and consultants, since they generally have a quality assurance background and have little or no environmental experience and training in environmental law. Numerous organisations have in fact been dealing with the problem of legal compliance in EMS, and guidelines have been issued by interdisciplinary groups. Nonetheless, the complexity of Switzerland's environmental policy and legislation prevents non-legal experts from gaining a deeper understanding of the subject. One can only hope that with the rapid expansion of the system, greater attention will be paid to the question of legal compliance, environmentally relevant data acquisition and to the purely system-relevant component.

The Swiss environmental protection authorities exercise a certain restraint towards ISO 14001. The EMS is appreciated as an enforcement tool and instrument to enhance environmental awareness among the private sector. However, emphasis is also rightly placed on the fact that the introduction of an EMS will not lead to any 'enforcement benefits', or ensure a countrywide environmental legal compliance. The executive authorities of the individual cantons are ultimately still responsible for enforcing Switzerland's environmental policy legislation. Whether a company adheres to a standardised EMS or not is actually irrelevant, because environmental legal compliance is legally prescribed in any case.

Finally, certain executive authorities also point to the fact that implementation of an EMS according to ISO 14001 would lead to a shift in the burden of proof. A company publicly registered as certified in legal compliance will at all times also have to provide proof of its continuing compliance. While in the past, proof of specific non-compliance had to be established, the certified company will henceforth and at all times have to assume responsibility for providing proof of its legal compliance. In future, this factor will gain importance in the context of civil liability.

In addition to the introduction of EMS according to ISO 14001, the signing of inter-sector and individual agreements between private parties and executive authorities on the meeting of environmental objectives has recently been observed (cf para 2.1.4 above). Such agreements are mainly based on Dutch and Danish models. However, they still form the exception to customary enforcement, and can barely be tolerated from a legal standpoint. Nonetheless, they contribute to a new understanding of the question of enforcement by the environmental protection authorities, and to more environmental self-responsibility by the private sector concerned.

4.3 Environmental due diligence procedures

In dealing with environmental risks in the context of business and business transactions, two major sources of information are generally required:

(1) A technical environmental due diligence audit.
(2) A legal environmental opinion.

The technical environmental due diligence audit is required for the determination of environmental risks and must be executed by expert environmental consultants. It is important to understand however, that the physical risks, once evaluated, must then be translated into the legal, regulatory and liability risks, a task for specialised environmental lawyers, since ultimately environmental risk is the risk of legal non-compliance and liability. Therefore, close co-operation between environmental consultants and environmental lawyers is a must. This co-operation enables 'crystal ball gazing' to evaluate the likelihood of future regulatory and liability developments. In the context of a major transaction this may be as important as evaluating existing legal risk.

In view of the described complexity of Swiss environmental law and relevant compliance risk, it is clear that extensive due diligence procedures are increasingly becoming standard practice in Swiss company and property transactions.

Based on the above, use of EMS in compliance with ISO 14001 will not be of great benefit in transactions. A far more important aspect is specific analyses of the general legal compliance of a company in the environmental field, with special emphasis on risks relating to contaminated sites. Independent of the scope with which the environmental due diligence analysis is conforming to the transaction, implementation of only a Phase I audit within the American Society for Testing and Material (ASTM) standard will rarely be sufficient in this country.

A specific soil investigation is usually required for each conducted transaction in the industrial sector, in commercial building transactions and in the overall field of property transactions and property development. This is of particular relevance if the object of any transaction is listed in the contaminated sites register. The methodology described in the Contaminated Sites Ordinance (CSO) (see para 2.3 above) will in such a case apply providing an established course of action leading generally to reasonable and objective results.

Business-specific checklists have been successfully used in practice to review overall legal compliance. Experienced environmental consultants jointly elaborate such checklists with legal environmental experts and adapt them to the specific transaction and to the constantly evolving environmental policy legislation. Due regard to the problems posed by electromagnetic compatibility (the so-called 'electrosmog) have increasingly been observed. Although this subject is also dealt with in the Federal Law relating to the Protection of the Environment (LPE, art 7, para. 1), it has so far only been reflected in a few court decisions and only recently perceived as a public health risk. Furthermore, special priority issues of the client can be taken into account or supplemented by additional elements, which are not necessarily covered by the actual Swiss environmental policy and legislation. Increased attention has recently been given to the problems of occupational safety and hygiene, general questions pertaining to the assessment of structural integrity of industrial buildings and to energy consumption studies.

4.4 Environmental provisions in transaction documents

As regards the legal structure of the transactions, it can generally be stated that the results of environmental due diligence procedures can have a significant influence on transactions. In particular, costs arising from non-compliance risks, which have to be solved by remediation measurements, can reduce the price significantly.

Due regard should be paid to some problems encountered at the interface between private and public law in the Swiss legal system:

(1) While legal claims for environmental restoration in compliance with LPE, arts 16 and 32 c, never become barred under the statute of limitations, express warranties and guarantees are generally limited to 5–10 years.
(2) According to LPE, art 32 d, para 3, it is also possible under public law to circumvent an express contractual warranty clause at a later date by a remedial cost distribution provision if due regard is not given in the contract to this peculiarity in Swiss law.

4.4 *Chapter 11*

(3) Elements of uncertainty may also arise in connection with an objectively formulated legal compliance warranty. This type of warranty can be far more comprehensive than the legal compliance required by Swiss environmental law. Actual and legally binding restoration liabilities do not simply arise from violating quality standards and the like, but follow from specific restoration provisions enforced by the executive authorities (LPE, art 16). Contractual law can, therefore, be more restrictive than public law. Environmental warranty clauses are becoming developed and standardised in Switzerland, although there are no Supreme Court decisions dealing with this issue. Merger and acquisitions warranties are usually formulated in more detail than in transactions of real property.

(4) Finally, LPE, art 46, provides the authorities with extensive powers to regulate the exchange of information wherein compliance can be waived only by professional secrecy or possibly by business secrecy. A correspondingly problematic situation may arise within the scope of a transaction if a comprehensive review of legal compliance has to be conducted in place of a mere contaminated site-oriented preliminary investigation in accordance with the CSO. This could subsequently provide the executive authorities with an easily accessible basis for enforcing comprehensive restoration provisions in all areas regulating environmental protection.

4.5 Practical points for transactions

The following general principles for management of environmental risk in business transactions in Switzerland should be considered:

(1) One must look for factors indicating potential environmental problems and develop a view on the appropriate amount of due diligence. Does the type of business in question create, or may it in the past have created, environmental problems? Is any real or personal property to be acquired likely to be contaminated? Are there any other hazardous substances such as PCBs (polychlorinated biphenyls), asbestos etc? The key is to inquire into past and present uses of the property. Interviews conducted with on-site personnel and inspection of records are essential.

(2) Deal with environmental issues early. Environmental risks should be dealt with from the onset of a transaction, before price and other central terms and conditions have been finally resolved. Environmental and hazardous substance risks can be deal-stoppers or at least may significantly affect the terms of a deal. Left unaddressed, they may threaten the very existence of the business involved. If the necessary environmental due diligence investigation has to be undertaken under pressure and without adequate time, it may not produce valid results. Where environmental issues exist, expert environmental lawyers and consultants should be consulted as early as possible.

(3) Deal with all of the environmental risks. A broad range of both regulatory and liability risks have to be kept in mind. Qualified lawyers and consultants work with comprehensive checklists, which are broadened or focused according to the individual deal.

(4) Keep the deal context in mind. The extent to which an environmental audit is pursued will vary with the physical environmental risk created by the acquired business, the legal structure given to the transaction, the specific value of the business and the general worthiness of the seller. While analysis of credit-

worthiness and business value is routine, identification of the physical environmental risks and analysis of the impact to the deal structure on the incidence of that risk is also important. One has to be aware that while managers take risks all the time, the mere existence of environmental risks seems to be much harder to assess and manage than the more familiar traditional business risks.

(5) Confidentiality is of the essence. Environmental due diligence audits can be powerful tools for gaining knowledge regarding liability but they also can generate sensitive information. Attorney–client privilege may apply to the communication of information between an attorney and a client or consultant, while the same does not hold true for in-house counsel or in-house experts under Swiss law. In order to protect the confidentiality of information given or received during and after environmental audits, channels of communication have to be structured carefully from the outset of the negotiations and confidentiality agreements should address these points.

(6) Use both locally and transaction experienced environmental consultants. Close co-operation between lawyers and consultants is mandatory to reduce legal and physical environmental risks. This kind of co-operation is hard to establish under the pressure of a specific deal. Rather look for experienced teams, which have a history of successful achievements.

(7) Beware of representations and warranties as to environmental cleanliness. Representations and warranties are more a tool of discovery and disclosure of information than a mechanism for recovering losses from unexpected problems. Even if drafted extensively, they may or may not shelter the corporation from environmental liabilities even if geared towards indemnification. Besides, indemnity provisions are, of course, only as good as the solvency of the indemnifier.

4.6 Environmental insurance

Swiss environmental impairment liability insurance covers damage only if it is attributed to a hazardous event. Coverage is not provided for emissions occurring during normal operations. Since liability insurance covers basically only damage to third parties, the damage suffered by the policy-holder is not the object of such insurance.

The insurance companies are mostly responsible for preventive measures against immediate and impending personal injury or material damage. Restoration costs of contaminated sites incurred, for example, by the disposal of contaminated material are not covered. Waste storage, treatment or disposal companies are excluded since 1989 from the general policy conditions.

All companies involved in an industrial activity and exposed to a certain potential risk are urgently recommended to effect an environmental impairment liability insurance.

5 CONCLUSION

Swiss environmental protection law originally operated primarily by means of coercive regulations, which was why the first signs of shortcomings were already becoming apparent in the early stages of its execution. In particular the effort to motivate industry on a widespread basis to act in a responsible and pro-environmental manner has proved unsuccessful. An appropriate supplement to environmental policy instruments with financial incentives was therefore urgently needed. In

4.6 *Chapter 11*

addition, the rapid acceleration of technical development made it imperative that new areas of regulation were incorporated into the law.

The revision of the Federal Law relating to the Protection of the Environment (LPE) is on the whole both appropriate and straightforward. It reflects new realisations and revised perceptions of efficiency and effectiveness in the attainment of the goals of environmental policy.

Following the July 1997 revision of LPE and its associated numerous new ordinances, no fundamental material changes are anticipated in the foreseeable future. Deviation from the current regulatory system to an actual liability regime in Swiss environmental law is not likely in the near future. In particular, the provision of a specific system of environmental criminal law is not under discussion.

Chapter 12

FRANCE

Christian Huglo and Francois Steinmetz

Huglo Lepage & Associés, Paris

1 INTRODUCTION

French people themselves usually consider that France is not very concerned by environmental issues.

However, beyond this 'cliché', the reality is very different. France has developed very important environmental legislation, including strict liabilities for industrial pollution. Even if the population is usually not aware of it, the government, through numerous departments and agencies, imposes strong controls over industry, and the *Procureur de la République* (the equivalent of the Attorney General) does not hesitate to prosecute polluters.

1.1 Origin of environmental law

1.1.1 Historical review

Environmental law first appeared in the 19th century, and the principles on which it is based were mainly enacted during the 19th and the beginning of the 20th century. For example, the critical Law on Classified Installations, dated 19 July 1976, is directly derived from the Decree on Insalubrious, Awkward or Hazardous Facilities (also known as classified facilities) dated 10 October 1810.

Environment regulations have developed alongside industrialisation. At first, environmental preoccupations were the consequences of city growth, and more particularly, the expansion of Paris. There were two themes arising from this: on the one hand, the reality of many people living at the same place creating a public health issue due to the accumulation of waste; on the other hand, the need to utilise waste in a socially beneficial way. In other words, since the very beginning, environmental regulations were aiming at recycling, although the recycling was only concerned with industrial waste.

Initially, environmental regulations applied to facilities, as opposed to populations. But environmental law slowly moved to a more general concept of the environment and now includes wider goals than regulating classified facilities, such as protection of landscape, fauna and flora, fresh water etc.

Today, environmental law in France is highly complex, comprising Laws, Decrees and Orders. It is applied by numerous administrations among which include the Environment Ministry and many independent agencies.

1.1 Chapter 12

1.1.2 Sources of French environmental law

There are three different sources of environmental law: international conventions, EU environmental law and national law.

(a) International conventions

France is a party to many international conventions. These conventions cannot be directly applied, but are often aimed at a substantial modification of French environmental law.

One of the best examples of a successful international convention is probably the Montreal Protocol. This convention is not enforceable by itself, either at an international level or at a national level. However, despite this, the Protocol has been completely transposed into French environmental law and, as a result, is now enforceable in France as any other environmental law.

Nevertheless, such success remains exceptional, and complete transposition of an international convention is unusual. International conventions are normally only incentives, and are often written as a declaration of principles.

(b) EU environmental policies

European Union environmental policies are much more constraining. As in every other member state's law, every EU directive must be implemented into French law. As arts 130r, 130s and 130t of the EC Treaty give the EU environmental competence, environmental legislation within the EU is constantly developing.

As a consequence, a part of French environmental law is simply the transposition of European regulation. However, it must be emphasised that implementation is a flexible mechanism that allows adaptations. France, with its practical vision of the protection of the environment, always takes into account its own environmental philosophy when transposing EU directives.

(c) National policies

As opposed to federal nations, such as the USA, and despite the 'decentralisation' reform of 1983, France remains very attached to the idea of a central administration.

It is thus the State, and only the State, that regulates the environment. However, laws can originate with the Parliament or the government, depending on the issue regulated and on the field of application of the law.

Usually, environmental laws give to local authorities, such as the Prefect *(Préfet)* or the Regional Prefect *(Préfet de Région)*, a wide discretion to adapt legal controls to specific situations. In addition, French environmental law delegates many competencies to these authorities. There are thus many Orders and Decrees completing and implementing environmental laws.

One of the major problems regarding environmental laws is the novelty of the concepts they refer to. For example, what is meant by 'quality of life'? To interpret these concepts usually requires a legal decision. France is a civil law country, and the judge is not a source of law, but by interpreting laws, judges can restrain or enlarge the impact of environmental laws.

It is important to be aware of this aspect of environmental law because, through judicial decisions, French environmental law became and remains a very practical law. Judicial decisions usually lead to effective protection of the environment, but still at the lowest possible cost.

Consequently, French environmental law is a mixture of international principles, implemented EU directives and national laws, complemented by numerous decrees and orders giving the final requirements regarding environmental protection and pollution prevention.

1.1.3 Structure of environmental regulatory agencies

In order to understand French environmental law, it is necessary to describe the organisation of the 'environmental administration'. This administration is divided into three types of institutions: the central administration (essentially the Ministry for the Environment), local administrations for the environment and agencies in charge of protecting the environment.

(a) Ministry of the Environment

Although environmental protection is a long-standing concern for the government, it was only in 1971 that the first Ministry for the Environment was created (art 1 of the Decree dated 2 February 1971). The idea was to create an institution to co-ordinate government action, but without transferring the other ministries' environmental competencies. As a result, the first Ministry for the Environment had very limited power. However, the new ministry has constantly widened its competencies, and has now merged with its oldest partner, and some times opponent, the Ministry for National Infrastructure *(Ministère de l'Equipement)*.

The ministry's current objective is to monitor the quality of the environment, protect nature, prevent, reduce or totally eliminate pollution and other nuisances, and enhance the 'quality of life'. With this in mind, it conducts two different types of actions:

(1) The preservation and protection of open spaces and species. This includes the prevention of pollution and of major risks, nature conservation, the protection of sites and landscapes and, last but not least, the management of water resources.
(2) The development of research, improvements in the knowledge of the state of the environment and consideration of environmental concerns at both the European and international level.

Both types of action also contribute to educating, training, heightening awareness and informing all who are able to contribute to the environment's protection.

To perform these aims, the ministry has a number of specific powers:

(a) the regulation and management of freshwater fishing, hunting and water resources;
(b) the regulation and control classified installations;
(c) the regulation, management and control of waste disposals;
(d) the control of noisy activities or devices;
(e) the creation and promotion of an environmental dynamic in the economic and social field.

Since the environment is a cross-sectoral issue, the Minister for the Environment shares a number of responsibilities with other ministers. Such responsibilities include decisions regarding planning and development, the management of water resources, energy, nuclear safety, health, transportation etc.

1.1 *Chapter 12*

The Ministry itself is divided in four main departments *(directions):*

(1) The Administration and Development Department *(Direction Générale de l'Administration et du Développement*—DGAG.)
(2) The Water Resources Department *(Direction de l'Eau*—DE).
(3) The Prevention of Pollution and Risks Department *(Direction de la Prévention des Pollutions et des Risques*—DPPR).
(4) The Nature and Landscapes Department *(Direction de la Nature et des Paysages*—DNP).

The Ministry for the Environment is assisted by a network of decentralised departments as well as the expertise of a number of attached organisations. This national network is constituted by 26 Regional Departments of the Environment *(Directions Régionales de l'Environnement*—DIREN), together with the Industrial Environmental Services of the 24 Regional Departments for Industry, Research and the Environment *(Direction Régionales de la Recherche, de l'Industrie et de l'Environnement*—DRIRE). These services are in charge, under the authority of Regional Prefect or the Prefect *(Préfet de Region* or *Préfet),* of local implementation of the policies defined at the national level.

In addition, at the department level, the ministry's work is carried out mainly by the Departments of Health and Social Affairs *(Direction Départementale de l'Hygiène et des Affaires Sanitaires et Sociales*—DDASS), the District Infrastructure Departments *(Direction Départementale de l'Equipement*—DDE) and the District Department for Agriculture and Forests (DDAF).

(b) Regional Departments

(i) Regional Environment Departments

The Regional Environmental Departments (DIREN) were established by a Ministerial Order of 4 November 1991. Their objective is to improve knowledge concerning the natural environment, relying on data collection networks, inventories and surveys.

DIREN work to ensure that environmental considerations are included in various development programmes, relevant contracts and various European projects. They also ensure that regulations governing nature conservation, protected sites and landscapes are applied. They contribute to preservation policies and to the improvement of the natural environment.

Each department has its own characteristics, depending on their geographical situation, and on the main features of the region (mountain, coast etc).

(ii) Regional Departments for Industry, Research and the Environment

The Regional Departments for Industry, Research and the Environment (DRIRE) are under the authority of the Prefect *(Préfet),* as opposed to the Regional Prefect *(Préfet de Région)* authority for the DIREN.

Since 6 July 1992, the DRIRE have had a Regional Service for Industrial Environment. The DRIRE's objective is to co-ordinate and lead inspections, and to ensure compliance, at a regional level, with legislation governing classified installations, air pollution (especially the implementation of warning and protection procedures) and waste (especially cross-border waste transfers, industrial waste, etc)

The DRIRE is in charge of supervising and directing the activities of other environmental organisations: associations managing air pollution networks, and the

France 1.1

Permanent Secretariats for the Prevention of Industrial pollution (*Secrétariats Permanents pour la Prévention des Pollutions Industrielles*—SPPPI).

(c) Specialised agencies

Alongside the Ministry for the Environment and the national network of local administrations and services, the 'environmental administration' includes some specialised agencies. These agencies may be described as state supervised or jointly supervised public corporations.

Some of these operate at the national level, and with a national jurisdiction such as the:

(1) French Environment and Energy Control Agency *(Agence de l'Environnement et de la Maîtrise de l'Energie*—ADEME*)*;
(2) National Agency for the Management of Radioactive Waste *(Agence pour la Gestion des Dechets Radioactifs*—ANDRA*)*;
(3) French Environmental Institute *(Institut Français de l'Environnement)*;
(4) National Institute for Industrial Environment and Risks *(Institut National de l'Environnement Industriel et des Risques*—INERIS*)*;
(5) National Museum of Natural History *(Muséum National d'Histoire Naturelle)*
(6) Fisheries Council *(Conseil Supérieur de la Pêche*—CSP*)*;
(7) National Hunting Office *(Office National de la Chasse*—ONC*)*;
(8) National Forestry Office *(Office National des Forêts*—ONF*)*;
(9) Conservatory of Coastal Areas and Lakeside Shores *(Conservatoire de l'Espace Littoral et des Rivages Lacustes)*.

Others operate at regional level, such as the Water Agencies *(Agences de l'Eau)* and National Parks *(Parcs Nationaux)*.

The main agencies dealing with industrial pollution and international transactions are the following: ADEME, ANDRA, INERIS, and at a local level, the Water Agencies.

The French Environmental and Energy Control Agency (ADEME) is an Industrial and Commercial Public Corporation *(Etablissement Public à Caractère Industriel et Commercial*—EPIC*)* established under the Law of 19 December 1990. It is under the supervision of the Ministry for the Environment. It carries out organisational projects on research, technical advice, heightening awareness and financial incentives in the following areas:

(a) control of energy and raw materials;
(b) development of renewable forms of energy;
(c) waste disposal and recycling;
(d) air and soil pollution control;
(e) development of clean technologies;
(f) noise control.

It has three technical centres and 26 regional offices.

The National Agency for Management of Radioactive Waste (ANDRA) is also an Industrial and Commercial Public Corporation. It has been transformed into an EPIC under art 13 of the law of 30 December 1991.

Under the supervision of the Ministry for the Environment, ANDRA is in charge of the long-term management of radioactive waste. It plays an active role in research and development programmes in the field. It manages long-term storage centres, and

1.1 *Chapter 12*

designs, and builds new storage centres. ANDRA also defines specifications for the packaging and storage of radioactive waste. It records the condition and location of all radioactive waste within France and publishes an annual inventory of radioactive waste.

The National Institute for Industrial Environment and Risks (INERIS) is an administrative public corporation established by the Decree of 7 December 1990 and is in charge of furnishing technical expertise to environmental organisations, in particular to the Ministry for the Environment. Its purpose is to forecast and to assess the consequences of industrial activities on the environment and people.

It has four principal activities:

(1) studies and consulting;
(2) testing and research;
(3) standardisation;
(4) certification and regulation.

At a local level, industrial companies often deal with one of the six Water Agencies. They were established in 1964 as administrative public corporations under the supervision of the Ministry of the Environment. In accordance with the guidelines established by the ministry, they implement the policies formulated by their respective Basin Committees *(Comités de Bassins)*. The Water Agencies are also responsible for creating and backing with financial and technical assistance, actions for controlling water pollution, ensuring a balance between users, reaching the objectives in the guidelines and finally, promoting studies and research in partnership with other organisations.

The Water Agencies' financial resources come from charges levied on water use and water pollution. Each Basin Committee comprises representatives of all the water users at the basin level and authorises the levying of these charges.

Four main advisory bodies are attached to the ministry:

(1) The National Council for the Protection of Nature *(Conseil National de la Protection de la Nature)*.
(2) The National Council for Noise Pollution *(Conseil National du Bruit*—CNB*)*.
(3) The National Water Committee *(Comité National de l'Eau)*.
(4) The High Council for Classified Installations *(Conseil Supérieur des Installations Classées)*.

Each of these is responsible for advising and assisting the Ministry in making decisions. This is the function of the French Sustainable Development Commission *(Commission du Développement Durable)*, attached to the office of the Prime Minister and which advises the authorities on the implementation of the decisions taken at the June 1992 UN Conference on Environment and Development in Rio de Janeiro.

This description of the French environmental administration is not exhaustive, and there are many other less important commissions, committees, and agencies dealing in one way or another with environmental issues or considerations.

2 OUTLINE OF ENVIRONMENTAL LAW RELEVANT TO MERGER AND ACQUISITION TRANSACTIONS

Merger and acquisition transactions involve civil law principles, laws protecting the environment in a general way and laws dealing with specific environmental concerns (water, air, waste etc).

2.1 Civil law principles and laws of general application

Civil law principles are of general application and for a long time were considered sufficient to regulate environmental matters. However, the government established new rules and principles through two main Laws protecting the environment and nature in a general way.

Since merger and acquisition transactions deal with liabilities, arts 1382 and 1134 of the Civil Code are applicable.

2.1.1 Civil Code, art 1382

This is the basis for civil liability:

> 'Every act of a man which causes injury to another obliges the one by whose fault it occurred to give redress.'

Applying this principle, every one committing a fault is responsible for the damage that occurs and which is a consequence of the fault. Under this article, any polluter is responsible for the damage caused by the pollution.

In theory, art 1382 is sufficient to regulate pollution situations. However, the claimant has to prove three different things: (1) the fault of the defendant, (2) the damage, and (3) the link between the fault and the damage. In the case of pollution damage, it may be very hard, if not impossible, for the claimant to establish such proof. That is mainly why claimants more often use the new environmental principles in their actions. Nevertheless, anyone suffering pollution damage can start an action under art 1382.

2.1.2 Civil code, art 1134

This Article is the basis for contractual liability and provides that a valid contract, between two parties, is as binding as the law itself. In addition, contracts must be executed in 'good faith'.

As a consequence, an action could be started under art 1134 if there are difficulties with a transaction with regard to environmental matters. But, once again, new environmental principles and laws make it easier to establish the liability of polluters, and actions are rarely started under art 1134.

2.1.3 New environmental principles

One of the most interesting developments in environmental law has been the emergence of new principles. This new approach has resulted in two important Laws: the Nature Law and the Barrier Law.

(a) Nature Law

The most innovative concept of the Nature Law of 10 July 1976 is the creation of an impact assessment (*étude d'impact*) duty. This new notion is more precisely defined in the Law's implementing Decrees, the Decree of 12 October 1977 and the Decree of 25 February 1993. The 1993 Decree modified the 1977 Decree in order to implement Directive (EEC) 85/337 of 27 June 1985 (the EIA Directive).

As a consequence, it is almost always necessary to include an environmental impact assessment in all projects, which is designed to give an overview of the effects the installation should have on fauna, flora and human health. The administrative decision to authorise or to prohibit the project will be based mainly on the impact assessment.

2.1 Chapter 12

There are actually two kinds of impact assessment. For some limited works, the administration will only require a notice. The notice on environment can be quite vague. Article 2 of the Decree of 12 October 1977, as modified by the Decree of 25 February 1993, requires only that the notice must state the project's potential impact on the environment and how the project addresses environmental concerns.

The assessment has to be much more detailed, and must cover:

(1) studies and consultation;
(2) an analysis of the initial state of the site and its environment;
(3) an analysis of the project's effects on the environment;
(4) the reasons why this specific project was chosen against alternatives;
(5) the measures that the applicant intends to take to preserve the environment, and an evaluation of the related expenses;
(6) the methods used and the difficulties met in this evaluation.

(b) Barrier Law

The Law of 2 February 1995 (also known as the Barrier Law) is especially remarkable because it established new principles of environmental law. First of all, it refers to the precautionary principle. Under this concept, there is no need to wait until damage actually occurs to take appropriate measures to protect the environment and people. The second fundamental rule established by this Law is that preventive actions should have priority over reparation.

The Barrier Law also refers to the principle of participation, under which the public has a right to be involved in any administratively imposed environmental inquiry, whether the inquiry is public or private and establishes the principle that the polluter pays.

Finally, the Law affirms the right of everyone to a healthy environment.

2.2 Specific environmental laws

The Nature Law and the Barrier Law are of general application. For this reason, it was necessary to enact other legislation to regulate specific activities or to protect specific aspects of the environment. Different kinds of regulation address various types of pollution:

(1) The Waste Law (1975).
(2) The Sea Pollution Laws (1976, 1977, 1983).
(3) The Law on Classified Installations (1976).
(4) The Sea Bed Mineral Resources Law (1981).
(5) The Public Inquiries Law (1983).
(6) The Noise Law (1992).
(7) The Water Law (1992).
(8) The Environment Protection Reinforcement Law (1995).
(9) The Air Law (1996).

The focus below will be on the laws relevant to cross-border transactions.

2.2.1 Contaminated land

There is no specific law protecting soil or addressing contaminated land issues in France. However, contamination of land is indirectly regulated by many laws. The simultaneous application of the Classified Installations Law, the Air Law, the Water Law and the Waste Law ensure appropriate protection of the soil, and prevent the contamination of land. However, the Classified Installations Law addresses this issue in the most direct way.

Classified installations are facilities officially listed because of the danger or the risks they pose to the environment. Land contamination is usually the result of an industrial activity. This is why the Classified Installations Law is the most efficient law in protecting soils.

The Classified Installations Law ensures protection in two different ways. First, before running a classified installation, operators need to make a declaration, or obtain an authorisation, depending on the potential seriousness of the environmental threat posed by the installation. The Prefect receives the declaration and delivers the authorisation. When doing it, he can make an order establishing specific rules that will regulate the pollution caused by the industrial activity. Prefect's orders are the first way of preventing land contamination.

The Classified Installations Law also imposes an obligation to restore sites. Polluters have an obligation to clean-up land and to restore sites used for a classified installation. This obligation applies on the closure of the installation, but it does not mean that the site has to be as clean as it was before polluting activities commenced. The operator has to comply with the restoration requirements imposed by the Prefect. These requirements will depend on many criteria including the surroundings of the site (any aquifer, fresh water sources etc) and the planned re-use of the site (construction of a road or a children's garden etc). This clean-up obligation is the second way for the Prefect to prevent permanent land contamination.

Since the operator has a restoration obligation, the Prefect, who is the local administration in charge of supervising classified installations, will usually not take any measure before the closure of the facility, unless the activity results in off-site pollution, or the operator does not comply with its preliminary orders (orders made at the beginning of any activity).

In many cases, contamination of the land may result in a criminal sanction or an administrative sanction pursuant to the Classified Installations Law. This combination of sanctions (criminal and administrative) is typical of French environmental law.

Under arts 18, 19 and 20 of the Classified Installations Law, anybody running a classified installation without the required authorisation can be sentenced to prison for up to 2 years and/or to a fine up to 1 million francs. The judge or the Prefect can also order the operator to stop the activity. If the operator is not complying with orders, administrative sanctions can be used, and the Prefect can order that the required work is undertaken at the expense of the operator.

Once again, there is no express sanction for ground pollution. All sanctions and responsibilities will be triggered through another regulation, the main law being the Law on Classified Installations.

As a consequence of France's industrial past, the administration is currently leading a national investigation on polluted sites. The DRIRE is in charge of conducting this investigation, and the goal is to classify polluted sites in accordance with their state of pollution. The investigation is called a simplified investigation of risks (*enquête simplifiée des risques*—ESR). It is therefore highly recommended to contact the DRIRE before any acquisition, to establish whether the target site has been investigated, and if it has, to obtain the result of the investigation. One of the principles of French public law is the free access to administrative documents.

2.2 Chapter 12

2.2.2 Pollution of water resources

There are two laws on water resources: the Law of 12 December 1964, which is the basis of the legislation, and the Law of 3 January 1992, which completed and modernised the 1964 Law. However, the 1992 Law is the main text regarding water resources pollution.

(a) Law of 12 December 1964

The purpose of 1964 Law is to regulate the balanced use of water. To do this, it created the financial basin agencies, which became, by application of an order of 14 November 1991, the Water Agencies. These agencies operate under the principle that the polluter pays.

The Water Agencies are funded through two specific water taxes. The first one is based on the quantity of water used (*redevance de prélevement*), the second one is proportional to the quality of water returned to the system after use (*redevance de pollution*). The taxes also finance loans and subsidies for both public and private measures to improve water quality.

(b) Law of 3 January 1992

The 1992 Law modernised the 1964 Law. It also created the General Scheme for the Use and Management of *Water (Schémas Directeur d'Aménagement et de Gestion des Eaux*—SDAGE*)*, the drafting of which is supervised by the Prefect. This new document established precise rules for the use of water. The main text, with its two implementing Decrees (93–742 and 93–743 of 3 January 1993) regulates the voluntary use and discharge of water.

All activities or works having an effect on natural surface or underground sources of water have to be declared or authorised. The expression 'having an effect' is intentionally an open notion. The Law clearly intends to include use and discharge, but also any unpredictable situation creating a risk for water resources.

One of the implementing Decrees, of 29 March 1993 lists the activities needing an authorisation or a declaration. It also establishes those activities that are not controlled. Domestic use of water and equivalent amounts (less than 40 m^3 a day) do not require an authorisation.

Articles L. 20 and L. 21 C of the 1964 Law establish protection perimeters around the most sensitive and fragile areas. There, the use of water is completely forbidden. The discharge of specific substances (eg non-biodegradable detergents), without consideration for where the discharge would take place, is totally prohibited.

As will be described below, the legislation is intended to prevent pollution and its purpose is to impose the best level of water protection at the lowest possible cost for companies.

However, due to the importance of water, the Law also includes significant criminal and administrative sanctions. Usually, administrative sanctions will be taken before any criminal action. Nevertheless, a significant pollution incident, with effects on human health, will definitely result in a criminal sanction.

Administrative sanctions will be taken when the operator does not comply with the Prefect's orders. As for classified installations, the Prefect can (but does not have to) order the carrying out of the required work at the expense of the operator. The Prefect can also order the operator to stop its activities until the completion of the relevant work.

The four main criminal offences are set out below together with the maximum penalties.

(1) running a facility without the required authorisation, which may result in a fine of 120,000 francs and/or a prison sentence of up to two years;
(2) running a facility in violation of a Prefect's order to suspend activities, which may result in a prison sentence of up to two years and/or a fine of one million francs;
(3) running a facility in violation of a Prefect's order requesting the operator to respect the terms of prior orders which may result in a prison sentence of up to two years and/or a fine of one million francs;
(4) attempting to hinder an investigation, which may result in a fine of 50,000 francs and/or a prison sentence of up to six months.

2.2.3 Authorisation for discharges to water and for taking water from natural sources

Since classified installations are regulated by specific legislation, they are not covered by the following procedure. However, when applying for an authorisation under the Nature Law of 10 July 1976, classified installations have to include, in their impact assessment, effects on water, and the Prefect can refuse the requested authorisation because the water pollution effects are not satisfactory.

For all other installations, the use or discharge of water is subject to a separate prior and specific authorisation or declaration. The application for an authorisation has to include the effects of the operation on water (taking account of climate variations) and will detail the effect on flora and fauna, on water quality, on water levels, and more generally on every element mentioned in art 2 of the Law of 3 January 1992.

2.2.4 Integrated pollution control

Integrated pollution control is regulated by the Integration Order of 2 February 1998 (*Arrêté Intégré*). This new Order institutes technical and general prescriptions applicable to classified installations. It also implements the last EU directives, and the Air Law. Its main effect is to modify the Prefect's power regarding emission limits and monitoring. Under the Integration Order, emissions limits are no longer imperative but only indicative. Thus, the Prefect can authorise a classified installation to exceed these limits when there is no real danger for the environment. In such cases, the operator has to prove with technical arguments, the absence of danger.

Otherwise, the Order strengthens obligations for monitoring pollution risks for aquifers, water resource protection (by imposing more stringent limits although, as described above, the Prefect can make exceptions), dust emissions and the obligation to provide good integration in the landscape.

However, the Integration Order does not include any provisions regarding criminal or administrative liability. Sanctions are within the relevant individual Laws.

2.2.5 Emissions to the atmosphere

The Law of 2 August 1961 was the first Law relating to air quality. It was completely modified and modernised by the Law of 30 December 1996 (the Air Law).

The new legislation is applicable to all discharges to air that are capable of:

(1) being a risk for human health;
(2) debasing biological resources or the ecosystem;
(3) influencing climate change;
(4) damaging goods;
(5) generating excessive olfactory problems.

2.2 Chapter 12

It essentially affects four matters:

(a) transportation,
(b) energy,
(c) health,
(d) air quality.

The Air Law establishes an outline structure for new legislation concerning air protection. It should be completed by implementing decrees which provide the details of control.

The Air Law starts with a statement that everyone has the right to breath air that does not damage their health. As a consequence, it establishes the principle of pre-set air quality standards. Under the Air Law, environmental agencies (DRIRE, DIREN, DDE etc) are responsible for controlling those standards. However, implementing decrees or orders will probably describe the exact competence of each agency.

Articles 12 and 13 establish emergency procedures, whenever a dangerous level of pollution is reached. The administration is authorised to restrict or suspend activities contributing to the pollution. There is also authority to reduce polluting emissions from fixed and mobile sources, including cars. In return, when the population cannot use cars, public transportation is free.

In the Ile de France region, Prefects can also forbid the use of specific combustibles, or suspend or restrict specific activities contributing sulphur dioxide to the atmosphere *(Arrêté Interpréfectoral 94–10504)*.

The Air Law also aims to improve air quality by a better and more rational use of energy. Article 21 allows the government to regulate the energy consumption of goods through the implementation of technical criteria.

The provisions of the Air Law do not include any sanctions. They only refer to the Classified Installations Law where pollution is generated by a classified installation. In such cases, administrative (as opposed to criminal) sanctions apply, and the Prefect can, at his discretion, order the required work to be done at the expense of the operator. He also has the power to close the facility down until the relevant work has been undertaken.

At the present time, there are no specific criminal sanctions. These sanctions will probably be instituted by implementing decree.

2.2.6 *Waste management including recycling/re-use obligations*

Waste is mainly regulated by the Waste Law of 15 July 1975.

Waste is defined as every residue resulting from a production, transformation or use and every substance, material, product or anything else that has been abandoned or that its owner intends to abandoned. Although this definition is different from the European legal definition, it remains the current French definition of waste.

Waste is classified into six different categories: domestic waste, regulated by Article 373–3 of the Local Bodies Code; waste generating pollution, as listed in Decree 77–974 of 19 August 1977; ultimate waste, as defined by art 1 of the Waste Law; industrial waste; domestic packaging waste, regulated by Decree 92–377 of 1 April 1992; and industrial and commercial packaging waste, regulated by Decree 94–609 of 13 July 1994. Industrial waste is similarly due to be regulated by decree.

The first obligation of anybody producing or owning waste is to make certain that it will be treated in an acceptable way as regards environmental and human health considerations. This does not mean that such persons have to treat the waste themselves, but that they are responsible for it. The producer's or owner's obligation is thus to make sure that his waste will be correctly handled by the appropriate professional.

The second obligation is one of providing information. The administration can ask producers or owners for details of the way in which their waste is treated. This information obligation is reinforced in the case of polluting waste.

In addition, producers of specific types of waste may have other obligations. These mainly concern used oil. This is regulated by Decree 79–981 of 21 November 1989, implementing Directives (EC) 75/439 of 16 June 1975 and 87/101 of 22 December 1987. These Decrees have been complemented by an Order of 21 November 1989 on used oil collection. Those holding such waste have an obligation to collect it and stock it in adequate conditions, until they have it treated by an 'authorised professional'.

There is also a recycling obligation for generators of domestic packaging waste. They must contribute to the reduction and elimination of this waste (in given proportions). To do that, they have two possibilities: (1) to collect and treat the waste themselves; or (2) to use the services of an authorised company.

Sanctions for not complying with waste regulations can be criminal, administrative or civil. Civil actions can be triggered by those suffering from the non-compliance, administrative sanctions can be taken by the Prefect, by application of the Classified Installations Law, and criminal sanctions can result in a fine of up to 500,000 francs, and/or a prison sentence of up to two years. Sanctions apply to those abandoning waste or treating waste without the required administrative agreement.

2.2.7 Land use planning/zoning

France does not have specific environmental land use planning. Land use planning is general and therefore requires that every construction must have a prior authorisation. The authority granting the construction permit (usually the Mayor) has an obligation to consider environmental issues.

However, there is a principle of 'regulation independence'. As a result of this principle, it is illegal for the relevant authority to refuse a construction permit on the basis of non-compliance with the Classified Installations Law. They can only refuse to grant a construction permit for non-compliance with the requirements of construction law. Any person building a classified installation will have to ask for at least two different authorisations. The first gives the right to run the installation. The second relates to the right to build the factory. The environmental issues considered when the operator asks for the second permit are mainly the aesthetic impact of the construction and the restrictions that apply to the land where the construction will be built.

Usually, where there is a residential area nearby, any activity representing a risk for people will be forbidden. The building permit can be refused on this ground.

2.2.8 Use and storage of hazardous substances including radioactive material

Decree 97–517 of 15 May 1997 lists hazardous wastes. The Decree explicitly states that the current list can be modified and completed in the future. The list does not expressly mention radioactive waste, but it includes carcinogenic waste. Thus, it can be said that it includes radioactive waste.

Producers and holders of hazardous waste have a reinforced obligation of information on the origin, nature, characteristics, quantity, destination and treatment method for the waste (Waste Law, art 8). This obligation extends to the waste they produce, the waste they transfer to an authorised person or the waste they handle for someone else.

The storage of radioactive waste is regulated by Law 91–1381 of 30 December 1991. This Law allows underground storage, but only for a limited period of time. This leaves a question, of course, of what will happen to the waste after this period of time.

2.2 *Chapter 12*

Currently, there is no answer. The government is conducting experiments on underground laboratories. These could result in a permanent solution for the storage of radioactive material. However, there is fierce opposition to this solution, because it would be a 'non-return' solution. Once the waste is underground, it would not be possible to recover it.

2.2.9 Noise and nuisance

Most significant is the Law on Classified Installations of 19 July 1976 and more specifically an implementing Order of 20 August 1985, as amended by the Integration Order of 1 March 1993, whereby such installations are compelled to meet certain preset noise standards. Failure to do so may result in sanctions.

In addition, on 31 December 1992, a Law on Noise Abatement was adopted. It is subject to several implementing Decrees, including a Decree introducing an airport tax to compensate residents in the vicinity of airports. It also increased the criminal sanctions to imprisonment for up to two years and/or 200,000 francs in fines.

The two last important provisions regarding noise are the Law of 29 March 1976 which forbids constructions in the proximity of highways and main roads, and Decree 95–408 of 18 April 1995. This decree modifies art R. 48–1 of the Human Health Code, and gives the limits beyond which a noise is considered as a nuisance.

Finally, the Mayor has important powers regarding policing of noise. He can make orders strengthening nationals rules in his town.

3 PARTICULAR ENVIRONMENTAL ISSUES RELEVANT TO TRANSACTIONS

3.1 Assumption of liabilities—routes and basis for liabilities

As stated above, French environmental law makes a distinction between three different kinds of liabilities: civil liability, administrative liability and criminal liability.

The only assumption of liability that exists concerns the operator of a facility. The law considers the person in charge of running a facility as administratively liable for the time he runs the facility. The main consequence of this assumption will occur at the closure of the facility. When the industrial activity ends, the operator will have an administrative obligation to restore the site, no matter if he is or is not the polluter. Thus, in the case of major pollution due to a prior operator, the last person running an activity on the site will remain responsible. However, even though the administration can take action against the last operator, it can also take action against the real polluters when they can be identified.

Another very important principle of French environmental liability is that even if an operator has an administrative permit to run a polluting activity, he can still be sued on the grounds of his civil liability.

3.2 Historical liabilities—past practices and procedures, including those of former site owners

The Classified Installations Law, which regulates administrative liability, makes a distinction between the operator of the facility, the owner of the facility and the owner of the polluted site. Administratively, the operator of the facility is considered as liable.

However, if this operator cannot assume the restoration obligation, or if he cannot be traced, the owner of the facility can be held liable, as opposed to the owner of the site, who is never considered to have administrative liability.

When neither the operator or the owner of the facility can be identified, the administration will search for the person responsible for the pollution. But, in this case, the administration has to prove the origin of the pollution and the identity of the polluter.

Civil liability is very different, in that even the owner of the site can be liable for damages. Article 1384 of the Civil Code is very clear:

> 'A person is responsible not only for the injury which he causes by his own act, but also for that which is caused by the act of persons for whom he is responsible, or matters which he has in his care.'

Land is considered to be such a matter. So, in the case of a pollution migration, the person owning the site which is causing pollution can be held liable for damage occurring. However, up to now, this route for liability has rarely been triggered.

3.3 Liabilities for off-site activities or impacts

This may include an escape of hazardous or polluting material or liability through the waste management chain.

Under the Classified Installations Law, companies have an obligation to discover any pollution accidents. This obligation, of course, extends to off-site pollution.

Any such accident will automatically result in administrative measures, but not necessarily in sanctions. The first administration aim will be to ensure the clean-up of the pollution, and as long as there is no permanent damage, the administration will not enforce sanctions. Of course, it would be different if the pollution was due to non-compliance with the Prefect's orders. In such a case, sanctions would be not only administrative, but also criminal.

In addition, if anybody suffers damage from the off-site pollution, that person would be entitled to sue the operator of the facility (Civil Code, arts 1382 and 1383), the owner of the facility (Civil Code, arts 1382 and 1383) and the owner of the site (Civil Code, art 1384).

3.4 Liabilities of directors and managers

Directors and managers will never be liable under civil law or administrative rules. Their responsibility will be of a criminal nature. However, the French criminal law has recently been significantly modified and companies can now be held criminally liable too. As a consequence, it is hard to say if the *Procureur de la République* will still prosecute managers or, instead, will prosecute companies directly.

In any event, managers remain responsible, as contributing to the commission of the offence (eg by giving orders) is considered as complicity. But managers can escape liability if they can prove that there was a delegation of powers. In such a case, the liable person is whoever was in charge, that is the person who was really managing the operation.

3.5 Liabilities of those financing businesses

Persons financing businesses are normally not liable for pollution caused by the financed activity. However, it is possible for a financier to face administrative,

3.5 Chapter 12

criminal and civil liability, if the financier not only finances the operation, but also intervenes in the management of the facility. By advising the operator, or by imposing its decision on the manager, the financier can become a manager itself, and can thus be liable just as the operator. Thus, any person financing a polluting activity must be careful never to impose its decisions (eg on how to handle waste). The financier should restrain itself from even advising the person running the facility.

In addition, it must be emphasised that the French equivalent of a mortgage, a 'hypothèque', cannot induce liability. A financier willing to sell a building on which he has a mortgage becomes, by operation of the mortgage, the owner of the building until he sells it. But the 'hypothèque' mechanism is different on that point, and the financier can proceed to sell the building although he never becomes the owner of it. As a result, where a 'hypothèque' exists there is no right of action against the financier for pollution problems.

3.6 Transferability of permits and licences

Transferability of permits and licences is an issue at the time of sale of the facility.

There are two ways of buying a facility. If the buyer purchases shares, he will become the owner of the company. Since the permits are granted to the company, the buyer will automatically benefit from these permits. However, a negative aspect is that if he purchases shares, he will not benefit from the vendor's 'discovery obligation'. The Classified Installations Law imposes on the vendor of a polluted site (as opposed to the vendor of shares), a duty to disclose to the buyer all the information he has or should have on the site (Classified Installations Law, art L.8–1). The buyer therefore knows exactly what he purchases and, in these circumstances, is considered to be responsible for any pollution. Since he was aware of this pollution (the vendor had to disclose it), by buying the site, he accepted liability for the existing pollution. The intention is that the buyer should negotiate the price of the site to take into account the existing pollution.

If the buyer purchases the site instead of shares, he will not automatically benefit from existing permits. However, if he wants to pursue the same activity, the Prefect will normally deliver the required permits.

4 MANAGING ENVIRONMENTAL ISSUES IN TRANSACTIONS

4.1 Current practice for assessment of risk

The most usual and efficient way to minimise environmental risk is to proceed with an audit of the site. At the end of the audit, the buyer should be able to answer at least the questions shown below. The list is not exhaustive but itemises those issues common to every environmental audit:

(1) Issues regarding the geographical site's situation:
    (a) What is the neighbouring population density?
    (b) Are there other classified installations next to the site?
    (c) What are the communication routes and rights of access, and what are the risks regarding those routes?
    (d) Are there any sites needing specific protection for historical or environmental reasons?
    (e) Is there any potable water source near to the site?

(2) Issues regarding town planning:
   (a) What is the applicable zoning plan?
   (b) What kind of buildings are allowed by the zoning plan next to the site?
   (c) What town planning rules could be applied to the site and to the classified installation?
   (d) What public service constraints apply or could apply to the site?

(3) Issues regarding the geological situation:
   (a) What is the hydrological and geological situation of the site, and the nature of the soil and sub-soil?
   (b) Is there any aquifer or any other undergroundwater?
   (c) If there was a previous classified installation on the site, how was the soil cleaned up on closure of the site, and is there any chance that the site is still polluted by any substances already released?
   (d) In the case of waste storage, what kind of waste was stored, and how was it done?

(4) Issues regarding the running of the facility, and its needs for natural resources, especially water:
   (a) Is it possible to provide the facility with its natural resource needs in a legal way?

By reviewing those questions, the buyer should try to determine the exact state of pollution of the site. It is also in the interest of the vendor to be able to prove that at the time of the deal, the site was not polluted, or that the pollution was at a given level.

4.2 Warranty or indemnity terms

Environmental risk is very different, depending on what the buyer purchases. If the purchase is of shares, the audit will have to be as precise as possible. The buyer must always be aware that he will be held liable for the past pollution as well as for his own pollution. He must also keep in mind that he is dealing with a vendor free of the disclosure obligation. This way of proceeding is obviously the one presenting the most serious risks. As a consequence, warranties will have to be drawn up to cover each and every possible pollution issue. They will also have to state explicitly that the vendor will have to compensate the buyer for any pollution discovered after the sale, and due to a prior activity.

4.3 Issues for those lending money to businesses—practice for ongoing management, reporting on the business and assuming management control

A financier may feel concern about the risk taken by its client in buying a polluted site. This risk may potentially affect the client's ability to discharge its obligations to the financier.

However, no specific audit is undertaken for financiers, since they are not liable as long as they do not act as managers, ie no liability arises as long as they do not take any decision regarding the running of the facility.

4.4 Insurance

The insurance industry is not very eager to insure environmental risks for a very good reason. This risk is highly difficult to evaluate and it is very likely that environmental standards will be harder to meet in the future.

However, an institute grouping of various insurance companies, ASSURPOL, has developed a model of contract. It is thus possible that insurance provision will develop quickly in the next years, especially if there is more data available to make a better evaluation of risks.

5 CONCLUSION

At this point, it can be said that environmental law is no longer just a national concept. National pollution in France is clearly regulated by numerous laws, Decrees and Orders and there is a complex and powerful administration applying and controlling the law.

In addition, the French practical attitude with regard to environmental issues allows economic development with quite strong protection of the environment, nature and human health.

The next challenge is the struggle against international pollution. CFC, greenhouse gases etc are now regulated by international treaties. These conventions will have a strong influence on the current environmental law. Hopefully, they will also lead to a strong and healthy improvement in environmental performance.

Chapter 13

PORTUGAL

Henrique dos Santos Pereira

Barrocas & Sarmento, Lisbon

1 INTRODUCTION

1.1 Origins and application of law

Portuguese law was influenced by Roman law, then by the Napoleonic codification and recently by German concepts. Portugal has a civil law regime and the national legal system is comprised of several codes and several separate statutes published daily in the official gazette called *Diário da República*.

Although the jurisprudence of the Appeal Courts and Supreme Court may have some relevance, common law principles are not applicable in Portugal. The relevance of jurisprudence only exists to the extent that lower courts, and usually the first instance courts, tend to interpret and apply the laws in the same way as the superior courts. However, there is no obligation of uniformity of jurisprudence. The most important source of law is the Constitution of the Republic of 1976. Article 66 of the Constitution relates directly to environmental issues. Paragraph one establishes the essential principle that all citizens have the right to a healthy and ecologically sound environment and that it is the duty of all citizens to protect the environment. Paragraph two comprises a list of the state's activities necessary to apply the principles of paragraph one.

The main statute specifically regarding environment is the Basic Law on the Environment (*Lei de Bases do Ambiente*—Law 11/87, dated 7 April 1987), which contains the essential principles on environment, and the Environment National Plan (*Plano Nacional da Política do Ambiente*) approved by Resolution 38/95 of the government, dated 21 April 1995.

Environmental law enacted by the Portuguese government is applicable in all Portuguese territory including the islands of the Azores and Madeira.

EU law issued as regulations is incorporated into Portuguese law automatically and EU directives are incorporated after being transposed into national legislation by a government Act.

1.2 Environmental policy formulation and regulators

The institutions or bodies responsible for applying environmental law are the following:

1.2 Chapter 13

1.2.1 Ministry of Environment and Natural Resources

This governmental department is responsible for the formulation and development of policies on the environment, natural resources and consumers' rights. It has two central departments:

(1) *General–Secretariat*: This is the central co-ordination service that supports all departments of the ministry in relation to human resources, budget control and general planning.
(2) *General Board for Environment*: This board provides support on all questions relating to the definition and execution of environmental policies and evaluates the environmental impact of projects with national ambit.

In addition to the above two central departments, the Ministry of Environment and Natural Resources has five regional departments covering different areas of the Portuguese territory.

1.2.2 Offices supervised by the ministry

The following offices also deal with specific environmental issues and operate under the supervision of the Ministry of Environment and Natural Resources:

(1) *Office for the Protection of Water Quality (Instituto da Água)*: This promotes and applies national policies on water resources and basic sanitation, eg by prosecuting water resources offences and applying fines and/or imposing clean-ups. This office is also responsible for issuing some permits related to the use of water resources.
(2) *Meteorology Office (Instituto de Metereologia)*: The Meteorology Office organises national activities on meteorology, seismology and air quality.
(3) *Office for the Conservation of Nature (Instituto da Conservação da Natureza)*: This promotes activities related to the conservation of nature and management of protected areas. In some cases, this office may prosecute offenders.
(4) *Office for Environmental Promotion (Instituto de Promoção Ambiental)*: The office develops education and information about environmental issues and also supports associations for the protection of the environment.
(5) *Office for Waste Management (Instituto dos Resíduos)*: This promotes the accomplishment of national policies on every aspect of waste, eg by issuing permits for discharge or transport of waste.

2 OUTLINE OF ENVIRONMENTAL LAW RELEVANT TO MERGER AND ACQUISITION TRANSACTIONS

2.1 Contaminated land

There is no legislation in Portugal specifically related to contaminated land. This issue should be considered in accordance with the general principles of law, mainly those established by the Civil Code, the Criminal Code and also the Basic Law on the Environment (Law 11/87, dated 7 April 1987). This Law establishes the main essential principles on environment all of them based on the basic principles that 'all citizens have the right to a healthy and ecologically sound environment', that 'it is the duty of all citizens to protect the environment' and that 'the State is obliged to improve the quality of life of citizens, both individually and collectively'.

In accordance with the general provisions established by the Basic Law on the Environment, anyone causing significant damage to land has to pay a fine up to P Esc 9 million and to indemnify the State as well as all third parties who are affected. Beyond this, the offender may also be obliged to clean up the pollution caused.

The person responsible for cleaning up contaminated land is its current owner, even if he is not the original polluter, without prejudice of the right of recourse against the latter. The general principles of law in this respect mean that the transfer of property results in the obligation to clean-up passing to the new owner. However, criminal penalties, if applicable, are not transferred to the new owner of the land.

Although, as stated above, there are no specific rules on contaminated land, there are a number of statutes applicable to the use of the soil and sub-soil:

2.1.1 The soil

The Basic Law on Soils (*Lei de Solos*), enacted by Decree–Law 794/76, dated 5 November 1976, defines the principle according to which the reasonable use of the soil in general is based and stipulates the conditions that must be observed when carrying out any activity that may produce harm to the soil. The aims of those conditions are to (1) ensure that agricultural land will not be used for any other purposes, (2) limit soil pollution and regulate the use of fertilisers and other chemicals and, finally, (3) ensure that all urban and industrial developments take into consideration the landscape, the fertility of the soil and the environment in general.

The occupation by private entities of land for public use is governed by Decree–Law 468/71, dated 5 November 1971.

Certain modifications to the soil and landscape are governed by Decree–Law 343/75, dated 3 July 1975.

The protection of forests is governed by Regulatory Decree 55/81, dated 18 December 1981.

2.1.2 The sub-soil

Any exploitation whatsoever of the sub-soil must take into consideration the conservation of the landscape and the environment in general as well as the effect on the sub-soil itself, in accordance with the rules established, for example, by Decree–Law 90/90, dated 16 March 1990. The preservation of the environment in general includes, inter alia, the protection of animal and plant species and their habitats.

The sources of all mineral and thermal waters are protected by law and those whose activities affect the landscape in an adverse way are obliged to return it to its original state.

2.2 Pollution of water resources

The protection, preservation and improvement of water quality are the objects of Decree 5787–4 I, dated 10 May 1919, the Basic Law on Water (*Lei das Águas*), Decree–Law 74/90, dated 7 March 1990 and Decree–Law 236/98, dated 1 August 1998, which are applicable to:

(1) inland surface and groundwaters;
(2) territorial maritime waters;
(3) waters in the exclusive economic zone;
(4) river beds and river banks;

2.2 Chapter 13

(5) lakes and their shorelines;
(6) the coastline.

The main principles of Portuguese laws on water quality are, inter alia, (a) to use the water reasonably, (b) to establish a seashore protection area, (c) to restrict the discharge of liquid waste into the sewage system, and (d) to introduce measures to reduce pollution caused by factories and other enterprises.

Any alteration to the quality or composition of the water caused by discharges of waste or radiation will be considered to be acts of pollution.

Any company that intends to discharge effluents or waste into water (including the sea and coastal waters) must receive a prior authorisation from the Office for Waste Management and the Office for the Protection of Water Quality and another authorisation from the same departments will also be necessary for the transport, treatment and storage of waste. However, an authorisation will not be granted in relation to toxic and hazardous waste.

The infringement of the regulations on the protection of water against pollution may result in the payment of a fine ranging between P Esc 500,000 and P Esc 10 million. Furthermore, the authorities are entitled to close the plant in question, either temporarily or permanently. Cleaning-up obligations may also be imposed to the offender.

Penalties for the pollution of sea water, beaches and shores are provided by Decree–Law 90/71, dated 22 March 1971. The maximum fine applicable in accordance with this Decree–Law is P Esc 1 million.

2.3 Authorisations for discharge to water and for taking water from natural resources

Authorisation from the Ministry of the Environment and Natural Resources is required before discharging any liquid waste into the sewage system. The applicant has to demonstrate that the limits determined by Law 74/90 for waste water will be achieved and must provide full technical specifications.

The discharge of urban waste waters is covered by Government Directive (*Portaria*) 624/90, dated 4 August 1990.

It is possible for the authorities to review at anytime the licence in order to protect the public and/or the environment.

The applicant must notify the licensing authority of any changes in the circumstances in which the licence was granted.

The authorities are allowed to inspect the installation at any time to confirm that the conditions of the licence are being discharged by the applicant and are also entitled to suspend or terminate the operation of any industrial plant until the source of any eventual pollution is identified and dealt with. The authorities are also entitled to seize any plant or specific equipment that is causing pollution. Beyond this, certain fiscal benefits can be withdrawn and licences to operate the plant can be cancelled.

Finally, anyone who infringes legal regulations and as a consequence of the infringement causes significant damage to the environment in general or, in particular, to water quality, is liable to pay a fine (of between P Esc 10,000 to P Esc 500 million depending on the circumstances of the case) and to indemnify the State as well as all third parties adversely affected. Furthermore, cleaning up obligations may be imposed.

If, for any reason (eg urgent need to avoid worse consequences) the authorities conduct the clean-up themselves, they are entitled to claim reimbursement—beyond fines, penalties, etc—from the polluter. This is a clear case of application of the polluter pays principle.

The use of water from any source for industrial purposes is also subject to obtaining a previous permission from the Office for the Protection of Water Quality which will stipulate all the conditions that must be met by the applicant.

2.4 Integrated pollution control

In accordance with the Portuguese Basic Law on the Environment, pollution includes all and any act which adversely affects human health or welfare, animal and plant species, landscape and the 'fragile balance that exists between the various ecosystems'.

There are no legal rules on integrated pollution control and for this reason each polluting act has to be considered and punished in accordance with the relevant applicable statute, ie the statute or statutes ruling each type of pollution.

2.5 Emissions to the atmosphere

Decree–Law 352/90, dated 9 November 1990, comprises the rules regarding the protection of the atmosphere. This Decree–Law incorporates into Portuguese law the following directives relating to air pollution: Directive (EEC) 88/609 on large combustion plants, Directive (EEC) 89/369 on prevention of air pollution caused by incinerators, Directive (EEC) 89/427 on limits for sulphur dioxide and particulates and Directive (EEC) 87/817 on pollution caused by asbestos.

Decree–Law 352/90 comprises all the rules for the licensing of activities that cause emissions to the air. Those licences, granted by the Ministry of the Environment and Natural Resources, are always necessary when constructing, managing or altering plants emitting any kind of substances to the air.

Failure to comply with the rules on protection of air quality set out in that statute (eg when exceeding the maximum levels of pollutants allowed by law) could lead to the forced shut down of the operations of the plant concerned, the imposition of fines (up to a maximum of P Esc 9 million) and the suspension or withdrawal of subsidies or of the operating licence itself. In the case of some infringements, the suppliers of water, electricity and gas may also terminate their supplies on instruction from the authorities.

The main principles established by Decree–Law 352/90 are the following:

(1) definition and application of the principle that those who pollute the air must pay for it (the so-called polluter pays principle, also applicable for other types of pollution);
(2) minimisation of emissions and discharges from industrial plants by establishing limits on all discharges;
(3) protection of the atmosphere in accordance with the specific measures provided for in the statute (eg pollutants must be emitted into the atmosphere through chimneys). The technical specifications for chimneys are detailed in the Decree–Law and the construction must be approved by the competent authorities;
(4) ban on the unauthorised burning of industrial waste;
(5) regulation of the disposal of toxic, dangerous and domestic waste and scrap that might affect the quality of the air;

2.5 *Chapter 13*

(6) fines to be imposed by the government on anyone unlawfully polluting the atmosphere. The proceeds should be reinvested by the government in further efforts to reduce pollution.

Monitoring of air pollution is undertaken by the Ministry of the Environment and Natural Resources, the municipal authorities and the police.

The Government Directive (*Portaria*) 286/93, dated 12 March 1993, amended by Government Directive 125/97, dated 21 February 1997, and by Government Directive 399/97, dated 18 June 1997, establishes limits for emissions of certain substances to the atmosphere.

Directive (EC) 93/59 of 28 June 1993 on measures against air pollution originated by motor vehicles was transposed into national law by Government Directive (*Portaria*) 53/94, dated 21 January 1994.

2.6 Waste management including recycling/re-use obligation

The law distinguishes between waste (both solid and liquid waste) and effluents (vapours and gaseous substances).

Portuguese legislation, eg Decree–Law 488/85, dated 25 November 1985 (establishing rules on solid wastes), provides for tax and financial incentives for the recycling of waste or for its use as a raw material or energy source.

There are no re-use obligations but any toxic waste produced must be eliminated or neutralised using clean technologies.

The management and disposal of waste originated by industrial plants is governed by Regulation 374/87 4 May 1987, and by Decree–Law 239/97, dated 9 September 1997.

The law distinguishes between 'industrial waste' and 'pollutant waste'. Industrial waste is defined as:

(1) solid, semi-solid and liquid substances, materials or products that, by their own nature, cannot be considered as sub-products and may not be discharged into the sewage system;
(2) hazardous waste that must be subject to special treatment;
(3) waste needing disposal deriving from the operation of any plant.

'Pollutant waste' is defined as waste that contains weak concentration of dangerous components but which does not require any special treatment.

The disposal of pollutant waste, as well as toxic and hazardous waste, ie waste with strong concentration of dangerous components, has to be licensed by the administrative authorities and must be eliminated or neutralised with the use of clean technologies.

The transfer of waste is governed by Decree–Law 296/95, dated 17 October 1995.

It is illegal in Portugal to dispose of waste by incineration, burial or discharge at sea and the infringement of those regulations will result in a fine of between P Esc 500,000 and P Esc 10 million. In addition, for serious offences, the authorities are entitled to close the activity of the plant concerned, temporarily or permanently.

Local authorities, companies and health care units are obliged to organise and keep updated a register indicating the quantities, nature, origin and destination of the waste produced or collected. When that waste is toxic or dangerous, the registration should also indicate the storage conditions, the exact place where the waste is stored and the methods that will be used for the elimination. This register must be provided to the competent regulatory authorities upon request.

2.7 Land use planning/zoning

Decree–Law 38.382, dated 7 August 1951, the General Rules on Urban Constructions (*Regulamento Geral das Edificações Urbanas*), regulates the construction of new buildings and development of infrastructures in order to protect the landscape. Furthermore, authorisation for any new urban settlement will not be granted if its area, profile, colouring, etc, does not blend adequately with the existing landscape.

The exploitation of natural resources through mining activities, landfills for waste and logging activities are subject to tight control. Special measures were enacted against the over-exploitation of natural resources, especially in order to protect those natural resources that are rare or of particular scenic or scientific interest. National Parks, nature reserves, protected areas and natural monuments are listed and duly protected by law against over-exploitation or any kind of exploitation depending on the characteristics of the protected natural resource. So, in these areas it is very difficult, if not impossible, to get permission to exploit natural resources.

As to industrial projects, the main applicable provisions are contained in Decree–Law 109/91, dated 15 March 1991 (the General Regime on Industrial Activity—*Regulamento do Exercicio da Actividade Industrial*), Regulatory Decree 10/91, dated 15 March 1991 and in Decree–Law 13/71, dated 23 January 1971. These statutes cover the following items:

(1) prevention and control of the hazardous effects of industrial activities;
(2) health of the public in general and the workforce in particular;
(3) health and safety of the workers in the workplace;
(4) security of people and assets;
(5) protection of the environment in general.

For initiating operations and for altering existing installations it is necessary to obtain a prior authorisation from the Ministry of Industry and Energy. In some specific cases, it is also necessary to obtain an authorisation from the Ministry of Agriculture. The ministry concerned must consult with the governmental departments or local authorities responsible for environment, health and working conditions before approving any application.

All applications for licences for this type of project must be accompanied by an environmental impact assessment and the applicant must indicate who will build the plant and furthermore who will undertake the operations at the plant. The rules on the assessment of the environmental impact of certain activities enacted by Decree–Law 186/90, dated 6 June 1990, amended by Decree–Law 278/97, dated 8 October 1997, which transposed Directive (EEC) 85/337 into national law, are fully applicable in these cases.

Finally, regional planning is ruled by Decree–Law 176–A/88, dated 18 May 1988 and municipal planning is governed by Decree–Law 69/90, dated 2 March 1990. The licensing of construction works is governed by Decree–Law 445/91, dated 20 November 1991.

All buildings must be licensed by the regional and/or municipal authorities. In addition to central government, the municipal authorities also have a very important role to play in implementing and enforcing environmental legislation, for example, through the approval of building construction. Beyond this, and in general, the municipal authorities have the power to impose fines for any infringement of any environmental laws.

Regarding specifically industrial plants, the municipal authorities can only give permission for construction if the owner of the plant concerned can produce a permit issued by the Ministry of Industry and Energy. Authorisation for the commencement of operations will only be granted if the owner of the plant complied with all the specifications and obligations determined by the authorities, both central and local.

2.7 Chapter 13

The violation of land use planning regulations regarding industrial plants may result in the imposition of a fine in the range of P Esc 50,000 to P Esc 500,000 if the owner of the plant is an individual, or P Esc 50,000 to P Esc 6 million if the owner of the plant is a company.

The authorities are allowed to cancel any subsidies that the company is eligible for (or is already receiving) and also to seize or remove the plant or equipment involved if there is any infringement of regulations, in addition to the fine. Finally, the authorities may also order the utilities and some suppliers (usually gas, electricity and water) to suspend supplies to the industrial plant in question.

2.8 Use and storage of hazardous substances including radioactive material

Specific measures to be adopted by plant managers to prevent serious industrial accidents are provided for by Decree–Law 204/93, dated 3 June 1993, transposes to domestic law EU Directive 88/610, dated 24 November 1988 (which amended EU Directive 82/501). All managers are obliged to identify any potential risks, establish measures for dealing with those risks and inform and equip adequately all those working in the plant. Any violation of these regulations may result in the payment of a fine ranging between P Esc 250,000 and P Esc 6 million. In addition to the fine, the following penalties may also be applied, depending on the circumstances of the case:

(1) withdrawal of subsidies or any other pecuniary benefits;
(2) forced closure of the premises;
(3) prohibition of carrying out a specific activity.

In these three cases, the penalty will last between 10 days and 2 years.

The imposition of such penalties is publicised in national and regional newspapers for at least 30 days. A copy of the penalties is also affixed to the front door of the building during the same period.

The system for notification, classification, packaging and labelling of chemical products is governed by Decree–Law 280–A/87, dated 17 June 1987.

The trade, handling and disposal of certain dangerous products is governed by Decree–Law 221/88, dated 28 June 1988.

Decree–Law 47/90, dated 9 February 1990, establishes limits to the use of certain hazardous substances and preparations.

The storage and burning of used oils is governed by Decree–Law 88/91, dated 23 February 1991.

2.9 Noise and nuisance

Noise pollution in general is covered by Decree–Law 251/87, dated 24 June 1987, the so-called *Regulamento Geral sobre o Ruído*, with the amendments introduced by Decree–Law 292/89, dated 2 September 1989. All sources of noise are subject to Decree–Law 251/87, including, inter alia, motor vehicles, motorcycles, industrial compressors, industrial plants, demolition equipment, etc.

The construction of buildings in general and of industrial plants in particular, is subject to the rules established by Decree–Law 251/87, in an attempt to minimise as much as possible noise pollution from construction.

This statute provides for the establishment of maximum permissible levels of noise, the reduction of noise levels through the determination of maximum levels applicable to the different sources, the introduction of new building requirements and the obligation to consult the public on certain specific sources of considerable noise.

An operating licence for a plant will only be issued if the plant is considered capable of adhering to the noise pollution regulations and will be retained only if it subsequently achieves these noise levels.

Anyone infringing legal regulations and as a consequence of the infringement causing noise pollution is liable to pay a fine up to P Esc 3 million and to indemnify all third parties adversely affected. The control of noise is undertaken by the police authorities.

Noise pollution originated by bars, discos, public shows and other specific activities are governed by Decree–Law 271/84, dated 6 August 1984, by Government Directive (*Portaria*) 879/90, dated 20 September 1990 and by Government Directive (*Portaria*) 77/96, dated 9 March 1996.

2.10 Miscellaneous

The law stipulates that adequate lighting levels should be provided in the workplace and in public places to ensure the comfort and welfare of all citizens. Consequently, there are some restrictions, eg on new buildings and illuminated advertisements as well as in and around 'green areas' and open spaces.

There are some measures safeguarding flora in general and forests, 'green areas' and plant species is particular provided in several pieces of legislation. Any act that may affect the normal development or recuperation of the flora in general or of species of plants which are of particular scientific, economic or scenic interest is punishable by law. Consequently, before granting any licence for constructing new buildings, the authorities must confirm that the construction will not affect, for example, rare trees or plants with particular scenic or scientific interest.

Further important statutes in force in Portugal governing other issues relating to the environment are the following:

(1) Decree–Law 28/87, dated 14 January 1987, with the amendments introduced by Decree–Law 138/88, dated 22 April 1988—trade and use of asbestos;
(2) Decree–Law 348/89, dated 12 October 1989—rules on protection against ionizing radiation;
(3) Decree–Law 8/90, dated 4 January 1990—prohibits the use of detergents which are less than 90% biodegradable and establishes rules on the labelling of detergents;
(4) Decree–Law 121/90, dated 9 April 1990—rules on the transborder shipment of dangerous waste;
(5) Decree–Law 186/90, dated 6 June 1990, amended by Decree–Law 278/97, dated 8 October 1997—rules on the assessment of environmental impact of certain activities and transposition into national law of Directive (EEC) 85/337 on environmental impact assessment;
(6) Decree–Law 322/95, dated 28 November 1995—transposes into national law EC Directive (EC) 94/62 on the management of packaging;
(7) Decree–Law 153/96, dated 30 August 1996—rules on the protection of people and environment against risks originated by the use of sealed radioactive sources.

3 PARTICULAR ENVIRONMENTAL ISSUES RELEVANT TO TRANSACTIONS

In accordance with the Portuguese Constitution, the Basic Law on the Environment and the Environment National Plan, all citizens have a right to a healthy and ecologically sound environment. If this right is infringed because of pollution, any citizen is entitled to demand the termination of the illegal pollution activity and claim compensation. Furthermore, where there is an infringement of environmental law, the State itself may also be entitled to compensation that may consist in the polluter paying all cleaning-up costs or, if it has not been possible to clean-up the pollution caused, in paying a pecuniary compensation. Finally, any fines or other penalties may also be imposed of the polluter.

There are two types of liability that may arise from infringements of environmental law: civil liability and criminal liability.

3.1 Civil liability

As to civil liability, the general principle is defined by art 483 of the Portuguese Civil Code as follows:

> 'Whosoever with intent or due to negligence unlawfully infringes the right of a third party or any legal provision established to protect the third party's right must undertake to indemnify the third party for the damage resulting from the infringement.'

Under environmental law, both fault-based liability and strict liability without intent or negligence are provided for.

Regarding vicarious liability, the following cumulative requirements have to be proved to succeed with a civil legal action:

(1) there must have been an act or a failure to act;
(2) that act or failure to act must have been contrary to the law;
(3) the act or failure to act must be attributable to the party that caused the pollution;
(4) it must be shown that damage was caused;
(5) there must be a causal link between the act or failure to act and the party that caused the pollution.

Only if all these requirements are satisfied will the party that caused the pollution be considered liable and responsible for indemnifying the affected third party.

Regarding strict liability irrespective of intent or negligence, art 41 of the Basic Law on Environment (Law 11/87, dated 7 April 1987) establishes the following:

> 'There is an obligation to indemnify, irrespective of any fault, whenever someone has caused significant damage to the environment as a result of a particularly dangerous activity, even though he has complied with the law and all technical rules that are applicable.'

The indeterminate concepts used in this article—'significant damage' and 'particularly dangerous activity'—are interpreted and applied by the courts in accordance with the circumstances of each specific case. There are no general definitions applicable to all cases as the aim of the legislator was exactly to allow the judges freedom to decide in each circumstance.

Except in these very exceptional cases of liability without fault (which is usually difficult to prove), all the five requirements above will have to be proved for a civil action to succeed. Furthermore, only damage which can be proved to be directly the result of an act or failure to act will be compensatable. The direct relation between the act and the damage exists in all cases where there is a clear cause–effect relation.

3.2 Criminal liability

One of the most important applicable principles of criminal law is that there are no environmental crimes or criminal sanctions except those expressly provided for in the law.

The relevant environmental crimes provided for in the Portuguese Criminal Code are the following:

3.2.1 Article 272

This creates offences in connection with the following:

(1) 'Relevant' fires in buildings or in any constructions, forests, woods or grain fields.
(2) All kinds of explosions.
(3) Emissions of toxic or asphyxiating gases.
(4) Emissions of radiation or radioactive substances.
(5) Floods and avalanches.
(6) Collapse of buildings or any other constructions.

If danger to the life of human beings, public health or significant damage to property belonging to third parties originates from any of these events, the person who committed the deliberate act is subject to between three and ten years' imprisonment. If the act is a result of negligence the imprisonment will be between one and eight years.

3.2.2 Article 273

If any of the acts defined by art 272 of the Criminal Code causes the emission of nuclear energy the applicable criminal sanctions will be the following:

(1) five to ten years' imprisonment in the case of an intentional act;
(2) three to ten years' imprisonment in the case of a negligent act.

3.2.3 Article 275

The acts of importing, manufacturing, storing, buying, selling, transporting or using explosive substances or substances capaable of producing nuclear or radioactive explosions without the proper permit are considered crimes. The applicable sanction is imprisonment up to three years.

3.2.4 Article 278

Whosoever, infringing the law, eliminates fauna or flora specimens, destroys natural habitats or exhausts sub-soil resources will be subject to imprisonment up to three years in the case of intentional acts or up to one year in the case of negligent acts.

3.2.5 Article 279

The pollution of water or soil, its contamination or poisoning, the commission of air pollution and noise pollution are also crimes. The sanctions applicable are of up to three years of imprisonment in the case of intentional acts or up to one year for negligent acts.

3.2 *Chapter 13*

3.2.6 Article 280

If any of the acts referred to in art 279 causes danger to human life or to public health or property, the applicable sanctions are of between one and eight years' imprisonment for intentional acts and up to five years' imprisonment for negligent acts.

3.2.7 Article 281

The following acts are considered by this art 281 as crimes: propagation of diseases, plagues and deterioration of animal foodstuffs. The applicable sanction is up to two years of imprisonment for intentional acts or up to one year if the act was performed with negligence.

3.2.8 Article 282

The deterioration of human foodstuffs and medicines is a crime subject to imprisonment for between one and eight years if the act was intentional or up to five years if it was negligent.

In addition to the general environmental crimes established by the Criminal Code there are others provided for by separate statutes, covering matters such as forest fires, illegal hunting of protected animal species, acts or omissions relating to public health and non-compliance with embargoes and conservation orders.

3.3 Other liability principles

Also of significance is art 42 of the Basic Law on the Environment which entitles any citizen to demand the immediate suspension of activities causing damage to the environment under *embargo administrativo* proceedings.

In accordance with art 43 of the Basic Law on the Environment, anyone undertaking activities that may have an adverse effect on the environment is obliged to have an insurance policy covering those risks.

Finally, art 44 of the Basic Law on the Environment provides that those who apply for compensation as a result of damage in connection with offences to the environment are exempt from paying legal costs in certain circumstances.

3.4 Historical liabilities

Regarding historical liabilities, there is a distinction in Portuguese law between an individual's liability and liability of a company. Individuals will always remain liable for all their acts damaging the environment, whenever the pollution was caused, and will retain liability for activities at a property they no longer own. Liability of a company will continue to apply to the company while it exists, irrespectively of its changing owners who will never be personally liable, except in the above cases.

3.5 Liability of directors, managers and shareholders

The directors, managers and financiers of a company will never be personally liable vis-à-vis any third parties for civil claims arising from the acts of the company. However, in those cases where criminal liability exists in addition to civil liability, the corresponding sanctions will be imposed on those individuals since companies cannot have criminal liability.

Two types of civil liability are considered here: (1) shareholders' liability and (2) liability of officials of the company. The liability of shareholders is limited, both in the case of a *Sociedade por Quotas* and of the *Sociedade Anónima* (the two types of limited liability companies) to the amount of subscribed capital. This means that if the capital is not fully paid up, the company as well as any creditor of the company, by way of legal subrogation, can demand that the shareholders pay up the capital for which they subscribed.

Whilst on the subject of shareholders' liability, the liability of directors of the *Sociedade Anónimas* and the managers (*Gerentes*) of the *Sociedades por Quotas* is of interest. As a general statutory rule, the directors and the managers must act with the care of a prudent and organised manager and have a fiduciary duty to act in the interest of the company, of the shareholders and of the employees. In case that duty is not properly accomplished, the Director or the manager in question will be liable vis-à-vis the company (but not vis-à-vis third parties) for any damage he or she may have caused.

All directors are jointly liable vis-à-vis the company except if they vote against an unlawful resolution which has been approved by a majority of the other directors and any clause in the articles of association which limits their liability is not valid.

3.6 Liability of financiers

There is no legislation in Portugal specifically related to liability of financiers. This subject should be considered in accordance with the general principles of law, mainly those established by the Civil Code and the Criminal Code. Following those principles, the banks and any other financial providers cannot become liable for any environmental problems arising in the business they financed. The law considers the investors as third parties for this purpose, ie parties not involved in the incorporation or management of the companies. Otherwise, the financiers would have to supervise constantly and daily all the businesses to which they invested.

So, if a Portuguese company causes any kind of pollution, no one would normally even consider the possibility of claiming liability from the bank that financed the company's activity. However, some extreme situations may occur in which the financier may be held liable, for example, if finance was extended for the illegal acquisition of substances to produce nuclear or radioactive explosions.

3.7 Transferability of permits and licences

In general, permits and licences are granted if all the requirements established by law are fulfilled. As a principle, the transfer of permits and licences is not allowed by law. However, if the ownership of a company is transferred, the permits and licences held by that company are also transferred.

4 MANAGING ENVIRONMENTAL ISSUES IN TRANSACTIONS

4.1 Assessment of environmental risks

Assessment of environmental risks in transactions is not commonly undertaken in Portugal, at least for the time being. Generally, only the largest companies address

4.1 *Chapter 13*

these risks, mainly those companies owned by foreign investors who are playing an important role in Portugal in changing attitudes to the need to protect the environment. In any event, usually only the most serious risks such as pollution of rivers are assessed.

4.2 Warranty and indemnity terms

Portuguese environmental law has no peculiarities which affect warranty or indemnity terms as long as the terms do not infringe the bona fide principle. In accordance with this principle, the parties to a contract must always act diligently, loyally and correctly. This principle is applicable not only in relation to all contractual duties and obligations but also in the exercise of all rights generally granted by law.

Also the principle of the freedom of the parties to determine their own obligations and rights is fully applicable in relation to warranty and indemnity terms. The general practice, at least for the time being and mainly in relation to transactions between Portuguese entities, is to disregard warranties and indemnities specifically related to the environment when drafting contracts. Nevertheless, this does not mean that the party that caused any damage is free from liability since there are general principles of law, such as the bona fide principle referred to above, which are always applicable to contracts irrespective of the specific obligations imposed on the parties.

4.3 Control by financiers

There are no relevant mandatory rules for those lending money to businesses and the practice for ongoing management varies from case to case, although generally lenders usually exercise little control over the environmental practices of businesses they lend to.

5 CONCLUSION

Portugal was one of the first countries to recognise that all its citizens have the right to live in a healthy and ecologically sound environment but since then implementation of the principles established by the Constitution of the Republic of 1976 has been slow. There are very few prospective legislative developments in the area of environmental law.

However, the Portuguese handicap is not the absence of legislation but, at least for the time being, a question of attitude. In fact, Portugal has still not fully appreciated the importance of protecting the environment and this affects not only the public in general but also those who have powers and duties to enforce the existing legislation.

To conclude, a final word of hope: young Portuguese people show much more interest in all questions related to the environment and it is expected that in the next one or two decades, the present situation will improve.

Chapter 14

GREECE

Christina Vlachtsis

M & P Bernitsas, Athens

1 INTRODUCTION

Greece does not have a legislative history for the prevention of environmental harm. Problems associated with the environment were not addressed until the 1970s and even then, were not attributed the priority required.

Public interest is unfortunately not great and the conventional approach of considering that interests of the economy and environmental protection can go hand-in-hand is insufficient to deal with the Greek environmental situation.

In recent years there has been increasing development of environmental law creating compliance and liability risks. However this body of law is still incomplete and its impact is undermined by inadequate enforcement.

1.1 Origins of environmental law

Environmental law in Greece primarily originates from the constitution and a landmark in Greece for the protection of the environment was the 1975 passage of the present constitution (as amended in 1986) whereby, pursuant to art 24, para 1, the constitutional protection of the environment was proclaimed:

> 'The protection of the natural and cultural environment is a duty of the State. The State is bound to adopt special preventative measures for the preservation of the environment.'

Environmental law also arises from international law and conventions. Article 28, para 1 of the constitution prescribes that:

> 'The generally acknowledged rules of international law, as well as international conventions from the time they are ratified by law and become operative according to the conditions therein, shall be an integral part of domestic Greek law and shall prevail over any contrary provisions of Greek law.'

The European Union also influences the creation and implementation of environmental law in Greece. Nevertheless, difficulties have arisen with implementation, namely delays in compliance and incomplete or incorrect transposition of EC law into national law.

Furthermore, administrative law and other areas of law have developed certain general principles that have had a bearing on judicial precedents of the Council of

1.1 Chapter 14

State and are often referred to for the purpose of correctly interpreting legislation. These principles have the force of law and are recognised as sources of environmental law.

Domestic legislation is also an important source and consists of:

(1) Acts of Parliament, passed by Parliament and published in the *Official Gazette*.
(2) Legislative Acts, issued by the President of the Republic after a proposal of the Cabinet (art 44, para 1 of the constitution).
(3) Presidential Decrees issued by the President of the Republic and counter-signed by the competent minister for the implementation of laws (art 43, para 2 of the constitution).
(4) Regulatory Decrees subsequent to a proposal of the competent minister, issued to carry out the intent of law. Administrative agents may issue regulatory acts in cases related to specific issues or issues of local interest or of a technical and detailed nature (art 43, para 2 of the constitution). The President of the Republic may likewise be authorised to issue Regulatory Decrees in order to regulate matters specified in legislation passed by the Plenary Session of Parliament (art 43, para 4 of the constitution).

The first specific provisions applicable to the relationship of individuals with the natural environment were enacted under Law 360/76. Until this date, environmental law was not an autonomous body of law and the regulation of environmental problems was inadequately covered by general provisions of law.

Although the measures adopted by Law 360/76 broke new ground, difficulties with enforcement aspects limited the effective protection of the environment and it became apparent that an additional legislative basis was required. In the meantime the inactivity of the legislature was confronted by judicial precedents of the Council of State confirming the view that in the event of the legislature's unjustified procrastination, the administrative authorities, in the light of art 24 of the constitution, are under an obligation to attend to the protection of the environment.[1]

Law 1650/86 on the Protection of the Environment was the long awaited legislation, authorising the issuance of Presidential Decrees and Ministerial Acts and Decisions for its implementation.

However, Law 1650/86 failed to provide a real impetus for the preservation of the environment and merely substituted the legislature's inactivity. Although Law 1650/86 pursues objectives of environmental protection, there is a conflict between these objectives and the inadequate means adopted for achieving these given objectives.

1.2 Institutions or bodies responsible for applying environmental law

The functions for the protection of the environment are distributed amongst central and regional administration as well as local government agencies (municipalities and communities) and various other independent public law entities.

At the central administration level, the protection of the environment is the responsibility of the National Council on Land Use Planning and Environment and the Ministry of Environment, Land Use Planning and Public Works in association with other ministries.

---

1 Council of the State 363/1990.

The National Council on Land Use Planning and Environment was established by Law 360/76 on Land Use Planning and the Environment and its composition was later modified by Law 1032/80 on the Establishment of a Ministry of Residential Planning and Environment. By virtue of Law 1558/85 on Government and Governing Bodies, the National Council on Land Use Planning and Environment was introduced into the Ministry of Environment, Land Use Planning and Public Works.

Pursuant to Law 360/76, the National Council on Land Use Planning is competent in the following areas:

(1) to take policy decisions in matters pertaining to land use planning and the environment;
(2) to approve master plans and programmes for the protection of the environment and the harmonisation of these plans with development programmes;
(3) to ensure compliance with master plans and programmes for the protection of the environment.

The Ministry of Environment, Land Use Planning and Public Works includes a General Environmental Department that is divided into two parts: the Directorate of Environmental Planning and the Directorate for the Control of Atmospheric Pollution and Noise.

The Minister of Environment, Land Use Planning and Public Works is competent, either alone or in association with other ministers, to take nearly all the decisions pertinent to the protection of the environment with the exception of certain competencies retained by other ministries for more specialised areas. In this context, the Ministries of Agriculture, Development, Health, Welfare and Social Security, Commercial Shipping and Transport and Telecommunications are worthy of note.

Functions that are exclusively exercised by the Ministry of Environment, Land Use Planning and Public Works or those exercised by that ministry in association with other ministries may be transferred to regional agencies or to Executive Committees for the Organisation of Planning in Athens and Thessaloniki (Law 1650/86, art 27).

The Prefect is the highest official of each regional agency known as the Prefecture and is competent for consenting to projects that are likely to have significant effects on the environment and for consenting to projects that do not have significant effects on the environment but are nevertheless subject to certain criteria and thresholds. Furthermore the competent Prefect, by drawing on the Prefecture's personnel, may decide to establish special units or detachments for the control of the quality of the environment, charged with ensuring that all measures regarding the assessment of environmental effects are complied with and for the purpose of enforcing legislation on the protection of the environment. For the carrying out of these controls, the special units are entitled to inspect installations when it is considered likely that their operation undermines the environment. Measures that should be adopted are then indicated and a report is prepared suggesting the sanctions that should be imposed. The special units have a right of access to installations provided that security measures are respected. Those responsible for the operation of the installations are required to provide any necessary information that will facilitate the inspection (Law 1650/86, art 26).

Local government agencies pursuant to the Code on Municipalities and Communities have powers to deal with drainage and sewerage systems, roads, squares, bridges and public utility areas and also for waste management, the control of atmospheric and water pollution, protection of forests and the use of less harmful forms of energy. Local government agencies are also competent to give consent to projects or activities that are likely to have less serious effects on the environment.

1.2   Chapter 14

An environment agency may be established by Presidential Decree with its seat in Athens. The environment agency is likely to have administrative and economic independence and to be controlled by the Ministry of Environment, Land Use Planning and Public Works. Regional departments of the environment agency may also be established by virtue of a separate Presidential Decree. The functions of the environment agency are intended to be consultative and supplementary in nature as opposed to decision-making. The environment agency shall have exclusive competence for implementing national networks, for measuring and analysing environmental effects and for co-ordinating the activities of other agencies charged with the same. The environment agency shall also be competent to supply appropriate information. However, the relevant Presidential Decrees for the establishment of the environment agency and its regional departments have not yet been issued and this is not likely to occur in the near future (Law 1650/86, art 25).

Finally, in the context of land use planning, mention should be made of the important role of the regional town planning offices that are assisted in carrying out their functions by the police authorities.

2   OUTLINE OF ENVIRONMENTAL LAW RELEVANT TO MERGER AND ACQUISITION TRANSACTIONS

2.1   The general protection prescribed by Law 1650/86

Law 1650/86 identifies the areas of environmental law subject to protection and authorises the issuance of Presidential Decrees and Ministerial Acts and Decisions for the purpose of implementing the necessary measures within the prescribed contexts.

Law 1650/86 makes provision for the possibility of adopting measures for the prevention of atmospheric pollution by authorising the implementation of emission limits and air quality values and for the protection of the aquatic environment by imposing limits on emission standards and quality objectives. The legislation also covers protection of the soil, particularly concerning the final disposal of toxic and dangerous waste and waste disposal deriving from mining and quarrying activities. Reference is also made to waste management, which is primarily the responsibility of local government agencies. The legislation also promotes the adoption of measures for noise protection and authorises the adoption of permissible noise levels. Special provision is made for the implementation of measures for protection from hazardous substances and radioactivity.

2.2   Contaminated land

Article 11 of Law 1650/86 provides for the adoption of measures relating to the protection of land from natural disasters and in particular from erosion, lack of aeration, dehydration, deterioration, salt, chemical exhaustion, excessive use of fertilisers or inappropriate uses thereof and the introduction of toxic substances into the soil as a result of the use of fertilisers and pesticides.

The competent ministries, subsequent to obtaining the opinion of local government agencies, may issue a decision for the determination of suitable disposal sites for toxic and dangerous waste and sludge. The competent Prefect, subject to an opinion of the local government agencies, may determine suitable disposal sites for waste. More particularly, waste resulting from mining and quarrying activities is dealt with in accordance with the legislation in force.

Article 11 also serves as a legislative basis for the introduction of measures on the use of natural fertilisers to protect plants and animals against diseases and the prohibition of the use of pesticides that result in contamination of the soil and methods, limits and restrictions for the use of residual sludge from the treatment of waste in agriculture. Ministerial Decision 16190/1335/1997 on the protection of waters against pollution caused by nitrates from agricultural sources (implementing Directive (EEC) 91/676[2]) provides that a code or codes of good agricultural practice shall be established under the supervision of the Ministry of Agriculture, to be implemented by farmers on a voluntary basis.

Provisions are also made for the protection of the soil from contamination in Ministerial Decision 221/1965 which prescribes that the discharge of urban or industrial waste waters into the soil, either at or below surface level, is subject to the observance of specific requirements and the granting of a licence. Liability is assumed under the relevant provisions of the Penal Code.

Admittedly, Greece has a less wide-ranging contaminated land regime than many other jurisdictions and this may to some extent be attributed to the fact that the Presidential Decrees and Ministerial Decisions necessary for implementing art 11 have not yet all been issued.

2.3 Pollution of water resources

Articles 9 and 10 of Law 1650/86 provide for the protection of the aquatic environment. Discharge limits have been prescribed with regard to mercury, cadmium and hexachlorocyclohexane in Ministerial Act 144/2/11/1987 (implementing Directives (EEC) 76/464,[3] 82/176,[4] 83/513,[5] 84/156[6] and 84/491[7]) and with regard to certain dangerous substances in Ministerial Act 73/1990 (implementing Directives (EEC) 86/280[8] and 88/347[9]). The Ministerial Acts apply to inland surface waters and internal coastal waters and the discharge of the substances prescribed is subject to prior authorisation which specifies emission standards. The Ministry of Environment, Land Use Planning and Public Works or competent Prefect, in the context of the approval of environmental conditions, may impose more stringent emission standards than those laid down in the Ministerial Acts.

Ministerial Decision 55648/2210/1991 (implementing Directives (EEC) 86/280[10] and 88/347[11]), as supplemented by Ministerial Decision 90461/2193/1994 (implementing Directive (EEC) 90/415[12]), prescribes the appropriate measures to be adopted

---

2 Concerning the protection of waters against pollution caused by nitrates from agricultural sources.
3 On pollution caused by certain dangerous substances discharged into the aquatic environment of the Community.
4 On limit values and quality objectives for mercury discharges by the chlor-alkali electrolysis industry.
5 On limit values and quality objectives for cadmium discharges.
6 On limit values and quality objectives for mercury discharges by sectors other than the chlor-alkali electrolysis industry.
7 On limit values and quality objectives for discharges of hexachlorocyclohexane.
8 On limit values and quality objectives for discharges of certain dangerous substances included in list I of the Annex to Directive (EEC) 76/464.
9 Amending Annex II to Directive (EEC) 86/280 on limit values and quality objectives for discharges of certain dangerous substances included in list I of the Annex to Directive (EEC) 76/464.
10 On limit values and quality objectives for discharges of certain dangerous substances included in list I of the Annex to Directive (EEC) 76/464.
11 Amending Annex II to Directive (EEC) 86/280 on limit values and quality objectives for discharges of certain dangerous substances included in list I of the Annex to Directive (EEC) 76/464.
12 Amending Annex II to Directive (EEC) 86/280 on limit values and quality objectives for discharges of certain dangerous substances included in list I of the Annex to Directive (EEC) 76/464.

so as to prevent the pollution of water as a result of dangerous substances contained in waste waters.

Ministerial Decision 26857/533/1988 on the protection of groundwater against pollution by certain dangerous substances (implementing Directive (EEC) 80/68[13]) provides that a permit is required for direct or indirect discharges into water. Prior to granting a permit, an investigation must be conducted into the risks of pollution. In the light of that investigation the Ministry of Environment, Land Use Planning and Public Works or competent Prefect will decide whether or not to grant authorisation. Discharge of dangerous substances is permissible on condition that all technical precautions are taken and monitoring arrangements for the discharge have been made.

Ministerial Decision 5673/400/1997 on urban waste water treatment (implementing Directive (EEC) 91/271[14]) regulates the collection, treatment and discharge of urban waste water and the treatment and discharge of waste water from certain industrial sectors. The measures prescribed are intended to protect the environment from the adverse effects of waste water discharges.

Failure to observe the provisions of these Ministerial Acts and Decisions results in the imposition of the sanctions provided under arts 28, 29 and 30 of Law 1650/86 (examined in more detail para 3.1.1 below).

Ministerial Decision 463/1352/1986 has set water quality levels for drinking and bathing waters and waters supporting fish life and shellfish (implementing Directives (EEC) 75/440[15], 76/160[16], 78/659[17], 79/923[18] and 79/869[19]).

The Ministry of Environment, Land Use Planning and Public Works, either independently or in association with other concurrently competent ministries, may serve a notice on any natural or legal person whose activities may endanger or undermine the legitimate use of surface waters. This notice will instruct that person to take appropriate measures for the protection of public health and the aquatic environment and to respect water quality levels. The above-mentioned natural or legal person is then required to submit a report annually informing the Ministry of Environment, Land Use Planning and Public Works and other competent ministries of the measures that have been taken.

The Ministerial Decision prescribes criminal and administrative sanctions for failure to comply with these provisions (art 9).

Furthermore, Ministerial Decision 221/1965 on the discharge of urban and industrial waste water into surface waters and the soil prescribes the required quality of surface water depending on its intended use (eg drinking, bathing or fishing waters). Urban and industrial waste are subject to treatment and discharge is effected in such a manner so as not to affect the use of receiving waters. A licence is also a prerequisite. Liability for non-compliance is assumed under the provisions of the Penal Code.

Mention should also be made of Law 1739/87 which contains the overall legislative framework on water resources. However, the necessary Presidential Decrees and Ministerial Decisions for its implementation have not yet been issued and the required administration has not yet all been put in place.

The Ministry of Development is the competent authority with respect to the management of water resources and their allocation. The Ministry of Environment, Land

13 On the protection of groundwater against pollution caused by certain dangerous substances.
14 Concerning urban waste water treatment.
15 Concerning the quality required of surface water intended for the abstraction of drinking water in the member states.
16 Concerning the quality of bathing water.
17 On the quality of fresh waters needing protection or improvement in order to support fish life.
18 On the quality required of shellfish waters.
19 Concerning the methods of measurement and frequencies of sampling and analysis of surface water intended for the abstraction of drinking water in the member states.

Use Planning and Public Works has competence for the protection of the quality of those water resources.

One problem that arises is the inadequacy of Law 1739/87 in conforming with the more recent initiatives of the EU. Endeavours to improve management of the quality and quantity of water resources at a national and regional level commenced in 1994 under the auspices of the Ministry of Environment, Land Use Planning and Public Works and the Ministry of Industry, Research and Technology (now the Ministry of Development). Two programmes, the Hydroscope and the Master Plan were introduced but were, unfortunately, of limited success.

As regards marine pollution, Presidential Decree 55/1998 codifies the provisions of Law 743/77 on the protection of the marine environment. The marine pollution legislation applies to the pollution of ports, shores and national waters from installations, ships or tankers under Greek or foreign control and from any other source. It also applies to pollution of the open sea from ships and tankers under Greek or foreign control after the application of any EU or international convention in force, according to the principal of subsidiarity.

Polluters are liable for restoration expenses involved in remedying the pollution they cause. Civil liability is joint and several, since not only the liability of the polluter but that of other persons managing the enterprise may be caught. Criminal liability is also possible and any person who wilfully causes serious environmental damage is liable to imprisonment for at least three months. Negligent polluters are also punishable by imprisonment. Furthermore, administrative sanctions may be brought against marine polluters by the competent port authorities and fines may be imposed. These are calculated for each day of delay in remedying any breach, once the date set for restoration has expired. An independent disciplinary action may also be brought against any polluter who is a Greek mariner. Finally, a vessel may be prevented from leaving a port until a letter of guarantee, issued by a bank operating in Greece, or a letter of undertaking, issued by the vessel's insurance company, is provided.

Marine pollution legislation also originates from the ratification of multilateral conventions. The International Convention of 1973 on the Prevention of Marine Pollution from Ships and its amendment by the Protocol of 1978 (internationally known as MAR-POL 73/78) were ratified by Law 1269/82. The International Convention of 1972 on the Protection of the Mediterranean Sea Against Pollution by Dumping from Ships and Aircraft was ratified by Law 1147/81 and the International Convention of 1976 on the Protection of the Mediterranean Sea Against Pollution and the relevant Protocols, signed in Barcelona, were ratified by Law 855/78.

2.4 Emissions to the atmosphere

Ministerial Acts implementing arts 7 and 8 of Law 1650/86 have determined emission limits and air quality values for lead (Ministerial Act 98/1987 implementing Directive (EEC) 82/884[20]), sulphur dioxide and suspended particulates (Ministerial Act 99/1987 implementing Directive (EEC) 80/779[21]), nitrogen dioxide (Ministerial Act 25/1988 implementing Directive (EEC) 85/203[22]) and asbestos (Ministerial Decision 8243/1113/1991 implementing Directive (EEC) 87/217[23]). Ministerial Decision 58751/2370/1993 has also implemented Directive (EEC) 88/609 with regard to the limitation of emissions of certain pollutants into the air from large combustion plants.

20 On a limit for lead in the air.
21 On air quality limit values and guide values for sulphur dioxide and suspended particulates.
22 On air quality standards for nitrogen dioxide.
23 On the prevention and reduction of environmental pollution by asbestos.

2.4 *Chapter 14*

The Ministry of Environment, Land Use Planning and Public Works must be satisfied, before a permit is issued for a new plant, that the operator has taken all appropriate measures to prevent air pollution including the best available technology not entailing excessive costs, that the plant shall not cause significant air pollution and that specified limits will not be exceeded. Appropriate measures have also been adopted for the gradual adaptation of existing plants.

The use of specified measuring methods and equipment to monitor emissions from combustion plants is now compulsory for new plants although at the discretion of the Ministry of Environment, Land Use Planning and Public Works for existing plants. Such monitoring is carried out at the operator's expense.

Ministerial Decision 11294/1993 sets limits on air pollution from industrial plants and Ministerial Decision 11535/1993 determines the types of fuel that may be used by industrial installations, the use of any other types of fuel being subject to the requirement of the submission of a technical report and the granting of an approval.

Disregard of the provisions prescribed in the above Ministerial Acts and Ministerial Decisions results in the imposition of criminal, civil and administrative sanctions provided in arts 28, 29 and 30 of Law 1650/86.

2.5 Waste management including recycling/re-use obligations

Pursuant to art 12 of Law 1650/86, waste should be disposed of without endangering human health or harming the environment and without causing a nuisance through noise or odours or adversely affecting the countryside or sites of special interest. The recovery, re-use and recycling of waste is encouraged with a view to extracting raw materials.

Local government agencies are responsible for waste disposal but may decline to accept certain waste, when by virtue of its composition, nature, quality or quantity, disposal cannot be effected along with domestic waste. In this event the producers of waste must dispose of waste themselves or employ specialist waste collectors. Any natural or legal person that carries out waste operations must obtain a licence from the competent Prefect. Waste disposal resulting from the working of mines and quarries is the responsibility of the operators of such activities.

Waste disposal at a national and regional level is effected in accordance with Plans relating to the manner of disposal and suitable disposal sites.

Persons responsible for waste disposal must draw up a plan including measures for the reduction of waste, the treatment of waste for its recycling and re-use, the recovery of raw materials and the production of energy from waste.

The previous legislative framework in force on the management of waste was Ministerial Decision 49541/1424/1986 (implementing Directive (EEC)75/442[24]) but was never really enforced in practice due to important inadequacies.

Ministerial Decision 69728/824/1996 on measures for waste management, complemented by Ministerial Decisions 114218/1997 and 113944/1997 (implementing Directive (EEC) 91/156[25]) prescribes licensing requirements for the disposal, recovery, collection, temporary storage, transport and transformation of waste.

The Ministerial Decision distinguishes between competent authorities responsible for waste management and those responsible for establishing the national policy for waste management.

The authorities competent for drawing up waste management plans and the manner in which such plans will be drawn up, approved and completed is also determined in

24 The Waste Framework Directive.
25 Amending Directive (EEC) 75/442 on waste.

the Ministerial Decision but implementation is in effect difficult due to the wide range of authorities that are attributed competence.

Ministerial Decision 69728/824/1996 additionally sets out the general policy measures for waste management that are prescribed in Ministerial Decision 113944/1997 and the technical requirements and waste management plans are determined in Ministerial Decision 114218/1997.

Inspections of undertakings managing waste are carried out by the competent environmental and health authorities of each Prefecture prior to their operation in order to ensure that the conditions of the relevant licence are respected and that the personnel is adequately trained. Undertakings managing waste are subject to periodic inspections by Prefectorial agencies and are also required to keep a record of the waste and to make this information available, on request, to the competent authorities and to forward this information on an annual basis to the competent Prefecture.

Criminal, civil and administrative sanctions pursuant to arts 28, 29 and 30 of Law 1650/1986 are imposed on any person who violates these provisions.

Ministerial Decision 72751/3054/1985 on toxic and dangerous waste and polychlorinated biphenyls (PCBs) and polychlorinated terphenyls (PCTs) (in compliance with Directives (EEC) 78/319[26] and 76/403[27]) provides that the holder of toxic and dangerous substances and PCBs is responsible for their management and disposal but may delegate these operations to a third party who has been granted a licence.

The disposal of toxic and dangerous waste and PCBs or PCTs is subject to the granting of a licence from the competent Prefect. Storage also requires a licence in accordance with the terms and procedures set out in Law 1360/83. In both cases the licence is only granted after a report has been made to the competent regional department of the Ministry of Environment, Land Use Planning and Public Works and after this ministry has obtained the opinion of the competent committee, which consists of numerous members, including members from local government agencies and ministries.

Anyone who produces, holds or manages toxic and dangerous waste and PCBs or PCTs is under an obligation to keep a record of the quantity and nature of that waste and the methods and sites used for disposal, including the dates of receipt and subsequent disposal. This information shall be available to the competent authorities upon request.

This Ministerial Decision prescribes the criminal and administrative sanctions that are imposed in the event of violation of its provisions (art 17).

Ministerial Decision 19396/1546/1997 covers the management of hazardous waste (implementing Directive (EC) 91/689[28]) and provides that hazardous waste must be managed in a manner so as prevent risk to water, air, soil, plants and animals, forests and fishing production. Furthermore, adequate measures should be adopted to ensure that there is no alteration of the landscape or areas of special ecological, historical, cultural or aesthetic interest. Hence, the Ministry of Environment, Land Use Planning and Public Works, in conjunction with other concurrently competent ministries, undertakes preparation of the National Plan for the Management of Hazardous Waste, taking into consideration technical, economic, environmental, planning and social requirements.

Any party wishing to manage hazardous waste should obtain a licence from the Prefect for the temporary storage, collection, transportation, transfrontier shipping, exploitation and disposal of the material. The prior negotiation and agreement of the environmental terms of the licence, in accordance with the provisions of Law

26 On toxic and dangerous waste.
27 On the disposal of PCBs.
28 On hazardous waste.

1650/1986, is necessary for the issuance of such a licence. If granted, the licence is valid for a period not exceeding five years.

Installations or undertakings that manage hazardous waste are obliged to employ specialised and technical personnel and to possess the necessary technical infrastructure. Failure to comply with these provisions incurs civil, criminal and administrative liability. Civil and criminal sanctions imposed are those prescribed in arts 28 and 29 of Law 1650/86, whilst special provision is made for the imposition of administrative sanctions in art 18 of this Ministerial Decision.

2.6 Land use planning/zoning

Article 24, para 2 of the constitution provides that the National Plan and the formation, development, town planning and expansion of towns and residential areas in general shall be under the regulatory authority and control of the State, with the objective of arranging the development of settlements and securing the best possible living conditions.

The basic legislation in force in the context of the planning of cities, towns and communes is the Legislative Decree of 17 July, 1923. The text prescribes the fundamental principles for the drawing up, approval and application of town plans and establishes the general terms of their development. The legislation authorises the issuance of Presidential Decrees restricting the development of cities, towns and communes and lays out the terms and conditions regarding the manner in which construction operations are carried out. These terms and conditions are dictated by considerations of hygiene, safety and aesthetic values. Law 947/1979 provides that failure to comply with these requirements may result in the imposition of administrative sanctions. The Legislative Decree also provides that any building under construction, any activity pertaining to construction and in general any construction or installation situated either within or outside cities, towns or communes is subject to state control. Moreover the erection, renovation or demolition of any building or more generally any construction or installation is subject to a permit granted by the competent Technical Department subsequent to the submission of a written application from the interested party and the necessary study of the project to be carried out. In certain cases the provision of a guarantee may be requested as a prerequisite to the granting of a licence. The execution of the project requires the appointment of a supervisor.

Any erection or construction carried out in disregard of the above provisions may be demolished by the competent authorities and depending on the gravity of the infringement, penal sanctions may additionally be imposed (such as imprisonment and confiscation of equipment).

All parties involved, namely the owner, the supervisor and contractor are jointly and severally liable for the payment of expenses incurred in demolishing the building or any other damage caused to a third party as a result of the intervention of the competent authorities.

Law 1337/83 on the development of town plans, settlements and zoning regulates matters pertaining to: (a) the development of approved town plans and settlements that have been in existence prior to 1923; (b) the introduction of town planning to settlements that have been in existence since 1923 and that have not been subjected to an approved plan and the development of such areas; (c) the introduction of town planning to areas for uses other than residential.

In relation to the introduction of town planning to any particular town or settlement or the development of that area, a master plan is prepared, subject to the issue of a Decision by the Minister of Environment, Land Use Planning and Public Works that is published in the *Official Gazette*. Law 2508/97 prescribes that the Master Plan shall determine areas of special protection that shall not be subject to town planning; areas surrounding towns or settlements requiring special supervision and restriction of their development; and all areas that are subject or that shall be subject to town planning in the future.

Law 1337/83 also provided for a procedure according to which buildings erected in disregard of permit requirements could be legalised subsequent to a declaration by the competent authorities and payment of an amount equivalent to 10% of the value of the building. This provision had only temporary effect but unfortunately resulted in the failure of much development to correspond to the submitted plans. Recently a draft law was submitted to Parliament with a similar objective but was dismissed.

Law 1577/85, referred to as the General Building Regulation, determines the special terms and conditions and any restrictions on construction within or without the approved town plans or settlements so that the natural, residential and cultural environment may be protected and so that public interest may be served.

Articles 18–22 of Law 1650/86 prescribe measures for the protection of nature and landscape and include the possibility of zoning of particular areas with the objective of preserving and protecting natural flora and fauna and wildlife.

Zones of Special Environmental Reinforcement refer to areas that present serious environmental problems justifying the adoption of appropriate restrictions in order to prevent environmental harm in these areas (Law 1650/86, art 23).

Zones for the Development of Productive Activities are designated in order to control the uses of land and are subdivided into 'zones of exclusive use' where any activity other than the permitted activity is prohibited and 'zones of principal use' where other activities are permitted but subject to terms and conditions (Law 1650/86, art 24).

2.7 Use and storage of hazardous substances including radioactive material

Article 15 of Law 1650/86 encourages the adoption of limits for storage and handling of hazardous substances and the implementation of a procedure for the use, transportation, storage, production and packaging of hazardous substances. Ministerial Decision 19744/454/88 on the supervision and control of the transfrontier shipment of hazardous waste regulates these shipments by introducing notification, consignment note and handling requirements (thus implementing Directives (EEC) 84/631,[29] 85/469,[30] 86/279[31] and 87/112[32]).

Ministerial Decision 18187/272/1988 (implementing Directives (EEC) 82/501[33] and 87/216[34] amending Directive (EEC) 82/501) on major accidents in the course of industrial activity defines 'industrial activity' as 'any operation carried out in an industrial installation . . . involving or possibly involving one or more dangerous substances . . . capable of presenting a major accident hazard, and including transport or storage carried out within the installation'.

29 On the supervision and control within the EC of the transfrontier shipment of hazardous waste.
30 Adapting to technical progress Council Directive (EEC) 84/631 on the supervision and control within the EC of the transfrontier shipment of hazardous waste.
31 Amending Directive (EEC) 84/631 on the supervision and control within the EU of the transfrontier shipment of hazardous waste.
32 Adapting to technical progress for the second time Council Directive (EEC) 84/631 on the supervision and control within the EC of the transfrontier shipment of hazardous waste.
33 On the major accident hazards of certain industrial activities.
34 Amending Directive (EEC) 82/501 on the major accident hazards of certain industrial activities.

2.7 Chapter 14

A 'major accident' is defined as 'an occurrence such as a major emission, fire or explosion resulting from uncontrolled developments in the course of industrial activity involving one or more dangerous substances, leading to a serious danger to human health and security, immediate or delayed, inside or outside the establishment and to the environment'.

A manufacturer or plant operator is required to notify the competent authorities of the substances it uses or handles, the location of the industrial plant, any possible impact on the environment as a result of industrial activities carried out, possible situations presenting potential risks of a major accident, preventive and security measures adopted and emergency plans. The manufacturer is exclusively responsible for the accuracy of the information supplied.

Manufacturers are also required to notify the competent authorities of certain dangerous substances involved or stored and to prove that they have identified existing major accident hazards, adopted appropriate safety measures and informed, trained and equipped persons working on the site in order to ensure their safety.

In the case of new industrial activities, the operator is required to notify the competent authorities and apply for a licence prior to commencing any industrial activity.

The information referred to in the notification made by the operator of new or existing industrial activities is received by the authority which is competent for granting the relevant licence, the Department of the Ministry of Development.

Copies of the information provided is then dispatched to the concurrently competent ministries who are required within five months to deliver their opinion. Supplementary information may be requested.

The Ministry of Environment, Land Use Planning and Public Works and other competent ministries ensure that an emergency plan is drawn up for action outside the establishment.

Pursuant to art 17 of Law 1650/86, radioactive substances or waste that emits radioactivity may be used provided that specified limits and prescribed measures are respected.

Buildings or departments of buildings where activities involving such substances are designed, built and used in compliance with special requirements may have their operation terminated when such requirements are disregarded. Constant supervision and measuring of emissions is also a prerequisite.

Failure to comply with these requirements entails the imposition of civil and criminal sanctions pursuant to arts 28, 29 and 30 of Law 1650/86.

2.8 Noise emissions

Article 14 of Law 1650/86 authorises the implementation of Ministerial Acts and Decisions for the determination and measurement of noise emissions and vibrations in residential and public utility areas and sound levels in anti-noise areas. These areas are designated with a view to protecting health.

Article 14 is the legislative basis for the adoption of provisions restricting the production and use of any appliance or machine creating excessive noise levels or any appliance or machine intended for the emission of noise. Article 14 promotes the fixing of permissible noise and vibration levels, noise measuring and approval procedures and associated restrictions or prohibitions.

Appliances and machinery may be exempted from these provisions in the case of large or special projects.

Further, the adoption of measures is also encouraged for the prevention or reduction of noise emissions from appliances or machinery that have already been introduced in Greece at the time of implementation of the above restrictions.

Ministerial Decision 69001/1921/1988 prescribes permissible sound power levels for machinery and appliances used on work sites (compressors and so forth) (implementing Directives (EEC) 84/533,[35] 84/535,[36] 84/536,[37] 84/537,[38] 85/406,[39] 85/407,[40] 85/408[41] and 85/409[42]) and Ministerial Decision 11481/523/1997 regulates the limitation of noise emitted by earth-moving machines (implementing Directive (EC) 95/27[43]).

Violation of the provisions regarding noise emissions results in the imposition of civil and criminal sanctions pursuant to arts 28, 29 and 30 of Law 1650/86.

Ministerial Decisions may impose restrictions and protective measures may be adopted in relation to projects and activities that could create noise. These include noise level limits, measuring techniques, measures for reducing vibrations, restrictions on hours of operation, the role of supervisory bodies and minimum distance requirements from residential or public utility areas.

Anti-noise areas may also be designated and criteria for the location of new installations or activities and terms and conditions for the further development of activities in such zones may be prescribed.

It should be noted, however, that all the Presidential Decrees and Ministerial Decisions required for the proper implementation of art 14 have not yet been issued.

2.9 Nuclear energy and radioactive waste

The construction and operation of radioactive installations requires prior authorisation and the granting of a special permit from the Ministry of Development (Legislative Decree 854/1971, art 2).

The permit is subject to the adoption of security measures determined by the Ministry of Development further to an opinion of the Greek Committee of Atomic Energy.

Any person who intentionally endangers the life or health of persons is punished by imprisonment of at least two years and a financial penalty and the court may additionally order the confiscation of the nuclear installation. The negligent committees of this offence is also punishable by imprisonment of up to two years.

The appropriate functions for matters related to nuclear energy have been decentralised to the Greek Committee of Atomic Energy. This committee has responsibility for the protection of the population and the environment, for issuing security manuals and for drawing up regulations for the operation of installations and machinery and for

---

35 On the approximation of the laws of the member states relating to the permissible sound power level of compressors.
36 On the approximation of the laws of the member states relating to the permissible sound power level of welding generators.
37 On the approximation of the laws of the member states relating to the permissible sound power level of power generators.
38 On the approximation of the laws of the member states relating to the permissible sound power level of powered hand-held and concrete-breakers and picks.
39 Adapting to technical progress Council Directive (EEC) 84/533 on the approximation of the laws of the member states relating to the permissible sound power level of compressors.
40 Adapting to technical progress Council Directive (EEC) 84/535 on the approximation of the laws of the member states relating to the permissible sound power level of welding generators.
41 Adapting to technical progress Council Directive (EEC) 84/536 on the approximation of the laws of the member states relating to the permissible sound power level of power generators.
42 Adapting to technical progress Council Directive (EEC) 84/537 on the approximation of the laws of the member states relating to the permissible sound power level of powered hand-held concrete-breakers and picks.
43 Amending Council Directive (EEC) 86/662 on the limitation of noise emitted by hydraulic excavators, rope-operated excavators, dozers, loaders and excavator-loaders.

2.9 *Chapter 14*

the granting, modification or revocation of permits for the production, possession, distribution and use of radioactive substances (Law 1733/87, art 28).

Presidential Decree 22/1997 implementing Euratom Directive 92/3 on the supervision and inspection of the transportation of radioactive waste provides that the owner of radioactive waste in Greece intending to transport it outside the boundaries of the country, is obliged to submit an application for the relevant licence to the Greek Committee of Atomic Energy. The latter forwards the application for approval to the competent authorities of the country of destination and to those of the country of transit of the waste in question. The required licence is valid for a period not exceeding 3 years. In the event that Greece is the country of destination of the radioactive waste, the Greek Committee of Atomic Energy may not impose conditions that are stricter than those in force for the transportation of radioactive waste within the Greek territory.

In relation to the import and export of radioactive waste to or from the EU, should Greece be the country of destination, then the recipient of the waste is required to apply to the Greek Committee of Atomic Energy in order to obtain the necessary licence. In addition, in the event that radioactive waste whose ultimate destination is a non-EU country is imported to Greece from a third country, thus rendering Greece the first member state of the EU in which material is imported, Greece shall be considered the country of origin for the purposes of transportation and the relevant provisions are applicable.

2.10 Environmental impact assessment

The basic legislative provisions on environmental impact assessments are Presidential Decree 1180/1981, which introduced environmental impact assessments for certain industrial activities, Law 1650/86 (arts 3–6) which is more extensive and which implements Council Directive (EEC) 85/337 and provides that environmental assessment is a condition for the granting of a licence for the creation, installation and operation of projects and activities and Ministerial Decision 69269/5387/1990 which regulates the application of the relevant provisions of Law 1650/86.

Law 1650/86 classes public and private projects into three categories in accordance with the effects that they have on the environment.

The first category includes projects that by reason of their nature, size or location are likely to have significant effects on the environment. The approval for projects and activities included in this category is granted by virtue of a joint Decision issued by the Minister of Environment, Land Use Planning and Public Works in association with any other ministries that are concurrently competent. These projects and activities are also subject to an assessment of environmental effects and to prior approval regarding the location of the installation or activity.

The second category includes projects that are not likely to have significant effects on the environment but are subject to criteria and thresholds. Projects and activities mentioned in this category are authorised by the Prefect and are not subject to an assessment with regard to their effects. The applicant is however required to complete a questionnaire and forward documents evidencing compliance with the provisions on environmental protection.

The final category identifies those projects that are only likely to have minor effects on the environment. Activities under the third category are approved by virtue of a decision of the competent mayor or president of the community and likewise the submission of documents assuring compliance with provisions on environmental protection is required.

Ministerial Decision 69269/5387/1990 divides the projects of the first two categories into two further categories (A and B). Category A has been subdivided into two groups (I and II).

Group I of Category A includes activities that have major effects on the environment such as crude oil refineries, thermal and nuclear power stations, installations for the storage or disposal of radioactive waste, cast iron and steel industries, installations for the extraction, processing and transformation of asbestos, chemical installations, construction of roads, railway lines, airfields and harbours and waste disposal installations of toxic and dangerous wastes.

Group II of Category A includes activities that have a reduced but not insignificant impact on the environment such as agriculture, the extraction industry, energy industry, metals processing, chemical industry, food processing, textile, leather, wood, paper and rubber industries.

Category B includes all other projects and activities whose installation and operation require the granting of a licence and that do not come within the above-mentioned groups.

Pursuant to Law 1650/86, the environmental impact assessment must include at least:

(1) a description of the project or activities comprising information on the site, design and size of the project;
(2) identification and assessment of the main effects on the environment;
(3) a description of the measures envisaged to prevent, reduce and remedy adverse effects on the environment;
(4) examination of alternative solutions and an indication of reasons for the choice of the solution preferred;
(5) summary of the assessment.

New projects, the extension or relocation of existing projects or activities identified in the previous categories are all subject to authorisation.

The application for authorisation for a private or public project is made to the competent authority and in effect consists of proposals that will ensure the protection of the environment. The approval of these proposals is a necessary prerequisite, in the context of the administrative procedure, for the granting of a licence to operate.

3 PARTICULAR ENVIRONMENTAL ISSUES RELEVANT TO TRANSACTIONS

The prevention principle is central to Greek environmental policy. The first principle is the adoption of measures to prevent detrimental environmental effects. The polluter pays principle is introduced at a later stage when the environment has already been harmed and focuses on repair and restoration rather than prevention. Polluters are charged with the costs of action to combat the environmental harm they cause.

3.1 Assumption of liability—routes and bases for liabilities

3.1.1 Environmental liability pursuant to Law 1650/1986

Environmental liability is regulated by arts 28–30 of Law 1650/86 and consists of criminal liability, civil liability and administrative sanctions.

3.1 Chapter 14

(a) Criminal liability (art 28)

Penal sanctions of imprisonment from three months to two years and a fine may be imposed on those who are found to have:

(1) polluted or damaged the environment by act or omission contrary to the requirements of Law 1650/86 or as prescribed in Decrees or Decisions implementing the same;
(2) operated without the required licence or approval or exceeded the limits defined in the licence or approval and impaired the environment.

In the event that these criminal offences are negligently committed, imprisonment of up to one year is imposed.

If by reason of the nature or quantity of pollutants or by reason of the extent and significance of the damage to the environment there is a risk of loss of life or personal injury, then imprisonment of at least one year and a fine is imposed. Where personal injury or loss of life has resulted, imprisonment of up to ten years is imposed.

Where the offender, prior to examination by the competent authority, voluntarily mitigates the pollution or environmental harm or by duly notifying the competent authority, effectively contributes to minimise the detrimental consequences, the court may impose a reduced punishment pursuant to art 23 of the Penal Code or even absolve the offender.

The injured party may bring a legal action claiming for the restoration of environmental damage to the extent that this is feasible.

(b) Civil liability (art 29)

Article 29 imposes strict liability but then establishes defences which, if the defendant can satisfy the burden of proof, will allow him to avoid liability. The common defences in this context are force majeure and fraudulent third party intervention.

(c) Administrative sanctions

Irrespective of criminal and civil liability, administrative sanctions may be imposed and consist of:

(i) Fines (art 30)

As regards natural or legal persons that pollute or undermine the environment, a fine of up to 10 million GRD can be imposed by a decision of the Prefect.

In the event of significant pollution or environmental harm and in particular if there is a risk of loss of life or personal injury or widespread ecological destruction, further to deferral of the case by the Prefect, the Minister of Environment, Land Use Planning and Public Works and, in appropriate cases, in conjunction with the concurrently competent minister, may impose a fine of up to 100 million GRD.

Fines of up to 250 million GRD are imposed for marine pollution following the issue of a joint decision of the Ministry of Environment, Land Use Planning and Public Works and Ministry of Commercial Shipping (Law 2508/97, art 30).

Derogations from these fines may be introduced in more specific legislation.

(ii)   Interruption of the operation of the enterprise (art 30)

Where an enterprise pollutes or impairs the environment, the temporary interruption of its operation can be required by the competent Prefect until appropriate measures are taken to avert these detrimental effects.

In the event of non-compliance with the necessary measures or where the adoption of effective measures is not feasible, the permanent closure of the operation of the enterprise may be imposed by a decision of the Prefect.

In exceptional circumstances and more particularly where by virtue of the nature or quantity of pollutants or significance of environmental harm, there is a risk of death or serious bodily harm, of widespread ecological disruption or destruction, the foregoing sanctions are imposed by the Minister of Environment, Land Use Planning and Public Works and in appropriate cases, in conjunction with the concurrently competent Minister. In addition to the prohibition to operate, a fine ranging from 10,000 GRD to 1 million GRD may be imposed for every day of infringement of the prohibition.

(iii)   Compulsory expropriation (art 22, para 2)

Compulsory expropriation of private land in favour of the State may be ordered provided that this is of the utmost necessity for the protection of nature and the landscape and serves the public interest. Compulsory expropriation is subject to the payment of compensation and other expenses involved.

(iv)   Sealing of buildings (art 22, para 5)

Buildings may be sealed when activities other than those prescribed in land use provisions are carried out.

3.1.2   *Codified provisions*

(a)   Civil liability

Environmental liability may also be assumed by application of the non-contractual civil liability provisions of the Civil Code. The remedies are provided for a broad range of cases and are applied on an analogous basis for the protection of the environment.

(i)   Liability pursuant to the provisions on the protection of the rights of the person

Article 57 of the Civil Code prescribes that any person who causes unlawful damage to the interests of another where the injury is to his person may be restrained by the court from committing or continuing such conduct. Fault-based tort liability may also be imposed pursuant to arts 914 et seq of the Civil Code. Article 59 of the Civil Code provides that further to an action brought by individuals to protect their persons, the court, after having assessed the nature of the damage, may decide to impose liability for moral damages consisting of either monetary compensation or of the publication of the infringement or of any other measure deemed appropriate.

Judicial precedents have interpreted art 57 in such a manner as to embrace preventative action prior to the realisation of environmental harm in cases where sufficient evidence indicates that damage will be caused in the future.

3.1 *Chapter 14*

(ii)   Liability assumed under provisions pertaining to the protection of ownership and possession in conjunction with the provisions of neighbour law

On the basis of provisions on the protection of ownership (arts 1000 and 1108 of the Civil Code) and possession (arts 984 and 989 of the Civil Code), liability may be assumed in cases of interference with the enjoyment of the environment connected to rights of ownership and possession.

Article 1003 of the Civil Code provides that the owner of property must tolerate emissions of smoke, soot and vibrations or other similar interference from neighbouring property to the extent that the degree of interference is reasonable having regard to the location of the neighbouring property. In this context, emissions or other activities exceeding the limits prescribed in art 1003 of the Civil Code found an action to restrain the offender from committing or continuing such conduct. Where the enjoyment of property has been interfered with, a nuisance action may be envisaged pursuant to arts 984 and 989 of the Civil Code. Irrespective of whether the use is normal with regard to the location involved, any activities endangering the human health of the owner of neighbouring property give rise to an action to restrain the offender from committing or continuing such conduct (arts 1000 and 1008 of the Civil Code in conjunction with arts 57 and 281 of the Civil Code and interpreted in the light of art 24 of the Constitution).

Enjoyment of the environment may also be protected pursuant to arts 1004 and 1005 of the Civil Code which complement arts 1003 and 1108 of the Civil Code.

Article 1004 of the Civil Code provides that an owner of property may prevent the construction or maintenance of installations on neighbouring property where damage to the owner's property can be envisaged with certainty. However, pursuant to art 1005 of the Civil Code, where the installation is constructed subsequent to the granting of a licence by an authority or further to compliance with special conditions set by law, an application for the removal of the installation can be requested only after the harmful effects have been caused.

(iii)   Fault-based tort liability pursuant to arts 914 et seq of the Civil Code

Liability to compensate requires illegal conduct (intentional or negligent fault), damage and a causal connection so that the damage suffered flows from the fault.

The extension of this rule to environmental cases is limited since it is often difficult to prove the requirements of fault liability and it has therefore been maintained that the burden of proof is reversed in relation to fault and therefore the offender has to prove that damage was not a result of his fault, the reversal of proof making it easier to establish liability.

Civil liability under the Civil Code is contingent on fault and is not objective as under art 29 of Law 1650/86. Therefore, liability under art 29 is primary as contrasted with liability under the Civil Code which is contingent or secondary.

(b)   Criminal liability

The Penal Code punishes, for example, disturbance of the peace by noise (art 417) and the violation of the provisions on cleanliness (art 427 includes the mention of waters), pollution (art 428) and contamination of water sources or foodstuffs (art 279).

3.2 Historical liabilities

It is generally agreed that the original polluter is liable. However practical problems often arise in applying the established polluter pays principle to historical contamination. For instance, in cases of change of ownership of land, although the original polluter is liable for damages and clean-up costs, such person may be unidentifiable.

Therefore for historic pollution, programmes should be established for the carrying out of remedial works by the State with procedures for recovery of the cost.

Several references to the position can be found in Law 1650/86.

Article 6, para 4 prescribes that 'the payment of charges may be imposed on undertakings in order to cover expenses . . . for projects and programmes for the protection of the environment'. These charges are allocated on the basis of the extent of pollution or quantity of waste involved.

Pursuant to art 13, para 2 of Law 1650/86, by Presidential Decree, special dues may be imposed in order to cover 'costs . . . for the protection of the environment' when waste produced from enterprises creates problems of waste management.

Furthermore, art 23, para 2 provides that it is possible by virtue of Presidential Decree to 'impose charges on natural or legal persons that are subject to the special restrictions that apply in 'zones of special environmental reinforcement'.[44]

3.3 Liability of directors and managers

Pursuant to art 28, para 4 of Law 1650/86, where the pollution or environmental harm derives from the activity of a legal entity, the court will impose liability on that legal entity for the payment of the penalty and will also impose liability on natural persons that represent the legal entity. Therefore liability is strict and the legal entity and the natural persons that represent the legal entity have a joint obligation for the payment of the penalty.

Article 28, para 5 provides that presidents of the board of directors, the special managing directors or general managing directors of limited companies, the managers of limited liability companies, the president of the board of directors of partnerships and persons that manage other legal entities of public or private law have a special legal obligation to ensure that the provisions pertinent to the protection of the environment are respected.[45] These persons may be punished as perpetrators for any act or omission of the legal entity irrespective of whether any other person is also criminally liable and irrespective of the civil liability of the legal entity, provided that such persons intentionally or negligently failed to fulfil their special legal obligation to comply with the relevant legislative provisions.

Liability of these persons is therefore fault-based (reference is made to intention and negligence) and independent of the liability of other persons who are only liable for a certain act or omission. In a decision of the Supreme Court of Greece (412/1997) the

---

44   Zones of special environmental reinforcement may be determined by virtue of Presidential Decree issued after a proposal made by the Ministers of National Economy, Finance and Environment, Land Use Planning and Public Works and are areas that present critical environmental problems and exceed air quality values set or limit values prescribed for the protection of the aquatic environment. Special restrictions for the use of land and a programme for the adoption of measures for the protection of the environment beyond the general restrictions in force may also be provided for in the Presidential Decree.

45   Presidents, special managing directors and general managing directors are members of the board of directors, which is authorised to represent and administrate the company's affairs. The general competencies of the board of directors are determined by Law 2190/1920. The general managing director is in effect the chief executive officer of the company.

view that criminal liability is fault-based was upheld ('the accused knew very well the negative impact that the operation of their factory would have on the environment...').

Article 28, para 4 embraces not only the persons managing the legal entity pursuant to authority vested by the articles of incorporation but also those who, even temporarily, are involved in the management of the company.

However, where the management of the legal entity has instructed employees, any act or omission in disregard of the directions and guidelines given cannot be attributed to the legal entity. The employee who disregarded the directions or guidelines can be criminally liable.

The managing directors of the company may be criminally liable when they acquire actual knowledge of the unlawful act or omission of an employee and, despite this, fail to comply with their special legal obligation to prevent what results (art 15 of the Penal Code). In such an event, both the management and the employee have acted in concert and accordingly will be jointly and severally liable.

3.4 Liability of those financing businesses

The liability of those financing businesses ultimately depends on whether they have become involved in the management of the company, even temporarily. Hence where the lender has a directorship he will be jointly and severally liable for environmental harm. Therefore, even where the lender has only briefly exercised management responsibilities, an action may be brought against him for the entire amount of any fine and this is particularly so when the lender is a large financial institution ('deep pocket' liability).

3.5 Transferability of permits and licences

Permit and licensing requirements do not prohibit any particular transaction but corporations making acquisitions will have to obtain or transfer all necessary permits and licences. An application for a modified permit is necessary in the event of extension or relocation of existing activities and future expansion may even be inhibited. Purchasers should also bear in mind issues relating to the validity of licences and compliance with environmental requirements.

A share purchase does not require existing permits to be transferred since they remain with the company. Similarly, in the event of universal succession as a result of a merger, absorption or spin-off, the successor acquires all of the predecessor's obligations and liabilities and therefore permits are not required to be transferred. However, in the case of a transfer of assets, permits will have to be transferred or new permits obtained.

In relation to permit transfer procedures, depending on the activity in question, some permits are transferable as of right (eg where the permit is granted with respect to a particular activity), whilst in other cases new permits must be obtained (eg where a mere personal permit has been granted).

3.6 Mechanisms for compliance cost increases

Compliance costs imposed by competent authorities essentially consist of costs of technology necessary to enable compliance and costs of penalties and fines for failure to comply with prescribed requirements.

However new regulations may alter compliance requirements thus rendering the determination of compliance costs more difficult. For instance Ministerial Decision 58751/2370/1993 on the limitation of pollutants into the air from large combustion plants implements strategies and measures for the gradual adaptation of existing plants to the best available technology therefore tightening compliance requirements that were in force when previous licences to operate were granted.

4 MANAGING ENVIRONMENTAL ISSUES IN TRANSACTIONS

4.1 Current practice for assessment of risk

Environmental risks in business transactions can to some extent be managed by 'due diligence'. Two types of risk must be addressed in any business transaction, compliance risk and liability risk.

The acquirer must initially identify environmental risk, namely any past or present environmental problems. Some activities may involve increased compliance requirements and therefore importance should be attributed to the impact of future developments. An audit serves to address both past and present operations and review future environmental requirements.

An assessment of the site is carried out in the context of the due diligence and involves the investigation of the physical condition of property in order to detect the existence of any contamination or potential contamination. It may also be prudent to investigate surrounding sites.

Physical inspection of the site or facilities is effected by engineering experts and the results of the inspection are subsequently evaluated in terms of liability by the purchaser's legal counsel, evidently a complex task.

The transaction may also require various permits and approvals with which its activities must comply.

Investigations are often time-consuming and therefore, depending on possible environmental problems involved, environmental investigations may consist of ascertaining present and prior operations of the property subject to acquisition and examination of its physical condition or may be more extensive involving soil, water and underground sampling. In the light of the extent of potential liability being assumed the purchaser, after consulting its legal advisers, decides on the degree of thoroughness of the investigation to be carried out.

In Greece the general practice is to limit pre-acquisition auditing to an examination of the physical condition of the property. However, where a site presents potential environmental problems, then a more detailed investigation would be required.

4.2 Warranties and indemnities

In most acquisition transactions, the transferee will require the transferor to give representations and warranties embracing the following matters:

(1) the availability of necessary permits and approvals;
(2) compliance with environmental regulations and restrictions;
(3) restoration and reparation obligations resulting from any infringement;
(4) the existence of hazardous or dangerous and toxic substances or PCBs or whether such substances have been collected, sorted, transported, recycled or deposited above or under the ground;
(5) the existence of under ground storage tanks or pipelines.

4.2 *Chapter 14*

The parties may sign an indemnification agreement but it is not certain that the courts will give full effect to these provisions in respect of past operations since criminal and civil liability is involved and administrative sanctions are imposed on 'natural and legal persons that pollute or undermine the environment'. Although an indemnity may be valid between the parties, initial liability under the legislative provisions in force still remains. For instance, an indemnification agreement to share liability would not necessarily relieve the transferor who polluted or undermined the environment.

4.3 Issues for those lending money to businesses

In order to avoid potential liability, lenders should take appropriate measures and look particularly to the wording of representations, warranties and undertakings so as to ensure compliance with environmental laws and regulations and so as to prevent their operations from being considered as management practices.

The lender should request from the borrower the following covenants, warranties and representations:

(1) that the undertaking in question is in conformity with all relevant environmental laws and regulations and that the borrower is in compliance with all necessary licensing requirements;
(2) that liability proceedings are not pending or are not in the process of being initiated against the borrower with respect to any violations;
(3) that past, present and anticipated future uses of the borrower's facility have been disclosed;
(4) that there are no contaminants, discharges into the aquatic environment, toxic and dangerous substances and hazardous waste in violation of environmental law provisions;
(5) that the borrower will undertake to carry out environmental auditing at regular intervals and the audit shall be disclosed to the lender.

The lender may also provide for events of default, namely:

(1) Failure to comply with environmental legislation and licensing requirements;
(2) Failure to notify the lender of any accidental pollution that is not authorised by the licence obtained;
(3) Failure to carry out environmental auditing in accordance with the intervals prescribed.

The lender should ensure that any covenants, warranties, representations and events of default cannot be interpreted in such a manner so as to infer that he has assumed management practices.

4.4 Insurance

Article 23 of Law 2496/97 regulating insurance contracts prescribes that unless otherwise agreed, insurance for environmental damage includes expenses for the reparation of damage to the natural environment and expenses for cleaning up contaminants from the resulting insurance risk.

Indemnification covers only expenses incurred provided that the damage arose from an unexpected event.

It may also be difficult to obtain unlimited insurance cover and even where this is available, insurance cannot be provided for historic pollution and this is essentially left to State initiative.

4.5 Structuring the management of companies

Liability for environmental damage is focused on the legal entity, directors and managers. Each party is jointly and severally liable and therefore where it is agreed that one party shall not assume environmental liability, such party should ensure that he shall not be regarded as a manager or director and therefore should not become involved in management practices even for a brief term.

However, where liability is apportioned amongst the parties, then the parties should be involved in management practices. They are responsible together and individually for environmental harm caused. The plaintiff can sue and recover from all parties involved or from one party alone.

5 CONCLUSION

An inherent problem for the less developed countries of the EU is the potential conflict between the protection of the environment and assuring the attainment of economical objectives, the latter necessarily entailing rapid development which is rarely compatible with requirements for the protection of the environment. The response to environmental problems in Greece is therefore hindered to some extent by prevailing financial issues.

The basic legislation, Law 1650/86 on the Protection of the Environment, is to some extent void of content since the implementation of its provisions is conditional and dependent upon the issuance of Presidential Decrees, Ministerial Decrees and Decisions. For instance it provides that environmental agencies may be established by the issuance of a Presidential Decree and to date this provision has not been implemented. Legislation with a more imposing content focusing on supervision aspects would be more effective in forestalling environmental harm and would enable the legislation to be more coherent.

Chapter 15

ISRAEL

Aner Berger and Maya Lakstein
Herzog, Fox & Neeman, Tel Aviv

1 INTRODUCTION

Environmental law in Israel is a relatively new subject in the Israeli consciousness and is in constant and continuous development. The Israeli authorities have declared their intention to increase the enforcement of environmental law. Israeli environmental legislation is comprised of special purpose legislation, based upon principles of the laws applying in the USA and in the European Union, as well as on principles of general tort and criminal law.

This chapter discusses significant areas of interest in connection with Israeli transactions. Such a discussion, by its nature, can present only a general overview of Israeli environmental laws, which are complex and subject to change.

1.1 Background information: the State of Israel

Israel is a parliamentary democracy having three central authorities: the legislature, the executive and the judiciary.

1.1.1 *The legislature*

Israel's legislative body is the Knesset, which consists of 120 members who are elected on a party basis once every 4 years.

1.1.2 *The executive*

The executive branch is the government, at the head of which is the Prime Minister, who is elected in direct elections (usually held in conjunction with the election of the Knesset). The Prime Minister appoints the members of the government and the ministers, including the Ministry of the Environment. The government depends upon the continuing support of the Knesset.

1.1.3 *The judiciary*

The judiciary is made up of a court system which is independent of the legislature and the executive.

1.1 Chapter 15

The court system includes the magistrates' courts, which deal with relatively minor civil and criminal claims. At present, most environmental issues are brought before the district courts, in which all the civil and criminal matters which do not fall under the jurisdiction of the magistrates' courts are heard and which also deal with appeals from the magistrates' courts, and the Supreme Court, the High Court of Justice which deals with administrative matters (including petitions against the Ministry of Environment) and which, in addition, serves as a court of appeal with respect to rulings of the lower courts.

Environmental issues are also dealt with by a small number of separate courts, with specific jurisdictions such as the water court and the local affairs court (which deals with matters relating to business licences).

1.2 Israeli environmental law—an overview

The subject of environmental protection in Israel is mainly regulated in primary legislation of the Knesset, accompanied by subordinate legislation. In addition, there are laws of the Mandate in this area, Hebrew versions of which were adopted by Israeli law after the establishment of the State. Certain areas are under the jurisdiction of the local authorities which promulgate byelaws applying to businesses located in their area of jurisdiction.

In addition to the legislative system, Israel is a party to several international treaties on the subject of environmental protection, such as the Vienna Convention for the Protection of the Ozone Layer, the Montreal Protocol on Substances that Deplete the Ozone Layer, the Rio de Janeiro Convention on Biological Diversity and the UN Framework Convention on Climate Change. Israel has bilateral agreements with a number of its neighbouring states as well as with the Palestinian Authority regarding protection of the environment (the Gaza–Jericho Agreement on Protection of the Environment, signed on 4 May 1994 and the Israel–Jordan Agreement on the Environment, signed on 19 July 1994). However, although these treaties require the government of Israel to act in accordance with the standards prescribed therein, they do not have binding legal status of Israeli law unless adopted through Israeli internal legislation.

It should be noted that Israeli law applies in the territory of the State of Israel and does not apply to the West Bank—Judea, Samaria, Gaza Strip or in the territory of the Palestinian Authority, except for the specific application of certain matters to Israelis located there.

1.3 Administrative authorities dealing with environmental issues

1.3.1 Ministry of the Environment

The primary authority is the Ministry of the Environment. It was established in 1988 as the government office responsible for advancing environmental protection in Israel. The Ministry of the Environment supervises legislative processes on environmental matters, is involved in standardisation of the subject and has certain powers to enforce environmental laws (as discussed below). The majority of the powers of enforcement in the area of environmental protection were transferred to the Ministry of the Environment, although a few powers remain in the hands of the Ministry of Health, the Ministry of Agriculture and local authorities.

The ministry operates supervisory units that are responsible for practical enforcement: the patrol unit for environmentalism, a supervisory unit for sea pollution and a unit for the supervision of toxic substances. The ministry is also responsible for operating a statutory system for granting approvals of licences for businesses.

The Ministry for Environmental Affairs works in co-operation with Environmental Units which operate under the auspices of local authorities and with city-based environmental organisations. The role of the Environmental Units includes the provision of advice and support to local authorities in environmental matters, especially with respect to sewage, disposal of poisonous waste, raising public awareness of environmental matters, advice to planning authorities with respect to environmental impact on planning matters and environmental advice in relation to business licensing.

The Ministry for Environmental Affairs is involved in the legislative process in respect of environmental issues and has legal powers to enforce the various environmental laws as will be detailed below.

1.3.2 Intra-Office Committee for Business Licensing

The Interior Ministry, which issues business licences, established an inter-ministry committee together with the Ministry for Environmental Affairs which examines environmental issues when granting a business licence.

1.3.3 Environmental patrolling

This is a body established by the Ministry for Environmental Affairs in order to supervise the enforcement of those laws which the ministry is responsible for. The patrolling body conducts supervision and tracking procedures for the purpose of gathering evidence and preparing investigations. The decision whether to open an investigation against a polluting party is a joint decision between the head of the patrolling body, the district head and the legal branch of the Ministry for Environmental Affairs.

1.3.4 Supervisory Unit for Sea Pollution

This is a unit within the Ministry for Environmental Affairs which supervises the enforcement of laws relating to protection against sea pollution.

1.3.5 Supervision of Poisonous Substances Unit

This unit is connected to the dangerous substances branch of the Ministry for Environmental Affairs and is entrusted with the supervision and enforcement of the proper disposal of dangerous waste, supervision of transport of dangerous waste across borders and supervision of carrying out of conditions attached to permits for the use of poisons.

In addition the following bodies have a significant influence in relation to environmental law issues:

1.3.6 Water Council

This body, which is appointed by the government in accordance with the provisions of the Water Act 1959, is responsible for advising the Agriculture Minister regarding water policy. In addition to the Water Council, the government appoints a Water Commissioner who is responsible for the management of all matters relating to water in Israel and acts as the vice president of the Water Council. As part of his role, the Water Commission is responsible for preserving water sources in Israel and preventing water pollution.

1.3 *Chapter 15*

1.3.7 Interior Ministry

This is a government ministry which acts in co-operation with the Ministry for Environmental Affairs in granting business licences.

1.3.8 National Planning and Building Board

This body is responsible for advising the government with respect to national building and development plans. In addition to the national board, there are district committees which are responsible for the granting of building permits which must take into account environmental matters when deciding to grant a permit.

1.3.9 Local authorities

Local authorities have a role in enforcing environmental laws on a number of levels. A local authority is authorised to attach conditions to the granting of a business licence which relate to the preservation of the environment. They are also authorised to establish by virtue of secondary legislation methods for collecting and disposing of waste and recycling sewage and industrial waste. In addition, local authorities are required to remove public nuisances and are entitled to enter into private places in order to undertake investigations and examinations in this respect, as will be detailed below. Local authorities are supported by the Environmental Units of the Ministry for Environmental Affairs which also act as advisory bodies to local authorities in respect of environmental matters.

1.3.10 Keren Kayemet Le'Israel

Keren Kayemet Le'Israel (Jewish National Fund (KKL)) is a Zionist national body established in 1901, long before the State of Israel, in order to purchase and develop land in Palestine. KKL owns a substantial portion of the land of Israel, especially the forests. KKL's activities are regulated by a convention signed between KKL and the State of Israel in 1968, which authorises the KKL to develop certain parts of the land of Israel and forests. As part of this role, KKL is responsible, inter alia, for the allocation of trees for felling and is involved in the enforcement of the Maintenance of Cleanliness Law 1984.

1.3.11 Restoration of Israeli Rivers Administration

This body was established by the Ministry for the Environment and Keren Kayemet Le'Israel with the participation of the Water Commission, the Interior Ministry, the Government Tourist Company, the Agricultural Ministry, the National Parks Authority, the Reserves Authority, the Nature Preservation Company and Tel Aviv University. It is responsible for the restoration of Israeli rivers and enforcement against river pollution. It advises the Environmental Patrolling Authority of any water pollution, which then opens an investigation against the polluting body.

1.4 Non-governmental organisations

In recent years several non-governmental organisations and action groups have commenced operation in Israel in order to protect the Israeli environment. These bodies play an important role and need to be considered. The activities of such bodies include aiding environmental legal actions, acting as government and local authority 'watchdogs', initiating individual citizen as well as class action suits against polluting bodies and lobbying for environmental issues in the Knesset and the executive.

2 OUTLINE OF ENVIRONMENTAL LAW RELEVANT TO TRANSACTIONS

Set out below is a review of various requirements in the area of environmental protection which have implications for the ongoing operation of a business and are relevant to possible Israeli transactions (especially mergers and acquisitions). This subject is dynamic and developing and therefore forthcoming legislation in these areas is anticipated.

2.1 Disposal of waste

2.1.1 Prohibition on the disposal of solid waste and provisions regulating the disposal of waste

In recent years, there has been a significant increase in the quantity of solid waste produced in all sectors of the economy in Israel. Israeli legislation deals with this subject both in terms of centralised collection of waste to regulated sites, and from the aspect of reducing the waste to be disposed of by encouraging the public to recycle waste.

Legislation prohibits the disposal of waste other than at specifically designated places and authorises local authorities to establish arrangements (by means of byelaws) regarding sites for the disposal or treatment of waste. (See the Law for the Prevention of Environmental Disturbances (Civil Claims), 5752–1992; the Law for the Preservation of Cleanliness, 5744–1984.) Burning of waste substances is also prohibited, unless in accordance with a licence given by a supervisor on behalf of the Ministry of Agriculture. Waste disposal may be by landfill, recycling or incineration. At the point of transfer to a designated place, as stated above, the originator of waste is no longer deemed responsible for its disposal.

The local authority may determine where a different type of waste will be treated at each site (eg building waste, 'domestic' waste, cuttings, tyres, etc). The disposal of waste at a place not properly designated by law constitutes a criminal offence.

There is a distinction between 'domestic' waste and industrial waste. 'Domestic' waste is disposed of by the local authority in the framework of the services which it provides to its inhabitants, without a fee. The proprietors of an industrial site must bear the costs of disposing the industrial waste.

There are hundreds of operational waste disposal sites throughout Israel. The Ministry of the Environment is moving towards reducing the number of waste sites and concentrating the disposal of waste in large sites at which supervision will be especially strict. It is expected that upon completion of the process of reducing the number of waste sites, the costs of disposing of waste will rise significantly.

2.1.2 Recycling waste

The local authorities are authorised under law to establish byelaws for the collection and disposal of waste for recycling in their areas. If they do not exercise this power, the Minister of the Environment may require them to do so (Law for the Preservation of Cleanliness, 5744–1984, s 8(3); Law for the Collection and Removal of Waste for

2.1 Chapter 15

Recycling, 5753–1993). A business located within the area of jurisdiction of a local authority which has established such byelaws, is obliged to install a container designed for removing the waste or a device for the purposes of recycling waste, in accordance with the relevant byelaw. The proprietor is required to maintain the recycling device or the container in an orderly state and to replace it from time to time and the appropriate type of waste must be disposed of in the appropriate device.

Waste which was disposed of in such a device or container is the property of whoever installed the container or the device and the waste for recycling which was collected and removed in accordance with an arrangement with the local authority will be the property of the local authority or its representative.

Where a local authority has established an arrangement for the collection and recycling of waste, waste must be removed solely in accordance with such arrangement (although the waste for recycling may be removed to a plant whose business is the recycling of waste).

2.1.3 Levy on packaging and on beverage containers

Israeli New Law (Beverage Container Deposit Law, 5757–999) imposes a levy (of NIS 0.25, approximately $0.06) on any beverage container (less on some recyclable containers). The law authorises the Minister of Environment to enact regulations to supervise the recycling of empty containers returned to the wholesalers.

A levy of 0.25% of total sales or imports is imposed on manufacturers and importers of beverage containers (Regulations for the Preservation of Cleanliness (Levy for the Preservation of Cleanliness), 5747–1987).

2.2 Hazardous substances

2.2.1 Chemicals and toxins

Hazardous substances are defined as chemicals or toxins listed in the addendum of the Hazardous Substances Law, 5753–1993. Any place selling a defined hazardous substance requires a licence under the Business Licensing Law, 5728–1968. Such licence may contain various conditions for storage and dealing with hazardous substances.

Much of the Hazardous Substances Law relates to toxins. It prohibits a person (subject to some exemptions) from dealing in toxins without a permit to do so from a body authorised by the Minister of the Environment. The toxins permit is limited in time and may be subject to conditions. Non-compliance with the conditions results in the invalidation of the permit.

The recipient of the toxins permit must comply with comprehensive requirements—such as proper, professional and safe storage of the hazardous substances, establishing emergency procedures and the training of professional teams to handle the substances, carrying out a risk assessment where there is an issue regarding public order or the environment as a result of the plant's activity or as a result of use and storage of hazardous substances in large quantities and other special requirements dependent on the activity of the party holding the permit.

If toxins are kept without a permit or contrary to the terms of the permit or in the event that toxins or toxin waste are disposed of on public property, the authorised body may order the owner of the toxins or the owner of the property in which the toxins are kept, or the party who improperly disposed of the toxins to arrange for the proper removal or disposal of the toxins in accordance with the provisions of the order.

Any office holder, including directors, of a corporation is obliged to supervise and do everything possible to prevent offences by the corporation or by its employees. Failure to do so is an offence. An office holder is defined as an active manager of the corporation, a partner (excluding a limited partner) or an officer appointed by the corporation to be responsible for the relevant activity.

Transportation of hazardous substances requires a transportation licence from the Ministry of the Environment (Transportation Services Law, 5737–1977; Aviation Regulations (Transportation of Hazardous Substances), 5743–1983).

2.2.2 Hazardous plants

The owner of a hazardous plant is obliged to take all necessary measures for handling the hazardous substances in his plant, according to the best know-how and accepted technologies and subject to the manufacturer's instructions. The language of the law does not contain any cost limit for such measure, although one may assume that all requirements have to be on reasonable grounds. The owner is required to ensure that only skilled personnel who have received appropriate training handle the hazardous substances and is required to maintain a file detailing the manner of handling malfunctions and incidents which are likely to occur as a result of operating the plant and which may constitute a danger to the public and to the environment (Business Licensing Regulations (Hazardous Plants), 5753–1993). A plant owner is one of the following: the holder of the business licence or the applicant for the licence, as the case may be, a person under whose control, supervision or management the business was operated, or the registered owner or occupant of the property on which the business is located.

2.2.3 Disposal of waste from hazardous substances

Every plant owner is required to dispose of waste from hazardous substances only to toxic waste sites in accordance with the instructions of the Ministry of the Environment. The ministry may approve disposal of the waste to another place for the purpose of recycling, re-use or any other purpose (Business Licensing Regulations (Removal of Waste of Toxic Substances), 5750–1990). The responsibility for complying with these instructions is imposed directly on the plant owner, who is obliged by the regulations to transfer the waste to the sites, and his responsibility continues until receipt of the waste at the designated site. The plant owner is obliged to keep receipts in relation to the disposal of waste to such sites and to present them to the licensing authority or a party on its behalf.

2.2.4 Prohibition on the import and export of hazardous substances

Israel has ratified the Basle Treaty dealing with the prohibition on the transfer of hazardous waste between countries. Regulations have been promulgated in Israel which prohibit the import or export of hazardous waste, unless in accordance with a permit certificate from the Minister of the Environment and under the terms of the permit. (See the Hazardous Substances Regulations (Import and Export of Waste of Hazardous Substances), 5754–1994.)

2.2.5 Pesticides

In the framework of handling hazardous substances, a special arrangement exists for pesticides (Hazardous Substances Regulations (Registration of Preparations for the

Extermination of Pests Harmful to Man), 5754–1994). Any preparation designed for the extermination of pests harmful to man which is either produced in or imported into Israel requires registration.

The requirements for registration are based on international standards. The factors examined are the composition of the preparation, its name, packaging, quality, safety etc The issuing of a certificate of registration is conditional upon compliance with all the decisions of the licensing authority in relation to the preparation, such as the issuing of a toxin permit, changes to the packaging and labelling, an undertaking to perform efficiency tests, etc

An additional special arrangement exists for preparations containing hazardous substances, which are intended for use in agriculture (Protection of Flora Regulations (Arrangement for Import and Sale of Chemical Preparations), 5754–1994). A manufacturer or importer who wishes to sell such a preparation is required to register the preparation at the Department for the Protection and Control of Flora at the Ministry of Agriculture and such application needs to be approved by several government offices. The certificate of registration is valid for 3 years. A preparation containing a hazardous substance, which does not have a valid certificate of registration, may not be sold. The permit is granted to the manufacturer and/or to the importer and any change in its details (including change of manufacturer or composition of the preparation) necessitates a new permit.

2.3 Pollution by radiation

The regulation of radiation pollution under Israeli law is divided into two types, ionizing and non-ionizing radiation.

2.3.1 *Ionizing radiation*

Any dealing with radiation, radiation devices, radioactive devices and products containing radioactive substances requires a permit by the Ministry of the Environment (Pharmacists Regulations (Radioactive Elements and their Products), 5740–1980). In the case of a substance containing radioactive material in a quantity exceeding those specified in the regulations, it is necessary to obtain a special permit from the Committee for Atomic Energy.

The insertion or dispersion of a radioactive substance in the ground, water or air and the mixing of a radioactive substance with other substances are prohibited unless carried out under a permit and in accordance with the terms of the permit.

It is possible to get an exemption when dealing with substances containing minimal quantities of radioactive material.

The authorised body operates a network of radiation supervisors who conduct inspections of installations dealing with radioactive substances and are authorised to issue safety instructions.

All the institutions, which use radioactive substances, may produce radioactive waste. Solid or liquid radioactive waste must not be removed other than to the designated radioactive waste site.

2.3.2 *Non-ionizing radiation*

Any installation which discharges radio radiation is required to comply with standards with regard to the nature and quantity of the radiation discharged during its operation (Planning and Building Regulations (Application for a Permit, its Terms and Fees),

5730–1970; Telecommunications Regulations (Standards and Specifications for Cable Networks), 5747–1987). The standards applying in Israel on this subject are based on the standard of the International Radiation Protection Association (IRPA). The IRPA standard has also been adopted in relation to the public's exposure to radiation by electrical and magnetic fields of network frequencies.

2.4 Water pollution

Israeli legislation prohibits the pollution of sea water and the pollution of Israel's internal water sources and various enactments exist in relation to each of these areas.

2.4.1 Sea water

(a) Prohibition on disposing of waste from vessels and aircraft

Waste must not be discharged into the sea from vessels or from aircraft and waste must not be loaded on to vessels or aircraft for the purpose of discharging it into the sea, other than under the terms of a permit from the Ministry of the Environment.

Israeli legislation precludes the owners or captains of vessels or aircraft from allowing waste to be discharged from their vessels or from allowing it to be loaded for the purpose of discharging it into the sea, unless they believe that this is in accordance with a valid permit. Certain types of substances will not receive a permit for disposal at sea by virtue of being hazardous substances (see the Second Addendum to the Regulations for the Prevention of Sea Pollution (Dumping of Waste), 5744–1984).

(b) Prevention of oil pollution to the sea

Israel is a party to the International Convention on Civil Liability for Oil Pollution Damage signed in 1969 in Brussels which deals with civil liability for damage to the sea by oil pollution. In accordance with the treaty, Israel has incorporated regulations, which prohibit pollution of the sea by oil (Ordinance for the Prevention of Oil Pollution to Sea Water (New Version), 5740–1980; Regulations for the Prevention of Oil Pollution to Sea Water (Implementation of the Treaty), 1987). The penalty of a fine may be imposed for discharge of oil to the sea.

When oil has spilled into the sea (or if in the opinion of the Minister of Transport, it is feared that oil will be spilled from a vessel into the sea) the minister may give written notice to the owner of the vessel requiring him not to move the vessel. The owner of the vessel or the captain who receives such a notice and does not execute it within the time prescribed is liable to a fine.

The above provisions apply to Israeli vessels (even when they are situated outside the coastal waters of Israel), and to foreign vessels located in Israel's coastal waters or which are located outside Israel's coastal waters, but which constitute a threat to Israel's coastal waters.

(c) Prevention of pollution of sea water from land sources

Israel is a party to the Protocol (to the Barcelona Convention) for the Protection of the Mediterranean Sea against Pollution from Land-Based Sources and Activities and it has adopted legislation, which corresponds to the provisions of this Protocol (Law for the Prevention of Pollution to the Sea from Land Sources, 5748–1988).

The provisions of the Law prohibit the dumping or discharge of waste or sewage from a land source for the purpose of disposal by sea, unless in accordance with a permit. Permits are granted by an inter-ministerial committee which deals with each case individually and which only grants a permit for discharge into the sea after it has been convinced that there is no reasonable land-based alternative to deal with the waste or sewage and that the best available techniques have been used in relation to the sewage to prevent pollution. Furthermore the applicant for the permit has to prove that no damage will be caused to the marine environment in the area of the discharge. For this purpose he is required to execute a control and follow-up programme in order to examine the effects of the discharge into the sea and on the environment. In general the institutions (plants and local authorities) which receive a permit for discharging sewage into the sea will be obliged to install a discharge pipe, in order to ensure that the sewage is discharged at least a few hundred metres from the coast line. It should be noted that there are substances whose discharge into the sea is totally restricted and prohibited (see Regulations for the Prevention of Pollution to the Sea from Land Sources, 5750–1990).

2.4.2 Internal water sources

Israeli legislation deals with water administration on a number of levels. The first level regulates the use of the State's water resources and the allocation of water quotas and the second level concentrates on the prevention of water pollution.

(a) Use of the State's water resources

The basic principle under Israeli law (The Water Law 1959) is that all of the State's water resources (springs, streams, rivers, dams and other surface and subterranean water, including drainage water and sewage water) are the public's property, under the State's control, and are reserved for the use of its inhabitants and for the country's development. The Commissioner of Water, appointed by the government to administer the State's water affairs, is responsible for regulating the use of water, including the establishment of water quotas for use in agriculture and industry. In addition, any person wishing to extract water from, or discharge a substance into, a water source requires a licence from the Commissioner of Water who is authorised to attach conditions to such licence.

The quality of Israel's drinking water is subject to regulations, which establish standards for the sanitary quality of the drinking water (Public Health Regulations (The Sanitary Quality of Drinking Water), 5734–1974).

There are special regulations as to manufacturing and marketing of mineral water, in addition to the provisions in connection with the licensing of businesses (Public Health Regulations (Mineral Water and Spring Water), 5746–1986).

(b) Prohibition on the pollution of water

A number of authorities in central as well as in the local government deal with prevention of water pollution. These include the Commissioner of Water, institutes for the purification of sewage, the Ministry of Health, the Ministry of the Environment, local authorities, city associations and specific river authorities.

Israeli legislation requires every individual to refrain from any activity which pollutes water or which is likely to cause the pollution of water, directly or indirectly, irrespective of whether or not the water source was polluted even prior to such action (Water Law, 5719–1959, s 20b; Penal Law, 5737–1977, s 221). Legislation uses the term 'is likely to cause' and therefore, it is not necessary to prove actual pollution of the water source. An action, which might cause the pollution of water in the future, constitutes a criminal offence under Israeli law.

The term 'water pollution' is defined in a broad fashion and includes a change in the attributes of water in the water source from a physical, chemical, organic, bacteriological, radioactive or other aspect, or a change which causes the water to be dangerous to public health, or which is likely to harm fauna or flora or to make the water less suitable for the purpose for which it is used or intended to be used.

Furthermore, Israeli water legislation prohibits the dumping or discharge of waste into a water source or in the proximity thereof and, in addition, waste may not be deposited next to a water source. In other words, even if no pollution was caused, no substance may be put into a water source, or even be placed in its proximity. Naturally, it is prohibited to discharge sewage or agricultural run-off into any water source, unless a special permit is granted. The Israeli Water Commissioner in the past has granted permits to discharge purified treated sewage into the land.

The Commissioner of Water may issue an order requiring the cessation of allocation of water or the cessation of consumption of water by a person who caused pollution. The Commissioner of Water also has emergency powers which enable him, in a situation of serious pollution of water or where there is a threat of such serious pollution, to adopt any measure he sees fit to cease the pollution or the results thereof (including use of force). In addition, the Commissioner of Water may require a polluter to carry out a clean-up operation. If the polluter does not do so, or does not do so to a satisfactory standard, the Commissioner may undertake a clean-up operation himself and the polluter will be liable for the costs incurred.

In addition to the general law prohibiting pollution of water by legislation, specific arrangements can be found which deal with activities particularly likely to pollute water.

(1) *Petrol stations*: Arrangements, based on European and US provisions, oblige operators of petrol stations to install various means at the station to discover, in good time, any leaking of petrol from tanks and from underground pipes. Similarly, there is an obligation to report any leaking of petrol, unsealed containers and the handling/removal of contaminated ground (see Business Licensing Regulations (Sanitary Conditions at Petrol Stations), 5729–1969).
(2) *Washing and cleaning*: There is a prohibition on the manufacture, import, distribution and marketing of products or preparations used for washing or cleaning, unless in accordance with a special permit (Water Regulations (Prohibition on Hard Detergents), 5734–1974).
(3) *Fumigation*: Fumigation is prohibited near a water source, or from the air where the weather conditions may cause the fumigating materials to be swept into a water source (Water Regulations (Prevention of Pollution to Water) (Fumigating in the Proximity of Water Sources), 5751–1991).
(4) *Salt*: Water Regulations prohibit the disposal of salts in water (Water Regulations (Prevention of Pollution of Water) (Reduction of the Use of Salts in the Refreshing Process), 5754–1994). In the process of softening water, salt waste is produced. These Regulations govern the proper disposal of such salt.
(5) *Sewage*: Sewage water of a sewage producer is required to undergo treatment to achieve a water discharge quality determined by instructions issued by the Ministry of Health (Public Health Regulations (Determination of Standards for Sewage Water), 5752–1992).

Sewage is also regulated by legislation concerning municipalities and local authorities. Examples of authorities and powers granted by the law to local authorities in this regard are shown below:

2.4 Chapter 15

(a) A municipality may demand that owners of land or premises build gutters, drains, lavatories, septic tanks, latrines or urinals and that the owner of land or any of the occupants maintain and preserve the installations in a clean state once built (Municipalities Ordinance (New Version), s 249(15)).

(b) A municipality may take action to stop an overflowing tank and claim the costs from the owner of the property (Municipalities Ordinance (New Version), s 255).

(c) An order of the Commissioner of Water imposes upon any person in possession of any asset whose operation or use require the discharge of sewage to submit to the Commissioner of Water a plan detailing the manner of removing such sewage, including all the relevant details with respect to the chemical and physical composition of such sewage for his approval.

(d) According to the Standard Byelaw for Local Authorities, which was adopted by approximately 40 municipalities and local councils, the owner or occupant of an industrial plant cannot discharge industrial sewage into the sewerage system in a manner, quantity and quality which may cause damage to the sewerage system or cause a nuisance or danger to the public (Standard Byelaw for Local Authorities (Discharge of Industrial Sewage into Sewerage Water), 5741–1981).

(e) Due to the administrative division between the powers of the various authorities, it is possible that an industrial plant in Israel may receive different and sometimes conflicting demands regarding the treatment of sewage from different authorities. In many cases the plant has to comply with the most stringent demands. At present there is no mechanism of co-ordination between the different bodies.

2.5 Nuisances

2.5.1 General

The general principles of Israeli tort law prohibit the creation of a nuisance to the individual and protect a person's entitlement to make reasonable use of and to derive reasonable pleasure from his land against disturbance by others (Torts Ordinance (New Version), s 44).

Similarly, Israeli law prohibits the creation of a public nuisance and protects the public's right not to have their life, safety, health, property or comfort endangered by unlawful disturbances (Torts Ordinance (New Version), s 45).

These concepts are derived from the British common law tort of nuisance, as interpreted by Israeli courts and subject to special purpose Israeli legislation described below.

Israeli law imposes an obligation upon municipalities and local authorities to adopt measures to remove a public nuisance, granting these authorities powers to enter public and private places in order to conduct inquiries and inspections for the prevention, discovery and removal of disturbances and hindrances (Regional Councils Order, s 63(c); Municipalities Ordinance (New Version), ss 235–242).

2.5.2 Noise and smell

In addition to the general provisions which prohibit the creation of nuisances, specific provisions exist to prevent a noise or a smell which is so strong or unreasonable that it disturbs or may disturb a person in proximity or a passer-by (Law for the Prevention of Disturbances, 5721–1961; Penal Law, 5737–1977, s 223; Public Health Ordinance 1940, s 53).

The system for preventing noise and smell and the parameters for unreasonable noise and smell are defined in various regulations enacted under the Law for the Prevention of Disturbances. However the Supreme Court has determined that even where the noise and smell are considered 'reasonable' under the standards prescribed by the regulations, there is still a possibility of proving that in the particular circumstances, the noise or the smell is not reasonable and the matter is left to the court's discretion.

Besides the provisions which prescribe general standards for unreasonable noise, there are provisions which regulate specific noise sources, such as building equipment and aircraft (see (Regulations for the Prevention of Disturbances (Unreasonable Noise from Building Equipment), 5739–1979; Aviation Regulations (Noise of Aircraft), 5737–1977).

2.6 Interference with sunlight

Israeli tort law prohibits interference with the enjoyment of a reasonable quantity of sunlight by the owner or occupant of land as a result of obstructing the sunlight or due to the creation of an interference in another manner. The reasonableness of the quantity of sunlight is examined while taking into account the location and nature of the land and subject to the provisions of the law (Torts Ordinance (New Version), s 48). However, there is a requirement that the owner or occupant of the land has consecutively enjoyed a reasonable quantity of sunlight, other than in accordance with an agreement or a contract, for at least 15 years prior to the obstruction of sunlight and/or the prevention of sunlight in any other manner.

2.7 Air pollution

Israeli legislation prohibits the causing of strong or unreasonable pollution of the air, from any source, if it disturbs, or is likely to disturb, a person in proximity or a passer-by (see The Law for the Prevention of Disturbances, 5721–1961; Penal Law, 5737–1977, s 222). (See also para 2.5.2 above).

The Ministry of the Environment has issued technical directives, as administrative guidelines, specifying suitable emission standards which are to be administered in Israel. These directives are taken into account in the framework of the conditions for granting business licences that are issued to plants and businesses causing air pollution. In addition, these directives are taken into account in surveys of the effect on the environment on behalf of planning institutions (see para 2.10 below).

The technical directives are based upon international standards in this area (mainly the regulations regarding emission for industrial plants which were published by the Federal Government of Germany, directives of the Air Quality Administration in Southern California and the Directive of the European Community on the Prevention of Air Pollution by Industrial Plants (Directive (EEC) 84/360 of 18 June 1984)).

In addition to these directives, there are standards prescribed in legislation for the permitted rate of emission of molecular substances into the air (Regulations for the Prevention of Disturbances (Emission of Molecular Substances into the Air), 5732–1972), for the concentration of substances causing pollution in the air (Regulations for the Prevention of Disturbances (Quality of the Air), 5752–1992) and for air pollution by motor vehicles (see Regulations for the Prevention of Disturbances (Pollution of the Air by Motor Vehicles), 5723–1963; Public Health Regulations (Emission of Pollution from Vehicles), 5740–1980; Operation of Vehicles Law

2.7 *Chapter 15*

(Engines and Petrol), 5721–1961; Operation of a Vehicle Motorised by Petrol Order, 5721–1961; Traffic Regulations, 5721–1961).

Israel is a party to international treaties on air pollution (the Montreal Protocol and the Kyoto Protocol to the UN Convention on Climate Change) and has undertaken some actions towards its implementation, such as restricting the import of substances harmful to the ozone layer and supervision of the application of the restrictions on the production of metal bromide. Israel is not defined as a 'developed country' under the Climate Treaty and the practical restrictions of greenhouse gases do not apply to it.

2.8 Business licensing

Almost any business in Israel requires a licence for its operation (Business Licensing Law, 5728–1968). Lack of such a licence is a criminal offence. One of the criteria prescribed by legislation for the definition of a business requiring a licence is protection of the environment and the prevention of disturbance and nuisance.

The Minister of the Environment has issued many regulations that establish conditions designed to protect the environment, with which a business owner must comply in order to obtain a business licence (see eg Business Licensing Regulations (Removal of Waste of Hazardous Substances), 5750–1990).

It should be noted that the need for a business licence is separate from and in addition to, any requirement for all other permits and licences previously referred to. However, there a number of provisions in those laws relating to such other licences which, if not complied with, may result in the cancellation of a business licence. The business licence requirement, therefore, serves as a device for enforcing legislative provisions dealing with the environment (see eg Law for the Prevention of Sea Pollution by Land Sources, 5748–1988, s 11). Operating a business without a proper licence or contrary to its terms is a criminal offence under Israeli law.

2.9 Land pollution

There is no specific legislation dealing with land pollution or the apportionment of liability for acts causing pollution to land. However, there are a number of provisions relating to those matters raised above, such as waste disposal and hazardous substances, which will have direct consequences on land pollution. Beyond specific legislation, however, only general common law principles such as negligence and nuisance may be relied upon.

2.10 Land use planning/zoning

2.10.1 *Planning and building institutions*

The planning and building institutions, established in accordance with the provisions of the Planning and Building Law 1975, are as follows:

(a) National Planning and Building Council

This contains 32 members, approximately a third of which are government members or their representatives, approximately a third are local government representatives and a third are professional or sector representatives.

The National Council advises the government on all matters relating to planning and building policy including legislation. The National Council has a role in approving national planning (which is a plan relating to the whole of the State of Israel) and, inter alia, the purpose and use of particular stretches of land, establishing major road networks, holiday areas, forestry, areas for factories and for public purposes with national importance and others.

(b) District Planning and Building Committees

Each District Planning and Building Committee has 17 members. Eleven members are government representatives. One member is a professional in the field of land use planning and five members are appointed by the local authorities within the boundaries of the district. Israel has five district committees: Jerusalem; the North; Haifa; the Centre; Tel Aviv; and the South. Once in every five years, the District Committee prepares a general plan for the National Council's approval. The purpose of this general district plan is to set the details required for carrying out the national plan within the district. In addition, the district committee is entrusted with supervising the local committees and acts as an appellate body for local committee decisions.

(c) Local planning and building committees

The Interior Minister is authorised to order comprehensive local planning. Where local planning falls within the borders of one local committee, the local authority will act as the local planning committee. Where the planning announced by the Interior Ministry includes more than one local authority, a separate local committee will be established with eight members appointed by the Interior Ministry in accordance with the recommendations of the relevant local councils. The local committee for planning and building is responsible for supervising the development of land within the expanse of local planning in accordance, with a general district plan. A person or body requesting to build a structure within a particular plan and/or to change the assigned purpose of specific land (eg a change in land designated for agriculture to a designation for industry) must request a permit from the local committee. In addition, a change to an existing structure requires a permit from the local committee.

In order to safeguard the environment, a system of reviews on the effect of planning and building proposals on the environment was established in Israel, based on the view that environmental aspects should be integrated into the decision-making process for planning projects (Planning and Building Law (Reviews of Effects on the Environment), 5742–1982). This is now arranged through an environmental impact review.

An 'Environmental Impact Review' is a document, similar to the environmental impact statement contained in the EU directive on environmental impact assessments (Directive (EEC) 85/337), which reviews the connection between the proposed project and the environment in which it is intended to be executed, including assessments of anticipated or projected effects of the project on the environment and a description of the measures required to mitigate negative effects.

2.10.2 Environmental impact study

In accordance with the provisions of the Planning and Building Law 1965, an environmental adviser (who is appointed by the Interior Minister with advice from the

2.10 *Chapter 15*

Agriculture, Health and Industry and Trade Ministers) is entitled to require that an environmental impact study be prepared when a plan is filed with the district committee. The provisions of the Planning and Building (Environmental Impact Study) Regulations 1982 establish types of plans which require the filing of a study and a number of types of plans where the filing of such a study is at the discretion of the environment adviser.

Those plans which require the filing of a study are:

(1) Power stations, airports, sea ports and sites for the disposal of toxic waste.
(2) Airstrips, moorings, national water supply channels, weirs and dams, waste purification factories, quarries and mines and places for the disposal of heavy waste (where the National Council or the district committee believes that their activity will have an impact on the environment).
(3) An industrial plant in an area which is not used, or is not intended for use, for industry which the National Council or the district committee which deals with planning believes may have an environmental impact beyond the local boundaries.

In addition to the plans listed above, the minister's representative on the planning institution (one of the three institutions mentioned at (a)–(c) above) with which the plan was filed may require the person filing the plan, which, in the representative's opinion, may cause substantial impact on the environment, to perform a study and file the same with the planning institution.

Factories, which are to be established in areas in accordance with approved plans for industrial structures, do not require change to the general plan. However, they do require a building permit. A building permit is granted by the local committee for the construction of a new structure or an addition to or demolition of all or part of an existing structure. Where a building is constructed without such a permit, the relevant authority is authorised to issue an order to demolish the property. As the requirement for an environmental impact study falls only on plans and not on building permits, factories situated in areas designated as industrial areas do not always undergo studies.

Currently, however, there is a call in government for the cancellation of the requirement to conduct environmental impact studies.

The decisions of planning authorities do not require the preparation of a study or do not take a study into account, where they may be appealed to the courts. Under Israeli administrative law, public bodies whose aim is to promote the quality of the environment may appeal to the courts regarding the reasonableness of the authorities' decisions from the aspect of protection of the environment. Likewise, in the case of the *Society for the Protection of Nature*, the court ruled that the dangers which the relay networks of radio stations in the Arava (southern Israel) posed to the environment had not been sufficiently examined by the National Council for Planning and Building and therefore the decision of the Council approving the construction plan of the stations was invalid.[1]

2.11 Taxes and levies

In addition to the restrictions imposed by legislation on various activities, Israeli law imposes a limited number of environmental taxes and levies.

---

1 HCJ 3476/90 *The Society for the Protection of Nature v The National Council for Planning and Building Takidan—Elyon*, vol 91(2), at p 53.

2.11.1 Levy for the preservation of cleanliness

As described in para 2.1.3 above.

2.11.2 Fee for preventing oil pollution of the sea

Certain fees and levies are imposed upon ship owners (including the lessee, the operator or the captain of the ship (or their agents)) and owners of terminals for transferring oil to and from ships. This fee is paid to a fund for the prevention of oil pollution of sea water and the fund is available for clean-up of the sea and to control potential pollution (Regulations for the Prevention of Oil Pollution of the Sea (Levy for the Preservation of Cleanliness), 5747–1987).

3 PARTICULAR ENVIRONMENTAL ISSUES RELEVANT TO TRANSACTIONS

Liability for the breach of environmental protection provisions is twofold: criminal and civil.

3.1 Criminal liability

Most environmental legislation contains criminal penalties for non-compliance. Generally, it is accepted that offences are of strict liability. There is no mental basis (mens rea) for the offence, and it is sufficient for the prosecution to prove the execution of the act or omission (actus reus). In offences of this type, the accused is presumed by law to be negligent and he is required to prove that even with the utmost caution and the strictest compliance, he could not have prevented the offence.

Criminal liability may be imposed on corporations when a person, such as an office holder, manager or director of the corporation has committed an offence during the course of fulfilling his role in the corporation. In an offence involving an omission, criminal liability will be placed on the corporation, where an express obligation of performance is imposed on the corporation by legislation and in such case there is no need to attribute the offence to any particular office holder of the corporation (Penal Law, 5737–1977, s 23).

In the majority of legislation in the area of environmental protection, the liability is placed not only on the corporation guilty of causing the pollution, but also on any 'office holder' of the corporation. An 'office holder' is commonly defined as one of the following: any active manager of the corporation, any partner (except for a limited partner) or an officer who is responsible, on behalf of the corporation, for the area in which the offence was committed (see eg Preservation of Cleanliness Law, 5744–1984, s 15; Law for the Collection and Removal of Waste for Recycling, 5753–1993, s 11; Water Law, 5719–1959, s 20(22) etc). The active manager or partner may be held liable even if environmental issues are not within his job description.

For most environmental legislation, the principle of the separate legal identity of the corporation and its managers on the one hand and the limited liability of shareholders on the other hand has been maintained. Therefore, in most enactments, the liability is imposed on the corporation and on the relevant office holders and not on the shareholders. There are two major exceptions to this rule: under a few enactments in which the liability is also placed on the owner of the plant/business (Law for the Collection and Removal of Waste for Recycling, 5753–1993; Business Licensing Regulations

3.1 Chapter 15

(Removal of Waste of Hazardous Substances), 5750–1990; Law for the Prevention of Sea Pollution (Dumping of Waste), 5743–1983; Ordinance for the Prevention of Oil-Pollution of Sea Water [New Version], 5740–1980). Furthermore, the new corporate code has embodied existing case law to the effect that the 'corporate veil' can now be pierced if, for example, the shareholders have become involved in the day-to-day management of the business.

The penalties imposed for committing an offence under environmental laws are imprisonment and/or a fine up to the level set by each law. As of 1998, the maximum rates of fines are between an equivalent to approximately \$10,000 (and for a corporation, a fine equivalent to approximately \$200,000) and an equivalent to approximately \$150,000 (and for a corporation, an equivalent of approximately \$300,000). Maximum prison sentences range between six months and three years.

When the offence is a continuous offence, the court is authorised to impose further imprisonment and/or fines for every day on which the offence continues after notice of the offence was received from the authorised bodies (see Public Health Ordinance 1940; Water Law, 5719–1959, etc).

Where the court decides that the person and/or the corporation convicted of the offence intended, as a result of the offences, to obtain a benefit for himself or any other body, the court may impose an alternative fine to those set above at a value of four times the value of the damage caused or the benefit obtained by virtue of the offence (Penal Law, 5737–1977, s 63(a)).

The sentencing policy of courts in Israel for environmental offences is quite lenient. The courts do not usually impose the maximum penalties and fines mentioned above. In the majority of cases, prison sentences have not been given and the rate of fines in practice is much lower than the maximum amounts prescribed by legislation. Set out below are a number of examples of fines imposed following environment-related indictments:

(1) A company which operates a light airplane service for insecticide spraying was indicted for polluting the air with insecticide waste. The court sentenced the company to a monetary fine of US\$2,000 and obliged it to provide a monetary undertaking of US\$25,000 that it would desist from committing similar offences over the course of 3 years.
(2) A municipality, its mayor and vice-mayor were indicted for operating a waste site in contravention of the Prevention of Damage Law. The municipality was fined US\$13,000 and each of the other defendants were fined US\$300.
(3) A company was convicted of polluting sea water over the course of 2 years. It was fined US\$20,000.
(4) A kibbutz was fined US\$16,500 for disposing of waste into the Alexander River. The court also required a monetary undertaking, in the amount of approximately US\$25,000, that the company would desist from committing similar breaches over the course of three years.
(5) A kibbutz was fined US\$38,000 for disposing of domestic and bovine sewage into a river. In addition, the kibbutz was obliged to give a guarantee, in the amount of US\$38,000, that it would not commit similar offences. The court also fined each of the kibbutz's works co-ordinators US\$1,200.
(6) A municipality, its ex-mayor and its chief sanitation manager were convicted of managing a waste disposal site in a way that failed to prevent air and smell pollution. The chief sanitation manager received 80 hours of community service in which he was obliged to lecture in schools about enviromental issues. The municipality received a fine of US\$17,000 and was obliged to give a guarantee, in the amount of US\$38,000, that it would not commit the same offences over the next 3 years. The ex-mayor received a personal fine of US\$750.

In addition to fines, most of the enactments in environmental law authorise the court to impose on the convicted party, obligations to pay clean-up costs, to remove the disturbance and to restore the situation to its former state. Where more than one person is convicted of an offence, the court may impose liability on all of them or on some of them, jointly and severally, or may divide the amount amongst them as the court sees fit (Water Law, 5719–1959, s 20(24); Preservation of Cleanliness Law, 5744–1984, s 14; Prevention of Sea Pollution (Dumping of Waste), 5743–1983, s 9; Law for the Prevention of Pollution of the Sea from Land Sources, 5748–1988, s 9 etc).

In addition to the penalties imposed under environmental laws, it should be noted that the court may oblige a person and/or corporation convicted of an environmental offence to pay compensation for the suffering caused (at present up to an equivalent of approximately $20,000) to any person who was harmed as a result of the offence (Penal Law, 5737–1977, s 77(a)). Similarly, the court is empowered to oblige the convicted party to give a monetary deposit held against an undertaking to refrain from committing an offence within a period prescribed by the court (3 years maximum). The deposit will be of an amount not exceeding the fine which may be imposed with respect to the offence in relation to which the party in question was convicted (Penal Law, 5737–1977, s 72).

There is also legislation which, importantly, places responsibility on owners of property from which pollution was caused, even if such pollution resulted from the actions of a third party. For example, the Prevention of Sea Pollution (Waste Disposal) Regulations 1984 place responsibility on the owner of a ship or aeroplane from which waste was illegally disposed. In this case, the owner of such ship or aeroplane has a duty of care to ensure third parties are prevented from causing such pollution.

Israeli criminal law implements the concept of *nullum crimen sine actu*. Thus, when a corporation or entrepreneur purchases land or a plant in order to continue operating such plant or to erect on the land a new venture, the purchasing venture is not liable for land pollution which was committed prior to the acquisition transaction.

However, in cases such as these, the purchaser may find itself in a situation in which it is required to make investments in order to change the state of the plant/land in order to obtain a permit to continue its activity. Thus, for example, a purchaser might purchase polluted land that requires him to carry out clean-up work involving high costs, in order to obtain a permit to continue its operations.

3.2 Civil liability

As has been mentioned above, there are specific civil wrongs, such as nuisance, the prohibition against causing unreasonable noise or smell and interference with sunlight, which may form the basis of a civil claim, together with general tort law principles such as negligence, trespass or breach of statutory duty. It should be noted that in the case of dangerous articles, case law has imposed a higher standard of care than would normally be required of a reasonable person.

Where a civil wrong has been committed in respect of an individual, such individual will be entitled to compensation for damage suffered and also, in general, to an order requiring the cessation and removal of the wrong (Torts Ordinance (New Version), ss 71, 74).

In addition to a claim based on a civil wrong of a nuisance to an individual, a person who was harmed or is likely to be harmed by an environmental disturbance, may apply for an order of the court. The court has the authority to grant diverse orders: to prevent an environmental disturbance, to terminate its occurrence and to repair the breach by restoring the situation to its condition prior to the breach. Where the court grants such an order, it must specify the time for executing the repair work and if the party who caused the disturbance does not execute the repair work in due time, the court may determine how the situation will be repaired and impose the costs involved in executing the repair work on the party responsible for the breach (Law for the Prevention of Environmental Disturbances (Civil Claims), 5752–1992, ss 2 and 8).

Before granting an order, the court will consider the degree of damage which was caused or is likely to be caused to the plaintiff or to the public or to the public interest, in comparison with the damage which is likely to be caused to the party causing the disturbance or to the public interest as a result of issuing the order. Israeli case law states that the court may grant, if it sees fit, a *quia timet* order which is an order to prevent an anticipated disturbance.

When the creation of an environmental disturbance is recurrent (eg the party causing the disturbance caused the same disturbance again, or failed to comply with an order to repair) the court may oblige the party causing the disturbance to compensate the plaintiff for the damage incurred by it due to the recurrent environmental disturbance.

3.3 Enforcement

The enforcement of environmental law is undertaken in three ways: administrative enforcement, criminal enforcement and civil enforcement.

3.3.1 *Administrative enforcement*

The regional branches of the Ministry of the Environment usually conduct administrative enforcement. These enforcement measures are based upon conditions in the business licence and the issuing of administrative orders. The Minister of the Environment may issue a personal order to a plant causing pollution instructing it to take steps to prevent the pollution produced by it. The provisions of the personal order include operational and technological steps, which are required of the plant in order to reduce the pollution which has been created in its operation (Law for the Prevention of Disturbances, 5721–1961; Water Law, 5719–1959). Non-compliance may be a criminal offence.

A further important means of enforcement is administrative cessation orders. The business licensing law empowers the Ministry of the Environment to issue administrative cessation orders, for the temporary cessation of the business' operation for the duration of up to 30 days. After the 30-day period has elapsed, it is possible to extend the administrative cessation orders for additional 30-day periods, provided that a criminal indictment is filed. The administrative cessation orders are subject to the powers of the court to cancel or change them (Business Licensing Law, 5728–1968, ss 20–22).

3.3.2 *Criminal enforcement by the governmental authorities*

Criminal enforcement includes the conducting of investigations under caution by supervisors of the relevant agency and the filing of a criminal indictment against the offenders. The criminal enforcement is mainly conducted by the Ministry of the Environment and by the so-called 'green police' units—the Environment Protection Agency, the Unit for the Prevention of Pollution to the Sea and Coasts and the patrol force of the Nature Conservation Authority.

3.3.3 Private/civil enforcement of environmental law

Israeli law enables, to some degree, the serving of criminal indictments by way of a private complaint (Law of Criminal Procedure, s 68). Such a complaint may be filed by any person with respect to an offence which was committed in his private domain or with respect to an offence which caused him damage. A local authority may also initiate criminal charges with respect to offences which were committed within its area of jurisdiction. In addition, there are laws that authorise public and professional bodies which operate for the protection of the environment to file complaints, as mentioned above (Law for the Prevention of Disturbances, 5721–1961, s 11e; Preservation of Cleanliness Law, 5744–1984, s 21a etc).

An injured person may sue an environmental wrongdoer in the courts. Furthermore, various enactments vest the right to institute a civil claim to registered non-profit organisations whose principal aim is protection of the environment, if at least one of its members is entitled to submit a claim in his name. Certain enactments allow the filing of a class action (see Law for the Prevention of Environmental Disturbances (Civil Claims), 5752–1992, ss 6 and 11). Although it is not a daily phenomenon, in recent years there has been an escalation of such civil claims.

3.4 Liability following a change in the shareholdings/ownership of a corporation

Israeli law adopts the principle of Anglo-American law according to which a corporation has an independent and continuous existence as distinct from its shareholders. As a result, both in the case where the shareholdings in a corporation have changed and where the controlling shareholders of the corporation have changed, a corporation faces exposure for offences which were committed prior to the said changes. The corporation will bear liability for the deeds of the past as long as the relevant period of prescription (commonly between 1 and 10 years) is still running.

As has been mentioned, in the majority of cases, the law imposes liability on the corporation and on the office holders and does not impose direct liability on the shareholders. However, there are a number of laws which impose vicarious liability on the owner of a plant/business, although this is not commonly exercised.

3.5 Transfer of permits and licences

As a result of the principle of the separate legal identity of the corporation, the permits and licences which are given to a corporation in the framework of environmental laws are given, in the majority of cases, to the corporation itself and not to its shareholders. Thus, the change in the shareholdings of the corporation does not affect the validity of the permits, which were given to the corporation, unless expressly determined otherwise in the permits themselves. However, if the transaction requires a change in the legal structure of the corporation (a merger, split etc), it must be ensured that all the permits and licences of the corporation in relation to which the change in structure was effected, are assigned (or, as the case may be, reissued) accordingly.

In general, Israeli legislation varies in its dealings with transfers of licences and permits. In certain cases, the legislation is silent, while in others, there are detailed transfer provisions. In general, a permit or licence may be transferred only with the approval of the issuing authority.

3.5 *Chapter 15*

The Hazardous Substances Law 1993, provides for a more detailed procedure whereby the transferee is required to request approval from the ministry of the Environment for the issue of a new licence or permit. Such application must include details of the licencee and the terms of the existing licence or permit. Upon receipt of such application, the ministry usually undertakes an examination to determine whether any change in operations will be implemented by the transferee. If the ministry is satisfied, it will issue a new licence or permit, which may include new terms. It should be noted that the transferor must provide written approval (which may be in the form of a signed agreement with the transferee) for the transfer of the licence or permit.

3.6 Liability of banks and lending institutions

It should be noted that banks and lending institutions do not assume responsibility for any environmental matters concerning their borrowers until they foreclose on a loan and take possession of, or otherwise become involved in, the polluting business or building. This matter may be significant at the point of lending, when a valuation of the business or building is made.

4 MANAGING ENVIRONMENTAL ISSUES IN TRANSACTIONS

Some general recommendations for preventive measures in order to minimise exposure in the area of environmental law are set out below:

4.1 Acquisitions

4.1.1 Environmental due diligence

At present, pre-acquisition environmental due diligence does not play an important role in commercial transactions in Israel. It is not common practice to take soil or water sampling before acquisition or to conduct historic land use searches. Since the concept of environmental liability for lenders does not exist in Israeli law, there is no environmental supervision by Israeli financial institutions,

There are no uniform (or generally accepted) due diligence standards for these matters. As a 'rule of thumb', when undertaking a due diligence of a company, investigation should be made as to:

(1) whether the company possesses the necessary approvals and the permits required in relation to the activity being undertaken as well as compliance with permit provisions and relevant regulations;
(2) the transaction will effect the need for a fresh consent or renewal of any applicable permit; and
(3) whether the company has an insurance policy (see para 4.2 below) and the level of the corporation's exposure in respect of environmental problems.

In addition, it is recommended that an expert in the area of environmental protection and compliance visits the relevant property or plant and undertakes a review (such as examination of the area in which the plant is located, the procedures used at the plant and any environmental management procedures in place).

4.1.2 Representations and indemnification terms

Checking compliance with substantial provisions of the regulations or permits is difficult. Israeli authorities do not issue certificates of compliance on a day-to-day basis. This issue is best addressed by the inclusion of representations by the vendor in the relevant agreement, as well as including indemnification in the event that such representations prove to be untrue. This is a matter of contract drafting and negotiation and is not regulated by specific disclosure laws (such as the CERCLA law in the US). At present there is no common accepted form or format of such representations.

4.1.3 Transaction structuring

In addition consideration must be given to the structure of the deal including whether it is asset or share purchase, bearing in mind the considerations outlined above.

4.2 Insurance and indemnification

Under Israeli law, Israeli corporations and/or office holders cannot be insured against sanctions under the criminal law, as insurance for these penalties would in effect cancel their deterrent ability. It is possible to insure against the costs of administrative, non-criminal measures, for example where required to undertake clean-up works.

Legal costs for criminal proceedings conducted against office holders of a company may sometimes be covered, provided that the corporate documents of the corporation allow this (power to effect insurance of office holders has to be contained in the company's articles of association) and provided that the matter was approved in accordance with the provisions prescribed in the Companies Ordinance or in any other enactment.

Therefore, coverage for legal expenses in criminal proceedings, which are conducted against the corporation or against an office holder of the corporation, may be included in a third party policy. This type of coverage is conditional upon the fact that the cause for filing the criminal indictment is a result of an insured incident under the policy.

For damages claims in torts, standard insurance policies for liability towards a third party normally include an exception with respect to claims dealing with the environment. Nevertheless, in most cases, this exception may be cancelled with respect to claims having their origin in accidental pollution.

In addition, coverage can be bought for environmental damage through a special policy, but this coverage is expensive, difficult to obtain and not commonly used in Israel.

With respect to indemnification of office holders, it is likely that under Israeli law an office holder cannot be indemnified by an Israeli company for a fine that was imposed on him by reason of an offence. Similarly, the common interpretation of Israeli law is that automatic indemnification provisions (even for expenses which are not fines) cannot be pre-determined and the question of whether it is appropriate to indemnify the office holder needs to be considered in each individual case upon its merits.

The office holder may be indemnified for civil liability imposed on him in favour of a third party, including the grant of a judgment, as a result of an act that he performed in his capacity as an office holder in the company.

4.3 Risk management

The following may be of use in managing environmental risks in practice:

4.3 *Chapter 15*

(1) The employment of specialists to manage the risks of pollution for plants dealing with substances and processes that have a high risk factor.
   This course of action is of benefit mainly in the practical and administrative area of managing the risks of pollution. The advantage in engaging specialists of this type is twofold:
   (a) a reduction of the risk of causing pollution, and
   (b) the very fact that specialists are engaged constitutes evidence that the company is operating in a responsible manner to prevent the risks of pollution and, in so doing, weakens any allegations of failure to take measures to control the risks of pollution.
(2) The engaging of employees who will be responsible for the environmental issues at the factory, such as a safety and control officer, who will be in charge of improving protection of the environment, including establishing work procedures and controlling their execution, procedures for handling malfunctions etc., and who are in contact with environmental regulatory bodies such as the Ministry of the Environment and representatives of the local authority.
(3) The adoption of appropriate measures and technologies for complying with the standards required by the Ministry of the Environment.

5   CONCLUSION

Public awareness in Israel of the importance of environmental matters has grown rapidly in recent years. However, it is likely to be a number of years before this awareness is given legal expression.

At the present time a degree of statutory regulation regarding environmental matters exist in Israel. This statutory framework includes rules of civil liability as well as criminal law, in particular in connection with nuisances, and as well as specific regulations regarding matters such as water pollution, dangerous substances, poisons, air pollution and so on.

There is an increasing trend to enforcement of the statutory provisions, both by governmental authorities and also by public non-governmental organisations. Israel has recently witnessed the beginnings of political activity on the part of environmental activists in the form of a 'green' party, and it can be assumed that such activity will enhance awareness and increase the level of enforcement of the statutory environmental regulation.

Nevertheless, particularly, when compared to the USA and Western Europe, environmental law in Israel is at a very early stage.

Both the legislature, as well as governmental bodies, are increasingly becoming exposed to, and aware of Western European standards regarding preservation of the environment. However, progress towards such standards will be a lengthy process, taking a number of years. At the same time, in the business community, there is a growing acknowledgment of the need to maintain ongoing environmental checks.

The concept of 'lender liability' in relation to harm caused by projects which have been financed by those lenders is not provided for in Israeli law. Theoretically, it is possible to arrive at such a result by means of general provisions of Israeli law, but there is currently no precedent in this regard.

Consideration should be given today to environmental issues at the time of implementing a transaction, on the assumption that the awareness of, and sensitivity towards environmental issues, and the enforcement of environmental laws will grow considerably in years to come.

Chapter 16

NORWAY

Geir Steinberg and Børge Krogsrud

Lowzow & Co, Oslo

1 INTRODUCTION

1.1 Norwegian law and jurisdiction

Norway is a unitary state. Law is approved by the Constitutional Assembly (*Stortinget*), according to the constitution.

Statutes are generally of common application for the whole country. However, within certain areas local authorities (*kommune/county kommune*) have been delegated the right to make regulations applicable particularly to the local environment. This includes certain questions concerning the usage of areas under the Planning and Building Act.

There are three judicial authorities within the Norwegian court system. The county court (*Byrett* or *Herredsrett*) as court of first instance, the Court of Appeal (*Lagmannsrett*), and the Supreme Court (*Høyesterett*) as court of the last instance. In special circumstances, a case may be referred directly to the High Court. Norwegian Supreme Court decisions are powerful precedents. In civil cases, judges in Norway are legally trained and appointed by the Ministry of Justice, except in special cases where judges in lower courts may be supplemented by expert judges appointed pursuant to agreement with the involved parties.

The government is composed of a number of ministries with environmental law falling under the auspices of the Ministry of the Environment (*Miljøverndepartementet*). This ministry is responsible for establishing national policy with regard to the environment. However, environmental regulations have also been promulgated by the Ministry of Agriculture (*Landbruksdepartementet*), the Ministry of Health and Social Affairs (*Helse og sosialdepartementet*), the Norwegian Maritime Directorate (*Sjøfartsdirektoratet*) and the Ministry of Local Government and Labour (*Kommunal og arbeidsdepartementet*).

In 1992 an article concerning protection of the environment was included in the constitution. Article § 110 b states that everybody is entitled to a healthy environment, the natural productiveness and diversity of which must be preserved. Natural resources are to be managed for the long term with a universal perspective that preserves the rights of future generations. The article also grants the right to information about environmental issues. It only has an impact on the interpretation of environmental laws, and will on its own not form the basis for any substantive legal claims.

1.2 EEA–EU

Norway is a member of the European Free Trade Association (EFTA) and party to the European Economic Area (EEA) agreement. Pursuant to the EEA agreement a large part of the existing EU regulations are binding in Norway. The environmental regulations applicable in Norway as a result of this are specified through referrals in the EEA agreement. The EEA agreement includes EU directives concerning production control and pollution, and EU directives concerning environmental research for public and private projects and the general public's access to information concerning environmental issues.

New regulations from the EU within the areas covered by the EEA agreement will be part of the EEA law after decisions made by the EEA committee. The regulations must be implemented by legislation in order to be binding in Norway. Before such implementation has been carried out, the regulations are binding as a national regulation, but do not have any internal effect for the citizens of the country.

1.3 Important environmental statutes

1.3.1 Pollution Control Act

The most important statute concerning pollution waste, the Pollution Control Act (*Lov om vern mot forurensning og om avfall*, dated 13 March 1981, no 6), has as its main objectives the restriction of new pollution, reduction of existing pollution, reduction of waste generation and encouragement of better waste treatment. The main focus of the Act is pollution from activities taking place in one location. The Act regulates pollution and waste in the external environment. Most types of pollution are covered, ie the Act includes licence requirements for polluting activities, an obligation to prevent and reduce waste and deals with liability for illegal pollution. A number of regulations have been issued under the Act.

1.3.2 Planning and Building Act,

The Planning and Building Act (*Plan- og bygningsloven*, dated 14 June 1985, no 77) sets out general rules concerning the use of land. It includes regulations concerning area planning and building permits, as well as regulations concerning consequential analysis.

Use of land in accordance with the Building and Planning Act must, among other things, consider environmental issues and ensure that polluting activities are located in a manner minimising their effect on other activities.

1.3.3 Neighbour Act

This Act (*Granneloven*, dated 16 June 1961, no 15) regulates an owner's right to use his own property in relation to neighbours. It prescribes a level of impact which a landowner must accept from activities which are inconvenient or damaging to his own property. Pollution issues in neighbour relationships can thus be regulated by the provisions of the Neighbour Act. It is particularly important with regard to air pollution and noise.

The Neighbour Act also stipulates a warning obligation to neighbours when initiating activity which may be inconvenient or damaging to the neighbouring property, such as digging, building and industrial activity. Activity in breach of the acceptance

Norway **1.4**

level stipulated by the Act may lead to strict liability (without negligence) for economic loss. A neighbour also has a right to have the activity changed or stopped. In certain cases compensation is payable.

1.3.4   Petroleum Act

Searching for and extracting oil and gas on the Norwegian continental shelf requires a licence pursuant to the Petroleum Act (*Petroleumsloven*, dated 29 June 1996, no 72). The Act also includes regulations with a view to avoiding serious pollution from oil and gas exploration and extraction, concerning standby requirements etc Incidents of pollution in connection with oil and gas exploration and extraction are, however, regulated by the Pollution Act. Liability in cases of damage caused by pollution is, however, covered by the Petroleum Act.

1.3.5   Maritime Act

The Maritime Act (*Sjøloven*, dated 24 June 1994, no 39) incorporates regulations concerning liability for damage caused by oil spillage from vessels. The regulations implement, among other things, regulations concerning strict liability, compensation and limitations in international treaties such as the Liability Treaty 1992 and the Fund Treaty 1992. Liability also includes expenses incurred in order to avoid or limit environmental damage. Limitation of liability in accordance with the Act is conditional upon the ship owner not having committed a fault or being negligent.

1.3.6   Other relevant Acts

The Product Control Act regulates pollution from moveable property. It also covers health risks from products and consumer services. It covers the whole lifecycle of a product, from raw material to waste.

The Local Community Health Services Act includes regulations concerning health and the environment. This includes pollution which may affect health. The regulations in the Local Community Health Services Act have particular importance as they give local communities a basis to act in the case of local pollution problems.

The Water Way Act includes regulations concerning the right of ownership with respect to waterfalls. This includes, among other things, the right to increase or decrease the water flow, and to put up fences or build in or over waterfalls. Pollution of waterfalls and requirements concerning pollution licences, are governed by the Pollution Control Act.

1.4   International treaties and associations

Norway is a member of the European Environmental Association and a signatory to most international environmental treaties,[1]

Because of this, the impact of legislation introduced by the EEA agreement has

---

1   The Esbjerg Declaration, OSPAR Convention, Basel Convention on Transboundary Movements of Hazardous Wastes and their Disposal, Agreement for Co-operation in Dealing with Pollution of the North Sea by Oil and other Harmful Substances, Convention concerning Occupational Safety and Health and the Working Environment, Convention Concerning Prevention and Control of Occupational Hazards Caused by Carcinogenic Substances and Agents, Convention for the Prevention of Marine Pollution by Dumping from Ships and Aircraft, 1991 VOC Protocol, ECE Convention on Long-range Transboundary Air Pollution, 1988 NOx Protocol, and the 1994 Sulphur Protocol.

1.4 *Chapter 16*

been limited. The new legislation mainly involves product control, imports, exports and labelling of hazardous substances.

1.5 Environmental agencies

The Ministry for the Environment is the supreme ordinary bureaucratic agency dealing with environmental issues. The ministry adopts and implements regulations, particularly within the field of pollution. Many complaints are also decided upon by the ministry.

Responsibility under the Planning and Building Act is split. Regulations concerning area planning are made by the Ministry for the Environment, whilst those concerning planning permission are made by the Ministry for Local Communities.

The Ministry for the Environment has established the State Pollution Control Board (*Statens Forurensningstilsyn—SFT*) which has a duty to protect the external environment from pollution, reduce existing pollution and promote better treatment of waste. The SFT issues licences, enacts regulations and sets threshold levels for pollution. The SFT has, among other things, the authority to grant permission for discharges from industry, including granting of permission to establish storage areas or facilities for treatment of special waste, production waste and furnaces for waste. SFT monitors industrial discharges and initiates criminal prosecutions where appropriate. The Ministry for the Environment handles appeals against decisions made by SFT.

The regional counties control area planning, but may be overruled by the Ministry for Local Government and Labour.

The authority of the regional governor concerning pollution is executed by the governor's Environmental Department. Among other things, the regional governor has authority to issue licences to establish facilities for treatment of production waste and sewage. The regional governor also handles appeals against decisions made by local governments concerning area planning and building permits. SFT handles appeals against decisions made by the regional governor.

Local government deals initially with area planning and building permits and also has a right to make decisions in certain pollution cases. Among other things, local government has the power to require clean-up of refuse and waste or cover the cost of doing so.

Organisation of environmental issues at local government level varies substantially. The Local Government Act 1992 allows the local government itself to determine its internal organisation.

Environmental crimes are prosecuted by a special governmental branch, the National Authority for Investigation and Prosecution of Economic and Environmental Crime (*Økokrim*). The policy of *Økokrim* is that fines should be linked directly to what an undertaking can save by ignoring environmental legislation. It has steadily increased fines for crimes against the environment.

2 OUTLINE OF ENVIRONMENTAL LAW RELEVANT TO MERGER AND ACQUISITION TRANSACTIONS

2.1 Dealing with pollution – the Pollution Act provisions

2.1.1 Prohibition against pollution

The Pollution Act contains a general prohibition against pollution in s 7. Therefore, anyone carrying out activities which may pollute must have specific legal authority to do so. This may be by virtue of the statutory limitations provided by Ch 8, decisions made pursuant to Ch 2, or special decisions pursuant to Ch 3.

2.1.2 What is pollution?

The definition of 'pollution' effectively describes the issues covered by the Act. The term is broadly defined and includes most forms of effect on the environment. Specifically it covers the emission of solid compounds, fluids or gas and includes noise. Effects from temperature resulting, for example, from the emission of heated cooling water, also fall within the definition.

In order for individual effects on the environment to be characterised as pollution, the pollution must be inconvenient or damaging to the environment. It is sufficient for there to be danger of inconvenience or damage.

Any inconvenience and/or damage must be taken into consideration when evaluating whether pollution has occurred, irrespective of whether it is people, animals or nature which are affected, and whether the damage or the inconvenience occurs in congested areas or in natural habitats. The damage or inconvenience does not need to have any economic effect in order to be considered as pollution under the Pollution Act. The evaluation takes no account of any property or country borders. It is no defence that the pollution only affects the property of the person responsible. However, damage or inconvenience which is of no consequence will be insufficient to satisfy the definition. This may apply, for example, to short-term noise issues or where the effect is otherwise severely limited. On the other hand, damage or inconvenience which on its own cannot be construed as pollution, may be considered as pollution if it results in a noticeable increase in damage or inconvenience or if the environment becomes more vulnerable as a result of the increased damage or inconvenience.

When considering whether pollution results from a particular activity or business, the pollution must be considered as a whole. It is possible for several types of pollution, which individually would be too insubstantial to fall within the Act, to be construed collectively as pollution within the meaning of the Act.

2.1.3 Pollution licence

A licence from the relevant authority must normally be obtained for any activity which may lead to pollution. The licensing authority is the State Pollution Control Board (SFT).

In certain cases a licence will not be necessary, for example for ordinary pollution from farming, fishing, residential property, hotels, shops etc, and pollution which does not lead to any noticeable damage or inconvenience.

However, usually anyone wishing to conduct polluting activities must apply for a licence. The applicant may be obliged to carry out an impact assessment. Whether a licence will be granted depends on a general assessment made by the authority. The Act does not stipulate any minimum requirements. Thus, there is no direct statutory protection of a set quality of the environment. However, great importance is placed on the consequences of any pollution which the activity may lead to, but the Act does not rule out also taking into account economic issues such as employment needs and the viability of the applicant's business, particular for ongoing activities.

The law sets out certain guidelines for licensing. The most practicable technology must be used to counter pollution. Further, pollution must be actively combated at source, preferably by use of environmentally friendly production methods, as opposed to cleaning up emissions. When restrictions on emissions are set, issues of importance

2.1 *Chapter 16*

are the vulnerability of the local environment and how much natural attenuation of any emissions may occur.

The decision of the SFT in relation to a licence applicable may be appealed to the Ministry for the Environment.

2.1.4 Licence terms

The terms of the licence may, among other things, impose conditions on the production process, protection and clean-up measures, recycling and internal control. Conditions may be made in respect of the nature of the emissions, quantity, concentration, time and place. The licence may also only be given for a limited period.

The licence may contain operational requirements, including provision of guarantees and insurance for possible liability under the Pollution Act. These are not standard terms, but are more common, for example, for activities involving special waste or import or export of waste.

2.1.5 Change or reversal of a licence

The SFT may in certain cases change or reverse an existing emission licence. This applies in respect of any licence obtained under the Pollution Act.

The right to change or reverse means that the terms of the licence may be replaced by more or less stringent terms, that terms may be removed or added and that the licence may be withdrawn. Other than in specified circumstances, a change or reversal may take place only after 10 years from the issue of the licence. The decision to change or reverse is at the discretion of the administration, but in the exercise of its discretion, the administration must consider the costs of the change or reversal for the polluter and the advantages and inconveniences a change or reversal may lead to.

For a reversal or change to be made before the expiry of the 10-year period, one of the alternative requirements set out in the Act with respect to reversals must be fulfilled. These requirements include cases where the damage or the inconvenience from the pollution are substantially larger or different than anticipated. A comparison must be made with the assumptions made at the time of the grant of the licence. It does not matter whether the increased or altered damage or inconvenience results from incorrect assumptions at the time of the granting of the licence, or whether the circumstances have later changed. The incorrect assumptions may be connected to new knowledge acquired at a later time concerning the consequences of substances. A change of circumstances may be based on changes in the receiving environment or a change in the emissions to that environment.

A change or reversal may also be made within 10 years where the damage or inconvenience may be reduced without undue cost for the polluter. This is particularly important where the pollution is as anticipated, but it is recognised that there is a need for improvement in the environment. The regulations cover circumstances where it is possible to reduce the pollution without major expense to the polluter, and where small inconveniences to the polluter may lead to substantial benefits for the environment.

If new technology makes it possible to decrease the pollution substantially, the licence may be altered to require the polluter to use this technology. Businesses must follow technological development not only with respect to new and better production equipment. They must also adapt to new possibilities which ensure their business is environmentally friendly. However, not all technological developments can form the basis for changes to the licence. The Act requires that the technological development must have substantial benefit.

For a change or reversal to be made prior to the ending of the 10-year period, a general evaluation similar to that mentioned above must be made. In this respect, due consideration must be had to the costs a change or reversal may inflict upon the polluter, and the corresponding benefits.

The licence may also be changed or reversed to the detriment of the polluter in accordance with generally accepted principles of administrative law, such as where the polluter breaks the terms of the licence and this constitutes a substantial breach of confidence.

The right to change or reverse is often exercised, particularly in order to impose stricter terms.

2.1.6 Lapse and loss of pollution licence

Licences pursuant to the Pollution Act may also lapse without changes or reversals being made by the authority. This will be the case if a licence has not been used and a long time has passed since it was issued. A new application will be necessary even though the activity is that for which the licence was originally granted.

In the case of a criminally sanctioned breach of licence terms or regulations, the right to conduct the polluting activity may be lost pursuant to the regulations in the Criminal Offence Act or non-statutory legal principles. If the polluter, by severe or continued breaches of the terms of a licence, has shown itself not to be competent to conduct the polluting activity, the licence may also be withdrawn.

2.2 Overview of regulations for certain types of polluting activity

2.2.1 Contaminated land

Pollution of the ground by spillage of any substances is generally prohibited pursuant to the Pollution Act, see para 2.1.2 above. Emission may only take place pursuant to permission from the pollution authorities. Concerning waste, see para 2.2.4 below.

2.2.2 Pollution of water resources

Pollution of water resources, ie sea, lakes and waterfalls, is prohibited under the general prohibition against pollution in the Pollution Act. The prohibition covers spillage not only of substances in water, but also covers changes of temperature in water, for example following a spillage of cooling water from industry. Emission may take place pursuant to licences from the relevant pollution authority.

Special Acts such as the Maritime Act and the Petroleum Act also regulate pollution of water.

2.2.3 Emission to the atmosphere

Emission of polluting substances to the atmosphere is prohibited pursuant to the Pollution Act. Such emission requires a licence from the relevant pollution authority.

CO_2 taxes have been in force since 1994 and cover approximately 60% of all CO_2 emissions. The tax rate varies considerably depending on the area of use. Some sectors are exempted from CO_2 taxes for reasons of competition.

2.2 Chapter 16

2.2.4 Waste management

The Pollution Act contains a general prohibition against littering and there are regulations requiring any breach of the prohibition to be remedied by means of clean-up. The law defines waste as discarded moveable property or substances. The definition includes solid waste and waste in the form of particles or fluids, such as paint residues or spilled oil. To the extent that waste disposal may lead to pollution, the regulations of the Act concerning pollution will be applicable in addition to the regulations concerning waste.

2.2.5 Land use planning/Zoning

Planning consent and building permits involve issues of environmental control. It is necessary to take into account the impact that any new building will have on the local waste and pollution problems.

2.2.6 Use and storage of hazardous substances, including radioactive material

There are special regulations concerning hazardous waste in addition to the regulation in the Pollution Act.

The regulations contain obligations to deliver, collect, receive and handle/use certain groups of special waste.

The law on radioactive activities imposes strict liability for any radioactive radiation from atomic accidents.

2.2.7 Transport of hazardous substances

The Pollution Act contains regulations concerning transport of waste. The pollution authorities give licences for such transport, including setting terms, see para 2.1.3 above.

Regulations in the Maritime Act, the Seaworthiness Act and the Road Carriage Act are also of importance for transport of hazardous substances.

Regulation (EC) 259/93 concerning transborder transport has been implemented in Norway. The Norwegian regulations include procedures for the approval of the import and export of waste.

2.2.8 Noise and nuisance

The prohibition against pollution in the Pollution Act also covers noise and vibration to the extent these are or may be damaging or inconvenient to the environment. A regulation of 30 May 1997 no 490 has been made under the Pollution Act concerning environmental quality standards for local air pollution and noise. Activities leading to noise and/or vibration which are considered as pollution pursuant to the Act must have a licence.

Binding environmental qualities standards of the EU are also applicable in Norway.

The Neighbour Act is also important in the control of noise and nuisance and is described at para 1.3.3 above.

2.3 Sanctions

Environmental law in Norway has no common sanctions for breaches. Under most legislation, breaches may be penalised by fees or charges. Limits may be imposed whereby a breach of the limit leads to an obligation to pay a certain amount, for example, for each day in excess of the limit.

Authorities may, in certain cases, carry out the individual polluter's obligations at the polluter's expense (Pollution Act, ss 74–76) and may issue fines.

Most of the environmental Acts impose a requirement for negligence or wilful misconduct as a prerequisite to the imposition of penalties. Regulations the Pollution Act stipulate that wilful or negligent pollution may lead to fines and/or imprisonment of up to 3 months. Any participation in creating pollution is also subject to penalties. A transgression of certain orders or obligations, including illegal handling of waste, is penalised pursuant to similar regulations. If a penalised action is carried out by anyone acting on behalf of a company, the company itself may be fined or the right to carry out the activity prohibited.

A breach of the terms imposed on emission licence under the Pollution Act may form the basis for the reversal or withdrawal of that licence . However, it is not usual for an emission licence to be withdrawn in its entirety as a result of a breach of its terms, although a change of its terms is normal.

3 PARTICULAR ENVIRONMENTAL ISSUES RELEVANT TO TRANSACTIONS

3.1 Assumption of liability

Liability in relation to pollution is largely dealt with under the regulations of the Pollution Act. A number of special statutes also have regulations concerning pollution liability and these take precedence within their fields. The Pollution Act does not directly interact with these statutes, but can in certain circumstances supplement them if similar regulations are not found.

Two types of liability exist under the Pollution Act: liability to limit and clean-up pollution and a strictly economic liability in respect of pollution damage.

3.1.1 Obligation to act

When there is a danger of illegal pollution, the polluter has an obligation to make efforts to limit any pollution. If illegal pollution occurs, the polluter has an obligation to make the necessary arrangements in order to stop the spillage and prevent it from spreading. The cost of such measures is, as a general rule, borne by the party responsible for the pollution.

This obligation to implement remedial measures is independent of any order by the authorities for clean-up. Factors to consider in determining whether there is an obligation to undertake remedial measures include the degree of risk of the pollution, as well as the extent of possible damage or inconvenience which may result. The risk of damage and inconvenience is weighed against the remedial measures which the party responsible can be obliged to undertake.

The amount of remediation depends on a variety of factors such as the extent of the environmental damage and the result of remedying that damage. The greater the damage or inconvenience that may occur, or the higher the likelihood of it occurring, the more comprehensive the measures which may need to be undertaken.

Where pollution has already taken place, the party responsible not only has an obligation to stop the spillage, but also to clean-up and undertake mitigating measures. This means that the pollution must be removed, and the situation remedied to as near as possible to its state prior to pollution.

3.1 *Chapter 16*

The environmental authorities may order the party responsible for pollution to take measures to combat the pollution. Although the authorities may stipulate the extent of measures necessary in an order for clean-up, their powers are limited. The order may specify what should be done and how it should be carried out. However the order can only include measures which are reasonable, based on the actual circumstances. If such an order is not complied with, the authorities may themselves carry out the measures and claim any expenses from the responsible party. Private individuals also have a right to carry out remedial measures and claim their expenses from the responsible party. The environmental authorities may ensure that such measures are carried out with the assistance of the courts. Non-fulfilment of an order may lead to criminal prosecution.

For lawful pollution, there is generally no obligation to undertake measures. The polluter is, however, not totally free from the obligation to consider the consequences of a lawful emission on the environment. If the conditions are satisfied for a reversal of an existing emission licence pursuant to the Pollution Act, the obligation to undertake measures to limit or contain any pollution generally applies.

However, it is doubtful that an owner of real estate or polluter can be ordered to undertake clean-up measures when the pollution is lawful.

3.1.2 *Liability*

The Pollution Act regulates liability in connection with pollution damage, which is defined as damage, inconvenience or loss resulting from pollution. Section 6 of the Pollution Act is the primary provision concerned with liability for pollution damage. This regulation is based on a broader definition of pollution than otherwise found in the Pollution Act. A number of matters which are not considered as pollution may, where they fall within the definition of the regulation, lead to an obligation to pay damages. Damage, loss or inconvenience caused to the environment resulting from light or radiation are considered pollution, irrespective of whether any administrative regulation specifically provides for this. Damage, loss or inconvenience resulting from waste falling within the regulation is also included as is pollution from individual means of transport.

Lawful pollution, ie in accordance with statutes, regulations or emission licences, will normally not lead to any liability. However, if the pollution is unreasonable or unnecessary (see Neighbour Act, s 2), it may lead to liability notwithstanding that it is lawful. Only losses resulting from exceeding the threshold provided by s 2 of the Act shall be compensated for.

The present owner is liable even for historic pollution, and the terms of his acquisition contract and general principles of contract law will determine whether he can claim indemnification for historic pollution, see para 3.2.8 below.

3.1.3 *Basis for liability*

The Pollution Act imposes strict liability for any damage resulting from unlawful pollution (s 55). This means that there is extensive employer liability. A business is liable for any pollution by employees, even if no responsible individual can be identified, and irrespective of whether the pollution is as a result of negligence from several employees.

There is an exemption from the rule of strict liability for pollution damage in respect of an 'indirect tortfeasor'. Under the Pollution Act, this means anyone delivering goods or services which as a result of faults etc are held to be a factor in causing pollution. Indirect tortfeasors are only liable if the damage caused results from wilful misconduct or negligence, unless they have a more comprehensive responsibility based on regulations found outside of the Act.

Despite the provisions of s 55, liability can be based on other grounds, even if these will normally not be of importance. For example, liability based on negligence under the non-statutory rules for strict liability, employer liability pursuant to the Tort Act, s 2–1 or the regulations of the Neighbour Act, may be applicable.

3.1.4 Burden of proof

If a polluting emission by its nature or extent (alone or together with other causes) inflicts damage, an injured party does not have to prove that the polluter is liable. The polluter bears the burden of proof.

3.1.5 The extent of the liability

The liability of the polluter extends to the economic loss and expenses related to restitution. With respect to restitution, compensation is not given for damage from lawful pollution not exceeding set tolerance levels or thresholds.

3.1.6 Liability under other regulations

Special rules concerning environmental liability are found in a number of other statutes.
Liability will normally occur irrespective of fault. Liability for pollution may also be based on normal non-statutory tort law. Typically this may be the case for items which are not considered as waste within the meaning of the Pollution Act, and which do not fall with any special regulations in other statutes.

3.2 Categories of liable persons

3.2.1 Liable persons under the Pollution Act

The regulations concerning liability under the Pollution Act are based on the principle that the polluter pays.
The regulations differ in terms of preventive measures and repairs on the one hand, and compensation on the other. It is therefore necessary to consider these categories separately.

3.2.2 Preventive measures and repairs

The obligation to undertake preventive measures against pollution is normally placed on the 'responsible person'. The responsible person is the person from whom the pollution originates. Normally this will be an owner. However, where a lessee is involved, the lessee will normally be liable. Other people with rights may, depending on the individual circumstances, be considered as liable under the Act. Several persons may be held liable if they each have a connection to the pollution incident occurring or having occurred.
The main issue is to determine the most appropriate party to take the necessary preventive measures against pollution. This will be based on an evaluation of several issues, including the party's connection to the activity and whether there is an economic interest in the activity leading to pollution.

3.2.3 Compensation liability

The Pollution Act is based on the principle of strict liability for pollution. The liability is linked to actual use of property or operation or of an activity.

3.2 *Chapter 16*

The relevant user is determined following a specific assessment. The owner is responsible provided he is also operating, using or in possession of the property etc If the owner is not in such possession, liability rests entirely on the person who is operating, using or in possession of the property etc Typically it will be the case that where the property has been leased, the lessee exclusively uses it. In such a situation the owner will not have control over the circumstances which may lead to pollution damage. The owner accordingly cannot be held liable, even where the user is insolvent and thus not sueable. Joint and several liability for the owner and the user occurs under s 55 however, where the pollution damage is due to matters for which the owner is also liable pursuant to other provisions concerning compensation.

Even indirect tortfeasors may be held liable under the regulations of the Pollution Act. This will typically apply to anyone supplying goods or services which as a result of fault or similar circumstances is a (contributing) cause for the pollution. Examples are suppliers of cleaning equipment or technical consultants.

3.2.4   *Several polluters—joint and several liability*

Sometimes the source of pollution may be difficult to ascertain. The damage will often be the result of several contributing sources. Where there are several tortfeasors, there may be joint and several liability for the pollution damage. Such liability may apply even if none of the tortfeasor could have inflicted the damage on their own.

In the case of several polluters, the Act does not specify how the obligation to undertake remedial measures or to provide compensation, shall be split between them. Therefore each individual tortfeasor must individually comply with the obligation to undertake remedial measures and provide compensation even if his activity alone would not have lead to this result.

3.2.5   *Liability for parent company or shareholder*

If the pollution is the responsibility of a company or another legal person forming part of a group of companies with a complex ownership structure, there may be a question as to whether the parent company is liable. This issue may be relevant in relation to a physical person owning all or the majority of the shares in the polluting company. The question may also arise in relation to the obligation to undertake measures or in respect of orders from authorities or liability. This issue is generally irrelevant in the case of limited liability companies. However, for unlimited companies it follows from the liability structure that the participants will have a direct liability.

An initial consideration is whether parent companies may be directly liable pursuant to the regulations of the Pollution Act.

The parent company is under an obligation to undertake measures or to receive orders from authorities if the parent company can be considered to be 'responsible for the pollution'. A complete evaluation must be made, where importance is placed on which company has the governing role. If the parent company has incorporated the polluting company as a pro-forma arrangement, but is still the governing company, the parent company will be considered liable. As a result of this, the parent company may have an obligation to undertake measures pursuant to s 7 of the Pollution Act.

A parent company may be liable pursuant to s 55 of the Pollution Act as the owner of the polluting activity, property etc Liability may also arise for a parent company as user where the parent company formally owns the polluting activity, but where it is mostly an 'empty shell' and where the activity is for all intents and purposes governed by the parent company. Also in other circumstances where the polluting company itself does not have control over the decisions made with respect to pollution, the parent company may be liable.

The application of the common law principle of 'piercing the corporate veil' may also result in liability for a parent company/shareholder. Liability on this basis will probably not include an obligation to undertake measures or be subject to orders for clean-up. However, the regulations in respect of compensation pursuant to s 76 of the Pollution Act will probably apply.

Under Norwegian law, the parent company will normally not be directly liable to the creditors of a subsidiary. The parent company is generally only liable through its capital contribution to the subsidiary. The same applies to shareholders who are physical persons. If the subsidiary itself does not have the economic means to cover the cost resulting from the obligation to undertake measures, orders, licence terms or liability, the parent company or the shareholder will as a general rule not be liable for more than its contributed part of the share capital. There are exceptions to this rule, although piercing the corporate veil under Norwegian law is relatively unusual. Situations which may lead to a possible piercing of the corporate veil include where it is deemed improper towards the creditors to uphold the subsidiary's limits of liability or where there has been little differentiation between the activities of the companies so that the formal incorporation structure does not deserve to be upheld. These two arguments must be considered together by way of an overall evaluation.

However, the fact that the parent company has a dominant position and/or that there is little differentiation between the companies is not a sufficient basis on its own for piercing the corporate veil, neither is the fact that the subsidiary company is under financed. There may be circumstances where the creditors' position is weakened in an improper way or other circumstances which lead to the conclusion that the parent company should not be exempt from liability. A subsidiary may be incorporated with an improper motive, ie that the subsidiary is incorporated with the intention of avoiding the risk for pollution liability, or where the parent company has a large degree of control over the subsidiary and hides behind the subsidiary in respect of its operation in breach of laws and regulations such as the Pollution Act.

The issue of whether the claim of a creditor is based upon contract or not may also be of importance. If a creditor has suffered accidental damage as a result of pollution, this is more likely to lead to liability for the parent company or a shareholder, than where the creditor has a financial claim against the subsidiary company based on contract.

3.2.6 *Liability for managers and directors*

Managers and directors can be liable. Where the action or inaction of the manager and director has caused the pollution, both the enterprise and the manager and director can be punished for a criminal offence. Any person may be subject to liability where they are in a position to influence risk of pollution or take necessary measures for avoiding pollution.

3.2.7 *Liability for those financing businesses*

The general rule under Norwegian law is that a lender will not be held liable for pollution damage. However, liability can occur if the lender has actual governance over the activity. This may lead to liability, both with respect to the obligation to undertake measures and as regards orders for compliance, as well as liability for damages. In relation to the obligation to undertake measures or being the recipient of orders, a lender may be held liable if, in connection with a default of the loan, he has actively participated in the administration of the activity in a manner whereby he has actual control over the administration of the activity.

However, it is clear that a lender will not be held liable as owner pursuant to the regulations of the Act, unless he has actually taken over the proprietary rights relating to the polluting activity. If, after evaluation, the lender is deemed as the party 'actually conducting, using or owning the property etc', he may be held liable as "executor" for the pollution damage as a result of circumstances occurring whilst he effectively had executive control. This may occur, for example, where the owner has been stripped of his proprietorship for the benefit of the lender, as a result of a default on the loan.

3.2.8 Liability upon transfer—division of liability between seller and buyer

Statutory protection exists for the buyer of shares and land.

If past pollution is known to the parties, it is possible to regulate in an agreement their liability with respect to costs for any orders or liability for damage. The agreement will only have relevance between the parties. In accordance with general principles, it will normally not have any relevance when considering who is subject to liability pursuant to the regulations of the Pollution Act, see para 3.2.9 below.

If it is unknown to the buyer that, for example, the property is polluted and there is the potential for orders concerning clean-up or liability for damage, this may provide a reason for default under the acquisition contract. However, strict liability under the Pollution Act for the owner of polluting real estate, property, construction or activity, will mean that the owner is liable also for pollution resulting from actions of previous owners, such as waste buried by previous owners. This applies even if the present owner has acquired the property or business in good faith. A new owner who himself has not contributed to the pollution in any way will, as a main rule, still be obliged to take preventive measures and clean-up pollution. In such circumstances, there is also an obligation to pay for any necessary measures.

Additionally, the liability of the previous owners with respect to the clean-up of illegal pollution will initially continue after the activity or the property has been transferred to others. Similarly, the liability for illegal pollution damage occurring as a result of activities conducted before the transfer of the property or activity, and which first manifests itself after the transfer, will rest with the perpetrator. As a general rule, a previous owner will be liable for activities after the transfer, on the basis that he is responsible.

The extent to which the new owner can obtain indemnification from the previous owners must be addressed in the transfer agreement, see para 4.2 below.

3.2.9 Private agreements concerning liability—relevance for the division of public law obligations

Where there are several possible responsible parties in respect of preventive or repairing measures or liability, these parties may agree among themselves who shall carry the costs. Such an agreement will, however, not be decisive with respect to the liability towards third parties. Even if an agreement exists, the pollution authority may still make an order directed towards the person who, pursuant to the Act, is considered as responsible. This is based on the principle that the regulations of the Act concerning liable persons cannot be set aside by way of an agreement where this may have consequences for an injured party. An agreement between the parties will, however, indirectly have importance as to whom shall be held liable. An agreed split of liability internally will be one of the issues considered in the legal evaluation of who shall be held responsible pursuant to the Act.

3.2.10 Liability for pollution pursuant to other statutes

The Neighbour Act imposes strict liability on persons 'responsible' for breach of the Act. The liability presupposes that the tortfeasor is linked to real property. The liability is primarily an 'owner liability'. The owner of a business will be held liable for damage and inconvenience resulting from the activity. The owner is also liable for damage caused by an employee, and this liability is not conditional upon any fault or negligence on the part of the employee. The regulation thus expands the normal employer liability pursuant to the Tort Act, s 2–1.

Liability pursuant to the Neighbour Act may also be imposed on an individual user, such as a tenant. The owner may, depending on the circumstances, be held jointly and severally liable.

The Petroleum Act imposes liability on the 'possessor of rights'. The possessor of rights is a person or company which has an extracting licence. If there are several possessors of rights, they are generally jointly and severally liable. However, a claim for damages shall, in the first instance, be made against the company which is the operator.

3.3 Liability for past practices and procedures—introduction of new regulations

The extent to which new and more stringent regulations are applicable to pollution or polluting activities originating before the regulations came into force are uncertain. A distinction must be made between claims arising from an existing activity and pollution already existing in the form of deposits etc. It is undisputed that stricter requirements may be imposed on an existing activity, such as on the reversal or change of an emission licence.

Where a new emission licence is granted to a company, terms may be set concerning past practices. A further issue is whether ownership of the property is in itself sufficient to be the subject of an order to clean-up pollution or waste deposits which were not unlawful at the time they took place or were established on the property. Generally, under the Pollution Act, the property owner is responsible for pollution and waste on the property. However, in respect of earlier permitted pollution or waste deposits, which were discontinued before the Pollution Act came into force, the issue has arisen as to whether the obligation to clean-up may be contrary to the constitutional prohibition against giving statutes retrospective application.

With respect to the obligation to clean-up in relation to waste which was lawful at the time the Pollution Act came into force, it is clear that this cannot be said to be in breach of the constitution. The same generally applies in respect of the obligation to clean-up polluted grounds or water.

The same applies where a new owner has acquired the property, activity etc before the law came into force, and himself has not polluted or contributed to the waste deposit. The fact that the new owner was not aware of the pollution at the time of the transfer of the property is of no relevance. However, in cases where the imposition of liability may be construed as unreasonable, it is possible that the new owner will not be held liable.

The previous owner who polluted or contributed to the waste, can initially be held liable in relation to the obligation to clean-up etc (see para 3.2.8 above). A further issue may be whether the previous owner may be subject to the obligation when the property activity etc was transferred before the Act came into force and thereby the pollution became illegal. These are problems which are particularly relevant when the new owner is unable to carry out clean-up or when the imposition of liability would be considered unreasonable. In relation to waste deposited on the property, the previous owner may as a general rule be ordered to clean up. However, it is doubtful whether this same rule applies in respect to other pollution of the ground or water. A legal argument has been put forward that the prohibition in the constitution against the retrospective effect of statutes is not applicable to the obligation of a previous owner to clean up polluted ground or water, even if the pollution was legal at the time it was carried out.

3.4 Transferability of permits and licences

Emission licences granted under s 11 of the Pollution Act will, as a general rule, follow the activity if it is transferred to a new owner.

The emission licence will normally include a standard formulation setting out an obligation to notify SFT within a specific time in case of transfer. If the SFT thinks it necessary in any case, it may undertake a new evaluation of the emission licence. The SFT can reverse, alter or set new terms, or withdraw the licence, where the requirements of s 18 of the Pollution Act are met.

As a general rule, the new owner will thus take over the licence and the obligations pursuant to it.

3.5 Other ways an investment may be prejudiced by environmental problems

3.5.1 Obligation to notify and undertake an impact assessment for activities which may have major pollution problems

An increase of activity which may lead to pollution must be notified to the pollution authority. The pollution authority may order the notifier to conduct an impact assessment in order to clarify the consequences the pollution may have.

An impact assessment includes a survey of the pollution danger, measures taken to reduce the danger, alternative location of production processes, abatement equipment etc and an overview of the effect of the activity in relation to local zoning plans. The assessment is comprehensive and may lead to substantial delays with respect to planning and expansion or changes of a polluting activity.

An impact assessment may be required only when the activity may lead to major pollution problems, where new activities are to be commenced and where there is substantial expansion or change in the activities.

3.5.2 Redemption of real property

Pursuant to s 17 of the Pollution Act, the pollution authority may require that the person 'responsible' remediates neighbouring real estate when pollution will render properties 'little suited' for the purpose intended. The term 'responsible' under s 17 is as described in para 3.2.2 above.

The owner of the individual property has no right to demand redemption. The pollution authority has a legal right to require redemption for affected owners, against the perpetrator being granted an exemption when the requirements of the Act have been fulfilled.

The requirement that the property is little suited to the purpose it has been used for does not mean the same as unsuited. Section 17 has been little used in practice. The

Ministry for the Environment, however, required Kværner Rosenberg Shipyard in 1996 to redeem several neighbouring properties. The requirement can thus have importance in any assessment made by an acquirer.

3.5.3 Environmental fees

Environmental fees in different forms have been continuously discussed in political forums. In particular, there has been much recent discussion in respect of fees connected to the emission of carbon dioxide. Any start-up of a business or acquisition should include an analysis as to the likelihood that such fees may be applicable in the case of pollution.

4 MANAGING ENVIRONMENTAL ISSUES IN TRANSACTIONS

4.1 Current practice for assessment of risk

There are no legal requirements to conduct environmental due diligence investigations. However, such investigations are usually conducted, particularly in the case of larger acquisitions and with respect to property used for industrial purposes.

It may be necessary to conduct surveys of ground and groundwater, control of spills, production equipment, standards of cleaning equipment, deposits etc. Legal due diligence must be co-ordinated with other investigations. Mutual exchange of information is important for the carrying out of the investigations instigated in order to survey the effect of the activity on the natural environment.

4.2 Warranty or indemnity terms

When the activity or real estate has been investigated, any environmental risk discovered will be relevant to whether the transaction should be completed.

Appropriate solutions will, among other things, be dependent on the stage in the transaction process at which the investigation has been conducted and whether the parties agree who should bear the risk. For example, the transfer agreement may have been entered into and the environmental survey together with the other due diligence investigations may lead to a reduction in a given part of the purchase price.

When the transferor and transferee do not agree as to who should bear the risk, a broad spectrum of alternatives for splitting the risk may be applicable. This can vary from the transaction not taking place at all, to the transaction taking place as planned without any special regulations connected to the environmental risk.

A number of alternative solutions may be agreed between the parties, such as:

(1) the property affected by the environmental hazard is not included in the transaction;
(2) the transferor is liable for satisfactory clean-up and sets aside funds to discharge this liability;
(3) the transferor is not liable for the environmental risk and the circumstances uncovered by environmental due diligence;
(4) the transferor shall indemnify the transferee against all costs related to any orders for remedial measures to be implemented or liability as a result of environmental damage or for any other economic consequence of the pollution or the danger for pollution.

4.2 Chapter 16

Contractual control of environmental risk varies greatly. The nature of the transaction will itself be of major importance, as will the negotiating strength of the parties and, generally, the desire to carry out the transaction.

In situations where the obligation to implement remedial measures or where the danger for pollution is evident, the main issues will be price and the acquirer's right to claim indemnification for the costs from the seller. In cases where the economic consequences of the environmental circumstances are uncertain, two evaluation mechanisms may be included in the contract guarantees and limitation of liability.

Most contracts concerning the transfer of major activities include warranty clauses whereby the seller guarantees certain issues in relation to the value of the company and the purchase price. Warranties form part of the so-called warranty catalogue, which includes a number of different warranties from the seller. Warranties related to the environment will normally be dependent on whether an environmental survey has been conducted or is to be conducted, how extensive it is and the results of the survey. For the acquirer, warranties are naturally of greatest importance when the environmental risk has not been investigated, where the investigation has not been comprehensive or where the investigation has concluded that there is environmental risk, but has not stated the content of the risk.

A comprehensive set of warranties will generally include:

(1) that the activity has the necessary emission licences;
(2) that the emission licences have been adhered to;
(3) that the activity has not resulted in any pollution damage;
(4) that all orders etc from pollution authorities have been adhered to;
(5) that specific information provided concerning the environmental issues connected to the activity is complete and accurate; and
(6) that no issues exist related to the activity which may lead to any danger of pollution etc

It is also important that a period is defined for the application of the warranties.

The consequences of a breach of warranty may vary. A breach of a warranty will mean a breach of contract and strict liability. Often where a contractual warranty is called on, the acquirer will as a consequence have a right to a reduction in price equal to the loss in value the breach of contract leads to. Such price reductions may be limited by maximum liability provisions.

Breach of warranty may also give a right to rescind the contract. The right to rescind may be linked to how substantial the breach of the warranty is, such as by reference to specified figures in respect of the economic consequences for the acquirer, or specified breach of specified warranties. Additionally, a breach of warranty may give the acquirer a right to require the seller to undertake to restitute, for example, by carrying out the remedial measures necessary or ordered pursuant to s 7 of the Pollution Act.

The fact that the acquirer should have discovered the actual and guaranteed environmental risk in his environmental survey will generally not impact on the liability of the seller. However, this should be clearly expressed in the relevant contract.

A limitation of the seller's liability may be formulated in different ways. A limited warranty may have the effect of limiting liability to those issues that have been uncovered in the environmental survey. A limitation may also prevent the acquirer from making any claims against the seller in respect of the effect of the activity on the natural environment etc The courts have on a number of occasions taken a restrictive approach towards the limitation of liability. Gross negligence will often not be covered by the limitation in liability. Comprehensive limiting wording, which otherwise generally would have lead to a substantial breach of contract, is often the subject for restrictive interpretation.

The fact that the seller has limited his liability in respect of environmental matters does not mean that the seller does not have an obligation to undertake remedial measures pursuant to s 7 of the Pollution Act.

4.3 Issues for those lending money to businesses

The requirements of a lender in relation to guarantees for the handling of pollution danger etc from the activity varies. A clause in a loan agreement may be:

> 'The Borrower shall in the ordinary course of its business conduct frequent reviews of the effect of Environmental Law on its business, operations and properties, and its employees, agents or representatives will always comply with Environmental Law presently in effect in zones where the Borrower operates, which can have a material adverse effect on the business, operation, financial condition or prospects of the Borrower.'

4.4 Role of environmental management systems (EMS)

EMSs have to date not been widely implemented in Norway. In any transaction it is necessary to ascertain whether the activity has an acceptable management process and how it has been implemented.

4.5 Insurance

There is no statutory requirement of insurance schemes for environmental damage in Norway. However, environmental insurance is in practice available for many activities.

4.6 Structuring the management of companies, ownership of assets and operation of businesses

Environmental risk may motivate the acquirer to conduct transactions in a manner which limits the risk of a company formally acquiring the target property or activity, where it may be under-capitalised to bear the costs connected to any possible orders for remedial measures. This may lead the environmental authorities to make any claim under the Pollution Act against the owner of the acquirer, typically the parent company within a group. It will also be important to avoid the corporate veil being pierced by an absence of differentiation between the activities of companies, meaning that the formal incorporation of the companies cannot be maintained.

The fact that a company is under-financed in respect of environmental risks in relation to past problems will generally not form the basis for piercing the corporate veil. Where there is an obligation to undertake remedial measures, piercing the corporate veil may be appropriate where the acquirer is a group which is aware or which should have been aware of the environmental risk and has chosen to let an under-capitalised company within the group be the formal acquirer of the property or the activity.

5 CONCLUSION

Acquisition of an activity in Norway may mean a substantial environmental risk. Any acquisition should include an investigation in respect of environmental risk. The investigation should be undertaken based on the relevant statutory regulation and should involve an investigation of the individual activity, and apportionment of the risk by way of contract. An unsatisfactory assessment of the environmental risk may lead to significant losses, and to the imposition of comprehensive responsibility by Norwegian pollution authorities.

CONTACT DETAILS FOR CONTRIBUTORS

Address	Phone	Fax	EMail
AUSTRALIA			
Mr Andrew Beatty Allen Allen & Hemsley The Chifley Tower 2 Chifley Square Sydney NSW 2000 Australia	00 61 2 9230 4000	00 61 2 9230 5333	Andrew.Beatty@allens.com.au
Mr Martijn Wilder Baker & McKenzie AMP Centre 50 Bridge Street Sydney NSW 2000	00 61 2 9225 0276	00 61 2 9223 7711	martijn.wilder@bakernet.com
AUSTRIA			
Messrs Paul Luiki & Gernot Thanner Bruckhaus Westrick Heller Löber Seilergasse 16 A-1010 Wien	00 43 1 515 150	00 43 1 512 63 94	

Contact details for contributors

Address	Phone	Fax	EMail
BELGIUM			
Mr Francis Van Nuffel De Bandt, van Hecke, Lagae & Loesch/Linklaters & Alliance Rue Brederode 13 B-1000 Brussels Belgium	00 32 2 501 9411	00 32 2 501 9494	fvannuffel@debandt.com
FRANCE			
Messrs Christian Huglo & Francois Steinmetz Huglo Lepage & Associes 40 Rue de Monceau 75008 Paris France	00 331 56 59 29 59	00 331 56 59 29 39	hugolav@imaginet.fr
GERMANY			
Drs Gerhard Limberger & Stefanie Birkmann Bruckhaus Westrick Heller Lober Taunusanlage 11 D-60329 Frankfurt Am Main Taunusanlage 11 Germany	00 49 69 27 30 80	00 49 69 23 26 64	

Contact details for contributors

Address	Phone	Fax	EMail
GREECE			
Ms Christina Vlachtsis M & P Bernitsas 5 Lykavittou Street GR-106 72 Athens Greece	00 30 1 361 5395	00 30 1 361 8789/ 00 30 1 364 0805	bernlaw@otenet.gr
ISRAEL			
Mr Aner Berger & Ms Maya Lakstein Herzog Fox & Neeman Asia House 4 Weizmann Street Tel-Aviv 64239 Israel	00 972 3 692 2091	00 972 3 696 6464	berger@hfn.co.il
NETHERLANDS			
Messrs Willem Th. Braams & Mark R Birnage Pels Rijcken & Droogleever Fortuijn Postbus 11756 2502 AT's-Gravenhage Netherlands	00 31 70 34 88 815	00 31 70 38 20 564	pelsbieb@euronet.nl.

Contact details for contributors

Address	Phone	Fax	EMail
NORWAY			
Messrs Geir Steinberg & Borge Krogsrud Lowzow & Co Raadhusgaten 27 PO Box 359 Sentrum N-0101 Oslo Norway	00 47 22 41 68 10	00 47 22 41 68 08	post@lowzow.no
PORTUGAL			
Mr Henrique dos Santos Pereira Barrocas & Sarmento Av Eng Duarte Pacheco Empreendimento das Amoreiras Torre 2, 16th Floor 1070-274 Lisboa Portugal	00 351 213 843300	00 351 213 870304	Barrocas@mail.telepac.pt
SPAIN			
Mr Bernat Mullerat Bufete Mullerat Av Diagonal, 640, 4a 08017 Barcelona Spain	00 34 93 405 93 00	00 34 93 405 91 76	b.mullerat@mullerat.com

Contact details for contributors

Address	Phone	Fax	EMail
SWEDEN			
Mr Rudolf Laurin Wistrand Advokatbyrå Lilla Bommen 1 SE-411 04 Goteborg Sweden	00 46 31 771 21 00	00 46 31 771 21 50	rudolf.laurin@wistrand.net
SWITZERLAND			
Dr Hans U Liniger Ecosens AG Grindelstrasse 5 Postfach CH-8304 Wallisellen	00 41 1 839 47 77	00 41 1 839 47 70	ecosens@access.ch
UK			
Mr Mark Brumwell SJ Berwin & Co 222 Gray's Inn Road London WC1X 8HB	0044 (0) 20 7533 2222	00 (0) 20 7533 2000	mark.brumwell@sjberwin.com
USA			
Mr Andrew A Giaccia Chadbourne & Parke LLP 1200 New Hampshire Avenue NW Washington DC 20036	00 1 202 974 5600	00 1 202 974 5602	andrew.giaccia@chadbourne.com

INDEX

Abstraction of water
France, **12**:2.2.3
Israel, **15**:2.4.2
Netherlands, **5**:2.2.3
Portugal, **13**:2.3
Spain
continental waters, **9**:2.3.1
generally, **9**:2.3
marine waters, **9**:2.3.2
Sweden, **8**:2.3
United Kingdom, **4**:2.3
Access to information
Belgium
Brussels Metropolitan Region, **7**:2.5.3
Flemish Region, **7**:2.3.3
Walloon Region, **7**:2.4.3
Acid rain permits
United States, **2**:2.2.4
Administrative liability
Austria, **10**:2.2.3, **10**:3.1.1
Greece, **14**:3.1.1
Air compliance reporting
United States, **2**:2.6.1
Air permits
United States
acid rain permits, **2**:2.2.4
federal permits, **2**:2.2.3
generally, **2**:2
local permits, **2**:2.2.6
operating permits, **2**:2.2.5
state permits, **2**:2.2.6
Air pollution
and see **Atmospheric emissions**
Austria
boiler facilities, **10**:2.5.3
emissions, **10**:2.5.2
introduction, **10**:2.5.1
other laws, **10**:2.5.5
ozone, **10**:2.5.4
Israel, **15**:2.7

Air pollution – *contd*
Switzerland, **11**:2.5
Air quality management districts (United States), **2**:1.4.3
Atmospheric emissions
Australia, **6**:2.4.4
Austria
boiler facilities, **10**:2.5.3
emissions, **10**:2.5.2
introduction, **10**:2.5.1
other laws, **10**:2.5.5
ozone, **10**:2.5.4
France, **12**:2.2.5
generally, **1**:2.5
Germany, **3**:2.1
Greece, **14**:2.4
Israel, **15**:2.7
Netherlands, **5**:2.3.2
Norway, **16**:2.2.3
Portugal, **13**:2.5
Spain, **9**:2.5
Switzerland, **11**:2.5
United Kingdom, **4**:2.5
Audits, environmental
Austria, **10**:4.1.2
Belgium, **7**:4.1
Germany, **3**:4.1
Netherlands, **5**:4.4.2
Australia
atmospheric emissions, **6**:2.4.4
common law liability, **6**:2.4.8
conclusion
anticipation of effects, **6**:5.5
generally, **6**:5
harmonisation of regulation, **6**:5.1
incentives, **6**:5.3
public accountability, **6**:5.2
standards, **6**:5.4
corporate structure, **6**:4.8
costs of compliance, **6**:3.7

357

Index

Australia – *contd*
  environmental laws
    general Acts, **6**:2.3.1
    generally, **6**:2.3
    licence compliance, **6**:2.3.2
    thresholds, **6**:2.2.1–2.2.2
  federal laws, **6**:1.3.1
  financiers
    liability, **6**:3.5
    role, **6**:4.4
  hazardous substances, **6**:2.4.6
  historic liability, **6**:3.2
  indemnities, **6**:4.3
  insurance, **6**:4.7
  introduction
    generally, **6**:1.1
    legal system, **6**:1.2
    regulatory system, **6**:1.3–1.3.5
  Inter-Governmental Agreement on the
    Environment, **6**:1.3.4
  issue management
    corporate structure, **6**:4.8
    financiers' role, **6**:4.4
    indemnities, **6**:4.3
    insurance, **6**:4.7
    introduction, **6**:4.1
    management systems, **6**:4.5
    reporting, **6**:4.6
    risk assessment, **6**:4.2
    warranties, **6**:4.3
  land contamination, **6**:2.4.1
  land use planning, **6**:2.4.9
  lender's liability, **6**:3.5
  liability
    financiers', **6**:3.5
    generally, **6**:3.1
    historic, **6**:3.2
    lender's, **6**:3.5
    off-site contamination, **6**:3.3
  licence
    compliance, **6**:2.3.2
    transfer, **6**:3.6
  local laws, **6**:1.3.3
  management systems, **6**:4.5
  marine pollution, **6**:2.4.4
  merger and acquisition transactions
    atmospheric emissions, **6**:2.4.4
    common law liability, **6**:2.4.8
    general regulation, **6**:2.3–2.3.2
    hazardous substances, **6**:2.4.6
    introduction, **6**:2.1
    land contamination, **6**:2.4.1
    land use planning, **6**:2.4.9
    marine pollution, **6**:2.4.4
    noise, **6**:2.4.7
    recycling, **6**:2.4.5
    specific industry issues,
      6:2.5
    thresholds, **6**:2.2.1–2.2.2
    waste management, **6**:2.4.5
    water pollution, **6**:2.4.2
  noise, **6**:2.4.7
  off-site contamination, **6**:3.3

Australia – *contd*
  permit
    compliance, **6**:2.3.2
    transfer, **6**:3.6
  recycling, **6**:2.4.5
  regulatory system
    federal laws, **6**:1.3.1
    generally, **6**:1.3
    Inter-Governmental Agreement on the
      Environment, **6**:1.3.4
    international laws, **6**:1.3.5
    local laws, **6**:1.3.3
    state laws, **6**:1.3.2
  reporting, **6**:4.6
  risk assessment, **6**:4.2
  specific industry issues
    merger and acquisition transactions, **6**:2.5
    transaction issues, **6**:3.
  state laws, **6**:1.3.2
  tax concessions, **6**:3.8
  thresholds for acquisition approval
    generally, **6**:2.2.1
    impact of proposals, **6**:2.2.2
  transaction issues
    costs of compliance, **6**:3.7
    financiers' liability, **6**:3.5
    generally, **6**:3
    historic liability, **6**:3.2
    lender's liability, **6**:3.5
    liability, principles of, **6**:3.1
    licence transfer, **6**:3.6
    off-site contamination, **6**:3.3
    permit transfer, **6**:3.6
    specific industry issues, **6**:3.9
    tax concessions, **6**:3.8
  warranties, **6**:4.3
  waste management, **6**:2.4.5
  water pollution, **6**:2.4.2
Austria
  administrative liability, **10**:2.2.3, **10**:3.1.1
  air pollution
    boiler facilities, **10**:2.5.3
    emissions, **10**:2.5.2
    introduction, **10**:2.5.1
    other laws, **10**:2.5.5
    ozone, **10**:2.5.4
  chemicals, **10**:2.8
  contractual provisions
    absence of knowledge statement, **10**:4.3.7
    bank guarantee, **10**:4.3.4
    definitions, **10**:4.3.2
    escrow of price, **10**:4.3.3
    generally, **10**:4.3
    guarantee, **10**:4.3.5
    indemnification, **10**:4.3.8
    purchase price, **10**:4.3.1
    statutory warranty period, **10**:4.3.9
    warranty exclusion, **10**:4.3.6
  corporate structure, **10**:4.4
  criminal liability, **10**:2.2.2
  directors' liability, **10**:3.3
  environmental audits, **10**:4.1.2
  environmental information, **10**:2.12

Index

Austria – *contd*
  financier's liability, **10**:3.4
  hazardous substances, **10**:2.8
  historic liability
    Civil Code, **10**:3.2.1
    Commercial Code, **10**:3.2.2
  impact assessment, **10**:2.11
  insurance, **10**:4.5
  introduction
    judicial system, **10**:1.5
    legal system, **10**:1.1
    policies, **10**:1.2
    regulatory agencies, **10**:1.4
    regulatory system, **10**:1.3
  issue management
    contractual liability, **10**:4.3–4.3.9
    corporate structure, **10**:4.4
    fraudulent conduct, **10**:4.2.2
    insurance, **10**:4.5
    risk assessment, **10**:4.1.1–4.1.2
    warranties, **10**:4.2.1
  land contamination
    civil liability, **10**:2.3.4
    clean-up, **10**:2.3.3
    introduction, **10**:2.3.1
    old waste sites, **10**:2.3.2
  land use planning, **10**:2.7.1–2.7.2
  legal system, **10**:1.1
  lender's liability, **10**:3.4
  liability
    administrative, **10**:2.2.3, **10**:3.1.1
    civil, **10**:2.3.4, **10**:3.1.2
    criminal, **10**:2.2.2
    directors', **10**:3.3
    financier's, **10**:3.4
    historic, **10**:3.2.1–3.2.2
    lender's, **10**:3.4
    principles of, **10**:3.1.1–3.1.2
    managers', **10**:3.3
  licence transfer, **10**:3.5
  managers' liability, **10**:3.3
  merger and acquisition transactions
    air pollution, **10**:2.5.1–2.5.5
    chemicals, **10**:2.8
    environmental information, **10**:2.12
    hazardous substances, **10**:2.8
    impact assessment, **10**:2.11
    land contamination, **10**:2.3.1–2.3.4
    land use planning, **10**:2.7.1–2.7.2
    noise, **10**:2.9
    nuisance, **10**:2.9
    offences, **10**:2.2.1–2.2.3
    other laws, **10**:2.10
    Trade Code licensing, **10**:2.1
    waste management, **10**:2.6
    water pollution, **10**:2.4
  noise, **10**:2.9
  nuisance, **10**:2.9
  offences
    administrative, **10**:2.2.3
    criminal, **10**:2.2.2
    introduction, **10**:2.2.1
  permit transfer, **10**:3.5

Austria – *contd*
  regulatory agencies, **10**:1.4
  regulatory system, **10**:1.3
  risk assessment
    audits, **10**:4.1.2
    generally, **10**:4.1.1
  soil clean-up, **10**:2.3.3
  transaction issues
    directors' liability, **10**:3.3
    financier's liability, **10**:3.4
    historic liability, **10**:3.2.1–3.2.2
    lender's liability, **10**:3.4
    liability, principles of, **10**:3.1.1–3.1.2
    licence transfer, **10**:3.5
    managers' liability, **10**:3.3
    permit transfer, **10**:3.5
  warranties, **10**:4.2.1
  waste management, **10**:2.6
  water pollution, **10**:2.4

Belgium
  access to information
    Brussels Metropolitan Region, **7**:2.5.3
    Flemish Region, **7**:2.3.3
    Walloon Region, **7**:2.4.3
  audits, **7**:4.1
  Brussels Metropolitan Region
    access to information, **7**:2.5.3
    environmental care, **7**:2.5.3
    groundwater pollution, **7**:2.5.2, **7**:2.5.3
    impact assessment, **7**:2.5.3
    integrated pollution control, **7**:2.5.1
    land use planning, **7**:2.5.3
    noise, **7**:2.5.3
    soil pollution, **7**:2.5.2
    waste management, **7**:2.5.3
    water pollution, **7**:2.5.3
  conclusion, **7**:5
  criminal liability, **7**:3.2.3
  directors' liability, **7**:3.2.4
  environmental care
    Brussels Metropolitan Region, **7**:2.5.3
    Flemish Region, **7**:2.3.3
    Walloon Region, **7**:2.4.3
  federal laws, **7**:2.2
  financiers' liability, **7**:3.2.5
  Flemish Region
    access to information, **7**:2.3.3
    environmental care, **7**:2.3.3
    groundwater pollution, **7**:2.3.2, **7**:2.3.3
    impact assessment, **7**:2.3.3
    integrated pollution control, **7**:2.3.1
    land use planning, **7**:2.3.3
    noise, **7**:2.3.3
    soil pollution, **7**:2.3.2
    waste management, **7**:2.3.3
    water pollution, **7**:2.3.3
  groundwater pollution
    Brussels Metropolitan Region, **7**:2.5.2, **7**:2.5.3
    Flemish Region, **7**:2.3.2, **7**:2.3.3
    Walloon Region, **7**:2.4.2, **7**:2.4.3

359

Index

Belgium – *contd*
  impact assessment
    Brussels Metropolitan Region, **7**:2.5.3
    Flemish Region, **7**:2.3.3
    Walloon Region, **7**:2.4.3
  insurance, **7**:4.3
  integrated pollution control
    Brussels Metropolitan Region, **7**:2.5.1
    Flemish Region, **7**:2.3.1
  introduction
    regulatory institutions, **7**:1.2
    regulatory system, **7**:1.1
  issue management
    acquisition structure, **7**:4.2
    audits, **7**:4.1
    insurance, **7**:4.3
    management systems, **7**:4.4
    soil testing, **7**:4.5
  land contamination
    Brussels Metropolitan Region, **7**:2.5.2
    Flemish Region, **7**:2.3.2
    Walloon Region, **7**:2.4.2
  land use planning
    Brussels Metropolitan Region, **7**:2.5.3
    Flemish Region, **7**:2.3.3
    Walloon Region, , **7**:2.4.3
  lender's liability, **7**:3.2.5
  liability
    criminal, **7**:3.2.3
    directors', **7**:3.2.4
    financiers', **7**:3.2.5
    lender's, **7**:3.2.5
    principles of, **7**:3.2.1
    strict, **7**:3.2.2
  licence transfer, **7**:3.3.2
  management systems, **7**:4.4
  merger and acquisition transactions
    Brussels Metropolitan Region, **7**:2.5.1–2.5.3
    federal laws, **7**:2.2
    Flemish Region, **7**:2.3.1–2.3.3
    generally, **7**:2.1
    Walloon Region, **7**:2.4.1–2.4.3
  noise
    Brussels Metropolitan Region, **7**:2.5.3
    Flemish Region, **7**:2.3.3
    Walloon Region, **7**:2.4.3
  permit transfer, **7**:3.3.2
  regional laws
    Brussels Metropolitan Region, **7**:2.5.1–2.5.3
    Flemish Region, **7**: 2.3.1–2.3.3
    generally, **7**:2.1
    Walloon Region, **7**:2.4.1–2.4.3
  soil clean-up, **7**:3.3.3
  soil pollution
    Brussels Metropolitan Region, **7**:2.5.2
    Flemish Region, **7**:2.3.2
    Walloon Region, **7**:2.4.2
  soil testing, **7**:4.5
  strict liability, **7**:3.2.2
  transaction formalities
    licence transfer, **7**:3.3.2
    permit transfer, **7**:3.3.2
    soil clean-up, **7**:3.3.1

Belgium – *contd*
  transaction issues
    criminal liability, **7**:3.2.3
    directors' liability, **7**:3.2.4
    financiers' liability, **7**:3.2.5
    generally, **7**:3.1
    lender's liability, **7**:3.2.5
    liability, principles of, **7**:3.2.1
    strict liability, **7**:3.2.2
  Walloon Region
    access to information, **7**:2.4.3
    environmental care, **7**:2.4.3
    groundwater pollution, **7**:2.4.2, **7**:2.4.3
    impact assessment, **7**:2.4.3
    operating permits, **7**:2.4.1
    land use planning, **7**:2.4.3
    noise, **7**:2.4.3
    soil pollution, **7**:2.4.2
    waste management, **7**:2.4.3
    water pollution, **7**:2.4.3
  waste management
    Brussels Metropolitan Region, **7**:2.5.3
    Flemish Region, **7**:2.3.3
    Walloon Region, **7**:2.4.3
  water pollution
    Brussels Metropolitan Region, **7**:2.5.3
    Flemish Region, **7**:2.3.3
    Walloon Region, **7**:2.4.3
Brownfield sites
  United States, **2**:2.1.3
Brussels Metropolitan Region
  access to information, **7**:2.5.3
  environmental care, **7**:2.5.3
  groundwater pollution, **7**:2.5.2, **7**:2.5.3
  impact assessment, **7**:2.5.3
  integrated pollution control, **7**:2.5.1
  land use planning, **7**:2.5.3
  noise, **7**:2.5.3
  soil pollution, **7**:2.5.2
  waste management, **7**:2.5.3
  water pollution, **7**:2.5.3
Bundesimmissionsschutzgesetz (Germany), **3**:2.1

Change-in-law risks
  United States, **2**:3.5
Chemical substances
  Austria, **10**:2.8
  Israel, **15**:2.2.1
  Netherlands, **5**:2.3.5
  Sweden, **8**:2.7
Chemical usage reporting
  United States, **2**:2.6.3
Comprehensive Environmental Response, Compensation and Liability Act (United States), **2**:2.1
Clean Air Act (United States), **2**:1.2
Clean Water Act (United States), **2**:1.2, **2**:2.1.6
Comparison of laws
  conclusion, **1**:5
  environmental laws
    atmospheric emissions, **1**:2.5
    generally, **1**:2.1

Index

Comparison of laws – *contd*
  environmental laws – *contd*
    integrated pollution control, **1**:2.4
    land contamination, **1**:2.2
    land use planning, **1**:2.7
    waste, **1**:2.6
    water, **1**:2.3
  introduction
    contractual rights, **1**:1.3
    enforcement, **1**:1.2
    origins, **1**:1.1
    structure, **1**:1.1
    third party rights, **1**:1.3
  issue management
    environmental management systems, **1**:4.4
    financiers' role, **1**:4.3
    indemnities, **1**:4.2
    insurance, **1**:4.5
    risk assessment, **1**:4.1
    warranties, **1**:4.2
  transaction issues
    corporate veil, **1**:3.3
    directors' liability, **1**:3.4
    financiers' liability, **1**:3.5
    foreign investment, **1**:3.2
    historical liability, principles of, **1**:3.1
    managers' liability, **1**:3.4
    ongoing compliance, **1**:3.7
    permit transfer, **1**:3.6
Compliance, costs of
  Australia, **6**:3.7
  Greece, **14**:3.6
  Spain, **9**:3.6
  Sweden, **8**:3.7
  United Kingdom, **4**:3.7
Contaminated land
  Australia, **6**:2.4.1
  Austria
    civil liability, **10**:2.3.4
    clean-up, **10**:2.3.3
    introduction, **10**:2.3.1
    old waste sites, **10**:2.3.2
  Belgium
    Brussels Metropolitan Region, **7**:2.5.2
    Flemish Region, **7**:2.3.2
    Walloon Region, **7**:2.4.2
  France, **12**:2.2.1
  generally, **1**:2.2
  Germany, **3**:2.4
  Greece, **14**:2.2
  Israel, **15**:2.9
  Netherlands
    introduction, **5**:2.1.1
    sale of contaminated property, **5**:2.1.3
    soil protection, **5**:2.1.2
  Portugal
    generally, **13**:2.1
    soil pollution, **13**:2.1.1
    sub-soil, **13**:2.1.2
  Spain, **9**:2.2
  Sweden, **8**:2.1
  United Kingdom, **4**:2.1

Contaminated land – *contd*
  United States
    brownfield sites, **2**:2.1.3
    CERCLA, **2**:2.1.1
    oil pollution, **2**:2.1.5
    RCRA, **2**:2.1.2
    remediation, **2**:2.1.3
    underground storage tanks, **2**:2.1.7
Contractual rights, **1**:1.3
Corporate structure
  Australia, **6**:4.8
  Austria, **10**:4.4
  Germany, **3**:4.3
  Greece, **14**:4.5
  Netherlands, **5**:4.6
  Norway, **16**:4.6
  Sweden, **8**:4.6
  United Kingdom, **4**:4.6
Costs of compliance
  Australia, **6**:3.7
  Greece, **14**:3.6
  Spain, **9**:3.6
  Sweden, **8**:3.7
  United Kingdom, **4**:3.7
Criminal liability
  Austria, **10**:2.2.2
  Belgium, **7**:3.2.3
  Germany, **3**:3.1.3
  Greece, **14**:3.1.1–3.1.2
  Israel, **15**:3.1
  Portugal, **13**:3.2–3.2.8
  Spain, **9**:2.10
  Sweden, **8**:2.4.9
  Switzerland, **11**:3.3
  United States, **2**:2.7
Development control
  Australia, **6**:2.4.9
  Austria, **10**:2.7.1–2.7.2
  Belgium
    Brussels Metropolitan Region, **7**:2.5.3
    Flemish Region, **7**:2.3.3
    Walloon Region, **7**:2.4.3
  France, **12**:2.2.7
  generally, **1**:2.7
  Germany, **3**:2.5
  Greece, **14**:2.6
  Israel
    impact studies, **15**:2.10.2
    planning and building institutions, **15**:2.10.1
  Netherlands, **5**:2.3.4
  Norway, **16**:2.2.5
  Portugal, **13**:2.7
  Spain, **9**:2.7
  Sweden, **8**:2.6
  Switzerland, **11**:2.7
  United Kingdom, **4**:2.7
  United States, **2**:2.4
Directors' liability
  Austria, **10**:3.3
  Belgium, **7**:3.2.4
  France, **12**:3.4
  generally, **1**:3.4

Index

Directors' liability – *contd*
  Greece, **14**:3.3
  Netherlands, **5**:3.4
  Norway, **16**:3.2.6
  Portugal, **13**:3.5
  Spain, **9**:3.3
  Sweden, **8**:3.4
  Switzerland, **11**:3.3
  United Kingdom, **4**:3.4
  United States, **2**:3.6
Disaster prevention
  Switzerland, **11**:2.11
Discharges into water
  France, **12**:2.2.3
  Israel, **15**:2.4.1
  Netherlands, **5**:2.2.3
  Portugal, **13**:2.3
  Spain
    continental waters, **9**:2.3.1
    generally, **9**:2.3
    marine waters, **9**:2.3.2
  Sweden, **8**:2.3
  United Kingdom, **4**:2.3
Disclosure requirements
  Australia, **6**:4.6
  Austria, **10**:2.12
  Netherlands, **5**:4.4.3
  United States
    air compliance reporting, **2**:2.6.1
    chemical usage reporting, **2**:2.6.3
    generally, **2**:2.6
    leak reporting, **2**:2.6.2
    securities laws, under, **2**:2.6.4
    spill reporting, **2**:2.6.2
    transfer notifications, **2**:2.6.5
    water compliance reporting, **2**:2.6.1
Due diligence
  Israel, **15**:4.1.1
  Switzerland, **11**:4.3

Emergency Planning and Community Right-To-Know Act (United States), **2**:2.6.3
Emissions, atmospheric
  Australia, **6**:2.4.4
  Austria
    boiler facilities, **10**:2.5.3
    emissions, **10**:2.5.2
    introduction, **10**:2.5.1
    other laws, **10**:2.5.5
    ozone, **10**:2.5.4
  France, **12**:2.2.5
  generally, **1**:2.5
  Germany, **3**:2.1
  Greece, **14**:3.1.1, **14**:2.4
  Israel, **15**:2.7
  Netherlands, **5**:2.3.2
  Norway, **16**:2.2.3
  Portugal, **13**:2.5
  Spain, **9**:2.5
  Switzerland, **11**:2.5
  United Kingdom, **4**:2.5
Enforcement, **1**:1.2
Environment Agency (United Kingdom), **4**:1.2

Environmental audits
  Audits, **10**:4.1.2
  Belgium, **7**:4.1
  Germany, **3**:4.1
  Netherlands, **5**:4.4.2
Environmental care
  Belgium
    Brussels Metropolitan Region, **7**:2.5.3
    Flemish Region, **7**:2.3.3
    Walloon Region, **7**:2.4.3
Environmental information
  Australia, **6**:4.6
  Austria, **10**:2.12
  Netherlands, **5**:4.4.3
  United States
    air compliance reporting, **2**:2.6.1
    chemical usage reporting, **2**:2.6.3
    generally, **2**:2.6
    leak reporting, **2**:2.6.2
    securities laws, under, **2**:2.6.4
    spill reporting, **2**:2.6.2
    transfer notifications, **2**:2.6.5
    water compliance reporting, **2**:2.6.1
Environmental law
  Australia
    general Acts, **6**:2.3.1
    generally, **6**:2.3
    licence compliance, **6**:2.3.2
    thresholds, **6**:2.2.1–2.2.2
  contractual rights, **1**:1.3
  enforcement, **1**:1.2
  issue management
    environmental management systems, **1**:4.4
    financiers' role, **1**:4.3
    indemnities, **1**:4.2
    insurance, **1**:4.5
    risk assessment, **1**:4.1
    warranties, **1**:4.2
  Netherlands
    generally, **5**:1.1
    sources, **5**:1.2
  origins, **1**:1.1
  outline
    atmospheric emissions, **1**:2.5
    generally, **1**:2.1
    integrated pollution control, **1**:2.4
    land contamination, **1**:2.2
    land use planning, **1**:2.7
    waste, **1**:2.6
    water, **1**:2.3
  structure, **1**:1.1
  third party rights, **1**:1.3
  transaction issues
    corporate veil, **1**:3.3
    directors' liability, **1**:3.4
    financiers' liability, **1**:3.5
    foreign investment, **1**:3.2
    historical liability, principles of, **1**:3.1
    managers' liability, **1**:3.4
    ongoing compliance, **1**:3.7
    permit transfer, **1**:3.6

Index

Environmental law – *contd*
United Kingdom
  enforcement, **4**:1.2
  generally, **4**:1
  origins of law, **4**:1.1
Environmental management
Netherlands
  audit, **5**:4.4.2
  certification, **5**:4.4.4
  generally, **5**:4.4
  management system, **5**:4.4.1
  outline licences, **5**:4.4.5
  reporting, **5**:4.4.3
Environmental management systems
Australia, **6**:4.5
Belgium, **7**:4.4
generally, **1**:4.4
Netherlands
  certification, **5**:4.4.4
  generally, **5**:4.4.1
  reporting, **5**:4.4.3
Spain, **9**:4.4
Sweden, **8**:4.3
Switzerland, **11**:4.2
United Kingdom, **4**:3.6
United States, **2**:4.5
Environmental Protection Agency (United States), **2**:1.2
Environmental reporting
Australia, **6**:4.6
Netherlands, **5**:4.4.3
Escrow agreements
United States, **2**:4.3

Federal laws
Australia, **6**:1.3.1
Belgium, **7**:2.2
Germany, **3**:1.1
United States
  approved programmes, **2**:1.2.1
  consistency of programmes, **2**:1.3–1.3.5
  enforcement, **2**:1.2.3
  generally, **2**:1.2
  non-conforming plans, **2**:1.2.2
  other plans, **2**:1.2.4
Financiers' liability
Australia, **6**:3.5
Austria, **10**:3.4
Belgium, **7**:3.2.5
France, **12**:3.5
generally, **1**:3.5
Germany, **3**:2
Greece, **14**:3.4
Israel, **15**:3.6
Netherlands, **5**:3.5
Norway, **16**:3.2.7
Portugal, **13**:3.6
Spain, **9**:3.4
Sweden, **8**:3.5
Switzerland, **11**:3.4
United Kingdom, **4**:3.5
United States, **2**:3.8

Financiers' role
Australia, **6**:4.4
France, **12**:4.3
generally, **1**:4.3
Greece, **14**:4.3
Netherlands, **5**:4.3
Norway, **16**:4.3
Portugal, **13**:4.3
Spain, **9**:4.3
United Kingdom, **4**:4.3
Flemish Region
access to information, **7**:2.3.3
environmental care, **7**:2.3.3
groundwater pollution, **7**:2.3.2, **7**:2.3.3
impact assessment, **7**:2.3.3
integrated pollution control, **7**:2.3.1
land use planning, **7**:2.3.3
noise, **7**:2.3.3
soil pollution, **7**:2.3.2
waste management, **7**:2.3.3
water pollution, **7**:2.3.3
France
abstraction of water, **12**:2.2.3
atmospheric emissions, **12**:2.2.5
civil law principles
  Civil Code, art 1134, **12**:2.1.2
  Civil Code, art 1382, **12**:2.1.1
  environmental, **12**:2.1.3
  generally, **12**:2.1
conclusion, **12**:5
directors' liability, **12**:3.4
discharges to water, **12**:2.2.3
environmental laws, **12**:2–2.2.9
financiers' liability, **12**:3.5
financiers' role, **12**:4.3
hazardous substances, **12**:2.2.8
historic liability, **12**:3.2
indemnities, **12**:4.2
insurance, **12**:4.4
integrated pollution control, **12**:2.2.4
introduction
  generally, **12**:1
  regulatory agencies, **12**:1.1.3
  regulatory system, **12**:1.1.1
  sources of law, **12**:1.1.2
issue management
  financiers' role, **12**:4.3
  indemnities, **12**:4.2
  insurance, **12**:4.4
  risk assessment, **12**:4.1
  warranties, **12**:4.2
land contamination, **12**:2.2.1
land use planning, **12**:2.2.7
lender's liability, **12**:3.5
liability
  directors', **12**:3.4
  financiers', **12**:3.5
  historic, **12**:3.2
  lender's, **12**:3.5
  managers', **12**:3.4
  off-site, **12**:3.3
  principles of, **12**:3.1
licence transfer, **12**:3.6

363

Index

France – *contd*
  managers' liability, **12**:3.4
  merger and acquisition transactions
    abstraction of water, **12**:2.2.3
    atmospheric emissions, **12**:2.2.5
    civil law principles, **12**:2.1–2.1.3
    discharges to water, **12**:2.2.3
    environmental laws, **12**:2–2.2.9
    generally, **12**:2
    hazardous substances, **12**:2.2.8
    integrated pollution control, **12**:2.2.4
    land contamination, **12**:2.2.1
    land use planning, **12**:2.2.7
    noise, **12**:2.2.9
    nuisance, **12**:2.2.9
    recycling, **12**:2.2.6
    waste management, **12**:2.2.6
    water pollution, **12**:2.2.2
  noise, **12**:2.2.9
  nuisance, **12**:2.2.9
  off-site contamination, **12**:3.3
  permit transfer, **12**:3.6
  recycling, **12**:2.2.6
  regulatory agencies, **12**:1.1.3
  regulatory system, **12**:1.1.1
  risk assessment, **12**:4.1
  sources of law, **12**:1.1.2
  transaction issues
    directors' liability, **12**:3.4
    financiers' liability, **12**:3.5
    historic liability, **12**:3.2
    lender's liability, **12**:3.5
    liability, principles of, **12**:3.1
    licence transfer, **12**:3.6
    managers' liability, **12**:3.4
    off-site contamination, **12**:3.3
    permit transfer, **12**:3.6
  warranties, **12**:4.2
  waste management, **12**:2.2.6
  water pollution, **12**:2.2.2

Genetically modified organisms
  Switzerland, **11**:2.12

Germany
  audits, **3**:4.1
  conclusion, **3**:5
  contamination
    land, **3**:2.4
    water, **3**:2.2
  criminal liability, **3**:3.1.3
  emission control, **3**:2.1
  federal laws, **3**:1.1
  financiers' liability, **3**:2
  hazardous substances, **3**:2.6
  historic liability, **3**:3
  indemnities, **3**:4.3
  insurance, **3**:4.5
  introduction
    legal system, **3**:1.1
    regulatory system, **3**:1.2
  issue management
    acquisition agreement, **3**:4.2
    audits, **3**:4.1

Germany – *contd*
  issue management – *contd*
    corporate obligations, **3**:4.3
    due diligence, **3**:4.1
    generally, **3**:4
    indemnities, **3**:4.3
    insurance, **3**:4.5
    management systems, **3**:4.4
  land contamination, **3**:2.4
  land use planning, **3**:2.5
  lender's liability, **3**:2
  liability
    corporate, **3**:4
    criminal, **3**:3.1.3
    generally, **3**:3.1
    historic, **3**:3
    lender's, **3**:2
    private, **3**:3.1
    public, **3**:3.1.2
  local laws, **3**:1.1
  management systems, **3**:4.4
  merger and acquisition transactions
    emission control, **3**:2.1
    generally, **3**:2
    hazardous substances, **3**:2.6
    land contamination, **3**:2.4
    land use planning, **3**:2.5
    noise, **3**:2.1
    nuisance, **3**:2.1
    waste management, **3**:2.3
    water, **3**:2.2
  noise, **3**:2.1
  nuisance, **3**:2.1
  permit transfer, **3**:5
  private liability, **3**:3.1.1
  state laws, **3**:1.1
  transaction issues
    corporate obligations, **3**:4
    historic liability, **3**:3
    lender's liability, **3**:2
    liability, **3**:3.1–3.1.3
    permit transfer, **3**:5
  waste management, **3**:2.3
  water, **3**:2.2

Greece
  administrative liability, **14**:3.1.1
  atmospheric emissions, **14**:2.4
  civil liability, **14**:3.1.1–3.1.2
  conclusion, **14**:5
  corporate structure, **14**:4.5
  costs of compliance, **14**:3.6
  criminal liability, **14**:3.1.1–3.1.2
  directors' liability, **14**:3.3
  financiers' liability, **14**:3.4
  financiers' role, **14**:4.3
  hazardous substances, **14**:2.7
  historic liability, **14**:3.2
  impact assessment, **14**:2.10
  indemnities, **14**:4.2
  insurance, **14**:4.4
  introduction
    generally, **14**:1
    regulatory agencies, **14**:1.2

Greece – *contd*
  introduction – *contd*
    regulatory system, **14**:1.1
  issue management
    corporate structure, **14**:4.5
    financiers' role, **14**:4.3
    indemnities, **14**:4.2
    insurance, **14**:4.4
    risk assessment, **14**:4.1
    warranties, **14**:4.2
  land contamination, **14**:2.2
  land use planning, **14**:2.6
  lender's liability, **14**:3.4
  liability
    administrative, **14**:3.1.1
    civil, **14**:3.1.1–3.1.2
    criminal, **14**:3.1.1–3.1.2
    directors', **14**:3.3
    financiers', **14**:3.4
    historic, **14**:3.2
    lender's, **14**:3.4
    principles of, **14**:3.1.1–3.1.2
    managers', **14**:3.3
    tortious, **14**:3.1.2
  licence transfer, **14**:3.5
  managers' liability, **14**:3.3
  merger and acquisition transactions
    atmospheric emissions, **14**:2.4
    generally, **14**:2.1
    hazardous substances, **14**:2.7
    impact assessment, **14**:2.10
    land contamination, **14**:2.2
    land use planning, **14**:2.6
    noise emissions, **14**:2.8
    nuclear energy, **14**:2.9
    radioactive material, **14**:2.7
    radioactive waste, **14**:2.9
    recycling, **14**:2.5
    waste management, **14**:2.5
    water pollution, **14**:2.3
  noise emissions, **14**:2.8
  nuclear energy, **14**:2.9
  permit transfer, **14**:3.5
  radioactive material, **14**:2.7
  radioactive waste, **14**:2.9
  recycling, **14**:2.5
  regulatory agencies, **14**:1.2
  regulatory system, **14**:1.1
  risk assessment, **14**:4.1
  tort liability, **14**:3.1.2
  transaction issues
    administrative liability, **14**:3.1.1
    civil liability, **14**:3.1.1–3.1.2
    costs of compliance, **14**:3.6
    criminal liability, **14**:3.1.1–3.1.2
    directors' liability, **14**:3.3
    financiers' liability, **14**:3.4
    generally, **14**:3
    historic liability, **14**:3.2
    lender's liability, **14**:3.4
    liability, principles of, **14**:3.1.1–3.1.2
    licence transfer, **14**:3.5
    managers' liability, **14**:3.3

Greece – *contd*
  transaction issues – *contd*
    permit transfer, **14**:3.5
    tort liability, **14**:3.1.2
    warranties, **14**:4.2
    waste management, **14**:2.5
    water pollution, **14**:2.3
Groundwater contamination
  Belgium
    Brussels Metropolitan Region, **7**:2.5.2, **7**:2.5.3
    Flemish Region, **7**:2.3.2, **7**:2.3.3
    Walloon Region, **7**:2.4.2, **7**:2.4.3
  Netherlands, **5**:2.2.3
  Switzerland, **11**:2.4
  United States
    CERCLA, **2**:2.1.1
    generally, **2**:2.1.4
    oil pollution, **2**:2.1.5
    RCRA, **2**:2.1.2
    remediation, **2**:2.1.3
    underground storage tanks, **2**:2.1.7

Hazardous substances
  Australia, **6**:2.4.6
  Austria, **10**:2.8
  France, **12**:2.2.8
  Germany, **3**:2.6
  Greece, **14**:2.7
  Israel
    chemicals, **15**:2.2.1
    disposal, **15**:2.2.3
    import/export, **15**:2.2.4
    pesticides, **15**:2.2.5
    plants, **15**:2.2.2
    toxins, **15**:2.2.1
  Netherlands, **5**:2.3.5
  Norway
    storage, **16**:2.2.6
    transport, **16**:2.2.7
    use, **16**:2.2.6
  Portugal, **13**:2.8
  Spain, **9**:2.8
  Sweden, **8**:2.7
  Switzerland, **11**:2.8
  United States, **2**:2.3.1
Health and Safety Executive (United Kingdom), **4**:1.2
Historic liability
  Australia, **6**:3.2
  Austria
    Civil Code, **10**:3.2.1
    Commercial Code, **10**:3.2.2
  France, **12**:3.2
  generally, **1**:3.1
  Germany, **3**:3
  Greece, **14**:3.2
  Israel, **15**:3.4
  Netherlands, **5**:3.2
  Norway, **16**:3.3
  Portugal, **13**:3.4
  Spain, **9**:3.2
  Sweden, **8**:3.2

Index

Historic liability – *contd*
  United Kingdom, **4**:3.2
  United States, **2**:3.3

Impact assessment
  Austria, **10**:2.11
  Belgium
    Brussels Metropolitan Region, **7**:2.5.3
    Flemish Region, **7**:2.3.3
    Walloon Region, **7**:2.4.3
  Greece, **14**:2.10
  Israel, **15**:2.10.2
  Norway, **16**:3.5.1–3.5.3
  Switzerland, **11**:2.10

Indemnities
  Australia, **6**:4.3
  Austria, **10**:4.2.1
  France, **12**:4.2
  generally, **1**:4.2
  Germany, **3**:4.3
  Greece, **14**:4.2
  Israel, **15**:4.2
  Netherlands, **5**:4.2
  Norway, **16**:4.2
  Portugal, **13**:4.2
  Spain, **9**:4.2
  United Kingdom, **4**:4.2
  United States, **2**:4.4

Insurance
  Australia, **6**:4.7
  Austria, **10**:4.5
  Belgium, **7**:4.3
  France, **12**:4.4
  generally, **1**:4.5
  Germany, **3**:4.5
  Greece, **14**:4.4
  Netherlands, **5**:4.5
  Norway, **16**:4.5
  Spain, **9**:4.5
  Sweden, **8**:4.5
  Switzerland, **11**:4.6
  United Kingdom, **4**:4.5
  United States, **2**:4.6

Integrated pollution control
  Belgium
    Brussels Metropolitan Region, **7**:2.5.1
    Flemish Region, **7**:2.3.1
  France, **12**:2.2.4
  generally, **1**:2.4
  Netherlands, **5**:2.3.1
  Portugal, **13**:2.4
  Sweden
    best location, **8**:2.4.5
    best possible technology, **8**:2.4.4
    burden of proof, **8**:2.4.1
    criminal liability, **8**:2.4.9
    generally, **8**:2.4
    knowledge, **8**:2.4.2
    precautions, **8**:2.4.3
    product choice, **8**:2.4.7
    reasonableness, **8**:2.4.8
    resource management, **8**:2.4.6

Integrated pollution control – *contd*
  introduction
    legal system, **8**:1.1
    regulatory agencies, **8**:1.3
    regulatory system, **8**:1.2
  United Kingdom, **4**:2.4

Inter-Governmental Agreement on the Environment (Australia), **6**:1.3.4

Israel
  abstraction of water, **15**:2.4.2
  acquisition agreement, **15**:4.1.1–4.1.3
  air pollution, **15**:2.7
  civil liability, **15**:3.2
  conclusion, **15**:5
  criminal liability, **15**:3.1
  discharges to water, **15**:2.4.1
  enforcement of liability
    administrative, **15**:3.3.1
    civil, **15**:3.3.3
    criminal, **15**:3.3.2
    generally, **15**:3.3
  financiers' liability, **15**:3.6
  hazardous substances
    chemicals, **15**:2.2.1
    disposal, **15**:2.2.3
    import/export, **15**:2.2.4
    pesticides, **15**:2.2.5
    plants, **15**:2.2.2
    toxins, **15**:2.2.1
  historic liability, **15**:3.4
  impact study, **15**:2.10.2
  indemnities, **15**:4.2
  introduction
    generally, **15**:1
    legal system, **15**:1.1–1.1.3
    non-governmental organisations, **15**:1.4
    regulatory agencies, **15**:1.3.1–1.3.11
    regulatory system, **15**:1.2
  issue management
    acquisition agreement, **15**:4.1.1–4.1.3
    generally, **15**:4
    indemnities, **15**:4.2
    risk assessment, **14**:4.3
  land contamination, **15**:2.9
  land use planning
    impact studies, **15**:2.10.2
    planning and building institutions, **15**:2.10.1
  legal system
    executive, **15**:1.1.2
    generally, **15**:1.1
    judiciary, **15**:1.1.3
    legislature, **15**:1.1.1
  lender's liability, **15**:3.6
  liability
    civil, **15**:3.2
    criminal, **15**:3.1
    enforcement of, **15**:3.3–3.3.3
    financiers', **15**:3.6
    historic, **15**:3.4
    lender's, **15**:3.6
    licence transfer, **15**:3.5

Israel – *contd*
  merger and acquisition transactions
    air pollution, **15**:2.7
    business licensing, **15**:2.8
    generally, **15**:2
    hazardous substances, **15**:2.2.1–2.2.5
    impact assessment, **15**:2.10.2
    land contamination, **15**:2.9
    land use planning, **15**:2.10.1–2.10.2
    noise, **15**:2.5.2
    nuisance, **15**:2.5.1–2.5.2
    radiation pollution, **15**:2.3–2.3.2
    sunlight, interference with, **15**:2.6
    taxes, **15**:2.11–2.11.2
    waste disposal, **15**:2.1.1–2.1.3
    water pollution, **15**:2.4–2.4.2
  noise, **15**:2.5.2
  nuisance
    generally, **15**:2.5.1
    noise, **15**:2.5.2
    smell, **15**:2.5.2
  permit transfer, **15**:3.5
  radiation pollution
    generally, **15**:2.3
    ionizing radiation, **15**:2.3.1
    non-ionizing radiation, **15**:2.3.2
  recycling, **15**:2.1.2
  regulatory agencies
    Environment Ministry, **15**:1.3.1
    Environment Patrolling, **15**:1.3.3
    Intra-Office Committee for Business Licensing, **15**:1.3.2
    Interior Ministry, **15**:1.3.7
    KKL, **15**:1.3.10
    local authorities, **15**:1.3.9
    National Planning and Building Board, **15**:1.3.8
    Poisonous Substances Unit, **15**:1.3.5
    Restoration of Rivers Administration, **15**:1.3.11
    Sea Pollution Unit, **15**:1.3.4
    Water Council, **15**:1.3.6
  regulatory system, **15**:1.2
  risk assessment, **15**:4.3
  transaction issues
    civil liability, **15**:3.2
    criminal liability, **15**:3.1
    enforcement of liability, **15**:3.3–3.3.3
    financiers' liability, **15**:3.6
    generally, **15**:3
    historic liability, **15**:3.4
    lender's liability, **15**:3.6
    licence transfer, **15**:3.5
    permit transfer, **15**:3.5
  waste disposal
    packaging levy, **15**:2.1.3
    recycling, **15**:2.1.2
    solid waste, **15**:2.1.1
  water pollution
    aircraft waste, **15**:2.4.1
    generally, **15**:2.4
    internal waters, **15**:2.4.2
    oil, **15**:2.4.1
    sea water, **15**:2.4.1

Issue management
  acquisition agreements
    Belgium, **7**:4.2
    Germany, **3**:4.2
    Sweden, **8**:4.2
    Switzerland, **11**:4.4
  Australia
    corporate structure, **6**:4.8
    financiers' role, **6**:4.4
    indemnities, **6**:4.3
    insurance, **6**:4.7
    introduction, **6**:4.1
    management systems, **6**:4.5
    reporting, **6**:4.6
    risk assessment, **6**:4.2
    warranties, **6**:4.3
  Austria
    contractual liability, **10**:4.3–4.3.9
    corporate structure, **10**:4.4
    fraudulent conduct, **10**:4.2.2
    insurance, **10**:4.5
    risk assessment, **10**:4.1.1–4.1.2
    warranties, **10**:4.2.1
  Belgium
    acquisition structure, **7**:4.2
    audits, **7**:4.1
    insurance, **7**:4.3
    management systems, **7**:4.4
    soil testing, **7**:4.5
  corporate structure
    Australia, **6**:4.8
    Austria, **10**:4.4
    Greece, **14**:4.5
    Norway, **16**:4.6
    Sweden, **8**:4.4
    United Kingdom, **4**:4.6
  escrow agreements
    United States, **2**:4.3
  financiers' role
    Australia, **6**:4.4
    France, **12**:4.3
    generally, **1**:4.3
    Greece, **14**:4.3
    Netherlands, **5**:4.3
    Norway, **16**:4.3
    Portugal, **13**:4.3
    Spain, **9**:4.3
    United Kingdom, **4**:4.3
  France
    financiers' role, **12**:4.3
    indemnities, **12**:4.2
    insurance, **12**:4.4
    risk assessment, **12**:4.1
    warranties, **12**:4.2
  Germany
    acquisition agreement, **3**:4.2
    audits, **3**:4.1
    corporate obligations, **3**:4.3
    due diligence, **3**:4.1
    generally, **3**:4
    indemnities, **3**:4.3
    insurance, **3**:4.5
    management systems, **3**:4.4

Index

Issue management – *contd*
Greece
corporate structure, **14**:4.5
financiers' role, **14**:4.3
indemnities, **14**:4.2
insurance, **14**:4.4
risk assessment, **14**:4.1
warranties, **14**:4.2
indemnities
Australia, **6**:4.3
Austria, **10**:4.2.1
France, **12**:4.2
Germany, **3**:4.3
Greece, **14**:4.2
introduction, **1**:4.2
Israel, **15**:4.2
Netherlands, **5**:4.2
Norway, **16**:4.2
Portugal, **13**:4.2
Spain, **9**:4.2
United Kingdom, **4**:4.2
United States, **2**:4.4
insurance
Australia, **6**:4.7
Austria, **10**:4.5
Belgium, **7**:4.4
France, **12**:4.4
Germany, **3**:4.4
Greece, **14**:4.4
introduction, **1**:4.5
Netherlands, **5**:4.5
Norway, **16**:4.5
Spain, **9**:4.5
Sweden, **8**:4.5
Switzerland, **11**:4.6
United Kingdom, **4**:4.5
United States, **2**:4.6
introduction
financiers' role, **1**:4.3
indemnities, **1**:4.2
insurance, **1**:4.5
management systems, **1**:4.4
risk assessment, **1**:4.1
warranties, **1**:4.2
Israel
acquisition agreement, **15**:4.1.1–4.1.3
generally, **15**:4
indemnities, **15**:4.2
risk assessment, **14**:4.3
management systems
Australia, **6**:4.5
Belgium, **7**:4.4
Germany, **3**:4.4
introduction, **1**:4.4
Netherlands, **5**:4.4–4.4.5
Norway, **16**:4.4
Sweden, **8**:4.3
Switzerland, **11**:4.1
United Kingdom, **4**:4.4
United States, **2**:4.5
Netherlands
corporate structure, **5**:4.6
financiers' role, **5**:4.3

Issue management – *contd*
Netherlands – *contd*
indemnities, **5**:4.2
insurance, **5**:4.5
management, **5**:4.4–4.4.5
risk assessment, **5**:4.1
warranties, **5**:4.2
Norway
corporate structure, **16**:4.6
financiers' role, **16**:4.3
indemnities, **16**:4.2
insurance, **16**:4.5
management systems, **16**:4.4
risk assessment, **16**:4.1
warranties, **16**:4.2
Portugal
financiers' role, **13**:4.3
indemnities, **13**:4.2
risk assessment, **13**:4.1
warranties, **13**:4.2
risk assessment
Australia, **6**:4.2
Austria, **10**:4.1.1–4.1.2
France, **12**:4.1
Greece, **14**:4.1
introduction, **1**:4.1
Israel, **14**:4.3
Netherlands, **5**:4.1
Norway, **16**:4.1
Portugal, **13**:4.1
Spain, **9**:4.1
Sweden, **8**:4.1
Switzerland, **11**:4.1
United Kingdom, **4**:4.1
United States, **2**:4.1
site assessment
United States, **2**:4.1
Spain
financiers' role, **9**:4.3
indemnities, **9**:4.2
insurance, **9**:4.5
management systems, **9**:4.4
risk assessment, **9**:4.1
warranties, **9**:4.2
Sweden
acquisition agreements, **8**:4.2
corporate structure, **8**:4.4
insurance, **8**:4.5
management systems, **8**:4.3
risk assessment, **8**:4.1
Switzerland
contractual provisions, **11**:4.4
due diligence, **11**:4.3
insurance, **11**:4.6
management systems, **11**:4.2
practical issues, **11**:4.5
risk assessment, **11**:4.1
United Kingdom
corporate structure, **4**:4.6
financiers' role, **4**:4.3
indemnities, **4**:4.2
insurance, **4**:4.5
management systems, **4**:4.4

Index

Issue management – *contd*
United Kingdom – *contd*
risk assessment, **4**:4.1
warranties, **4**:4.2
United States
escrow agreements, **2**:4.3
generally, **2**:4
indemnities, **2**:4.4
insurance, **2**:4.6
management systems, **2**:4.5
site assessment, **2**:4.1
warranties, **2**:4.2
warranties
Australia, **6**:4.3
Austria, **10**:4.2.1
France, **12**:4.2
Greece, **14**:4.2
introduction, **1**:4.2
Netherlands, **5**:4.2
Norway, **16**:4.2
Portugal, **13**:4.2
Spain, **9**:4.2
United Kingdom, **4**:4.2
United States, **2**:4.2

Judicial rulings
United States, **2**:1.6

Land contamination
Australia, **6**:2.4.1
Austria
civil liability, **10**:2.3.4
clean-up, **10**:2.3.3
introduction, **10**:2.3.1
old waste sites, **10**:2.3.2
Belgium
Brussels Metropolitan Region, **7**:2.5.2
Flemish Region, **7**:2.3.2
Walloon Region, **7**:2.4.2
France, **12**:2.2.1
generally, **1**:2.2
Germany, **3**:2.4
Greece, **14**:2.2
Israel, **15**:2.9
Netherlands
introduction, **5**:2.1.1
sale of contaminated property, **5**:2.1.3
soil protection, **5**:2.1.2
Norway, **16**:2.2.1
Portugal
generally, **13**:2.1
soil pollution, **13**:2.1.1
sub-soil, **13**:2.1.2
Spain, **9**:2.2
Sweden, **8**:2.1
Switzerland
restoration, **11**:2.3
soil protection, **11**:2.2
United Kingdom, **4**:2.1
United States
brownfield sites, **2**:2.1.3
CERCLA, **2**:2.1.1
oil pollution, **2**:2.1.5

Land contamination – *contd*
United States – *contd*
RCRA, **2**:2.1.2
remediation, **2**:2.1.3
underground storage tanks, **2**:2.1.7
Land use planning
Australia, **6**:2.4.9
Austria, **10**:2.7.1–2.7.2
Belgium
Brussels Metropolitan Region, **7**:2.5.3
Flemish Region, **7**:2.3.3
Walloon Region, , **7**:2.4.3
France, **12**:2.2.7
generally, **1**:2.7
Germany, **3**:2.5
Greece, **14**:2.6
Israel
impact studies, **15**:2.10.2
planning and building institutions, **15**:2.10.1
Netherlands, **5**:2.3.4
Norway, **16**:2.2.5
Portugal, **13**:2.7
Spain, **9**:2.7
Sweden, **8**:2.6
Switzerland, **11**:2.7
United Kingdom, **4**:2.7
United States, **2**:2.4
Leak reporting
United States, **2**:2.6.2
Legal system
Australia, **6**:1.2
Austria, **10**:1.1
Belgium, **7**:1.1
Germany, **3**:1.1
Israel
executive, **15**:1.1.2
generally, **15**:1.1
judiciary, **15**:1.1.3
legislature, **15**:1.1.1
Netherlands, **5**:1.2
Norway, **16**:1.1
Spain, **9**:1.1
Sweden, **8**:1.1
Switzerland, **11**:1.1
United Kingdom, **4**:1.1
United States, **2**:1.1–1.4.3
Lender's liability
Australia, **6**:3.5
Austria, **10**:3.4
Belgium, **7**:3.2.5
France, **12**:3.5
generally, **1**:3.5
Germany, **3**:2
Greece, **14**:3.4
Israel, **15**:3.6
Netherlands, **5**:3.5
Norway, **16**:3.2.7
Portugal, **13**:3.6
Spain, **9**:3.4
Sweden, **8**:3.5
Switzerland, **11**:3.4
United Kingdom, **4**:3.5
United States, **2**:3.8

Index

Liability
  administrative
    Austria, **10**:2.2.3, **10**:3.1.1
    Greece, **14**:3.1.1
  Australia
    financiers', **6**:3.5
    historic, **6**:3.2
    lender's, **6**:3.5
    off-site contamination, **6**:3.3
    principles of, **6**:3.1
  Austria
    administrative, **10**:2.2.3, **10**:3.1.1
    civil, **10**:2.3.4, **10**:3.1.2
    criminal, **10**:2.2.2
    directors', **10**:3.3
    financier's, **10**:3.4
    historic, **10**:3.2.1–3.2.2
    lender's, **10**:3.4
    managers', **10**:3.3
    principles of, **10**:3.1.1–3.1.2
  Belgium
    criminal, **7**:3.2.3
    directors', **7**:3.2.4
    financiers', **7**:3.2.5
    lender's, **7**:3.2.5
    principles of, **7**:3.2.1
    strict, **7**:3.2.2
  civil
    Austria, **10**:2.3.4, **10**:3.1.2
    Greece, **14**:3.1.1–3.1.2
    Israel, **15**:3.2
    Portugal, **13**:3.1
  criminal
    Austria, **10**:2.2.2
    Belgium, **7**:3.2.3
    Germany, **3**:3.1.3
    Greece, **14**:3.1.1–3.1.2
    Israel, **15**:3.1
    Portugal, **13**:3.2–3.2.8
    Spain, **9**:2.10
    Sweden, **8**:2.4.9
    Switzerland, **11**:3.3
    United States, **2**:2.7
  directors'
    Austria, **10**:3.3
    Belgium, **7**:3.2.4
    France, **12**:3.4
    Greece, **14**:3.3
    introduction, **1**:3.4
    Netherlands, **5**:3.4
    Norway, **16**:3.2.6
    Portugal, **13**:3.5
    Spain, **9**:3.3
    Sweden, **8**:3.4
    Switzerland, **11**:3.3
    United Kingdom, **4**:3.4
    United States, **2**:3.6
    Norway, **16**:3.2.7
    joint and several, **16**:3.2.4
    lender's, **16**:3.2.7
    managers', **16**:3.2.6
    parent company, **16**:3.2.5
    principles of, **16**:3.1–3.1.6

Liability – *contd*
  directors' – *contd*
    purchasers', **16**:3.2.8
    shareholders', **16**:3.2.5
    strict, **16**:3.2.10
  financiers'
    Australia, **6**:3.5
    Austria, **10**:3.4
    Belgium, **7**:3.2.5
    France, **12**:3.5
    Germany, **3**:2
    Greece, **14**:3.4
    introduction, **1**:3.5
    Israel, **15**:3.6
    Netherlands, **5**:3.5
    Norway, **16**:3.2.7
    Portugal, **13**:3.6
    Spain, **9**:3.4
    Sweden, **8**:3.5
    Switzerland, **11**:3.4
    United Kingdom, **4**:3.5
    United States, **2**:3.8
  France
    directors', **12**:3.4
    financiers', **12**:3.5
    historic, **12**:3.2
    lender's, **12**:3.5
    managers', **12**:3.4
    off-site, **12**:3.3
    principles of, **12**:3.1
  Germany
    corporate, **3**:4
    criminal, **3**:3.1.3
    generally, **3**:3.1
    historic, **3**:3
    lender's, **3**:2
    private, **3**:3.1
    public, **3**:3.1.2
  Greece
    administrative, **14**:3.1.1
    civil, **14**:3.1.1–3.1.2
    criminal, **14**:3.1.1–3.1.2
    directors', **14**:3.3
    financiers', **14**:3.4
    historic, **14**:3.2
    lender's, **14**:3.4
    principles of, **14**:3.1.1–3.1.2
    managers', **14**:3.3
    tortious, **14**:3.1.2
  historic
    Australia, **6**:3.2
    Austria, **10**:3.2.1–3.2.2
    France, **12**:3.2
    Germany, **3**:3
    Greece, **14**:3.2
    introduction, **1**:3.1
    Israel, **15**:3.4
    Netherlands, **5**:3.2
    Portugal, **13**:3.4
    Spain, **9**:3.2
    Sweden, **8**:3.2
    United Kingdom, **4**:3.2
    United States, **2**:3.3

Index

Liability – *contd*
  introduction
    directors', **1**:3.4
    financiers', **1**:3.5
    historic, **1**:3.1
    managers', **1**:3.4
  Israel
    civil, **15**:3.2
    criminal, **15**:3.1
    enforcement of, **15**:3.3–3.3.3
    financiers', **15**:3.6
    historic, **15**:3.4
    lender's, **15**:3.6
  lender's
    Australia, **6**:3.5
    Austria, **10**:3.4
    Belgium, **7**:3.2.5
    France, **12**:3.5
    Germany, **3**:2
    Greece, **14**:3.4
    introduction, **1**:3.5
    Israel, **15**:3.6
    Netherlands, **5**:3.5
    Norway, **16**:3.2.7
    Portugal, **13**:3.6
    Spain, **9**:3.4
    Sweden, **8**:3.5
    Switzerland, **11**:3.4
    United Kingdom, **4**:3.5
    United States, **2**:3.8
  managers'
    Austria, **10**:3.3
    France, **12**:3.4
    generally, **1**:3.4
    Greece, **14**:3.3
    Netherlands, **5**:3.4
    Norway, **16**:3.2.6
    Portugal, **13**:3.5
    Spain, **9**:3.3
    Sweden, **8**:3.4
    Switzerland, **11**:3.3
    United Kingdom, **4**:3.4
  Netherlands
    directors', **5**:3.4
    financiers', **5**:3.5
    generally, **5**:3.1
    historic, **5**:3.2
    lender's, **5**:3.5
    managers', **5**:3.4
    off-site contamination, **5**:3.3
    ownership of land, **5**:3.7
  Norway
    directors', **16**:3.2.6
    financiers', **16**:3.2.7
    joint and several, **16**:3.2.4
    lender's, **16**:3.2.7
    managers', **16**:3.2.6
    parent company, **16**:3.2.5
    principles of, **16**:3.1.1–3.1.6
    purchasers', **16**:3.2.8
    shareholders', **16**:3.2.5
    strict, **16**:3.2.10

Liability – *contd*
  off-site contamination
    Australia, **6**:3.3
    France, **12**:3.3
    Netherlands, **5**:3.3
    Sweden, **8**:3.3
    United Kingdom, **4**:3.3
  parent company
    Germany, **3**:4
    Norway, **16**:3.2.5
    United States, **2**:3.6
  Portugal
    civil, **13**:3.1
    criminal, **13**:3.2–3.2.8
    directors', **13**:3.5
    environmental, **13**:3.3
    financiers', **13**:3.6
    historic, **13**:3.4
    lender's, **13**:3.6
    managers', **13**:3.5
    shareholders', **13**:3.5
  shareholders'
    Norway, **16**:3.2.5
    Portugal, **13**:3.5
    United States, **2**:3.6
  Spain
    criminal, **9**:2.10
    directors', **9**:3.3
    financiers', **9**:3.4
    historic, **9**:3.2
    lender's, **9**:3.4
    managers', **9**:3.3
    principles of, **9**:3.1
  strict
    Belgium, **7**:3.2.2
    Norway, **16**:3.2.10
  successor
    United States, **2**:3.7
  Sweden
    criminal, **8**:2.4.9
    directors', **8**:3.4
    financier's, **8**:3.5
    historic, **8**:3.2
    lender's, **8**:3.5
    managers', **8**:3.4
    off-site, **8**:3.3
    principles of, **8**:3.1
  Switzerland
    criminal, **11**:3.3
    directors', **11**:3.3
    financiers', **11**:3.4
    lender's, **11**:3.4
    principles of, **11**:3.1
    managers', **11**:3.3
  tortious
    Greece, **14**:3.1.2
  United Kingdom
    directors', **4**:3.4
    financiers', **4**:3.5
    generally, **4**:3.1
    historic, **4**:3.2
    lender's, **4**:3.5
    managers', **4**:3.4

371

Index

Liability – *contd*
  United Kingdom – *contd*
    off-site contamination, **4**:3.3
  United States
    directors', **2**:3.6
    historic, **2**:3.3
    lender's, **2**:3.8
    parent company, **2**:3.6
    shareholder, **2**:3.6
    successor, **2**:3.7
Licence compliance
  Australia, **6**:2.3.2
  United Kingdom **1**:3.7
  United States, **2**:3.2
Licence transfer
  Australia, **6**:3.6
  Austria, **10**:3.5
  Belgium, **7**:3.3.2
  France, **12**:3.6
  generally, **1**:3.6
  Germany, **3**:5
  Greece, **14**:3.5
  Israel, **15**:3.5
  Netherlands, **5**:3.6
  Norway, **16**:3.4
  Portugal, **13**:3.7
  Spain, **9**:3.5
  Sweden, **8**:3.6
  United Kingdom, **4**:3.6
  United States, **2**:3.4
Local laws
  Australia, **6**:1.3.3
  Germany, **3**:1.1
  United States, **2**:1.5

Management systems (EMS)
  Australia, **6**:4.5
  Belgium, **7**:4.4
  generally, **1**:4.4
  Germany, **3**:4.4
  Netherlands
    certification, **5**:4.4.4
    generally, **5**:4.4.1
    reporting, **5**:4.4.3
  Norway, **16**:4.4
  Spain, **9**:4.4
  Sweden, **8**:4.3
  Switzerland, **11**:4.2
  United Kingdom, **4**:4.4
  United States, **2**:4.5
Managers' liability
  Austria, **10**:3.3
  France, **12**:3.4
  generally, **1**:3.4
  Greece, **14**:3.3
  Netherlands, **5**:3.4
  Norway, **16**:3.2.6
  Portugal, **13**:3.5
  Spain, **9**:3.3
  Sweden, **8**:3.4
  Switzerland, **11**:3.3
Marine pollution
  Australia, **6**:2.4.4

Merger and acquisitions transactions
  Australia
    atmospheric emissions, **6**:2.4.4
    common law liability, **6**:2.4.8
    general regulation, **6**:2.3–2.3.2
    hazardous substances, **6**:2.4.6
    introduction, **6**:2.1
    land contamination, **6**:2.4.1
    land use planning, **6**:2.4.9
    marine pollution, **6**:2.4.4
    noise, **6**:2.4.7
    recycling, **6**:2.4.5
    specific industry issues, **6**:2.5
    thresholds, **6**:2.2.1–2.2.2
    waste management, **6**:2.4.5
    water pollution, **6**:2.4.2
  Austria
    air pollution, **10**:2.5.1–2.5.5
    chemicals, **10**:2.8
    environmental information, **10**:2.12
    hazardous substances, **10**:2.8
    impact assessment, **10**:2.11
    land contamination, **10**:2.3.1–2.3.4
    land use planning, **10**:2.7.1–2.7.2
    noise, **10**:2.9
    nuisance, **10**:2.9
    offences, **10**:2.2.1–2.2.3
    other laws, **10**:2.10
    Trade Code licensing, **10**:2.1
    waste management, **10**:2.6
    water pollution, **10**:2.4
  Belgium
    Brussels Metropolitan Region, **7**:2.5.1–2.5.3
    federal laws, **7**:2.2
    Flemish Region, **7**:2.3.1–2.3.3
    generally, **7**:2.1
    Walloon Region, **7**:2.4.1–2.4.3
  France
    abstraction of water, **12**:2.2.3
    atmospheric emissions, **12**:2.2.5
    civil law principles, **12**:2.1–2.1.3
    discharges to water, **12**:2.2.3
    environmental laws, **12**:2–2.2.9
    generally, **12**:2
    hazardous substances, **12**:2.2.8
    integrated pollution control, **12**:2.2.4
    land contamination, **12**:2.2.1
    land use planning, **12**:2.2.7
    noise, **12**:2.2.9
    nuisance, **12**:2.2.9
    recycling, **12**:2.2.6
    waste management, **12**:2.2.6
    water pollution, **12**:2.2.2
  Germany
    emission control, **3**:2.1
    generally, **3**:2
    hazardous substances, **3**:2.6
    land contamination, **3**:2.4
    land use planning, **3**:2.5
    noise, **3**:2.1
    nuisance, **3**:2.1
    waste management, **3**:2.3
    water, **3**:2.2

Index

Merger and acquisitions transactions – *contd*
  Greece
    atmospheric emissions, **14**:2.4
    generally, **14**:2.1
    hazardous substances, **14**:2.7
    impact assessment, **14**:2.10
    land contamination, **14**:2.2
    land use planning, **14**:2.6
    noise emissions, **14**:2.8
    nuclear energy, **14**:2.9
    radioactive material, **14**:2.7
    radioactive waste, **14**:2.9
    recycling, **14**:2.5
    waste management, **14**:2.5
    water pollution, **14**:2.3
  Israel
    air pollution, **15**:2.7
    business licensing, **15**:2.8
    generally, **15**:2
    hazardous substances, **15**:2.2.1–2.2.5
    impact assessment, **15**:2.10.2
    land contamination, **15**:2.9
    land use planning, **15**:2.10.1–2.10.2
    noise, **15**:2.5.2
    nuisance, **15**:2.5.1–2.5.2
    radiation pollution, **15**:2.3–2.3.2
    sunlight, interference with, **15**:2.6
    taxes, **15**:2.11–2.11.2
    waste disposal, **15**:2.1.1–2.1.3
    water pollution, **15**:2.4–2.4.2
  Netherlands
    atmospheric emissions, **5**:2.3.2
    hazardous substances, **5**:2.3.5
    integrated pollution control, **5**:2.3.1
    land contamination, **5**:2.1.1–2.1.3
    land use planning, **5**:2.3.4
    noise, **5**:2.3.6
    nuisance, **5**:2.3.6
    sources, **5**:1.2
    waste management, **5**:2.3.3
    water contamination, **5**:2.2.1–2.2.3
  Norway
    atmospheric emissions, **16**:2.2.3
    hazardous substances, **16**:2.2.6–2.2.7
    land contamination, **16**:2.2.1
    land use planning, **16**:2.2.5
    noise, **16**:2.2.8
    nuisance, **16**:2.2.8
    pollution provisions, **16**:2.1.1–2.1.6
    radioactive material, **16**:2.2.6
    sanctions, **16**:2.3
    waste management, **16**:2.2.4
    water pollution, **16**:2.2.2
  Portugal
    abstraction of water, **13**:2.3
    atmospheric emissions, **13**:2.5
    discharges to water, **13**:2.3
    hazardous substances, **13**:2.8
    integrated pollution control, **13**:2.4
    land contamination, **13**:2.1–2.1.2
    land use planning, **13**:2.7
    miscellaneous, **13**:2.10
    noise, **13**:2.9

Merger and acquisitions transactions – *contd*
  Portugal – *contd*
    nuisance, **13**:2.9
    recycling, **13**:2.6
    waste management, **13**:2.6
    water pollution, **13**:2.2
  Spain
    abstraction of water, **9**:2.4–2.4.2
    atmospheric emissions, **9**:2.5
    civil offences, **9**:2.11
    classified activities licence, **9**:2.1
    criminal offences, **9**:2.10
    discharges to water, **9**:2.4–2.4.2
    generally, **9**:2
    hazardous substances, **9**:2.8
    land contamination, **9**:2.2
    land use planning, **9**:2.7
    noise, **9**:2.9
    radioactive material, **9**:2.8
    waste management, **9**:2.6
    water pollution, **9**:2.3–2.3.2
  Sweden
    abstraction of water, **8**:2.3
    chemical products, **8**:2.7
    discharge of water, **8**:2.3
    hazardous substances, **8**:2.7
    integrated pollution control, **8**:2.4–2.4.9
    land contamination, **8**:2.1
    land use planning, **8**:2.6
    waste management, **8**:2.5
    water pollution, **8**:2.2
  Switzerland
    air pollution, **11**:2.5
    disaster prevention, **11**:2.11
    environmental protection, **11**:2.1.1–2.1.5
    genetically modified organisms, **11**:2.12
    groundwater, **11**:2.4
    hazardous substances, **11**:2.8
    impact assessment, **11**:2.10
    land use planning, **11**:2.7
    noise abatement, **11**:2.9
    restoration, **11**:2.3
    risk management, **11**:2.11
    soil protection, **11**:2.2
    surface waters, **11**:2.4
    waste disposal, **11**:2.6
  United Kingdom
    abstraction of water, **4**:2.3
    atmospheric emissions, **4**:2.5
    discharges into water, **4**:2.3
    generally, **4**:2
    hazardous substances, **4**:2.8
    integrated pollution control, **4**:2.4
    land contamination, **4**:2.1
    land use planning, **4**:2.7
    noise, **4**:2.9
    nuisance, **4**:2.9
    recycling, **4**:2.6
    waste management, **4**:2.6
    water pollution, **4**:2.2
  United States
    air permits, **2**:2.1–2.2.6
    criminal liability, **2**:2.7

Index

Merger and acquisitions transactions – *contd*
  United States – *contd*
    environmental disclosure, **2**:2.6–2.6.5
    generally, **2**:2
    groundwater contamination, **2**:2.1–2.1.7
    land contamination, **2**:2.1–2.1.7
    land use planning, **2**:2.4
    noise, **2**:2.5
    nuisance, **2**:2.5
    waste management, **2**:2.3–2.3.4
    water contamination, **2**:2.1–2.1.7
    water permits, **2**:2.1–2.2.6

National Pollutant Discharge Elimination System (United States), **2**:2.1

Netherlands
  abstraction of water, **5**:2.2.3
  atmospheric emissions, **5**:2.3.2
  audit, **5**:4.4.2
  chemical substances, **5**:2.3.5
  conclusion
    legal developments, **5**:5.1
    practice developments, **5**:5.2
  directors' liability, **5**:3.4
  discharges to water, **5**:2.2.3
  environmental law
    atmospheric emissions, **5**:2.3.2
    hazardous substances, **5**:2.3.5
    integrated pollution control, **5**:2.3.1
    land contamination, **5**:2.1.1–2.1.3
    land use planning, **5**:2.3.4
    noise, **5**:2.3.6
    nuisance, **5**:2.3.6
    sources, **5**:1.2
    waste management, **5**:2.3.3
    water contamination, **5**:2.2.1–2.2.3
  environmental audit, **5**:4.4.2
  environmental management
    audit, **5**:4.4.2
    certification, **5**:4.4.4
    generally, **5**:4.4
    management system, **5**:4.4.1
    outline licences, **5**:4.4.5
    reporting, **5**:4.4.3
  environmental reporting, **5**:4.4.3
  financiers' liability, **5**:3.5
  financiers' role, **5**:4.3
  groundwater, **5**:2.2.3
  hazardous substances, **5**:2.3.5
  historic liability, principles of, **5**:3.2
  indemnities, **5**:4.2
  insurance, **5**:4.5
  integrated pollution control, **5**:2.3.1
  introduction
    generally, **5**:1.1
    regulatory authorities, **5**:1.3
    sources of law, **5**:1.2
  issue management
    corporate structure, **5**:4.6
    financiers' role, **5**:4.3
    indemnities, **5**:4.2
    insurance, **5**:4.5
    management, **5**:4.4–4.4.5

Netherlands – *contd*
  issue management – *contd*
    risk assessment, **5**:4.1
    warranties, **5**:4.2
  land contamination
    introduction, **5**:2.1.1
    sale of contaminated property, **5**:2.1.3
    soil protection, **5**:2.1.2
  land use planning, **5**:2.3.4
  lender's liability, **5**:3.5
  liability
    directors', **5**:3.4
    financiers', **5**:3.5
    generally, **5**:3.1
    historic, **5**:3.2
    lender's, **5**:3.5
    managers', **5**:3.4
    off-site contamination, **5**:3.3
    ownership of land, **5**:3.7
  licence transfer, **5**:3.6
  management system
    certification, **5**:4.4.4
    generally, **5**:4.4.1
    reporting, **5**:4.4.3
  managers' liability, **5**:3.4
  noise, **5**:2.3.6
  nuclear accidents, **5**:2.3.5
  nuisance, **5**:2.3.6
  off-site contamination
    hazardous material, **5**:3.3.1
    third party property, **5**:3.3.2
    waste management, **5**:3.3.3
  oil pollution, **5**:2.3.5
  radioactive material, **5**:2.3.5
  recycling, **5**:2.3.3
  risk assessment, **5**:4.1
  sources, **5**:1.2
  surface water, **5**:2.2.2
  transaction issues
    directors' liability, **5**:3.4
    financiers' liability, **5**:3.5
    historic liability, principles of, **5**:3.2
    lender's liability, **5**:3.5
    liability, principles of, **5**:3.1
    licence transfer, **5**:3.6
    managers' liability, **5**:3.4
    off-site contamination, **5**:3.3
    ownership of land, **5**:3.7
    permit transfer, **5**:3.6
  underwater soil, **5**:2.2.1
  warranties, **5**:4.2
  waste management, **5**:2.3.3
  water contamination
    abstraction of water, **5**:2.2.3
    discharges to water, **5**:2.2.3
    surface water, **5**:2.2.2
    underwater soil, **5**:2.2.1

Noise
  Australia, **6**:2.4.7
  Austria, **10**:2.9
  Belgium
    Brussels Metropolitan Region, **7**:2.5.3
    Flemish Region, **7**:2.3.3

Noise – *contd*
  Belgium – *contd*
    Walloon Region, **7**:2.4.3
  France, **12**:2.2.9
  Germany, **3**:2.1
  Greece, **14**:2.8
  Israel, **15**:2.5.2
  Netherlands, **5**:2.3.6
  Norway, **16**:2.2.8
  Portugal, **13**:2.9
  Spain, **9**:2.9
  Switzerland, **11**:2.9
  United Kingdom, **4**:2.9
  United States, **2**:2.5
Norway
  atmospheric emissions, **16**:2.2.3
  conclusion, **16**:5
  corporate structure, **16**:4.6
  directors' liability, **16**:3.2.6
  financiers' liability, **16**:3.2.7
  financiers' role, **16**:4.3
  hazardous substances
    storage, **16**:2.2.6
    transport, **16**:2.2.7
    use, **16**:2.2.6
  historic liability, **16**:3.3
  impact assessment, **16**:3.5.1–3.5.3
  indemnities, **16**:4.2
  insurance, **16**:4.5
  introduction
    legal system, **16**:1.1
    regulatory agencies, **16**:1.5
    regulatory system, **16**:1.2–1.4
    sources of law, **16**:1.2–1.4
  issue management
    corporate structure, **16**:4.6
    financiers' role, **16**:4.3
    indemnities, **16**:4.2
    insurance, **16**:4.5
    management systems, **16**:4.4
    risk assessment, **16**:4.1
    warranties, **16**:4.2
  land contamination, **16**:2.2.1
  land use planning, **16**:2.2.5
  legal system, **16**:1.1
  lender's liability, **16**:3.2.7
  liable persons
    compensation, **16**:3.2.3
    directors, **16**:3.2.6
    financiers, **16**:3.2.7
    generally, **16**:3.2.1
    joint and several liability, **16**:3.2.4
    lenders, **16**:3.2.7
    managers, **16**:3.2.6
    parent company, **16**:3.2.5
    preventive measures, **16**:3.2.2
    private agreements, **16**:3.2.9
    purchasers, **16**:3.2.8
    repairs, **16**:3.2.2
    shareholders, **16**:3.2.5
    strict liability, **16**:3.2.10

Norway – *contd*
  liability
    directors', **16**:3.2.6
    financiers', **16**:3.2.7
    joint and several, **16**:3.2.4
    lender's, **16**:3.2.7
    managers', **16**:3.2.6
    parent company, **16**:3.2.5
    principles of, **16**:3.1.1–3.1.6
    purchasers', **16**:3.2.8
    shareholders', **16**:3.2.5
    strict, **16**:3.2.10
  liability, principles of
    basis, **16**:3.1.3
    burden of proof, **16**:3.1.4
    extent, **16**:3.1.5
    generally, **16**:3.1
    miscellaneous regulations, **16**:3.1.6
    obligation to act, **16**:3.1.1
    relevant damage, **16**:3.1.2
  licence transfer, **16**:3.4
  management systems, **16**:4.4
  managers' liability, **16**:3.2.6
  merger and acquisition transactions
    atmospheric emissions, **16**:2.2.3
    hazardous substances, **16**:2.2.6–2.2.7
    land contamination, **16**:2.2.1
    land use planning, **16**:2.2.5
    noise, **16**:2.2.8
    nuisance, **16**:2.2.8
    pollution provisions, **16**:2.1.1–2.1.6
    radioactive material, **16**:2.2.6
    sanctions, **16**:2.3
    waste management, **16**:2.2.4
    water pollution, **16**:2.2.2
  noise, **16**:2.2.8
  nuisance, **16**:2.2.8
  parent company liability, **16**:3.2.5
  permit transfer, **16**:3.4
  pollution provisions
    generally, **16**:2.1.1
    lapse of licence, **16**:2.1.6
    licence, **16**:2.1.3
    pollution, **16**:2.1.2
    terms of licence, **16**:2.1.4
    variation of licence, **16**:2.1.5
  radioactive material, **16**:2.2.6
  regulatory agencies, **16**:1.5
  regulatory system
    EU law, **16**:1.2
    international treaties, **16**:1.4
    statute, **16**:1.3.1–1.3.6
  risk assessment, **16**:4.1
  shareholders' liability, **16**:3.2.5
  sources of law
    EU law, **16**:1.2
    international treaties, **16**:1.4
    statute, **16**:1.3.1–1.3.6
  strict liability, **16**:3.2.10
  transaction issues
    directors' liability, **16**:3.2.6
    financiers' liability, **16**:3.2.7
    historic liability, **16**:3.3

Index

Norway – *contd*
  transaction issues – *contd*
    impact assessment, **16**:3.5.1–3.5.3
    lender's liability, **16**:3.2.7
    liable persons, **16**:3.2.1–3.2.10
    liability, principles of, **16**:3.1–3.1.6
    licence transfer, **16**:3.4
    managers' liability, **16**:3.2.6
    parent company liability, **16**:3.2.5
    permit transfer, **16**:3.4
    principles of, **16**:3.1–**16**:3.1.6
    shareholders' liability, **16**:3.2.5
    strict liability, **16**:3.2.10
  warranties, **16**:4.2
  waste management, **16**:2.2.4
  water pollution, **16**:2.2.2
Nuclear accidents
  Netherlands, **5**:2.3.5
Nuclear energy
  Greece, **14**:2.9
Nuisance
  and see **Noise**
  Austria, **10**:2.9
  France, **12**:2.2.9
  Germany, **3**:2.1
  Israel
    generally, **15**:2.5.1
    noise, **15**:2.5.2
    smell, **15**:2.5.2
  Netherlands, **5**:2.3.6
  Norway, **16**:2.2.8
  Portugal, **13**:2.9
  Switzerland, **11**:3.2
  United Kingdom, **4**:2.9
  United States, **2**:2.5

Off-site contamination
  Australia, **6**:3.3
  France, **12**:3.3
  Netherlands
    hazardous material, **5**:3.3.1
    third party property, **5**:3.3.2
    waste management, **5**:3.3.3
  Sweden, **8**:3.3
  United Kingdom, **4**:3.3
  United States, **2**:3.2
Oil pollution
  Netherlands, **5**:2.3.5
  United States, **2**:2.1.5
Oil Pollution Act (United States), **2**:2.1.5
Ozone Transport Commission (United States), **2**:1.4.2

Parent company liability
  Norway, **16**:3.2.5
  United States, **2**:3.6
Permit transfer
  Australia, **6**:3.6
  Austria, **10**:3.5
  Belgium, **7**:3.3.2
  France, **12**:3.6
  generally, **1**:3.6
  Germany, **3**:5

Permit transfer – *contd*
  Greece, **14**:3.5
  Israel, **15**:3.5
  Norway, **16**:3.4
  Portugal, **13**:3.7
  Spain, **9**:3.5
  Sweden, **8**:3.6
  United Kingdom, **4**:3.6
  United States, **2**:3.4
Portugal
  abstraction of water, **13**:2.3
  atmospheric emissions, **13**:2.5
  conclusion, **13**:5
  criminal liability, **13**:3.2–3.2.8
  directors' liability, **13**:3.5
  discharges to water, **13**:2.3
  environmental liability, **13**:3.3
  financiers' liability, **13**:3.6
  financiers' role, **13**:4.3
  hazardous substances, **13**:2.8
  historic liability, **13**:3.4
  indemnities, **13**:4.2
  integrated pollution control, **13**:2.4
  introduction
    regulatory agencies, **13**:1.2.1–1.2.2
    sources of law, **13**:1.1
  issue management
    financiers' role, **13**:4.3
    indemnities, **13**:4.2
    risk assessment, **13**:4.1
    warranties, **13**:4.2
  land contamination
    generally, **13**:2.1
    soil pollution, **13**:2.1.1
    sub-soil, **13**:2.1.2
  land use planning, **13**:2.7
  lender's liability, **13**:3.6
  liability
    civil, **13**:3.1
    criminal, **13**:3.2–3.2.8
    directors', **13**:3.5
    environmental, **13**:3.3
    financiers', **13**:3.6
    historic, **13**:3.4
    lender's, **13**:3.6
    managers', **13**:3.5
    shareholders', **13**:3.5
  licence transfer, **13**:3.7
  managers' liability, **13**:3.5
  merger and acquisition transactions
    abstraction of water, **13**:2.3
    atmospheric emissions, **13**:2.5
    discharges to water, **13**:2.3
    hazardous substances, **13**:2.8
    integrated pollution control, **13**:2.4
    land contamination, **13**:2.1–2.1.2
    land use planning, **13**:2.7
    miscellaneous, **13**:2.10
    noise, **13**:2.9
    nuisance, **13**:2.9
    recycling, **13**:2.6
    waste management, **13**:2.6
    water pollution, **13**:2.2

Index

Portugal – *contd*
noise, **13**:2.9
nuisance, **13**:2.9
permit transfer, **13**:3.7
recycling, **13**:2.6
regulatory agencies, **13**:1.2.1–1.2.2
risk assessment, **13**:4.1
shareholders' liability, **13**:3.5
sources of law, **13**:1.1
transaction issues
  civil liability, **13**:3.1
  criminal liability, **13**:3.2–3.2.8
  directors' liability, **13**:3.5
  environmental liability, **13**:3.3
  financiers' liability, **13**:3.6
  generally, **13**:3
  historic liability, **13**:3.4
  lender's liability, **13**:3.6
  licence transfer, **13**:3.7
  managers' liability, **13**:3.5
  permit transfer, **13**:3.7
  shareholders' liability, **13**:3.5
warranties, **13**:4.2
waste management, **13**:2.6
water pollution, **13**:2.2

Radioactive material
and see **Hazardous materials**
Greece, **14**:2.7
Netherlands, **5**:2.3.5
Norway, **16**:2.2.6
Spain, **9**:2.8
United States, **2**:2.3.4
Radioactive waste
Greece, **14**:2.9
Radiation pollution
Israel
  generally, **15**:2.3
  ionizing radiation, **15**:2.3.1
  non-ionizing radiation, **15**:2.3.2
Recycling
Australia, **6**:2.4.5
France, **12**:2.2.6
Greece, **14**:2.5
Israel, **15**:2.1.2
Netherlands, **5**:2.3.3
Portugal, **13**:2.6
United Kingdom, **4**:2.6
United States, **2**:2.3.2
Regional laws
Belgium
  Brussels Metropolitan Region, **7**:2.5.1–2.5.3
  Flemish Region, **7**: 2.3.1–2.3.3
  generally, **7**:2.1
  Walloon Region, **7**:2.4.1–2.4.3
United States
  air quality management districts, **2**:1.4.3
  generally, **2**:1.4
  Ozone Transport Commission, **2**:1.4.2
  River Basin Commissions, **2**:1.4.1
Regulatory authorities
Austria, **10**:1.4
Belgium, **7**:1.2

Regulatory authorities – *contd*
France, **12**:1.1.3
Greece, **14**:1.2
Israel
  Environment Ministry, **15**:1.3.1
  Environment Patrolling, **15**:1.3.3
  Intra-Office Committee for Business Licensing, **15**:1.3.2
  Interior Ministry, **15**:1.3.7
  KKL, **15**:1.3.10
  local authorities, **15**:1.3.9
  National Planning and Building Board, **15**:1.3.8
  Poisonous Substances Unit, **15**:1.3.5
  Restoration of Rivers Administration, **15**:1.3.11
  Sea Pollution Unit, **15**:1.3.4
  Water Council, **15**:1.3.6
Netherlands, **5**:1.3
Norway, **16**:1.5
Portugal, **13**:1.2.1–1.2.2
Spain
  autonomous communities, **9**:1.4.2
  generally, **9**:1.4
  local authorities, **9**:1.4.3
  state, **9**:1.4.1
Sweden, **8**:1.3
United Kingdom, **4**:1.2
United States, **2**:1.8
Regulatory system
Australia, **6**:1.3–1.3.5
Austria, **10**:1.3
Belgium, **7**:1.1
France, **12**:1.1.1
Germany, **3**:1.2
Greece, **14**:1.1
Israel, **15**:1.2
Netherlands, **5**:1.2
Norway
  EU law, **16**:1.2
  international treaties, **16**:1.4
  statute, **16**:1.3.1–1.3.6
Spain, **9**:1.1
Sweden, **8**:1.2
Switzerland
  history, **11**:1.2
  structure, **11**:1.3
United Kingdom, **4**:1.1
United States, **2**:1.1–1.4.3
Remediation
Switzerland, **11**:2.3
United States, **2**:2.1.3
Reporting, environmental
Australia, **6**:4.6
Netherlands, **5**:4.4.3
Resource Conservation and Recovery Act (United States), **2**:2.1.2
Reuse of materials
France, **12**:2.2.6
Greece, **14**:2.5
Israel, **15**:2.1.2
Netherlands, **5**:2.3.3
Portugal, **13**:2.6

377

Index

Reuse of materials – *contd*
  United Kingdom, **4**:2.6
  United States, **2**:2.3.2
Risk assessment
  Australia, **6**:4.2
  Austria
    audits, **10**:4.1.2
    generally, **10**:4.1.1
  France, **12**:4.1
  generally, **1**:4.1
  Greece, **14**:4.1
  Israel, **15**:4.3
  Netherlands, **5**:4.1
  Norway, **16**:4.1
  Portugal, **13**:4.1
  Spain, **9**:4.1
  Sweden, **8**:4.1
  Switzerland, **11**:4.1
  United Kingdom, **4**:4.1
  United States , **2**:4.1
Risk management
  Switzerland, **11**:2.11
River Basin Commissions (United States), **2**:1.4.1

Scottish Environmental Protection Agency (United Kingdom), **4**:1.2
Securities laws, reporting under
  United States, **2**:2.6.4
Shareholders' liability
  Norway, **16**:3.2.5
  Portugal, **13**:3.5
  United States, **2**:3.6
Site assessment
  United States, **2**:4.1
Site contamination
  United States, **2**:3.1
Soil clean-up
  Austria, **10**:2.3.3
  Belgium, **7**:3.3.3
  Switzerland, **11**:2.2
Soil pollution
  and see **Land contamination**
  Belgium
    Brussels Metropolitan Region, **7**:2.5.2
    Flemish Region, **7**:2.3.2
    Walloon Region, **7**:2.4.2
  Switzerland, **11**:2.2
Soil testing
  Belgium, **7**:4.5
Solid waste
  United States, **2**:2.3.3
Sources of law
  France, **12**:1.1.2
  Netherlands, **5**:1.2
  Norway
    EU law, **16**:1.2
    international treaties, **16**:1.4
    statute, **16**:1.3.1–1.3.6
  Portugal, **13**:1.1
  Spain, **9**:1.3
  United Kingdom, **4**:1.1

Sources of law – *contd*
  United States
    federal laws, **2**:1.2–1.3.5
    judicial rulings, **2**:1.6
    local laws, **2**:1.5
    other, **2**:1.7
    overview, **2**:1.1
    regional laws, **2**:1.4–1.4.3
    regulatory agencies, **2**:1.8
Spain
  abstraction of water
    continental waters, **9**:2.3.1
    generally, **9**:2.3
    marine waters, **9**:2.3.2
  atmospheric emissions, **9**:2.5
  classified activities licence, **9**:2.1
  conclusion, **9**:5
  costs of compliance, **9**:3.6
  criminal liability, **9**:2.10
  directors' liability, **9**:3.3
  discharges to water
    continental waters, **9**:2.3.1
    generally, **9**:2.3
    marine waters, **9**:2.3.2
  financiers' liability, **9**:3.4
  financiers' role, **9**:4.3
  hazardous substances, **9**:2.8
  historic liability, **9**:3.2
  indemnities, **9**:4.2
  insurance, **9**:4.5
  introduction
    associate jurisdictions, **9**:1.2
    regulatory agencies, **9**:1.4–1.4.3
    regulatory system, **9**:1.1
    sources of law, **9**:1.3
  issue management
    financiers' role, **9**:4.3
    indemnities, **9**:4.2
    insurance, **9**:4.5
    management systems, **9**:4.4
    risk assessment, **9**:4.1
    warranties, **9**:4.2
  land contamination, **9**:2.2
  land use planning, **9**:2.7
  lender's liability, **9**:3.4
  liability
    criminal, **9**:2.10
    directors', **9**:3.3
    financiers', **9**:3.4
    historic, **9**:3.2
    lender's, **9**:3.4
    managers', **9**:3.3
    principles of, **9**:3.1
  licence transfer, **9**:3.5
  management systems, **9**:4.4
  managers' liability, **9**:3.3
  merger and acquisition transactions
    abstraction of water, **9**:2.4–2.4.2
    atmospheric emissions, **9**:2.5
    civil offences, **9**:2.11
    classified activities licence, **9**:2.1
    criminal offences, **9**:2.10
    discharges to water, **9**:2.4–2.4.2

Index

Spain – *contd*
  merger and acquisition transactions – *contd*
    generally, **9**:2
    hazardous substances, **9**:2.8
    land contamination, **9**:2.2
    land use planning, **9**:2.7
    noise, **9**:2.9
    radioactive material, **9**:2.8
    waste management, **9**:2.6
    water pollution, **9**:2.3–2.3.2
  noise, **9**:2.9
  permit transfer, **9**:3.5
  radioactive material, **9**:2.8
  regulatory agencies
    autonomous communities, **9**:1.4.2
    generally, **9**:1.4
    local authorities, **9**:1.4.3
    state, **9**:1.4.1
  regulatory system, **9**:1.1
  risk assessment, **9**:4.1
  sources of law, **9**:1.3
  transaction issues
    costs of compliance, **9**:3.6
    directors' liability, **9**:3.3
    financiers' liability, **9**:3.4
    historic liability, **9**:3.2
    lender's liability, **9**:3.4
    liability, principles of, **9**:3.1
    licence transfer, **9**:3.5
    managers' liability, **9**:3.3
    permit transfer, **9**:3.5
  warranties, **9**:4.2
  waste management, **9**:2.6
  water pollution
    continental waters, **9**:2.3.1
    generally, **9**:2.3
    marine waters, **9**:2.3.2
Spill reporting
  United States, **2**:2.6.2
State laws
  Australia, **6**:1.3.2
  Germany, **3**:1.1
  United States
    contamination reporting, **2**:1.3.2
    enforcement, **2**:1.3.5
    generally, **2**:1.3
    permit procedures, **2**:1.3.4
    remediation standards, **2**:1.3.3
    transfer notification, **2**:1.3.1
Stormwater permits
  United States, **2**:2.2.2
Strict liability
  Belgium, **7**:3.2.2
  Norway, **16**:3.2.10
Successor liability
  United States, **2**:3.7
Surface water
  Netherlands, **5**:2.2.2
  Switzerland, **11**:2.4
Sweden
  abstraction of water, **8**:2.3
  chemical products, **8**:2.7
  conclusion, **8**:5

Sweden – *contd*
  costs of compliance, **8**:3.7
  criminal liability, **8**:2.4.9
  directors' liability, **8**:3.4
  discharge of water, **8**:2.3
  financier's liability, **8**:3.5
  hazardous substances, **8**:2.7
  historic liability, **8**:3.2
  insurance, **8**:4.5
  integrated pollution control
    best location, **8**:2.4.5
    best possible technology, **8**:2.4.4
    burden of proof, **8**:2.4.1
    criminal liability, **8**:2.4.9
    generally, **8**:2.4
    knowledge, **8**:2.4.2
    precautions, **8**:2.4.3
    product choice, **8**:2.4.7
    reasonableness, **8**:2.4.8
    resource management, **8**:2.4.6
  introduction
    legal system, **8**:1.1
    regulatory agencies, **8**:1.3
    regulatory system, **8**:1.2
  issue management
    acquisition agreements, **8**:4.2
    corporate structure, **8**:4.4
    insurance, **8**:4.5
    management systems, **8**:4.3
    risk assessment, **8**:4.1
  land contamination, **8**:2.1
  land use planning, **8**:2.6
  lender's liability, **8**:3.5
  liability
    directors', **8**:3.4
    financier's, **8**:3.5
    historic, **8**:3.2
    lender's, **8**:3.5
    managers', **8**:3.4
    off-site, **8**:3.3
    principles of, **8**:3.1
  licence transfer, **8**:3.6
  management systems, **8**:4.3
  managers' liability, **8**:3.4
  merger and acquisition transactions
    abstraction of water, **8**:2.3
    chemical products, **8**:2.7
    discharge of water, **8**:2.3
    hazardous substances, **8**:2.7
    integrated pollution control, **8**:2.4–2.4.9
    land contamination, **8**:2.1
    land use planning, **8**:2.6
    waste management, **8**:2.5
    water pollution, **8**:2.2
  off-site contamination, **8**:3.3
  risk assessment, **8**:4.1
  transaction issues
    costs of compliance, **8**:3.7
    directors' liability, **8**:3.4
    financier's liability, **8**:3.5
    historic liability, **8**:3.2
    lender's liability, **8**:3.5
    liability, principles of, **8**:3.1

Index

Sweden – *contd*
  transaction issues – *contd*
    licence transfer, **8**:3.6
    managers' liability, **8**:3.4
    off-site contamination, **8**:3.3
    permit transfer, **8**:3.6
  waste management, **8**:2.5
  water
    abstraction, **8**:2.3
    discharge, **8**:2.3
    pollution, **8**:2.2
Switzerland
  air pollution, **11**:2.5
  conclusion, **11**:5
  criminal liability, **11**:3.3
  directors' liability, **11**:3.3
  disaster prevention, **11**:2.11
  due diligence, **11**:4.3
  environmental protection
    co-operation principle, **11**:2.1.4
    generally, **11**:2.1.1
    polluter pays principle, **11**:2.1.3
    pollution control system, **11**:2.1.5
    prevention principle, **11**:2.1.2
  financiers' liability, **11**:3.4
  genetically modified organisms, **11**:2.12
  groundwater, **11**:2.4
  hazardous substances, **11**:2.8
  impact assessment, **11**:2.10
  insurance, **11**:4.6
  introduction
    effect of regulation, **11**:1.4
    legal system, **11**:1.1
    regulatory system, **11**:1.2–1.3
  issue management
    contractual provisions, **11**:4.4
    due diligence, **11**:4.3
    insurance, **11**:4.6
    management systems, **11**:4.2
    practical issues, **11**:4.5
    risk assessment, **11**:4.1
  land contamination
    restoration, **11**:2.3
    soil protection, **11**:2.2
  land use planning, **11**:2.7
  legal system, **11**:1.1
  lender's liability, **11**:3.4
  liability
    criminal, **11**:3.3
    directors', **11**:3.3
    financiers', **11**:3.4
    lender's, **11**:3.4
    principles of, **11**:3.1
    managers', **11**:3.3
  management systems, **11**:4.2
  managers' liability, **11**:3.3
  merger and acquisition transactions
    air pollution, **11**:2.5
    disaster prevention, **11**:2.11
    environmental protection, **11**:2.1.1–2.1.5
    genetically modified organisms, **11**:2.12
    groundwater, **11**:2.4
    hazardous substances, **11**:2.8

Switzerland – *contd*
  merger and acquisition transactions – *contd*
    impact assessment, **11**:2.10
    land use planning, **11**:2.7
    noise abatement, **11**:2.9
    restoration, **11**:2.3
    risk management, **11**:2.11
    soil protection, **11**:2.2
    surface waters, **11**:2.4
    waste disposal, **11**:2.6
  noise abatement, **11**:2.9
  nuisance, **11**:3.2
  restoration, **11**:2.3
  regulatory system
    history, **11**:1.2
    structure, **11**:1.3
  risk assessment, **11**:4.1
  risk management, **11**:2.11
  soil protection, **11**:2.2
  surface waters, **11**:2.4
  transaction issues
    criminal liability, **11**:3.3
    directors' liability, **11**:3.3
    financiers' liability, **11**:3.4
    lender's liability, **11**:3.4
    liability, principles of, **11**:3.1
    managers' liability, **11**:3.3
    nuisance, **11**:3.2
  waste disposal, **11**:2.6

Tax concessions
  Australia, **6**:3.8
Third party rights, **1**:1.3
Tortious liability
  Greece, **14**:3.1.2
Transaction issues
  administrative liability
    Austria, **10**:2.2.3
    Greece, **14**:3.1.1
  Australia
    costs of compliance, **6**:3.7
    financiers' liability, **6**:3.5
    generally, **6**:3
    historic liability, **6**:3.2
    lender's liability, **6**:3.5
    liability, principles of, **6**:3.1
    licence transfer, **6**:3.6
    off-site contamination, **6**:3.3
    permit transfer, **6**:3.6
    specific industry issues, **6**:3.9
    tax concessions, **6**:3.8
  Austria
    directors' liability, **10**:3.3
    financier's liability, **10**:3.4
    historic liability, **10**:3.2.1–3.2.2
    lender's liability, **10**:3.4
    liability, principles of, **10**:3.1.1–3.1.2
    licence transfer, **10**:3.5
    managers' liability, **10**:3.3
    permit transfer, **10**:3.5
  Belgium
    criminal liability, **7**:3.2.3
    directors' liability, **7**:3.2.4

Transaction issues – *contd*
  Belgium – *contd*
    financiers' liability, **7**:3.2.5
    generally, **7**:3.1
    lender's liability, **7**:3.2.5
    liability, principles of, **7**:3.2.1
    permit transfer, **7**:3.3.2
    strict liability, **7**:3.2.2
  corporate veil, **1**:3.3
  costs of compliance
    Greece, **14**:3.6
    Spain, **9**:3.6
    Sweden, **8**:3.7
    United Kingdom, **4**:3.7
  directors' liability
    Austria, **10**:3.3
    Belgium, **7**:3.2.4
    France, **12**:3.4
    generally, **1**:3.4
    Greece, **14**:3.3
    Netherlands, **5**:3.4
    Norway, **16**:3.2.6
    Portugal, **13**:3.5
    Spain, **9**:3.3
    Sweden, **8**:3.4
    Switzerland, **11**:2.4, **11**:3.3
    United Kingdom, **4**:3.4
    United States, **2**:3.6
  financiers' liability
    Australia, **6**:3.5
    Austria, **10**:3.4
    Belgium, **7**:3.2.5
    France, **12**:3.5
    generally, **1**:3.5
    Germany, **3**:2
    Greece, **14**:3.4
    Israel, **15**:3.6
    Netherlands, **5**:3.5
    Norway, **16**:3.2.7
    Portugal, **13**:3.6
    Spain, **9**:3.4
    Sweden, **8**:3.5
    Switzerland, **11**:3.4
    United Kingdom, **4**:3.5
    United States, **2**:3.8
  foreign investment, **1**:3.2
  France
    directors' liability, **12**:3.4
    financiers' liability, **12**:3.5
    historic liability, **12**:3.2
    lender's liability, **12**:3.5
    liability, principles of, **12**:3.1
    licence transfer, **12**:3.6
    managers' liability, **12**:3.4
    off-site contamination, **12**:3.3
    permit transfer, **12**:3.6
  Germany
    corporate obligations, **3**:4
    historic liability, **3**:3
    lender's liability, **3**:2
    liability, **3**:3.1–3.1.3
    permit transfer, **3**:5

Transaction issues – *contd*
  Greece
    administrative liability, **14**:3.1.1
    civil liability, **14**:3.1.1–3.1.2
    costs of compliance, **14**:3.6
    criminal liability, **14**:3.1.1–3.1.2
    directors' liability, **14**:3.3
    financiers' liability, **14**:3.4
    generally, **14**:3
    historic liability, **14**:3.2
    lender's liability, **14**:3.4
    liability, principles of, **14**:3.1.1–3.1.2
    licence transfer, **14**:3.5
    managers' liability, **14**:3.3
    permit transfer, **14**:3.5
    tort liability, **14**:3.1.2
  historic liability
    Australia, **6**:3.2
    Austria, **10**:3.2.1–3.2.2
    France, **12**:3.2
    generally, **1**:3.1
    Greece, , **14**:3.2
    Israel, **15**:3.4
    Norway, **16**:3.3
    Portugal, **13**:3.4
    Spain, **9**:3.2
    Sweden, **8**:3.2
    United Kingdom, **4**:3.2
    United States, **2**:3.3
  introduction
    corporate veil, **1**:3.3
    directors' liability, **1**:3.4
    financiers' liability, **1**:3.5
    foreign investment, **1**:3.2
    historical liability, principles of, **1**:3.1
    managers' liability, **1**:3.4
    ongoing compliance, **1**:3.7
    permit transfer, **1**:3.6
  Israel
    civil liability, **15**:3.2
    criminal liability, **15**:3.1
    enforcement of liability, **15**:3.3–3.3.3
    financiers' liability, **15**:3.6
    generally, **15**:3
    historic liability, **15**:3.4
    lender's liability, **15**:3.6
    licence transfer, **15**:3.5
    permit transfer, **15**:3.5
  lender's liability
    Australia, **6**:3.5
    Austria, **10**:3.4
    Belgium, **7**:3.2.5
    France, **12**:3.5
    generally, **1**:3.5
    Germany, **3**:2
    Greece, **14**:3.4
    Israel, **15**:3.6
    Netherlands, **5**:3.5
    Norway, **16**:3.2.7
    Portugal, **13**:3.6
    Spain, **9**:3.4
    Sweden, **8**:3.5
    Switzerland, **11**:3.4

381

Index

Transaction issues – *contd*
  lenders' liability – *contd*
    United Kingdom, **4**:3.5
    United States, **2**:3.8
  managers' liability
    Austria, **10**:3.3
    France, **12**:3.4
    generally, **1**:3.4
    Greece, **14**:3.3
    Netherlands, **5**:3.4
    Norway, **16**:3.2.6
    Portugal, **13**:3.5
    Spain, **9**:3.3
    Sweden, **8**:3.4
    Switzerland, **11**:3.3
    United Kingdom, **4**:3.4
  Netherlands
    directors' liability, **5**:3.4
    financiers' liability, **5**:3.5
    historic liability, principles of, **5**:3.2
    lender's liability, **5**:3.5
    liability, principles of, **5**:3.1
    licence transfer, **5**:3.6
    managers' liability, **5**:3.4
    off-site contamination, **5**:3.3
    ownership of land, **5**:3.7
    permit transfer, **5**:3.6
  Norway
    directors' liability, **16**:3.2.6
    financiers' liability, **16**:3.2.7
    historic liability, **16**:3.3
    impact assessment, **16**:3.5.1–3.5.3
    lender's liability, **16**:3.2.7
    liable persons, **16**:3.2.1–3.2.10
    liability, principles of, **16**:3.1–3.1.6
    licence transfer, **16**:3.4
    managers' liability, **16**:3.2.6
    parent company liability, **16**:3.2.5
    permit transfer, **16**:3.4
    principles of, **16**:3.1–3.1.6
    shareholders' liability, **16**:3.2.5
    strict liability, **16**:3.2.10
  off-site contamination
    Australia, **6**:3.3
    France, **12**:3.3
    Netherlands, **5**:3.3
    Sweden, **8**:3.3
    United Kingdom, **4**:3.3
  ongoing compliance,
    United Kingdom **1**:3.7
    United States, **2**:3.2
  parent company liability
    Norway, **16**:3.2.5
    United States, **2**:3.6
  permit transfer
    Australia, **6**:3.6
    Austria, **10**:3.5
    Belgium, **7**:3.3.2
    France, **12**:3.6
    generally, **1**:3.6
    Germany, **3**:5
    Greece, **14**:3.5
    Israel, **15**:3.5

Transaction issues – *contd*
  permit transfer – *contd*
    Netherlands, **5**:3.6
    Norway, **16**:3.4
    Portugal, **13**:3.7
    Spain, **9**:3.5
    Sweden, **8**:3.6
    United Kingdom, **4**:3.6
    United States, **2**:3.4
  Portugal
    civil liability, **13**:3.1
    criminal liability, **13**:3.2–3.2.8
    directors' liability, **13**:3.5
    environmental liability, **13**:3.3
    financiers' liability, **13**:3.6
    generally, **13**:3
    historic liability, **13**:3.4
    lender's liability, **13**:3.6
    licence transfer, **13**:3.7
    managers' liability, **13**:3.5
    permit transfer, **13**:3.7
    shareholders' liability, **13**:3.5
  shareholders' liability
    Norway, **16**:3.2.5
    Portugal, **13**:3.5
    United States, **2**:3.6
  Spain
    costs of compliance, **9**:3.6
    directors' liability, **9**:3.3
    financiers' liability, **9**:3.4
    historic liability, **9**:3.2
    lender's liability, **9**:3.4
    liability, principles of,
      9:3.1
    licence transfer, **9**:3.5
    managers' liability, **9**:3.3
    permit transfer, **9**:3.5
  strict liability
    Belgium, **7**:3.2.2
    Norway, **16**:3.2.10
  Sweden
    costs of compliance, **8**:3.7
    directors' liability, **8**:3.4
    financier's liability, **8**:3.5
    historic liability, **8**:3.2
    lender's liability, **8**:3.5
    liability, principles of, **8**:3.1
    licence transfer, **8**:3.6
    managers' liability, **8**:3.4
    off-site contamination, **8**:3.3
    permit transfer, **8**:3.6
  Switzerland
    criminal liability, **11**:3.3
    directors' liability, **11**:3.3
    financiers' liability, **11**:3.4
    lender's liability, **11**:3.4
    liability, principles of, **11**:3.1
    managers' liability, **11**:3.3
    nuisance, **11**:3.2
  tax concessions
    Australia, **6**:3.8
  tort liability
    Greece, **14**:3.1.2

Transaction issues – *contd*
  United Kingdom
    costs of compliance, **4**:3.7
    directors' liability, **4**:3.4
    financiers' liability, **4**:3.5
    generally, **4**:3
    historic liability, **4**:3.2
    lender's liability, **4**:3.5
    liability, principles of, **4**:3.1
    licence transfer, **4**:3.6
    managers' liability, **4**:3.4
    off-site contamination, **4**:3.3
    permit transfer, **4**:3.6
  United States
    change-in-law risks, **2**:3.5
    directors' liability, **2**:3.6
    generally, **2**:3
    historical non-compliance liability, **2**:3.3
    lender's liability, **2**:3.8
    off-site contamination, **2**:3.2
    parent company liability, **2**:3.6
    permit restrictions, **2**:3.4
    shareholder liability, **2**:3.6
    site contamination, **2**:3.1
    successor liability, **2**:3.7
Transfer notifications
  United States, **2**:2.6.5

Underground storage tanks
  United States, **2**:2.1.7
Underwater soil
  Netherlands, **5**:2.2.1
United Kingdom
  abstraction of water, **4**:2.3
  atmospheric emissions, **4**:2.5
  conclusion, **4**:5
  contamination
    land, **4**:2.1
    water, **4**:2.2
  directors' liability, **4**:3.4
  discharges into water, **4**:2.3
  environmental law
    enforcement, **4**:1.2
    generally, **4**:1
    origins of law, **4**:1.1
  financiers' liability, **4**:3.5
  historic liability, **4**:3.2
  indemnities, **4**:4.2
  insurance, **4**:4.5
  integrated pollution control, **4**:2.4
  introduction
    generally, **4**:1
    origins of law, **4**:1.1
    regulatory agencies, **4**:1.2
  issue management
    corporate structure, **4**:4.6
    financiers' role, **4**:4.3
    indemnities, **4**:4.2
    insurance, **4**:4.5
    management systems, **4**:4.4
    risk assessment, **4**:4.1
    warranties, **4**:4.2
  land contamination, **4**:2.1

United Kingdom – *contd*
  land use planning, **4**:2.7
  liability
    directors', **4**:3.4
    financiers', **4**:3.5
    generally, **4**:3.1
    historic, **4**:3.2
    lender's, **4**:3.5
    managers', **4**:3.4
    off-site, **4**:3.3
  lender's liability, **4**:3.5
  licence transfer, **4**:3.6
  management systems, **4**:4.4
  managers' liability, **4**:3.4
  merger and acquisition transactions
    abstraction of water, **4**:2.3
    atmospheric emissions, **4**:2.5
    discharges into water, **4**:2.3
    generally, **4**:2
    hazardous substances, **4**:2.8
    integrated pollution control, **4**:2.4
    land contamination, **4**:2.1
    land use planning, **4**:2.7
    noise, **4**:2.9
    nuisance, **4**:2.9
    recycling, **4**:2.6
    waste management, **4**:2.6
    water pollution, **4**:2.2
  noise, **4**:2.9
  nuisance, **4**:2.9
  off-site contamination, **4**:3.3
  permit transfer, **4**:3.6
  recycling, **4**:2.6
  risk assessment, **4**:4.1
  transaction issues
    costs of compliance, **4**:3.7
    directors' liability, **4**:3.4
    financiers' liability, **4**:3.5
    generally, **4**:3
    historic liability, **4**:3.2
    lender's liability, **4**:3.5
    liability, principles of, **4**:3.1
    licence transfer, **4**:3.6
    managers' liability, **4**:3.4
    off-site contamination, **4**:3.3
    permit transfer, **4**:3.6
  warranties, **4**:4.2
  waste management, **4**:2.6
  water
    abstraction, **4**:2.3
    discharges, **4**:2.3
    pollution, **4**:2.2
United States of America
  acid rain permits, **2**:2.2.4
  air compliance reporting, **2**:2.6.1
  air permits
    acid rain permits, **2**:2.2.4
    federal permits, **2**:2.2.3
    generally, **2**:2
    local permits, **2**:2.2.6
    operating permits, **2**:2.2.5
    state permits, **2**:2.2.6
  air quality management districts, **2**:1.4.3

Index

United States of America – *contd*
  brownfield sites, **2**:2.1.3
  change-in-law risks, **2**:3.5
  chemical usage reporting, **2**:2.6.3
  conclusions, **2**:5
  consistency of programmes
    contamination reporting, **2**:1.3.2
    enforcement, **2**:1.3.5
    generally, **2**:1.3
    permit procedures, **2**:1.3.4
    remediation standards, **2**:1.3.3
    transfer notification, **2**:1.3.1
  contamination
    brownfield sites, **2**:2.1.3
    CERCLA, **2**:2.1.1
    groundwater quality, **2**:2.1.4
    oil pollution, **2**:2.1.5
    RCRA, **2**:2.1.2
    remediation, **2**:2.1.3
    underground storage tanks, **2**:2.1.7
    water, **2**:2.1.6
  criminal liability, **2**:2.7
  directors' liability, **2**:3.6
  environmental disclosure
    air compliance reporting, **2**:2.6.1
    chemical usage reporting, **2**:2.6.3
    generally, **2**:2.6
    leak reporting, **2**:2.6.2
    securities laws, under, **2**:2.6.4
    spill reporting, **2**:2.6.2
    transfer notifications, **2**:2.6.5
    water compliance reporting, **2**:2.6.1
  escrow agreements, **2**:4.3
  federal laws
    approved programmes, **2**:1.2.1
    consistency of programmes, **2**:1.3–1.3.5
    enforcement, **2**:1.2.3
    generally, **2**:1.2
    non-conforming plans, **2**:1.2.2
    other plans, **2**:1.2.4
  financiers' liability, **2**:3.8
  groundwater contamination
    CERCLA, **2**:2.1.1
    generally, **2**:2.1.4
    oil pollution, **2**:2.1.5
    RCRA, **2**:2.1.2
    remediation, **2**:2.1.3
    underground storage tanks, **2**:2.1.7
  hazardous waste, **2**:2.3.1
  historical liability, **2**:3.3
  indemnities, **2**:4.4
  insurance, **2**:4.6
  introduction
    consistency of programmes, **2**:1.3–1.3.5
    federal laws, **2**:1.2–1.2.4
    judicial rulings, **2**:1.6
    local laws, **2**:1.5
    other sources, **2**:1.7
    overview, **2**:1.1
    regional laws, **2**:1.4–1.4.3
    regulatory agencies, **2**:1.8

United States of America – *contd*
  issue management
    escrow agreements, **2**:4.3
    generally, **2**:4
    indemnities, **2**:4.4
    insurance, **2**:4.6
    management systems, **2**:4.5
    site assessment, **2**:4.1
    warranties, **2**:4.2
  judicial rulings, **2**:1.6
  land contamination
    brownfield sites, **2**:2.1.3
    CERCLA, **2**:2.1.1
    oil pollution, **2**:2.1.5
    RCRA, **2**:2.1.2
    remediation, **2**:2.1.3
    underground storage tanks, **2**:2.1.7
  land use planning, **2**:2.4
  leak reporting, **2**:2.6.2
  lender's liability, **2**:3.8
  liability
    directors', **2**:3.6
    historical, **2**:3.3
    lender's, **2**:3.8
    parent company, **2**:3.6
    shareholder, **2**:3.6
    successor, **2**:3.7
  local laws, **2**:1.5
  management systems, **2**:4.5
  merger and acquisitions transactions
    air permits, **2**:2.1–2.2.6
    criminal liability, **2**:2.7
    environmental disclosure, **2**:2.6–2.6.5
    generally, **2**:2
    groundwater contamination, **2**:2.1–2.1.7
    land contamination, **2**:2.1–2.1.7
    land use planning, **2**:2.4
    noise, **2**:2.5
    nuisance, **2**:2.5
    waste management, **2**:2.3–2.3.4
    water contamination, **2**:2.1–2.1.7
    water permits, **2**:2.1–2.2.6
  noise, **2**:2.5
  nuisance, **2**:2.5
  off-site contamination, **2**:3.2
  oil pollution, **2**:2.1.5
  other sources, **2**:1.7
  overview, **2**:1.1
  Ozone Transport Commission, **2**:1.4.2
  parent company liability, **2**:3.6
  permit restrictions, **2**:3.4
  radioactive material, **2**:2.3.4
  recycled materials, **2**:2.3.2
  regional laws
    air quality management districts, **2**:1.4.3
    generally, **2**:1.4
    Ozone Transport Commission, **2**:1.4.2
    River Basin Commissions, **2**:1.4.1
  regulatory agencies, **2**:1.8
  remediation, **2**:2.1.3
  River Basin Commissions, **2**:1.4.1
  securities laws, reporting under, **2**:2.6.4
  shareholder liability, **2**:3.6

Index

United States of America – *contd*
site assessment, **2**:4.1
site contamination, **2**:3.1
solid waste, **2**:2.3.3
sources of law
  federal laws, **2**:1.2–1.3.5
  judicial rulings, **2**:1.6
  local laws, **2**:1.5
  other, **2**:1.7
  overview, **2**:1.1
  regional laws, **2**:1.4–1.4.3
  regulatory agencies, **2**:1.8
spill reporting, **2**:2.6.2
state laws
  contamination reporting, **2**:1.3.2
  enforcement, **2**:1.3.5
  generally, **2**:1.3
  permit procedures, **2**:1.3.4
  remediation standards, **2**:1.3.3
  transfer notification, **2**:1.3.1
stormwater permits, **2**:2.2.2
successor liability, **2**:3.7
transaction issues
  change-in-law risks, **2**:3.5
  directors' liability, **2**:3.6
  generally, **2**:3
  historical non-compliance liability, **2**:3.3
  lender's liability, **2**:3.8
  off-site contamination, **2**:3.2
  parent company liability, **2**:3.6
  permit restrictions, **2**:3.4
  shareholder liability, **2**:3.6
  site contamination, **2**:3.1
  successor liability, **2**:3.7
transfer notifications, **2**:2.6.5
underground storage tanks, **2**:2.1.7
warranties, **2**:4.2
waste management
  hazardous waste, **2**:2.3.1
  radioactive material, **2**:2.3.4
  recycled materials, **2**:2.3.2
  solid waste, **2**:2.3.3
water contamination
  CERCLA, **2**:2.1.1
  generally, **2**:2.1.6
  oil pollution, **2**:2.1.5
  RCRA, **2**:2.1.2
  remediation, **2**:2.1.3
  underground storage tanks, **2**:2.1.7
water compliance reporting, **2**:2.6.1
water permits
  generally, **2**:2
  NPDES, **2**:2.2.1
  stormwater permits, **2**:2.2.2

Walloon Region
access to information, **7**:2.4.3
environmental care, **7**:2.4.3
groundwater pollution, **7**:2.4.2, **7**:2.4.3
impact assessment, **7**:2.4.3
operating permits, **7**:2.4.1
land use planning, **7**:2.4.3

Walloon Region – *contd*
noise, **7**:2.4.3
soil pollution, **7**:2.4.2
waste management, **7**:2.4.3
water pollution, **7**:2.4.3
Warranties
Australia, **6**:4.3
France, **12**:4.2
generally, **1**:4.2
Greece, **14**:4.2
Netherlands, **5**:4.2
Norway, **16**:4.2
Portugal, **13**:4.2
United Kingdom, **4**:4.2
United States, **2**:4.2
Waste disposal
Switzerland, **11**:2.6
Waste management
Australia, **6**:2.4.5
Austria, **10**:2.6
Belgium
  Brussels Metropolitan Region, **7**:2.5.3
  Flemish Region, **7**:2.3.3
  Walloon Region, **7**:2.4.3
France, **12**:4.2, **12**:2.2.6
generally, **1**:2.6
Germany, **3**:2.3
Greece, **14**:2.5
Netherlands, **5**:2.3.3
Norway, **16**:2.2.4
Portugal, **13**:2.6
Spain, **9**:2.6
Sweden, **8**:2.5
Switzerland, **11**:2.6
United Kingdom, **4**:2.6
United States
  hazardous waste, **2**:2.3.1
  radioactive material, **2**:2.3.4
  recycled materials, **2**:2.3.2
  solid waste, **2**:2.3.3
Water, abstraction of
France, **12**:2.2.3
Israel, **15**:2.4.2
Netherlands, **5**:2.2.3
Portugal, **13**:2.3
Spain
  continental waters, **9**:2.3.1
  generally, **9**:2.3
  marine waters, **9**:2.3.2
Sweden, **8**:2.3
United Kingdom, **4**:2.3
Water contamination
Australia, **6**:2.4.2
Austria, **10**:2.4
Belgium
  Brussels Metropolitan Region, **7**:2.5.3
  Flemish Region, **7**:2.3.3
  Walloon Region, **7**:2.4.3
France, **12**:2.2.2
generally, **1**:2.3
Germany, **3**:2.2
Greece, **14**:2.3

Index

Water contamination – *contd*
Israel
aircraft waste, **15**:2.4.1
generally, **15**:2.4
internal waters, **15**:2.4.2
oil, **15**:2.4.1
sea water, **15**:2.4.1
Netherlands
abstraction of water, **5**:2.2.3
discharges to water, **5**:2.2.3
surface water, **5**:2.2.2
underwater soil, **5**:2.2
Norway, **16**:2.2.2
Portugal, **13**:2.2
Spain
continental waters, **9**:2.3.1
generally, **9**:2.3
marine waters, **9**:2.3.2
Sweden
abstraction, **8**:2.3
discharge, **8**:2.3
pollution, **8**:2.2
United Kingdom
abstraction, **4**:2.3
discharges, **4**:2.3
pollution, **4**:2.2
United States
CERCLA, **2**:2.1.1
generally, **2**:2.1.6
oil pollution, **2**:2.1.5
RCRA, **2**:2.1.2
remediation, **2**:2.1.3
underground storage tanks, **2**:2.1.7
Water, discharges to
France, **12**:2.2.3
Israel, **15**:2.4.1
Netherlands, **5**:2.2.3
Portugal, **13**:2.3
Spain
continental waters, **9**:2.3.1
generally, **9**:2.3

Water, discharges to – *contd*
Spain – *contd*
marine waters, **9**:2.3.2
Sweden, **8**:2.3
United Kingdom, **4**:2.3
Water usage
Germany, **3**:2.2
United Kingdom
abstraction, **4**:2.3
discharges, **4**:2.3
Water compliance reporting
United States, **2**:2.6.1
Water permits
United States
generally, **2**:2
NPDES, **2**:2.2.1
stormwater permits, **2**:2.2.2

Zoning
Australia, **6**:2.4.9
Austria, **10**:2.7.1–2.7.2
Belgium
Brussels Metropolitan Region, **7**:2.5.3
Flemish Region, **7**:2.3.3
Walloon Region, **7**:2.4.3
France, **12**:2.2.7
generally, **1**:2.7
Germany, **3**:2.5
Greece, **14**:2.6
Israel
impact studies, **15**:2.10.2
planning and building institutions, **15**:2.10.1
Netherlands, **5**:2.3.4
Norway, **16**:2.2.5
Portugal, **13**:2.7
Spain, **9**:2.7
Sweden, **8**:2.6
Switzerland, **11**:2.7
United Kingdom, **4**:2.7
United States, **2**:2.4